Letters 1913–1956

Bertolt Brecht Letters

Translated by Ralph Manheim
and edited with commentary
and notes by John Willett

METHUEN

First published in Great Britain in 1990
by Methuen London Ltd, Michelin House,
81 Fulham Road, London SW3 6RB
by arrangement with Suhrkamp Verlag, Frankfurt am Main,
based on the original work published by
Suhrkamp Verlag in 1981 as *Brecht Briefe*

Printed in Great Britain
by Richard Clay, Bungay, Suffolk

ISBN 0 413 51050 6

A CIP catalogue record for this book
is available from the British Library

Contents

The man with a load of mischief 3

1 The formative decade.
Bavaria 1913–1924 11

2 Brecht finds his place.
Berlin 1924–1933 89

3 Exile and the approach of war.
Svendborg 1934–1939 157

4 The Second World War.
Sweden, Finland, America 1939–1947 307

5 Last years in a divided Europe.
Zurich and East Berlin 1947–1956 431

Editorial Notes 567
Notes on Individual Letters 567
Book List 692
List of Common Abbreviations 694
Index 696

1 Bavaria
1913-1924

The man with a load of mischief

We need only look at our own daily correspondence, whether it gets filed or goes into the wastepaper basket, to see that it can include anything from declarations of income to declarations of love. Editing some forty years of it, then, is bound to be a hit or miss affair. This is especially so when the correspondent was working in an ephemeral art, moving from one country to another, threatened by his own government and forced to allow for the interception of his letters by political police of various colours. But even in more normal lives no selection of letters can be all that coherent or balanced. The people the letter-writer knows and loves best, those with whom he or she discusses what really matters, are as a rule too close to need to be written to. Everything in a correspondence depends on who was where when; on whether they needed to be informed, amused, convinced, comforted, cajoled, flattered, choked off, bargained with, used as a verbal punch-ball or kept in the dark. The correspondence of a genius makes a particularly fascinating rag-bag, but rag-bags – even the most catholic of poetry anthologies, for instance, like the alphabetically-ordered Auden-Garrett *The Poet's Tongue* – need some principle of arrangement if they are to function as a book.

The present selection of Brecht's letters, based on Günter Glaeser's annotated East-West German edition of 1981–3, is unilateral; that is to say, only Brecht's side of the correspondence is given, though letters addressed to him are often cited in the notes. In order to pick out some of the concerns that run through it, and to recall those historical, political and cultural changes by which it was so largely conditioned, we have divided the great pile of letters into the five main periods into which they (and with them Brecht's activities as a whole) seem to fall, prefacing each section with a broad account of the background of events and the development which was taking place in the writer's own affairs. Thus first come the eleven years before he settled in Berlin, including his first play, his first marriage and the First World War. Then Berlin from the currency stabilisation to Hitler's Third Reich: years of the works with Kurt Weill, of the 'Lehrstücke' and the shift to militant Communism. Third comes the emigration which cut Brecht off from the German theatrical and publishing 'apparatus' and brought him together with others in the same boat, right across the globe. Then the Second World War, culmination of the fears of anti-Nazi exiles everywhere, which for Brecht lasted until his return from America to Europe in 1947. Finally there are the last nine years, covering his interlude in Switzerland as he felt his way back, followed by his historic campaign to rebuild the German-language theatre from a base in the Soviet-influenced portion of his country and of its devastated capital.

Among Anglo-American critics who do not like Brecht it has become common to speak of him as a 'survivor': a little sneeringly, as if cutting a path through the bloody jungle of his times were not a very creditable thing to have done. But the issue in these letters, surely, has to do less with the survival of any individual, however gifted, than with the transmission against all odds of those ideas, influences and values – of the particular tradition, in fact – that is able to survive with him. This is the overriding theme which links the first three divisions of the book with the last two, for the pile does seem to have its centre at that halfway point: the start of the Second World War, the writing of *Mother Courage*, the tailing-off of the Svendborg poems, the loss, too, of a certain vitality in the letters, which are written with a growing reluctance. Letter-writers alter with age: Brecht was by then over forty and, particularly for the professional author, the sheer fun and momentum of bursting into unpaid words to a new addressee is likely to pall after that. But for anybody concerned with the development of post-war Germany on the one hand or that of the arts on the other there is a fascinating story here: the persistence of Brecht's intention, however his country might evolve, to act as a messenger from the avant-garde theatre before Hitler to the culture of our second half-century. In that sense he was as much a survivor as is the hero of any cliff-hanger. Except that, unlike Sherlock Holmes at Reichenbach, he ensured that his rucksack came back with him.

*

Before 1939, then, what we get here is a constellation of pointers to his creativity, his combativeness and his long-term importance. We meet him before the First World War, already enjoying his skill with words: a middle-class provincial member of that extraordinary generation of the 1890s to which Weimar culture owed so much of its energy and its determination to absorb each new technical and social experiment. The German theatre into which he forced his way during the 1920s was far in advance of any other, remaining even sixty years later in some respects – its treatment of opera, for instance – a model for the rest of the world; again there is an infectious fizz to be found in his letter-poems to that dubious ally Arnolt Bronnen (scattered between Letters 64 and 87) or in the outline plan for *Happy End* which he made for Elisabeth Hauptmann (Letter 146), while his reservations about the Berlin State Theatre and his early co-operation with Piscator's politico-technical theatre are evidence of the road he would take. Likewise the political forms evolved in the Weimar Republic's last phase between 1929–33 are still seminal today. But Brecht was not going to have these forms laid down for him – which is what makes his letters to such independent Marxists as Korsch, Benjamin and Brentano of interest, particularly where they relate to the plan for a review to be called *Crisis and Criticism*. Here we find the beginning of those differences with Georg Lukács (see the draft Letter 156), which would be important for the rest of his life.

Then comes the emigration and the Nazis' exclusion from the German theatre of Brecht, Piscator and other such pioneers. If the English theatre is still in the age of the oil lamp, he tells George Grosz in Letter 245, the Germans of the Third Reich have gone back to torch-light. The letters conjure up various aspects of exile and of its literature: the problems of publishing and of dealing with scattered groups of anti-Nazi actors, the almost complete break in correspondence with those left in Germany, the anxious waiting for visas and permits, the effort to make the Communist movement understand the extent of its defeat. Since London is a 'wicked hard-bitten town' full of vicious inhabitants – e.g. the porter of the Savoy Hotel (Letters 234–5) – the choice in the long run is between New York and Moscow. The former, as Brecht experiences it in 1935, is the liberal city of Roosevelt's New Deal and the various Federal arts projects – something much closer to the radical Weimar culture than anything he would encounter there later. Yet even so he could not work in the American 'left' theatres except by establishing that 'nice little dictatorship' (Letter 276 to his wife back in Denmark) which made him so disliked; and in Letter 282 he expressly warns Piscator against them, saying 'you're better off with Shubert', in other words with commercial Broadway.

Like Piscator then, he looks to the USSR, with its still functioning avant-garde (Okhlopkov, Tretiakoff, Eisenstein, the journalist Mikhail Koltsov) and its sizeable German communities, and, although he never quite goes along with Piscator's unreal scheme for a great émigré theatre in the Volga German Republic, he maintains his Soviet connections well into the Stalinist reaction of the later 1930s, by which time Piscator has left the USSR and all such international operations have been halted. The ups and downs of Koltsov's German magazine *Das Wort* until Koltsov himself was shot are of particular relevance; Brecht was nominally one of its editors, but much of the evidence about its demise was long swept under the mat. The disillusionment provoked by this generally shabby story (e.g. Letter 375) coincides with his decision to move – as Piscator, Grosz, Kurt Weill and Hanns Eisler had done before him – to the United States.

In one sense this was a climax, since the pivotal years 1938–41 saw the completion of those five great plays – from *Galileo* to *Arturo Ui* – which would remain virtually unknown until Brecht's return to the German theatre after Hitler's defeat. In another it was almost the opposite, because throughout most of the 1940s the USSR simply drops out of his correspondence; he is trying to establish himself on what to us is more familiar ground in California and New York, and in the process some of the spontaneity of the earlier letters seems to seep away. For much of the American period we are dependent on letters to his Danish mistress, Ruth Berlau, many of them setting her tasks in connection with his work: letters that bear primarily on contacts and contracts, money and translations.

Here his fitful judgements of the work of such collaborators as Alfred Kreymborg, Hoffman Hays, W. H. Auden and Eric Bentley show how unsure of these matters a displaced writer can be; moreover at the same time he has the successful and helpfully-disposed Kurt Weill pressing him to use Ben Hecht and other word-fixers who might help him to climb on the great Broadway stage-coach – something he never manages to do. Along with these and the rather more considered letters to Isherwood's old mentor Berthold Viertel (who became important to him in the US context and later) there are insights into his political work as a member of the Council for a Democratic Germany, a Communist-supported body presided over by Thomas Mann's brother Heinrich (see Letter 498 for the latter's function, 495 for Brecht's sceptical view of Allied intentions and 477 for his attempt to win Thomas over). Then, with Hitler's defeat, come various indications of

Brecht's plans for a return to Berlin: an allusion to mysterious discussions back in Finland (Letter 506), a formal offer of alliance to
Piscator (534–5) and a batch of crucial letters to Caspar Neher (529–
532), the first correspondence with his old friend, confidant and designer
for many years.

Already in this fourth section – and even more so in the final one,
once Brecht has left the United States with three more big plays and the
Laughton *Galileo* in his sack – the focus of attention is likely to shift
from his evolution as a writer to the dear old points of controversy so
often stressed by his personal and political critics: the great Austrian
passport saga, the mystery of the Swiss bank, the *Lucullus* issue, and his
supposed rejection of the 17 June Rising. On all these matters (of which
only the last two can be considered as worth serious attention) the
letters contain evidence that helps to make them credible and sets them
in a wider context: e.g. that of the prevailing travel barriers and the
interests of the new Berliner Ensemble. For if Brecht's main concern in
America was the adapting, translating and recommendation of his
plays with a view to gaining a place in the US theatre, once back in
Europe he was for the first time essentially a director, and one who was
planning, training and promoting (while his wife was organising and
leading) a new company devoted to his own notion of a post-Nazi
German theatre and its repertoire.

Many of his later letters, then, are concerned with detail: with
requests and persuasion, whether of actors or of official bodies. And
because the company was a subsidised one, dependent on a government that, for better and worse, was far from indifferent to the arts,
he came to find himself increasingly an establishment figure, helping
to conduct the affairs of the revived Academy of Arts, taking an
interest in the schools curriculum and issuing the occasional statement
on public affairs. That being so, much of the interest lies in his
resistance to the imposition of any kind of officially preferred aesthetic
principles or forms, along with his considerable success in shaking up
the arts administration (for instance by Letter 732 to the responsible
minister). All this is intercut with such long-running problems as the
production of his plays elsewhere, the *Threepenny Opera* situation and
the more or less disastrous plans for filming *Puntila* and *Mother
Courage*.

*

Students of the great Brecht jigsaw will find a lot of missing pieces of all sizes and shapes in these pages, some of them pointing to new areas of puzzlement (like Letter 287 to Lee Strasberg of Actors' Studio fame). But then they will no doubt long since have spotted them in the original German edition. Those readers more generally interested in the extraordinary cultural history of the period – a period with so much to suggest to us today – will come away with a vivid if spotty picture of the Weimar Left, its experience during twelve or more years of emigration, East and West, and its relation to the two Germanies of 1949. One sees some of the writer's problems (for instance in Brecht's nagging correspondence about the typography of the *Threepenny Novel*) and gets a new insight into the shifting relations between the different émigrés: Brecht and Grosz, Brecht and Piscator, Brecht and Becher (a 'du' intimacy full of ambiguities). There are also the productive, really creative, letters like some of the early ones to Caspar Neher (notably Letter 62 about Brecht's third play *In the Jungle*) or those to Dudow about *Carrar* and *Fear and Misery of the Third Reich* in 1930s Paris.

There are memorable descriptions, such as those of the Bavarian summer in the early letters to Neher and to Bie Banholzer, or of the junk mania which hit the septuagenarian Karin Michaelis at a Hollywood lost-property auction (Letter 487). And then there is an intriguing, very uneven sprinkling of letters to the women he loved. A few of these, near the start, are to Bie (Paula) Banholzer, his Augsburg sweetheart, along with those letters to Neher where he talks about their relationship. Four, added evidently at a late stage, are to his first wife, the Gauguinesque Marianne Zoff; about a hundred more have now been released by their family and will appear in German too late for inclusion in this volume. Seven are to Dora Mannheim, a short-lived Berlin affair of 1920; seven to the reticent Elisabeth Hauptmann ('Bess') all connected with work; nothing to the almost equally important Margarete Steffin (though there are references to her introduction into his household in 1932 and to her death nine years later in Letters 162–3 and 428–9 respectively, while some fifty hitherto unpublished letters may be added in the next German edition). There is only a single letter to his younger companions in East Berlin. Among the fifty-seven addressed to Helene Weigel, his wife and partner, there are certainly some that touch on the most personal matters (including an important one at the time of Steffin's arrival).

But the real serial story, from 1942 to the end of Brecht's life, is the relationship with the difficult, demanding, sometimes hysterical Ruth

Berlau, recipient of sixty-five of these letters, most of them signed with private marks of love. 'Do you really want to turn our exile into an interminable Lovestory', he asks despairingly at one point in mid-1942, using the kitschy script-writer's word. The worsening problem which Berlau represented for herself and him (to say nothing of the long-suffering Weigel) has never been so clearly conveyed. This flood of letters to her is one of the factors that may have determined certain omissions in the German edition. Just because she became the most troublesome, it would not do to suggest that she was also the central woman in his life. But be that as it may there are quite a lot of important letters that have been published or paraphrased elsewhere – e.g. in Yuri Oklyanskii's novel about Margarete Steffin – yet left out of the authorised selection. To say nothing of the very copious business correspondence, which Dr Glaeser has on the whole consciously ignored.

All this should be remedied in the new collected (Frankfurt and Weimar) Brecht edition, but it still presents a problem for us today. Another is that the original selection seems to have such a long and diminishing tail, particularly for the non-German reader, who will have no idea who half the addressees are. Far be it from us to suggest that what matters in the special context of the German Democratic Republic is of no interest outside it, since it is a country and a society of great importance and many fine qualities, which Western propaganda has done too much to obscure. All the same, quite a lot of the later letters hardly seem worth printing by any standard – like the one to an unidentified reader called Carl-Emil Binkenstein which goes simply 'Dear Mr Binkenstein, I think one should only use the term "novella" if one is prepared to allow the novella to change. With best greetings, yours . . .' And so we have left them out. They do however figure in the notes, together with the gist of what they say, and the same is true of such omitted letters as have come to our attention; we have insinuated these into the German edition's numbering sequence and given them an x, xx, or xxx to show that they are extra to it. In both categories the relevant numbers are prefixed with an asterisk, signifying that they will not be found in the main text.

The notes themselves have been rewritten to allow for the particular interests and limitations (such as not knowing Mr Binkenstein) of the Anglophone reader. This is mainly a question of supplementing the very extensive information given in Dr Glaeser's German notes, and at the same time condensing it as best we can. All the spadework is his. We aim, however, to avoid his solution of publishing notes and indexes in a separate volume from the letters themselves; moreover we have used running heads to the pages to help clarify the passage of time and the sequence of events. Footnotes marked with an asterisk were added by Brecht himself; short explanatory footnotes by the editors are numbered on the page. The main Editorial Notes at the end of the book act also as a chronological list of the letters, including those omitted by us which are in the German editions. The Index is a general one, and mainly uses letter numbers rather than page numbers so as to refer simultaneously to the letters themselves and the corresponding notes in this volume, and also to the German text in the Suhrkamp and Aufbau editions. There is a key to initials or abbreviations, and a short book list giving some of the main biographical sources in German and English.

John Willett
Ralph Manheim

The formative decade

When Brecht wrote the first of these letters – in ebullient doggerel verse – Queen Victoria's nephew Wilhelm II was still the Emperor of Germany, and Bavaria, under its Stuart-descended kings, was the largest and least Prussianised section of his confederated Reich. Munich at that time had almost as much claim as Vienna to be the cultural capital of a great German-speaking world whose language, theatres and artistic institutions dominated the whole of central and south-eastern Europe right up to the First World War. Not only did its tradition of court patronage (as seen particularly in Ludwig II's relationship with Wagner) elevate it in many respects above Berlin, but a conflux of new ideas coming from France with Wedekind, from Scandinavia with Ibsen and Bjørnson, from Russia with Kandinsky, had made it into a centre of attraction for the generation immediately before Brecht's. The Mann brothers and Lion Feuchtwanger in literature, Richard Strauss and Hans Pfitzner in music, the Blaue Reiter and the Neue Künstlervereinigung in art, along with the magazines *Jugend* (which gave its name to a whole new style) and *Simplizissimus*, plus a lively fringe or near-fringe theatre ranging from the cabaret acts of Wedekind, Mühsam and Ringelnatz to the private Kammerspiele directed by Otto Falckenberg, all turned it into much more than a great European city. Right through the 'Wilhelmine' period it was a warm, beautiful, lively, stimulating sorting-house for new developments in many fields, at a time when militarised Prussia was felt to have little to offer but the marvellous theatre of the Austrian Max Reinhardt, then at the peak of his energies and inspiration.

The story, therefore, of Brecht's development between the ages of fifteen and twenty-six is interwoven with that of Munich's swift change, first into a conservative city, a centre of slightly mad nationalism and resistance to the Socialist-dominated Berlin of the early 1920s, then in due course to Hitler's 'Capital of the Movement', with its Brown House, House of German Art, Feldherrnhalle and other shrines of Nazism. Before 1920 there is no sign that the young poet was particularly aware of Berlin, and when he eventually moved there in 1924 he was very much the provincial: indeed not so much a Münchner, even, as a young man from Augsburg: 'The Augsburger' as he would call himself in the original version of his *Messingkauf Dialogues*. For Augsburg is where he was born in 1898, not long after his parents had come to Bavaria from the Black Forest so that his father could take a job there in the Haindl paper mills: a Roman city some forty miles from Munich, made famous by the Fugger banking house at the end of the Middle Ages, and now a flourishing manufacturing centre of about 100,000 inhabitants with a Catholic cathedral, a daily paper and a 1300-seat municipal opera-cum-theatre. The Haindls had started their firm around 1850; they claimed to have been the first producers of newsprint reels, and by the end of the century had 300 employees. Brecht's father and his Reitter uncle (recipient of the first letter) worked for them, as later did his brother Walter. Both families lived in company houses in the north-eastern outskirts, and some of Brecht's early writings (notably his first play *Baal* in 1918) were typed for him in his father's office, sometimes through the mediation of Marie Roecker the family housekeeper.

After those two letters to the Reitters Brecht's family drops out of the correspondence until his first marriage in November 1922. (In all his published letters there are none to his mother, none to his brother, one to his father, nothing more to his uncle and cousins.) Up to the First World War the focus is rather on his Augsburg school friends and the kind of life and activities that are so vividly reflected in the early poems and diaries, the different versions of *Baal* and the wonderfully evocative accounts given us by Hans-Otto Münsterer and Walter Brecht. The school was the Royal Real-Gymnasium (or boys' modern secondary school), where Brecht was educated in history, religion, German, Latin, French, English, physics and chemistry up to the middle of 1917 – the first four of these subjects being his best. Among the friends, several of whom had by then volunteered or been drafted into the war, much the most significant was the prospective artist Rudolf Caspar Neher, a local schoolteacher's son who had joined Brecht's class in 1911 and would eventually be the closest of all his theatrical collaborators. Neher became a gunner in a Bavarian field artillery regiment in the middle of the second year of the war (at one point he functioned as post corporal), fought on the Western Front and at Verdun, was wounded and buried alive. The letters show Brecht not only treating him as a 'brother *in arte*' and intimate confidant but also working to keep up his friend's spirits in a war about which both boys became increasingly sceptical.

Brecht never went to the war, though he had to register on leaving school. Called up a year later, he had by then completed a semester at Munich university, where he went over ostensibly to medicine; and this choice of subject, coupled with his weak heart and a formal request from his father, restricted his actual war service to a few weeks as a medical orderly in a local hospital. Where others of his generation, therefore, suffered those appalling war traumas that so influenced the culture of the Weimar Republic, Brecht enjoyed an exceptional freedom to develop in every direction in an atmosphere of (occasionally some-what bewildered) parental sympathy, wide skies and great natural and architectural beauty. This climate of what Münsterer – himself a partici-pant and observer – described as 'Baal-ish feeling for the world' domi-nates Brecht's summers from 1917 to 1920: the whole transition from war to peace, from Reich to Republic and (on the personal level) from adolescence to manhood which lies at the back of *Baal* and, roughly speaking, of the first hundred pages of the collected *Poems* in the Methuen edition. During that four-year period with its songs, its excursions, its scrubbed wooden inn rooms, its flirtations and fairground amusements, Brecht was publishing his first poems and theatre criticisms in local papers, planning *Baal* and other projects with Neher, listening to the great heretic Wedekind and attending his funeral, learning what he could from the theatre professor Artur Kutscher and the then Expressionist Hanns Johst; and also playing a very minor part in the local revolutionary Soldiers' Council (something that is not reflected in his letters). Crucially too, in July 1918 he enjoys 'it' with Paula Banholzer whom he calls 'Bittersweet': his first major sexual experience, leading rather too soon to his first experience of fatherhood.

It is the Neher letters (along with the *Diaries*) that show us something of the development of the young Brecht's literary, artistic and theatrical judgement. Hamsun, Shakespeare, Kipling and Villon figure among his early influences; Hodler and Goya among those whom he recommends to his friend (whose own work he admired and did his best to promote); Albert Steinrück and Paul Wegener as actors who impressed him. Of the Blaue Reiter and other avant-garde painters he seems to have known little or nothing; it was only many years later that he wrote in defence of Franz Marc and his blue horses. Nor did Expressionism as a whole appeal to him, as we can see from Letter 33: on this point, and in regard to his own use of 'very old material', his attitude never greatly changed. Once Neher too left the army and began working at the Munich

Academy – first as an illustrator, with Klee and George Grosz among his influences, and then as a painter – Brecht kept drawing him into his film and theatre concerns, treating him always as a creative partner rather than a pure designer. So he enlisted Lion Feuchtwanger (known at that time as a playwright rather than a novelist) to recommend Neher to the State Theatres and the Kammerspiele as a potential scene designer, tried to get his *Baal* drawings published, and during 1921 collaborated with him in writing a number of film treatments which the two of them tried vainly to sell to Joe May, producer of the 'Stuart Webbs' thriller series. The following year he hoped to associate Neher with his own theatrical breakthrough with *Drums in the Night*, but was unable to get the beautiful little drawings accepted.

Brecht first visited Berlin in February 1920 some two months before his mother died. In Munich the short-lived Bavarian Soviet had been toppled; there had been murders and executions, and the writers Ernst Toller and Erich Mühsam were serving long jail sentences for their involvement. Now there was a right-wing coup in Berlin, headed by an obscure nationalist called Wolfgang Kapp, causing Brecht to return hurriedly to Munich; the coup soon failed, but in Munich the moderate Socialists resigned in favour of a conservative government, and from then on reactionary Bavaria became, if not actually separatist, at any rate largely independent of the government in Berlin. There is no sign that Brecht was at all moved by these events, but he found the Berlin theatre exciting and in November 1921 returned there to spend the winter in a deliberate effort to get himself and his work accepted in that stony city which he had begun calling 'cold Chicago'. By then he was deeply involved in his obsessive love affair with Marianne Zoff, an opera singer at the Augsburg and subsequently Wiesbaden theatres whose brother Otto was a dramaturg at the Munich Kammerspiele; and very soon Paula Banholzer (and all too often their son) became forgotten in a whole tide of changes to Brecht's life.

This centred on the many new contacts which he was making in Berlin, notably with Herbert Jhering, critic of the Berlin *Börsen-Courier*, the local equivalent to the *Financial Times* thanks to its strong arts coverage; with the young Austrian playwright Arnolt Bronnen and the budding impresario Moritz Seeler, who was just setting up his 'Junge Bühne' series of one-off performances of new plays. Seeler was persuaded to let Brecht direct Bronnen's 'black expressionist' play *Vatermord* ('Parricide') as his opening production, and although the cast rebelled (so that Berthold Viertel had to take over) Jhering for one was convinced that Brecht, Bronnen and the 'Junge Bühne' were the beginning of an important new wave.

Brecht fell seriously ill that winter and was taken to the Charité hospital, but when he returned to Munich at the end of April he had contracts with Kiepenheuer the Berlin publisher and with the film producer Richard Oswald, had appeared briefly in the 'Wilde Bühne' cabaret and, above all, had completed his third play *In the Jungle*. Within weeks this had been accepted by the Bavarian State Theatres (where Jacob Geis was dramaturg), while the Kammerspiele agreed to stage *Drums in the Night* at the start of the coming season. And so it all started. Jhering came from Berlin for the opening of *Drums*, and though Falckenberg and his designer Otto Reigbert gave it a conventionally Expressionist production the critic not only welcomed it as a striking departure from that school of playwriting but chose it for the Kleist Prize, a much respected award whose judge he was that year.

This immediately established Brecht as a new dramatist to be reckoned with, and performances all over Germany followed, notably a production at Reinhardt's Deutsches Theater in Berlin by the same director and designer, with Alexander Granach playing the half-crazed, morally shabby soldier. Brecht maintained his alliance with Bronnen, several of whose plays were staged in Berlin in the first half of the 1920s; worked inconclusively on adaptations and film projects with him and hoped to direct his late-Expressionist play *Anarchie in Sillian* (also known as *Verrat*); later, as Bronnen showed himself to be a Nationalist, they drifted apart. In Munich Brecht became an assistant dramaturg at the Kammerspiele, where he directed and (with Feuchtwanger) co-adapted Marlowe's *Edward the Second* for production in March 1924, by which time *In the Jungle* too had had its première; both these performances were reviewed by Jhering and other 'national' critics and led to productions in Berlin and elsewhere. It was a time when the Berlin theatre generally was looking desperately around for new talent and new plays, and following the reception of the Munich *In the Jungle* not only its director Erich Engel but also Brecht and Neher were signed up by Felix Holländer, Reinhardt's stand-in at the Deutsches Theater. Erich Engel began work there late in 1923, the others at the end of the following summer. Jhering was right; and from then on the three young men formed the kernel of a new movement in the Berlin theatre.

The whole balance and character of the Weimar Republic was decided

by a series of events in the autumn of 1923, and although there is no
allusion to these in the letters their result was to be decisive both for
Germany and for Brecht. First came the disastrous inflation of the
mark, itself aggravated by the Rhineland resistance to French military
government (subject of the first of Bronnen's nationalist plays); then the
Comintern called for a German revolution that November; then Hitler
in Munich got in on the act by staging his attempted putsch at that very
moment; then both left- and right-wing revolts fizzled out, while the
currency was stabilised by the far-sighted conservative Gustav Strese-
mann, who thereafter normalised Germany's relations with her former
enemies and managed (under the Dawes Plan of 1924) to get American
and other foreign backing for the new economy. Not only did this mean
an end to Bavarian separatism and to all freelance military adventures,
but the theatre and opera apparatus benefited from the new prosperity,
and the closures and takeovers that had taken place at the height of the
crisis were followed by a period of investment, whether in building
works or in increasingly elaborate productions and stage machinery. At
the same time the period of Germany's post-war isolation was at an end:
'Americanismus' became increasingly fashionable, while foreign plays
(like those of Galsworthy, O'Neill and Pirandello) once again became
prominent, particularly in the repertoire of the Reinhardt theatres,
where Reinhardt's own interest and presence were now only fitful.

So Brecht found that in addition to his self-imposed mission to renew
the theatre in Berlin he and his collaborators would be given the
opportunities and facilities for doing so. Everything looked more promising than in Munich, and the circumstances of his private life altered to
match when he started his important new relationships with Elisabeth
Hauptmann, henceforward his regular and intimate collaborator, and
the actress Helene Weigel who bore his son Stefan soon after his arrival.
He had married Marianne Zoff in Munich in 1922, about a month after
the première of *Drums in the Night*, but despite the birth of their
daughter Hanne he was no longer in love with her, and with the move
to Berlin this too was put behind him. Thereafter it is Weigel, not he,
whom we find taking an interest in his two elder children. Neher was
still an essential colleague and friend, and in many other respects his
earlier contacts remained valuable, not least when those concerned had,
like Feuchtwanger, also moved to Berlin. But broadly speaking on the
eve of the so-called 'golden twenties' he was in the position of Garga at
the end of *In the Jungle*: 'the chaos has been used up'.

1 To the Reitter family

Augsburg, July 1913

Reitters dear,
Yesterday some 7 hours before midnight
We got in here
The sky was clear
The sun was bright
And as some of us felt a touch of cramp
We put our feet up and reclined
Then thought we'd better set out and find
A flat where we could camp.
Well . . . It had of course crossed our mind
That the place might be fairly chock-a-block
But finding it all booked out was a bit of a shock.
So . . . What do you think we did?
We leapt around and a mere two hours after that
We had succeeded.
We'd actually managed to get a flat.
Admittedly Mama didn't think it was quite what was needed
But it was all there was to be had.
Beggars can't be choosers, so they say.
And anyhow *I* think my room isn't bad
Though it does seem rather a long way
To go if you want to take the waters.
Well then, having by now settled into our new quarters
We went out for a spot of exercise
And to try this town for size
And really one has to recognise
The place seems pretty good.
So 4 weeks here should prove quite agreeable
Fine gardens with benches and pergolas
Nothing locked up, they don't seem nervous of burglars
Concerts galore, and the theatre too may be seeable
And there are nice walks to be had in the wood
If you're in the mood.
But what gave me the greatest pleasure
And removed the last traces of gloom
Was that I could spend my leisure

In the public reading room.
Then at supper last night
The helpings were splendid
We sat down and ate them
And once it was ended
We couldn't forget them.
So that was all right.
But –
When this morning we opened our eyes
And drew back the curtain
There were clouds in the skies
Copiously spurting.
And you could see for certain
It was going to rain all today.
If not tomorrow too.
Well, it's not very gay
Sitting around wondering what on earth to do.
It's raining cats and dogs, that's the long and the short of it
So keep a stiff upper lip and see the thing through.
All right, but just
Suppose it decides to rain on *you*.
I'd laugh myself fit
To bust.
Et finio meam epistulam
voluntate, esse peius apud nos.
Id putarem certe priusquam
calamitatem scripsitis nos –
nam malum cupiit bos!

> Greetings and kisses by the dozen
> from your loving nephew and cousin
> Eugen

[Additions from father and mother Brecht follow]

2 To the Reitter family

Steben July 1913

My dear Reitters,

> 'It rains till it can rain no more
> And then it really starts to pour'

There's my motto. True, the sun peers bashfully through the clouds from time to time. Then we have two hours of fair weather. Then it starts raining again. Never mind, we're having a pretty good time. The food is good and the lodgings pleasant. We can pay our devotions under the colonnade and drink the water, which is as sweet as ink. We bathe every other day. Afterwards we lie in bed for two hours *without reading*. We eat and we're bored.

We've received your first letter. Fritz of course is a genius. What purity of speech! So many different registers! (Etc.!) It gave us an exact picture of your present life. Really, everything that happens to you is in it.

The only thing of interest here is the music. Morning and afternoon the fine Casino orchestra gives a concert. The conductor sits opposite me in the dining room. He eez a Hongarian and eats wid heez hands. The refined people at the table look at him aghast. – Yesterday evening I went to a symphony concert at which Beethoven, Mozart and Haydn were played beautifully. The day before yesterday went to the theatre, where they did Bahr's *Concert*, a charming comedy. We laughed a lot. But I must close, Mama wants to add something.

Best regards from your cousin and nephew Eugen

[Postscript from Brecht's mother follows]

3 To Caspar Neher

My dear Rudolph Neher,

Thank you for your visit last Sunday. Unfortunately I was in the cemetery when you arrived. So I'll write what I have to say.

Thanks again for the *Faust* colour sketch. On studying it a second time, I thought: composition excellent. But I wouldn't have taken your view of the apparition. All Goethe says is that the spirit appears in a 'reddish flame'. – Faust himself might (perhaps) better be shown in profile. (Leaning on his desk?) The windows and candlesticks are *very* beautiful . . .

As a friend, not as a critic (because to that I can lay no claim), I advise you not to overdo your treatment of light, in other words to avoid unlikely light effects. So far, it is true, your handling of light conveys an extraordinarily poetic mood, but . . .

But a poet (and a painter in my opinion) is dependent on reality. To combine fidelity to nature with idealism – that is art. 'Reality is the great poet's bed, on which he dreams his dreams.' (G. Hauptmann has mastered this art of exalting everyday happenings to spiritual heights. Just read the last act of *Michael Kramer*, the finest thing ever accomplished by a naturalist – Shakespeare excluded.)

Your subject matter needn't be distinguished by outward beauty. You don't need kings for your heroes, you don't need poets or philosophers. (Or Antigone or Faust.) The life of a washerwoman (Mother Wolffen in [Hauptmann's] *Biberpelz*) can be tragic (hence (?) beautiful). What matters is the mind *of the artist*, who transfigures the object, permeates it with his being. Meunier's workers are superior to Kaulbach's vacant-faced bodies, and Leo Putz's grimacing whores perhaps superior to Thoma's peasant women. (I hate Defregger!)

A modern painter must read Zola.

Because the place of the great (pictorial) naturalist is still vacant. The soul of the people has not yet been explored.

Theme: The accident.

Night. Torchlight. A crowd has gathered around a hole in a winding street. Mute. Black. Pressed close together. Pale faces. *Horror* . . .

Oh, I forgot I was writing to you and not in my diary. So let's get back.

Have you read the latest issues of *Jugend*? They contain some full-page pictures (by Staeger), or what amounts simply to poems framed in allegorical borders.

I have a poem of that kind.

Theme:

In the afternoon the enemy is defeated. The telegraph wires announce the event.

On one side: Joy, jubilation, prayers.

On the other side: Fear, despair, hate.

The dead are buried during the night. The telegraph wires carry the news:

This is a night when mothers weep.
On *both* sides

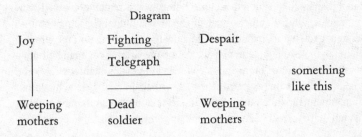

Diagram

Joy   Fighting   Despair
             _____

             Telegraph
             _____   something
                                            like this
             _____

Weeping   Dead   Weeping
mothers   soldier   mothers

If the thing interests you, bring me a sketch when you come here. I
hope you come in any case.

If I'm really not home, leave word where I can find you.

> Greetings from your
> brother *in arte*
> B. Eugen Brecht

Augsburg 10 November 1914

NB I've just noticed that this letter looks like a picture album. Not a
comic one, I hope.

4 To Heinz Hagg

Dear Heinz,

It's all settled. Today Monday 6 p.m. the ice cream shop across from
Heiligkreuz Church in Kreuzstrasse, meeting of the Sylvester[1] spooks.
Have you got any essence of punch? Requisite: drinking cup. (Sled)
Wood (in your knapsack). Harmonica. Humour. Cigarettes. Well-
ingtons. Feeling for romance and fun. Aim: Relaxation. Bobsledding
by the light of the stars. Tea in the woods. Single combat with doormen.
So don't forget, 6 o'clock, my lovely.

> B. Brecht

[Undated note; presumably written in Augsburg. Early January 1917.]

[1] New Year's Eve.

5 To Max Hohenester

Dear Max Hohenester,

Many thanks for your letter. Our letters seem to have crossed. But I'm writing again today because I unfortunately have time. About two weeks ago I retired to my sunny room on the second floor (acquired in February 1917) and for these two weeks I have been taken up 18 hours a day with some kind of cramp in the stomach muscles, which strikes the doctor as odd and me as painful. So, I've had lots of bellyache in my sunny room and I smile painfully at the dim consolation that everything connected with me is so original and incomprehensible, even my ailments.

Neher has been to see me from time to time. Army life has turned him into quite a character. He makes himself ridiculous by complaining about women for hours. Here and there in our conversations a significant phrase is spoken, as is bound to happen between two men who know all there is to know about life and, thanks either to their temperament or to stomach trouble, despise it. The business with Paula ended ingloriously and absurdly. After I'd given her up, delivered two furious harangues and smilingly flung my blessing at her, [–] that commercial school student stepped in and 'replaced me'. It's a funny feeling when you can't help being ashamed of a ruin that once seemed beautiful – in fact you didn't even know it was a ruin until you got this commercial school student to look at it. All the same, I didn't come off too badly. Do you know my story about the Zulu Kaffir who got thinner and thinner from day to day until, when drink didn't help any more, he turned to religion? So he went to the medicine man, who advised him to make himself a living god. Possibly because of some tender childhood memory, the man took a wild pig for his god. And you can't accuse him of making light of the matter or of not believing. So he worshipped the wild pig and dreamt of it and sacrificed the best of the best to it, all the last bites that he forced himself to save. And yet he grew thinner and thinner.* Finally, in his despair, he began to suspect that the god couldn't help him. This made him so angry that he went home one dark night in the rainy season and killed his god and ate the pig. For fear of his ritual murder being discovered, he ate all night and consumed the whole pig. As a result, he was fat in the morning, as fat as a eunuch, as fat as a bagpipes, miraculously fat, divinely fat. And even though in the course of the morning the man exploded in a thicket and died in a state of beatitude, it was a fat man who died. So the story can be cited as a pious refutation of the tendentious view held by certain unbelievers that what saves is faith and not the god. You see that my life is not terribly amusing, I have come to be as alone as you are unalone. – Two painful states of affairs amid shellfire or bellyache. The incomparable Pfanzelt, chief of the Augsburg dog police, still goes strutting about with my mother's poor lonely son in the summer glories of the Wolf-zahn, and we philosophise about death.

I'm sending you three stories by Hamsun. You will receive my whole *Summer Symphony* when it's finished, in return for your assurance of definitely being able to return it. Otherwise I have nothing, assuming that you know *The Song of the Vulture Tree*. I haven't been reading much. Most recently *Coriolanus*. Wonderful! I hope to receive something from you as soon as possible. If I can ever do anything for you here, just let me know.

When the content permits, I pass your letters on to my mother, who enjoys reading them because she has a feeling for poetry and for you. My mother's card was an act of gratitude for your beautiful letter about the flowering meadow. So if there is one, I'll gladly do you the favour if my health permits. Best regards and many thanks for the beautiful pictures.

Yours,
Bert Brecht

Ausburg, in der Wolfshöhle, 8 June 1917.

*The god throve and grunted, sang with well-being; the god grew fatter and fatter, the man thinner and thinner.

6 To Caspar Neher

Dear Cas,

When are you coming home?

Why are you coming so late? Everything I send you keeps being returned. And besides you seem to have run out of patience. You promised to send a diary and there hasn't even been a letter. Have you done everything (everything) possible towards getting home?

Your old

Bert Brecht

[Augsburg] about 20 August 1917.

7 To Caspar Neher

Early September 1917

Dear Cas,

You are a great man. But a lieutenant looked at the stars and said to them: 'Well, you stars are something and I'm something too. Each in his own way.' I'm a tutor. I'm a tutor in Tegernsee. For three hours a day I try to drum in knowledge, after that I'm lord of the manor. I sit in my room and write, I read Schopenhauer or play the lute; or I lie in a meadow under the trees, as full of melancholy as a hollow tree is of honey. At night I go rowing, it's as beautiful as the Plärrer. Rosa has written to me and stuck the stamp on crooked. I asked a girl in the Thelott quarter to track down the vanished Sophie. The first person she asked was her milk woman, who was able to supply information: Sophie is her daughter.

Many thanks for the sketches. I like the others, the first and the 'last' man more and more. But who is this 'English poet'? He's excellent. You man of mystery! You inspired symbolist! Kipling, Shaw, Shakespeare – one of those? Whom do you mean?

What have you been 'up to'? Write, but more legibly. I'll send you reading matter from Augsburg. You eternal student!

A few themes:
Girls have no use for us poets – we merely *write*
About love, for the fun of it. A scandal . . .
What's more, they aren't brilliant. True, they shed *some* light
But all the light *they* can use is – a candle.
And our dreams only prove that we know how to sleep
And that only in dreams, not – with *them*. And it's funny
But we're too slack to work and too slack to keep
And we're much too extravagant to make any money.
Our foreheads are pallid and riddled with thought
Our esteem they find loathsome – so chilling.
Our eyes, from observing, get tired and distraught
And too much observing leaves no room for feeling.
Young wives have no use for us writers – we're poets

We don't deceive their husbands, we deceive *them* instead.
When we pray it's *our words* we believe. And they know it's
Quite pointless to have high ideals when in bed.

The girl that listened to the Romance in F:
After he lost her, all the pain that ensued
Made him keep silent as the grave –
His songs revealed it, lurching, drunk and crude.
And on the crest of the music's wave
A girl swam nude.

Paula!
Just do your exercises – and you'll get a horse.
Your father said so. Sooner not be tied?
But P T's a fine thing. You must be fit of course
And, Paul, some women *must* have a horse
To get a man who'll ride.

Anyway doing a shit is more constructive than doing nothing.

The strongest men are scared of babies.

This in thanks for the sketches, in so far as a beggar can thank a king.
I'm looking forward to your sketches and to Hamsun's next book.

When I get to Munich, I'll buy some frames. But you'll probably
have to send me money for them, because when I'm there I have to
strain my budget buying books for my New Life. But we'll arrange for
that.

> In the meantime, regards.
> Yours,
> Bert Brecht

> Tegernsee, Villa Kopp (until 12 September)

Regards from Müller-Otto, who was here for a few days. Could you
find out through your sister how his stock stands at present?

8 To Caspar Neher

Dear Cas,

I have less time than God himself, and if He were in my situation He wouldn't be able to write any more often. He needed thousands of years to write his one and only book, and that's why the end of it is entirely different from what the reader and God himself supposed at the outset. In the course of writing, God grew old and mellow. There's nothing divine about assiduity.

But your caricatures, you big childish cynic you, are very, very good. Really. You seem to be trying to caricature souls, whereas others have only caricatured expressions or minds or bodies. You must draw as much as possible and give me everything you do. This is essential. Please write me a special letter telling me I can keep them. Otherwise I'll have to pray for you to die soon. If I go to Argentina, I'll carry them in my feed bag or my belly band, which I mean to keep for that purpose.

Did you get my last letter?

Once again, a bit of verse in lieu of thanks.

If you knew what torture it is to copy poetry, you'd send me lots of drawings. And learn a good deal in the process . . .

> A woman said, as we were starting to go through the motions:
> I'll tell you what it is about artists that I detest
> They talk about love such a lot the woman gets forgotten.
> You offer us incense. Incense and candles. How rotten
> That instead of arousing your sensations
> We awaken your interest.
> Well, people without principles . . . I said.
> She broke in: Are like a naked man in bed.
> In public one would sooner he wore clothes of course.
> I said: Your lot wants the jockey to be whipped by the horse.
> She said: A whip's what a competent jockey doesn't need.
> So: If you've retained principles indeed
> You're not in love the whole way through
> And she won't give herself to you.

To Caspar Neher:

> Nauseous creatures, these artists. They live by abuse and disorder.
> Offer the citizen pain in exchange for the coins in his pocket. –
> Vultures have shat on a tree, thinking their droppings would choke it.
> Sneering, it welcomed their dung – never bore heavier fruit.

Wherewith many kisses, O divine Rosa Maria, and to you best regards, dear Cas Par

> from your affectionate Bert Brecht

> Tegernsee, September 1917.

Just write to Augsburg, Cas, I'll be back there shortly.

9 To Caspar Neher

Dear Cas,

You're really an idiot even though you do such wonderful drawings that I pray you'll die so I can keep them. Now I know why you fail to get promoted, thereby heaping shame and worry on your poor parents, which is less humane than running after soldiers with the mailbag. Because that's the reason. Müller heard that the captain told someone that as long as you do everyone's dirty work and volunteer for details that are ordinarily assigned to the lowest of the low, you won't be officer material. Otto Müller heard that from the Weidemanns. It's true that I know you pretty well, dear, childish, doublecrossed Cas, the Cyclops with the sinful brain and virtuous heart, it's touchingly kind of you to make sure that the poor devils out there get their mail as quickly as possible and that your heart will be completely exhausted by Christmas from running and hauling, but it took all my imagination to glean this from the wild talk that's going around; because the profanum vulgus says you do it for the money. They're a lot of idiots, though they don't do such wonderful drawings as the ones you'll soon send me, Sergeant Neher.

> Your worried
> Bert Brecht
> Who is not at all pleased with you.

I've rented a room at your aunt's.

I'm writing a play called *Alexander and his Soldiers*. Alexander the Great. Without iambics. And his soldiers without cothurni. I want it to be immortal.

But I also want you to become a sergeant.

Got it?!?!

> [Munich], September 17

10 To Caspar Neher

Dear Cas,

The new drawings are *very* good. The 'Juno' is enchanting, a splendid companion piece to your earlier sketch signed 'I'. Forgive me. What have you been up to all this time? Please write to me about it legibly, because I have to tell your aunt. She sends her regards. I'll probably show her your drawings one of these days when I want something from her. So you're a lance-corporal now. In case you didn't know it, you must behave accordingly. I expect you to become a general. With your sense of humour ... You never write me anything about my stories and aphorisms, it's as if you'd rather not mention them. I've never been in favour of pulling punches. You brute. I'll write you something coherent about your sketches another time. I'm going to take them to *Simplizissimus* when I'm in Munich. This isn't the right terrain for them. Especially 'The People' is wonderful. But wouldn't you like to do something political? In the extended sense, I mean, something symbolic à la Goya? About the *Nationalverein* which is collaborating with Wilson in trying to save peace from premature birth!?

Please write soon and send me lots of drawings.

Your loving Bert Brecht

Address: M[unich], Maximilianstrasse 43/III

[circa October 1917]

11 To Caspar Neher

Dear Baron Cass,

Might your Grand Mogulic grace summon up the kindness to send your most submissive belly dancer a few lines concerning the well-being of your beatific corporeity, in other words, pick up a piece of lead (plumbum Pb) in your filthy claws and throw my paltry nonentity into a state of frenzied jubilation by daubing a series of organised lines on a sheet of paper. Your eminent and brilliant laziness stinks to high heaven, in fact, they say it's getting unbearable up there.

Deign to accept the respects of an incurably hopeful subject of whom long ago your mellifluous cherubic voice was kind enough to deign to condescend to speak in flattering terms.

Mu[nich], 26 October 1917

(NB: The drawings aren't bad.)
I'm moving on the 27th. For the present address your next hundred or
so letters to Augsburg.

B

12 To Caspar Neher

Dear Cass,

Thank you for your excellent letter and for the shipment of paper.
Your thanks for my paper, which you do not wholly reject, has moved
me deeply. You have always been courteous when it doesn't cost you
anything. To me you have never been courteous. Oh, great Cas, your
irony is significant, your style personal and trenchant. I'd welcome
more of it. That's how I've always been. – All your heroes do too *much*,
always just a bit more than they are capable of, hence their goitres.
Adam is marvellous; his lack of neck shows me right off that you don't
regard him as a genius; the ingratitude of genius, my dear Cas. Eyes
looking piously upward, in which they are impeded by no forehead –
ethical sentiment. This piece is outstanding. Unfortunately. The knight
is chaster than you, but my grandmother prayed more fervently than the
unprepossessing fellow with the sunflower, who has again been dedicated to me of all people. The storyteller is excellent, I'm only afraid the
pencil lines will rub off. Do please use ink and wash as much as possible
for your drawings. I don't dare apply fixative to the things. Anyway,
you'll never get them back – except perhaps as a loan. But now an order!
1) Please a cartoon for Rosmarie. Rosa Maria.
2) The sweet dream of my cold night doesn't love me. Nothing helps.
You must write to her. Tell her I'm in despair. Or better still, draw my
picture for her! But don't make me ridiculous. I'm counting on you for
that. Or vulgar . . . Hmm. Make me big, eternal, immense, ironic. Etc.
But: don't draw me in the nude. Or her either. Or I'll have to wring
your neck. Wring. Your neck. Can I see the drawing first? Because
afterwards I want *you* to send it to her from the trenches. Bitschlier-
strasse 4. Sophie Renner. They're respectable people. Not naked.

So greetings, Auf Wiedersehen, Thanks, Please.

Bert Brecht

Write again. Very soon and to the new address: Adalbertstr. 12/1
I've moved. It was too much out of the way. Otherwise, I was sorry.

One more thing: return this letter with your answers in the margin. I don't have to tell you why. You know me. Thanks.

[Munich], 8 November 1917

13 To Caspar Neher

M(unich) 23.11.17

Dear Cas,

Many thanks for your letter and especially for the drawings. I wasn't just teasing you, my boy. I didn't want *my* letter back, I only wanted to force you, in a tender kind of way, to keep looking at it while you were writing to *me*, because then I'd get some sort of *answer*. Well, it was a failure. Something else has been a failure. I took a morning off and went to Neuhausen. But that Simpl[izissimus] they said the things were very good but not right for the *Simpl*. Main reason: not topical enough. But I think they find them too radically human. But that's just what makes them so good. *Jugend*, where I went next, wouldn't let me in, but in the shape of a doorman asked me to leave them. I wasn't prepared to do that. So should I send them in? I think that outfit stinks. Besides, these formats are unacceptable. Write to me about it. For the Kunstverein I especially need *The Kiss*. But I think I can see so much progress in the things you've done since, that I'm against that sort of interim show. And incidentally, I've never believed so staunchly and defiantly in your triumph than on my way back from the *Simpl*. The new things are good. In *The Apostle* you show an intuitive grasp of the typical. (In his classes Kutscher has the same soul – he *is* the Apostle!) In *Suicide* there's something extremely vital about using such an enormous amount of energy to kill oneself, something paradoxically wasteful. *The Logical Man*. In *The Man of the People*, what enormous effort combined with minimal mental development. I wouldn't want to entrust these things to the vagaries of editorial chance. – I don't remember what annoyed you in my last letter but one. It must have been a joke. I hope you're not losing your sense of humour. I know you might be better off. But I also know that you're better off than anyone else. Basically, that is. 'Nothing can happen to us.' From Hohenester I hear nothing but complaints. I'm sorry for him. I comfort him. I respect his *distress*. (Seriously!) Should I feel sorry for you too? It's better to respect *people*.

Yours,
Bert Brecht.

Please write again. I'm practically drowning in banality. I'm very fond of your letters. When I can read them.

Russia seems to be getting sick and sensible. It would be wonderful if we could be here together. Working! We wouldn't need any other people. I'm full of ideas that are all languishing. I don't want to make friends with anybody here. They are all terrible windbags in spite of their cultivated manners. I'd just like to see your grin once again or your way of sniffing. Just as a mural decoration in my room, you'd be incredibly stimulating. If you get shot dead I shall be an ordinary singular of people. So please *don't*!

Bert Brecht, Munich, Adalbertstrasse 12/I
[Return address on Armed Forces Letter].

14 To Heinz Hagg (Postcard)

Dear Heinz,

It's high time I wrote to you again. Not that there's anything doing here. It would be awful if I had time to think about it. But I'm always busy. 8 to 11; 12 to 1; 3 to 6:30; 7 to 10:30 – in the lab, at the university, at the theatre. Every day. I gobble up everything within reach and read an incredible amount. I'll digest it all in the army. + + + I'm always glad to go to Augsburg, where I can be lazy for a day and a half. Here I'm caught up in a system of always being late. By six in the morning I'm almost 24 hours late. By 11 at night, 24 + 15 hours. One of these days I'll just stop getting up in the morning. Basta. I hope to see you in Augsburg. Life is a toboggan slide. Better look for a place at the ticket office [?] !!! Please convey to your sister and dear Emil my most unctuous regards.

Yours,
B. Brecht

Munich, 23 November 1917
Adalbertstrasse 12/I

15 To Caspar Neher

Dear Cas,

Many thanks for the letter and sketches. Didn't I thank you for the colour sketches? Sorry. *The Walker* is magnificent. Inexorably, he walks, immense, dark, driven by his will, as though by a taskmaster . . . It's a good caricature of me – or what *we* obstinately persist in calling a caricature: the perception and representation of the inherently absurd in the relatively rational, or the justification which the individual, by *being* absurd, gives to absurdity. The amazingly vital idleness of this excreted group of men, who stretch out their legs and *exist*, partakes of this comedy of despair. I take it that you're not as happy as you think. Don't you agree? I'm not quite right in my saddle either, or am I asleep in the saddle? I will *not* kiss Rosmarie, since somebody else is kissing her. This insignificant development plagues me, though it's immaterial in view of the World War or if one contemplates the inexorable sum of phenomena. Right? Think of a strong, healthy brute of a body that has a tiny festering wound, in the arse for instance, where it interferes with only one thing . . . And this big man loses all feel for the workings of a sound organism, all the joy of breathing, eating and sleeping, merely because of this little festering sore, which only impedes one thing. Funny, isn't it? Wipe that grin off your face.

I rise from my affliction and call your attention to the problem of the never-again-possible. That we ourselves die is really of no importance. But that others die . . . That everything else dies before us, with us, after us. If it doesn't give you the shudders, dwell on it for a while. Torment is a good thing, one never feels better than when suffering. So I can't kiss Rosmarie any more (she has soft, moist, full lips in her pale, thirsty little face). I can kiss others, of course. In my mind's eye I see a hundred mouths; they will waste away without my kiss. I give myself thirty years and five continents. But as for Rosmarie, I can't . . . Damn it all! What are a hundred possibilities beside *one* impossibility. Forgetfulness is power = flight by reason of weakness. The best one can do is to take what one can. But the rest? The rest that one cannot take . . .? 'There can't be a God, because if there could be, then I couldn't bear *not* to be a God.' Who can help laughing at that? (Laughter, too, is a strength of the weak.)

Rosa Maria is not pretty. That was a legend invented by *me*. She is pretty only from a distance or when I ask: 'Isn't she pretty?' – Her eyes are dreadfully empty, small, wicked, sucking whirlpools, her nose is turned up and too wide, her mouth too big, red and fat. The line of her neck is not pure, her posture is idiotic, her gait scatterbrained and her belly protuberant. But I'm fond of her. (Though she's not bright and not nice.) I'm still very fond of her. What disgusting nonsense. Am *I* pretty?

Please write me what you think. Nobody has been really horrid to me for a long time. The young people around me are so polite. (And I'm so crude – but very bashfully, pianissimo, psst!)

Many thanks for the new sketches. *The Eternal Kiss* is beautiful and strong. But Rosmarie? Oh good God Neher! What a big deceiver *I* must be!

Please send your next things – as soon as possible – to Augsburg, Bleichstrasse 2. I'll be home over Christmas. But I won't kiss Rosmarie!
    Bert Brecht

        Munich, Wolf's Den, 18 December 1917,
        The day I received yours of 15 December.
        Happy Christmas! Peace! So long.

16 To Caspar Neher

        29 December 1917

Dear Cas,

Many thanks for your letter with the waitress motif. Unfortunately I feel the same as you do. Only I'm not as crazy about lechery as I am sick of waitresses. There's a lot of snow on everything. I skate and I eat ice cream. So do Hohenester and Gehweyer. But I hardly know them any more. All the death out there has made them fat. Hohenester is like Jehovah and Fritz is a sergeant. Dear Cas, don't get fat. I've been thinking about a critique of God and the Devil. God is so ignorant, Science keeps contradicting him. Besides, He's a sadist. I'm also going to write a book about good manners. There's nothing much doing in the arts. I think the theatres should be closed on artistic grounds. There won't be any art until the last theatregoer hangs himself with the bowels of the last actor. Politics is beginning to revolve around facts rather than speeches. Once the diplomats, the military and the capitalists go to hell, the only obstacle to peace will be spinelessness. The papers write that victory is certain by early June. I can't think of anything else to write despite the lovely stationery but these lines from my *Winter Song*:

> When you see their chalky faces
> As blankly white as a hospital wall
> Instead of singing you can vomit

Because you pity the bastards after all.

Yours, Bert Brecht

Permit me to wish you a good New Year.

17 To Caspar Neher

Dear Cas,

Gehweyer and Hohenester are home on leave; jubilantly welcomed by me, they arrived; cautiously avoided by me, they will leave. Max is a poor soldier and Fritz a good one. They've come a long way! I've been thinking about *you*. For a long time we strode side by side, and I must have been useful to you before you were useful to me. Am I right? But what happened then? You conjured up my renaissance and gave me more than anyone else. I have to write you that, otherwise I'll forget it, and it's so terribly important. Now I'm in your debt, so watch out. Our fields are so far apart that we can't crowd each other out of the sun. As long as we stay friends, we can afford the most outrageous pessimism. Couldn't you write and tell me what you think of me? I've given you opinion after opinion about you, but you've never written to me about me. If you think I should be satisfied with your writing to me at all, that will be a bitter pill for me to swallow. Do you take me for an art critic? And nothing more? It's not just vanity that makes me ask. But it's so quiet all around me. I hear nothing but my own voice. It's in danger of going hoarse. I don't say that something can come of nothing, but from little a great deal can develop. I don't believe you can know whether there's something there or nothing. So you may as well give me your *sincere* opinion. I don't want to know what I am, I want to know what you think of me. Please write to me about it. Various things are driving me a little crazy.

Yours,
Bert Brecht.

30 December 1917

18 To Caspar Neher

Early February 1918
Augsburg

Dear Cas,

Many thanks for your letter. I didn't mean to offend you with my remarks about the profession of drawing teacher, 'which undoubtedly presents certain advantages'. I've just pinned your *Walker*, *Life*, and the enormous frieze with the golden arc in yellow and blue on the walls of my room. I'd be very grateful if you'd also send me some coloured pictures, so you don't get out of practice. Couldn't you put some colour into your wonderful soul portrait of my paltriness as a tramp with endless knees in a flowery meadow? That would be wonderful, because I don't want to hang the pencil sketch, it might fade. I'm afraid this request means a lot to me.

Do all you can to wangle some leave. I'm always home these days. In the morning I write songs for the guitar, and have no one to sing them to in the afternoon. Paul Bittersweet is wonderful of course. The ice is no good by now. I'll have to start eating ice again. Unfortunately little Rosmarie (the boomerang, I've been calling her lately) said in the ice-cream shop (I must warn you against getting in a family way): In sexual matters I wouldn't be too particular. It's awful that children develop into people, but alas it's even worse that children develop out of people. I used to think her feverish little face was a symptom of consumption. Now I know that quite on the contrary it conceals a much more dangerous reproductive urge. Too bad I'm so crude.

Though your writing is not as legible as it used to be, it does look as though you weren't getting on very well. Please pull yourself together. You must bear in mind that most soldiers get killed while running away. Maybe you think it's easy for me to talk. I don't know your life. But I know the value of your life. Listen to me. I've thought about it at length. It's out of the question that the war will hurt your art. You are now planting trees that you'll harvest in twenty years. The most important part of an artist is the human being. Even if you sometimes have or think you have an empty stretch now (your letters indicate the contrary), you mustn't forget that at home you'll find a different atmosphere. Sometimes – even without the war – I'm so sober that I regard art as a hoax. But when that happens I'm not happy.

When you come home, we'll work hard together. For that you'll certainly come. You can become a drawing teacher after all. I'll let you if you're good.

Yours, Bert Brecht

Do you want a photo of Paul?
Müller sends regards, he's a recruit in Depot 2.
Pfanzelt sends regards.
My mother sends special regards.

19 To Caspar Neher

Dear Cas,

Many thanks for your letter. Congratulations. I'm on holiday, but I'm happy enough even so. Writing biblical stories. Starting with 'Susanna'. You must do a watercolour. In addition, I'm doing songs for the guitar, characterised by great emotional depth and unwholesome crudeness. When are you coming home?

Now Bittersweet loves me. That's my name for Paul. She's wonderfully soft and spring-like, shy and dangerous. Day after day, I lead myself into temptation to deliver myself from evil. But I don't want to do what I want to do? But what if *she* does? Write to me, Saint Cas, what will happen then? If someone is better than me, on him will I cast the first stone.

Your handwriting is terrible. Couldn't you dictate your immortal thoughts to one of your Hanesses [?]? I'll send you a picture of Bittersweet later.

Yours, Bert Brecht

Augsburg, Zwinger, 24 February 1918

20 To Caspar Neher

Dear Cas,

You don't seem to have got my last letter. So I'm writing you another. Though I don't know much. I'm on holiday, living all alone in my Zwinger surrounded by your paintings, making up grotesque songs to the guitar. I often meet Bittersweet (Paul) and we go for a stroll in the evening on the grey heath to the right of the Lech. The atmosphere is sensual. But now that I've heard what certain people have to say, I'm more or less immune. Once in a while Geyer comes over to play Haydn. I'm beginning to like him better, though. Strange to say, George misses you very much. He often speaks of you. – The ice fairy, the big bony beast with the red hands in the ice-cream shop, the frozen-blue consumptive male nude with the hungry little face, also asks about you. I always say you'll be here soon.

I want to write a play about François Villon, a fifteenth-century murderer, highwayman and writer of ballades in Brittany. When you come home, you must also take an interest in the *dance*. Didn't Michelangelo arrange masked processions and ballets? Write again, just a few lines if you're very busy.

All the best,
Bert Brecht

[Augsburg] Zwinger, March 1918

21 To Caspar Neher

Augsburg, Zwinger, mid-March 1918

Dear Cas,

This is my *third* letter. Here the spring is coming in. TB wind and blue sky. Dry ground, quite all right to sit down. You can even lie down ... On Saturday night Ludwig Prestel and I strolled along the Lech. Since we'd taken the guitar we stopped by the weir and I sang a few of Frank Wedekind's songs. The next morning I read that he had died. On Tuesday I went to his funeral. I even saw him in his coffin. One of the biggest surprises I've ever had: around the mouth he looked like a little boy. Gone were the self-satisfied, precious line of the lips, the surfeited, cynical look. At first, he seemed to be smiling; but then one saw that he had 'kicked the habit' of smiling. – Unwilling to lead the half life of a cripple, he had submitted to an operation that wasn't strictly necessary. Six weeks ago, I heard him singing to the lute at a bar where we members of Kutscher's seminar had met to celebrate the end of term. He looked as if he couldn't possibly die. He was a personality like Socrates or Tolstoy.

Can't you wangle some leave?

Geyer comes here from time to time. If his fingers are as light and nimble in his surgery as in playing Haydn, I'll let him cut everything out of me that I can manage without. A pure pleasure, I'm sure.

Someone took my death mask. It was most unpleasant, you think you're going to suffocate.

I've composed some guitar songs for you. When are you coming home? I'm being called up in May. – Are you drawing? Are you growing? Are you awake?[1] You mustn't fall asleep. Why have you stopped writing? Haven't you got my letters? But even if you haven't you should write. I could be ill, after all. Or my letter might have gone astray. Bez[old], Müller and all the others are falling away like leaves. Pfanzelt's clothes grow with his body. He is wonderfully resigned. At night under the still-bare tree cascades we joke about God and the anarchists. He had heart trouble and may not live very long. His brothers and his father died young. Yet I've never seen him sad. – I mean to send you some photos, but not until I know you're getting my letters.

I gave Bittersweet a little ring. She trembled and kissed me. We didn't say anything. I'm filled with desire to gallop to Asia. I wish I could see you now. I'm almost entirely well. Sometimes at night I'm afraid for you. We mustn't let anyone talk us into believing that art is a hoax. *Life* is a hoax. Art is simpler. More orderly. More meaningful. Stronger. There will be another Renaissance. When we're dead, that is. But then there won't be anything new about it. There is so much ahead of us. To sail on a ship, morning, noon and night. Under burning white tropical canvas tents. And at night in a crow's nest under Orion. On skins in Tibet. At the Moulin Rouge in Paris. In the morgue. In Valhalla. But you must come home. For good!

                              Yours, Bert Brecht

22 To Caspar Neher

My dear Cas,

I wish I knew where the pastel (?) *The Kiss*, with the magnificent tree is. And how I can borrow it. I've decided to take various things to the Kunstverein after all, mostly caricatures. But first I'll consult the critics I know on the Augsburg newspapers. What would *you* like me to enter? Let me know. Proviso: it must be something the public will like. (Because of your father.) If I can possibly manage it, I will write the most conspicuous review in the *Neueste Nachrichten*. But don't get your hopes up. It just *may* be possible. – Hardly anything going on here. Bittersweet is crushing me. Her holiday was wonderful and very strenuous. At present only distance can preserve our love. Did you get the little picture of Rosmarie? Please let me know.

---

[1]The connection between growing and waking is that in German the words look alike except for an umlaut: *wächst, wachst*.

Yours,
Bert Brecht

Augsb[urg] 10 April 1918

23 To Caspar Neher

Dear Cas,

Many thanks for letter and sketches. Incidentally, I've already written to you, twice. Once with a photo of little Rosmarie. Didn't you get it? Please let me know if you did. Now I'm sitting in my kennel with Geyer, because I went for a walk with Bittersweet and missed the Munich train. The Plärrer is magnificent. How are you? The Plärrer is the most beautiful thing in the world.

> A child that I saw there
> Has hair of shining gold
> And eyes that become her
> A wonder to behold

It's getting strangely springlike. Bittersweet may be home alone over Whitsun. Write me something on the subject.

Farewell to you (for whose sake I sometimes believe in God, so as to be able to pray, seriously).

Yours, Bert Brecht

[Augsburg] 13 April 1918

[handwritten regards from Georg Geyer]

24 To Caspar Neher

Dear Cas,

Many thanks for the Easter greetings. How was Easter? Here we had good weather for Easter.

I'm burgeoning. But luckily for me I miss you. You could paint Bittersweet. Against a pale-blue sky, you know. I'm not doing much. Either Bittersweet is here. Or she's not here. Then I'm waiting for her. Gondola ride on the pond with Chinese lanterns. I wonder if this thing will ever ebb away. Pray, Kaspar Rudolf. Or I'll fall apart. Doesn't Rosa Maria look sweet in the photos? But she's out for seduction like a bitch on heat. She lay in my arms like gelatin (liquid); she flowed into the creases. Too bad I didn't take her before I thought of it. Would *you* have done? On a bench in the park? 'I love you so! Up skirts! Get fucking!' Ugh!

My brother has been assigned to the infantry. That raises him above me. He's swimming in bliss. Ludwig Prestel to the artillery. Not swimming. Paddling like a dog at the most.

I'm being called up in the merry month of May. But my heart is bad. I run too much. I think too much. I would wreck our offensive.

Your old Bert Brecht

George sends regards

A[ugsburg], April 1918

25 To Caspar Neher

My dear Cas,

Letter received. Thanks. I admire your 'humour in the hour of death'. Something could have been done here in the Plärrer, but I made a mess of it. The girl maligned me. To get even I wrote a poem. The evening paper is paying five marks for it. Just five marks. I'll see the little thing again at the Auer Dult. The dancer Leistikow is here. I was swimming in bliss. I wrote a review, but the *Neueste* [*Nachrichten*] wouldn't print it, because my imagination 'had played tricks on me'. It had dancing trees and fountains in it. That won't do. Our girls have too many limbs, that's why they're so clumsy. Some have graceful legs, Leistikow has no legs at all – only a body. A divine bum – I wrote a poem to her and sent it to her. (But nothing happened in it.) I compared her with a lot of things. End:

> Out of night wind and morning light
> God made you, the old sot.
> If you can prove that I'm not right
> Then I'm an idi-alist.

These are heavenly days (call-up on May 1st). At night we sing songs by Goethe, Wedekind and Brecht. Everybody loves us. And I love everybody – except Bittersweet. I'm sick of her. Rosi [Rosmarie] hasn't been in her status quo ante for a long time. Superior disjecit (a salesman with lecherous fingers). I shall pray that you will not moulder away.

And you won't. I need you. I'm glad you've finally come to the conclusion that you must come back. I'd sooner have victors than victory. There are lots of things you must do when you're here. If you're a bit tired I'll whip you, you will never have sung more sweetly, every day you'll let go with a swan song, you will mess up enormous areas of canvas and knead your visions into mountains. You will conquer the world and listen to my teaching, and you will die old and surfeited with life like Job who was admired by 100 camels. And then, together, we shall reform hell and make something of it. Now you know your prospects and have an aim in life. On top of that you are, I hope, in good health and (in the higher sense) happy. When in distress one must look round for allies. Are your lungs all right? Your head? Your hand? Is there a tree where you are? Do you see clouds? Do you recognize faces? Do you want anything? Have you a great friend? Are you necessary? See? Smooth out your tunic, Caspar.

> As ever,
> Bert Brecht

At Wedekind's funeral:

> Baffled, they stood there in top hats
> Like crows around a vulture's feast
> With sweat and tears they tried their best
> But couldn't lay that old wizard to rest.

> Augsburg, end of April 1918

26 To Hans Otto Münsterer

Dear Herr Münsterer,
Many thanks for your kind visit; I'm sorry not to have been home. I'd be very glad to see you again down here. Would you have time on Thursday by chance? My *Baal* comedy is half finished. Have you done anything new? I wish you would write to me here in Munich. Have you any theatrical plans?

> With regards,
> Yours, Bert Brecht

> [Munich] May 1918

27 To Hans Otto Münsterer

Dear Herr Münsterer,

I very much regret not having heard from you again. What are you doing? How is your *Faust* coming along? I wish you would write to me. People like you and me get their best ideas while writing. – There's quite a lot going on in Munich at the moment. The theatres are doing guest performances. On Monday I'm seeing a private performance of Wedekind's *Samson* that has been suppressed by the SPCA. I now have a (good?) title for *Baal*: Baal eats! Baal dances!! Baal is transfigured!!!

What do you think of it? Have you a better one? Some idea about *Baal*? *You should write to me.*

Bert Brecht

[Munich] Kaulbachstrasse 63 A/II c/o Dr Krautloher
[5 May 1918]

28 To Caspar Neher

A[ugsburg], Zwinger, 11 May 1918

Dear Cas,

Many thanks for letters and sketches.

I've been waiting day after day for your answer whether it's better to be an artilleryman or a headquarters medic. My only consolation, since my second hope, namely that I'll get some leave, is highly unlikely, is that I'll at least, so it seems, be sent to the front. Please write and tell me what kind of life the medics have there. Write immediately, it's high time.

There's nothing doing here except the spring. Everything is fine. Munich is amusing. The people there are horrible. I miss you badly. Your letter before last was absolutely incomprehensible, even where it was legible. What are you driving at with your irony? I don't know what you mean with this irony. It's not my fault if I'm not badly off. In that respect there will soon be a change for the better no doubt. Now I often have eight hours of class a day and not a single friend. When I get to Augsburg, my whole room is full of it, and Bittersweet and I haven't a corner where we can discuss certain things in the dark. So at night we light Chinese lanterns and go through the city to the beautiful girls and make music and howl with the wolves. This is because I am *without* a bellyache at the moment and you must purge your memory of all trace of pain.

I imagine you're having a bad time. You should write to me about it. I fervently hope you're keeping a diary. It would be shameful not to. You must write down the important things. Philosophy, people, marches, the dead, guns. When a notebook is full, please send it to me. To keep it from falling apart, use as thin ones as possible. You can seal them, then I'll never open them – until your death. Should I send you a notebook? Two? You have a wonderful chance to do something big and powerful just by writing things down. Remember that Lionardo [sic], whom I dearly love, was also a prolific writer. He never did anything without reason.

Some letters from me must be on their way. I wish you the best possible Whitsun. Won't you ever be looking at my face again? It's worth while.

As ever, Bert Brecht

The photos will get there now that I know you receive them. I didn't know you had the ones of Rosa M[aria]. If you can get your picture taken at the front, please do. You, too, have a beautiful face.

Please write to me at once about my military career.

Artillery or medical corps?

Come to think of it, I'd rather collect feet etc. than lose them.

B

29 To Caspar Neher

Augsburg, 17 May 1918

Dear Cas,

Your last letters to Geyer and me paint an alarming picture of a broken man. Apart from the fact that the mess is illegible – you seem to have arrived at a threshold. Have you summoned up your whole stock of humour and thrown it into the breach? Your concern for your skin is probably justified and worthy of respect, but your worries about your art are perfect nonsense. Forgive me. Not only does a man who is always sitting in the dark not see the sun, but with the help of a philosophical system he can also lose his sense of humour to such a degree that he begins in all seriousness to doubt the existence of the sun. You probably can't even imagine any more what it's like when you're here with me. Then, dear Cas, the sun will warm you through and through. Remember, when you're having a bad time, that life (elsewhere, of course) is beautiful, wonderfully beautiful and decorated with adventures, full of colour and illusion, with all the room in the world for grandiose gestures etc. But really, you'll make it if you grit your teeth and keep your chin up. Don't fall by the wayside, that's all. I have enormous respect for what you've accomplished up to now and I thoroughly envy you your past. You've undoubtedly learnt more than I. *Your* afflictions at least spring from substantial causes, for which you are not responsible. The obstacles in your path are purely external and you will surmount them. So show your teeth and think of the beauties of the world. Certain of my letters can't have reached you yet; please keep a diary (your notebooks should be as thin as possible) and let off steam. And write me something realistic now and then. What you're doing and what's going on. Your drawings are excellent, and no one I've shown them to thinks your powers have diminished. They all see that you're making great strides even under the present repugnant conditions. Don't worry. You're just having to pay in advance. You'll get in.

> Now pay attention. Nicknames for me:
> Lup (Wolf)
> Chancre (cancer; pronounced Tschanzer)
> What do you think?
> I've been dancing with Bittersweet.
> Maypoles are in bloom. The grass smells.
> The wind is rolling through the leaves of my chestnut trees.
> Bittersweet . . .

> Bert Brecht

[A postscript by Otto Bezold follows]

30 To Caspar Neher

Dear Cas,

Your letter is amazing. I like the seriousness you show in it. Let me throw off my mask; I'm not a pessimist. Pessimism is too much of a strain on for me. I'm doing all right and I'm not a poseur. My bowels are functioning perfectly. They were in bad shape long enough. I have no desire to investigate your pessimism. Just entrench yourself behind your haughty pessimism Ltd. One of these days someone will find you there all squashed and drag you out. It seems to me that a man who curses his mother, the sun and the world because he had a bellyache or a man who takes a dark view of beds because he has had to lie in one for a long time has no right to infer from his misfortunes that someone whom God has favoured with a holiday must be shallow. The analogy is pretty tortuous. But it applies. I take what is available and if I'm pleased with it, I'm not necessarily pleased with myself. You've written a disgustingly rude letter. I'm not an optimist. I don't know if you'll ever come home. I don't give a hoot for your childlike harmony (if you want to know, you big pessimist). I'm glad I can drop the pretence. Forgive me for having thought it necessary. That's the one thing I must ask you not to do, O great Rudolf Neher! When I write my letters I'm not in the mortal danger you are in when you read them. If you stick to your 'new' attitude – you can base it on this letter – I shall have prayers said for you and stop playing the clown in the circus I have directed up until now. You don't seem to be able to stand tickling any more. Are you sick of *grinning*? What else are you sick of? I *don't* thank you for your advice about my military affairs, which you don't give a damn about. Anyway, I'm not going to throw myself into some buggy and go twittering around in the blue sky with sound feet – a vehicle rolling into your sacrosanct harmony. Your advising me to let myself be guided by the kind of uniform that little girls like best looks to me like your last spark of humour. That, among friends, is a joke that hurts.

Now, I believe, we have restored a wholesome foundation of seriousness and truth between us. So just go paddling on calmly and boozily in your beloved harmony, praise the Lord, be thorough in your pessimism, dance round the scalps of your friends, and despise me amply. I won't interfere with your shameless megalomania. The devil take you, dear Cas. How old are you?

As ever, Bert Brecht

Mr Devil[1] can leave his drawings here.
[Probably May 1918]

---

[1]In the original an arrow stands for 'Devil'.

31 To Paula Banholzer

Dear girl,

I'll have to make it fast. As quickly as possible I'll write down the thoughts that come to my mind during a lecture on land reform. Yesterday was a very long day. It went on from five in the morning till twelve at night. Motored here with Ehrenberg, who's a bastard, but I'll introduce him to you soon. Then plunged into a cataract of lectures on marriage, contracts, infant mortality, tuberculosis, music, chemistry, etc., etc. For lunch potato dumplings. In the evening theatre. Today again four hours of classes, with reading room, ticket buying, essay writing in between. What are you doing? You are the bright star above the waterfall I am standing under. You are the eternally sunlit top of the tree, whose eel-smooth trunk I am climbing through darkness etc. There are more such metaphors . . . If you ask me, that good Werrenreth girl is a poor thing and without a chance of happiness. But her husband is probably an even poorer thing; he has every chance of *un*happiness. Last night, incidentally, sitting on my window sill, I added something to a few scenes in a play. From which you may gather some day that I love you very much. What else can you expect me to write here? There's so much going on. I've transferred to medicine, a terrible run-around. Now it's midday. This afternoon three hours of classes, then potato dumplings and theatre. Four hours of *Palestrina* (standing). But all this is wonderful. There's a freshness about it. Everything goes swimmingly. Hoopla, in disregard of all sorts of petty comforts. In the evening I'm dog-tired but cheerful all the same, and before I fall asleep you come to me with a rudimentary halo around your prim little head and plant a tender motherly kiss on my overheated brow. Then I fall asleep happy.

I kiss you vigorously, rumple (in spirit) your mop of hair, and squint towards the door – the postman is coming.

Yours, B

I may not get there until about 7.30 p.m. (like your sister the other day). Then I'll go straight down Kreuzstrasse and hope to see or be told where to go. But probably I'll arrive at midday.

[Munich, May 1918]

32 To Caspar Neher

Dear Cas,

Thank you for your last letter and the good, strong diary pages. And

I beg forgiveness for *my* last letter, which I wrote in anger. You're a periodic griper; now and then you stamp on a fellow's belly when it's full, then observe the psychology of his facial muscles. I realise now that my last letters were bad, because I tried to amuse you by writing feature articles. When a child I had to walk through a dense black forest, I whistled as loudly and cheerfully as I could – but only because I was afraid. And the less I believed in your idea of harmony the more I clung to it. It's alien to my nature. It takes all the playfulness and cruelty out of life and leads us firmly by the hand. I want to be able to die when I feel like it – even at the risk of having to do it some day when I don't feel like it – I'm well and trying my best to be happy. It's not so simple. Even so, I've attained a certain level. I'm working on a comedy: 'Baal eats! Baal dances!! Baal is transfigured!!!' There's a bandit in it, a monstrous hedonist, a dumpling, a May-crazed man with immortal bowels!

As I write, the mail brings your pictures. They are magnificent. The colour is really breathtaking. Do you paint with your elbows? There's summer in these things, force and discipline. Did you know that Hodler is dead? There's another who managed in his own way to get the better of life. Yet the one thing that counts is what kind of life you have, whether it's naked, severe and terrible enough. It's more important than ever that you should get some leave. There's so much in the air. (Mostly English steel as far as you're concerned, I suppose?) We swim in the Lech, in the whirlpools. Rushing down on your back (I've probably written you this before; it's a feeling of infinity) you see the naked sky, open, hungry, eternally silent, in the daytime with metallic rays, in the evening they're violet. And then you can climb the trees in the Wolfzahn-au and swing *naked* in the green tree tops that swing in the noonday wind. Then the wind cuts through you; it's indescribable. Otherwise there's not much passion here. I'm studying medicine. The theatres are playing rubbish. They're waiting . . .

Thanks again for the letter and pictures.

And I beg forgiveness.
I'm a periodic griper.

Yours, Bert Br.

Augsburg, Corpus Christi, May 1918

Under separate cover I'm sending you a new notebook. It's a thin one, that way it will soon be full, then we can move it somewhere for 'safe keeping'. I couldn't get hold of better paper. It would be a good idea to write legibly and date all your entries.

33 To Caspar Neher

Dear Cas,

Thanks for your letter. I swallow your irony with pleasure as Pyrrhus swallowed the Attic poison. The boredom here is sickening. Pessimism often clogs me like coal dust, but on the whole I'm bearing up. I've switched to medicine, but that's of no interest. The only thing that really disgusts me is the new art. This Expressionism is horrible. All feeling for the beautifully rounded or splendidly crude human body languishes like the hope of peace. The intellect crushes vitality all along the line. Mystical, clever, consumptive, ecstatic pretentiousness runs rampant, and it all stinks of garlic. I shall be banished from the heaven of these noble, intellectual idealists, from the Strindhills and Wedebabies, and then I'll have to write books about your art. All right, I'll stand on my own feet and spit, I'm sick of the new. I'm starting to work with very old material that's been tested a thousand times over, and I'm doing what I want even if what I want is bad. I'm a materialist and a lout and a proletarian and a conservative anarchist, and I don't write for the press but for myself and you and the Japanese. You should know that you have to be better than your best work – or it won't be good. A man who just wants something new will come to the idiotic conclusion that railways are progress and the piano the cause of Beethoven's sonatas. The worst of it is the symbolism. Draw batteries moving up to the front, [?] in the wind, clouds wanting to move on and soldiers *not* wanting to move on; things with as much motion as possible in them. Use pencil or charcoal. Do a bang-up job, draw ten batteries and not just one. You've got to be hungry. Disgust too, is hunger, only in reverse. Draw plenty of life, especially horses, with gusto and true. No sleight-of-hand. Draw a field gun as if it were a girl called Bittersweet, talk with the gun about its mistakes and that kind of thing, love it and make discoveries with its help. Otherwise you'll never be able to draw a girl. Am I talking nonsense? Write something.

Yours, Bert Brecht

Have you received the notebook? Do you want anything else? Write and tell me.

Munich, 18 June
Kaulbachstrasse 63a/2

34 To Caspar Neher

Dear Cas,

The most tremendous things are happening.

1) My comedy:

> *Baal eats! Baal dances!! Baal is transfigured!!!*
> *What does Baal do?*   *24 scenes*

is finished and typed – an imposing tome. I hope to get somewhere with it. Of course I can send it to you only if you'll absolutely promise to return it.

2) The Bittersweet affair is nearing some kind of catharsis, which ought to be over by the time you read this. It's churning me up pretty deeply. Now she seems to want 'it'. May God and I help her!

I've seldom missed you *so much*. Last summer I had a bellyache and never felt quite right. Now I can see how admirable your drawings are. The expression on the whore's face is marvellous. More knowledge in it than in thick volumes of psychology. The rest is a triumph too. Take care of your fingers. First rate, I believe.

Your grateful
Bert Brecht

Mid-June 1918
Munich, Kaulbachstrasse 63a/2

35 To Caspar Neher

Dear Cas,

I take the opportunity to write you a harsh letter. Sit down.

Hohenester is furious. Because he hasn't had any leave since Christmas. You haven't had any for a year. Are you furious? Do you know what? You are (I think) an *idiot*. But that wouldn't matter much. If it just weren't so *criminal* in your case. You have only yourself to blame for anything that happens to you in the time that you could be spending here. When *you* get here, *I*'ll have been called up long since. 15 August is the latest possible date. If I haven't been called up, we won't be much good to each other because in the army I'll only be half a man. Why aren't you doing everything in your power to get away? You are *not* doing everything in your power. Dammit. You *must*. Understand? You won't be able to hold out till then. (Neither will I). Please for once don't just let things ride. Get away!!!! Make up your mind. Stop giving in. Just manage to be here next week. It can be done. I've asked everywhere. It must be done. A year in the field is too much. Make a stink. Good God, man. Don't let them push you around. I won't have it. I hope you'll finally give me an explanation. I refuse to wait any longer. Do you hear? I *refuse*. Here everything is glorious: beautiful, hot, blue sun! Sky! By night the smell of jasmine. The Great Bear swinging in the top of the lime tree. Then swimming in the Lech. Wolfzahn! Woods! Forest path! My room at night! Don't you want to sit on my sofa? I'll tune my guitar. The ice-cream shop! Chinese lanterns! Bittersweet! (She's all mine now. Cas, what shall I do if 'it' has consequences? Christ! Write to me about it! Talk to me about it! Come home!) And then there's art: My comedy! Songs! Stories! I need title pages! And I need you! What's the matter with you? Take the obstacles by storm. *With* your shield or *without* it. But come! Do you remember what a café looks like, or George Pfanzelt? The city park at night with music? Are we, or are we not the king of Spain? I'll choke you! (If only you were here to let me.) I'm sick of it all!

So what's it to be? See you *next* week! Next week! The very next!
Yours, Bert Brecht

Are you sitting in the train? Are you riding through yellow fields to the city of Augsburg? I want you to see the Ulm railway station! And the trees on Bahnhofstrasse here! – And me!

Isn't all that enough? Then to hell with you! Do you hear? Do you hearrr?

Early July, 1918, Munich

36 To Casper Neher

Thank you for the two pictures, *Dancer* and *Temptation*. I think they show *genius*. Where did you get the touch? It's wonderful, the way those muscles live. Geyer and I were in the Glaspalast today and left with the conviction that you can compete with *anyone* there. Some of those people have a certain ability. But they don't *amount* to anything. It's all artificial, kitschy, stupid, humourless and without seriousness. If only you could *come*! You're needed here. There's been a stupid business with little Bittersweet. It's not quite over yet. I'm very fond of her. We were in the mountains by the Starnberger See together, whole days and nights. One night a storm blew up on the lake, and I carried her to the window that looked out over the lake, because she was terribly tired. For three days she was a duchess, and then came wretched fear, because she didn't get her period. It still hasn't come, it's been three days now, I'm waiting for her to wire, I hope you're not grinning as you read this. I won't let God mess up the miraculous thing we had to steal from him. But it's horribly boring here when I'm waiting for telegrams and the sun is shining to no purpose and someone is playing the piano next door, and someone upstairs will soon start practising the violin. I hope you're praying for me, because I really wouldn't know how to cope with a baby ... The scandal wouldn't help, for one thing because it would go on too long and I might have to go to India with you. As you know. But I'm just talking to make the time pass till the telegram comes. I'm very much afraid that you're laughing, but I'm even more afraid that *I won't* be able to laugh. Naturally I took no precautions, none at all, it would have spoilt our pleasure, it would have been unaesthetic, and anyway, I couldn't have. I'm not a tarock player, I can't hold back my trumps. You know. Damn it to hell, why the swearwords? You know, I'm only afraid for Bittersweet. I made her very brave, I didn't tell her any lies, I didn't ever hide anything from her, and she didn't say one word of reproach. Though she didn't want 'it' and put up quite a struggle. But it was so beautiful. There was nothing mean about it and I loved her a lot more afterwards than before. And I carried her to the window to see the storm and I stretched out her hand for her to feel what a storm is like. She has a face like a small child's when she's scared or pleased. And she has that face (a bit too) often now. When are you coming? What nights we're having! Deep blue and full of music! The moon like a greenish cucumber! The willows by the Lech like grey dancers too old to dance, and the Great Bear swinging comfortably in the chestnut trees in the garden. I can't wait for you to get here.

> Yours gratefully
> Bert Brecht

> Munich, 22 July 1918

If you're coming and know it well in advance, write and tell me. It will make my pleasure last long. But if you find out only a short time in advance, surprise me. Then I won't have to wait so long.

37 To Paula Banholzer

Ziesler Waldhaus
10 August 1918

My dearest girl,

I'm writing today because after tomorrow I won't get much chance to. Nearly 12 (twelve) hours in the train. A short hike. Now I'm alone with Fritz in a wooden shack in the middle of the woods. I'm writing on a bench. Fritz is dancing around some Maggi soup and tea. Gloomy clouds overhead. Maybe a storm tonight. Then you'll be sleeping peacefully in the light of the almost full moon, oh how touching! And I'll be in the midst of raging storms, oh how terrifying! The trees keep roaring around us. If only you were here, dear girl. Our room, all wood, is very crude. Two snow-white beds. A wobbly table. In the evening we play the mouth organ. And before going to bed I tell the story it took me twelve hours to dream up, about a man who fell out of an express train and ran behind it shouting: 'I'm so sorry, I fell out.' Fritz complains because it doesn't make sense. And then the candle burns a while, while we're turning in. Once the candle's gone out, we lie for ten minutes in the room, which is bathed in a blue twilight, and I think of you. – Tomorrow we're going into the woods bright and early. – 10 p.m.

6 a.m.

That was written in the evening. The night was cold. We had very thin blankets. Water and trees roared all night. And brother wind came creeping over our beds. Give Hartmann my best regards. Will I see him in Munich at the 'Franziska'? I hope he stays that long.

4 p.m.

Walked through the woods this morning. There are big fallen trees lying flat with their roots all full of earth. Over them moss and ferns. Water trickling in between. Afternoons we lie for three hours in the sun, which comes pouring through a wide gap in the foliage. For lunch I'm cooking – Fritz has gone out – old Fritz's favourite dish, smoked pork and cabbage, all by myself. A work of art.

I'll stop now. We're going to walk all night, the whole time in woods. Maybe the stars will be out. And now I kiss you.

> Yours,
> Bert Brecht

Give my friend Oskar my regards if you see him. Also Fräulein Wiktor. You're the first human being to hear from me. I won't write to my parents until tomorrow. Isn't that marvellous? Now and then I feel like kissing you immensely, and when I think of your trouble I want to cry. But it can't be done in the sun and wind, on a half-empty stomach.

> 4.30 Sunday morning
> *High up* on the Arber [12 August]

Dearest girl,

Now the sun is rising.

We hiked all night. Slept two hours in the hay, in a windy hut. Then through woods the whole time. Our rucksacks rammed us into the ground. And our sticks carried on when our feet wanted to stop. Now it's wonderful. A strong wind blowing over the summit. Grey wooded hills down below. The moon going down like an orange-yellow lamp shaded in silk.

Yesterday I was almost ill. The old trouble again. It was bad. Not a village within seven hours. We lay in the woods and let the raspberries hang down into our mouths. Now the trouble is over and I'm laughing again. What are you doing? Are you dreaming of me? I'm the wandering Jew.

Yesterday I played the guitar in a pub in the woods. In return they gave us milk and butter, which are *very* rare here. I sang perfectly in tune, much better than at home.

Of course I'll be glad to get back. Last night I started writing a ballad, in which the fires of passion flare up; it's so romantic you wouldn't understand it.

Now the sky is turning red. Yes, now the heavens are aflame.

All the same, I'd gladly give you a kiss, my fresh little peach blossom. But the sun is lovely too, when it's rising.

This letter is very romantic. On the other hand, the sun is just rising over the highest mountain in the German Mittelgebirge. Not much point in complaining that no matter how divinely happy one is, one can still confuse two things: a hot kiss and a hot cup of coffee?!

Now the mountains are darkening and the wind is freezing my back. My fingers are stiff. I keep thinking of the look of astonishment my mawkishness will put on your face and love you more and more.

Now the moon is down and dismissed. All night it shone so snootily between the black tree trunks. The stones I'm sitting on are getting colder and colder, and your face is becoming dearer and dearer in my memory.

Now the sun is rising. Already I love you more than words can tell. The wind is making music and cold. The pencil is falling from my hand and my eyes are closing. But now the sun is rising.

Today we may go as far as the Bohemian Forest. Possibly I'll come home tomorrow. As I choose. The sun and wind are wonderful. There's nothing more glorious on earth. But a warm meal after so much cold food will also be very very beautiful. And one has no right to be tired in the sun and wind. But I am. Now the sun is up.

Many many kisses.

Your Bert Brecht

Don't forget the notebook

38 To Caspar Neher

Beloved!

Art thou angry, blessed one? Can I do anything about the Armed Forces Postal Service? This country is a pigsty without a Circe. My existence is disorganised. I'm lazy and tired and bored. I lie on the bed the whole time thinking of Canada and a roaring blue sky. Aren't you ever coming home? Bittersweet is away and it doesn't matter and I can't work and the sky is a hole I can't spit into, and you aren't saying anything, and German literature is trash, and I'm trash too, and always having to get dressed in the morning and the waiting, and the lousy feeling that nothing matters and that nothing can happen to me except precisely that nothing more can happen to me . . . It's enough to make the Devil weep. Where are you staggering around? Accursed Devil! Heavenly Devil! (God puts up with everything. He's in a bad way.)

And so is Bert Brecht

Augsburg, 26 August 1918 [Postmark]

39 To Hans Otto Münsterer

Dear Herr Münsterer,

Many thanks for your letter. Here we've just had the Plärrer! I've worn myself out on the swingboats. How can anyone work much when the summer is so damn beautiful? What are you doing? I'm eating ice cream, playing the guitar, awaiting my death sentence, and swinging at the Plärrer. And working now and then on a new play for the theatre of the future, entitled

'The Fat Man on the Swingboat'.

Please write to me about Corpse-Kutscher. He wrote me something about *Baal*. He's the shallowest individual I've ever run into.

> Regards,
> Bert Brecht

> Augsburg, August 1918

41 To Jacob Geis

Dear and esteemed Herr Geis,

Many thanks for your kind letter. I also thank you very much for your efforts. I'm sorry I can't do so by word of mouth. I've had a fall off a horse and am half lame at the moment. That gives me time, in between cursing and groaning, to rework *Baal*, I'm just sorry I've had to do so without your advice. But perhaps you will let me bother you with it all the same. At any rate, *Baal* has benefited a good deal, especially in structure, but also in detail, some scenes have been changed completely, others thrown out, a few added. Now at last it is playable. So it distresses me that Herr Steinrück should have the 'Ur-Baal', which is absolutely unplayable and can only put people off. He won't read the thing twice, that would be too much to expect. Next week I'll send you a new copy. Perhaps I'll be able to bring it myself. (The play is now pretty well purged of Verlaine and Johst. As for the latter, what's left is just the antithesis.) Might you still be able to wrest the 'Ur-Baal' away from Steinrück? I'd be grateful to you again, just as I shall always be grateful to you for giving it to him in the first place.

> Yours faithfully,
> Bert Brecht

> Augsburg, Bleichstrasse 2. 28 April 1919

42 To Caspar Neher

Dear Cas,

I was very much looking forward to you and Ma and the Chinese lanterns by night, but now I have to leave town. It's disgraceful but I am innocent. Your sister never phoned. Too bad. For my mouth was sweeter than honey with wisdom. But your sister, whom I have renamed Ma, who rides a grey elephant, lovely and pale and swathed in seven veils, doesn't see the beggar who sits in the dust and knows songs about the clear sky. She's as beautiful as the morning light on wide streets before the dust comes, and she rides like a young panther, but where is she riding to? Etc. I am looking forward to your Baals. Leave them here. I'm coming to Munich next week and will attend to them. Regards to Georg and to your sister, who didn't ring up and didn't worship the light, though it was right there, but persisted in sitting in darkness . . .

> Your dear
> Bert

> Augsburg, May 1919

43 To Hanns Johst

I feel greatly humiliated that you haven't written me anything about *Baal*. I sit in my dark room, it's raining, and suddenly it occurs to me that you're not saying anything and that I was expecting something or other. I can easily believe that you didn't like *Baal*, yet without despairing in it or you. Perhaps you've been put off by the fact that in places I used the same model as you in *Der Einsame* [The Lonely One], though in my play I haven't stressed it and if you like I can bite off the umbilical cord completely by throwing out those scenes (though a vestige is bound to remain, but *Peer Gynt* and various others would have that). But I'm sure it can't be that. So then I thought you may have taken my Düsseldorf review amiss, though I really treated those people with kid gloves. But it would be too bad if we quarrelled over someone like Boetticher, whose *Friedrich* I've read carefully; I'll say no more about him. I'll understand perfectly if you say *Baal* and everything else I'll ever write is rubbish, but if you don't say anything I'll think you must want me to feel offended. Please forgive this letter because it's raining.

> Yours,
> Bert Brecht

[December 1919-January 1920]

44 To Hanns Johst,

Dear Hanns Johst,

Thank you kindly for your letter, which gave me great pleasure. In the meantime, I've reworked my play and, for instance, thrown out all the scenes with the mother. This pretty well relegates the ghost of *Der Einsame* to the periphery. I'd be very glad to discuss dramaturgical matters with you and will visit you in Oberallmannshausen as soon as I can. I'll bring the whole mess (which I'm beginning to feel heartily sick of) with me.

I thank your wife for her regards.

Cordially yours,
Bert Brecht

Munich, Paul Heyse 9/4 (nine)
[January-February 1920]

45 To Hanns Johst

Dear Hanns Johst,

I am now in Berlin and I like it here (as I do almost everywhere). The ballyhoo seems to be worse here than anywhere else and to be taken more seriously. But now I must ask you to send me the two *Baal* MSS, which you still have, I hope. I have to make the most of my chances. You might mention the matter to your wife, in whom I have a great childlike confidence with regard to such matters and in general.

It's a pity I couldn't get out to see you before Berlin. If you like, I'll come when you're home again. Or will you be coming back by way of Augsburg? That would be splended.

You haven't forgotten Bi's business?

Warm regards to you and your wife.

Your devoted
Bert Brecht

Eislebener Strasse 13, Berlin W
c/o Frank Warschauer
Berlin, 21 February 1920

46 To Caspar Neher

Dear Cas,

First the pleasant part:

Feuchtwanger tells me on the phone that he has shown the drawings to Falckenberg and Pasetti, who like them *very much*. You can always be able to come learn something at the Kammerspiele and do sets for them as soon as you've mastered the technical end. When I get back to Munich, let's go and see Feuchtwanger, old boy.

And now the unpleasant part:

I have to go to Berlin on Saturday. The train starts at Munich. It's the 7.30 a.m. express. I must ask a great favour of you: take this train and get in early enough to find a seat. When you get to Augsburg put something on the seat and whistle for me. (You pay the express supplement at the unnumbered window – first window on the *left*, not the usual one on the right, where you'd have trouble.)

Dearest Cas, in case you can't make it on Saturday wire me at once or simply telephone (4083), but I'd be *very* grateful. (Otherwise I'll have to stand for twelve hours!) A good seat will rate a kiss.

Herewith emphatic greetings.

Stay fat and regulate your bowel movements.

Yours, Bert

Finish the *Baal* designs.

Could you get my umbrella and opera glasses from the [*Pension*] Trommer? I'll pick up the suit myself some time.

I may come to Munich on Thursday. So if possible ring me at the Pension at three in the afternoon.

Bert

[Augsburg, February 1920]

47 To Caspar Neher

Dear Cas,

Berlin is wonderful. Couldn't you steal 500 M somewhere and come? There's the Underground and Wegener, for instance. Everything is jam-packed with bad taste, but on what a scale! Man, can't you . . .

Of course I have a favour to ask.

In fact, two:

1) Could you go to Müller's (Production manager Engelmann) and ask him if *Baal* is being printed in *Munich*? If so, I'd like you to go there – I give you full powers – and see about the type face. But you can attend to that even if the printing press is somewhere else. Just say: Whom do you take Brecht for? If necessary, phone Feuchtwanger (51370). This means a lot to me.

2) Would you, friend of my heart, get Trommer's bill and send it to me. (It has the price of two night's lodgings upstairs for Bi; I'll have to erase that without Trommer finding out.) That would be wonderful of you.

And then please give my regards to Orge and Otto.

My head is full of new things. I'm going great guns now. We'll show the world.

Cas, I hug you.

Bert

Berlin W 30
c/o Frank Warschauer
Eislebenerstrasse 19

If you can lay hands on the MS at the printers', please change the last lines in the Night, Wind, Willows scenes (The drowned girl): 'We lie in the willows' (more or less) to 'the hazel bushes' (more or less) and in the title of the next scene 'willow' to 'hazel bush'.

(February 1920)

48 To Jacob Geis (Postcard)

29 February 1920

Dear Herr Geis,

The ballyhoo in Berlin is distinguished from all other ballyhoo by its shameless grandeur. The theatres are wonderful. With thrilling verve, they engender small kidney stones. I love Berlin, but with limited liability.

See you soon and best regards

Yours
Bert Brecht

Berlin W 50, Eislebenerstrasse 13
c/o Warschauer

56 To Hans Otto Münsterer

Dear Hans Otto,

Thank you for your letter. I have greatly sinned, but my heart is contrite, so you must forgive me. I wrote you a card saying I had written you a letter. But then I found the letter all ready to send and the card had vanished and they both lay there. A wind had passed over and the two bits of paper lay in the corner like two rotting eggs. I got out of there as fast as I could. But my enemy in me laughed as he did the last time we were in Munich together when we separated in Perusastrasse because Hedda wanted to go to the opera, and I let you go and felt sorry and ran away from her and after you, and then at the Starnberg Station I heard the train was an hour late and you hadn't a roof over your head. *That* hour, too, is lying in the corner. But now you must forgive me; I'll reform. I'm going to Munich next week and will probably see you then. I don't know yet where I'll be living, but Hedda Kuhn lives at Adalbert 42, care of Däumling. Thanks again, I press your hand.

Bert

Augsburg, early May 1920

57 To Hans Otto Münsterer

Dear Hans Otto,

I'm sitting quietly on my island, it's pleasant here, and here I'll stay until all the food is gone. Once in a while I shoot at birds that are trying to fly away from me, and eat them again, and once in a while I repaint the sky, perhaps flea-colour or embahuba-tree brown, and sometimes I play with Buja Bu, the billiard beast in the attic.

I'm looking forward to seeing you again.

Bert Brecht

Augsburg [probably summer] 1920

58 To Caspar Neher

Dear Cas,

At seven thirty I'll be going to the Steinicke Gallery (Adalbertstrasse-Frisch), where R. J. Becher is to read poems that are of interest.

My dear boy,

You can get in by showing your student card. Yours or Georg's, or will Georg be with you? It's sure to be interesting. Enjoyment of literature for 50 pfennigs or one mark.

> Greetings Bert

> [Munich, 7 July 1920]

59a To Marianne Zoff

Dear Marianne,

I've been working for four days and nights now. I'm writing a play, it's going easily, everything flows into it, but now I'm shattered. All this time I've been waiting for letters, but you have 'many friends' and 'little time', and I haven't had anything from you. The two lawsuits are coming up tomorrow, and I can't avoid them, though these last days have given me a fever and I've forgotten what they're all about. What is Recht doing? Have you written to him? I'm sitting here as on an island, it's all right when I'm working, but I never sleep and food repels me. What are you doing with your evenings?

My head is all inflamed, I feel as if I had gravel in my mouth. I'm getting deep into 'Jungle', I'm practically in tatters. And in addition I'm afraid of some kind of fever that will wipe out the whole thing.

> Why don't you write?

> [Augsburg, 19 September 1921]

60 To Paula Banholzer

My dear little nanny goat,

Thank you for your letter that took so terribly long in coming and for the photograph, in which you look so nice and stupid. I have all your pictures here – except the one at Otto's, in your kimono by the curtain, couldn't you send me that one for a while? I always see you, many times a day, when I open my file of letters. It's cold here, now it's raining besides, and I have to run around so much – rehearsals with Reinhardt, etc. I'll probably sign an exclusive contract with the Erich Reiss Verlag, but I have my choice between them and Kiepenheuer. This is a very important consequence of my trip to Berlin. And I'm making lots of contacts, everybody is reading my story in the *Merkur* and talking about it and they all want to help me. Often its the kind of rat race you would like, but I am really fed up. Take last Monday for instance (an especially full day, it's true): Until ten in the morning I worked on a film scene. Then I ran to the university, then to the Deutsches Theater for rehearsals. At three I grabbed something to eat standing up somewhere, then I met Klabund at a café, he's trying to wangle a contract with Reiss, we chewed the fat until six about publishing business, meanwhile stopping at three liqueur bars with a young fellow who had been paid an advance and treated us to liqueurs, then took the Underground to the Scala, where Matray and Katta Sterna were dancing, then drove with Warschauer, Matray and Katta Sterna to Warschauer's, stayed there for two hours, during which I 'supped' and drank wines, plural, then went with Matray to the Maenz Restaurant, where Granach introduced me to a whole crowd of theatre people, and then at two a.m. toddled home with a cigar. And all these people push each other, write about each other, envy, despise and ridicule each other!!! And the girls, the Lord have mercy on them. Wise-cracking, highly strung, dissipated geese, whorish and ill bred, and so stupid, so stupid! Not one real woman, one real person, oh, how I love you, Bi! Dear nanny goat, good nanny goat, I love you. You must write more often. What are you doing the whole time? You mustn't buy me anything for Christmas, it would have to be something of *yours*, but I *too* have no money, and you'll have to content yourself with very little this year, *next* year I'll be making money. Why do you always return the bit of money I send you? It's horrid of you, quite seriously horrid. You can use it for Frank, send him chocolate, or save it up, it's so little, but it's all I can manage now. And I can't understand why there's such a wall between us, it's horrid of you. After all, I come to you when I need money and take it from you when you have some, or don't you want to give it to me? I love you too much to scold you properly and I'd rather kiss you, but it's not right for you. I kiss you anyway, but I won't any more if you do it again. You're my little wife and you must 'obey' me, or I'll beat you, I will.

But now I kiss you, because you're a silly little nanny, whom I love too much.

Yours, Bert

I *must* have a letter the day after tomorrow. Must! Must! Must!

[Berlin, early December 1921]

61 To Casper Neher

Make it snappy, boy

First class
Work
desired!

Dear Cas,

I've been to see the Matisses, I'm going to the Cézannes. I'm doing a play, 'Pope Joan' for Tilla, I'm working on three different film treatments. I'm going to read 'Garga' to some theatre people (A-1) as soon as you've corrected it. I may sing in a cabaret. I've got matches that can be lit on the sole of your shoe!

Katta Sterna and Matray (dance team) have asked me (!) if I knew of a highly talented young painter. I didn't keep my knowledge to myself. I've been to see Gurlitt, I have to go again, but send something more I can show, something grotesque, decorative with costumes: there lie fame and dough, they dance at the Scala.

What you've written on the MS is excellent. Thank you. We are not from Göggingen. Please do a little more. Especially Scene 2, Shlink's office, it had a few Kaiserisms and Shlink is not visible enough (the shrinking, the mud, the sinister, pantherlike, mysterious quality). In general: the mimicry, the many metamorphoses of the characters, all the snakiness, the cold laughter, the coarseness, the cynicism (but no insolence!) Please make it as quick as possible, because I have a lot of good opportunities for reading here. You can keep *one* copy and make changes in it at your leisure (Doesn't it amuse you? Man, in that case it's work.), i.e., please, bring it first to Fräulein Roecker to have it mimeographed in the shop. Send me the other straight away.

Tell me, where does Lilli live?

Have you stopped doing portraits?

(You must learn sculpture, go to Port, don't put it off. It's terribly important. One must know how 1) to do many things, 2) to make money.)

I kiss you carefully.

Bertie v.d. Sch

If it's beneath you to enter all the corrections on the still uncorrected copy, then put your *new* corrections on the unprinted one, send me that one and give the one I corrected to Fräulein Roecker with your additions. But I'd rather you sent the corrected one with additions to me and worked over the uncorrected one afterwards and gave it to

Fräulein Roecker. Your corrections mean a hell of a lot to me, my boy, but you know that.

Kisses

B

[Berlin, December 1921]

62 To Caspar Neher

D C [Dear Caspar]

Do send me as soon *as possible* the first half. Keep two of the typed copies for yourself; Otto should take another to Feuchtwanger. You can give one to Orge if he feels like reading it. (Because he's so high class.) You can, should (are requested to) keep on correcting one copy.

On p. 2 of the scene before last (Wooden Shack in the Jungle) you have crossed out 'the vision of cold Chicago' after 'Garga . . . I have no use for revenge'. This, I think, is a pity because this major chord is needed here, if only because of Garga's metamorphosis in this scene. Won't you give it to the young lady at Haindls's after all?

It should be:

'. . . just the same. I'm taking over the lumber business. I'm a Catholic: you can't run a business without ideals. I won't sit still.

SHLINK: Never, That could cost you your neck.

GARGA: Not yet, Shlink. The uproar on Milwaukee Bridge has not died down, neither has the stamping of good carthorses, nor the icy rain on butchers' carts, nor the screeching of the streetcars on iron tracks strewn with cattle salt. The teamsters' oaths drive the streetcar galleys into the daily battle, the mooing of the indigestible rabble gets up every morning and the fresh, round chest of cold Chicago takes mighty breaths, it always has plenty of morning air.

SHLINK: Twenty years ago I was a streetcar conductor in Chi. It was just as you describe it. I became as you see me now. Since then a good many ice blocks have flowed down the black rivers, and the bridges don't find them very interesting (amusing?) any more. But that's no business of yours.[.] (Silence)

It would be good to give indications about the sets for certain scenes, the material at least. But you can do that better than I. Please make sure the typed MS looks as good as possible and is complete. I have good hopes of a Reinhardt or Jessner production. Then you'll have to do the sets. And another point: I think the play is at least as strong as *Baal*, and in addition more mature. Write me your opinion. Am I on the right track? Please give this thing all you've got.

>Bert

[Berlin, winter 1921–1922]

64 To Arnolt Bronnen

May 22

Dear Arnolt,

Here is *The Second Flood*. It would be good, though, if in typing you could make the human events a little more complicated.

I hear from Kasack that you want to give *Baal* and 'Garga' (Haven't you got Wegener's copy, the second is with Dr Lipmann at the Staatstheater) to Jhering. Why? I hope you've made it clear to him that you're not satisfied with half the prize. In any case you must tell him that I *definitely* am not, we must each get the *whole* prize successively. (Since the whole thing has only publicity value, our beautiful gesture of envylessness is a waste, because the beast *in me* will grunt that *no one* deserves the whole prize!) But I am eagerly awaiting your letter, which you had better send to Augsburg, Bleichstrasse 2.

If you see Jacob, give him my regards and tell him he should definitely send the manuscript of *A Mean Bastard* (*Der Schweinigel*) to me in Augsburg. With my fee. Please! What are you doing otherwise? When will you be on the move?

>I embrace you
>Bert

65 To Arnolt Bronnen

Dear Arnolt

But I'm enjoying the Czech cooking, my dear fellow, but there are white and pink fruit trees, my little pigeon, but I can't get the top hat off my neck, my Ottokar.

None the less, what about the two films for Kyser? 'Garga' and *Vatermord* (*Parricide*)? And what about your latest trip with Stefan Grossmann?

Let the Afterword alone, it's needed, if only as to protect the idea.

I'll send you the second film by tomorrow's post. Send me your curses (abridged) here, my dear friend.

> Gre-gre-greetings
> Bert

[In Marianne Zoff's hand]

Ugly Marianne sends best regards.

[In Brecht's] (She is mostly to blame, of course,)

(May-June 1922)

68 To Arnolt Bronnen

September 1922

Dear Arnolt,

What is a murderer's conscience compared to the stinking dung pit in the back of my head?

But I only received your telegram yesterday.

But today Neher has turned up with a kiss on the hands for you.

I've rewritten *Drums* and spoken with Marianne.

That's all.[1]

But of course I need the flat, and it's got to be warm.

The fifteenth will be all right though. I'll probably arrive sooner, but I can camp somewhere until then.

Just throw those Servaes bedbugs out of those rooms bodily. Raze them to the ground, besiege them, spit in their coffee, shut off their heating, bore holes in their shoes, provoke them, spit at them.

If Biti is cold, Biti will go home to Dad.

Call Dr Feilchenfeldt at Cassirer Verlag and ask him if he knows of a flat.

In the meantime, I've been pestering everybody to find us lodgings in Munich for January February.

I don't know what has stopped you from looking for a flat.

True, I find here a letter to you, unposted. But even so.

As for the bedbugs, nail a bloater under their table, a roe-herring, then they'll stink like the plague and get evicted like lepers. Be good to Cas and show him cold Chicago.

Rub him with snow if he's cold and in the evening if he discovers wounds, sprinkle salt on them.

So as to make his nose learn to smell even though it's pounded flat and teach him to restore it from memory.

In short, initiate him with piss into the secrets of cold Chicago and
   wipe his little arse with a grater.
To make him sit up and take notice.
But grant me absolution because you are a sinner.
And how is Gerda, my big sister?
Put pepper in her whiskies lest the theatre die out. Amen.
As for the bedbugs, shame them with kindness and screw them with
   guile, to make them go away like tape worms.
And take my blessing for all this, my son, O thou cynosure, navel of
   bliss, smoked meat.

> Yours,
> b

> Augsburg

[1]English in original.

69 To the Lessing Theatre (Berlin)

Dear Herr Berstl,
   The Drei-Masken agency informs me that the Lessing Theatre is
interested in *Drums in the Night*. I have offers from other theatres, but I
would be very glad to see the play on your stage, especially as my friend
Alexander Granach could then play the part of Kragler, and I attach
great importance to that. The play has been rounded out a little in the
course of rehearsals here; also cuts have been made and I have no
objection to its being adapted to each particular theatre. But if you are
considering major cuts, I would like you to call my attention to them. I
shall be in Berlin at the beginning of October. Nevertheless, would you
please give me definite word whether you are considering the play,
because I should like to conclude arrangements for Berlin before the
play is put on here (on the 29th). If you yourself have ever had a play
open here, you know how unfavourable the terrain is for anything
unusual. I expect to hear from you very soon.

> Yours faithfully,
> Bert Brecht

> Münchener Kammerspiele
> 22 September [1922]

And please tell me if Blandine Ebinger might be available for the part
of Anna, which has been added to substantially.

70 To Herbert Jhering

Dear Herr Doktor Jhering,

I wish to thank you for your review in the *Börsen-Courier*, on the strength of which the Lessing Theatre has written to me about *Drums*.

I've told the Drei-Masken people quite a few things that they're not likely to stick in their mirror. I've asked them a number of times to get a move on and send you *Drums* and *Jungle*. It's loathsome having to depend on these operetta peddlers.

Now I have an unusual request that I hardly dare to make: could you attend my opening, which will be on 29 September (Friday)? I know how much I'm asking of you, but it means a great deal to me. Since Berlin has stopped taking chances, it's very difficult to get serious criticism at a time when one needs it most.

> With best regards.
> Yours,
> Bert Brecht

> Munich, 22 September 1922

71 To Arnolt Bronnen

Dear Arnolt,

Many thanks for the telegram.
Drums went off well, it didn't rain in the theatre.
I'm all skin and bones.
I'm glad you have a flat. Is it warm?
Feet under table, snuff in nose, an insolent look on one's face.
For such people all things must prosper.

I'll probably arrive Monday morning, by sleeper, I hope. You'll get a wire.

Could you go and see Klöpfer and light a fire under his arse, because the Deutsches Theater is supposed to do *Baal*, and [Heinrich] George is supposed to play the part, but he promised, you were there, he's just gone back on his word, dammit, deserted in the face of the enemy, I can't understand him. – I've wired Kiepenheuer not to sign a contract without Klöpfer.

Tell Viertel too.

How are you looking?
I want you to look red. Have you been eating enough veal?
How's it going with Polish Gerda?
How she sings!!!
I'm bringing a Chinese lantern for the trousseau, plus my guitar and
    typewriter.
You must bring humour, Gerda's singing, cigarettes.
I'm also bringing projects and a fig leaf.
And a top hat, boy oh boy.

       Bert

               3 October 1922
               Augsburg

72 To Arnolt Bronnen

Dear Arnolt,

1

In my cradle they'd sing me to sleep at night
Redskins used my scalp for toilet paper
Amongst willow nymphs in the grey-green half-light
I saw myself coming like some hirsute ocean creature.

Those were the days when syphilis swept
Through the cities, apes lost their hair, became a friendly race.
We smoked, read papers, drank brandy, shat, slept
Shut out the heavens and grew commonplace.

2

How are you?
My stomach is weak, mamma
I've got the horizontal position for that, and everything would be all
    right except for the rats in the corners, the bad dreams.
Have you got your flat?
Write and tell me what you think should be in a 'Hannibal'.
Use an encyclopaedia.
And kindly send Biti's films to Kasack, who prints films. But use the

typewriter for telling me about Hannibal, so that some of it unlike your emotional effusions can be read.

But have you been drinking enough cocoa?

?

Regards to my sister from her big brother.

Has she been drinking? Has she been drinking too much? Has she been sleeping?

Are we to fight like vultures over the funeral oration?

Have you told Klöpfer that he must play Kragler?

Can I have the copy of *Verrat* (Treason) soon?

What does Gerda say about it?

Tomorrow I'm going to talk to them about the comedy in Munich.

With devil's tongues and bronze gullet.

And now, I kiss your hands.

> Your
> B

Augsburg, 22 October [1922]

73 To Herbert Jhering

Dear Herr Jhering,

First I roamed around Munich, it was bitter cold, yet people kept lifting their hats. Revolting.

But now I'm sitting in my kraal again, I can smoke and let my hair grow and write to thank you.

I have a warm room, I can sit with my back to the stove and keep my trap shut. I have rescued your face from all that confusion.

Now, from time to time, when I feel like it, I work on *Hannibal*, but, I repeat, only when I feel like it, and that's something I hadn't been able to do for a long time. Actually, I feel like it rather often.

In this one I can proceed a little more classically, without a cookingpot, with a tightly drawn bow, and as soberly as possible.

The voilà at the end is rather offensive, don't you think?

Incidentally, I want to direct *Hannibal* myself, because the present style of acting can't go on for ever, otherwise it will turn out to be a Boche business, civilised. When there are no stars on the programme, the people chew their toenails for boredom. Begging your pardon.

I'd be awfully pleased if you'd write me a few lines on my island.

With kind regards,
Yours faithfully,
Bert Brecht

Augsburg, Bleichstrasse 2,
Mid-October 1922

74 To Herbert Jhering

1

I first saw the light of the world in 1898. My parents hail from the Black Forest. Elementary school bored me for four years. In the nine years of my pickling at the Augsburg Realgymnasium I made no great contribution to my teachers' advancement. They never wearied of pointing out my penchant for idleness and independence. At the university I read medicine and learned to play the guitar. At secondary school I went in for all kinds of sport and developed a heart condition, which familiarised me with the secrets of metaphysics. During the war, I served as an orderly in a military hospital. After that I wrote a few plays, and in the spring of this year I was taken to the Charité hospital because of undernourishment. Arnolt Bronnen was unable to help me substantially out of his earnings as a sales clerk. After twenty-four years in the light of the world I have grown rather thin.

2

I'm certain that the present Brecht boom, no less than the slump that will follow, is the result of a misunderstanding. In the meantime I'm lying peacefully enough on the horizontal, smoking and keeping quiet.

It's a good thing that *Hannibal* isn't being produced straight away. Reich is a Reich [realm] of darkness and this *Hannibal* is a warning to sergeants. And I'll be able to smoke a few more cigars in peace. Regardless of whether anything comes of it.

The ballads are in the *Hauspostille* [Devotions for the Home], which has not yet been published. As soon as there's a copy, you'll get one. I delight in every line I receive from you.

Cordially yours,
Bert Brecht

Augsburg [October] 1922

75 To Alexander Granach

Dear Alexander Granach,

Forgive the typewriter, I'm not good at it, but you'll read me more easily.

I was fed up with the city, so I cleared out. Here the wind is blowing and there's snow on the ground; that makes for lightness.

I'd have been glad to see you, you know that. Even from here I can see your Kragler. In among the little houses at nine in the evening you give one a lease on heaven. I can hear you.

Thank you for Kragler.

It's such a childlike business, you know.

Marianne sends best regards.

> Yours,
> bert brecht

Please give the others my regards.

> Augsburg, Christmas 1922
> Bleichstrasse 2

76 To Arnolt Bronnen

Dear Arnolt,

A letter to you and Cas has been returned. I'm sending it back to the same address. I'm sitting on an island, my boy.

I've reread *Verrat* very carefully and I have all sorts of ideas. I regard it as extremely important that we should discuss it again in great detail.

Boldly familiar (when only twelve I suffered a demonstrable heart seizure thanks to my daring) with the theatre from childhood on, I should like to suggest that you once again rework the play, in a fresh revolutionary way.

Pin down the setting geographically, demystify it, make it more real, root the characters, including Gerda, in their habitat and dialect, so they won't be such anonymous vehicles of ideas, motivate and shape the incidents, the arrival of Gerda for instance, more realistically, etc.

In short, serve up the rich new material in the more sinister and carnal envelope of *Vatermord*.

Since you are a doubting Thomas, you will think I have doubts; no, I'm just working.

Most of all, I absolutely need the pictures, the whole material.

I attach great importance to Ebinger playing Cel. I've studied the part carefully. It needs machine-room atmosphere and originality, and it would make things a lot easier for me. Try and swing it. In any case keep the possibility open until we see each other.

Steinrück is really needed. We must absolutely have actors with atmosphere. We must definitely speak to each other.

Incidentally, do you know why they've taken off *Drums?* It's monstrous.

Up till now, Friday evening, no sign of Cas. If he's not here by tomorrow, Reigbert will do *Jungle.* Just in case, try and find someone other than that traitor for *Verrat.*

> I embrace you
> Your
> b

I'll be in Augsburg until the fifteenth. Then at the Kammerspiele.

> [Augsburg, 12 January 1923]

77 To Arnolt Bronnen

Dear Arnolt,

Thank you for the reprieve. I'm spending part of my time in bed but I keep my top hat handy.

The air in my room is good, the bedbugs are having their spawning season, and if Gerda could sit here for a day, it would be pleasant. Please give her my regards with a gesture expressive of real devotion.

As for Cas, the thought of him appreciably darkens my mood. I believe this Berliner's name might soon look well on the blacklist.

Success affects the ovaries.

Isolated successes in big cities last two winters.

Put that in your scrap book.

Ebinger's health interests me. Why, you old sensation monger, do you supply details only under pressure, you swine?

Please smile at Grossmann. I'm going to describe him one of these days.

About Neher: This kind of thing exasperates me in the extreme. Any entente with him is unthinkable as long as he behaves in this way. In my opinion you should be looking around for another designer for *Verrat,* just in case. I refuse to be dependent on a character who promises to be available from the eleventh to the twelfth and then arrives on the fifteenth. I mean this very seriously (I've had more experience with him than you) and advise you to take it into consideration. Perhaps nothing is more important at the moment. But now, pleasant journey. When will you be in Munich? And what about Oswald?

I press you to my paternal bosom.

b

Augsburg, January 1923

Can you get me a copy of *Verrat* with room for notations? In any case you'll need *complete* copies for the actors, with plenty of room. And the stage directions small, in brackets. And where is my copy with the cuts in it? All this is very urgent. After all, son, I want to read the play before directing it.

78 To Arnolt Bronnen

Dear Arnolt,

What are you doing?

There's lots of water between the islands.

What about *Verrat*?

When you've finished your film that the great Cas has been going on about, couldn't you send it to us?

Or another one? The treatment of the circus film, for instance.

Can't you come here, you old roué?

Your presence is desired. You will be received with honour.

I'm planning to put on *Excesses* at the end of March.

How is our big sister?

She is supposed to come down here in April or May and do *Verrat* and *Penthesilea*.

How about a little letter to your friend Bidie on the southern island?

Bidie with the slightly disreputable exterior?

His kidneys aren't so hot, but his heart is golden.

When he and his friend Cas smoke, they dream of their brother in the asphalt jungle, and their eyes grow moist.

Feeling!

Say it with feeling, your Eminence!!

Bert

Akademiestrasse 15/0

Tomorrow the film will be finished and we'll take a bath.
We've learnt our lessons and in the summer we'll do something, eh?
Couldn't you come here soon?
Nur wer die Sehnsucht kennt . . .

[Munich, probably February 1923]

79 To Herbert Jhering

Dear Herr Jhering,

Your letter gave me great pleasure. I'd be very glad to see you again.
What I'm doing here? Chewing gum.

No room to turn round in this town, and the people are so stupid it strains one's sense of humour and puts one in a bad mood. It's all because of the bad water.

Apart from that, I'm doing some little films with Engel, Ebinger, Valentin, Leibelt and Faber.

In the theatre here they're not cooking watery soup but soupy water. It's a varnish factory.

So Hollaender has throttled *Drums*. The man has a black heart.

God will sit in judgement on him. That will be unpleasant for him. But I too will sit in judgement and that will be more unpleasant. I'll send you a little collection for the *Courier* one of these days. A few poems if you like.

Jungle has been postponed till March. Now they're doing *Die Nibelungen*. That's a bit different from the dead soldier.

Every line from you gives me great pleasure and I press your hand.

Cordially,
bert brecht

Munich, Akademiestrasse 15
February [1923]

80 To Herbert Jhering

Munich, 27 March 1923

Dear Herr Jhering,

I've had a few bad weeks and besides I've been meaning to go to Berlin any day. Besides the ballads were in Augsburg and I had to send for them, and the ones I expected didn't come. So please forgive me, you know that German art is a *long* art (Mozart). I hope to see you in Berlin next week. I don't seem to have *The Ballad of Mazeppa* any more.

> With kind regards
> Yours,
> bert brecht

81 To Arnolt Bronnen

Dear Arnolt,

It's beastly cold, and suffering from stomach cramps I've been battling nothingness between lavatory walls.

Because literature is the only hope of populating the planet.

(Professional secret.)

I wrote to you a week ago.

Once Marianne is delivered, I may come for a fortnight.

Bathing, screaming, drinking cocoa.

Friedrichstrasse, Aschinger, Charité.

Gleisdreieck, UFA, Wannsee.

Gerda.

But couldn't you speak to Klöpfer some time?

About *Baal*.

What about *Verrat*?

Oh, it's so boring here. The people drink dishwater (warmed up) and their shit is almost odourless.

No use for the top hat here, son.

Oh Java, Java, Java.

And these cavalcades of sullen dogs.

And Hitler on the Monopteros shitting on Moses Iglstein.

And the varnish factory in Augustenstrasse.

Oh Ganges in the early morning wind.

By Tagore.

Couldn't you come here for a few days?

> bert

[Manuscript postscript by Marianne Zoff]
[Then Brecht]

To set your mind at rest about *Olympia*, it's hysterical cowpat.

The same is true of 'God's Clown', which is the work of a billygoat.

The 'Olympia' production will be a great day for the Romanisches Café.

Allah il Allah.

The second augur.

[Munich, March 1923]

82 To Barrett O. Clark

Munich, 26 April 1923

Dear Mr Clark,

The Munich Kammerspiele is planning to produce a number of American plays and as agreed would be extremely grateful if you could come here to talk the matter over and stay a while. It is very difficult to communicate with the American Play Company without your help. Our repeated attempts to do so have been fruitless. We therefore ask you to inform us of your time of arrival.

> Yours very truly,
> [Stamp] Office of the dramaturg, Munich
> Kammerspiele
> bert brecht

83 To Arnolt Bronnen (postcard)

Dear Arnolt,

Wednesday *Jungle* première. (If the date had been known sooner, I'd have written sooner!!!) You must positively come. It is possible, in fact probable, that your fare will be paid by the O. C. Recht-Verlag, as there may be a good piece of business connected (M 400,000 monthly etc.).

> Affectionately
> bert

If you have to go straight from the train to the theatre, ask for Herr Geis at the theatre.

Munich, 4 May 1923 [postmark]

84 To Herbert Jhering (postcard)

Akademiestrasse 15

Dear Herr Jhering,
I've been wanting to write to you all along, but I've been up to my neck in *Jungle* and didn't know the opening date. It's *Wednesday the ninth*. It would be wonderful if you could come, I think it will be a good performance and you'll see Engel, Faber etc.

With best regards,
Yours,
bert brecht

In case you have to come directly from the train to the theatre, please see Herr Geis junior about your seat.

Munich, 5 May 1923 [postmark]

85 To Arnolt Bronnen (postcard)

Dear Arnoltscoundrel,
from now on you will be called
Arne, for you have forfeited the 'olt'
through mutiny.
You flimflam scoundrel.
You cow's suppuration.
You anise-hole
Of course you'll stay with us, partly in Starnberg, partly in Munich, just as you please. But take the next train, you scum.
I embrace you

biddi
bert

Arrange to stay a while.
Jungle at the beginning of June.

Munich, 19 May 1923 [postmark]

86 To Arnolt Bronnen

Dear Arnolt,
I'd forgotten, but you can do me a great favour. I have now completed

two acts of *Gösta*, which is to have three, but so far I have had no contract with Frau Ellyn Karin, who holds the authorisation from Lagerlöf. In other words, we don't know how the royalties are to be split.

Since there's bound to be some kind of trade-off, we can't put it into writing. Karin is a shrewd old cow, and you'll have to speak to her.

(1) Find out whether – since she has thus far favoured me neither with a word nor a line – she mightn't sell me the authorisation outright (for that you'll have to summon up all the horsepower you've got), and for how much.

(2) If not, how much of a royalty she thinks she can decently expect. I don't know how much Kiepenheuer is claiming, but she won't get more than 25% of *my* share in any case, and of course you must start by offering 10%!!!

(This amount in settlement must of course be paid by Kiepenheuer!) If she absolutely won't play ball, you might draw up two contracts for (1) and (2), in other words, either/or.

You can always brandish the threat that I won't write another word until I'm in Berlin myself.

She belongs to the species of vulture who use contracts as a means of living on other people's work.

If she should threaten to withdraw her offer to me, tell her my first act and prologue have already been set in type and that she herself has accepted an advance for *Gösta* from Kiepenheuer!!

Please handle this as shrewdly and quickly as possible. Otherwise I'll have worked all summer for nothing because I need the money for Marianne.

I press your hand.

> Your
> Bert

And please tell Viertel about Baal*!*
Kiepenheuer has copies now!
It was a confounded mistake not making a deal with that old crow at the start.

Her address is:

> Ellyn Karin, Belle-Alliance Strasse 46-A
> [July 1923]

87 To Arnolt Bronnen

The Lord of the South Sea to the Lord of the North Sea

Deign, dear brother, to hear that the shit is too thick.
When the most pressing stupidities were out of the way, the most remote were tackled. Now they are almost done with. What then???
Your brother '*That's all*'[1] has been working like a beaver.
Literature is one thing, bacon is another.
Mahagonny has been deporting all Bavarians.
Can I have your little drawing room play?
I am still interested in your literary experiments.
I am holding back *Jungle* in Berlin. Actually it has been promised to Engel.
I'd be glad to look into your Aryan face again.
As long ago in May.
What aren't you doing?
What kind of wife have you got?
Your meals.
Your film.
Hitler.
But where is one to get the gold marks?
Right?
But apart from that, something tells me better weather is on its way.
Your hand, sovereign of the North Sea.

[Probably end of July 1923]

87a To Marianne and Hanne Brecht

Dear Marianne,
    I never write but I sometimes wait for letters.
    I keep myself very busy, but I am disarmed against my pathological boredom. Most evenings I sit backstage at the theatre, listening to the dirty jokes the stage hands tell me. You will be amazed at the upheavals in the Western regions, and if you haven't been good, you will suddenly be in the wrong.
    It's high time you came home with the sublime Hah-neh. The leaves

[1]English in original.

are turning yellow and your husband has started smoking a pipe and has learned some more philosophy.

His stomach does not take to the rough cookery of the pueblo or to the drinks that intoxicate people who are not used to them. Solitary drinking is unseemly. Your bed stands empty and I sleep alone under the red blanket.

> b

Dear Hah-neh, sweet one,

How goes it?

Are you planning to stay in Pichling much longer?
Your room is full of tobacco smoke, sweet one, and seven devils seem to be singing next door.

The furniture is on strike, you ought to straighten things out.

Don't you want to see your sire again, regardless of how he looks, your black sire, Hah-neh????

He's been spitting into the corners and has acquired seven million disgusting habits. You'll have to straighten things out.

When he enters your room, he says Salaam, Sublime One, which is sacrilege, because you are not there.

And besides, he is pale, because between kitchen and hallway he has seen a ghost that was washing nappies and reminded him of a woman he once knew.

There is cold water for that kind of thing, but I think you ought to straighten things out.

I kiss you on your second little face, providing it is freshly washed, which our town does not doubt.

> b

Your father's address is Akademiestrasse 15.
The city is Munich, the country Bavaria, the planet Earth.

[Munich, September–October 1923]

88 To Herbert Jhering (postcard)

Dear Herr Jhering,

I'd be very grateful if you could publish the following in the *Börsen-Courier*:

that I have been working for some time, in collaboration with Lion

Feuchtwanger, on an adaptation of Marlowe's *Edward II*, which I shall produce at the beginning of the season in Munich and then in Berlin.

If you wish, I can make parts of the manuscript available to you for publication.

With best regards from Feuchtwanger and myself,

> Yours,
> bert brecht

Munich, 17 October 1923 [postmark]

89 To Alexander Granach

Dear Alexander Granach,

I'm writing this to you, because I know you best, but it's for your theatre.

All of a sudden I read in the *Börsen-Courier* that you are going to do *Edward*, which I've been working on for the last three weeks, because I mean to do it at the *Kammerspiele* here.

It's a good play but you'll have a hell of a time with the middle. It's given my mother's son a nasty lot of work and will cost you more sweat than you possess, you can count on that.

The lyrical element is magnificent, but the rest is very old, as you will soon notice.

So be nice people and leave poor *Edward* to me. Because I'd like very much to direct it both here and in Berlin. It's a brand new play, and with it I'll crush you and your old translation as surely as I am more alive than your great-grandfather, against whom I won't say another word.

No need to write to me about the manuscript if you won't let me direct it myself. I'm sure you know how I feel. In that case I won't let you have it.

I hope you understand that this letter and this suggestion are not aimed at [Karl-Heinz] Martin. Not at all.

Cordially and fraternally yours,

> brecht

[Munich]Akademiestrasse 15
[Probably autumn 1923]

89a To Berthold Viertel

Dear Herr Viertel,

I hear at the Kammerspiele that you're planning to put on *The Emperor Jones*. I don't know whether you have an actor for the title role. If not, I cannot recommend Oskar Homolka, who has been rehearsing the part with us, too highly. He is from Vienna, and I might mention in passing that when he was playing *The Last Days of Mankind* Karl Kraus singled him out for special praise in *Die Fackel*. I have to tell you, however, that from January to mid-March Homolka will be working on a big project with me here. In addition, I have definite plans for Homolka for the next season in Berlin, and these I must ask you to respect. I am writing because I think I may be doing you and Homolka a favour. Of course you would have to decide soon, because Homolka is on the point of signing some important film contracts, but he would let them hinge on whatever decision you may take, because he attaches great importance to the part.

> Cordially yours,
> bert brecht

[Munich, October/November 1923]

90 To Helene Weigel

Dear Helletier[1]

I am bound by contract to prepare two plays for publication by mid-January, to negotiate with the Deutsches Theater in Berlin, to get *Edward* ready for production here by 20 January, etc. etc.

And tomorrow I'll try to get a passport.

Write and tell me how long you will be there and wire if you are going to leave suddenly. I'd have been glad to go to Paris just for a week. If you like, come immediately by way of Munich.

I'm sick of snow.

Are you alone?

I kiss you

> bert

[Munich. End of 1923]

[1]Helle for Helene, Tier = beast.

91 To Herbert Jhering

Dear Herr Jhering,

Thank you for your letter to Feuchtwanger about the *Edward* business. Feuchtwanger is willing to forgo the mention of his name, but points out that since a great many people know of our collaboration we should have to expect violent attacks on me.

Nevertheless he refuses to let his name be mentioned in such a way as to belittle his contribution.

I should suggest the following on the reverse title: 'This play was written in collaboration with Lion Feuchtwanger.'

He rejects a dedication as damaging to him.

So what should I do?

I understand your arguments better and better. Everybody keeps on saying what you told me you were going to say (caution: bad syntax).

Please let me know what you think.

The rehearsals are most instructive. Opening in mid-March at the latest.

> With best regards,
> Yours,
> bert brecht

I have rejected Feuchtwanger's suggestion of a second book page making mention of continuous productive collaboration and saying that it is no longer possible to distinguish who wrote what.

In that case I'd prefer two names.

[Munich, February 1924]

92 To Herbert Jhering

Dear Herr Jhering,

I thank you for your letters to Feuchtwanger.

On the title page and the programme there will be only my name.

But on the second book page:

'I wrote this play with Lion Feuchtwanger. b.b.'

That's good, don't you think?

I'm in the midst of rehearsals, but it's easier to cut paving stones with one's teeth than to do this kind of thing. These people have no basic feeling for the theatre. These actors have imagination in any number of fields, but in the theatre, no. The fantastic, incredible fact that people with painted faces and speeches learnt by heart should appear on a platform and re-enact scenes from human life amid the inexplicable silence of a crowd of people is lost to this generation, which has invented the dilettante as functionary.

But lemonade with cognac is almost as good as whisky, and red hessian to cover walls with can be bought all over for a few pfennigs. It might be a good thing to excavate this stinking theatrical museum like Tutankhamun's tomb.

What is the tsetse fly beside these hundreds of dug-up corpses!!!

It's a good thing the winter is hanging on.

With best regards.

Yours,
bert brecht

Edward will probably be on Saturday fortnight. You *will* be able to come?

[Munich, late February–early March 1924]

2 Berlin
1924–1933

Brecht finds his place

Even after becoming assimilated in 1920s Berlin, with his close-cropped hair, leather jacket and nasty small cigars, Brecht was still recognisably the Augsburger, returning to his home town and to the Bavarian countryside in his holidays, though his circle of friends there had by now largely dispersed. But now he was also the 'dweller in cities' of his new cycle of poems (*Poems 1913–1956*, pp. 131–150), unrhymed, austere and rhythmically irregular, and so he began by planning a series of plays on the theme of humanity's rush to settle in those huge hostile centres. *Baal* became shortened and stripped of some of its poetry; in the 1926 version the poet is shown as an unemployed mechanic living in a garage. *In the Jungle* lost much of its atmospheric symbolism and became *In the Jungle of Cities*. The Munich project *Galgai*, for a play of identity set in Bavaria, materialised as the Anglo-Indian *Man equals Man*, Brecht's major work after the move to the capital. Likewise his interests shifted: a new world of business and technology, of skyscrapers and automobiles, of boxing and the Salvation Army, began to invade his writing with fresh terms and images, many of them Anglo-Saxon like the expression 'cold Chicago' itself. He started to dramatise Frank Norris's novel of the Chicago wheat market *The Pit* (under the title *Joe P. Fleischhacker*), he read about the great American buccaneering entrepreneurs – men like Dan Drew around whom he began to plan a play – and in 1926 he came on the ideas of Karl Marx.

To start with, he was a trainee director at the Deutsches Theater under Reinhardt's aide Felix Holländer who, besides Engel and Neher, had also engaged the young writer Carl Zuckmayer from Mainz. At the same time Brecht was getting advances from Kiepenheuer for the publication of three overdue books: his first book of poems (*Devotions for the Home*) and the final texts of *In the Jungle* and *Man equals Man*. The Deutsches Theater's production of *In the Jungle* in October 1924 had only a handful of performances, after which it seems that he saw his work as having little prospect there and felt that Leopold Jessner's Prussian State Theatre offered a better chance. He attended some of

Reinhardt's rehearsals (which in that season included Shaw's *Saint Joan* with Elisabeth Bergner, and Pirandello's *Six Characters*); he helped adapt *La Dame aux Camélias* for Reich to stage (again with Bergner) and was in some measure involved in the impressive *Coriolanus* which Engel directed for Reinhardt that winter in Neher's sets. Apart from that he took his job none too seriously, and his real work, whether in playwriting or in poetry, was done outside. Not surprisingly, his contract was not renewed at the end of the theatrical year, and from the summer of 1925 he was on his own.

Or rather: he started forming that Brecht collective (as it became called) which operated productively until Hitler came to power at the end of January 1933. This had germinated in the winter of 1924/25 when Elisabeth Hauptmann, a freelance writer and English teacher, was hired by Kiepenheuer to help Brecht complete the three overdue books, soon to be reinforced by the young Munich writer (and boxer) Emil Hesse Burri. The books were handed in, though the matter was complicated by the conservatism of Kiepenheuer's new backers, who would not publish Brecht's antimilitarist 'Legend of the dead soldier', with the result that all three books were transferred to Ullstein under a new contract of 1926. Hauptmann lost her job, but continued working on *Man equals Man* and the various 'American' projects – her mother was half-American – with a somewhat haphazard share of Brecht's earnings, plus what she could earn by her own stories and translations. And so not only Brecht's range of interests but also his women partners changed, for along with Helene Weigel, whose son had been born a few days after the Berlin opening of *In the Jungle*, Hauptmann seems virtually to have obliterated Brecht's former loves both from his correspondence and (Marianne's divorce proceedings apart) from his conscious life.

Despite Germany's increasingly spectacular economic revival, the year 1925–6 was a difficult, transitional one not only for Brecht and his collaborators but also for the Berlin theatre, whose future development in the direction of topical documentary themes, sober reality and a new musical theatre was still far from clear. This was when Brecht started contributing polemical statements – often in the name of 'the younger generation' – to the Berlin press, particularly to Jhering's paper the *Berliner Börsen-Courier*, in the course of which he managed to offend Jessner and thereby to ruin *Man equals Man*'s best chance of a Berlin production. Already he was trying to formulate the principles of that 'epic theatre' which Piscator had claimed to inaugurate with *Fahnen* (by

Alfons Paquet) at the Volksbühne two seasons earlier, and it was this that gave him a common interest with the older novelist Alfred Döblin. None the less he kept up his association with the 'Junge Bühne', for whom he staged the revised *Baal* in February 1926 (Weigel playing a small part) and helped it to secure first plays by Burri and the young Marieluise Fleisser. The Bronnen bubble, which had reached its climax in 1924, had already been deflated, though Brecht was slow to abandon his friend even after the hysterical nationalism of his *Rheinische Rebellen* at the State Theatre in May 1925. Nor was he quick to see the significance of Zuckmayer's conversion to a more popular, undemanding form of theatre with *The Cheerful Vineyard*, the smash hit of Christmas 1925.

For him the crucial change came after the Darmstadt production of *Man equals Man* at the start of the following season. For with this rambling Kiplingesque farce Brecht not only established himself with the theatre/opera directors Ernst Legal and Carl Ebert – both of whom were to become important in Berlin – but also slotted into the new sobriety or 'Neue Sachlichkeit' which had been promulgated by an art exhibition under that title the previous year, and was now being recognised as the overall successor to the Expressionist movement. (Characteristic artists were Grosz, Dix and Rudolf Schlichter, whose portrait of a leather-jacketed, crop-haired Brecht would be shown in 1928). Jhering and others pressed for the play to be staged in Berlin, and in March 1927 there was a broadcast which was enthusiastically reviewed by another exponent of the new trend, Kurt Weill. This was followed by a meeting between author and critic, who soon decided to collaborate on a musical work, to be based partly on Brecht's plans with Hauptmann for a play about the destruction of a city (Sodom or Miami) by natural forces (a hurricane, the Flood), and partly on the 'Mahagonny Songs' which they had added to the newly-published *Devotions for the Home*. The full opera which he and Weill had in mind was not realised till some three years later, though the experimental 'Songspiel' known as 'The Little Mahagonny' was ready for production at Hindemith's music festival that summer, where it delighted Otto Klemperer, drew Brecht into the new movement for functional music theatre, and gave a first showing to the talents of Weill's young wife Lotte Lenya.

Around the time of the first Brecht-Weill meeting Piscator left the Volksbühne with the intention of setting up his own Communistorientated theatre. Brecht, who can hardly have envisaged what that meeting was going to lead to, agreed to become one of his 'collective' of dramaturgs, working with Felix Gasbarra and Leo Lania on the plays *Rasputin* and *Konjunktur* and, much more radically, on the 'epic' dramatisation of Hašek's *The Good Soldier Schweik*, an experience that he never forgot. Meantime he continued working on his own *Joe P. Fleischhacker* play, which Piscator now intended to produce, and also on the equally unfinished project known as *Fatzer*, a play to be set in post-war Germany. There was some question too of a revival of *Drums in the Night* in a more documentary form and of a Brechtian production of *Julius Caesar*, two schemes which he discussed with Piscator and a new friend, the Marxist sociologist Fritz Sternberg. Early in 1928 however he was approached in a Berlin restaurant by E. J. Aufricht, another newly fledged impresario, who was taking over the Theater am Schiffbauerdamm and wanted a new play with which to open. Brecht appears to have shown him his current projects without getting much response, then mentioned a German translation of *The Beggar's Opera* which Hauptmann had been making. Influenced no doubt by the success of that work in London, Aufricht decided to stage it if Brecht wrote the songs, which Weill would compose. This proved to be the end of Brecht's involvement with Piscator, for the new play, provisionally entitled *Gesindel* (or Scum), demanded his entire concentration. By the time it began its year's run (and worldwi- de success) as *The Threepenny Opera*, Piscator's 1927–28 company had gone bankrupt and the 'dramaturgical collective' was no more.

Instead, Brecht now had a double involvement: on the one hand his partnership with Kurt Weill, initially to complete the *Mahagonny* opera but also to produce more peripheral works, starting with the radio cantata *Berlin Requiem*; on the other, his influential role at the Theater am Schiffbauerdamm, which he came to treat as 'his' theatre. Both involved Neher as designer and visualiser, as well of course as Hauptmann, to whom he now gave the task of writing the main text of *The Threepenny Opera*'s intended successor – which again was to have Brecht/ Weill songs and an Engel production – under the title *Happy End*. At the same time he was part of Aufricht's team, and as such he was closely concerned during spring 1929 with putting on Marieluise Fleisser's splendid second play *Pioniere in Ingolstadt* and P. M. Lampel's *Poison Gas over Berlin*, a work which was banned at the insistence of the General Staff. Whether or not Brecht was meant to, he took a hand in the direction of such works, and even in the casting, incidentally giving Peter Lorre his first significant Berlin parts. Not surprisingly his plans to write major plays for the 'straight' theatre rather stagnated, and of the two which he managed to complete before the Nazis took over in 1933 neither could be performed in Germany until the late 1950s.

Happy End, with its brilliant songs and frivolous gangster-cum-Salvation Army story, was an almost instant failure, and following it Brecht largely lost interest in *Mahagonny*, which eventually had its première in an orthodox opera house in March 1930. Hauptmann's text, which in contrast to her *Beggar's Opera* translation had been left virtually unrevised by Brecht, was then cannibalised to help make the collective's major play *St Joan of the Stockyards* and the unfinished *The Breadshop*, while at the same time Brecht's main interest switched to the development of a new form of didactic music theatre which Hindemith and he had called the 'Lehrstück'. Weill at first sampled this genre with him in the school play *Der Jasager* and the 'radio Lehrstück' *Lindbergh's Flight* (based on Charles Lindbergh's solo flight across the Atlantic), then concentrated on further exploration of the opera medium, initially with Neher as his partner. Brecht, who wanted to apply the new form to political themes, found a like-minded composer in Hanns Eisler, a Schönberg pupil who was brother to two well-known Communists, and with him wrote his major political-didactic works: the staged cantata *The Decision*, the agitational play *The Mother* and the film *Kuhle Wampe*. For these the collective was reinforced by the Bulgarian stage and film director Slatan Dudow and (for the film only) the Communist writer Ernst Ottwalt. At the same time, besides *St Joan*, Brecht was engaged on the adaptation of *Measure for Measure* for one of the actors' collectives that had emerged from the wreckage of Piscator's first company. This remained unstaged, and was later reworked to make *The Round Heads and the Pointed Heads*.

The fiasco of *Happy End*, like the almost simultaneous final collapse of Piscator's West End theatre, was just one aspect of the crisis that put paid to the so-called 'golden twenties', the boom period that had culminated in Klemperer's Kroll Opera, *The Threepenny Opera*, Piscator's *Schweik* and the Schiffer/Spoliansky revue *Es liegt in der Luft* in which Marlene Dietrich made her name. Though the real economic crisis and the revival of the Nazis only became apparent following the Wall Street crash that October, a revived nationalism was in the air and the polarisation of both politics and culture had already begun. So 1928 saw the end of the 'Junge Bühne', the splitting of the workers' theatre movement and the rise of agitprop and of Communist-led actors' collectives. Then in July 1929 the Communist Party congress accepted the concept of 'social-fascism' – the view that the German Socialists were merely preparing the road for the Nazis – which was emotionally based on the events of May 1st, when the Socialist-led Berlin police had killed some twenty-five Communist demonstrators. It seems to have been at this moment that Brecht, who had been watching the demonstration with Fritz Sternberg, decided to associate himself – informally, as it turned out, but definitively – with the Communist Party, who now for the first time started to treat him as something more than a bourgeois *enfant terrible*. This led not only to his new didacticism but also to a certain detachment from what he and Eisler saw as 'the apparatus' of established theatre and opera. He became in effect a Communist intellectual, attending classes at Johann Schmidt-Radvanyi's Marxist Workers' School (given among others by the dissident Marxist Karl Korsch) and planning a critical journal with Walter Benjamin and the journalist Bernard von Brentano. Like Piscator, however, he steered clear of the Party's 'League of Proletarian Writers' led by the former Expressionist poet Johannes R. Becher, and its journal *Die Linkskurve*, though he seems to have been on good enough terms with some of its members such as Kurt Kläber and Otto Bihalji-Merin. Nor did he find he could co-operate with the Marxist philosopher Georg Lukács, who had arrived from Moscow to keep them all on aesthetically conservative lines.

To some extent Brecht was prepared for Hitler's emergence as Chancellor on 30 January 1933, even if the violence and thoroughness of the repression following the Reichstag Fire a month later were more than he expected. Like the KPD itself, he saw the arrival of Fascism as a last desperate throw of the real rulers – the capitalists, landowners and military – in their effort to delay the inevitable working-class revolution which that party, supported by its Soviet friends, would soon lead. Given the Nazi detestation of works like *Mahagonny* and the 'Legend of the dead soldier', exile would have been unavoidable even had Weigel been a pure Nordic blonde; but at least it was an acceptable challenge which he was now placed to meet. Hauptmann, whose personal relations with him had been seriously shaken when he married Weigel in 1929, stayed on in Berlin for a year as an illegal member of the KPD, then went to join her family in America. Her place in his life was taken by the tubercular working-class Communist Margarete Steffin who had played the servant girl in *The Mother* and subsequently been sent for treatment and convalescence in Switzerland at Brecht's and Eisler's expense. Brecht himself had immediate work in Paris, where he and Weill were to write the ballet *The Seven Deadly Sins* (originally called Anna-Anna) for the eccentric English art patron Edward James. By July he was negotiating to write the *Threepenny Novel* for an advance which largely covered the price of the Danish cottage where he eventually settled. It seems that his father let him have the rest.

One of his strengths in this situation was that he soon saw that the Nazis were not without working-class support in Germany, and would not be easily dislodged. This gave him his impetus not just to write most of his anti-Nazi poems (of which only three date from before the takeover) but also to join in such practical work as the organisation of broadly-based meetings and the preparation of the *Brown Books* directed by Piscator's old administrator Otto Katz. More important however was his recent experience in alternative theatre, which would soon allow the German theatre in exile – much of it drawn from agitprop, cabaret and Communist collectives – to put his work to more striking and effective use than that of more orthodox playwrights. By now he had visited Moscow for the première of *Kuhle Wampe* and established some apparently promising connections there: notably with Tretiakoff and Mikhail Koltsov, then two of the most influential Soviet literary figures. Already a number of German theatre and film people had gone to work in the USSR, Piscator and Eisler among them, and in the autumn of 1933 Weigel too went on a tour which was cut short by illness. There was thus some sense in the Brechts' settling on the Baltic, within reach of Leningrad as well as of their own sadly estranged country. At that time, a year before the First Soviet Writers' Congress, the Russians still showed a strong sense of sympathy with the persecuted German Communists and a comparatively open attitude in the arts.

93 To Helene Weigel

Dear Helle,

I put on my leather gloves, lit a match, smoked a cigar, jotted something down, ate chocolate, blew my nose, and now I'm tired.

But most of all from the trip to Berlin with you.

I'm cheerful and in good shape and if Arnolt turns up, I'll probably stay with him.

He's supposed to be coming soon.

When will you have some free time again ???

Will you sleep as well as I want you to and be merry?

Not too merry though, but a little.

I am permanently devoted toward you, Madam and me.

          bidi
          (written with crayon)

[Probably first half of 1924]

94 To Helene Weigel

Dear Hellebeast,

The grand manitou is sitting again in a cloud of Dutch tobacco smoke blinking when light shines through the tent flap and listening to the gramo-beast [?] which is moaning 'Oh by Jingo'.[1]

What are you doing?

How much of you has come to Berlin and how much of me?

Have you already had your bath?

What is Arnolt, the black panther, doing?

And little Peter?

Oh by Jingo.[1]

And amen.

[Probably first half of 1924]

95 To Helene Weigel (postcard)

Naples 18 June [?] 1924

Dear Helle,

I am in Capri with Marianne, who is not at all well. Please write and

[1]English in original.

tell me all about what's going on in Berlin and how you are doing. I'll be here for about another week. I think I'll be able to work. How was Esther? I am looking forward to Berlin and Spichernstrasse. *Don't* be silly. No reason!!!

biddi

Marina piccola di Capri
Pension Weber

[on sealed envelope]
I'll be finished in about a fortnight.

96 To Helene Weigel

Dear Helle,

> The drink is revoltingly blue.
> Half an hour's bathing and kayak paddling.
> Two hours' eating in all.
> Smoking, lemonade, sixty-six, total four hours.
> And then.
> But now Cas has arrived and tomorrow we'll be descending on Naples.
> Where there are drinks, music and syphilis.
> I expect to be in Germany in one or two weeks.
> Marianne is feeling much better now.
> She'll be staying on in Capri.
> It's a good thing I brought her here.
> Then she'll go to Mondsee in Austria.
> Where her mother and child are, for the summer.
> By then she'll be fully recovered.
> It's good for the lungs here, but the landscape and inhabitants make you throw up.
> And everything is expensive and bad and the meat inedible. What are you doing?
> I'm looking forward to seeing you and Pietro.
> Is he getting big and fat and jolly?
> His mother is the apple of our eye.
> And does he sing 'I have no bananas'?
> And keep his father's bed ready, as it is written?

And does he know what's what and is he acquainted with the *Song of Songs* especially Chapter 2, Verses 10–15?

Wherewith a kiss on the neck, under the chin, you know.

[Capri, June–July 1924]

97 To Helene Weigel

Dear Helle,

Why no answer?

I still go for walks on the Kastanienallee and am not without occupation. I have now completed about four acts in rough draft. What I have is tolerable, some of it good.

I'll be there by the middle, at latest the end, of next week.

It's very boring here except for working hours, which are unbearable.

No news from the Staatstheater. What rudeness.

Write me all the rumours about *Jungle*.

Who's playing Jane? Binder???

It's hard staying here.

I'm still moderately devoted to you and to your mysterious contents.

A letter costs ten pfennigs.

Respectfully

[Late August–early September 1924]

98 To Herbert Jhering

Dear Herr Jhering,

I am now going to put down the substance of nearly all the conversations I have had with you this and last year, because in my opinion one of the best things about the present day is that we view as much as we can in a historical light. The bone I have to pick with you is that you sacrifice the drama to the theatre, specifically, the drama of our generation, to the theatre of the older generation. As I see it, you either gloss over or fail to notice the fact that this theatre is the theatre of the older generation. Writing in the high-flown manner of a Piloty, you hailed the *Wallenstein* production as a historical event and prevented me from showing my production of *Edward* in Berlin. You stood by in silence while my play, which you say is good, was punctured by the theatre that you say is good and in the same way let *The Rhenish Rebels* be punctured, nor have you ever appraised the ability of the theatre, which according to you 'shows the way', to produce the plays of this generation or to move the writers of this generation to write plays in its style.

I hope that in judging the thought underlying this letter you will bear the following in mind: – I am well aware that you have built up my own position practically single-handed and that you are the foremost critic of our day.

Yours

(1925)

99 To Helene Weigel

Dear Helli,

It is hard to write when one has sunk into a morass of gloom. I have had endless trouble with the car, and it still isn't ready. Besides, the money won't stretch. I'm planning to go to Vienna on Monday or Tuesday, but now it is so late that I doubt if I can be back at the same time as you. I hope to get the car in ten days, when I shall be able to pay the bill, the exact amount of which is not yet known. It would be nice if you could find out what the test costs in Vienna and whether I could take it there. Here it's expensive and I might come off more cheaply there.

With much nicotine I've turned out few sonnets. The boredom is unbearable, at the same time a catastrophic lack of money is keeping me from going to Vienna soon. But next week my father is shutting up the house for the holidays, so I'll have to leave. I'm awfully looking forward to seeing you.

bert

Don't let this letter spoil what's left of your good humour after my silence. But now Orge has gone off to Paris. I've exhausted the lending libraries. My brain isn't even halfway equal to the job of supporting me. If I had two selves, I'd murder one of them.

[Augsburg, June 1925]

100 To Helene Weigel

Dear Helli,

I've been in Vienna since yesterday. You wouldn't let me come by way of Munich. You don't even tell me why. It's so terribly boring everywhere. I'll be going to Augsburg in the middle of July. The flat is closed now, my father is away. I'll write to you in plenty of time about a room. I want to work as much as possible this summer. Here I have a secluded room all to myself out of town. In the afternoon I visit Hanne, who is wonderfully sweet to me. What are you doing? How was *Wozzek*? How were the notices? I wish I could read them. Bronnen is here. Kortner was. Homolka is. When will you go to see your parents? My address until July 1st is Mozartgasse 25, ground floor.

Do you miss me??? Are you reserved in your dealings with gentlemen? Do you behave yourself early and late??? I don't wish to be told things.

And now I kiss you, Helli.

> bidi

My regards to Otto and to Pappa George if you see him.

Marianne will be in Münster from mid-August on. I've signed with Ullstein. A great triumph. I don't want you to have any worries about the winter. One way or another, everything will be all right, Helli. Please write and tell me how you and Step are doing. Is he fat? Is he grinning again? What did he say when he saw me? Write and tell me.

[Vienna, June 1925]

101 To Lutz Weltmann

Dear Herr Doktor,

After long deliberation I have found it impossible to frame a more pleasing statement than the enclosed which struck me instinctively as the only possible answer to your question concerning the problems of the present-day theatre. To tell the truth, I am convinced that you are basically of the same opinion and I should not take it at all amiss if you were to regard this view of ours as unfit to print just now and unsuited to your purpose. In this case, please regard my lines as a private answer, which I feel I owe you in view of your kind invitation.

> With best regards

[August–September 1925]

101a To Marianne Brecht

Dear Mariandl,

I've finished *Galgei*[1] and am very much relieved – also *Jungle* and *Devotions for the Home* [Hauspostille].

---

[1]Provisional title of *Mann ist Mann*, first version.

For the last three days I've been driving with Otto; now I'm an expert.

You're opening (I read) on the 20th. I'll then be in Münster.

First of all, I'm going to Berlin tomorrow (I can go by sleeper and from Berlin to Münster it's only six hours) and I'll send you whatever you want.

I'm awfully looking forward to seeing you and to hearing all that Hanne can say now. I've got very skinny again, but I'm well.

> Your bert

> [Augsburg, October 1925]

101b To Marianne Brecht

Dear Mariandl,

It's awful, I'm up to my ears in work because I first have to block *Baal* myself (Viertel *can't*) and as usual I don't yet like the text.

What are you people doing? Thanks very much for your letter. Do write more often. Have you time to rest and for Hanne? Please write, I'm always thinking of you even when I don't write.

On Friday I'm going to Munich for two days (with a quick side trip to Augsburg) to take a look at an actor for Galy Gay.

Baal on 7 February (Sunday morning). You must come.

Please write, dear Mariandl, and tell me how you are. Are you well? And cheerful? And with Hanne?

> Yours, bert

What about Hanni? Has it gone away? Please tell me!!! And what other news?

> Berlin, January 1926

103 To Fritz Kortner

Dear Kortner,

Believe me: the theatre is really dead. And for people whose favourite way of spending their evenings is the theatre nothing can be worse than to believe it's still alive. This would be the extreme nihilism that would inevitably destroy what hope is still left. It's bad enough having to do things when we know we could do better. But all is not lost if we do them without knowing this.

In order to express my confident, optimistic view that we still know what theatre is and therefore have a chance of creating it, I have judged what has been termed the foremost achievement of the modern theatre, in other words the one that provides the best possibility of appraising the present state of the theatre. So I mentioned *Herodes und Mariamne*.

I think you know as well as I do that this was not living theatre (for living is not just a question of level); anyway I hope so. I confidently believe (and without this belief I could not work properly) that anybody worth bothering about has recognised that it's dead, and I think you yourself knew it. You yourself have done incomparably better things, and it is imperative that you know that. Naturally the perpetual school-boys and their wives who make up the audience today chew patiently and obediently on these big third-rate hams. We mustn't let that influence us.

What ought you to do? You must do as well as you can what is demanded of you, what you are permitted to do, what you want to do and what you can do better, and you must allow a few people to tell you what's what and shield you when you are told that the theatre is dead and that you are part of it.

I have been too lazy to make a complete statement for the general public unfortunately (perhaps). It shows my esteem for you, Kortner, that I do it just for you.

Your devoted

Berlin, early April 1926

104 To Leopold Jessner

Dear Herr Intendant [1]

I hear you are indignant over my remarks in the *Vossische Zeitung* about the death of the drama. The *Vossische Zeitung* asked me whether the drama was dying out and I replied that a certain variety of drama, the dominant variety, is already dead. I pointed out that the younger generation are left dissatisfied by the production of *Herodes und Mariamne*, a play which the leading critics are agreed in terming a classic and the production of which by a contemporary theatre may be regarded as

[1] Theatre manager.

exemplary and representative. If the best possible production cannot bring a work back to life, that work may be put down as dead. But if you produce works which are actually dead and in which the younger generation, unlike the dominant generation, can no longer find meaning, if you represent such works as outstandingly good and alive, you will lose the younger generation for the theatre. It seemed to me that these points were important enough to us all, to you as well as to me, to be taken into consideration even if they seem harmful to the theatre industry of the moment. I say 'seem' because the overwhelming majority of critics have commended this play to the public with such enthusiasm that one solitary reference to its rather depressing effect on people who in fact seldom go to the theatre is unlikely to affect box office receipts. Considering my positive view of the Staatstheater as the representative German theatre and how glad I am to be having my *Drums in the Night* performed there, I see no reason for you to suppose that I would wish to harm the Staatstheater.

With kind regards,

Yours truly devoted
bert brecht

[Berlin], 10 April 1926]

106 To Leopold Jessner

Dear Herr Intendant,

I very much regret your inability to receive me. I shall now have to give my publisher free hand to offer the production rights of my comedy *Mann ist Mann*, and this I cannot do without once again expressing my regret at not having been able at least to describe the play to you, so as to spare you the need to read it. In view of the present situation of the German theatre, it would have meant a great deal to me if you had seen fit to produce the play at the Staatstheater. I see few artistic possibilities in this country for this particular play, to which I attach special importance.

Respectfully yours,

Berlin, mid-May 1926

107 To Leopold Jessner

Dear Herr Intendant Jessner,

Although, as you know, I am very much opposed to your opinions, it seems important to me to ask you not to let your understandable feelings of revulsion deter you from fighting for your position. I think we all consider it necessary that you should continue with your artistic work in this city, for it is necessary and irreplaceable. I believe this frank declaration from the mouth of an enemy (whatever you may think of him) must prove to you that in such a struggle with worthless mediocrities all those for whom theatre is a passion are on your side.

                    bert brecht

                            [Towards the end of the twenties]

108 To Herbert Jhering

Dear Herr Jhering,

If you possibly can, please print these lines in as prominent a position as possible. It is exceedingly important that the few people who work for us in the Reich should find especial recognition in the *Börsen-Courier, when they do good work*. Hardt's production, though its style may be somewhat too monumental for my taste, was one of the best I have ever seen of one of my plays. *Müthel absolutely amazing, a feast for you.*

                    With best regards,
                    Yours,
                    bert Brecht

I'm writing this on the train to Paris

                            [End of May–beginning of July 1926]

[Enclosure follows]

In view of the Babylonian confusion of styles in the contemporary theatre, a playwright should be just as much entitled to call attention to significant productions of his plays as an engineer to write in specialised periodicals about the technological application of his work. In the two and one-quarter hour *creative* production of *The History of Edward II of England* by the poet Ernst Hardt in Cologne, which illumines the thought structure of the play in exemplary fashion, the outstanding stature of the actor Lothar Müthel was – by no means unexpectedly –

made manifest. The admirable charm of his acting enables him to be absolutely faithful to his role. As can be observed in every moment, he imponderably, with perfect clarity, enacted the imponderable drama of Edward's life, working almost with the precision of a physicist. The death scene was pure ivory in its majesty . . .

                     Bert Brecht

109 To Herbert Jhering

Dear Herr Jhering,

   More than six hundred kilometres from Berlin, digesting last winter's cement dinners on short motor tours, I am slowly beginning to grasp the real difficulties of the fight for this generation's theatre. I very much want to influence you with this letter, but that would be impossible if you thought I felt dissatisfied or something even worse. Thanks to my contract with Ullstein, which was due to you more than to anyone else, the year 1925 ended with a surprising success for me. The only thing I could possibly feel dissatisfied about is other people's visible satisfaction. I must own that it does indeed trouble me that you yourself may not be entirely dissatisfied (not of course with my success, but with that of my generation in its battle for the theatre), and I believe this would inevitably spoil everything. I know that you, far more than I, are always having to take a position, that you do not take this obligation lightly, and that consequently it is hard for you to see how little has been accomplished in this struggle, all the more so since your method of goading the theatre to outdo itself has often been successful. True, this may have had the effect of hastening the theatre's exhaustion. In my opinion, it proves nothing to say that many talents are at work, since it is open to question whether they are talents and quite certain that they lack direction. At the time of the Thirty Years' War, the initiative of a thousand small towns undoubtedly presented an impressive picture of healthy striving. And even if you believed that the one and only attempt to frame a theory of the theatre, i.e., Jessner's, may lead to something in the nature of a new theatre adequate to the cities of our century, you would have to pay for this opinion by renouncing the creation of new plays; for up until now this style has impoverished (not changed) older works beyond recognition and made new ones look as old as the hills. The principle of doing everything on as broad a front as possible is good provided you know where you are going, but I am very much mistaken if we are not approaching the time of visible weakening, where opposition is the only way of not being thrust aside. Nothing is more dangerous than wasting new principles on hopeless old bankrupts or the obsessive continuation of a tradition based on the classics. There is nothing to save in the present-day theatre and the relatively better it functions the more absolutely it must be combated. In writing this, I trust in your passionate objectivity, and it gives me some satisfaction to have provided a notion of 'Tantae molis erat' [how difficult it was] if only for the years to come.

[Paris, early June 1926]

110 To Herbert Jhering

Dear Herr Jhering,

I am back from Paris and in Augsburg.

It is a great disappointment to me that the *Börsen-Courier* should have totally disregarded the Cologne success of *Edward*, my first in a long time, a play that was deliberately massacred in Berlin. Had you any special reason for ignoring even my few lines? There has been something of a vacuum around my affairs these last few years.

Yours,
brecht

Augsburg, 10 June 1926

112 To Willy Haas

Dear Herr Haas,

In the August issue of *Uhu* there was something by Thomas and Klaus. It would be nice if you could make room in the *Literarisches Echo* for a melancholy little meditation on the subject. Only I would ask you to place it a little better than the last (about crime novels), which was really put in a bad spot. Would you be so kind as to let me know straight away and to return the article to me in Augsburg if you don't want to publish it. Though that would be too bad.

With regards,
Yours,
bert brecht

Augsburg, Bleichstrasse 2,
2 August 1926

117 To Emil Hesse-Burri

Dear Hesse,

The 'Junge Bühne' is rehearsing your *Amerikanische Jugend* [American Youth]. Did you know that? I ask because on one occasion you were not notified. And you'd better take a firm stand because the 'Junge Bühne' is really the most dangerous and corrupt enterprise of the Berlin theatrical bourgeoisie. And I'm sure you will never get Herr Seeler to utter the generous words of the Arab fishmonger: 'It's not the fish that stink, it's me.'

Cordially yours

[Berlin], Spichernstrasse 16
9 April [1927]

118 To Emil Hesse-Burri

Dear Hesse,

Many thanks for your letter. Enclosed a letter from me to Jhering. If you really want to stop the production (you might be giving up an opportunity), the only way will be to write to the actors. You would have to write that you don't wish your play performed by the 'Junge Bühne' because in your opinion the most important thing about it is that it offers the possibility of a new theatrical style, and beg them not to support anyone in an action against the play, and you can't help regarding a production by the 'Junge Bühne', however aesthetically successful, as just such an action. You could even say that as a stranger to the Berlin theatre, you attach sufficient importance to my opinion that the 'Junge Bühne' is a bourgeois institution for the sabotage of the living theatre, etc. I believe such a letter would be a means of utilising the one opportunity offered by the 'Junge Bühne's' projected production. I am writing you this letter only because I know you will not regard it as meddling and that you know where I stand and how much I expect of you.

Cordially yours

You had better send a letter to the actors through me. Possibly a duplicate later to Jhering, with the remark that of course you will take no steps apart from this letter, but wanted him at least to know your view of the matter.

[Berlin, April 1927]

119 To Herbert Jhering

Dear Herr Jhering,

I am writing about Burri. From Burri's letter I learn that he himself had no idea that his play was to be produced by the 'Junge Bühne'. Neither the 'Junge Bühne' nor Kiepenheuer Verlag communicated with him. He writes that he will do what he can to stop the production, which is just what I think he should do. In the interest of the theatre, I cannot approve the policy of making dramatists who should be encouraged available to a theatre that should be abolished, unless an adequate check is kept on the production. Critical comment is not sufficient. It comes too late to influence the production and cannot benefit the theatre as such, if only because the critics take the attitude that the performance of a new work is in itself an achievement. But actually such performances merely bolster up the older theatre, which should be abolished. Creation is impaired because the element that is most essential in the present period, namely, the element conducive to a new theatre, is sabotaged and rendered ineffectual. I have always taken this attitude and wish it to be put on record in the present situation (for the sake of good order, so to speak).

With best regards,
Yours,
brecht

13 April 27

122 To Helene Weigel

Dear Helli,

I've recovered the car just in time, the papers had been sent to the wrong address. Big success here. Fifteen minute uproar. When are you coming back?

bert

What news of Steff?.

Going back to Augsburg today. Then probably for two days to see Geis at Puch [?] on the Ammersee.

[Baden-Baden, July 1927]

123 To Felix Gasbarra

Dear Gasbarra

It's pretty boring here, so perhaps more than anyone else I am almost exclusively dependent on the statements – plentiful, I'm glad to say – that the Piscator Bühne sends to the bourgeois press. In my opinion a collective requires consensus up to a certain point. Largely for that reason, I am glad to say that I am in full agreement with you – half the battle is won if we get the public to expect as little as possible. The surprise will be all the greater. It will be achieved at one stroke if we can set up a theatre collective (which will kill seven or eight other birds besides). Another important task must be to keep the organisation as loose as possible but from the very start to make the strong hand behind it clearly visible. I must admit that at first, when I read Herzog's note thanking me for my collaboration (which was forced on him), I was unable to repress a certain anxiety. But your note about setting up the collective has reassured me; evidently you have persuaded him to work with me. Unfortunately, Toller still seems to be hesitating. He has only made a working arrangement with Erwin Piscator. Of course, since he is the only dramatist whose work it is planned to produce, he has to be very careful. It is especially unfortunate that the collective has issued this statement, because until the collective gets some practical work to do its sole function will be to take responsibility for producing the first play, and possibly giving the theatre a name. Most welcome at present would be a short statement to the effect that the Piscator Theatre has now organised a collective of theatregoers. [Followed by the names]

> With warm regards to all, including
> the boss who is doubtless still at the lakeside.
> Yours,
> B

[Augsburg, early August 1927]

124 To Erwin Piscator

Dear Piscator,

As you may have heard from Gasbarra, one of my eyes turned distinctly bilious when it first fell on a certain news item.

I'll make you a proposition: You abandon the literary character of the collective and make it political, start a 'Red Club' (R.C.) and call the theatre R.C.T. ('Red Club Theatre'). At first this club, which quite frankly would use the theatre only for political purposes, would include only the names already mentioned (plus of course such people as Jhering, Grosz, Schlichter, Weill, Sternberg etc.). But later – as soon as possible, that is – members of the audience should be enabled to join. This club could really play a political role, issue political pamphlets, etc. Then, and only then, would meetings be held in the theatre.

This is a personal idea of mine, please don't misunderstand it. I am not prepared to work under Gasbarra's *literary* direction, but under his political leadership I would be. I may be your comrade, but I am definitely not your dramaturg, etc.

Please think my proposal over. It would be easy to implement, and would give the whole affair an incomparably newer and more impersonal look.

> Cordially yours,
> brecht

[Augsburg, early August 1927]

125 To Herbert Jhering,

Dear Herr Jhering,

I don't believe the present setup of the Piscatorbühne is all that fortunate. In particular, the note about the dramatic collective under the 'direction' of Gasbarra (who is basically a *very* good man) is not much to my liking. I have now made Piscator an important proposal. I have written him a letter advising him to give up the idea of a literary theatre and make it political, to found a 'Red Club' and call the theatre the R.C.T. ('Red Club Theatre')! Then we shall have a political club that will use the theatre for its purposes, turn out pamphlets and hold meetings on its premises. That will give it an impersonal, functional character. From the very start interested members of the audience will be accepted as members, so that a real contact is established between audience and stage, and above all so that the work of the theatre is turned to political use. The first members will not be rather depressing literati but people like Grosz, Weill, Sternberg, etc. It will be possible to send groups into the provinces to make political propaganda on Sunday mornings in the theatres or concert halls. You, no less than myself, would be able to join this club. You would not have to sacrifice your objective critical attitude nor I my ideas as a playwright and so on. But even if you did not wish to join, you and anyone else would find a far more favourable situation if you went to this theatre. This would make it something much more than an experiment aimed abstractly at the rebirth of the theatre. How do you feel about it?

> Cordially yours,
> brecht

Augsburg, 6 August 1927

126 To Helene Weigel

Dear Helli,

Thank you for the letters. I've written to Steuer and will write to Kanter today. So bring Frau Kaiser the photograph, it will give you a chance to visit her. I'm working on *Fatzer*, very slowly but not badly. Apart from that, as usual when idle and orphaned, pornographic sonnets. I'll be there for your last rehearsals unless I'm desperately bogged down in *Fatzer*. If you hear anything about a studio renting for no more than about fifty marks a month, write to me and take it. Then I'll put Hesse up in Hauptmann's room. Also phone Ullstein (royalties department) immediately and tell them to send my instalment here. Don't let Steff run around in the sun too much and don't smoke cigarettes. I'm sure you have plenty of time to fill pipes. There's a picture of me in *Uhu*. Read *Tampico* (*Novels of World Literature*) and the new [Jack] London and send me all the Marxist literature you can lay hands on. Especially the new issues of the history of the revolution. Also call Koch and find out why he hasn't sent any answer to Baden-Baden, and inquire if possible about Cas, Moltkestrasse 10. If in addition to all that you take Steff's picture (in the sun 1/25 second exposure, lens half closed), you'll be as right as rain.

> I kiss you
> b

[Augsburg, August–September 1927]

127 To Erwin Piscator

Dear Piscator,

I'm writing instead of talking to you, because it's about an interesting and really important point. I'm obliged to give you a refusal which has cost me more thought than the hardest work would have done. So far I've been working on that ballad by [Upton] Sinclair, the one about the roses on the grave. I've begun translating it seven or eight times. The results are so dismal I wouldn't want you to see them. Naturally I've tried to find the reason (*since there was no lack of interest*) and to you it must be obvious that I did *not* put the blame on my incompetence. Even so, I want to tell you the result of my meditations on my failure: the poem, I believe, is not a good one. It's pretty, it's touching, the theme is objectively sound, but believe me, there's not an ounce of revolutionary feeling in it, in fact it's very much like those wretched working-class songs that cry out for pity (whose?). Imagine a whole house full of grown men bathed in tears and singing a four-part plaint to the effect that everyone and everything, even the roses on their graves, are persecuting them. The truth is that this is a historic genre painting, poetic in expression and embarrassing in effect. I'm going into it at such length because it typifies a certain weakness in socialist literature; I can get along without [Gerhart Hauptmann's] *The Weavers* and *Henschel* as well, which ain't doing so good either.

I hope you won't start regarding me as one of those people who are always theoretically willing to do practical work but in practice say they can't be bothered with theories (even their own).

Cordially yours,

In Oldenburg all of a sudden, 1927

128 To Ernst Hardt

Berlin W 50, Spichernstrasse 16
18 October 1927

Dear Herr Hardt,

Thank you for the regards Herr Braun has passed on to me and for the magazine with the article on *Mann ist Mann*. Forgive me for taking so long to write, but I was submerged in work all summer and for the last few weeks I've been laid up.

I'd have liked to talk with you about the possibility of a real radio play. I've sketched one out in the naive manner, it's called *The Story of the Flood*. Some fairly modern big cities are swallowed up in it. But it's hard to write something when there's no guarantee of its ever being used, and for which, even if it is broadcast, the pay is likely to be ridiculously low. (Which in part no doubt is because radio still has no repertory with possibilities of repetition. This kind of play should be produced each year on a certain day.) Though I have excellent connections both in Berlin and in Breslau, I should first like to ask whether you can create an opening for this sort of play in Cologne. I'm sure it would be a big thing, the first of its kind. It might even be entitled 'The Cologne Flood'. Incidentally, the project means a lot to me, but there's no hurry.

Cordially yours,

129 To Verlag Williams & Co./Edith Jacobsohn

Berlin W 50, Spichernstrasse 16,
16 December 1927

Dear Frau Jacobsohn,

I have just heard that you wish to pay me M 100 for the right to reprint a prose work of mine in your *Young People's Anthology*. When Herr Koch told me you wished to compile an anthology for young people I had no objection to being represented in it. If you had asked me then, I should have told you my price straight away, even if you had told me only that you wished to reprint this particular work. This price is and remains M 250. Unfortunately I get the impression that you wish to produce your book rather cheaply when you tell me you paid no more for a previously unpublished work by [Else] Lasker-Schüler! I must say that this news, far from reassuring me for myself, dismays me for Lasker-Schüler. I consider it totally inadmissible to pay her such a fee.

May I ask you to attend to this small matter.

Yours faithfully

Frau E. Jacobsohn
Berlin W

130 To the Wilmersdorf-Nord Finance Office

Berlin W 50 Spichernstrasse 16

Ref. 5/587, Room 801
To Finance Office Wilmersdorf-Nord, Wilmersdorf
Dear Sir,

I have received another summons to file a tax return and wish to explain to you why I regard myself as tax-exempt.

I write plays and, apart from a few poorly paid incidental jobs, live exclusively on publishers' advances, which are paid to me in the form of loans. Since *for the present* I earn next to nothing with my plays, I am up to my ears in debt to my publishers. I am living in a small studio in Spichernstrasse and, should you suspect the presence of wealth, invite you to call on me.

Yours faithfully,
Bert Brecht

132 To Erich Engel

Dear Engel,

It is true that intellectually developed persons have poor memories – yet I have a distinct (though not necessarily reliable) feeling that towards the end we gazed upon each other with friendly eyes.

If we failed to exchange the courtesies, which are always to be recommended, this should be taken as an expression of the unshakeable solidity of our relationship; so it's quite possible that we did.

I wanted to write you something very specific, but now, after so many sentences, no longer remember exactly what it was. As I'm not all that pedantic by nature or, as I hope, too calculating, such a lapse of memory doesn't trouble me very much, especially since I am probably more aware than most people of the constant flux of things and the incredible speed with which thoughts and feelings grow old. It is hard for an intelligent man, still capable of learning, to remain unreservedly committed to an idea until he has uttered the last word of his sentence. And another thing: the slightest effort we make in any direction wrecks the outcome. The one thing that worries me may be this: that what I have undertaken (without success) to write to you may derive a disproportionate and ostentatious importance from the very fact that I have not written it and you may need this very warning. But with true satisfaction I note that now, at the end of my letter, the feelings towards you with which I began it are almost unchanged, namely, favourable – undoubtedly a rare instance of constancy among humankind.

> Yours,
> Brecht

[Middle to end of the twenties]

133 To Erich Engel

Dear Engel,

I thought from the first that you would immediately consider the play complete if it might cost you money not to. When there were certain indications that it might cost you money, your refusal to rehearse this text gave way to the assurance that you could do so. In other words you regard this text as the right one and yourself as the right man as soon as a different opinion (your own previous one for instance) implies a loss of money. I don't think you are avaricious but a passive dependence on money (and possibly on prestige) has sufficed to make you incapable of artistically or intellectually responsible work. Obviously you yourself can no longer stage this simple play, which ventures only very timidly into new territory. For the mere sake of money and fame you would make old theatre of this play, and you know it. So ends our collaboration of several years, with which, regardless of the trouble it cost me and of the results, I was quite satisfied as long as I was able to believe that it served a creative purpose.

> Yours,
> Brecht

[Middle to end of the twenties]

135 To Ferdinand Reyher

> Berlin, Spichernstrasse 16
> 9 May 1928

Dear Herr Reyher,

No, I have never tried to do anything with my things in America. I'd be glad if you mentioned them occasionally. When will you be coming here again? It's mostly because of your play that I ask. This is how things stand: We've shown it to two publishers. After vain attempts to read it, both returned it and asked for a synopsis, because they were unable to read it. Elisabeth Hauptmann quickly did a sort of résumé. We didn't give it to the publishers, though, but to Erich Engel, who is the top director at the Staatstheater and undoubtedly our best director. (Next winter he'll be doing two of my plays and before that *The Beggar's Opera*). Engel liked it enormously, he said the play should be translated, it would definitely be produced. Then we got Kortner, the most influential actor at the Staatstheater, interested, and he liked it a lot too. He has always wanted to do a play about boxers. So the play has to be translated, then we must show it to Engel and Kortner, then we'll approach a theatre, after that a publisher.

As regards the translation, the simplest course would be if you and Hauptmann could sit down together; that way it could be done quickly and reliably. That's why I ask you if *you'll* be coming over again. Otherwise Hauptmann wants to try doing it with Samson-Körner. In that case, it might be a good idea for you to send a short list of words and phrases that you consider hard to translate, along with rough translations, which we will always be able to straighten out. I imagine you have a pretty good idea what these words and phrases are. There are some that would look quite harmless to us. If you don't think this advisable, we'll do it with the help of Samson and someone else who knows the field. Most important: all this must be done very quickly.

Tomorrow I shall be going to a place near Marseille for few weeks. Letters will reach me via Berlin. In mid-June I'll be back in Berlin for a fortnight. I won't be settled in Berlin until about 20 August. Will you attend the opening of your play in London? When is it to be?

Write as soon as you can.

> Yours,
> brecht

Enclosed E. Hauptmann's résumé. She would like you to tell her if she has misunderstood anything, and to write her a few lines explaining the swindle in the second act.

136 To Willy Haas

Saint Cyr, 6 June 1928

Herrn Willy Haas, *Literarische Welt*

After brief annoyance that [Stefan] George should not even have succeeded in keeping his sixtieth birthday a secret, I hasten to answer you, for I regard it as my duty to be present at certain reactionary events.

This author is one of those men who, because of their isolation in an age now regarded as inglorious, are believed to stand in contrast to that age. Thus they benefit from a sympathy which is in essence no more than a revulsion from the imperial age, until in the end it becomes clear that at bottom they were part and parcel of that age. And since such dissenting opinions as are still discernible are so very trifling or are situated in such very unimportant domains, one cannot fail to suspect that these men owed their isolation solely to their vanity or to their domineering ways. With the help of your questionnaire, I hope, you will discover that this author has had very little influence on the younger generation, though of course you will find this out only if you have canvassed the right people. My own criticism of George's poems is not that they seem empty. I have no objection to emptiness. But their form is so bombastic. His views strike me as irrelevant and incidental, as being originality for its own sake. True, he has absorbed piles of books that have nothing to commend them but their binding, and associated with people who live on their investments. He thus creates the impression of an idler rather than of the seer as which he has been trying to masquerade. The pillar this saint has been standing on was chosen too knowingly; it is situated in too populous an area, and is much too picturesque . . .

Brecht

137 To Ferdinand Reyher

Berlin W 50, Spichernstrasse 16,
July 19th, 1928[1]

Dear Mr Reyher,

I cabled yesterday: 'Please cable authorisation to give play to greatest Berlin publisher. Letter mailed. Brecht.'

You will remember I told you that here plays are given to so-called Bühnenvertrieben that manage and control all performances both in Berlin and in the provinces (Hamburg, Köln, Frankfurt, Leipzig, etc. –

[1]This entire letter is English in the original.

performances in which towns are with regard to reputation and royalties nearly on the same level as in Berlin – and the whole lot of smaller stages). Already for the 'Beggar's Opera' we got the greatest Berlin publishers (Bühnenvertrieb) Felix Bloch Erben, Berlin-Wilmersdorf, Nikolsburger Platz 3. They control the dramatic works of Hauptmann, Sudermann and what is perhaps more all the big 'Schlager' [hits] of the last season and the coming.

They read the play and were delighted and would take it at once 'to work' with it. This is the first of the four plays dealing with boxing that come over from America for the next season they said and we have a big chance. They have the best personal connections with our Berlin theatres and I think we could manage together with them a good performance. I promised them to let them have the play 'on hand' and to cable for your authorisation. As soon as they have it they will draw up a contract and send it to you. I asked Mr Rowohlt and he said I should give it them at any rate, for here the first chief thing is to have a good Bühnenvertrieb for a play which is a guarantee to get a good performance.

What about the New York performance?

> With best wishes
> yours sincerely
> brecht

138 To Helene Weigel

Dear Helli,

At last I am on the road to Utting again. Please forgive me for not writing. I've finished 'Beggar's Opera' etc. and have been almost uninterruptedly out of sorts because it has been too hot. Now, by way of Heidelberg where *Jungle* is being produced, I'm going direct to Augsburg, hence Utting. I expect to get there Monday. The Piscators are probably coming down too. Gottron hasn't found anything more. The performance of *Kalkutta* was abominable, Forster was awful, an eccentric salesman – but the box office seems to be good. The films of Steff and Hanne are wonderful. I think you'll be able to act quite a lot next winter. *Jungle* on Saturday, until then I'll be at Sternberg's in Hamburg.

> Kisses
> b

Best to Steff

[July 1928]

140 To Bernard von Brentano

Dear Brentano,

I'd be very grateful if you'd write me something in private about the congress of proletarian literature proprietors, for one thing because in an official report you'll be more likely to make up something favourable than to dig out anything unfavourable. You see, apart from themselves, those people hardly have any enemies left, and since that's their greatest weakness, why provide them with an enemy free of charge? Nor will a congress do what their productions don't, that is, prove that they deserve to be taken seriously as enemies of the bourgeoisie. They are just enemies of bourgeois writers, and they hope with the help of their congress to corner the proletarian market – their pen is to them what the safety match is to Kreuger. Since as literature owners they regard 'their' readers purely as customers (this stuff is good enough for the proletariat), they never detect the illiteracy behind the rabble's ability to read the newspaper. Should we blame them for not learning how to write, when they are guilty of the far greater crime of not teaching people how to read? It's a consumer co-operative. And not, as Lenin, whom they are constantly evoking, demanded, 'a component of organised, systematic Social Democratic party work'. No, it's proletarian culture, a hideous little superstructure, an ornament, bourgeois in character and taste, and for us consequently not an aim but a field of operations. This superstructure is exactly what is bound to develop, given this situation and this class, and these writers must be regarded as rabble and not as leaders of the proletariat. (You could say that what goes before this army is not a pillar of fire but the grey smoke that rises from field kitchens.) Strange as it may seem, the dominated class brings forth only bourgeois culture from its own womb and proletarian culture from the womb of the bourgeoisie. But enough of that.

If possible, start our dialectical activity by rigorously suppressing your private Brentanoan (or Brechtian) feelings and objections, which are not improvements such as can be instantly organised (by *us!*), and make use of your position to establish contacts, chiefly by praising, that is, praising *individuals*. Above all, personal contact. If possible, write to me beforehand, to tell me how you feel about it.

As for our business: Could you help me to compile a short syllabus for use by an intellectual wishing to learn the fundamentals of dialectical materialism? A list perhaps of the various passages scattered through Hegel, Marx, Engels, etc. That is the first thing to be done.

If you can, and you feel like it, take Suhrkamp with you (you can get his address from Hauptmann). He can write it up for the B[erliner] T[ageblatt]. But talk it over with him after the meeting.

> Affectionately,
> your old brecht

[September–October 1928]

141 To Erwin Piscator,

Dear Pis,

Thanks for your letter. I hope the *3-Penny Opera* doesn't sound too provocative at a distance. She hasn't an ounce of falsehood in her, she's a good honest soul. Her success is most gratifying. It refutes the widespread view that the public is incapable of being satisfied – which comes as something of a disappointment to me.

Four weeks in Berlin are enough to convince anyone that the city has recovered. Now that it's all over, it's plain that there's no cultural life apart from the revolutionary movement.

The last pathetic vestige: While *The Red General* was playing, catcalls (that no one wanted to acknowledge) were heard from Brecht's box, where a young Marxist by the name of Sternberg is thought to have been sitting.

The thirty-year-olds have liquidated the revolution, maybe the forty-year-olds will take it up again. But the trouble with intellectuals is that what starts as feelings ends in a hangover. Frankly: disillusionment is an adequate reason for getting oneself shot. Actually these revolutionaries have never gone beyond the Marxism of the Gracchi and now there will be long years of waiting. This is the very best time for any kind of serious work. You're sure to have time this winter.

I heard Mehring read his *Kaufmann* [*The Merchant of Berlin*]. It starts with a good character and a good setting, but then unfortunately he depicts the Jews as tragic. From the second scene on, it's idiotically romantic, with the technique of free association (which I condemned to death five years ago) and impressionistic colour. (The audience is requested to piece the tatters of mood together so as to form an 'impression'.) Too bad.

On the other hand, an excellent Russian film, *Shanghai*, is coming out at the end of October.

You must absolutely come by way of Augsburg. There's a first-rate hotel here that's not too expensive. And above all, time!

                      Shakehands[1]
                      b

                   Augsburg [September–October 1928]

142 To Helene Weigel

Dear Helli,

The photos are very nice. You must take some more. Were they taken with your camera? Here it's boring enough to drive one to despair and work!! *Fatzer* is a tough nut. I'm still tinkering with the framework. What do the two of you do when it's raining? Couldn't you amuse yourself some time shearing Steff bald with 3–5 millimetre clippers? That will get him used to the shape of his head. Please send me Döblin's address (it's in the phone book) and in general write more often, don't be so lazy.

                    b

                 [Augsburg, September–October 1928]

144 To Alfred Döblin

Dear Doctor,

re Diebold: Regardless of what he himself thinks, he needs advice. It should be easy to understand, stimulating, friendly in tone, but firm. Advise him, for instance, to refrain from appraising my talent, such advice would be worth its weight in gold to him. After all, there are other reasons for writing than trying to determine whether or not one is the new Shakespeare. If (because the questioner is lacking in imagination) the question of talent cannot be avoided, it should be made clear that it is me and not Herr Diebold who is being consulted about the drama.

Of course, in so far as Herr Diebold is the new Lessing, he can

[1]English in original.

demonstrate *his* talent by interpreting my reply (as embodied or implied in my plays) for the benefit of the theatrical public. It would be splendid if you could find another comparison to point up the difference between D's aims and wishes and mine (in certain points perhaps yours as well). I myself can't think of any such metaphor.

At this point I see to my horror how arrogant and inhuman my tone becomes when I think of the press. Please forgive me, but literary criticism seems inseparable from the 'German justice' complex . . .

Thank you for inviting me to read my poems in the Herrenhaus, but I have serious misgivings, because my poems have so much to answer for that for some time now every rhyme has stuck in my craw. The trouble is that my poetry is the most telling argument against my plays. The reader heaves a sigh of relief and says my father should have brought me up to be a poet and not a dramatist. As though my singular distaste for the existing 'drama' didn't argue in my favour. After all, I'm only trying to develop a form that will make it possible to accomplish on the stage what distinguishes your novels from Thomas Mann's. In view of the extremely recalcitrant nature of the dramatic medium, I don't know whether this endeavour comes through clearly enough; more often than not the audience's reaction is one of abject fear. Consequently, I don't know whether you yourself, for instance, could say at the present time whether this type of theatre would be more likely than the old variety to do justice to *Wang-lun* or *Wallenstein*. A statement by you in the affirmative (however hesitant) would of course be most helpful to me. It would amount to a condemnation of the Diebolds and others of his ilk, who do not regard such material as suitable for the stage and reject my ideas as 'not utilisable for the drama'.

It would be wonderful if we could have our weekly evenings again this winter. I got a good deal out of them. I have always known that your kind of writing can express our new picture of the world, but now it has also become clear to me that it fills the gap which, precisely, has been opened up by the current Marxist view of art.

Please forgive this theoretical letter, but the name of Diebold has rather thrown me off.

Cordially,
brecht

Augsburg, Bleichstrasse 2,
October 28

145 To Herbert Jhering

Dear Herr Jhering,

I have written to Piscator a few times about *Drums*, and I'd be glad if you could help me persuade him to produce it. At the present time, the mere fact of our collaboration would have an important effect on the public. But it would be a good thing in itself, because the example of a play, which in a sense marked the start of an era, would highlight the general transformation that has taken place since *Drums* was first shown. This would publicise at least one of the successes achieved by our eight years of work. I have done some careful thinking, and the realisation of this project is by far the most important thing I can conceive of for this winter. Objectively it just means work for me, it won't heighten the success of *The Threepenny Opera*, and I don't need to 'deepen' it. *Fatzer* (which can't possibly be put on until next year) is coming along nicely, and I can't make any more money out of *Drums*. But it would be so important. Could you write me a few words about it?

> Cordially yours,
> brecht

Augs[burg], Oct 28

Could you get Piscator to show you my last letter to him? There's something in it about my way of looking at *Drums* today.

146 To Elisabeth Hauptmann

Dear Bess,

Today it struck me that you might like to take a hand in the Massary business. I'd give you a plot, etc. and you'd hammer out a little play, something very loose and sloppy, you could do it piecemeal if you like. Something heartrending and at the same time funny, for about 10,000 marks. You'd have to put your name to it, but it would do you a lot of good.

Because the thing could be made quite acceptable by simple frankness and a kind of touching modesty.

Here, roughly, is the plot.

Setting: Salvation Army and gangsters' dive.

Content: Battle between good and evil.

Moral: Good triumphs.

A horrible gangsters' dive (a caricature of course, this kind of thing: Hey, Jimmy, Bob's finger that was shot off three days ago is still lying around. I suppose he got on somebody's nerves and all hell broke loose!), where Dick Ecclesia is going to the dogs (the worst criminal in all Chicago, very much feared, this kind of thing: Can we smoke, Dick? Well, we thought you wouldn't mind. Why don't he say nothing, that's a bad sign, Dick. Have you got something against us? Take the cigar out of your mouth, Bob, Dick don't like it, he don't like people to smoke in his presence . . .). One evening, enter with drum and saxophone, a Salvation Army detachment, among them Mimosa Bess, the proverbial Salvation Army lass ('You can't undress/Mimosa Bess') and a Chicago free-for-all begins. The boys put on a repentance act and narrate their shameful deeds, etc.

With the wolves howling around them, the Army people huddle together and sing the 'Song of the Brandy Peddler' (*Postille*). A silence follows, during which the gangsters wait for Dick Ecclesia to explode. (Dick hasn't said a word so far. Never mind. He'll send them packing! Already he's ice-cold with rage. Take it from me: blood will flow before the day is out.)

But behold, the girl steps up to him and asks: Whom are they talking about? Who is this Dick Ecclesia? Is it you? (All: Nothing like this ever happened before. Nobody ever dared!) But Dick is silent, ominously, as you can imagine. And again she speaks: If you don't want to talk, you don't have to. Then you won't say the wrong thing. Is this your home here? Do you really like it here – that kind of thing . . . And then she provokes him so blatantly that her comrades try to hold her back, and the gangsters retreat like cowards to escape from the line of fire, taking the other Salvation Army people with them. But Dick just says: Carry on.

The dancing starts up again with 'What's the matter with Dick? Is he sick? Has he got some secret sorrow?' etc., and Mimosa Bess sits down behind a glass of whisky and looks in his direction (I forgot to say that she has said *she wasn't afraid of him*), and it's him who sent her the whisky.

[Following page missing]

[Middle of 1929]

148 To Ernst Hardt

Dear Herr Hardt,

I've been thinking about the radio broadcast of *Lindbergh's Flight*, especially the planned public rehearsal. It could be used for an experiment, a way of showing, at least visually, how listener participation in the art of radio could be made possible. (I regard such participation as necessary if the radio play is to become an 'art'.)

I suggest the following little stage set for this demonstration:

The enclosed statement of principles concerning the use of radio is projected on a large canvas. This projection remains in place during the whole play. On one side of the stage (with the screen behind them) are the broadcasting apparatus, the singers, musicians, speakers, etc.; on the other side, screened off so as to suggest a room, a man sits at a desk in his shirt sleeves with a musical score and hums, plays and sings the part of Lindbergh. *This is the listener.* Since quite a few specialists will be present, it will probably be necessary to have on one side a sign saying 'The Radio' and on the other a sign saying 'Listener'. Before the thing starts, I should like to ask you, dear Herr Hardt, to say a few words about this experiment and the theory behind it, a statement of which I enclose and which we shall have an opportunity to discuss. This is a bother for you, but I know of no one else who could do it.

> With best regards,
> Yours,
> brecht

Enclosed also the complete manuscript.

The new parts are not set to music, they are just recited. The speaker of Lindbergh's part makes a caesura at the end of each line!

[July 1929]

149 To Gerhart Hauptmann

Baden-Baden, 27 July 1929

Dear Herr Doktor Hauptmann,

I am much obliged to you for your kindness in signing my appeal on behalf of Henri Guilbeaux and would be delighted if tomorrow, Sunday, you would attend an experiment of Paul Hindemith's and mine, a *Lehrstück* to be performed at the Stadthalle at 8 p.m.

                              Yours respectfully,
                              bertolt brecht

Because of the late date, I have asked Herr André Germain to bring you
this letter.

151 To Emil Hesse-Burri

Dear Hesse,
    I'll be in Augsburg Thursday and could start working straight away
if you could come. We ought to start on *Aus nichts wird nichts* [Nothing
comes of nothing] and the Daniel Drew thing, and possibly *Fleischhacker*
– the *Weizen* [Wheat] play. I think Aufricht would let you go for eight
or ten days, after all you'd be getting work done, though on a long-term
basis.* What are you doing? I've pretty well recovered and you can
safely blame my stilted handwriting on my pen and the desire to write
legibly.

                              Cordially,
                              brecht

                              Augsburg, Bleichstrasse 2
                              [probably late 1929 or early 1930]

    *Of course I'd take it as a favour on Aufricht's part and gladly return it.

153 To Hanns Eisler

Dear Eisler,
    I've finished with Schmitt and by early next week I'll have finished
with the Mediterranean as well. I've done a little work, but not on *Die
Massnahme* [The Measures Taken] it's too Babylonian-southern here for
that (in spite of Engels's *Dialectics of Nature* on my table under the
[Edgar] Wallace). I'll be going to the Ammersee next week. It would be
wonderful if we could see each other there and attack *Mann ist Mann* etc.
I have pretty well worked off my obligations to the publishers, so we'll
have the autumn for ourselves. I was delighted by our 'triumph' with
the Neue Musik. Weren't you? Could you write me something about
this mammoth flop? I'm looking forward to new work.
                              As ever,

brecht

[Le Lavandou, June–July 1930]

155 To Bernard von Brentano

Dear Brentano,

Please forgive my silence. Lots of work.

As regards the magazine, I have no idea, I haven't discussed it with Rowohlt and all I know is what Jhering and Benjamin have told me. But a conference is planned for the beginning of next week. Hessel, of course, would be only a nonvoting compiler, a technician put in by the publisher to cut down on editorial costs.

So far no agreement has been reached about the actual editorial board. I would suggest Jhering, Benjamin (whom Rowohlt wants and who would fully support us), you and myself. What do you think? Incidentally, I'll be going to Frankfurt (radio) on the 30th. *Die Massnahme* will go off to you tomorrow. It's disgusting that you're away, I'd have liked to talk with you, and not only about my lawsuit. What can we do to bring you to Berlin?

As ever,
brecht

I'd like to go to Paris next week. Couldn't you get yourself sent there?

[Probably autumn 1930]

156 To Georg Lukács

D L [Dear Lukács]

I very much regret that work on the magazine seems to be at a standstill. It is quite true that at the (few) conferences which, I might add, have been held only in response to our constant urging, both Brentano and I have been sceptical from the start about the propaganda *methods* you propose, and are also opposed to your over-abstract definition of 'intellectual', which struck us as impractical (i.e. politically, from the standpoint of influencing said intellectuals). It seemed to us that a magazine in the form you recently proposed would be ineffectual and perhaps even harmful. A purely didactic approach, putting too much stress on our superiority, is ill advised, even if we know that thanks to the disruption of their economic foundations some intellectuals are now open to discussion.*

Dear Lukács, you have made even us, Brentano and myself as well, only too well aware of your superiority, and Brentano's outburst, when he insisted on your listening to his arguments, has shown you how far one can go in dictating to him. This scene (in itself of no importance) would not have occurred if we [Here the text breaks off]

*It is undoubtedly a mistake to suppose that because intellectuals have been jolted by the crisis the slightest push will send them toppling like ripe pears into the lap of Communism. [Brecht's note.]

[End of 1930–beginning of 1931]

157 To Karl Klammer

Berlin, 16 February 1931

Dear Herr Ammer,

Many thanks for sending me your excellent book. Please forgive me for taking so long to write. I have not been very well and have been hard at work. I am sending my most recent volume, containing new work. I prefer to send you the *Threepenny Opera* songs when they are printed in an edition of the opera itself, as they soon will be.

With best regards,
Yours,
bertolt brecht

158 To Helene Weigel

Dear Helli,

Here I am at Le Lavandou, staying at the Hotel Provence, where the Weills are staying too. Hesse and Hauptmann are staying at a private pension, I don't think there can be any such gossip. The Weills are staying at the Hotel Provence.

What about Feuchtwanger? Would you notify Neher? The weather is bad. Wind and rain. What are Steff and Barbara doing? Living at the hotel is not as pleasant as the bungalow last year, no snacks between meals, and no fixed rallying point for us all. A suggestion: Would you care to spend three or four days with me in Paris?

What's happening with Dudow's film? He doesn't write. Please write.

Did you have any notices in Frankfurt?

Have you got Tretiakoff's photos of Barbara?

[Le Lavandou, May 1931]

159 To the Proletarian Theatre, Vienna

Dear Comrades,

We have studied your cuts very carefully, as one has to in a work of this kind. To make this production possible for our Austrian comrades we are prepared for a maximum of concessions. If we cannot agree to certain of your suggestions, it is because we are afraid they would alter the basic stance of the work, in which we find its essential value. The blue lines mean that these passages can be dropped. We fail to understand why the chorus, lines 104–119, cannot be entitled 'Praise of the USSR'. A praise that doesn't name the praisee is logically unjustifiable and artistically ineffectual. I am sorry to say that the Control Chorus, lines 178–184 (p. 334) cannot under any circumstances be dispensed with. If the young agitator were not given this lesson, there would be no justification whatever for his four comrades' taking him with them to have his errors criticised by the Control Chorus. Eisler, in particular, insists on Chorus lines 684–698 (p. 348); to delete them would detract seriously from the musical substance of the work. As for lines 988–994, they contain the explanation (and hence justification) of the killing. To omit them would give the whole play a character of repugnant brutality. And in our opinion the deletion of lines 1002–1041 would endanger the deeper effect of the work. The killing is only the metaphoric expression of the fact that the young comrade has done so much harm with his mistakes that the fight can be carried on more effectively without him than with him. We beg you not to turn a deaf ear to our arguments. We understand your difficulties, but we believe they can be overcome on the basis of our cuts. If this should not be the case, please explain your misgivings. Then perhaps something can be accomplished by *changes* rather than out-and-out deletion.

With revolutionary greetings

[August–September 1932]

160 To Hanns Eisler

Dear Eisler,

I am now at Utting, the next village after Schondorf. I've heard nothing about the film. It seems to be a typical million-dollar project without the millions. Unfortunately for mankind, such mammoth plans usually come to grief for lack of the train fare. But it's too bad that you yourself are so tied down. How about a little trip here? A room is available. Wouldn't you like to look into Grete's blue eyes? The *Measure for Measure* adaptation is ready and has turned out well (unperformable). I hope you will be one of the three readers who will read the work (while observing the necessary precautions). To think this too was conceived as a gold mine! Oh fleeting hopes!

As ever,
brecht

[Utting, summer-autumn 1932]

[Hand-written greetings from Margarete Steffin follow.]

161 To Helene Weigel

Dear Helli,

I'm writing instead of talking, because it's easier. I have such a distaste for talking that it's always a struggle. This is how it usually is with us: Small psychic upsets, which can have many causes and are largely inexplicable, sometimes brought on by misunderstandings and sometimes by the fatigue or irritability that comes of work, in other words by external causes, give rise to big, impenetrable upsets. When that happens, I am unable to repress a disagreeable and undoubtedly wounding tone, and you make forbidding or tragic faces. I have often thought one should try not to attune the body to the mind, since the body supplies more naive and more carefree reconciliations. And indeed it is always a mistake to blame the body (when something goes wrong). I know that in this I am always close to you, despite and even during upsets. If it doesn't look that way, don't forget that at present (and as a rule) I am doing difficult work and if only for that reason unable to express myself mimetically etc., and that I dread private conflicts, scenes, etc., which wear me out. But I am not leading a dissolute life. Nothing of the kind. I know that almost everyone insists on celebrating the day of his birth, explicitly taking leave when going away, saying hello on arrival, explicitly saying last words when dying, explicitly speaking his mind when there's something on his mind, and making it very plain when he's happy or out of sorts, in short, doing everything explicitly, couching it in words, putting in the full stops, beginning new sentences with capital letters – even when they know that they neither wish nor have any reason actually to change anything. This is so universal that you can't really blame anyone for being used to it, but how much more pleasant it would be if this were not so. What do you think?

b

[Probably 1932]

162 To Helene Weigel

Dear Helli,

Here is a street ballad that I wrote for *Uhu*. It goes to the tune of 'Henry slept beside his Newly-wedded' and should be sung in front of a primitive signboard with pictures at which the singer can point his stick. The pictures could be done by Otto or little Roth, who is very badly off.

Greetings,
b

I also have a song in the latest *Rote Post*, but I don't want to sign it. 'March into the Third Reich'. Tune: 'It's a long way to Tipperary'. This too could be sung with a pointer in front of projected photos.

You needn't worry any longer about Grete. She's at the Charité for observation.

[Late 1932–early 1933]

163 To Helene Weigel

Dear Helli,

There's no reason why we should unnecessarily widen an unnecessary rift. And I've told you in all sincerity, putting up Grete was a purely practical matter. Not for a moment was I concerned with having her near me, but only with putting her up. I'd have very much preferred it, and it would have been much more practical if you had put her up somewhere. It isn't as though her sickness were contagious. But even now I must ask you not to find fault with me for putting her up in Hardenbergstrasse, but to help me if it should again become necessary to put her up somewhere. She is now at the Charité, and then she's going to Russia, to the Crimea. She can't go back to Hardenbergstrasse, because it would be unhealthy for her and dangerous for me, but as you know, I'd like to help her (as long as it doesn't cost too much). And in between the Charité and the Crimea she may have to stay somewhere. Where?

Dear Helli, you mustn't make a big thing of this. I can't bear to let myself be influenced by gossip or having to make allowances for the fantasies of a few old maids, you know that. But I am as fond of you as ever.

[Late 1932–early 1933]

165 To Thomas Mann

Dear Herr Doktor Mann,

Permit me to inform you of the profound and sincere respect with which your statement in favour of the German working class has been received by friends I have spoken to in Berlin, Prague, Vienna and Zurich. I am writing you this because, as is widely known, your statement, which has preserved the good name of German literature, has brought you numerous enemies and no doubt endangered you personally as well, and because, what with the total intimidation of the progressive bourgeoisie, I assume that you cannot have heard much about the effect you have produced by coming out in support of the oppressed majority of our people.

Yours respectfully,
bertolt brecht

Lugano, End of March [1933]

167 To Helene Weigel

Dear Helli,

Early this morning in Zurich I read in the paper that Döblin is signing books somewhere this afternoon. I ring him up. A voice from the room next door sings out: Can that be Brecht by any chance? I say: it might be. It's Kurt Kläber. They were going to Lugano that same morning, they have a house on the lake. And then I met Döblin and Seghers with Mann. We decided to try and find something for all of us on Lake Lugano. The Kläbers are looking into it. It's said to be very cheap. I'm going there today. (I came to Lugano yesterday afternoon). Feuchtwanger arrives here tomorrow. Please write to me *poste restante*, Lugano, the hotel is too expensive, I'm moving as soon as possible, perhaps to the Kläbers'. But that's pretty far from Lugano, at Carona, where Feuchtwanger wants to be. Write at once. What news of Barbara? I hope to have something in two or three days. Every night at the hotel etc. is a dreadful expense. I want to have something definite for you when you arrive. One can't buy anything here. It would be best to have everything sent from Berlin.

And bring Steff with you.

> I kiss you
> b

Ratz has been asked to give you the 'Legend of the Unknown Soldier beneath the Triumphal Arch' and 'The Ballad of Paragraph 218' from Eisler's files. Give them to the *Arbeiterzeitung* (Braunthal). Because that will mean money!

[Lugano, March–April 1933]

168 To Helene Weigel

Dear Helli,

I've been running round quite a lot. But now I think it would be best for you yourself to come at once with the children, or maybe first with just Steff. It's easy to get cheap lodgings here for a few days, and then I'll show you what I've found. There's no point in a long-term rental until you get here. Of course I'd like to know how it is on Lake Zurich. Döblin and Seghers are there and besides it's a German city. Still, I think Lugano is cheaper than a few days in Zurich with a family and no flat, and later on we'd be able to take a trip there with this as a base. At present the weather here is better and a lot warmer. *We will need bed linen.* Has my father sent money? Seghers would like to have you in Zurich. If only they at least would come here. Schmidt is no Marx, but even so . . .

Where the Kläbers are, near Carona, there are good cheap places to live, but you can get there only three times a day by bus, which is rather expensive and the last one leaves at six p.m. Perfect with a car. (Maybe Brentano will bring his, but we'd better not count on him.) I'd be happy if we were all together. The currency control isn't bad. Sternberg could live cheaply here, Brentano writes from Basel that it's sinfully expensive. And by the way, tell Höllering to lend Alexander a copy of *The Pointed Heads* and tell him the text can be modified for an English edition. And from Kiepenheuer's stockroom I need a copy of Korsch's *Kapital*.

Please write to me. I kiss you.

b

Lugano, Hotel Bellerive [March–April 1933]

I see now that househunting is pretty hard work.

169 To Margo von Brentano

Dear Frau Brentano,

Many thanks for the letter and package. Mostly books were taken from my flat (when the police searched the place, only the janitor was present). Which ones I don't know, probably my collection of books on the war. As far as I know, [Elisabeth] Hauptmann hasn't been bothered yet. The Ottwalts seem to be having trouble again, Frau Ottwalt has been let out. I've been in Paris where Weill and I had a job to do; but I saw only Eisler and Seghers. There are very nice cheap flats there, and as I was busy this time, I liked the city a lot; we'll probably go there in the autumn after all. Switzerland is too expensive and has no cities; it's a stage set (but without stage hands). Please tell Brentano to let me have Neurath's book to read, I've promised him an answer. What are you people doing in Zurich? Have you been seeing anything of Döblin? Remember me to him.

With best regards,
brecht

Carona, April [1933]

Thank you for your letter and address. Now at last I can post this.

Couldn't Brentano come here one of these days? It would be important, especially as Kläber, who has full powers from the firm, is already here.

170 To Sergei M. Tretiakoff

Dear Comrade Tretiakoff,

Since giving Richter a letter and a play (*The Round Heads and the Pointed Heads*) for you, I have heard nothing from you. I've been in Switzerland for about four weeks, before that I was briefly in Prague, somewhat longer in Vienna, and a week in Paris. Among the comrades, I've found considerable confusion everywhere; after so short a time we have friction, distrust, scepticism or illusions. Almost all the professional revolutionaries seem to have stayed in Germany, but there is very little communication with them; up until now the existence of the party seems to have impaired rather than fostered cohesion among the refugees; they're waiting for directives, party lines, arbitrations etc. Everything is centralised, and the centre doesn't answer.

[Carona, April 1933]

171 To Helene Weigel

Dear Helli,

I've arrived here safely and am already hard at work with Weill. It will go quickly, I hope. If everything turns out right, I'll also get royalties from the London production. – It's very warm here, everything is already green. Haven't run into any friends yet. – Flats are cheap but unfurnished, I'll take a look at some tomorrow. If only we knew how much it would cost to move the furniture here. At least it's a big city, cinemas, theatres, inhabitants, cars, etc. And possibilities for making money. Ballet, film, theatre. Living (housekeeping) *very* cheap. We'd have to come in October more or less. – I hope to be able to send you money tomorrow. *At the latest* the day after tomorrow. (The business manager is still in London.) How are you people doing? I miss the lovely evenings in Carona. Steff ought to learn French.

> I kiss you
> b

But write! Hotel Splendide Etoile.

[Paris, May 1933]

172 To Helene Weigel (postcard)

Dear Helli,

The ballet went very well, though it wasn't all that significant. I expect to be there in about a week; I may get a commission to do a film (there may be a part for you, in the autumn, it's not impossible.) Then I'll negotiate with Aufricht for a *Round Heads* production in Paris. When are the Ottwalts coming? What about the car? What's it like at Thurö? Please write.

> I kiss you
> b

> Pension de Famille, 269 rue Saint-Jacques

Best to Marie, Steff and Barbara, also to M[aria] Lazar and Frau Michaelis.

Paris, 10 June 1933 [postmark]

173 To Johannes R. Becher,

28 June 1933

Dear Becher,

Now that I've been in Prague, Vienna, Zurich, Paris, Lugano and Denmark, I've begun to see more and more clearly how vitally necessary it has become to hold an authorised conference among a few colleagues, at which we would arrive at a definite decision concerning the scope and methods of our future work.

Almost everywhere I have found extreme discouragement and confusion. Cut off from the proletariat, kept increasingly busy earning a bare living, which is made possible only by compromise in all important matters, scattered among many widely-dispersed cities, proletarian writers will find it very difficult to keep up their revolutionary production. Already they're planning innocuous children's books, 'camouflaged' novels for bourgeois publishing houses, trashy films for bourgeois producers, etc. A few seem to cherish the hope that some yet-to-be-founded proletarian publishing houses will keep them above water.

The left bourgeois writers seem in general to be preparing for a *long* period in exile; they also seem to be considering possibilities of return, and have no orientation with regard to the fight against fascism. The fact that their names are borrowed for some cause now and then does not give them an orientation. Yet some seem painfully aware of their helplessness and disorientation and this gives us a real chance (though probably not for long) to win them over. The thesis that we should leave them in peace for fear of alienating their sympathies has never been more mistaken than now. Now, if ever, they would be accessible to a real political education.

Ottwalt's stories from Germany coincide alarmingly with my experience outside Germany; both point to a rapidly diminishing understanding of the difficulties facing the [Soviet] Union and of its progressive character. I'm afraid you people don't really take this into account, but this would be a very bad time to bury our heads in the sand. Of this, one example: I have spoken with members of the French delegation to the Theatre Olympiad and gained a devastating impression of their mood. What distressed them most was the absence of slogans. They had the impression that for practical purposes the leadership has ceased to exist. It is not uninteresting to note that the usual and inevitable complaints about the character of one slogan or another have given way to complaints about the absence of any slogan.

You must absolutely press for the conference and see to it that really authoritative friends attend it (for instance, Radek, Koltsov, Tretiakoff, Dinamov, etc.). I happen to know that apart from me and *independently* of me, Kläber and Ottwalt among others as well as Trude and Otto in Germany, are also demanding such a conference.

As ever,

By the way, when will you be passing through Denmark, Thurö for instance?

174 To Felix Bloch Successors, Theatrical Agents

Dear Herr Wreede,

I must first contradict certain points that you make in your last letter. You complain that in addition to writing plays I have turned out other literary works that you cannot handle. That is true. You knew, however, that I did this well before the contract I signed with you, that I was never a mass producer for the theatre, and that my luxury (as you put it) activity, embracing didactic plays, poems, prose works, and the creation of a new dramatic style, understandably redounded to my reputation as a writer and therefore served your interests as well. You have often assured me that you favoured such a view of my literary activity and approved the specific nature of my working methods. Moreover, even if I had completely given up all work not directly related to the stage, I could not have turned out more plays. Our contract provided for a minimum of three over a period of seven years, and I have delivered two within four years. You raised no objection to these when I delivered them. They were my principal work during that time, and I devoted great care to them. (Money, too, I might add, for I passed on a large part of my receipts to my co-workers.) I have heard no one say that these works indicated a decline of my talent. Ideological reasons alone prevented them from being produced at once, and you told me many times that you had no doubt of their success if the political situation should improve. And you, too, believed there would be such an improvement. Production in Germany is now out of the question, but the foreign market remains. As for the royalties paid me by your firm, they can have had no other source than the two plays. At our last interview, you made it very clear to me that if these payments should cease you would 'obviously' have to leave me free to dispose of my further production (which is all I have to live on). You told me explicitly that your receipts from *The Threepenny Opera* would serve exclusively for further payments to me. As for the advance on *Happy End*, I definitely did not receive a 'large share' of it. I was given the privilege of contributing my songs, in return for which I was to receive a share of the royalties. I passed the advance on to Frau Hauptmann with the understanding that she would settle up with me later. I am not responsible for a repayment of the advance, and I doubt if such repayment can be demanded. Nevertheless, if you should still think it would be useful to rework this play, I remain at your disposal, not only for the sake of the songs or because of my collaborator E. Hauptmann, but also for your sake, out of loyalty and because this contract, as explicitly stated, had nothing to do with the other contract, which is the only one we have been talking about. And another thing, to depart for once from a 'strictly legal point of view', I am not interested solely in defending my own interests, for I don't believe my interests are all that radically different from yours. A while ago I proposed certain projects to you that I thought financially promising. (The adaptation of *Measure for Measure* was one, I honestly thought so and I hope you do not doubt me.). I offered you my help with an adaptation of *Gösta Berling*, etc. I was not indifferent to your losses, though I never regarded them as irretrievable, nor am I today (when they are certainly not irretrievable). Of course you must do your best to place your plays, if not in then outside Germany. If, under the existing conditions, which are at least as hard on me as they are on you, you wish to discuss further work with me, you will find me prepared for financial concessions that will demonstrate my loyalty to you. Of course I have to live on my present and future work, but I don't need to tell you that. I don't believe I can owe you anything apart from your share in the two plays (assuming that in view of your nonfulfilment of our contract, I really do owe you this share). But over and above my legal obligations, I shall be glad to do what I can to help compensate for your loss as *quickly* as possible. What can I do? I would not like you to think me indifferent to your interests.

Yours faithfully,

Thurö per Svendborg, Denmark
End of June 1933

175 To Karl Kraus

Dear Herr Kraus,

I hope this isn't you! This item and in the *Wiener Tag* has given us a terrible fright. – For some weeks we have been on the small island of Thurö, a flat, green little island, with woods and bathing. There is a small town nearby, not bad at all. And it's amazingly cheap, much cheaper than Austria. If you are really going to northwestern France, couldn't you take a ship to Denmark on your way back? True, it's pretty far to Austria.

With warmest regards
your devoted
bertolt brecht

Thurö per Svendborg, Denmark
Beginning of July, 1933

Helli sends regards.

176 To Karl Kraus

Dear Herr Kraus,

It's been a long time since we heard from you. Since *Die Fackel* stopped coming out, there's been no way of knowing how you are. One can ask certain people, but the information obtained is not authentic.

I'd like to urge you again to do the study of language we once spoke of. (You know, the Chinese have a story that when Lao-tzu was leaving China to escape the stupidity and wickedness of his compatriots, a customs officer pleaded with him to write down a few more of his thoughts. The philosopher complied. It was thus that he came to write the *Tao Tê-Ching*, thereby showing the ages to come that such pleas are in order.)

For many years only the refinements of language were thought to be of interest. Only when 'used' by artists did language become an object of critique. No one who spoke without special pretension had to fear that his language would be examined through a magnifying glass. And yet the most frightful devastations have been caused by language. You have disclosed the atrocities of intonation and created an ethics of language; for you grammar has become a branch of ethics, and you have convicted criminals by using their language as evidence. I won't go into this too deeply, because I don't know where this letter will find you; I only want to say that this period, unhappy in so many respects, would be a good one in which to continue your study of language. I'm sorry to have to bring in another Chinese; maybe it's because the Chinese writers not only were concerned with recording manners and customs but also seem to have paid close attention to language. Confucius is said to have achieved great things just by replacing a few words in a common calendar with other words, e.g., by changing 'Such and such a prince murdered the emperor' to 'Such and such a prince executed the emperor'. That, too, was 'only' a matter of language.

[Fragmentary; probably mid-thirties]

177 To Sergei M. Tretiakoff

Thurø per Svendborg, Danmark, 11 July 33

Dear Comrade Tretiakoff,

I don't know whether you've received my last letter. I'm in Denmark now and am able to work quite well here. As before, I would be glad to work in Russia for a while some time in the autumn. Perhaps we could carry out the plan we made with Eisler.

But now I'd like to ask you to look among your things and see if you find that rather illegible typescript of my play *Mann ist Mann*. I can't lay hands on any other copy and would be grateful if you could send it.

What else is going on? Ottwalt is here too. Slatan has been arrested, but will probably be released and deported. He'll have a hard time, because he can't go back to his own country. Do you think he could possibly go to the USSR?

How is *St Joan* coming along? And, incidentally, have you any news of the actress Carola Neher, who hasn't been in Germany for the past six months and is thought to be in Russia? From what I've heard, she first went to Odessa. She has learnt Russian and joined the German party. Maybe you could ask the Germans about her (Piscator, for instance). She would be a wonderful Joan. If the part is already taken, perhaps she could understudy it.

At Becher's request, a short manuscript of mine, 'Songs of Proletarian Mothers', is soon being sent to *International Literature*. As Becher is away, it will be addressed only to 'the editors' of *I.L.* I'd be grateful if you would ask about it when you get a chance. I'm enclosing Eisler's music, I'd like them to print it so the songs can be sung.

    Yours cordially,

178 To the International Association of Revolutionary Writers

       [Thurö], July 13, 1933

Dear Comrades,

As agreed with Comrade Becher I am sending you the enclosed contribution to *International Literature*. Please print Hanns Eisler's music along with the poems, so as to give them use value.

Please send the fee agreed upon with Comrade Becher to:

    Margarete Steffin
   Beauchamp (Seine et Oise) France
    36, avenue Morère.

Please acknowledge receipt of the songs.

    With Com[munist greetings]
    bertolt brecht

179 To Otto Neurath

Dear Herr Neurath,

I've read your *Empirical Sociology* with great profit and jotted down a few notes and questions. These I hope to ask you in person one of these days. But at the moment I wish to inform you of a project with which a few friends and I are busying ourselves. This autumn, probably in Paris, we want to form a small association, whose members, working closely together, will try to draw up a *Catalogue of operative phrases*. By 'operative', of course, we mean 'affecting the structure of social life'. Our collaboration is to be governed by new methods of collective thinking; by which I mean specifically that our methods themselves will at every step be an object of inquiry. In your book you show how the possibility of achieving certain insights is contingent on certain social transformations. The association I'm speaking of, which is to bear the name (that you will not, I hope, find too distressing) of *Association for Dialectical Materialism,* will attempt to derive certain insights and potential insights from social transformations while helping as it were to bring these transformations about. Various phrases to be collected by or submitted to the Association, correlated with social attitudes, are to be analysed in such a way as to throw light on their origin, their effectiveness, and their dependence on other phrases. In addition to certain prognoses, we hope in every case to indicate the attitudes that make these phrases effective or ineffectual. Our catalogue is thus expected to combat metaphysics of every kind and at the same time to carry a concrete organisational force. The purpose of this (hastily written) letter is to ask you whether you would be interested in working with us and if so, to ask you to suggest further names among your acquaintance. It goes without saying that we are not interested primarily in a collection of flawless phrases, but rather in teaching flawless thinking by dissecting a catalogue of seeming truths, lies, infamies, and metaphysicisms. Such a work, including the most general as well as the most specialised phrases (including those of the scientist, since our phrases can of course be drawn from all walks of life . . .

[following page is missing]

[Probably summer of 1933]

180 To Hermann Kesten

Thurö per Svendborg, Danmark,
[20 July 1933]

Dear Kesten,
    Thank you very much for your letter. But in the meantime, probably

at your instigation, Landshoff has written to me. On his advice I have written to Kiepenheuer-Verlag about the rights and remaining stocks of my *Versuche*. With de Lange I have only a contract for one novel, but for reasons of loyalty, if I obtain their stock of the *Versuche* I shall tell him about it. On the other hand of course, I should be glad to work with Landshoff, who has always been helpful to me.

Your suggestion of arranging for an edition of my poems strikes me as a very good one, but before going ahead, we shall have to clear up the question of where we stand with the rights of those of my books which the German publishing houses have almost if not entirely ceased to distribute. My poems, for example, are in the hands of Ullstein. Of course they are nowhere to be had, but does that mean I can publish them somewhere else? What happens, for instance, if the publisher takes the attitude that there has been no demand for them? This question, of course, affects us all equally. How do you feel about it? Has any decision been handed down? Has any precedent been established? What do we do if not?

Do you happen to know where Kiepenheuer is? I'd like to write to him. Do you at least know how he is doing? Is there anything we can do to help him?

Please forgive all the questions.

> With best regards,
> Yours,
> brecht

181 To Johannes R. Becher

Dear Becher,

No news of you for a long time. But B. was here for two days and we were able to discuss a good many things. He wanted me to ask you about the *Neue Deutsche Blätter*, he himself didn't know too much. I wrote to Wieland, telling him that if only because of the 3000 kilometres between us I did not want to join the editorial board. I said I might contribute. B's sample case contained an excellent assortment, and I hope he did not find ours entirely empty. We agreed that our collaboration would have to be systematised and that preparations should be made for each successive step. This applies in particular to the projected magazine, which must be really well done if it is to be effective. In my opinion there could be more humour and less gossip. But this only in passing. Comrade Grete, who looks after my affairs in Paris, writes that the business of a proposed agency for placing stories and articles in newspapers, so as to make some money and get the pot boiling again, has given rise to all sorts of malicious gossip. Please do what you can to stop it. Kläber, Anna, and to some extent Balk, are in the know. It's an economic enterprise. Anyone who is against fascism and wants to sell articles can participate. If the club[1] goes in for something of the same sort, we can work together. Actually the whole thing is not very important, just one among many attempts to sell literary work under the present difficult conditions. I hope of course that you yourself will participate, that is, send some work. It's too bad you can't go back via Svendborg, but we'll see each other even so. There seems to have been all sorts of gossip about the plan we made in Vienna for a permanent meeting place in Paris, but I think B. realises that they will have to supply us systematically with material, advice and collaboration from over there.[2] Ottwalt has more or less completed his pamphlet, it will be sent out in the next few days, so I think I can regard the job here as done. As soon as I have carbon copies, I'll send them to the addresses we agreed on. (I know that Anna has already sent off the rough material, this I have not done because we expressly agreed to send only the formulation that promises to be more effective.) Such vacillations annoy me, and I am especially annoyed by the ghastly atmosphere of distrust and slipshodness that keeps taking over. Why must that be? You, too, must do something to stop it. On the whole, I'm thoroughly optimistic about the possibilities for meaningful work. Even from Germany I hear good things from all sorts of people. Copenhagen is interesting too and can contribute quite a lot.

Cordially

[Thurö, probably July–August 1933]

183 To Helene Weigel (postcard)

Dear Helli,

Good (and long) trip. Visa (Belgian) expired but not needed. Paris

[1] i.e., the Party.
[2] i.e., the Soviet Union.

hot and complicated. Will soon go on to Lio, the Lion. Please send the
second volume of *Versuche*. Preferably direct to the south. (I can start
someone off on the translation.) What's Barbara doing? Don't let the
walls get too [illegible]. Write to me here poste restante, Paris, 25 rue de
Danton. The first hotel I stopped at is too hot.

> I kiss you,
> b

> Paris, 11 September 1933 [postmark]

184 To Helene Weigel

Dear Helli,

Did you get my letter and the money (10,000 francs)? I've had no
answer so far and haven't received the *Versuche* either. It's boring here
on the Mediterranean. I'm at the Hotel La Plage (Sanary). The refugees
here are not a very pleasant sight. Döblin horrified me in Paris by
proclaiming a Jewish state with its own homeland, donated by Wall
Street. Out of fear for their sons, they are all (including Zweig here)
relying on the Zion Real Estate speculation. So Hitler has fascised not
only the Germans but the Jews as well. No one here cares about what's
really going on in Germany. Heinrich Mann is imitating Victor Hugo
and dreaming of a second Weimar Republic. – How about the house?
I'm looking forward to it, I don't think I'll be away for long. I'm
getting ahead with the novel. I've made a lot more changes in the first
half because of the end. – Actually you should have left by now, but I
don't see how you can make it. If you can't we'll leave together later.
I've suggested *Mann ist Mann, Dreigroschenoper*, and *Spitzköpfe* as a play
volume to Illés. For the translation what I'd like best, maybe you could
tell them over there, I haven't written, would be to have the German
printed and the Russian underneath or on the opposite page, then the
readers will learn a little German and those who can will make com-
parisons. And the Germans over there will learn some Russian. – I've
written to Tretiakoff and the Reichs about you. – What's Barbara
doing? Who'll go on studying Danish with Steff? Have you heard from
Martha? From the professor? Has Ottwalt a contract? – You can make a
lot of friends if you take 50 marks worth of merchandise with you. And
making friends is the main thing, don't quarrel and don't let yourself be
drawn into arguments. It would be a good thing if you could stay with

Tretiakoff or the Reichs. You can invite Tretiakoff [to visit us]. If he travels on a Russian ship, he won't need any hard currency.

Dear Helli, I kiss you

b

[Sanary, September 1933]

185 To Bernard von Brentano

Dear Brentano,

Unfortunately I haven't received your pamphlet. Did you actually send it? In ten days I'll be back in Paris and will expect to see you there soon. In December I intend to go back to Denmark, where it's a lot cheaper.

Korsch arrived there after I had left. He is living with us. And now a question: Can you do anything for him with the Büchergilde there? You know, from Korsch I'd always wanted something scholarly but accessible to the general reader, about the dialectical method, derived from *Das Kapital* etc. Do you think the Büchergilde would commission, i.e. publish a work about unknown Marxism? It would be extremely important. By way of introducing myself I'm sending you a poem for the Büchergilde Magazine you once told me about.

What are you doing otherwise?

Another thing. Could you ask Hartung, whom I know well, if he's interested in the *Measure for Measure* adaptation? If so, I'll send it to him. (I have only a few copies.)

I'm eagerly looking forward to your book. Even parts of it would interest me. Of course you can publish any of my poems you like, without a footnote. A reference somewhere to the, as you rightly say, totally unknown place where they were published would be helpful of course.

My work is getting ahead. I have some connections with Dutch publishing houses. Naturally, they're at your disposal.

In choosing a permanent residence you must absolutely keep Denmark in mind. During the summer I had a steady stream of visitors from Germany and students from Copenhagen. These last are very lively and they all understand German. Denmark is closer to Germany, Berlin that is, than Switzerland. Copenhagen is a big city with a good library.

> Yours cordially,
> brecht

> Sanary (Var)
> Hotel de la Plage
> [September 1933]

186 To Gérard de Lange

> Sanary (Var), 9 October 1933
> Hotel de la Plage

Dear Herr de Lange,

   I haven't been able to answer your letter any sooner. I must own that I do not understand it. It seems to change our contract by demanding that the publisher have a right of political censorship. Obviously I cannot accept such a right to censor the philosophical and political content of my work – nor can any other writer with convictions. Quite apart from the fact that I cannot acknowledge a new obligation not contained in our contract, I find it hard to believe that imposing such an obligation on me can benefit the publishing house. The Hitler regime is now trying to introduce a censored literature in Germany; any such attempt is doomed to failure.

   My work on the novel is going well and I hope to deliver it well before the agreed deadline.

> Yours faithfully,
> Bertolt Brecht

187 To (?)

Dear Herr Doktor,

   Would you be kind enough to let me know how Herr K. is getting along? We spent the whole summer in Denmark. Out of an advance I have bought a small fisherman's house not far from Frau Karin Michaelis in Svendborg, a small seaport. If the situation in Austria, which it is quite impossible to judge from here, is no longer to Herr K's liking, we should be very glad to see him up north. It's not too unpleasant. Perhaps, when the time comes, you could remind him of this. – I myself shall be back at the end of November. At present only my wife and children are living there. Until then I shall be in Paris.

With best regards,
Yours

[Autumn 1933]

188 To Helene Weigel

Dear Helli,

Borchardt brought me your letters, and all (3) together, only today, because he was ill and is rather addled. I sent the money in exact accordance with O's instructions, that is, via the State Bank. I wrote to Zurich expressly, telling them to send it in such a way that you don't receive roubles. Hasn't it come *yet*? I also received the telegram late, the postal service here, like various other things, has not progressed beyond the last century. The whole thing has been a mess. I'd be glad to come, but the first thin threads are just beginning to connect here, and besides, the people from the old study group have saddled me with a small but important job. The best would be if Tretiakoff could go with you and then stay a while. Have Asja Lacis and Reich turned up? I've written to them. – Most important, you mustn't do too much, you must take proper care of yourself. I'm still trying to work out how I myself could go there, if only it weren't so far and I had Paris behind me. I shudder at the thought of coming back here. I hope the fever isn't something bad that you've picked up. It would be nice if you wrote to me regularly. Dear Helli.

I've heard from Mari that they're all right. I've written to the professor and sent a lot of newspapers. You must try and get complete sets of Lenin and Marx, also the three or four volumes of the *Banner of Marxism*.

I kiss you
b

Have you got very thin? Those gatekeeper's houses are pleasant but treacherous.

[Paris, October 1933]

189 To Helene Weigel

Dear Helli,

At last I have a place to live. Pleasant room, view of rooftops, telephone, in big hotel, price 2.20 (marks) a day. I don't expect to be here more than three weeks. I hope we arrive home at the same time. The operation gave me a bad scare in spite of Ottwalt's cautious way of writing about it. – The novel is almost finished (in rough draft). – I've sent money. I hope you can get proper care. Tell the Ottwalts to write as often as possible with news of how you are. If you can, write yourself. I'm a little uneasy. Steff has written to me. I hope he doesn't make so many mistakes in writing Danish. – By the way, I haven't got Motesitzky's new address. Have you? – We're awfully far apart, Helli.

b

Eisler is sending a few compositions.

[Paris, October–November 1933]

190 To Helene Weigel

Dear Helli,

You write that I should start writing to Svendborg. Were you able to travel so soon? I'd be very glad if you were: you could convalesce much better there. And now a question: How soon do you think you might possibly be able to come here? About 10 December they're putting on a soirée at which you could recite. I don't really see how you can. You won't be well enough. A production of *The Mother* is planned for the end of January or the middle of February; that seems more likely. Anyway, when you feel well enough, write and tell me how many actors are needed for *The Mother*. I've forgotten. – I've also been talking over the *Medea* idea with Eisler; I think it can be done. The production too. I'm going to Belgium for a day or two at the end of the week to see about it. I'll be coming home soon. Please tell me straight away how you are. I hope the trip home wasn't too bad.

I kiss you
b

Regards to all
I thank Arno[?] for *The Exception and the Rule*.

[Paris, November 1933]

191 To Helene Weigel

Dear Helli,

I wanted to go to Dunkirk today, but then Walter's father had someone phone that he would meet me in Strasbourg, so now I'm sitting in the train to Strasbourg. So I won't be home until the 18th. Has Karin received a shipment of dishes from Berlin? It contains some manuscripts that I hope you've found.

I kiss you

b

[December 1933]

192 To Hermann Kesten

Dear Herr Kesten,

I'm afraid there are some misunderstandings in your letter confirming our recent conversation.

I started from the assumption that it might not be good for me to let my further relations with the Allert de Lange Verlag ('further' in so far as you would make it possible for the firm to publish further works of mine) hinge exclusively on your approval of such works. You once intimated to me that Allert de Lange, whom I do not know personally, is dependent on you for his judgement of literature, since he himself, for instance, was unacquainted with my name before concluding the *Dreigroschenroman* [*Threepenny Novel*] contract. But you yourself did not know whether I was capable of writing novels. Since in my case it is possible to contract for novels, as happened in the case of the *Dreigroschenroman*, *without* previous scrutiny, as also in the case of other authors of my rank (I have mentioned one of these to you), I dismissed the possibility of further contracts with de Lange. From reading two of your books and from some discussions I have concluded that our opinions regarding the aims of literary work and hence the standards by which it is to be judged are far apart. I could not help fearing that the works I submitted to you as reader would be judged by you as novelist. But the rejection of an unfinished work could be extremely damaging to me, for as long as a work is not available to the public, the opinion of an initiate, if it becomes known, is damaging because it cannot be tested. In dealing with the de Lange Verlag two possibilities were therefore open to me: I could write to them that they should not have the book read before signing a contract, or at least not by you; or I could make sure of your loyalty. I would not have expected you to promise to praise a work of mine that you don't like to a publishing house to which you are under obligation to give your true opinion. But I did have to hear from you whether it was really in your intention to tell the publisher that he must not sign a contract with me unless my work was submitted to and approved by you. Such an attitude on your part would have made it impossible for me to put a book into your hands. But you were free to take a different attitude. You could tell the publisher that there are great differences between your literary standards and mine, so that you must decline to judge certain of my literary works. You could tell the publisher what you told me, to wit, that my literary stature in general justified publishing works of mine. You could tell the publisher, for instance, that you had read a chapter and found it generally readable (not an essay in disguise or an unsaleable editorial etc.) or you could have let me show you as much of the *Dreigoschenroman* as I had already written and dispel the publisher's fears that *nothing* had been written. You could have said: Brecht has his own conception of literature, which I do not share, which I even oppose, but what he writes is definitely literature; I will not judge his individual works, since they do not fall in with my conception, but I recognise that he is a writer of a certain stature and not a dilettante. I told you that if I had been a reader I would have proceeded in this way with Döblin or Feuchtwanger for instance, whose works do not fall in with my conceptions but whom as a whole I accept to the extent that I would always say they should be published and discussed and that goes for everything they write. This is not a business pact, it is a tacit understanding between writers and is not directed against publishing houses. And it seemed to me that such an agreement had been reached when you told me that your attitude towards me was roughly as indicated above.

[Paris, December 1933]

193 To Sergei M. Tretiakoff

Dear Comrade Tretiakoff,

I want to thank you and your wife very much for the trouble you have gone to and your friendliness in looking after Helli.

I was almost beginning to hope that you were coming here. You must if you possibly can. I'm sorry to hear that you are often ill. You could convalesce here and we could meanwhile work over various things.

I completed a volume of poems while in Paris. It is being published by [Editions du] Carrefour, I'll send it as soon as I get proofs. A good part of the edition is being sent to Germany. The songs from *The Mother* were to be done over the radio in Hilversum (Holland), but the broadcast was forbidden at the last moment. That would have been a good opportunity to make myself heard in Germany, there are so few. You must pay close attention to Radio Moscow. If the songs from *The Mother* could be done there, it would be very important, because a good many workers here tune in. I could send you an introduction I did for Hilversum. I think I'll go there in April, Eisler is coming along, he's doing much too much music for films in Paris, it would be good for him to do something big. You ask why I don't take a prominent part in Antifa[1] action. The answer is simple. The time for spectacular proclamations, protests etc. is over for the moment. What is needed now is patient, persistent, painstaking educational work as well as study. Among other things, we (Kläber, myself and a few others) have tried to set up an archive for the study of fascism. Of course it's all very difficult. I keep hearing that I've become a fascist or Trotskyist or Buddhist or God knows what. Such nonsense keeps cropping up at present like mushrooms after rain. I'm very much looking forward to seeing you again.

As ever,
b

[Probably December 1933]

194 To Walter Benjamin

Dear Benjamin,
The address for the books is: Maria Lazar, Skovsbostrand per Svendborg. I was unable to pay the hotel bill, because it wasn't ready when I left. Please send it to me. Then I'll send the money. Incidentally, I must have left a horsehair cushion (flat, with white stitching), it may be upstairs. It is pleasant here, not cold at all, much warmer than in Paris. Helli thinks you could manage here on 100 Kr (60 RM, 360 francs). Moreover, the Svendborg library will get you *any* book. We have radio, newspapers, playing cards, your books soon, stoves, small cafés and an

---

[1] Antifascist

uncommonly easy language, and the world is expiring *more quietly* here.

As ever,

brecht

Skovsbostrand per Svendborg
Denmark
22 December 1933

195 To Karl Korsch

Skovsbostrand,
End Dec. 33

Dear Comrade Korsch,

It's really too bad I couldn't get there in time to see you. I was detained by a number of jobs which, if left unfinished, would have obliged me to come back to Paris, and also by my father's asking to see me in Strasbourg. Now of course I'm terribly sorry I wrote so seldom and superficially because I was expecting to see you soon in the flesh. I can only hope you don't think me too rude, all the more so as I'm about to ask you to come back here from Sweden. On hearing that you were planning to go straight back to Germany, my feeling was one of unmingled concern. It would be so much better if you at least postponed this project. For our sort of people, to judge by everything I've heard, living in Germany just now would mean only one thing: to *lose* contact with the working-class movement. Only an organisation might benefit by direct advice; anything else one might offer would first have to be made, and that is best done where it is most practical. The confusion is enormous, and going to Germany might in all seriousness be termed running away. Let me repeat: You will be exceedingly welcome here, as welcome as the exploited to the exploiter. I didn't find Paris very pleasant. Nothing but small groups, or rather, clumps. No perspective! The question is: how long will 'it' last? Otherwise, the usual shouts of betrayal. I understand your distaste for emigration perfectly. Perhaps you could get yourself an official alibi here in Denmark, some fictitious address, so you could go back at any time.

I'm enclosing the books you asked for. I couldn't get them any sooner. That Bauer! Not even Ibsen could have invented him.

With best wishes and regards to you and your wife,

Yours cordially,

197 To Otto Katz (?)

Dear K.,

So I was ten per cent right. The fact is it's not so easy to force whole classes into line. And to think that Bü hasn't been arrested yet. If you ask me, the legendary blood soup of the Spartans also had lots of water in it, it was really water soup. Those people are really out of luck with Bü. What makes them hire pickpockets for a burglary? As if criminals didn't have their specialities. There's something good in Bü, just as there is in the Prussian police, but he simply isn't a conjuror.

Now of course we must put more energy than ever into exposing the notoriously shaky juridical foundation of the anti-Communist campaign. What's needed most is documents, simple montage. Let the facts speak for themselves. No more appeals to sentiments. The tree of indictment will be gradually but all the more effectively stripped bare.

1) Public assertions and measures based on them.

2) Bill of indictment, dropped as a result of the preliminary investigation; a few of its assertions retained, however, and supported by witnesses.

3) Refuted by trial proceedings. New points raised in the indictment.

4) Dropped on the strength of the verdict.

5) What was left? The certainty that van der Lubbe could not have acted alone. The underground passage. Etc.

6) Herr Göring's confession. Motive: the hesitations of the Prussian police.

7) List of measures, court sentences and murders based on the false indictment.

Middle or introductory chapter: 'The Fight for a Book'. Or: 'A Book Fights'. Reference to that ass Shaw. (All those who protested before the verdict made fools of themselves.) A man says: 'A murder is due to be committed over there tonight. Go and prevent it.' The men go and wait for the murderers with searchlights. When they fail to appear, someone says: 'You . . .
[The next page is missing]

Skovsbostrand

End 1933/Beginning 1934

3 Svendborg
1934–1939

Exile and the approach of war

By the beginning of 1934 Brecht was settled in the thatched house at Skovsbostrand, overlooking the Svendborg Sound, where he would remain until four months before the Second World War. Leaving Elisabeth Hauptmann in Berlin (whence she emigrated to work as a teacher in the United States), he had acquired an apparently permanent replacement in the shape of Margarete Steffin, who came to Denmark with him from Paris in December 1933. He had also just met the Danish actress/journalist Ruth Berlau with whom he was to conduct an intense but often problematic love affair for the rest of his life; and from now on both women were attached to the nuclear Brecht family. Friends came to stay or found accommodation in the neighbourhood, among the most frequent being Hanns Eisler, Walter Benjamin and Karl Korsch the philosopher, a thinker who had taught at the Marxist Workers' School but was not otherwise accepted by the KPD. Brecht too began to travel, notably on a more extended stay to the USSR, several times to Paris and for the first time to London and to New York, to the second of which cities, despite a disastrous experience in the theatre in 1935, he became increasingly attracted. From now on most of his links with Germany were cut, even so close and hitherto essential a friend as Caspar Neher no longer figuring in his correspondence. Publishing was difficult, dependent on exiled firms and more or less short-lived German magazines issuing from Prague, Paris, Amsterdam or Moscow. Since Vienna, the home of Helene Weigel's family, now became sadly reactionary both in the cultural and in the political sense, Brecht's only outlets to the German-language audience in this period were through small émigré groups of a cabarettistic, semi-amateur kind.

But there was no lack of subject-matter or incentive. From the beginnings of his collaboration with Eisler, notably on *The Decision* and *The Mother*, Brecht had become a most committed poet who saw every reason, in the desperate campaign against the triumphant Hitler, to meet the tasks set by his party. This did not mean that he did nothing else, nor that his attitude to party policy was free of criticism (as his letters to the more conformist Johannes R. Becher interestingly show);

but it did mean that he could write. Moreover, because the theatrical form which he had evolved over the last years was marginal to the established theatre 'apparatus', he was better placed than most writers to work through such outlets as were available. Initially the policy of the Communist International had been to treat Hitler's dictatorship as evidence of an impending revolution, and this misjudgement – along with their unchanged hostility to the European Socialist parties – was confirmed by the Comintern's Moscow executive in December 1933. But already the international cultural secretariats had become less short-sighted, following the lead of Willi Muenzenberg's IAH organisation (originator of the *Brown Books* and publisher of Brecht's *Songs Poems Choruses* in 1934), until by the beginning of 1935 the KPD was accepting the need for a broad front against Fascism. This was formally proclaimed by Dimitroff at the International's Seventh Congress that summer.

To start with, Brecht busied himself completing the major works in hand, whose conception dated back to before his exile. There were the *Threepenny Novel* and the play *The Round Heads and the Pointed Heads*. Both were finished in the second half of 1934, the latter following an extended visit by Hanns Eisler to set the songs. From then on, however, both Brecht and Eisler began gearing their creativity more closely to the new circumstances, thereby not only modifying the scale and direction of their work but also developing the forms required by such Moscow bodies as MORT, the former International Association of Workers' Theatres, of which Piscator became president that same year, with Bernhard Reich as his deputy, and the International Music Bureau which Eisler chaired from summer 1935. So the short quasi-Chinese 'Lehrstück' *The Horatii and the Curiatii* was (rather amazingly) commissioned by the Red Army; the surprisingly Schönbergian Lenin Cantata (or Requiem, opus 59) by the State Music Publishers, supposedly for the twentieth anniversary of the October Revolution in 1937. The very minimal 'German War Primer' poems were written from 1935 on and became the equally atonal theme and variations *Gegen den Krieg* (opus 55) in 1936. The 'German satires' were written for the German Freedom Radio, that early example of 'black' radio which was set up also in 1936 and supervised from Paris by Eisler's brother Gerhart. The one-acter *Señora Carrar's Rifles* was commissioned by Slatan Dudow and the SDS (or German Writers' Defence League) for the exiled groups to tour in support of the

Spanish Popular Front; while the succession of short plays which Brecht began writing in 1935 and later combined to make *Fear and Misery of the Third Reich* relate to one of Piscator's MORT schemes and could well (in Reich's opinion) have been inspired by a meeting with Vilis Knorin of the Comintern presidium, who insisted on the need for the exiled writers to oppose Hitler's drive to war.

Like several of his fellow-writers, including such non-Communists as Plievier, Toller and Oskar Maria Graf, Brecht was invited to the 1934 Soviet Writers' Congress at which the Stalin-Zhdanov doctrine of Socialist Realism was forcefully, if none too lucidly proclaimed; but he felt too unwell to go. He did however accept Piscator's invitation to attend the 'fifth international decade of revolutionary art' in Moscow the following spring, when he saw Tretiakoff and the outstanding newspaper man Mikhail Koltsov, went to a number of performances including an Okhlopkov production in the round and a one-man show by the Chinese Mei Lan-fang, and learnt apparently for the first time of the Formalist concept of the 'Alienation effect', an expression which he subsequently adapted to his own ends. He appeared on Moscow radio, and the German colony both there and in Leningrad staged programmes of his work, including readings by himself and some of the Eisler songs. At least among the international Communist community he was being presented with various openings – including the possibility of a post as dramaturg to Piscator's planned German theatre in the Volga Republic – though the Russian theatre proper remained unreceptive, as it had done ever since the Moscow Chamber Theatre's *Threepenny Opera* production of 1933.

Yet even at this high point of his reputation in the USSR he stood a little outside all officially favoured groups, and as a result the various collective efforts which he tried to launch were all doomed to fail: the plan for a theatre review with Reich and Piscator, the scheme for a new Communist encyclopaedia which he discussed with Koltsov and others (notably during the first International Writers' Congress in Paris that summer), finally the attempt to set up his own international 'Diderot Society' which would re-found 'theatrical science' in the spirit of the great encyclopaedist. The Lenin Cantata was neither published nor performed, and only in 1936 did he achieve some kind of status as an honorary editor of Koltsov's German-language magazine *Das Wort*, by which time it was too late for him to have much influence in the Soviet sphere.

Not that he had any greater success in New York, where he went at the invitation of the Communist-led Theater Union company some six months after getting back to Denmark. For whereas both George Grosz (who paid a short visit to Svendborg in July 1935) and Eisler (then about to start teaching at the New School) enjoyed many aspects of American life, particularly in the New Deal period, Brecht was struck above all by the persistence in the New York theatre of a crampingly old-fashioned Stanislavsky-based realism. It was this that in his view wrecked the Theatre Union production of *Mother*, and since he had no hesitation in saying so, and was even prepared to call in the American Communist Party to enforce his and Eisler's rights, he largely destroyed such reputation as he had in American 'liberal' circles, with lasting effects. About the only positive benefits of the twelve weeks which he spent there were his encounters with the Blitzsteins and Max Gorelik, his visit to Odets's *Waiting for Lefty*, his attendance at a few rehearsals by Lee Strasberg of *Die Massnahme* and the publication of an article by him in the *New York Times*. The main lesson which he seems to have learnt was that Stanislavsky's ideas had to be combated, whether through the proposed MORT review or by means of some new grouping; (see his subsequent letters to Gorelik and the magazine *Theatre Workshop*, Nos. 310–11).

In 1936 the Popular Front policy seemed to be succeeding, with the advent of broad-based anti-fascist governments in Spain and France – though Hitler's remilitarisation of the Rhineland and Franco's launching of the Civil War showed that the process was not going to be easy. Eisler worked on his vast project for a 'Concentration Camp Symphony'; *Das Wort* was founded in Moscow as an anti-fascist magazine following discussions in France and London between Brecht, Feuchtwanger, Koltsov and his German wife Maria Osten; in Denmark Brecht saw much of Karl Korsch, and at last got *The Round Heads and the Pointed Heads* staged, in a small Copenhagen production with a Danish cast. Under the surface, however, a great deal was happening to affect his future intentions, particularly in so far as they involved the various international organisations in Moscow and the whole Soviet attitude to such creatively radical artists as Eisler and himself. This began with the comprehensive purge of Soviet life prompted by Sergei Kirov's murder and the growing fear of invasion, and burst spectacularly on the outside world with the first 'show trial' of Zinoviev, Kamenev and others that August. Piscator, who was on MORT business in Western Europe, decided on Wilhelm Pieck's advice not to return. The arrests of foreigners gathered pace, not sparing the highest levels of the Comintern. The campaign against 'formalism' in the arts and in favour of a strict Socialist Realism had received a fresh impetus from the Kremlin; bodies like MORT itself were wound up. By the end of the year it was clear that all the most significant of Brecht's Moscow friends and acquaintances were living in danger, even if they had not – like Ernst Ottwalt and Carola Neher – already been put away.

The immediate impact on Brecht can be traced from around Letter 300. From then on there is no more talk of plans involving Russia or MORT or the Mezhrabpom film studios or the foreign-language publishers VEGAAR. *Das Wort* now 'stinks' (letter 298); the alliance with Piscator becomes closer; till by mid-1937 Brecht can tell his friend Borchardt (who got out of Russia early) that he too would like to be in the US. The 'coded', critical, long-unpublished *Me-Ti* aphorisms begin, the only reference to them here start in a letter to Korsch of winter 1936/37. The disagreements with Georg Lukács start to matter, now that he has become the accepted interpreter of Socialist Realist doctrine and the gospel of 'cultural heritage' for the Moscow German-language press, not even excluding *Das Wort*. Partly to maintain the appearance of a common front, but partly too perhaps because (as Brecht told Benjamin) 'every one of their criticisms embraces a threat' Brecht never went publicly into print to defend his own choices of form. Along with the unpublished articles (from 1938 on) the relevant passages in the diaries, the references in the letters of these years to Lukács and the Moscow 'Hungarian clique' of Andor Gábor and Julius Hay are correspondingly important.

It was only in 1938 that Brecht seems once more to have shifted gear as a writer, following the completion and first performance (by Dudow in Paris that May) of *Fear and Misery of the Third Reich*. From then on his work for the old Communist cultural International was finished: it was made no better in his eyes by the fact that Lukács had rather condescendingly approved of it, and in any case the organisations and even the individuals who had stimulated it had mostly disappeared. This is when he compiled the *Svendborg Poems* and wrote a number of those great poems which are that collection's glory, including the Lao-Tse poem and 'To those born later'. From now on, too, he virtually gave up tailoring his plays to the needs and limitations of the émigré theatre groups and left-wing amateurs in other countries, embarking instead on that succession of large-scale plays which remained mainly unperformed till after the Second World War. Since the *Julius Caesar* project (Letters 344ff.) was never completed, the first of these was *Galileo*, which he began writing with a view to the American cinema, following a visit from the Hollywood writer Ferdinand Reyher, whom he had known in Berlin. It was finished that autumn, just when Piscator in Paris was negotiating with Gilbert Miller for a New York production of the *War and Peace* adaptation on which he himself had worked for about a year. Piscator moved to America at the end of December. Eisler was already there as a regular teacher at the New School, and would henceforward remain unavailable for work with Brecht in Europe.

By now Brecht had begun writing of 'the dark times', an expression which we find first in a poem written in 1937 (and here translated by Humphrey Milnes):

> They won't say: when the walnut tree shook in the
>   wind
> But: when [Hitler] crushed the workers.
> They won't say: when the child skimmed a flat stone
>   across the rapids
> But: when the great wars were being prepared for.
> They won't say: when the woman came into the room
> But: when the great powers joined forces against the
>   workers.
> However, they won't say: the times were dark
> Rather: why were their poets silent?

Much of this darkness is familiar history. The French Popular Front government fell in July 1937; the Front itself disintegrated soon after. Franco that year conquered all northern Spain. The Japanese took Shanghai and Nanking. In March 1938 Hitler annexed Austria; then in September, by a shameful agreement with Britain and France, the German-speaking parts of Czechoslovakia. A year later the rest of that country fell to the Nazis; a victorious Franco entered Madrid; Italy invaded Albania. Throughout the summer of 1939 Hitler was preparing for the invasion of Poland, which would open on 1 September and lead to the Second World War. The whole disastrous programme was enthusiastically supported by the majority of Germans, including many workers, and viewed from his Danish island with more or less impotent horror by Brecht.

Hence his decision to leave Denmark, which was now prepared to make a pact with Nazi Germany, and move on to Sweden, which was not. After that, as he told Korsch that February (Letter 380) he too would like to come with his family to the United States. For there was another aspect to the darkness, as close friends like Benjamin and Korsch knew from their talks with him in Svendborg. This lay in the steady deterioration of the situation in the USSR, marked not only by the continued arrests and the enforced aesthetic conformity but also by the increasing abandonment of the old internationalism. Brecht's mounting concern, both broad and in detail, about these things emerges at several points from Letters 300 to 400, which chart the monopolising of *Das Wort* by the 'Moscow clique' up to its absorption in Becher's *Internationale Literatur* (Deutsche Blätter) in spring 1939; the efforts made by him on behalf of Borchardt, Ottwalt and Carola Neher (who is supposed finally to have been shot in June 1942); the holding of the second show trial in Moscow, with Karl Radek as chief defendant, and the arrests of Tretiakoff and Koltsov (both shot). These tragedies overlap the productions of *Carrar* and *Fear and Misery*, the attempt to set up the Diderot Society and the correspondence about Brecht's earlier plays, all of which figure in the same letters but had their origins in a much earlier phase. Undoubtedly this second layer of darkness contributed to the almost resigned state of pessimism that can be detected in 'To those born later', greatest of all his exile poems:

> Our forces were slight. Our goal
> Lay far in the distance
> It was clearly visible, though I myself
> Was unlikely to reach it.
> So passed my time
> Which had been given to me on earth.

That goal did remain visible to Brecht, who was much too obstinate to abandon or deny it. But it no longer seemed quite so close as it had done in Berlin in the winter of 1932/33.

198 To Ernst Ottwalt

Dear Ottwalt,

These last weeks in Paris have been very upsetting, and I also had a cold, that's why I wasn't able to answer you before. The *Neue Deutsche Blätter* need you badly. You will have your work cut out. It will take two or three good issues to make people forget the first ones. Unfortunately, it would be hard for me to send anything more. There is really no good reason why they should treat me worse than the Kestens etc. I can take full responsibility for my contributions ... The reworked version of my poem that finally appeared does not seem very successful to me. More than ever I think you must publish your peasant stories; undoubtedly you can find a form that would make some of them (or even all, but that isn't necessary) publishable in Germany. This simple story – what is really to blame, and what is *un*important? is so good. And I'm also interested in your other novel, but there you have subject matter that's really on its way out. Are you planning to stay in Prague? I hope Prague won't mean too great an interruption of your literary work. Here it's not bad even in winter. Paris *is* bad though, even if there are possibilities (very few) of work. Can you find out something about Slatan [Dudow]? I don't know anything about him except that he is still in Germany and was selling ice-cream. Kurt and Otto are opening an institute with Lex in [Paris], you've probably heard about it. It's hard work. Otto B, in his manifestation as a young and pious Protestant theologian, must make a strange impression on the Gauls, they must be sorely tempted to invite him to a whorehouse ... Do write to me.

My regards to your wife and Johnny.

As ever

[Late 1933–early 1934]

199 To Allert de Lange Verlag

Gentlemen,

At your request I am sending you the introductory chapter of the *Dreigroschenroman* for promotion purposes. It is very hard for me to let you have it before the whole novel is finished. I very much hope, but I am not sure, that no further changes will be made in the final draft.

The first version of the novel is finished, so you needn't worry about my meeting the deadline. The first version comes to about 250 pages – 280 of the size of page I am sending you. The final draft may be longer but will certainly not be shorter. I'm telling you this to help you select typeface and format. It would be good to provide for *comfortable* reading, since parts of the book are quite dense. I would appreciate a sample of the printing.

As Dr Landshoff has probably told you, I have a charming little photo of Carola Neher as Polly Peachum for the jacket. I am arranging to have it sent from Berlin. If you are in a *great* hurry, I shall have to send you something else, to wit, a water colour by Caspar Neher, which I have here. But the photo would be better.

As for the title, please make it just *Dreigroschenroman*, without the article. The chapter I am sending is an introductory chapter, that is, it precedes Book One; the novel is divided into books.

Yours faithfully

200 To Karl Korsch

Skovsbostrand, Svendborg, 25 Jan

Dear Comrade Korsch,

Letters have their drawbacks and a talk would help at a time like this when thoughts come as a reaction and surface in no particular order. To commit them to writing at this point is to fixate them prematurely. All the same, here you are, however roughly.

With Otto Bauer's speech in mind (and having just read the announcement in *Neues Vorwärts* of a short article by Kautsky on the question of a new programme) I reread your splendid critique of Kautsky. In their desperate search for ways of getting into any kind of parliament, the reformists are trying to persuade doctors (including many of the dismissed Jewish doctors) to take up new professions and even attempting to concoct social-revolutionary programmes with a view to restoring democracy. They want us to make up for the omissions of 1918 and give democracy a solid foundation by dispossessing the junkers and industrialists. Democracy, in other words, calls for bloody sacrifice.

His disciples must feel vastly better, you can sense their relief. Kautsky, convinced that it could never have worked the last time – at which the disciples express their pious agreement – hopes that everything will be better next time: democracy will be established, of course it will, and the foundations will be better, perhaps not entirely sound, but better. Anyhow, democracy through socialisation, socialisation as a means of promoting democracy! What can one say to that? Nothing, it seems to me, has ever brought out more clearly the profound wisdom of the [Marxist] classics in leading the proletariat to see revolution as the means of transforming material production. Material production is not only the historical basis of state systems, not just their starting point, their 'lever'; it is itself the goal. That is the crux. Everything else is secondary, derivative and free to take its own form. The state form resulting from such a genuine, basic, radical transformation may be democracy – provided the word continues to be used after the content has undergone a complete change. Then the struggle for democracy becomes a mere matter of tactics: people fight for it because they expect it to bring about the transformation of material production; in which case democracy becomes the 'lever'. I think this way of looking at it can have certain results. Then the concept of democracy ceases to be an aim and becomes a formal matter, which indeed it is. Viz. the criticisms levelled against the Russian setup, deploring the absence of democracy but never saying how and to what extent its presence might promote that productive process from which alone the proletariat can expect any change to its advantage.

That's as far as I had got when your letter arrived. I see that I have already dealt with its first point, however vaguely.

As for point 2), the outlook: the essential, as I see it, is to observe the convergence of factors – unevenness of development and other such differences and displacements making themselves felt within world capitalism. A good many people expect the 'leading' nations to enter a completely fascist phase, blandly overlooking their different rates of development. I don't believe in the advent of total fascism, but even if it occurred, the outlook would still be determined by the sequence of events, in other words, by interactions. We have a fascist Germany and a not yet fascist France, and then the 150 millions (I believe) in the smaller countries, some of which have gone fascist, others not, and if the former then at varying tempos and with varying degrees of success; and on top of that (as in any process of rationalisation) the international situation makes such success depend entirely on whether or not a country is *exclusively* fascist! Anyway, as I've said, I see no real reason for a trend towards total fascism. There are compelling reasons for German fascism, which do not apply to other countries. The bourgeois democracies may look wistfully at the way in which wages can be cut in Germany and the unemployed enslaved, but they also see drawbacks (and France, for instance, has a bare 200,000 or so unemployed). Fascism is a stiff drink; you have to be chilled to the bone, and a *quick* coup must have prospects of success. Unfortunately, we still haven't the faintest idea of the significance of the World War. Its origins remain shrouded in dense fog. The 'salvation of Germany' could never have been achieved in the old democratic form. Regimented as it was, the proletariat was no longer capable of either a foreign or a domestic policy. Hence its avoidance of battle. That of course is a very special situation.

Enough of that. What I've written may be imprecise, but at least it shows where my sole hope lies, namely, in a strictly concrete study of our situation. We must see to it that our tools are in working order. Good old dialectics, as I see it, are far from obsolete; I believe they will have to fight the working class's entire war, and that if they are under a cloud today it is only because the movement has been temporarily weakened. They have rarely been applied – on two occasions, I believe – and both times have emerged clouded. We are in the midst of great changes, but that is no reason for suddenly choosing to turn back to the Stone and Ice Ages.

I would very much like to resume last winter's simple exercises. It is true that everything (i.e., the human material) has been dispersed, but that in itself is all the more reason for clarifying our methods, if we are not to be deprived of all possibility of coordinating our work on the various points that have to be tackled.

In any case, please don't be short of time when you come. In the meantime my *Neue Zeit* has come; that's not much but it's something. Steff and Barbara look forward to seeing the Professor.

> Most cordially yours
> brecht

> Danish Siberia, Jan 34

Just as I feared, it all sounds so dogmatic. Not that I could write a book, let alone two pages.

201 To Bernard von Brentano

Dear Brentano,

Thank you for the book and your last letter. The man is interesting, i.e. boring, i.e., one must read it. As soon as I am in Copenhagen, I shall pass your book on; from here it's difficult, I'm not on mailing terms with many people. I have not yet received the promised contribution by Schwerdt. Do send it. I hear indirectly that you're thinking of coming to our Danish Siberia. That would be splendid. (Next door to us there's a house with about five rooms, annual rent 7–800 crowns or 420–480 marks; it's unfurnished though. You'll be able here as well as anywhere else to follow the intellectual struggles going on in Germany over the radio and read tempting political programmes in the *Neues Vorwärts*. About the squabbles among refugees, it's true, we learn next to nothing here, but that only means that we learn little about nothing. In May, when the trees blossom, I'll be going over there to have a serious word with Uncle Joe under 150,000,000 eyes. In the name of the Association for Clergymen in Distress. What news have you of Fritz St[ernberg]? I no longer have his address. I suppose you have no news of Slatan either. Do ask K[esser] to write me something about his visit. What does Herbert [Jhering] live on anyway? Not, I trust, on any hope of my coming back soon. If he sends me word that he liked the latest drama, I'm sure it's just to make me hurry back. It looks like blackmail to me. Or did you think that up to make me unhappy? That wouldn't be nice of you. Another thing: How can I get hold of Silone's *Fascism* without its costing me a fortune?

Forgive this muddled letter, it's meant mostly as a sign of life. Regards to your wife, I'm so very sorry she's not well. Helli has been ill too, rather seriously in fact, and in Moscow to make matters worse. Here, thank the Lord, there are very good doctors and a good climate, the latter at least on Fyn.

As ever,
b

Danish Siberia, January 1934

202 To Kurt Kläber

Dear Kläber,

It would be marvellous if you should really turn up. I think the quiet here would be good for your health. You would certainly be able to work, and for reclining, walking and reading this place has no equal. But best of all we'd be able to talk things over. But why wait until March? Why not February? Helli will write to you about the economic side of things. She didn't see much in Moscow, she was ill much of the time and when she was more or less well again it was time for her to leave. But they were wonderfully nice to her.

[Lisa] Tetzner, whom you know slightly, writes that she may come here in the spring, which provokes general rejoicing. O pioneers, the finest pastures are still available, there are veins of gold just below the surface, building lots are awaiting your initiative. Those who come first will grind exceeding small and those who come last will be devoured by the dogs, as witness the example of the Institute. The radio enables us to listen in on the intellectual battles being fought in our distant homeland. We see Boniface bracing himself for a blow against the Hitler oak and we accompany him (though only in spirit) to the concentration camp. The priests and *our* godless ones are still standing in any case. Have you read that the ECCI regards the situation in Germany as eminently revolutionary? The latest *Vorwärts* with the new SPÖ programme is also stirring. For the sake of a little old-style democracy, they are prepared to make all sorts of concessions. They're even thinking of nationalising the mines for instance. That should be done by a *strong* elected government. The ballots, it's true, would probably be submitted in a revolutionary way, that is, by force. System is to be introduced into the economy, and then the arts and sciences will thrive. The programme is seductive, especially for old gentlemen. But apparently it is still meeting with opposition. I think the clergy are against it. If you come here, we must discuss it over a game of 66. But do come.

> As ever
> b

> Danish Siberia, January 1934

204 To Walter Benjamin

Dear Benjamin,

In my opinion you should always insist that you're a bibliographer, i.e. a scholar, and ask if there isn't some organisation you can join. That way, you will at least gain time. The stupid part of it is that I don't know (do you?) whether your publishers in Germany would make it a rope to hang you with if you signed. It's possible, but it would be nothing less than Maulerism. There is no real reason why you shouldn't join an obligatory organisation; but the later you do it the more likely you are to be accepted (see *Pointed Heads*), that is, if you haven't broken off the connection.

I'd completely forgotten about the hotel bill. But the money is being sent now. Forgive me. I hope it hasn't been too embarrassing for you.

As ever
b

I still think the best thing for you would be long monographs on Innovative City Builders, i.e. inventors of harness for draught oxen. You could become a new Plutarch.

[Skovsbostrand, early 1934]

206 To Karl Korsch

Dear Comrade Korsch,

Two more questions that strike me as especially important: (1) What Marxist-Leninist methods and constructions seem to you to have taken on an ideological character, i.e. to have detracted from the solution of certain questions and the launching of certain operations, and which methods and constructions have (to the detriment of the revolutionary movement) been discontinued? (Including of course all methods of struggle, party forms etc.)

2) What has been the experience of the working class in its attempts to make political use of its place in the productive process (strikes, union contracts, sabotage, etc.)?

(What capitalist countermeasures has it provoked? How has it dealt with these?)

What would you think of doing a critique of Stalin's *Problems of Leninism*?

I am still up to my neck in work on the *Pointed Heads*. When that's done I'll get back to the novel.

How are you lodged? How is your work going?

[Skovsbostrand, April–May 1934]

207 To Karl Korsch

Dear friend,

Our letters crossed. The reason for my silence was a last straining of energies on *Die Rundköpfe*, which, once Madame Lou was put to flight, we were able to whip into shape. Not long ago I heard our Henry VIII play *Macbeth* over the radio: excellent. If I were in London I'd try to interest him in doing Mauler in *Joan*.

I'm sorry about the Partos letter, I thought it was an issue of PAG that I had already sent you.

To judge by everything I hear from Lima, it might be a good idea to put out a trenchant, realistic, eight-page pamphlet, examining, on the basis of the principal Czuch claims, the changes that have actually occurred in the conditions of the tenant farmers as well as the facts indicating an absence of change in other spheres. In so doing, we should exercise as much dialectics (made recognisable as dialectics) as possible and save as much tradition as can be saved. Today tradition is all the tenant farmers have got left, and to make matters worse, it is often a false tradition. It is always a good method to defend what one's arch-enemy attacks most violently and to accentuate his most repulsive aspects. As for dialectics: *Where* is there still a parcel of such neutral soil? And have we not here an excellent tradition? The struggles for it are always connected with transitional phenomena (ghastly expression!): the essential here is always to intensify, to crystallise out the revolutionary core, etc. I am eagerly awaiting your circular letter.

> Yours cordially,

I am glad to hear about the beastly questions you speak of. Perhaps you hate apparatuses more than I do, but ought I to know them better? You won't begrudge my little triumphs?

> Auf Wiedersehen!

> [Skovsbostrand, May–June 1934]

208 To Hanns Eisler

Dear Eisler,

I must say your letter came as a big disappointment to us. I worked out the Copenhagen schedule as closely as possible. A chance such as we were dreaming of is now available. The Dagmar Theatre is putting its playbill together, and we should come first. The outcome of the negotiations is of course not 100% or even 80% certain, but they can't be postponed any longer. When I went to Copenhagen just now to gain time for you, I found that interest had flagged. I was able to revive it. Per [Knutzon] was concentrating on *Die Rundköpfe*, Gelsted was getting ahead with the translation. Per relied completely on your coming, which I represented as absolutely certain – and to the lawyer as well. I see Copenhagen as the only real possibility of getting it off the ground. And besides, it doesn't endanger any other possibility. Everything else can and must wait, especially as there are no translations. A few days at least. I can't see why you now withdraw your firm undertaking to come at once and not spend more than a week in Paris. The whole future of our work together may depend on it. Anyway, it's the eleventh hour for us and we know it. It's essential that they should hear the music. I am obliged to hold you wholly responsible if it all falls through.

Yours

Monday, 30 April 1934
Skovsbostrand

209 To Per Knutzon

Dear Per,

I hear you are afraid that R. may refuse to participate in a production of *Round Heads* because he does not wish the Jewish question to be discussed at all. I can't imagine how he can be so wrong about the effect of the play. It certainly does not tend to provoke a discussion of the Jewish question. It would do so only if it depicted the unjustified sufferings of the Jews. What it does show is that the 'Jewish factor' plays no part in the way National Socialism (and other reactionary systems, e.g. Tsarism, Pilsudskyism, etc.) exploit the racial question politically. The audience will not say: The Pointed Heads are good or bad, they are treated justly or unjustly, they will say: There is no real difference. If the play is done right, the audience will laugh, and that always clears the air. Anything specifically Jewish is avoided. After ten minutes the audience will see only Round Heads and Pointed Heads and laugh, just as they would if the new governor had in all seriousness broken down the population into bicyclists and pedestrians. Bear in mind that Isabella (the 'Jewess') actually goes into a convent. It's simply a *different* race. There might be ground for misgiving if, as in Bruckner's play *Rassen* or Feuchtwanger's novel, the audience were asked to side with the Jews. But there's no question of that. If the play produces any effect, I hope it will be more like that of in Indian fairy tale à la *Vasantasena*, a gentle mockery of human simplicity. And the music too will count. For instance, there isn't a single song about the racial question, we simply weren't thinking about it. As a socialist, for one thing, I'm not interested in the racial question as such; on the stage, everything connected with it would have a comic effect. The social question, on the other hand, has an effect of seriousness. The music shows that clearly. If R. is really worried, I think you need only give him this explanation. Watching a single scene in rehearsal would convince him.

As ever.

[May 1934]

210 To Walter Benjamin

Dear Benjamin,

Many thanks for the article. It reads splendidly and says more than a good 400-page book. What are your plans for the summer? Here everything is green and pleasant; but you must have rooms, that is, reserve them; otherwise they're not so cheap. We could help each other out, I think. Have you seen Eisler? Get him to show you the songs.

As ever,
brecht

[Skovsbostrand, probably spring 1934]

211 To George Grosz

The Lord of the Straw Hats to the Lord of the Skyscrapers.

Companion of Happy Days. For some months your friend has been living in a thatched rectangular house on an island with an old radio. Like many another, he has been washed away by the *anger of the people*. Though his nose has a bridge and his hair doesn't curl at the back, he has been obliged to shake the golden dust of his homeland off his feet. Gone are the days of asphalt literature. The Society for the Promotion of Moderate Progress Within the Limits of the Permissible has disbanded as has the Society of the Friends of Armed Insurrection. And our friend Borchardt the teacher and patriarch has gone to Minsk to teach the barbarians German culture. I saw him in Paris where the leading charitable organisations gave him a wide berth because of his views on morality. Your own decision to become a patron of the arts rather than remain an artist was a wise one. I read that our enemies reckon the longevity of their rule at about 30,000 (thirty thousand) years, some more cautiously at 20,000. Until then our works will have to remain in drawers which according to optimists will last five years. So far the refugee newspapers have kept us going; we are delighted to learn from them that our compatriots are not happy without us. Culture seems to be in a bad way. This gives us hope that they will soon bring us back.

Summer is coming, the water is warming up. It will soon be time for your annual trip to Europe, friend. Arise, embark. Room and board here cost four crowns (two marks forty). A small Ford from olden days makes life easier. Nowhere will you be closer to your homeland.

As ever,

Skovsbostrand, per Svendborg
May 1934

212 To Allert de Lange Verlag

Sygehus Svendborg, 23 June 1934

Gentlemen,

I am sending the first of the three books of the *3 Groschen Roman* under separate cover. There has been a slight delay because a painful kidney complaint put me in hospital.

The part I am sending today is roughly [–] of the whole novel. Slightly hampered by my illness, I am giving the other two parts a final reading. But you can expect them soon.

I think it would be advisable to consider illustrations. These could be done by Caspar Neher who, to the best of my knowledge, is now working at the Stadttheater in Essen, or by Th. Th. Heine in Prague. They should, in my opinion, be full-page illustrations with a sentence from the novel underneath, as was customary in books of the 1890s.

On a separate sheet I am enclosing a few indications for the compositor, which I should like you to look at.

Yours faithfully,
Bertolt Brecht

213 To Lion Feuchtwanger

Dear Feuchtwanger,

. . . Why shouldn't we just accept the term 'asphalt literature'? What is there against asphalt except those incurables that no amount of 'Heil!' can heal? Only the swamp complains of its great black brother. Of asphalt, so patient, clean and useful. We really are in favour of cities, though perhaps not in their present condition – and by 'present' I definitely don't mean just the last two years. We certainly expect no help from the soil, and we are well aware that the 'Blubo' people don't exactly regard the vast wheat fields of Ohio and the Ukraine as soil, but we, without a moment's hesitation, would prefer it to the meanly and jaggedly parcelled fields of our backward German agriculture, which take so much out of its tillers that they look like old men at the age of forty. Of course we can grant the name of 'asphalt literature' only to works embodying at least a minimum of the bourgeois-rational common sense that so eminently distinguishes the works of Swift, Voltaire, Lessing, Goethe etc. You see my point: for a time we would have to call all true literature 'asphalt literature'. – We would have to say that gruesome, cramped, irrational, formless and untalented works have nothing in common with asphalt literature. Obviously not a single one of the present legally printed products of the Third Reich, that pathetic branch of the international narcotics trade, can be termed asphalt literature. Nothing connected with the 'blood' that is shed and will have to be shed, or with this 'soil', which is of course the good old ground of cold facts, on which the oppressors' brain-gang take their stand, can ever be asphalt literature. Cases of imitation must be mercilessly unmasked and punished, for certain writers today employ forms and means of expression taken from asphalt literature, in other words from literature as such, from the great European literature that has developed historically over the last centuries.

bertolt brecht

[June–July 1934]

214 To Bernard von Brentano

Dear Brentano,

I haven't yet received the story you announce. But things from England have also failed to arrive.

I hope the rubbish about you in *International Literature* doesn't make you too angry, it doesn't mean a thing. Malice without power. As for your question: Do I defend the appointment of second-raters to important positions?: You know that I regard this as a secondary question, but of course we can discuss it. By and large the CP has taken a proletarian line in consulting the C[ommunist] I[nternational] in cases of disagreement between leaders. I know of no instance where this paralysed a revolutionary action and favoured a counter-revolutionary one. Take the RGO-policy and consider it now. How different they look! The withdrawal of the Communists from the unions, which was really brought about by the pressure of the revolutionary elements in the working class, is now revealed to be one of the measures resulting from the weakening workers' revolutionary élan in consequence of the world crisis (at a time when the SPD was strong). The united front! Was it really necessary to pry the workers away from the SPD leadership to win them for the struggle? In the days of the Kapp Putsch, the general strike supported a government that had the police and some of the military behind it. And that government still had something to offer. It was not a time of crisis. There was no way of changing its foreign policy and on the whole, I believe the following is true: few of the many anti-CP tendencies and measures would have produced a revolutionary effect if they had been successful; when they were not successful, their effect was counter-revolutionary. It's too bad we can't discuss this by word of mouth.

I don't have to tell you that Ottwalt hasn't a scrap of any letter that was not addressed to him. You wrote to him too. I read very little of your letter. I'm sure there was plenty in it that he could 'use'. The truth is that nothing helps but real work, usefulness. There's really no point in fighting unless you have power behind you, power you can use for the cause if you have been proved right. Believe me, this is not opportunism.

You must write to me more often and send me your writings.

As ever,

Concerning overleaf: Take another look at [Eugen] Varga, *Probleme der Kriegswirtschaft*, Chap. 7, 'Ausblicke' in *Neue Zeit*, 33, Jahrgang, I. Band, p. 449 (Heft 15)!

[June–July 1934]

215 To Bernard von Brentano

Dear Brentano,

I've been in a nursing home in Svendborg for about four weeks (kidney stones). But the trouble began before that. This is the reason for my silence, for which I apologise all the same. As for Hitler, of course he has plenty of moves left, he can still make himself useful to the dominant clique in a number of ways; still, his possibilities are limited: the revolutionary demands of the SA probably boiled down mostly to *paid* holidays, and when they get them they'll have nothing to wear but their uniforms. To forbid the wearing of the uniform under these circumstances amounts to nudism. On the whole the ruling apparatus is consolidating itself, growing stronger but more isolated, losing its metastases in the 'people', becoming something more and more extraneous, a foreign body. Undoubtedly this is a good thing. And the process is a rapid one. The regime is indeed growing stronger, but regardless of how it solves the employment problem, it is drawing on the budget of the future. What do you think? Incidentally, I'm afraid a letter from me to you has got lost. In that letter I asked you if you had read (and forgotten) Leschnitzer's rubbish. Perhaps it would be a good idea – think it over – for you to get back into the good graces of the Club, so as to shut those windbags up. Otherwise I hear good things about the Party; it is still weak but making a name for itself. The *Rundschau* (latest number (has an excellent programmatic proclamation of the CC [Central Committee], and the *Runa* reports are excellent (for a correspondence). – Pollock's article appeared in his old *Journal for Social Research*, about six months ago. What is Sternberg doing anyway? And what are you doing? Your book? Do you see Kläber? Give him my regards if you do? Won't you be coming here some time? It's beautiful and cheap. I doubt if I can get to Paris very soon. It's most annoying that they haven't sent you my poems, I'm sorry. You will get them of course.

How's your wife?

As ever,

b

Skovsbostrand, Svendborg
July 1934
Provisional address: Sygehus Svendborg, Danmark

216 To Karl Korsch

Dear Com[rade] Korsch,

I'm having a bit of trouble with my kidneys, I have to lie down and am taking advantage of the time and the lack of crime stories to read all the debates about war in the *Neue Zeit*. All grist to my mill. Most Social-

Democrats (virtually all the active members) – pure National Socialism: they actually use the term. The Kautskys and Mehrings are fighting against it. Feebly, of course, but the points that tell are those that invalidate the theoretical position they themselves have been taking for the last twenty years. Their good arguments are in fact Marxism. With such revolutionary substance as they had preserved, they managed (more or less) to survive the war but not the revolution. And yet the proletariat's few great practical insights – the Marxist ones, that is – had a tremendously revolutionary impact. For their purpose was not exhausted. Their causes were still operative.

I am still thinking about your notion of defining Marxism as a relatively short-term phase. That can't be right if you see this phase as already past. What change has there been in the conditions on which it is based? For the proletariat, I mean. They paid dearly for their experience in following Marxist methods, following them rather feebly, often neglecting them, then taking them up again. Thinking people tend to become impatient at the failure of any repeatedly and exhaustively tried method, and to want to discard it entirely; such impatience is dangerous. In any case, the proletariat won't find it easy to make a 'fresh start'. Perhaps after century-long phases of Caesarism, but there's nothing at present to suggest that. The World War having failed is to be repeated. As if it failed only because of the 'mistakes' that were made. The Marxist movement is to be pushed back into illegality. Its legal, collaborationist, gradualist, stoolpigeonish aspects are termed superficial, then discarded in a very practical sense.

We ought now to be concentrating. With difficulty the workers, and only a minority at that, have learned to speak. We need to make use of their speech, along with the images and metaphors derived from their (conscious) life. Traditionally, theory is a kind of weapon, at least in the field of organisation.

[mid-1934]

217 To Allert de Lange Verlag

Skovsbostrand per Svendborg
20 July 1934

Gentlemen,
I received the first sheets of the *Dreigroschenroman* today. I am rather

unhappy about the printing. My Danish friends, to whom I showed the proofs and who know German well, assure me that for them the type is almost illegible. And at present foreign readers are extremely important. In Copenhagen, for instance, my *Versuche*, though hard to get hold of, have sold surprisingly well. The fact is that even for a German reader it's not so easy to follow the very small print in the relatively wide lines. I realise of course that you are trying to give the book a distinctive look. The page as a whole looks good. But the print is *very* small and the bold type gives it a heavy look, which detracts from the unassuming character of the story. Of course I don't know if it's too late to choose a different typeface, but if the cost is not *very* great, I would strongly recommend it. As an example of print that I should like very much for the *Dreigroschenroman* I am sending you the fine Insel edition of [Rilke's] *Malte Laurids Brigge*.

I would also be very much obliged if you would send me galleys instead of page proofs. There are occasional changes which it would be much easier to make in the galleys.

> With best regards,
> Yours

218 To Allert de Lange Verlag

> Skovsbostrand per Svendborg
> (Danmark) 23 July 1934

Dear Dr Landauer,

I have now received the first proofs of the *Dreigroschenroman* and between you and me I am rather horrified at the typeface. I must admit that it is attractive as such and that might be regarded as all right from a certain point of view. But this typeface stresses the solemnity of the book in a most undesirable way. The reader is warned off, so to speak, before starting to read. It is such a solemn, long-bearded, dignified typeface. Of course I too am very much in favour of giving the story a 'distinctive' character. I've sent the Insel Verlag edition of Rilke's *Malte Laurids Brigge* as a model. That would be the right thing. Might it not be possible to reset it? It would really make a difference in the sales (and not only the sales).

As for the translation rights, I have, as I've already told you, certain obligations to Alexander. And in Paris a big French publishing house offered a long time ago to publish the book. I have taken no definite steps in either connection.

With regards,
Yours

219 To Allert de Lange Verlag

Skovsbostrand per Svendborg
23 July 1934

Gentlemen,

I am enclosing the first batch of corrected proofs. The failure to indent the first lines of paragraphs makes for an attractive page but unfortunately obscures the paragraphing. Where a paragraph ends with a full line, the next paragraph is not recognisable as such. But to me it is extremely important that the paragraphs should be clearly separated. So please indent the first line of every paragraph.

As for the italicised passages: because the roman typeface is so bold, they look too small; they are hard to read, and above all they produce the effect of more or less unimportant inserts. The opposite should be the case. You might try one point larger. I hope that won't clash too much with the overall effect.

In the meantime you have no doubt received the little model I have sent you, i.e. the Insel edition of Rilke's novel. In my opinion this format and this typeface would offer great advantages.

The second book and the material for your catalogue also go off to you today.

With best regards,
Yours

Enclosure

220 To Allert de Lange Verlag

Skovsbostrand per Svendborg,
3 August 1934

Gentlemen,

The third part of the *Dreigroschenroman* goes off to you registered by the same post. That leaves only the last chapter, which I shall be sending in the next few days.

Thank you for agreeing to indent the paragraphs and to give the italic passages greater emphasis by means of a different typeface. Perhaps you could send me a sample soon?

Above all I should like you to send the jacket. Once I see it I may find it easier to concoct an introduction.

By when do you need the photo?

With best regards,
Yours,
Bertolt Brecht

221 To Allert de Lange Verlag

Skovsbostrand per Svendborg
Danmark, 15 August 1934

Gentlemen,

The corrected proofs will come in steadily from now on. You needn't worry.

I've noticed a few more points.

The numbers look terribly prominent where the text is printed in italics; in one spot where the number is also italicised the effect is much better.

The spaces between sub-chapters (see, for example, pages 112 and 118) seem much too small, since there is a radical change of scene in these places.

'TSV' and 'ZEG', the abbreviations of the companies, should not be letter-spaced. At present they are sometimes normal and sometimes letter-spaced. After the chapter numbers please no full stop. Or after headings.

The new italic type is most attractive and the print in general looks neat and finished.

Many thanks for returning the Rilke and the picture of Polly. (Were you able to use the latter for the jacket?)

With best regards,
Yours,
Bertolt Brecht

P.S. You needn't bother to return my manuscript, I have another copy for comparison. On the other hand, I'd appreciate it if you sent *several* copies of the first set of galleys.

222 To Allert de Lange Verlag

Skovsbostrand per Svendborg,
18 August 1934

Gentlemen,

In correcting the proofs I see that the printer is still disregarding the paragraphing. This means a lot to me. Obviously the paragraphing is as much a part of the novel as the headings and mottoes; it is even more important. Please instruct the printer to observe the paragraphing scrupulously.

Another thing for the printer: at the beginning I wrote 'Blumsbury' instead of 'Bloomsbury'; please make the spelling consistent, using whichever form gives you the least trouble.

By the same post I am sending you more corrected proofs. I shall send the rest of what I have here on Monday.

With best regards,
Yours,
Bertolt Brecht

223 To Allert de Lange Verlag

Skovsbostrand per Svendborg
(Danmark) 23 August 1934

Gentlemen,

By the same post I am returning all the proofs I had. It's a pity you haven't sent more, because it holds me up and I would like to complete this work soon.

With best regards,
Yours Bertolt Brecht

N B At the front of the book, before the Copyright, I would like you to put: 'This novel is based on the stage play *The Threepenny Opera* and on John Gay's *The Beggar's Opera*.'

The title *Dreigroschenroman* might be more effective if it were printed in one line.

224 To Allert de Lange Verlag

Skovsbostrand per Svendborg
(Danmark), 26 August 1934

Gentlemen,

Many thanks for the last of the proofs.

I don't care for the new italic typeface. From a purely aesthetic point of view it is attractive, but it blends too well with the typography as a whole, and that is a big mistake. It doesn't give the impression that something is being *quoted*, that certain sayings and phrases are being put on *display*, as in the italicised passages in Book Two, on page 306 for example.

Please leave the italics as in Book Two. They are excellent and perfectly suited to the purpose. The book looks fine and can bear the slight blemish, or rather the somewhat unconventional appearance, of the quotations. The new italic typeface is a compromise solution. The reader will tend to ask: What is the purpose of this? The type area is splendid, I hope the pages won't have to be trimmed too severely.

I shall send all the rest of the proofs off to you tomorrow. Would you please have five copies of the last (second) set of proofs run off for me; I can do the work much more quickly if I have them read by several persons at once. And please send the first set at the same time.

With best regards,
Yours,
Bertolt Brecht

P.S. I can't wait to see the jacket.

225 To Allert de Lange Verlag

Gentlemen:

I'd be very sorry if you really decided to use the newly selected bold-face type for the italicised passages. The italicised passages must give the impression of quotations, the thought 'quotation' must spring to the reader's mind. The bold-face type does not meet this requirement. True, it fits into the overall picture, but for that very reason seems quite arbitrary. The reader must think: why suddenly a different typeface? With the light-face italics the intention was clear. With the new typeface I get the feeling that the main purpose of the typography is lost. The question should not be approached from a purely aesthetic standpoint; it should not be supposed that the overall impression has to be absolutely harmonious. It is not enough that the print should be attractive or even clear. It must look like a quotation. Moreover, it must not be smaller than the other print, for then the reader would be led to take the passage as an addition of minor importance. It would be wrong, for example, to print the punch line of a joke *smaller* than the rest.

Please believe me that I wouldn't dwell so long on this question if it were not important; I am reluctant to be so stubborn in view of the obvious pains you have taken.

With best regards,
Yours

Skovsbostrand, Svendborg
1 September 1934

226 To George Grosz

[Skovsbostrand],
2 September 1934

Dear George,

The island of Fyn is known as the garden of Denmark. As far as the eye can see, everything is green and, more important, these people have good commercial contracts with England. The branches of the fruit trees have to be propped, the fishermen thrust spears into the waters of the Sound and a few hours later pull out dozens of eels. I live well, I've written a 500-page novel, and what's more, I have a good commercial contract with a Dutch publishing house. Nevertheless, I am constantly planning blows against the criminals who dwell in the south, if you see what I mean. I listen to all their speeches over the radio, read their draft laws and collect their photographs.

I recently took another look at your drawings for *Three Soldiers*, and a little while later I saw a big Chinese painting on paper, about 3 metres by $1\frac{1}{2}$ (vertical format), apparently representing life in the Golden Age, trees, old men, girls, buildings. The figures are about [–] tall and there are more than forty of them. Even so, the painter has found a way to leave large spaces between them. There are whole oceans between groups (there are six groups and only three isolated figures). In addition, there are tall trees, a small half-flooded temple, a palace, a garden, clouds above it, and only then does the sky begin. And nothing looks small. Four old men are sitting round a table in a garden, playing a board game, and not far from them three others are showing each other the plan of a building. One old man is coaxing a fish out of the water, but this fish, green and about a centimetre long, seems to give him a negative answer. Half a dozen people are sitting on a piece of land that has broken loose in the flood; they are burning incense paper in honour of the gods (who are sitting high up, busy with their toilet) and are engaged in a discussion, probably about historical materialism, One with a fat belly is standing in a dance-like pose on a barrel in the water, holding an umbrella and wearing a splendidly painted carmine coat: a rogue! Etc.

[Rest of letter missing]

227 To Helene Weigel

Dear Helli,

Unfortunately the Dutch money hasn't come. I wired at once but I have to wait for it. Disgusting.

I'm sending you the *Rundköpfe* for Per. It's the only copy with the changes. As I need it for England, it must be handled with care. Maybe Per should first have the whole new Scene 7 typed, so as to have copies both for the translation and for me (I need at least five).

Also tell Per about the idea of the screens to the right and left of the stage. He must again, it's very important, compare the whole Danish text with mine. A good many changes have been made.

Mari thinks it's all right for you to come back this week. There are hardly any cases and those are very light (without paralysis). I also think it's all right for you to come back. I'll send you some money as soon as it comes.

I kiss you

b

[Skovsbostrand, September, 1934]

228 To Gustav Kiepenheuer

Dear Herr Kiepenheuer,

You will agree that for more than a year and a half the distribution of the *Versuche* has been in a very bad way. Some numbers are sold out and have not been reprinted, and the booksellers have been unable to lay hands on the others, etc. I therefore wish to relieve you of all obligations towards me and in turn to be relieved of all obligations towards the Kiepenheuer Verlag. I hereby retract the rights of all the dramatic texts, poems etc. that have appeared in the *Versuche* series. *If* you have any requests, please let me know as soon as possible. If I don't hear from you by 15 October, I shall assume that you agree to this settlement.

> With best regards,
> Yours faithfully,
> Bertolt Brecht

> Skovsbostrand, Svendborg, Denmark
> 26 September 1934

229 To Helene Weigel (postcard)

Dear Helli,

Please send the scene of the *Round Heads* that is only typed – I hope you have received the money in the meantime. I phoned Amsterdam. – What are the children up to? – How's the chess? – I'm feeling fine. Septum all right. – I'm staying at a pension, without meals, Korsch is living over me. The theatres are antediluvian.

> I kiss you,
> b

> London, 13 October 1934 [Postmark]
> 24 Calthorpe Street,
> London W C1

230 To Helene Weigel (postcard)

Dear Helli,

I would much rather you didn't travel until *after* Christmas. Anyway this is the worst time to see about spring and the following season. Better if you picked me up here. I haven't yet been all of four weeks in London. De Lange has only sent 1800 crowns, he's sure to send more. Couldn't you send me at least 200 crowns? Has Mari received the poem? And Steff my letter? I've written to Pappa and sent Mari's poem.

I scratch your back,

b

London, 7 November 1934 [Postmark]

231 To Helene Weigel

Dear Helli

I was rather late in receiving your first letter, telling me you had already left and the address. En route perhaps you can recruit a few people for Svendborg. (The Kläbers, the Brentanos.) Have you seen Sternberg? What's going on with the *Round Heads*? What about Gasbarra? Disgraceful his never writing. You're sure to run into Kraus in Vienna. Don't avoid him. He's bound to find out. I hear that he is (was?) rather ill. Phlebitis. If I were you, I'd be nice to him. You can tell him that I've been upset by his coming out against workers who were defending themselves (and for the agents of the entrepreneurs, bankers and landowners). Ask him if he has received the poems I sent Jaray for him. Also inquire in Vienna whether it's really possible to acquire Czech citizenship. I've heard it is. But in Berlin I don't know anyone but Camill Hoffmann. Kraus's friends probably know more people. I'd be glad to have Kraus's Shakespeare adaptations, which you can get at Lanyi's. – The ten pounds have come, also two copies of *Three Soldiers*. Thanks. Now all I need is *Joan*. Give your father my best regards. Invite him. Give Frank my best, too. How will you go back? If by way of the Saar, I'll send you Eisler's and my last Workers' Songs with music. (Simple marching songs.) Here things are improving slowly, but on the move. I'm trying to do some stories for the cinema, it would bring in some money. But I'm gradually getting fed up with London. Write to my father from down there.

I kiss you,

b

Just received telegram and letter. I don't know the Vienna address. Kiepenheuer has relinquished the rights to *me*. No one else has any rights. Please go and see. If anything whatever has been reprinted, we'll have to sue. I haven't got the letter to [Heinrich] George here. Dammert has it. (He's probably in Paris)

[London, November 1934]

233 To Stefan S. Brecht (postcard)

Dear Steff,

Here's a pretty card with an old Chinese picture, children playing theatre. Look closely at the play they're doing. I think it will strike you as very modern. What is your theatre doing? Thanks for your letter.

As ever,

bidi

London, November 27, 1934 [Postmark]

Regards to Marie

The picture would look good on the wall.

234 To Princess Elisabeth Bibesco

Dear Madam,

It was like arranging to meet a drop of water in the ocean when you invited me to the Savoy on Tuesday. A man of ministerial rank was standing in the entrance to the lobby; he began to question me in one of the languages that are regarded as English in these parts. Unfortunately, he did not recognise me as a man of lofty intellectual stature, a true socialist, etc., but let my exterior mislead him into regarding me as a dangerous individual, or anyway one who would poison the atmosphere of the Savoy. I felt certain that if I had mentioned your name to him, he would instantly have called the police and my intentions towards you would have been exposed. I tried to get into that Tower of Babel by yet another entrance. But there I was buffeted by such a stream of lofty, richly adorned persons, persons who have obviously made their way over dead bodies, that I gave up hope. The feeling was just too strong in me that I was attempting something forbidden. It was clear to me that without the help of at least fifty heavily armed dockers I could not hope to extract you from that building. I left in dismay, for I would very much have liked to talk with you.

[London, late 1934]

235 To Margot von Brentano

Dear Frau Margot,

Many thanks for your letter and the review from the *National*. The two of you should really decide to come up here for a few months. On the 20th I'm going back to Danish Siberia. London is a wicked hard-bitten town. The natives here are among the most vicious in Europe. There is a high culture of corruption, which is all but closed to the tourist. Did you read that on the occasion of a marriage in the Royal family[1] the London unemployed gave the prince a wedding present? Can the Stavisky case hold a candle to such corruption? – What are the Brentanos doing? And your husband's work? What can I read of it? One of these days I'll send him some theses by a young man who smuggled them out of prison. – M.'s address is Miss Mynatt (not Mynotti)!!!

> Affectionately,

> [London, December 1934]

236 To Johannes R. Becher

Dear Becher,

I have a slight horror of get-togethers for the sake of being together. You count the heads of your dearly beloved and assure yourself that all are of one mind etc. It would be very different, of course, if one of these congresses met to discuss a plan for a definite project. Let's say publishing an encyclopaedia, a literary work that might be brought out in fascicles by the members of a kind of academy, which however would have to be organised very loosely. Four or five writers would at the same time put down their opinions on certain topics, watchwords, political slogans, maxims such as 'public need before private greed', either with or without knowledge of what the others are writing. (The Communists, of course, would have to know what the others are writing.) I'm thinking of men like Wells, Shaw, Gide, etc. For the most important topics, of course, material would have to be made available to the writers if they wish – or even if they don't. The result would be a sort of reference work, a compendium of the opinions of antifascists. The greatest freedom could be allowed provided the articles were good. Such a plan would be a more effective means of organising people than any memorial services, celebrations, etc. Of course there's no point in approaching people until the spade work is done, I mean until either German, English or French publishers are found or all that is arranged

[1]The Duke of Kent and Princess Marina of Greece were married in November 1934.

over there. (It would be good if the names aroused a certain amount of interest.) Just now a conversation between Stalin and Wells published in *The New Statesman*, followed by some effusions of Shaw and Keynes, has been making a big stir in England. At present, I believe, a kind of Lexicon is being published over there, but it's scientific and in Russian. What I have in mind is something lighter, something accessible to the general public. The one would not interfere with the other. What do you think?

At the same time I'm sending you an article for *Der Schriftsteller* [*The Author*]. It contains the arguments published in the *Pariser Tageblatt* but carries them further. It is long, but you could run it in instalments. The material strikes me as important.

The *Dreigroschenroman* was sent to your address in Moscow, a long time ago in fact.

Couldn't you visit Copenhagen one of these days and pass through Svendborg?

Cordially,

Skovsbostrand, Svendborg
End of December 1934

237 To Bernhard Reich

Dear Reich,

Please pass the enclosed card with the poem on to Carola Neher. Why are you so hard on the Saar song? Ten thousand copies of it have been distributed in the Saar, it has been published in all the antifascist papers, even in England, and is more important than half a dozen plays. Can you print music in the MORT magazine? – [Unfinished]

[Late 1934–early 1935]

238 To Paul Hindemith

Dear Hindemith,

I hear you have been having serious conflicts with government circles. And I hear that some texts you set to music long ago are being held against you. The worst of them are by me. I hasten to confirm that it was not the 'destructive' tendencies in my poems that led you to work with me. You often told me that you could not regard socialist ideas as material for music. I therefore presume that what attracted you to me was a certain poetic talent and nothing else. I was not able to convince you that this poetic talent is absolutely inseparable from my socialist ideas. You took the attitude that 'under pressure' (and there was plenty of that) one could set a telephone directory to music. But even if I had written a directory for you, it might have led to conflicts with certain government circles – think what professions I might have attached to some of the names, just to lend them a poetic ring . . .

After the outbreak of the third of our calamitous German Reichs, you seem to have tried to set phone books to music. They should have given you high marks for that. It was most obliging on your part. But now we hear that even your musical talents are inseparable from certain ideas.

Those newspapers that are friendly to you stress that even your adversaries don't doubt your musical talent. This is said in a tone implying that this musical talent would have spoken in your favour when certain other things were brought up against you. In reality your musical talent was and remains the main argument against you. For whether or not you write a certain kind of music is not just a question of good will, but also of ability. Like it or not, you are unable to write the kind of music that is demanded in Hitler Germany. It won't help you to set *Mein Kampf* to music, a book whose author counts the top leaders of the police among his friends. You won't fool anyone. I can't help laughing when I read that you are accused of composing 'music of movement'. How are you going to stop that? Naturally they don't want that. Not in any field. Not under any pretext. Why should you of all people be permitted to move? A music that really reflects the world of the twentieth century – an undoubtedly confused, complicated, brutal and contradictory world – can expect no mercy. But what else should it reflect? The contention of a few holders of power that they have put the world in order, turned it into a little pasture full of lambs under a Führer? You can raise your hand in the Hitler salute – maybe they can force you to do that – but the moment you raise a conductor's baton, your competitors will be on the spot and will bring the police along. Music is not an ark in which to survive the flood.

Philosophy, literature, architecture, science or music – all these branches of culture participate in the development of the society to which they belong. Since this society has progressive and regressive trends, music like every other product of the human spirit will embody one or the other trend. The progressive elements of the people will not need the same kind of music as the regressive ones, and progressive music (for music of course has a development of its own) will have these progressive elements of the people as its hearers and practitioners, and in any case as its beneficiaries. The gentlemen in brown are quite right in thinking that your music cannot serve their cause, which is the cause of regression, and that musical talent is unacceptable for their purposes unless it is a talent for regression.

[Late 1934–early 1935]

239 To Johannes R. Becher

Dear Becher,

I hear that Kantorowicz, who in *Unsere Zeit* [*Our Times*] characterised my *Dreigroschenroman* as an idealistic book, which 'does not meet the requirements of realism', is your secretary. That gives his attack an official note.

This attack was made in a representative periodical and in the most virulent form, for the slimy friendliness in which it is wrapped is absolutely uninteresting in view of the central indictment of the novel as idealistic and not realistic.

The attack is made in a slipshod, frivolous way. Such accusations, regarded as lethal among Marxists, are not proved at all; the author has chosen the fine mixture of apodictic and slipshod which is justified in unimportant matters. This in respect of work on which I worked long and intensively.

It is assumed that all novels which are not realistic are therefore idealistic; this might be open to discussion if it were not that only novels devoid of invention are regarded as realistic. All satire would thus be banned as unrealistic. I rallied to the banner of 'realism' because I felt justified in calling Swift and Cervantes realistic authors. And I believed that a work is idealistic if consciousness is represented as the factor determining the reality of social institutions. Having shown in my novel that an individual's ideas are essentially determined by the economic situation and by the class he belongs to, I thought I had written a materialistic novel. Because, since there is no point in interpreting the world and the essential is to change it, I represented reality in such a way that causes and effects are clearly discernible and that action becomes possible, I thought I had written a novel for realists and not merely a novel in which reality plays a part.

Well, you people have taught me better.

I only wish it hadn't been done in such a superficial and arrogant way.

[Early 1935]

241 To Bernard von Brentano

Skovsbostrand, January 35

Dear Brentano,

Thank you for your letter. Your sentence about the advantages of monitoring seems to mean that the K[antorowicz] review is an unfortunate accident and that the monitor has hastened to tell me about it. So while awaiting rectification, let's forget about the review. The sentence provoked by this incident also suggests a certain resentment against supposedly free opinions and evaluations such as Kantor[owicz]'s. Furthermore, to come to the point that is of importance to you, it contains microscopic particles of totally free criticism. I think you know I feel friendly towards you, and not just for the sake of your good looks, but also despite some of your cherished opinions. I share your doubts as to the validity of opinions professed by persons who without said opinions would suffer material loss. But you will agree with me that such opinions may nevertheless be sound. Sound as well as unsound opinions can be bought. I do agree with you about the possibility of substantial reservations with regard to personal opinions and judgements where great tasks are being carried out by a small number of people. In the organisation of great social changes it is necessary on the one hand to make (and break) alliances in many quarters and to allow our like-minded allies considerable freedom in matters that have no bearing on the common aim. (The battle must *somehow* be won.) On the other hand, we must drastically restrict the freedom of opinion of a small nucleus. A party without strict discipline cannot enter into alliances. You tend, it seems to me, to forget how very limited the Russian revolutionaries are in number and how small their social base is. And what an enormous class struggle they are engaged in. And how isolated the Russian industrial proletariat is, how much hatred and how many adversaries they must contend with in building their industry, from which they expect everything. Only this revolutionising of the productive process can solve all problems, the distribution of commodities, the relations of people to one another, the creation of individual freedom. (Creation, not preservation.) It is not possible to bring about a radical change of this kind without repressing those who resist it and in some measure those who favour it. Such repression, we see, sometimes takes on a private character. I do not share your opinion of Stalin. The adulation of the sycophants and the attacks of those who (voluntarily or involuntarily) have withdrawn from the Russian struggle obscure the picture. He is not a brilliant writer. His toleration of a certain deification argues bad taste. But liking to hear himself called 'the great' does not make him little. The assertions of the 'bureaucracy' also have a character of struggle. They are addressed to those who have no confidence, who do not believe in the Party leadership and the necessity of all the effort and hardship (without necessarily being better leaders themselves). And of these there are many. Just consider the makeup of the Russian population, the numbers of peasants, white collar workers, technical intelligentsia of all sorts, of workers, of those who have only recently become workers, etc. Even if you think I am wrong about all this – even then there is one fact that ought to take the ground from under your feet. Your fight against a bad form of state becomes a fight against the highest form of state thus far developed. How can you call the Bolsheviks fascists? Do fascists abolish the private ownership of the means of production? Do fascists establish and maintain the dictatorship of the proletariat? You might as well say that a few individuals, aided by a few policemen, have seized power by violence (in line with Dühring's theses). Without a class base.

I know, Brentano, that if you start collecting arguments against these statements you will manage to refute them. E.g., there are contradictions between the interests of the various European proletariats, and some things are more important than others. Action requires an ability to handle contradictions.

I hope you will take this letter as it is intended, as a small labour of friendship.

242 To Bernard von Brentano

Dear Brentano,

No, my letters are not angry, a little impatient perhaps, because I think you are studying in the wrong direction, with zeal, with so much zeal. In my opinion, your thinking rests too much on purely political considerations, on programmes, tables of law, utopias, ideas. It's hard to understand how socialism is being built; seen from outside (and we are not inside), it looks as if orders, plans based on principles, etc. were being carried out. But the emergence of productive forces is a complex process; it calls for a complex description, and building itself is becoming more and more complex. From outside we discuss plans, nothing but plans and principles. Why do we so overrate plans? Why do we not simply (as every science does) state the facts: Here productive forces that were formerly chained are developing headlong; the proletariat, the industrial workers are creating their methods of production, the development is proceeding in such and such a way, under such and such political and cultural forms. Everything seems contradictory, so we say: Such and such are the contradictions. The proletariat is building; it must pay interest on foreign money that is invested in machines; it must procure bread, revolutionise agriculture first by force, then gently; here indulging old vices, there creating new virtues. For every month of its rule it must fight the predatory states round about; it must haggle and crawl. It must harness and sometimes even sacrifice its friends; it must employ repression [even] towards itself, a sliding scale of coercion; it must carry on the class struggle, build, spend and save. It hopes to obtain everything (but everything) from the development of productive forces, and only later to win leisure, individual freedom, a life worth living. Compare this with that other wretched conception: a small clique of power-hungry individuals, who can only rule, increase their power, and indulge their brutal instincts by forcing other men to do an enormous amount of building. The second conception can easily accord with the first, but the first can never accord with the second. You must see that. In one country the workers of the world have undertaken a vast effort; they are suffering there, they are paying for what is happening there, they are pinning their hopes on it.

I hope you see that I am not writing because I want to quarrel with you. It is all so hard to understand, believe me, we don't know the whole story yet. Not to fear too much from a handful of politicians means not to expect too much of them. A campaign has been won by the enemy, an important campaign almost without a battle. It was not just a matter of a few rulers. Look at history, the history of the masses. Two wars, brought on by the same complex of causes, one past, the other yet to come. The first, ending in national collapse, with a social impetus from below, a dampened sort of impetus that could not be organised in haste but could be disorganised by the rigid old organisations. Where was Communism? Then the convulsions, the idiosyncratic wage curve after the inflation, the rationalisation of unemployment, the world crisis, all in a bare decade and a half. Only a small part of the industrial proletariat [?] revolutionary. Almost inconceivable. No adequately trained teaching cadres. And it was always the duty of the German Club leaders to bear the *whole* in mind; because Germany had become the vanguard, and while carrying on the struggle had to provide for building in its rear. And no trained cadres. And no experience of illegality. Everything learned more or less cold. Who knew exactly what a party is? Who felt the need of one? In the main, the people who walked out were regarded as anarchists or Mensheviks, libertarians or Forty-eighters. Apart from that, there was disagreement about tactics. And all the critics employed such tactics that they inevitably cut themselves off from the masses. Lenin was a practical thinker, not an innovator. There's something hopelessly utopian about all renegades, they'll never be anything but renegades. Well, enough of that.

If the critics are to be believed, a thriving, powerful, class-conscious movement was browbeaten, obstructed, destroyed by a handful of apparatuses imposed from outside. But where was the movement? Such as it was, it was after all brought into being. So it wasn't powerful, it wasn't thriving? So much the worse. You should really read Martov and Zinoviev on the Russian Social-Democratic Party. I'm now reading what Lenin wrote about it. Yes, many things about that type of party are exceedingly unbourgeois, hard for intellectuals like us to swallow. There isn't much of what you say that Martov didn't say. As early as 1904 and then again in 1920. He hasn't exactly been proved right . . . [Incomplete?]

[Probably 1935]

243 To Bernhard Reich

Skovsbostrand, 18 January 1935

Dear Reich,

Here is a contribution to the *Theatre Review*. I have chosen this particular subject for various reasons. In Switzerland a Hans Otto festival has attracted a good deal of attention.

A bit of advice: you absolutely must publish short résumés of plays, those being performed in Moscow for instance. Then you can follow up with articles about principles of direction (contents of stage scripts). You must pile up material, not evaluations. Also needed: a short article about a certain variety of mass criticism.

Open an inquiry on the theme of Socialist Realism and theatre. Analyses of famous old plays from the technical angle would be excellent. Construction of *Hamlet*, etc.

Don't be too flashy. Theatre magazines without nudities and gossip don't belong on the boulevard. Six good issues with plenty of material – that's what is needed.

A collection of famous ripostes. Quotable passages from recent plays. New characters (Schweik, Pelagea Vlassova). Actors on the study of parts. Public discussions from the theatre director's angle. Examples of dramatised courtroom scenes, political discussions, interviews (on the left the authentic scene, on the right the dramatic interpretation). Contests for the best such dramatisation.

244 To Lion Feuchtwanger

[Skovsbostrand], 18 January 1935

Thank you for the invitation. If I can possibly make it . . .

Your novel on the glowing prospects for peace will probably be published at a time of great wars.

(It's really too bad you've stopped writing satire. Still, Kortner, too, has always wanted most to do something serious, such as Hermann the Cheruskian.)

Incidentally, take care not to make 'Josephus' too much like Schwarz-schild, who would like nothing better than to show the French general staff the way to Berlin (Berläng), so that, after his entry through the Brandenburg Gate (on horseback), European peace can be ushered in. But enough of my blasphemous jokes.

I hear that Weill, in collaboration with Reinhardt and Werfel, who seems to be back in favour again, is working on a justification of Jewish history for America. They all aspire to the honorary title 'Justamentus'. I wonder what would happen if I [were to glorify][1] the march of the Cheruskians through Teutoburg Forest . . .

Have you heard anything from Döblin?

[1] The verb, which in German comes at the end of subordinate clauses, is lacking in the original.

Zweig's article in *Neue Deutsche Blätter* is very decent. Now *there*'s a front-line soldier!

245 To George Grosz

Dear George,

I'm *very* glad to hear you're doing the drawings for the plays. That will give the whole edition a special quality. It's exceedingly difficult to *read* the plays, which are actually nothing more than prompt books. Most readers haven't seen the intimations of new theatre that we once staged (with Aufricht and Katzenellenbogen footing the bill). So they can't imagine what the things are like on the stage. I've just been in *old merry England*[1] lately but only for three months (which reminds me that you mustn't forget the land of your origins), the theatres there are still in the oil-lamp age. In Germany they're back to performing by torch-light.

I enclose a few notes.

As ever,

Skovsbostrand, January 1935

Threepenny Opera:
Main theme: *Bandits and bourgeois.*

The beggars have bank books in their pockets. So have the gangsters. So have the whores. The table for the wedding banquet could be a plank on top of an old gunpowder barrel. Gallows 'lent by X & Co.'. Peachum keeps his Bible on a chain for fear of its being stolen. Macheath's ledger (Scene 4, Mac and Polly) begins with 'By the grace of God'.

Macheath opens Polly's heart with a skeleton key, so to speak.

Round Heads and Pointed Heads:
Central theme: untenable classification, by races.

Tenable: by classes. Round Heads just as comical (misshapen) as Pointed Heads.

Of course you can add variations. For instance (just by way of an example) 'People looking at the government's racial charts.' In front of one chart showing 'scientific' head shapes (Homo pointokephalos and Homo roundokephalos) a crowd of people sneaking glances at each other's heads.

[1]English in original.

Short digression on the epic theatre (patent applied for):
The incidents are not self-evident; on the contrary, they are 'incredible', 'only too understandable', amazing, extremely striking, of historical interest, disturbing, giving ground for opti- (or pessi-) mism, 'will sooner or later come home to roost', are depicted onesidedly, tendentiously distorted, etc.

Hence no identification, no empathy, no going along. On the contrary: criticise, risk predictions, shake your head.

Thus the incidents are set up (naturally as naturally as possible), just as in scientific experiments the most ideal conditions possible are provided.

Pictures of manners and customs preferred. Motto: I saw it!

Individual sentences (and gestures) seen historically. ('That kind of man would not have said that kind of thing ten years ago.')

[The following was probably enclosed in Brecht's letter to Grosz.]
It would be a good thing – and part of the same job – if your drawings could also deal with the theatre, but the real theatre. For instance, a conference is shown (there must be an invisible pointer) two persons are seated as far as possible from each other on the stage (if they are not far enough apart, it means that there are listeners, not that the drawingroom chairs can't be moved) in the attitude of persons talking to each other, that is, performing very definite gestures. I have always had great difficulty in keeping groups together on the stage. To attract the notice of the director and to be seen by their admirers, the fellows were always wanting to scatter all over the stage instead of sticking together like the figures on old candlesticks. How otherwise can you see what's going on, who relates to whom? If for instance four men are talking with one man, the four must appear as four, each one is a quarter of one partner; there are two partners in all. If for instance we have the (historical) scene: 'Czuch landlords hand over their Czich fellow landlords to Iberin's gangs', we need no less and probably no more than the following: the rich Pointed Head being dragged away by thugs (who have their eyes on his fine clothes, watch, etc., while the Pointed Head implores them with his upraised fettered arms), and the three other rich men (one Pointed Head among them) turning a blind eye, looking in the air, for instance, but keeping together, and one onlooker looking on with curiosity (the invisible pointer).

246 To Robert Storm Petersen

Dear Mr Storm Petersen,

It has given me great pleasure to learn that you will be designing the jacket for my novel. Without wishing in any way to pin you down, I should like to tell you briefly what I have been thinking.

In Danish translation the novel should be titled *One must live well to know what living is*. This, I believe, fits in pretty well with the Danish mentality. On the jacket you could have the figure of Jonathan Jeremiah Peachum, a bald man in shirt sleeves with a stiff black hat perched on the back of his head. In one of his outstretched hands he is holding a small sailing boat, in the other his daughter Polly, as though offering them for sale. Both these articles could bear price tags. The (very old) sailing tub costs £15,000, the (pretty) daughter £7000.

I don't know if my idea will appeal to you, perhaps you'll choose something different. But a small picture of this kind would give a good idea of the content of the novel.

> With best regards,
> Yours sincerely,
> bertolt brecht

Skovsbostrand, Svendborg January 1935

I enclose a short characterisation of Mr Peachum.

247 To Walter Benjamin

Svendborg, 6 February [1935]

Dear Benjamin,

If you cling to the Institute's artificial silk heels, you'll soon land up in Hawaii. Here the ground is covered with snow, that white, granular, cold substance. Helli and Steff are playing chess, but chop-chop, I tell you. Hauptmann is waiting for your article for America, and it would be a good idea for you to write chop-chop (see above); because *Die Sammlung* [The Collection] may not be appearing for ever . . .

> As ever
> b

250 To Helene Weigel

Dear Helli,

The trip went off smoothly. Tretiakoff met me here. They send love. Beds of that kind [?] can be had here for a few rubles, they were innocently surprised that we should imagine they were living in an uncivilised country. Actually I'm amazed at how many things are available here. Through the MORT (Piscator), who's been very nice, I found a room at the Novaya Moskovskaya Hotel. Lunch at the Russian Writers' Club. I've already seen a good many plays and films. Plenty of confusion. Mei Lan-fang is here, the greatest Chinese actor. Please write to me every week, really. Is K. still there? I really forgot to post the Finnish letter.

There is some prospect of a German theatre here, but only a feeble one. Maybe I can strengthen it. We'll wire Karin. But according to the Almanach she's sixty-three. We just won't mention the figure.

It's not cold here. It would be good to arrange something for the autumn here for you to act in, perhaps I would direct, or something with the cinema.

> I kiss you
> b

How are Steff's eyes?
Thanks for your letter.
Could you ask K. the name of the author of the American book about violence (*Oskawa Case*)? Give him my regards.

[Moscow, March 1935]

251 To Helene Weigel

Dear Helli,

Thanks for the letter. I've sent you seven registered packages of books. If they don't all reach you, please write me the numbers of the ones that do. Unfortunately I have a rheumatic headache at the back of my head on the left, most annoying. I've seen the Chinese actor Mei Lan-fang with his troupe. He plays girls' parts and is really splendid. Except that every time I move my head it hurts. The Ottwalts are staying at this hotel. As usual, Ottwalt has a finger in every pie, he's always losing things and has got nothing. Tretiakoff is managing Mei

Lan-fang, so he hasn't got much time but he's very nice. They've all been asking about you, I tell them you'll be coming here with me in the autumn at the latest. But now in my mad struggle to get you a film part all I've found is an old woman in a German-language film about Dimitrov (directed by [Joris] Ivens; scenario unfortunately by Wangenheim). It's said to be a very good part. Maybe you won't want to do it, but I'd like them to offer it to you. Then you'd have to come here straight away. German theatre is in bad shape. Very few actors, all bad except Neher, and they don't think very highly of her. (Her child is hefty; she herself is rather stout and very nervous.) Please write now and again. About the children and yourself.

I kiss you
b

Have you picked up the *Me-Ti?* Did they do a good job? Best to Korsch. He should leap before he looks. And don't pound my typewriter to smithereens.

[Moscow, March–April 1935]

252 To Helene Weigel

Dear Helli,

Thanks for the package and letter. I had a bit of flu and spent more than a fortnight in bed for fear of complications. Now I'm all right except for an occasional slight headache. The only trouble is that I haven't seen very much. I'm planning to leave here at the beginning of May (the 3rd or 4th) – I wanted the photos because there was a (vague) prospect of a film part with Ivens; but as Wangenheim has done the scenario nothing will come of it. He's been behaving unforgettably disgustingly. About the offer at the German-Russian city (I hear Trepte has written to you about it): I've told them the most you could do would be to go somewhere for about eight weeks (August–September), look things over and rehearse *The Mother*, and possibly something else. No longer, if only because of the family. Besides, we don't know what it's like down there, and of course it's not a first-class setup, more like third class. But here there are absolutely no acting possibilities. Neher has had no luck at all. Still, there's talk of a German theatre, possibly for the autumn. Piscator would be involved, so we could join. Your coat is already hanging in my place. I can't go by way of Austria, too much of a

detour and too expensive. Why won't Marianne come to Denmark?
About Dudow: Hasn't Ruth tackled the Royal Theatre? She promised
to, and she has a letter from me about it. Of course something should be
done, it's very important. But what? Tonight I'll be speaking over the
radio for the second time, maybe you'll hear me, but it's not the big
transmitter. I'll be glad to return to the green island.

> and I kiss you, dear Helli

How's your back doing?

> [Moscow, April 1935]

254 To Paula Grosz, née Banholzer

> [Skovsbostrand], 29 May 1935

Dear Bi,

On my return from a trip I learn that you've taken Frank to live with
you in Augsburg. It's just a pity that he can't really stay with you or his
grandmother and that you can't get him an apprenticeship. At the
moment my economic situation is such that I can't possibly provide you
with as much money as he would need to study dentistry; quite apart
from the fact that that is hardly a suitable profession for Frank. I can
send you 50 marks a month for a year at the most, and even that is not
entirely sure, though I'll do my best. So it's extremely important for
Frank to learn a trade that will enable him to make some money. I'm
sorry to hear that his health hasn't been good and I hope the medical
treatment he had in Vienna can be continued. We have always been
assured that with proper care and medical supervision puberty will
bring an end to his trouble, or at least a significant improvement. It was
for medical treatment that he was taken to Vienna and his condition did
improve considerably there. Of course I'm glad Frank is with you now.
Because of the unfortunate circumstances you have had to take on
responsibility for him. The moment my circumstances improve, I'll help
you again. Best wishes to Frank and to you from

> [unsigned]

I'm sending you the first instalment. The rest, if my father agrees,
will be sent to him.

255 To Mikhail Koltsov

Dear Koltsov,

I can't be sure yet whether I'll be able to get away in June, as among other things I have an opening night that's important for me in Copenhagen; true, it's not till September, but the preparatory work is starting now. My trip to the USSR was refreshing in every respect, I can see that in my work. At the end I spent a few days in Leningrad, where I was also given an uncommonly friendly reception. And on the trip home, too, everything went well.

In Paris I think you should try to involve people in work: a writer is mostly interested in writing. (He'd have no objection to the end of the world if he could be sure his book about it would still manage to appear.) For instance, under the motto: 'Against systematic intellectual befuddlement by etc.' you could bring out a *New Encyclopaedia* of the best authors, a series of publications in which they could attack the slogans of fascism and militarism, each in a two- to ten-page article, in other words, ten to fifteen writers would comment simultaneously on every stultifying thesis put forward by the fascists. Such an encyclopaedia would be a rallying point and would soon attract specific groups of readers. – Your *Day of the World* is also in line with this sort of collective work.

Will you be coming back via Denmark as you promised?

Yours cordially

Please give my regards to Maria and to Feuchtwanger.

[Skovsbostrand, late May–early June 1935]

256 To Alfred Döblin

Dear Doctor,

I returned a few days ago from the USSR, where I'd been for more than two months. I hear from the director of the State Publishing House that you have some 15,000 roubles lying there, from *Alexanderplatz*, I believe. That's quite a bit of money. If you felt like going over there, it would keep you in comfort for half a year. You can buy everything there and the place is full of life. I've wired Querido for your new novel, but they haven't sent it. If you could send me *Wang-lun*, I'd give it to someone over there, there would be a lot more roubles, which you may need some day.

I'd be awfully glad to see you, but travel is expensive. These are ugly times. And you and I would have fitted so beautifully into the Age of Pericles. I'm sure we agree about that.

Last autumn I was in London. No one was interested in the culture that was too good for Herr Hitler. Only Toller gets by with his preaching. Not all that many people are willing to pay for the pleasure of getting indignant. And when a man has that kind of an audience, he holds it fast and won't let anyone come near it, he's funny that way.

The Third Reich doesn't seem to be collapsing for want of decent literature. The ancient Romans after all had . . .

Have you heard from Brentano again? From Sternberg? Have you read his book?

How are your wife and my typesetter? And how are you?

> Yours, brecht

> Skovsbostrand, Svendborg
> Early June 1935

257 To Thorkild Roose

Dear Mr Roose,

Of course I'd have no objection to putting off the interview proposed by you until the autumn. I believe you overestimate the amount of preliminary work required for a production of *Joan*. I have already done the inserts intended to help the audience understand the business deals that figure in the plot and I can let you have them. It's not true that the choruses are just sketches. Staging them is a purely technical job that can be worked out in rehearsal; ample experience in the German theatre convinces me that it's no great problem. And the changes of scene are easy to handle with a revolving stage. Only five basic sets are necessary. I'm writing you this because I wouldn't want it thought that my play is unfinished. It's fully worked out. If the scenes are not described in detail, that is in line with my artistic intention.

> With best regards

> 12 June 1935
> Svendborg

258 To Walter Benjamin

Dear Benjamin,

I'll be coming to the Writers' Congress (with Karin Michaelis). I'm taking the boat on Saturday (15 June, the day after tomorrow) and will arrive at the Gare du Nord at 11.36 p.m. I've also notified Dudow who, I believe, is staying at the Hotel Kensington (79 Avenue de la Bourdon-nais, Paris 7ᵉ). For Karin and myself I need two not too expensive but bug-free rooms in your hotel or Dudow's. You might give him a ring. If you have time on Sunday evening, your talents as a guide will be appreciated. I'll be there a little more than a week. What about your summer? Couldn't you come back with us?

As ever, affectionately
brecht

[Skovsbostrand, 13 June 1935]

259 To Karl Korsch

Dear K K,

Every evening we hear steps and think it must be you. But it isn't. Old merry England[1] is proving to be an unreliable ally to us as it is to everyone else.

Couldn't you encourage our friend the definitor, to settle in our neighbourhood? We'd have some good talk.

Will you bring Hobbes with you, *Leviathan* and the other animal? Many thanks for sending the Chinese cards so promptly.

As for me, I've been at the Writers' Congress where I collected quite a lot of material for my *Tui* novel. Heinrich Mann, for instance, submitted his paper on *Human Dignity and Freedom of the Spirit* to the Sûreté before delivering it. It's depressing how few ideas come to one.

Cordially looking forward,
b

I saw friend P. several times in Paris. He was able to help me with my paper, and I was glad to see him.

[Skovsbostrand, late June–early July 1935]

[1] English in original

260 To Berthold Brecht (Brecht's father)

Dear Herr Brecht,

Since you refuse to correspond with Herr Bert Brecht, I have the honour to inform you of the following at his behest.

Though Herr Bert Brecht would have preferred to spare your feelings, he could not possibly have abstained from making public statements against the National Socialist regime. As you know, he has never shared your political opinions. He could not possibly have kept silent. It would have meant abstaining from all literary work. It has come to his ears that you threatened some time ago to disinherit him, if you have not already done so. He has asked me to tell you that it would take more than this to deter him from expressing his convictions. He renounces his inheritance. Nevertheless, he asks you to bear in mind that his daughter, Hanne Brecht, who is still living in Germany, is not responsible for such of his behaviour as you disapprove. In conclusion he wishes to assure you that his feelings of gratitude towards you and his love for you are unchanged.

[Mid 1935?]

262 To Ernst Bloch

Dear Bloch,

To get back to the problem of the infrigidation of social life. Of course I realise that you have no intention of converting the study of society into a study of sociability, especially now that sociology has become a refuge for so many elements that are breaking with the bourgeoisie and joining up with the proletariat. 'Neue Sachlichkeit' came in with the rationalisation of industry through the establishment of the big monopolies. That was reinforcement by collapse (inflation: flight into 'real' values). When rationalisation threatened to collapse in its turn, we soon got a new irrationality; coolness in music and imaginative writing died out or was discarded. Up to a point we respected rationalisation as a technical development; monopoly can also be seen as failed economic planning. The unmistakable cooling-off that has taken place in people's personal relationships is merely symptomatic, secondary. Those who profit by this social constipation accept it only too willingly. Fascism has put a stop to the appalling competitiveness among individuals in the labour market, where labour was freely sold as a commodity – that ghastly race for the dwindling prospect of being exploited – by instantly closing the free market in labour. Winter Aid and National Community, along with 'Strength through Joy', replenished our emotional life. The coldness between the major classes became all the more relentless. We laughed at kindness, dragged humanity through the mud. That was *before* our defeat. Now we howl with pain and beg for democracy as for alms.

(About 1935?)

(Incomplete?)

263 To George Grosz

The Lord of the Still Water to the Lord of the Flowing Water
Dear brother,

I learn to my chagrin that the ship which brought me carried you away. Nevertheless, I can give you a vital piece of information. We have just rescued culture. It took 4 (four) days, and then we decided that we would sooner sacrifice all else than let culture perish. If necessary, we'll sacrifice ten to twenty million people. Thank the Lord, enough of the persons prepared to shoulder the responsibility for this were present. We proceeded at once boldly and with caution. Our brother Henricus Mannus submitted his oration in favour of free speech to the Sûreté before delivering it. A slight incident attracted notice. Towards the end, brother Barbussius devoured brother Andreus Gideus whole on the open rostrum. The episode ended tragically, for I'm told that an onlooker committed suicide out of boredom. – Fascism was unanimously condemned. What for? For its *unnecessary* cruelties.

I am eagerly looking forward to enfolding you in my arms, and will do so on Saturday unless you phone to put me off. (Christensen, merchant, Skovsbostrand, Brecht *personlik*).

As ever,
bertolt

[Skovsbostrand, probably July 1935]

264 To Johannes R. Becher

Dear H,

If you use the following please do so in toto. Here I can't find out much about the public reaction to the Congress. However, two articles of some length in the Basel *National-Zeitung* (whose attitudes tend to be typical) suggest that it was well received. A lot more could be accomplished by publishing the speeches in book form and distributing the book properly. It must absolutely be sent to the big papers. But there must be no repetition of what happened in the *Rundschau*, where my little talk, for instance, was completely distorted. I did not say what they printed there and what I said they did not print. (I have just sent Kantorowicz my speech, carefully reworked.)

It is important that the Club should acquire an organ and start functioning as a literary association, i.e. producing and publishing literary work. Obviously, occasional collections of signatures cannot hold such organisations together. A publicistic infrastructure must be ready for the grave times ahead. A book (or pamphlet) is a more reliable instrument than appeals to the press. (As the Congress seems to have shown, the latter are usually unsuccessful.) I regard a periodical as less effective, because only mediocrities contribute regularly. A process of *communication among writers* must be created. The Congress was undoubtedly a beginning. But only a beginning.

If we could announce a series of publications in the major languages, we should really be far advanced. The publications can be small, as a general principle we should change over to small doses of quality material.

To sum up: On the whole I regard the Congress as a success, indeed, what with the limited funds available and the short period of preparation, as an outstanding success, but I believe it will take hard work to exploit this success to the full.

With regards and express willingness to work

Yours cordially,

Skovsbostrand, Svendborg, July 1935

265 To Alfred Döblin

Dear Doctor,

I must again apologise for not getting in touch with you before leaving [Paris]. I caught sight of you in the lobby of the meeting hall: I was called to the door and when I came back I couldn't find you. (Most likely you had incautiously listened to what was going on in the auditorium and rushed away . . .) I'm sorry to say that I've received neither your last novel nor *Wang-lun*, nor for that matter the article on the epic. Could you send it to me? I'd send it over there as soon as I've read it, and the last novel as well. You know that I've promised them to people there.

K[arl] K[orsch] is here. Still depressed about last spring. His residence permit in London has not been renewed. Some hysterical women of both sexes are showering him with all the filth they can lay hands on. And in the circumstances he couldn't possibly have given this wretched private affair a political slant. Once again we see that people are anything but helpful, noble and good. As a rule they're lacking in common decency.

Sometimes I'm inclined to doubt that we saved culture by our recent efforts. Just another illusion perhaps. Anyway, it was too hot.

Please give your wife and the jacket designer my regards.

> Yours cordially,
> brecht

> Skovsbostrand, Svendborg
> 31 July 1935

266 To Wieland Herzfelde

Dear Wieland,

If I were you, I'd write and tell H.K. that it's hard to say anything about his talent because his little play is so stereotyped – unless this stereotyped quality is simply taken as an indication of a lack of talent. You could illustrate the point by a sentence in his covering letter to the effect that he wrote his four-acter with his *heart's blood*, an expression reminiscent of the handicrafts age when boots were made with the heart's blood. (Certain people in the Third Reich still find fault with machines for their lack of heart's blood.) Most stereotyped literature is written *exclusively* with the heart's blood. The only possible indication of talent is his repeated insistence that the play be read two or three times. I always insist on that myself. According to my non-Aristotelian theory of the drama, one must know how the thing ends if, when seeing the play on the stage, one is to recognise all the characters' blunders as blemishes rather than strokes of genius. Only I'm afraid H.K. has other motives for asking us to make two or three attempts to follow the flights of his fancy. It's really no good, in fact it's worse than most agitprop plays.

Böff expects to deliver [his drawings] in October. You'll get the second volume as soon as we get a copy of *St Joan* [*of the Stockyards*] from the publisher.

As for my little speech at the Writers' Congress, I hope you've used the last version, which differs from all those thus far published in the mimeographed magazines (minutes). The last version is the one with the motto at the top, the one I sent you in typescript.

I've also read the Langhoff now, but I'm for Bredel. Langhoff's book might be titled: 'How I fell into the hands of a savage tribe'. Bredel's book is a militant book. You know the gag line: 'If Hitler knew . . .!' Well, if Adolf were to read Langhoff's book, he'd say: 'These are indeed superfluous excesses. Such things shouldn't be allowed.' If he read Bredel's book, he would say: 'All that is much too mild. Why, we haven't got that bastard down!' Etc. . . . So: Publish Bredel, here on our green islands as well. Have you written to Copenhagen?

> Yours cordially,

[Skovsbostrand, late July–early August 1935]

267 To Hanns Eisler,

> [Skovsbostrand], 29 August 1935

Dear Eisler,

Re our disagreement in the matter of the Lehrstück *The Horatians and the Curiatians*, I should like once again to state my position briefly.

Work on the Lehrstück was begun on your initiative (though I was up to my ears in work on my play), because it had been commissioned by the Red Army and could have considerable propaganda value if performed in the left-inclined schools of America, England, France and the Scandinavian countries. If you hadn't gone to Prague, your holiday would have left you ample time in which to complete the short play and work out the main musical problems. I myself recognised from the start that the trip to Prague was necessary, but I refused to believe it should automatically stop our collaboration on the Lehrstück. I thought you should try your best to make use of the time remaining between the Prague Music Festival and your trip to America for the Lehrstück. I expressed my readiness to put aside my work on the play for the time being, and suggested that in the five days before you left for Prague we rough the whole thing out together. Then, I thought, I'd get ahead as fast as possible with the text and let you know in Prague whether I was far enough advanced that we could use the rest of your holiday here or, if it would save you time or trouble, meet in Copenhagen for a final editing (testing of the political line, musical form, possible changes for the sake of the musical form). It seemed to me that even a few days of such final editing were important, that we should content ourselves with what time we had left but use every scrap of it to the full. (If you took the boat in Dunkirk on 17 September, you'd be here on the evening of the 18th. That would give us until the 25th.) When we discussed the matter, you argued that this arrangement would be too hard on you and that the Lehrstück wasn't all that important. You thought we should drop the final editing and offered to write me your criticisms from America. I admitted that the trip via Copenhagen instead of London would be hard on you (though it wouldn't have cost any more, probably less, and anyway you were going to be reimbursed for your trip back) and that the time saved would be short, perhaps too short. I also admitted that you couldn't be sure of not being held up longer in Prague. I only wanted you to say that you'd *try* to come. Considering the enormous difficulties of life in exile, a work that is both political and artistic demands a great effort. What with the objective difficulties, there was no guarantee, not even with your consent to what I asked of you, that our work on the didactic play would be completed, but without it there was no point at all in my going on with the work. I doubt if you would persist in your contention that you were not really needed for the text nor I for the music. True, you can say that I was expecting too much of you. But considering the importance of every least bit of political art, I believe such demands, regardless of who makes them, are justified. In any case, your disgruntlement over my demands in the last days before your departure to Prague was no justification for dropping the work, which I immediately went on with. I very much regret this quarrel, and continue to hope you will do your best in the time you have left to participate in the creation of this Lehrstück. I was glad you came here in spite of the difficulties, and it would be a great pity if we were not to derive the maximum benefit from your stay. Mutual disgruntlements really shouldn't be allowed to affect our work.

268 To Hanns Eisler

Skovsbostrand per Svendborg
Early September 1935

Dear Eisler,

We have made haste with the Lehrstück. The rough draft is finished, eighteen typewritten pages, but there may be two more in the end. Now you and I absolutely must talk the whole thing over. For the present I have only put as much into the choruses as is necessary for the action. Some bits might still be added. The musical question is really not simple in this case; for some spots I haven't got the form yet. In its present shape it's all singable. But music is needed throughout, because the movement of the 'armies' must be fixed with precision. If you can spare the time, it would really be worthwhile for you to travel via Denmark. Since actual invention is no longer needed, we could get a lot done in a short time if necessary.

The American protests against the Comintern seem to be more a matter of form than anything else, but of course those people may scrutinise new arrivals rather closely. If you run into difficulty I'd be delighted to have you come here.

Regards

269 To George Grosz

Skovsbostrand per Svendborg
Early September 1935

Dear George,

I'd have liked to see you again before you left for America. It's very quiet here. Wieland has been after me, he wants to know what we agreed on and when he can expect the drawings. I know you're on holiday and don't want to get too deeply involved in work sessions, but perhaps we could discuss certain things in passing, though the essential, I think, is settled. Above all, we could listen to the Party Congress of Freedom on the wireless. The children would also be welcome here, though, I'm sorry to say, your wife has left. Eisler was here, we had a bit of a quarrel. Now he's gone, hastening with giant strides to his professorship. Piscator's letters reveal an intense longing for you. Drop him a card sometime (Moscow, Hotel Metropole).

Cordially,

270 To Erwin Piscator

Svendborg, Skovsbostrand (Danmark)
25 September 1935

Dear Pis,

If you take a holiday, I hope (again and still) that you'll spend it here.

I'll be glad to write something for BK, but not a pamphlet because as you know I suffer from a grave pamphletophobia. If one could jot down the stories he told us on that really lovely evening! Is any material available about it?

Did you get back the 300 roubles you sent to Grete and that never reached her?

Helli is dejected because she hasn't heard any more about Dnepropetrovsk. If you really do the *Rundköpfe* in the Jewish Theatre (are you going to?), couldn't she play Mrs Cornamontis? I'm sure she could learn those few pages in Yiddish.

What about the film we were going to do? I've had a few ideas, we'd have to thrash that out together. I've written to Held, but so far no answer.

Cordially,

271 To Fritz Sternberg

Dear Sternberg,

I've read your book – with great profit, I think, there's solid substance in it (for lack of which most analyses have such an aura of metaphysics). (You know the old saw: 'Everything hinges on economics but that just happens to be our weak point.') It's a pity that in certain important passages, in the second half, you wax so 'political', almost metaphysical. In a world war, after all, the proletariat is mobilised in many entirely different places for very different purposes, outside Russia for imperialistic purposes; but the imperialist powers are widely divergent complexes, and in certain contexts the end results vary even if the aims do not. (That's why the workers, as they repeatedly make clear, are so reluctant to ally themselves with antiimperialist organisations . . .) Moreover, wars have different phases, a beginning, a middle and an end at the very least, and the weight of the proletariat varies with these phases. Under certain circumstances victory of France allied with the USSR would mean a victory for the German proletariat, which would endanger certain of France's imperialist aims but put those of its proletariat within reach so to speak. If France allied with the USSR were to lose, there'd be a separate peace (1000 to 1); this, of course would be opposed by the French proletariat, and a sort of Commune situation would arise. A good slogan might be 'Defence of the Soviet Union can never be stultifying for the French proletariat'; besides, it's a flexible slogan and revolutionary in every phase of the war. War would offer the French proletariat a rare opportunity for almost legal revolutionary action and reinforce it greatly and quite openly. The crux of the matter is that there is hardly any government today that would survive defeat in a war. And some could not survive victory. Do dictate something on this point to Erna for me. Your secret script is too impenetrable.)

As ever

[Probably September–October 1935]

272 To Paul Peters

Skovsbostrand per Svendborg
(Danmark)
End of August 1935

Dear Comrade Peters,

Many thanks for sending your adaptation of *The Mother*. I'm sure you'll understand that it's hard for me to be fully satisfied with it. I'd taken particular pains to avoid naturalism, because it seemed to me that the working-class movement needs bold, simple forms. I'm always afraid to make the milieu too overwhelming, because then the spectator attributes the characters' actions to the milieu, and the subjective factor in political behaviour – whether correct or incorrect – is lost sight of.

I gather from your adaptation and Comrade Standen's letter that you don't think the American worker can do without naturalistic form. I suppose you are furious that I am nevertheless unable to countenance a naturalistic production of the play. As a matter of fact, though, I believe that – in New York as in Berlin – whether a non-naturalistic play like *The Mother* can be performed for a working-class audience depends entirely on the way it's performed. In Berlin too it was a gamble, and in

Berlin it succeeded. I'd hate you to be put out with me, but I must stand by my work. Of course it's a pity you've put so much into it. If I'd known before it was finished, I'd probably have had no difficulty in reaching an understanding with you on the principles involved. If I come to New York, I'll be glad to discuss it with you even if there's no more chance of a production.

>With best regards,
>Yours,
>Bertolt Brecht

P.S. Could you possibly send me your plays? They'd interest me very much.

273 To Victor Jerry Jerome

>Skovsbostrand per Svendborg
>(Danmark), Early September 1935

Dear Comrade Jerome,

I've discussed the Theatre Union matter in detail with Eisler, and as things stand we see no alternative but to call off the production. Of course we are not indifferent to your theatre's difficulties, as it's a workers' theatre. They were caused by the fact that without my knowledge the theatre had the play completely reworked, unfortunately in a naturalistic way that completely distorts the style. I foresaw from the start that it would be hard to stage the original play and realised that directors would be likely to help themselves out by adding background material and concocting a naturalistic atmosphere. That is why I offered to direct the play, and I still think you might cover the expense of my trip by advancing my share of the estimated royalties. Unfortunately, I have the impression that the difficulty is not so much the expense as the fact that the theatre doesn't think the original play effective enough and either fails to understand its unaccustomed style or has no confidence in it. But on this score I can't give in. The political content of the play cannot be fully brought out in any other way; if I thought it could, I myself would have chosen a different style. You may know that I have already had a bad experience with a play in New York. Done in the wrong way, *The Threepenny Opera* was not at all successful. The theatre is taking the attitude that the New York audience is different from the Berlin audience. That is a ridiculous platitude. Of course it's different.

Of course the difference must be taken into consideration. But the adaptation I have before me (the quality of which I am not questioning) is not strikingly American, it is strikingly naturalistic. It is almost identical with what was wanted in Berlin and thought to be the only way of making the play effective and intelligible to the audience. In Berlin, too, all sorts of objections were raised against the style of the original play. The reception of the play showed, however, that workers – not because they were Berliners but because they were workers – understood perfectly the way in which the dominant political line was brought out, the absence of sentimental background painting, and the absence of an old-fashioned plot. The workers responded to almost every line, and the discussion after the performances was a political discussion. I'm sick and tired of the old naturalistic foolishness. It's right for oil lamps but not for electric light. The adaptation looks to me as if someone hitched horses to his motorcar because he couldn't find the ignition key. In short: I won't have it. I'd rather wait. If the theatre wants to produce *The Mother*, then, precisely because it's a workers' theatre, it should produce the original *Mother*. I'm still willing to come over and direct the play provided only that my travel expenses are paid. I'm also prepared to pay them back out of whatever share of the royalties I can expect. I don't think it would take us long to make such changes as are needed for America. As for the cast, I've worked for years with all sorts of actors, the most famous stars as well as proletarian agitprop performers. It has never been easy to teach actors this style, but it has always worked out in the end.

I'm enclosing our copies of the correspondence for your information and trust you understand that I am motivated by something more than irresponsible obstinacy.

> With best regards,
> Yours,
> Bert Brecht

274 To Paul Peters

> Skovsbostrand per Svendborg
> (Danmark), 3 October 1935

Dear Comrade Peters,

In my talk with Comrade Gomez I insisted primarily that *The Mother*, which is a historical play, must not be presented as a work of fiction. If the direction were to overemphasise the role of Pavel, the result would of course be a mother-son play, and the end would have to be dropped. And that is just what should not be done. The Mother must go on living after her son's death, and this must not only be stated, but also shown. I believe, though, that we've found a solution which gets a strong effect out of the mother's carrying on the fight. On Pavel's return from Siberia, where in the present version he has completed his term (he leaves at once for his agitational work) mother and son work together once again, agitating against mobilisation for the war of 1914. So now your scene in the railway carriage, which I liked, can take place at the time of this mobilisation. Then comes the Bible scene, in the course of which the Mother learns of her son's death. While talking with the women, she stands erect, she even propagandises them, but at the end of the scene she collapses. Then comes the projection OUTBREAK OF THE WAR and the scene numbered 13 in the original version, in which the Mother, while lying ill at the teacher's house (she has done no Party work since her son's death), learns that the Party is being severely persecuted. The news puts her back on her feet. In the next scene (No. 12 in the original) she is again engaged in antiwar propaganda. The workers are in despair and are no longer willing to take the leaflets of the Bolsheviks. The answer to their fear that the aims of the Bolsheviks will never be realised is supplied by the last scene (Demonstration), which is introduced by a projection: IN NOVEMBER 1917 THE RUSSIAN PROLETARIAT TOOK POWER. These last scenes must show the Mother lonely and aged but still indefatigable. The historical character of the play must be brought out, chiefly by projections, which play an important part; texts for them are indicated in the notes to my edition of *The Mother*, p. 65. I'd be much obliged if you'd translate these notes, especially the first three chapters, i.e. pp 65–69 for the director and stage designer. In Berlin we got a strong and pure effect with a stage set consisting entirely of canvas. We used lots of light, which made the figures, surrounded by graffiti and projected photographs, stand out clearly.

I enclose a few pages in which you will find my suggestion for a slight reworking of your railway scene, necessitated by the transposition described above. I have had to make a slight change in the propaganda, because now the scene takes place not after three years of war, but during the mobilisation.

You will also find my suggestions for the other acts. Please don't take offence at the rather abrupt formulation, I wanted to keep the notes as succinct as possible.

Another thing: Comrade Gomez spoke of two letters you had written me. I've only received one. I'm looking forward to seeing you in New York and have great hopes for our work together. Please remember me to Eisler.

> With best regards,
> Yours,
> Bertolt Brecht

275 To Helene Weigel

Dear Helli,

Crossing rather rough at first, then fine. No trouble getting acquainted. Your Jewish descent is a big help. Here everything is all right. Nice people. Rehearsals hadn't begun yet. Text: mine (?). But the Mother is terrible. Will probably be recast. But so far they haven't found a replacement. Even harder to find than in Berlin. It won't be easy to find anyone on this planet to play your parts. In spite of the identical blocking, nothing is recognisable. *You really ought to learn English.*

I'm living in the same building as Eisler, in a small flat of my own, not too expensive. Food is cheap. Clothing too warm. Climate here like in Naples. Too bad the trip costs so much. We could manage here because of the cheap food.

How did it go in Copenhagen?

What are the kids doing?

What about K.K.'s book? Are the sentences still nice and short?

I need the *Round Heads badly*.

Address: Union Theatre, here all day.

(Home Address: W 69 Street, 225 Wilsonhouse [sic].)

> I kiss you, Helli
> b

Hauptmann is passing through New York next week. Then she's going on to the USSR.

> [New York, October 1935]

276 To Helene Weigel

Dear Helli,

I'm deep in rehearsals. Original version fully reinstated. Nice little dictatorship. But the cast is very very weak. Don't know yet how the Mother will be. Old woman, very intelligent. Thanks for *Round Heads*. Please don't get too skinny on me. We open on the 19th. But four nights of public previews first.

> I kiss you
> b

You should really learn English.

Regards to K.K. How's the book coming along? Can't some of it be sent to me?

When is Hanne arriving?

[New York, October–November 1935]

277 To the Theatre Union

[New York]
225 West 69th Street,
9 November 1935

To the Theatre Union
103 West 14th Street
New York City

I hereby inform you that I reserve the right to take all steps that seem necessary in connection with:

1) the state of the music and your refusal to carry out Eisler's suggestions;

2) the fact that I have been unable to set foot in your theatre since a pianist with your connivance threatened me with violence after I had justifiably criticised him, and the related fact that I cannot give the director the instructions I have contracted to supply;

3) your decision to make cuts without my consent and contrary to our contract.

> bertolt brecht

Enclosure

278 To the Theatre Union

[New York]
225 West 69th Street,
9 November 1935

Dear Comrades,

First I must express my amazement at your cavalier reaction to an insult offered me in your theatre. I must obviously insist on my right to protest energetically against amateurish distortions of a work which is to be presented to the public under my name. In a work of political art quality counts for so much that every detail demands the most exacting attention. I am still convinced, for instance, that your pianist is making a mess of Eisler's extraordinary music, and, as we heard today, Eisler is of the same opinion.

Yesterday's rehearsal showed that despite Mrs Cook's great talent and the largely satisfactory blocking a great deal remains to be done. This is particularly true of the Third Act, but elsewhere as well. In spite of all the difficulties (time wasted in fruitless discussions – and so hard to make up for; the inadequate translation; the poor actor material; the same actors playing two or three parts; the hopeless state of the music), I had the impression yesterday that the production might still be straightened out if the last days of rehearsal can be kept free of incompetent interference. The nervousness of the permanent supervisory committee, under whose surveillance (as the director testifies) it is difficult to work in any event, a nervousness which expresses itself in a barbaric outcry for cuts at any price, is something that should definitely be kept out of the theatre. Instead, positive suggestions should have been made. In these rehearsals, which were bound to be difficult under present conditions, it is utterly irresponsible and unprofessional to allow some individual unknown to anyone here to break in constantly with remarks emanating from an entirely different conception of drama.

A theatre's lack of funds need not be an obstacle to achievement, provided sufficient understanding, hard work and discipline are invested. If you should really see no possibility of granting me a few last *undisturbed* rehearsals, I shall feel obliged to oppose the performance of the play. And you force me to take the same step if you cannot give Eisler the assurance he demands, which is indispensable if his music is to be effective.

brecht

279 To the Theatre Union

225 West 69th Street
New York City
15 November 1935

To the Theatre Union
103 West 14th Street,
New York City

I was informed yesterday that the first performance of *The Mother* before an audience of workers was poor, technically inadequate, and at many points amateurish. This falls in with my impression at the dress rehearsal. Apparently with your encouragement Director Wolfson, who at first, in view of his inexperience, contented himself with carrying out my instructions, has recently declared his 'independence'. He has given a considerable number of amateurish directions that show a gross ignorance of the style and political content of my play. In view of the inability he demonstrated last night to direct so difficult a play on his own, it would be politically and artistically unthinkable for you to continue – after so much time has been stolen from me by the un-professional behaviour of the theatre management – to deter me from straightening out the production. If this should be your intention, you will bear responsibility for a great artistic and political outrage.

brecht

280 To the Theatre Union

[New York]
17 November 1935

Dear Comrades,

We have made some suggestions today and are awaiting your decision. Let us know the result of your deliberations. We shall then help you to carry them out.

Under no circumstances may any changes whatever in the text or music be made without our consent.

Signed
Bertolt Brecht   Hanns Eisler

I continue to insist on the reinstatement of those passages in the Bible and copper kettle scenes, the complete inclusion of which was

guaranteed by Comrade Jerome's decision.
> Signed
> Bertolt Brecht

281 To the Theatre Union

> [New York]
> 21 November 1935

Dear Comrades,

1. Considering that our political and artistic instructions and suggestions were given little or no consideration in the rehearsals of *The Mother*,

2. Considering that the production, for which you took political and artistic responsibility was a political and artistic failure,

3. Considering that this production in its present inadequate political and artistic state is to be presented to tens of thousands of workers, we suggest once again that now at long last you allow us to improve the production.

We know that once the press has delivered its verdict a bourgeois theatre usually stops work on a production. But since the central purpose of our play is to exert a political influence on the toiling masses, we believe that more work must definitely be invested in the production.

In practical terms, this means that you should finally give us the opportunity, for which we have so repeatedly asked, of putting the play into politically and artistically acceptable form.

> Signed:
> bertolt brecht   Hanns Eisler

282 To Erwin Piscator

> 225 West 69th Street
> NYC
> 8 December 1935

Dear Pis,

The Mother has been badly butchered here (stupid mutilations, political ignorance, backwardness of all kinds etc.) The Club took our part but without success. My worst difficulty here is getting decent translations.

One thing I can tell you: steer clear of so-called left-wing theatres.

They're run by small cliques dominated by hack playwrights who have the manners of the worst Broadway producers without their know-how, which doesn't amount to much, but even so. Even so, you're better off with Shubert, though of course you must read your contract very carefully. A fortnight ago I intervened actively. When I couldn't get anything out of Kertesz I went to Shubert himself, because I heard that the rehearsals of the A.T. under Shubert's management had been definitely set for the following Monday. He told me (Eisler was there) that he had a contract with Dreiser who held the rights to the play, and that he didn't need you. He said you had hesitated too long to accept his offers and the play was going into rehearsal, so it was too late. I politely expressed certain doubts about the regularity of the contract and mumbled something to the effect that I couldn't believe Dreiser would 'sell another man's hat' and that I hoped there wouldn't be a public scandal. Shubert seems to have taken this to mean that I myself as a friend (and author) would publicly discuss the merits of the case, and the upshot was that the rehearsals were postponed for six weeks and new negotiations with Dreiser begun. At this point Franz Höllering turned up. He has the same agent as Dreiser, a Mr Greenburger. This Mr. G. had drawn up the contract between Dreiser and Shubert. Apparently (one can't get to see the contract) there's nothing in the contract about your consent being necessary, but Dreiser has told Kertesz, and this is confirmed by Höllering, that Dreiser will stop the play if Pis does not give his agreement. Since we had reason to believe that Dreiser would do his best to get Shubert to re-engage you (because not to do so would have been 'selling another man's hat') but would never admit in Shubert's presence that he had sold another man's hat, I stopped Kertesz from going there (he's a rather uncouth son of the Puszta). But Höllering was there and they seem to have decided that Shubert would offer you another contract as director. We're waiting for it now, prepared, if it comes, to say no more about selling another man's hat or, if it doesn't come, to say plenty. As for your directing contract, less importance should be attached for the present to the amount of money you'll be making (though of course it should be fairly decent) than to a clause making it clear that you don't have to direct plays you don't like and will be permitted to direct plays you do like somewhere else if Shubert turns them down. In any case, there have been endless telephone calls and conferences about this in the last fortnight. I've turned myself completely into an agent, and Eisler is constantly being dragged all over the place too. But I can't stay here much longer, it's too expensive.

About filming *Die Rundköpfe*. Mezhrabpom has long had permission to pay authors royalties on foreign receipts. I think we must insist on this. If you could do the *Rundköpfe* at the Jewish theatre it would be really splendid, because a magnificent American tour could be organised with it. (Don't forget Weigel for Mrs Cornamontis.)

> Shakehands[1]
> brecht

The article in the *Times* on Sunday occupied a prominent place and seems to have convinced a good many people.

[A handwritten postscript by Hanns Eisler follows]

283 To Stefan S. Brecht

Dear old Steff,

This year you must play the head of the family and be strict. On my behalf you must kiss Helli and tell Barbara a story (perhaps the one about Joseph in Egypt). At bedtime. I'll bring a few things with me. The Groszes send regards.

> I shake your hand.
> bidi

New York, December 1935

284 To Helene Weigel

Dear Helli,

I've tried my *level best* to get away from here, but it would have been *too* stupid because negotiations over the novel and *The Round Heads* are still 'pending'. So I won't be able to get away for another fortnight or at the most three weeks, in other words I'll be in Svendborg by the middle of January. That means a dismal New York Christmas in the bosom of the Eisler family. Of course we'll make up for it with a Svendborg Christmas, I'll bring the trappings with me. I already miss Steff and Barbara terribly and I can't even remember a Christmas tree without you; it's always been a pleasant evening and a good night, *dear Helli*. It's

---

[1] 'English' in original

not very cosy here to begin with, and then there's Uncle Otto! He *must* come to us in January. Have you been eating enough? Don't smoke too much, and keep the house good and warm. Don't forget me (and write '*deine*' at the bottom of your letters).

I kiss you

b

[New York, December 1935]

285 To Maxim Gorky

225 West 69th Street,
New York City
18 December 1935

Dear Comrade Gorky,

The dramatisation of your novel *The Mother*, which I wrote in the winter of 1931/32 for Berlin was produced here beginning on 19 November by the Theatre Union (103 West 14th Street), with music by Hanns Eisler and in a translation by Paul Peters, a member of the Theatre Union. The Theatre Union is the only permanent workers' theatre in New York. The production ran until 15 December, performances being given every night and some afternoons, playing almost exclusively to working class audiences. As you can see from the enclosed accounts, the total receipts are as follows:

Previews (14–17 November)	$1782.52
19–23 November	$2506.02
23–30 November	$3717.38
1–7 December	$3148.47
7–14 December	$3791.85
15 December	$1084.85
	————
	$16,031.09

Total: $16,031.09

The Theatre Union pays a royalty of five (5) per cent of the gross receipts, which in this case comes to $801.56.

Of these five per cent the American translator and Hanns Eisler received three-tenths (3/10) each, for a total of six tenths. This leaves a remainder of four-tenths (of $801.56) which is due to you and me. In other words, our joint share comes to $320.64. Please tell me how much of this I should send you. I'd appreciate it, however, if you would bear in mind that to make the production possible (because of its style the play is hard to stage) I travelled to New York and that only my travel expenses and not my stay during the rehearsals was paid for. And various refugees have taken the greater part of my receipts.

The production sparked off quite a discussion of stagecraft, political theatre, etc. The immortal figure of Pelagea Vlassova, however, transcended all discussion and even the bourgeois press spoke respectfully of the novel as a classic.

> Yours sincerely,
> bertolt brecht

286 To Helene Weigel

Dear Helli,

Thank you for your wire and letter and Steff's drawing (beautiful). Poor Barbara. I can easily believe the cracking of her collarbone could be heard all the way to Odense. I broke mine once. Now I'm definitely leaving here on the 29th. (I've already got my ticket.) It's boring here, I spend most of my time playing chess with Eisler, and every day we go to the cinema, which is very cheap here – fifteen cents. I'll be glad to get home. It's very hard working here and it's more boring than Skovsbostrand. Christmas was horrible. Eisler and I spent the evening with people who had no children, and somebody went on and on singing Scottish ballads. I'd have liked to put you to bed, Helli, the same as other years.

> I kiss you
> b

Best regards to Steff and Barbara

Could you send Weill, *Hotel St Moritz, Central Park South, New York*, a *copy* of my *Threepenny Opera* contract – if it's still there.

And maybe the clause in the other (the general contract) saying that the general contract does not cover *The Threepenny Opera*.

[New York, late December 1935–early January 1936]

287 To Lee Strasberg

Dear Mr Strasberg,

Unfortunately we had to cease rehearsals on the *Massnahme* for political reasons. It is a great pity, because I had the impression that we worked very well together. In general it was not very easy for me to express what I thought necessary for saving the theatre here from bourgeois drug traffic and emotions racket. The few rehearsals with you and your group have at least shown me that a revolutionary pedagogic theatre is possible here too.

I owe you many thanks and I beg you to express my thanks to the actors too.

> Yours,
> bertolt brecht

New York City, 27 January 1936

288 To Victor J. Jerome

Dear Comrade Jerome,

Arrived back at my Danish Siberia, I think with pleasure of our last day in New York, one of the few days that were too short. Among other things, we didn't get round to a talk about American literature or at least dramatic literature. The case of Odets strikes me as most typical. That someone as intelligent and open-minded as Eva Goldbeck should think so highly of *Paradise Lost* points up the need for a thorough discussion of the matter. What an insidious step from *Waiting for Lefty* (that I think highly of) to *Paradise Lost*. From pity for the taxi driver to pity for those who will soon be unable to afford a taxi – for which accursed capitalism is to blame. The invisible enemy of the small capitalist is the big capitalist. The next play will show that the Rockefeller family suffers from *moral insanity*[1] or some other kind of insanity, and that the only possible doctor is Communism. As though all these symptoms wouldn't vanish instantly if fascism won out – pretty much in the same way as the symptoms of secondary syphilis disappear after a few shots of salvarsan. Instead of joining up with small gangsters, the son will join up with big ones, and the family won't refuse the big gangsters' money as it did that of the small ones. The sleeping sickness

---

[1] 'English' in original.

patient will be sterilised and family ties will be reinforced. After all, Hearst has taken to intoning 'something is wrong' day after day, but he knows what to do about it, and unlike Odets he says so plainly. It's imperative, I believe, that you discuss such matters in a column appearing regularly – if only once weekly or even monthly – I can think of no one else able and therefore under obligation to do so. That would be much the best way for the young people who come to the movement from the cultural 'Something is wrong' side to learn about the movement.

What about a few little discussions about Nat Turner on my green island?

Eva Goldbeck has that little 'Difficulties when writing the Truth' pamphlet and the children's book.

[Skovsbostrand, February 1936]

289 To Walter Benjamin

Dear Doctor,

When are you coming here? Remember your books, the chess, the Führer's voice over the wireless, the oil lamps, and the son of the great old [?]

> Yours,
> brecht

[1935–1936?]

290 To Walter Benjamin

Dear Benjamin,

Alerted by Korsch, who spoke of it with great enthusiasm, I read your article on linguistics and I too was enthusiastic. It is written in a grand style, it gives a broad view of the material, and shows that present-day scholarship should be approached with reserve. That is just how a new encyclopaedia should be written.

I wish I had a copy, because otherwise I'll have to steal Korsch's and that wouldn't be nice.

Thanks to some old friends I've been privileged to take a small part in the international narcotics trade. I'm polishing up film dialogue in the hope of getting the Svendborg pot boiling again. My immediate aim is to acquire a small hand press so I can print short things myself: both as author and typesetter, you are invited here for the summer. My work makes me think of Köhler's intelligence tests for anthropoid apes, in which the animals can reach certain fruits only if they swivel away from the barred window, turn their backs to the fruit for a moment, and choose the door.

Have you read Brentano's book? I think it's better written than the books of the Glaesers, Regers, Roths, Kestens and company, but it doesn't amount to much more than the old lament that the bourgeois revolution cannot be carried through on a basis of democracy in the form of party rule. Well, Hitler operates without parties . . .

So what about the summer? I'll be back in June. Shall we see each other? I doubt if we'll be able to play chess under the apple trees for many more summers.

> As ever,
> b

[London, April/May 1936]

291 To Johannes R. Becher

[London], 29 May 1936

Dear Comrade Becher,

I just got your wire, but unfortunately I haven't yet received any of the galleys, though I attach the utmost importance to having them sent to me, because of the changes that must not under any circumstances be forgotten (I indicated them to Wieland a long time ago). When I do get them, I'll return them to you at once. Please make sure I get them soon. Also my contract. Didn't you get my last letter that Comrade Steffin wrote you?

> With best regards,
> Yours,
> Bertolt Brecht

293 To Erwin Piscator

Dear Pis,

Max Gorclik (whom I wrote to you about from New York) needs your help badly. He designed the sets for *The Mother* and is both technically more advanced and politically closer to us than any other stage designer. He has now been given a grant to write a book about the European theatre. For this he must go to Moscow and Leningrad, and this is evidently being made very hard for him. He can't get an answer from anyone, because no organisation takes an interest in him. It's really disgusting. Please do something for him; he is stuck in Stockholm and is kicking his heels. Address: Max Gorelik, Stockholm, c/o American Express Company.

As ever,
brecht

[London, May 1936]

294 To the International Association of Writers for the Defence of Culture

London, 21 June 1936

Dear Comrades,

I regret to say that I was unable to attend the Congress yesterday, Saturday, because some work for which I was under contract kept me out of London. With regard to today's afternoon session, I wish to inform you that I am very much interested in the topic under discussion: Publication of a new encyclopaedia. Over a year ago I sent Comrade Becher detailed proposals in this connection. Unfortunately, I haven't got my material here. If I had heard about the Congress earlier than the evening before it opened, when I learnt of it by pure chance, it would have been easy to send for this material. In the absence of my material, I must ask you to inform the plenum of the existence of such material and at the same time let them know that I should like to collaborate in this undertaking.

With comradely greetings,
bert brecht

295 To Erwin Piscator

Dear Pis,

Your letter took a long time to reach me. I had come to London, here I had twice moved house, in the meantime my post was sent back to Svendborg, etc. The worst of it is that I can't leave here now. I have a little contract with a film company, which good old Kortner got me, one of the few odd jobs that still exist. The pay isn't at all bad. So I turn out a few pounds worth of evening entertainment to get the kettle boiling again. While I'm at it, I may be able to investigate the prospects for Anglo-Soviet co-productions. If you could get me a bit of documentation, I'd start in. There are distinct possibilities for that sort of thing here. Should I suggest *War and Peace*? That could *only* be done in the USSR, and we're the only people who could do it. By and large I like the Volga-German plan. Of course we'd first have to build up some foreign connections, so as to get on the world market and give guest performances of plays. Why does it always have to be Tairov? And another thing: Couldn't you arrange for Weigel to come and look around? For a few months I could always go there by myself, but for a longer stay we'd have to know how it would be with the children etc. From America I hear that the (bourgeois) press reacted very positively to *The American Tragedy*, that publicly our people are putting a good face on it, but taking it badly in their inner councils. How are your finances? Enough for a trip to America or at least to London? (Very cheap from Leningrad.)

About the Volga plan: Scharrer once told me some very interesting details about the place down there, wonderful visual anecdotes. What do you think of Dudow for dramaturg? He helped me a lot with the *Threepenny* film. True, his real ambition is to direct. But I don't think his Paris operation is doing very well.

I'd have been glad to do it. But there are so few opportunities to make a little money. I hope you realise that.

Otherwise, it's grey here. There's no theatre. My entertainment consists in playing chess with Eisler.

What has become of MORT? What's Reich doing?

Write to me.

It was nice of you to look after Grete. Thank you.

As ever
b

Brecht
London
148 Abbey Road
Telephone: Maidarvale [Sic] 3815

Dudow's Address
Paris 7^e
79 Avenue de la Bourdonnais
[June 1936]

296 To Erwin Piscator

Dear Pis,

Did you get my letter?

Grete has told me about the Engels plan. The idea of creating a big experimental theatre, where we can resume and amplify our theatrical explorations, seems splendid to me. I saw in New York how eager a whole lot of people are to take up everything connected with the new techniques. They are beginning to see more and more clearly that the new problems can no longer be solved with the old methods and the meagre ideological equipment at their disposal. I'm sure we'll never find actors better suited to our experiments than the ones who would be available to us there.

Why don't you discuss it with me on the green island of Fyn over a cigar or two? You could swim and drive around in my old Ford. There are newspapers and books, and you'll have a pleasant room. The programme changes twice a week at the two cinemas and they show nice American films. Of course we could work together too. It's a big mistake not to make propaganda for our ideas about theatre and cinema. We should write articles and possibly put out a pamphlet with photographs; it's high time we made all this material usable by putting it into coherent form. I've read Stanislavky's *My Life in Art* with envy and anxiety. The man put order into his system and the consequence is that the Stanislavsky school has swept Paris and New York. Must that be? We are really unworldly dreamers.

The trip to Denmark would be so very simple for you. You board ship in Leningrad and land in Copenhagen. Then you have a few hours in the train or someone meets you with a car. You don't need a visa. You may have to show the customs people some money, but I can send you that to the boat. Here you won't need any money.

I myself shall be back in Svendborg in two weeks at the most. Then we can travel back [to the USSR] together, possibly with a film in our pocket. *If it would make things easier for you I'd be glad to forgo royalties in hard currency for any work we did together.*

As ever,

brecht

[London, July 1936]

297 To Otto Bork (Foreign Workers' Publishing House)

London West Hampstead.

148 Abbey Road

20 July 1936

Dear Comrade Bork,

Thanks for your letter of 13 July. But I haven't received the letter mentioned in it – from your publishing house about outstanding questions.

As for the poems, I'll straighten the matter out in Denmark in the next fortnight. I'd like to edit them myself. Of course I have no objection to Becher, but they are being published in the German language and in German my name is sufficiently known.

With regard to a preface for a possible re-edition of the novel, I hear that such a preface is being written for the Russian edition. Perhaps we should wait for it. In any case, don't do anything in that connection without speaking to me about it again.

I'd appreciate it if you could send me Huppert's article.

Please send twenty copies of the *Dreigroschenroman* to me in Svendborg and charge them to my account.

But now to the main point: I haven't yet received any proofs of the play volumes and am very much afraid they'll be printed before I've read the proofs. And, as I've repeatedly written to you people, everything isn't quite right yet and most of these plays are being published for the first time. You know how meticulous I am about my texts. I could never allow a book to be published without reading the proofs, and it does say in our contract that I must receive proofs on time. I'm sure you realise that it's not bloody-mindedness that makes me insist on your sending proofs. The fact is I'd be obliged to *oppose* publication of a book for which I have not read proofs. Not only in the West but in the Soviet Union as well. I cannot stress this point enough. I'm writing this because I wired eight weeks ago, begging you to send the proofs, and

I've asked for them half a dozen times. I can imagine that you suddenly find yourself short of time, faced with the dilemma of either publishing the book without having the proofs corrected or missing an advantageous publication date. You must not do the former *under any circumstances*.

It would put my mind at rest if you were to send me the proofs and write to me about them immediately. From 23 June on my address will again be

Denmark, Svendborg, Skovsbostrand,

> With warm regards,
> brecht

297x To W. H. Auden

Dear Comrade Auden,

Before I left London I made a small arrangement with an American literary agent by which he would pay you an advance of £25 for an English version [*Nachdichtung*] of one of my plays. It's not a large advance, but it's something. One of them, *Die Rundköpfe und die Spitzköpfe* [*The Round Heads and the Pointed Heads*], is probably going to be produced in Copenhagen this autumn. If you came to see me you could see one or two of the rehearsals. I hope you haven't forgotten your promise to come? I would be very glad if you did.

> yours cordially,
> bertolt brecht

298 To Erwin Piscator

Dear Pis,

Thanks for the letter. I'm now rehearsing *Die Rundköpfe*. Even if you don't come until November, you'll be able to see it. But you must definitely come. And allow yourself a little time here. Recreation.[1] You'll have a pleasant room etc., and we'll have a number of things to talk about. You know, I think, that you can count on me, and I'm expecting you. God knows there's no rush of people. By the way, couldn't you write something for *Das Wort* to make it a little better? It stinks. I'm absolutely, positively expecting you to come. You must.

> As ever,
> brecht

[12 October 1936]

[1]English in the original.

299 To Per Knutzon

Dear Per,

While wondering how it might be possible, despite the hostility of the press, to gain as large as possible an audience for *Die Rundköpfe und die Spitzköpfe*, I came across a long poem about Lulu in the Sunday edition of a Copenhagen paper; it shows how popular she is. I am convinced that we should exploit this fact as quickly and thoroughly as possible, by featuring Lulu Ziegler in the role of Waitress Nanna in the advertisements for *Die Rundköpfe und die Spitzköpfe*, and highlighting her in the posters too. This may be at variance with your usual methods and your ideas about collective work, but if so I'm bound to disagree with you. The collective to which you belong, to which one might say you have the honour of belonging, is bigger than the number which emerges when you count the members of your troupe: it is a broad front against barbarism. This production is a brave attempt to enlist the forces of the theatre in the great cause of humanity. Such a cause must be endowed with every possible public appeal. You must absolutely exploit the popularity of your actors to the full. You are working in the midst of an ultra-capitalist society and can't afford to act as if you were in a different society. However useful and valuable the product you have to offer, you must offer it as a commodity on the capitalist market, and the better you understand this the more useful your work will be. I am saying all this because I can imagine that in a theatre like yours, where you all work so splendidly together, you find it hard to put one individual forward. But you must. In Germany, whenever we put on unconventional plays, we never scrupled to advertise names. We printed the names of such actors as Pallenberg, Carola Neher, Durieux, Wegener, etc. in big letters on our posters.

Yours cordially

Svendborg, November 1936

301 To Otto Bork (Foreign Workers' Publishing House)

[Skovsbostrand] 30 November 1936

Dear Comrade Bork,

I've sent you two-thirds of the first volume of plays; have you received them? About the rest, that is, *Die Rundköpfe und die Spitzköpfe*, here is how things stand.

If you wire, you can have it straight away, the play is finished. But I'd be glad if you could let me keep it another week while I make a few changes and write an epilogue and possibly the biography you asked for. Then I'd send you the picture too. Unfortunately, quite a few changes have been necessary, I've just directed the play here and in so doing made – I think – a good many improvements, which is important in such timely plays. There is always so much room for political misunderstandings etc.

I'm sorry to be giving the publishing house so much trouble. I won't excuse myself by referring to the old story I wrote last May (I wish you'd send the galleys because of changes) as compensation. I'd rather you deducted from my fee whatever you think proper of the extra costs entailed by resetting. But if you are too pressed for time I suggest that instead of *Die Rundköpfe* you include *St Joan of the Stockyards* in the first volume, though I'd absolutely need at least one set of proofs, which I'd return to you within five days.

I've kept you waiting a long time, I know that, but in addition to this opening, which gave me an enormous lot of work, I had a spate of bad luck, my Gr[ete] St[effin], who is much better at reading proofs and typescripts than I am, was ill in hospital for months. But she'll be out in a few days now, and you can be sure that everything will be punctually attended to.

Dear Comrade Bork, I'd be *very* grateful if you could help get the new *Rundköpfe* into the volume after all; please send me an air mail letter at once or a telegraphed letter to let me know. I'm looking forward to the edition, and of course I want to do my part in making it as good as possible. You realise that refugees write more or less for some distant date. So the materials used must be as durable as possible.

Thank you very much for the second shipment of the *Dreigroschenroman*. It's beautifully printed, much better than the Dutch edition.

> With warm regards,
> Yours,
> brecht

302 To Walter Benjamin

Dear Benjamin,

What are you up to? What has become of your second Paris Letter? The first, it seems to me, is in No. 5. I'd like to have the next one. I haven't been told yet when your long article ('The Work of Art in the Era of its Technical Reproducibility') is to appear.

Could you get me Gide's little book? Do you know anything about his motives? Did the trial have anything to do with it? How did our people take it? I've read a virulent article in *Pravda* and something nastily triumphant in the *Basel National-Zeitung* (with quotations: it seems that the workers are short on refinement and the government is to blame).

How's your health? How about a trip to the northland? The chess board lies orphaned; every half hour a tremor of remembrance runs through it; that was when you made your moves.

> Cordially, as ever,
> brecht

[Skovsbostrand, early December 1936]

303 To Karl Korsch

The first chapter strikes me as *excellent*. It's really a paragraph. It ends when you exhaust the subject. But there are other subjects and paragraphs. 2) The writing is succinct and serene. 3) This paragraph imprints itself on the memory because counterclaim and wishes to the contrary are immediately acknowledged. 4) With this way of writing, any corrections can be made within our own ranks and the enemy won't profit from it. 5) Obviously the book contributes to the establishment of a whole new literature; there will be other books on the subject but this one holds the kernel of what they will contain. Other writers will be able to add to it. The paragraph is complete in scope but not in depth or rather density. It merely sparks off decision. Others will be able to go on writing (that's what counts!). In this field the proletariat needs a compact, coherent literature. (The bourgeoisie produces only sporadic works, which always start from scratch and never come to an end.)

I'm writing all this to give you an idea of my first impression.

[Skovsbostrand, probably 1936]

304 To Karl Korsch

Dear Comrade Korsch,

Many thanks for your detailed letter with the odyssey of your Marx book. Anyway, Nausicaa hasn't waited in vain.* By now you must have seen how ground rent has 'shot up' in Manhattan, so perhaps I can come out with one more request. I want to go on with the book written in Chinese style, the one containing maxims, some of which you know. In looking through the material, I came across the enclosed maxims: they are so useful that I would like to ask you for more. You know, they can be incomplete, taken out of context, put into artificial contexts, etc. Couldn't you send me a handful? They need only be sketched in, I don't ask for guarantees, they can be scientifically irresponsible. You see what I mean. I'd use them as raw material. Of course we're all eager to hear your new impressions and to know what use you'll make of your new perspective (as seen from the USA). I can read English much more easily now. So your material will be extremely welcome. As you see, I'm always asking for something. About this place there's not much to tell you. I couldn't help being glad they renewed my residence permit after *Die Rundköpfe*. Actually, quite a few of my friends say I should choose either a reactionary content or a reactionary form, that both at once would be too much of a good thing. And a prominent Communist said: If that's Communism, I'm no Communist. Maybe he's right.

W D has sent a short article (not very scientific unfortunately, vaguely leftwing, but that was probably inevitable). I sent it straight on to *Das Wort*. I hope they publish it. (Of course it's a lot better than the other stuff.) I miss our talks and arguments.

Cordially as ever,
b

Regards to your wife and Barbara.

[Skovsbostrand, late 1936/early 1937]

*The copy hasn't come yet, not even parts [?] of it. And I need the book. [Brecht's note]

305 To Bernard von Brentano

Dear Brentano,

I've received your letter, but I don't understand it ('don't understand' shouldn't be taken to mean anything diplomatic). As I see it, some bourgeois newspapers accuse you of denouncing Ottwalt to the Soviet government for writing pro-Hitler letters. But how could such information have reached these papers from a 'Russian source'? The Russians could hardly have found fault with you for that. Or are you only trying to tell me that you can't be expected to testify against Ottwalt, since you received no such letters from him? In any case, I haven't heard from any Soviet source anything to suggest that you are believed to have counter-revolutionary letters from Ottwalt in your possession, and as far as I know no reference has been made to statements by you. True, I'm not very well informed. I've also heard that Ottwalt has been arrested, but nothing more. And this news also seems to have originated in bourgeois papers. I myself haven't corresponded with him for years. I still believe that the Bolshevik party is deeply rooted in the Russian proletariat and that the Russian economy is engaged in a great revolutionary process. I definitely do not regard *Le Temps* and *The Times* as suitable platforms for disagreements with the Bolshevik party.

If you don't mind I'll wait till we get some authentic information about the Ottwalt business. (Ottwalt is a party member, which I am not), and then, if you still want me to, tell the editors of *Das Wort* that you have never received any pro-Hitler letter from Ottwalt and that you have sent no material to any Russian or allegedly Russian organisation. You know that I respect you, that I take a friendly view of anything that comes to me from you, and respond in the friendliest way I can.

Cordially, as ever,

[Skovsbostrand] early February 1937 (dating: Steffin)

307 To George Grosz

Dear George,

I don't know if you people can get Weil or Pollock to do something for old Borchardt, but obviously we can't abandon him in his bog. Of course I've asked a few people (Arnold Zweig, for instance) to appeal to the New York Jews, but B. is in the most dreadful situation. Some say: Why don't the Berlin Jews do something for him? And others: Why did the Communists expel him? The 'some' and the 'others' are often the same people. On the one hand, his going back to Germany made people say that he seemed to have connections there, and on the other hand he's been locked up – I've learnt in the meantime that old man Ruehle is in Mexico; you know, the man who is said to have explained Marx on the basis of his chronic constipation. I don't know if it's true, but I hear that he's now in the Mexican Ministry of Culture. Maybe you know him, he was once a Communist and he's said to be a decent sort. Perhaps he could offer Borchardt a job, I remember vaguely that B. knew him. Could you write to him if you know him? You might write to him even if you don't know him, he certainly knows you. Remember me to your wife and if you have a sad moment one of these days, drop me a few lines, they're sure to reach me in a sad moment.

> Cordially as ever,
> b

> Skovsbostrand, Svendborg, February 1937

309 To [?]

> Svendborg, Skovsbostrand

Dear friends,

I've just heard from the wife of the writer Hermann Borchardt, an old friend of mine, that he's in a concentration camp (Dachau), and could be released if someone can get him a written offer of work or even an invitation from some foreign country. Frau B. has urged me to see about it. Well, I heard last year that B. had been expelled from Minsk, where he had a teaching job after leaving Germany. (He was a Jew, a pacifist, and the Social Democrat Kawenauer's right hand man.) Why he was expelled I don't know. Frau B. claims (so I've heard indirectly) that they objected to his way of teaching and that he refused to exchange his German passport for a Russian one, but that he was not accused of any political offence. Of course he was left free to choose where he wanted to go from the USSR. Like a fool he went back to Germany, apparently in a state of total confusion and nervous collapse. His wife still had her parents there, and it seems that he expected them to help him and his family financially. He ended up in a concentration camp. I'd be very grateful if you could tell me more about their reasons for expelling him and whether there is any reason why we shouldn't try to get him an invitation that would get him out of the concentration camp. It seems to me that considering where he is one can hardly refuse to help him.

Please let me know by return of post.

> With best regards
> Brecht

> [Probably March 1937]

310 To Max (Mordecai) Gorelik

Dear Gorelik,

Many thanks for your letter.

Your finding your little family alive and well struck us as a stupendous stroke of good fortune, considering how worried you were. As if you had shipped them off to some wilderness inhabited by bandits and murderers; though maybe it really is that sort of country.

I read the two issues of *Theatre Workshop* with great interest. In this journal the first wave of Russian theatre seems to have reached the States. It's a pretty muddy wave, the only progressive thing about it is probably a certain sort of system, a few precepts and a bit of technique. But what a vocabulary! Art is still (or again?) 'sacred'. An actor is supposed to 'serve'. Whom? Art. A work should be 'creative'. The 'Creator' has always been God. The actor should be metamorphosed, just as in the Mass the bread is metamorphosed into the body of Jesus. What happens on the stage must be justified at the Last Judgement. 'Concentration' is the 'self-absorption' of the mystic. The actor should play as if there were a fourth wall in place of the audience; he is 'alone' with his God, art. His aim is 'the' truth, he finds it through 'right feeling', which can be induced by Jesuit-style 'exercises'. The public must be hypnotised, made to stare at the stage as though 'spellbound'. And people have a 'soul'. Not a word about classes, not a word about society, not a word about economics, and the revolution just hasn't happened. The whole technique goes back to the days of Little Father Tsar. Meyerhold is only a late offshoot, a kind of excrescence, and what was revolutionary about him, his subject matter, isn't mentioned. Agit-prop and TRAM don't exist, Okhlopkov doesn't exist. Those people are really incorrigible intellectuals, dyed-in-the-wool bourgeois. Naturally, I don't hold this against *Theatre Workshop*, which deserves credit for publishing such articles, a first step in the right direction. And it's important that you should remain on the board.

I'm glad about the connections you've made with a view to the 'Society'. It may turn out to be important. We should make it clear, though, that we are not interested only in long, well-rounded, representative articles, because otherwise we won't get anything. Sometimes a single page, or even half a page will do. Especially in the present pioneering period, when we're just starting in. We need short, fresh, spontaneous notes on a few experiments, fragmentary problems, a brief suggestion for a new technical term, a simple account of the application of Piscator's treadmill stage or of how some lighting effect can play a crucial role in a certain situation. This would make our work lively and concrete – a science begins to be scientific when it is broken down into partial fields and becomes concrete. And another thing: we should include in our listings certain articles that might belong to our collection and have appeared somewhere else, with the author's approval of course. Such listing is very important for the sake of continuity. I will get hold of a (lengthy) work by a German director working in Moscow, *Reich*, a study on Shakespeare, and send it to you, also an essay, 'The Effect of technical reproducibility on the arts'[1] by Benjamin, in which he shows the revolutionary effect that the possibility of mass reproduction (photography, cinema, etc.) has had on art and attitudes towards art. My article on stage construction isn't ready yet, I'll send it when it is. Thank you for the letter to the *Times*.

With best regards to you and the family[2]
Yours

Early March 1937
Svendborg

311 To 'Theater Workshop' (New York)

Dear friends,

As far as I can see, the intense seriousness and meticulous care with which you approach the theatre make your review unique, and not only in English-speaking countries. *Theater Workshop* can not only claim the high distinction of having set forth the principles of the great Russians more completely than has ever been done anywhere else in Europe or America, but also deserves special praise for not hesitating to take note of certain theoretical or practical experiments – which amount to a critique of the broadly speaking unparalleled achievements of the Stanislavskys and Vakhtangovs, and an attack on their basic tenets. For that is just what is achieved by the experiments with epic theatre and non-

[1]Brecht paraphrases the title of Benjamin's essay *Das Kunstwerk im Zeitalter seiner technischen Reproduzierbarkeit*.
[2]English in original.

Aristotelian drama that are discussed by M. Gorelik in *Theater Workshop*. What makes your objectivity all the more noteworthy is that those experiments that have been put into practice (the productions of the Schiffbauerdamm Theatre and of Piscator's Nollendorf Theater in Berlin) are little known in Germany, while those which were purely theoretical took the form of short comments on productions, despite the fact that this experimental work aimed at nothing less than to call into question what had hitherto been regarded as the unshakeable foundation of all play writing and acting, namely, the phenomenon of *empathy*.

The epic theatre and the non-Aristotelian theory of drama are the products of attempts to counter certain difficulties facing the construction and performance of dramatic works during the last few decades. They originated in Germany. Theatre and drama have long played a special role in Germany (and a few northern countries having cultural ties with Germany). For more than a century drama was regarded as the highest of all literary forms. Theatres were subsidised by the state. G. E. Lessing, the father of German literary criticism, was a theatre critic. Thus the difficulties that arose in the last decades in connection with the construction and performance of plays seem to have been felt more acutely and discussed more seriously in Germany than anywhere else. An outward indication of these difficulties was how quickly the manner of writing and producing plays changed. Dramatists of one and the same generation employed such an extraordinary diversity of styles that diversity of temperament could hardly account for it. One and the same dramatist might have recourse to several entirely different styles, shifting between one work and another from the French convention (three- to five-act plays) to the English (a loose sequence of an indeterminate number of scenes) and back. One and the same theatre would use stylised sets for one play and naturalistic sets for another. At the same time there were open-air festivals of special types, religious festival plays harking back to an old tradition and in recent years extremely active working-class groups. And these theatres as well, some very old and some very new, were constantly changing their styles.

After the World War, which in Germany was followed by a revolution which despite its political weakness gave a powerful impetus to public and cultural life, the theatre knew a tempestuous development. Yet this does not mean that it was particularly easy to write or produce plays. On the contrary, it proved to be increasingly difficult. What happened was simply this. Playwrights discovered that the old, traditional form of drama was no longer equal to the task of portraying the life of people together.

The dramatic representation of a simple incident in daily life, no less than of the so-called 'great' themes, met with amazing difficulties. It made no difference how the dramatist attacked his theme. If he tried to construct an effective play (with a strong plot and striking roles) based on timely themes, he discovered – or his critics discovered – that the reality portrayed had been distorted, mutilated and rendered almost unrecognisable. If he tried to put as much as possible of that reality on the stage, to represent it with as little falsification as possible, then all his stage effects and his whole dramatic technique seemed distorted and mutilated. As for the acting, the great actors achieved their greatest success in the worst plays, the deepest psychological effects were obtained on the unworthiest occasions.

[Fragmentary]

[Skovsbostrand, probably middle of 1937]

312 To Bernhard Reich

Svendborg
Skovsbostrand
2 March 1937

Dear Reich,

I've just received copies of the Russian edition of *Die Rundköpfe*, and I hope the Russian comrades will read the play with a little more understanding than our Hay gang. It may interest you to know that [Julius] Hay (who can no more keep an opinion to himself than any old philistine with an opinion) raises mainly two insidious objections. *First*: the play brings grist to the fascist mill with the fascist assertion that Aryans have visibly (and anatomically) different racial characteristics from Jews. Obviously it is no more fascist to take note of racial differences than to contend, as some Jews do, that no such differences exist. It wouldn't do the oppressed Negroes in the United States much good if someone were to demand equal rights for them on the ground that they are white. *Secondly*: I was not giving a picture of fascism, because fascism can't happen in an agrarian country. This is true as far as it goes; since my purpose was to depict racism, I was able to get by with my camouflage (an agrarian setting). Racism is used to deceive the people, not only by German fascism (which in this, incidentally, differs from Italian Fascism) but also by other reactionary governments, and has been since time immemorial (formerly in Poland and Armenia, in America etc.)

I hope you haven't got yourself into too much trouble with your letter on anti-fascist drama in *Das Wort*. If you ask me, these people, who in such a situation refuse to talk about anything but form and are ready to pick the worst sort of quarrels on that score, are formalists of a most unpleasant kind. Or isn't it formalism to take ancient and outmoded forms, forms obviously inseparable from their erstwhile content or social function, and try to impose them at all costs on everything new?

How are you and how is Asja? It wouldn't hurt you to write now and then.

I've been working on an opera with Eisler and doing various other things. Don't forget to send me your Shakespeare studies. I'd like to have them for *Das Wort* (a few excerpts at least if they're too long), but also for American magazines (if I can swing it, I have some influence).

Cordially

313 To Julius Hay

Dear Comrade Hay,

I must have expressed myself badly if you have understood that I wished to suppress all criticism of any of my works or theories. If you write an informative article, free from invective, it can be as critical as you like of my works and still appear in *Das Wort*, just as your dramatic works were able to appear, regardless of what I thought of their form. But when you say that epic theatre (as developed by myself, Piscator, Wangenheim and the agitprop groups) is merely a degenerate form of the bourgeois theatre or 'establish' that Reich lacks the elementary requirements for a theoretician and that his writing is dismal and grotesque, etc., such undocumented allegations are pretty well bound to meet with my opposition. When you attack a play like *Die Rundköpfe*, I have to make sure that your attack is substantial enough, I mean that it contains enough substance, to warrant a substantial answer. And when, 'for the deepest political reasons', you attack the use of the 'Trojan Horse' technique in the theatre, you had better be very careful. For even the Communist members of the editorial board are bound to wonder whether this particular question should be fully aired. I advise you not to publish this particular article; it does not serve our common cause, and if I were you I would not make an issue of it.

[Skovsbostrand, March 1937]

314 To Johannes R. Becher

Svendborg, Skovsbostrand
(Danmark)
2 March 1937

Dear Becher,

I'd like to ask your help in an annoying matter. An article by Reich on an anti-fascist theatre (which incidentally I had not read beforehand) appeared in *Das Wort*; it so infuriated Julius Hay that he has submitted an article rich in direct invective and poor in content. I wrote Hay a friendly letter, rejecting his article. The article is an attack on all camouflage in the theatre; he just won't let Dimitrov's Trojan Horse appear on the stage. Since he attacks me by name, I should have answered, but I was more afraid of the violence of my counter-attack than of the attack itself. In view of present political circumstances, I have always refrained from stating publicly what I think of Hay's dramatic technique, but the main point is that if I write camouflaged plays and have them produced here in a democratic country, I can't very well state publicly that I am making use of camouflage and for what purpose. Hay and his likes have let their formalistic interests blind them to the practical side of the real struggle. As you can imagine, it hasn't been easy for me to confine myself to playing the editor and mumble such phrases as 'the tone doesn't seem quite right' or 'we can't tear each other's hair out in public', and, by simply rejecting his article, to throw away such a beautiful occasion to *write* what I think. Now in a rather outspoken letter, proclaiming his intention to pick a fight at all costs, Hay assures me that his opinion 'is shared by all the comrades he has consulted'. Since I hope he hasn't spoken to you yet, I'd like you to tell the comrades how things stand and make it clear to them that what stops me from publishing Hay's article is not abject fear that the world may learn the awful truth about my inferiority as a dramatist from Hay's mouth. We must do everything in our power to prevent a public quarrel about literary form, which, as Hay's article shows, would undoubtedly become most acrimonious, and must stop him from denouncing and sabotaging literary attempts to smuggle in the truth about the enemy in camouflaged form. (In short, we can do without Hay fever.)

> With warm regards,
> Yours

315 To Erwin Piscator

Dear Pis,

Thanks for your letter. The trouble with the flies we eat in hard times[1] is that they're so small it takes an awful lot of them to make up a medium-sized chop. I'd like to go and see you, but I'd have to finance the trip with some job and that's not easy just now. Couldn't you get away and come here? Mexico would be nice. We could become professors, that's not so bad. Mostly to show you my sympathy I'm enclosing a page with a little film plot (laid in France), which is not my very best oeuvre, but at least leaves room for some interesting shots (how Paris was saved in 1914).

Write to me again.

> As ever,
> b

Das Wort has sent me a disgusting little article by Hay on anti-fascist theatre, containing violent attacks on Reich, me, and (camouflaged) you: (the old song, familiar to us from Auntie Voss about 'bad directors who tear a play (shit) to pieces, etc.'). Did you ever tread on his toes? Disgusting rubbish. I hope I can block it. Why don't you write something for the rag, it pays in convertible currency and is sorely in need of good contributions.

Skovsbostrand, [probably March] 1937

316 To Erwin Piscator

[Skovsbostrand] 16 March 1937

Dear Pis,

Enclosed a few theses as a basis for a small society we hope to found,

[1]German proverb: 'In time of need, the Devil eats flies.'

to consist exclusively of productive people. I'm also sending them to Auden, Isherwood and Doone in England; to Burian in Prague; Gorelik and MacLeish in America; Moussinac and Renoir in France; Per Knutzon, Nordahl Grieg and Per Lindberg in Scandinavia. Eisler will also belong, and perhaps you can give us a few more names, but only the very best. Among the Russians I thought of Eisenstein, Okhlopkov and Tretiakoff. Let me know what you think.

As you will see, the theses are being kept as mild as possible. Please read them through and add what you think necessary.

If you're too busy, I can send you a few short notes on Piscator's Innovations, because they must undoubtedly provide the substance of the first publications.

Let me know as soon as possible if you are agreed. I believe we see eye to eye about the need for this sort of *productive* society as opposed to the many societies that are merely representative.

Among the Germans I'd prefer to have only your name, mine and Eisler's for the present. We can add others later on the strength of good work, *if* any is submitted. How do you feel about it? Incidentally, I think our correspondence on the subject should be kept private.

as ever,

b

317 To Jean Renoir

Svendborg
Skovsbostrand
Danmark
17 March 1937

Dear Renoir,

We are starting a small society, to which you absolutely must belong. But don't be frightened: in joining us you'll be taking on no obligations whatever, and there will be no ballyhoo. We hope in the course of time to receive contributions of varying length (some no more than a single typewritten page). Since we are enlisting only productive people, it will take some time, but little by little the concept of a new, social and antimetaphysical art will take form.

I'm writing at the same time to Auden, Isherwood and Doone in England, Gorelik and MacLeish in the USA, Eisenstein, Okhlopkov and Tretiakoff in the USSR, Burian in Prague and Knutzon, Nordahl Grieg and Lagerkvist in Scandinavia. Perhaps you can put me on to a few productive and experimental people in France.

> With best regards,
> Yours,
> Brecht

318 To Max Gorelik

> Svendborg (Skovsbostrand)
> Danmark

Dear Gorelik,

Enclosed a short draft introduction to the aims of our projected *Society*. I would now suggest calling it the Diderot Society. The great Encyclopaedist wrote about the theatre philosophically in the sense of materialist philosophy. From a bourgeois standpoint, of course, but that of the revolutionary bourgeoisie. If you have any objections, let me know straight away. I thought of just using a name, because any definition in the title would sound either banal or precious. I mean to send the prospectus to

Jean Renoir, Paris
Moussinac, Paris
Doone, London
Auden, London
Isherwood, London
Burian, Prague
Piscator, Paris
Eisler

Later we can send it to

Knutzon, Copenhagen
Per Lindberg, Stockholm
Okhlopkov, Moscow
Tretiakoff, Moscow

In the USA, I'd like you to give it to MacLeish and anyone else you think suitable. Please let me know immediately what you think. It would be good if we could get the thing started as quickly as possible.

Incidentally, it would give me pleasure if you'd send me as much of your book as you have done, even parts. It interests me very much. Regards to your family.[1]

>Yours

19 March 1937 (dated by Grete Steffin)

[1]English in original

320 To Robert Hale & Co. Publishers

Dear Mr Hale,

I don't know who was responsible for the rumours that your English edition of the *Dreigroschenroman* was mutilated. I'll be glad to confirm the fact that when we were drawing up our contract you readily agreed to make no changes in my book without my consent. And the fact of the matter is that nothing has been changed and nothing of any political importance omitted in the English edition.

>With best regards,
>Yours

[Skovsbostrand, March 1937]

322 To Erwin Piscator

Dear Pis,

Just a brief note in haste (Easter holidays): I think the film idea is wonderful. Of course I'll be ready to work with you at any time. Just write to me.

>As ever
>b

[Skovsbostrand], 4 April 1937

323 To Erwin Piscator

>[Skovsbostrand]
>21 April 1937

Dear Pis,

Many thanks for your outline 'How Long should a Film Be.' Obvi-

ously that kind of thing would be just right for the Society. I'd be glad
to add your name to my invitation to join, i.e. along with my own and
that of the young American stage designer Gorelik, with whom I've
discussed the whole thing. Of course these letters of invitation could be
very much improved, but how can we do it by post? Still, they cover the
main points, I hope. Write and tell me if you agree.

Grosz's address is: 202 Shore Road, Douglaston, L.I., New York.

What's happening with *Schweik*? You mustn't do it without me on
any account. Incidentally, I advise you to drop in on my old friend
Bartosch (Paris 6, rue du Vieux-Colombier) and take a look at the trick
film he made from a book of Masereel's graphic work. He has a very
original (and cheap) technique.

Tell Brachfeld to write and tell me in what way the article he wants
about you should differ from the one in the *New York Times* and what
it's for.

By the way, 'Potato Jones' – the sea captain who keeps trying to
break through the 'Spanish' blockade of Bilbao and being turned back
by *English* ships – is a wonderful idea for a film. The longer his potatoes
rot, the more eager he becomes to carry potatoes to the children of
Bilbao. At first he must have been afraid of getting there too late,
because of the Nationalist boast that Bilbao would be taken in a matter
of hours. But there was no need to worry about that. I assume that the
British fleet keeps him away for fear he'll notice that there's not a single
Spanish ship afloat. When the English officers board his ship, what
lovely conversations they could have with him about peace, nonintervention and neutrality. And through it all they have to hold their noses
because of the rotten potatoes in the hold. 'John Bull Never Dies', 'The
Flying Potato Man', 'Don Quixote of Plymouth', 'Odysseus and his
Potatoes', 'Michael Kohlhaas in the Bay of Biscay'. Five actors, a
freighter, and a few hundred feet of Spanish newsreels. That's all you'd
need.

As ever

324 To Erwin Piscator

Dear Pis,

I've read the *Schweik* film treatment carefully and of course I see what
you're driving at. The war must be attacked, made to seem arbitrary,
unpopular, 'unjustified', so that Schweik can really represent the people.

Yes, of course. But then the beginning has to be more serious, we don't want an operetta, the war shouldn't be made to look ridiculous, it must be a terrible calamity, that bursts in on that quiet, peaceful creature Schweik. We need poetic images picturing the peace that has been demolished. In a prefatory text (which is always permissible) we can say that it's a wretched peace, that menacing things were happening on all sides, etc., but that war nevertheless 'bursts in' unexpectedly. (I believe that even the workers who are now turning out shells in G won't be surprised when the next war starts.) Schweik's actual adventures can easily be made cinematic; your treatment isn't bad, but the whole thing should be lighter, more elegant. If you need a love story (the Americans manage without one in their comedies and war pictures), it will have to take place among Schweik's class of people, otherwise he will look like too much of a faithful servant, too much of a toady. And with all his good nature, he mustn't be a Mr Fixit, on the contrary, he messes things up, which may be the ideal way to fix them. Above all, you must bring out the exemplary, crassly typical aspect of the Schweik figure, or else the meaning will be lost, the audience will take him for a sort of village idiot, of the kind met with commonly in army barracks and played by [Jacob] Tiedtke. Actually he is a dictator's nightmare, a man capable only of 'low' thoughts, deaf to higher things, a mass-produced man, a flawed sacrificial animal, whose bungling wrecks the best-laid plans. If we could talk it over, I think we'd hit on something. I'm afraid the Marshal won't do as a foil. But you know that yourself. When the time is right we'll just have to get moving. It'll be worthwhile.

I've waited so long before answering because it's so hard to express oneself in writing about something that's in the making. Everything I say sounds so hypercritical and negative, and of course you've thought things over and have got your reasons. And it's so impractical to make suggestions from outside, because I don't know enough about the conditions imposed on you. For the ending, I see something like this: Schweik should be made to flit, singly or in a thousand different forms, through all the war preparations now under way in all the different countries: warships full of beaming Schweiks, masses of men with Schweik faces, raising their arms in the fascist salute (in front of the Palazzo Venezia), bombing planes full of Schweiks, etc. (Would it be too dangerous to make these Schweiks suffer all sorts of mishaps?)

But maybe this whole ending is dangerous. On the other hand, why do Schweik at all if he's not to be dangerous? But that, of course, is just the trick of it.

Regards
b

Your letter has just come. Please forgive the delay.

[Skovsbostrand, June 1937]

325 To Walter Benjamin

Dear Benjamin,

Helli may come to Paris in June. Anna Seghers has written to her about the Laterne Cabaret. (I think that's the name). Could you find out something about it?

1) How many times a week do they play?
2) Where and to what sort of audience?
3) Where could Helli stay? How expensive? How hot?
4) Can she live outside Paris? How late at night does the Cabaret close? Would the trains still be running? Could she stay with Anna Seghers, i.e. would the train service make it possible?

We'd appreciate a prompt answer. When are you coming here?
Everything's green and no heat.

Cordially, as ever,
b

Did you get the money for your second letter?

[Skovsbostrand, April–May 1937]

326 To Walter Benjamin

Dear Benjamin,

I've re-read your study of Fuchs and liked it more than ever. This declaration will leave you cold, but I believe your limited interest in the subject of your work helped you to handle it so economically. There's not a bit of ornament, but the whole piece is graceful (in the good old-fashioned sense, and the spiral is never prolonged by a mirror. You always stick to your subject, or else the subject sticks to you.
[Probably unfinished]

[Skovsbostrand, towards the middle of 1937]

327 To Lion Feuchtwanger

Dear Doctor,

I wish I'd been over there with you. Did you get my letter that Maria was supposed to give you? We enjoyed hearing your voice on the wireless and would be even more delighted to hear you tell some more stories. I've long been hearing a good deal about *Success* and the real success it's been having in the Soviet Union and I'm delighted even though the book contains those hideous caricatures of Hitler and me. Incidentally, could you do something about Neher? She is said to have been jailed in Moscow, I don't know why, but I really can't think of her as a danger to the survival of the Soviet Union. Maybe some sort of love trouble. In any case she is not a worthless person, but I doubt if they know it in the USSR, she hasn't had a real chance to show what she could do. I'm sure it will help her if you just make enquiries. All my own questions have gone unanswered and that worries me. Perhaps you, being on the spot, can find out something, and I'd appreciate a few lines from you. People are always asking me for information about her.

[Skovsbostrand, May 1937]

328 To Lion Feuchtwanger

Dear Doctor,

Do you think you might approach Stalin's secretary for information about Neher? In view of the only too well justified countermeasures against Goebbels's networks in the USSR, a mistake is always possible. Gorky, you know, has intervened from time to time on behalf of artists and scientists. If Neher has actually been involved in treasonable machinations, there's nothing we can do to help her, but perhaps by calling attention to her great talents as an artist, one might get them to speed up proceedings and give her case special attention (which in view of her reputation in Germany, Czechoslovakia and Switzerland, would be a good thing for the Soviet Union). A simple (unofficial) inquiry would call attention to her importance as an artist without complicating the work of the judicial authorities. Incidentally, please treat this request of mine confidentially, because I neither want to sow distrust of the Soviet system nor give certain people a chance to accuse me of doing so.

My coming to Paris depends on whether Piscator's present film plans materialise, and that's rather doubtful. Paris is hot and expensive now, and I have nothing to exhibit at the World Fair. By the way, I feel I ought to warn you not to regard everything that appears in *Das Wort* as Marxist. Its policy is to print non-Marxist material as well. I should hate to have you regard capitalism as something best symbolised by a provincial Lucrezia Borgia. I assure you that Hay can't claim Marx as his authority for that. The poor peasant girl who risks the salvation of her soul to get hold of a farm is a better illustration of the Bible verse: 'For what should it profit a man if he shall gain the whole world' etc. than of anything in *Das Kapital*. How many times your wife and I have tried to explain to you that when Goethe said the whole world was out for money it hardly made him a Marxist. I say this not without an element of reproach.

> Cordially as ever
> b

> [Skovsbostrand, June 1937]

329 To Martin Andersen-Nexö

> [Skovsbostrand]
> 5 June [properly: July] 1937

Dear Comrade Nexö,

Unfortunately I can't attend the Congress, I'd very much have liked to, but it was only on 26 June that I received a wire telling me I had to be in Paris on 30 June (at the latest), which was impossible; you yourself know how bad the boat connections are between here and France. It's really scandalous inviting me so late. This is the second time. In London the German section didn't invite me at all, though I was there at the time.

I wish the Congress every success and send greetings to the comrades.

> With best regards,
> Yours,
> Brecht

330 To Hermann Borchardt

Dear B.

I'm awfully glad to hear that you're out. When you've recovered you must tell me about your odyssey. Maybe you make too many pacts with God. (You know, Lloyd's has stopped insuring contracts with that unreliable partner.)

Did you manage to save your novel?

What are your plans for the future?

I wish I were in the USA myself.

[Skovsbostrand, probably mid-1937]

331 To Hermann Borchardt

Dear Borchardt,

Thanks for your letter and thanks again for the plays, which gave me great pleasure whether you intended it or not. To tell the truth, I sometimes think the keen intellectual pleasure they give me prevents me from saying anything about our enormous differences, which I really should do, since I'm devoted to you. When one approaches a literary work from an aesthetic point of view (even if one takes the 'content', the message etc., into account) one is always tempted – undoubtedly a Satanic temptation – to regard the work as a natural phenomenon, some sort of immutable monolith: that's how our aesthetic sense works. And of course it's all wrong, or, as I said before, Satanic. The question I think you should look into is this: Don't you, when you write, unsuspectingly slip into a certain role; in other words, doesn't a theatrical impulse take hold of you completely? Don't you become, let's say, the Adversary, the Advocatus dei, the Provocateur without fear and without reproach? I think we agree that, seen in a purely legislative light, the moral schema of 'good versus evil', doesn't amount to much, is not very productive, I mean. Often in our discussions, you put me in a most uncomfortable position, which isn't nice of you, by leaving it to me to say the things that are banal, boring and unattractive, but as it happens true. Actually I have no right to complain once I've taken, or let myself be taken by, the despised role of enlightener.

[First half of the forties]

332 To Slatan Dudow

Dear Dudow,

Thanks for the information. In the meantime I've had an answer. Now to my question.

1) Could you find out from Aufricht (Jasmin 4748, Paris 16, 25 Avenue de Lamballe) when he's starting to rehearse *The Threepenny Opera*? He was going to invite me to the rehearsals, and he really should, there's a good deal I could do. I don't think a two to three week stay would cost him too much. And he's putting a lot of money into the thing anyway. If possible, the Spanish play should be rehearsed at more or less the same time. I'm no longer rich enough to be able to finance trips and stay abroad so easily.

2) There are (German) phonograph records of gunfire. I imagine you've thought of them. Helli could bring one with her from Copenhagen. Your idea for the ending is good. Maybe I can think up a few lines of verse for it.

I think the production should be very simple. Sharply modelled figures against whitewashed walls, groups carefully composed as in paintings. No hysteria, quiet, well thought-out realism. Humorous details, never too heavy. Effective breaks.

3) Helli should have about two weeks of rehearsal. She can come at any time.

4) If you call in Katz (6579 Vaugirard), I'm sure he could do a lot, prise [Ernst] Busch loose for instance. I doubt if we can get anyone from Zurich, the season there is just beginning. Gretler would be best. And being Swiss, he won't have any trouble getting back. Aufricht may know of somebody. Still, you could be thinking of guest performances for Helli, possibly in Prague and Zurich. Of course we'd have to wait till after Paris.

At the moment I'm writing a series of short plays (10 minutes). The *Spiritual Upsurge of the German People under the Nazi Regime*. Along with the Spanish play, they would add up to an evening. Minimal cast. You see, I too am beginning to do little things.

Have you heard anything more about the *Satires*? I mean, the reactions. Our speech went well. Thanks to you.

Have you read Feuchtwanger's little book about the Soviet Union? Very interesting, I think.

About the *Grenzbestimmungen* Demarcations it would be best if we could discuss all that together. Since you will be defending my interests as well as your own – they are essentially the same – I can just as well put the whole thing in your hands. Only I must be able to tell you as much about the situation as I know. To the best of my knowledge next to nothing theoretical about literature and related fields has been appearing in the Soviet Union. (In *Das Wort* I've been blocking all attempts in that direction, because, it seems to me, they'd antagonise all sorts of people, including myself). (We read *Literaturnaya Gazeta* as well as *Pravda* and *Izvestia*). Now and then Lukács takes up formal questions; at present he's writing something rudimentary about the technique of the novel, always clinging fast to particular novels by Zola or Balzac or Tolstoy or Gorky). In my opinion, every form, naturalistic or otherwise, which derives not from the subject matter – the state of contemporary knowledge, or the needs of the class struggle – but from aesthetic postulates, is formalistic. I'm convinced that from this point of view we can launch your *Grenzbestimmungen* with little difficulty. But, as I said, I leave it to you, we'll just have to discuss the situation and you must listen to my analysis of it.

Cordially as ever

(Skovsbostrand, July 1937)

333 To Slatan Dudow,

A few more thoughts that have occurred to me in connection with your *Grenzbestimmungen*.

Ad 1) Word diplomacy. It seems to me that the best style in which to couch polemics, estimates of progress, contradictions etc. has been developed by the modern sciences, especially physics, but also biology, etc. Perhaps you can get hold of one of Eddington's or Russell's books somewhere; these men, active in a field where everything is in constant flux, have an excellently cautious style, the cautious style of science itself, they contradict an opponent (or the adherent of a superseded opinion) in the same way as they contradict themselves in the course of their research. Russell would express one of your ideas roughly as follows: Given the existence of the cinema, Brecht's attempts to liberate a radically realistic manner of writing from all naturalism takes on a new meaning. It could be shown that Piscator had merely overstepped boundaries and in a most instructive way, capable of arousing in the audience a first awareness of the boundaries. The advantage of this mode of expression (which I have somewhat exaggerated here) is that it takes production as its starting point and always remains practical. After all, and this is the diplomatic side of the matter, no one can sue for damages because someone has proved to him that his sodium sulphate is not sodium sulphate, but he can sue if someone tells him that he's bankrupt because his sodium sulphate is not sodium sulphate. Bacon, as he himself was proud to state, never went in for polemics, yet no one attacked scholasticism as violently and successfully as he. We unfortunately must go in for polemics; at least (thank God), we are not forbidden to (though admittedly I have no authority over *Das Wort*). However, after long meditation and a number of false starts I have found out that it really is more appropriate to say that something has gone wrong with empathy or even that it is experiencing a crisis than to speak of its definitive demise. Incidentally, no one I know has done so much for my ideas, all the while sticking to the facts, bearing in mind the consequences and aiming for maximum effect, as you, Dudow. When one is in the embarrassing position of being obliged, as we are, to assign ninety-nine hundredths of all plays, nine-tenths of all films and at least a third of all anticipated television, to the junk heap, one should at least wear one's Sunday best and play down one's opinions about the creations of the Hays and Wangenheims.

Ad 2) Discussion: It should be pointed out that the rudiments of drama and the novel are foreign bodies in the cinema. For though, generally speaking, cinema takes over the functions of these arts, it cannot do so by adapting their forms. I believe you agree with me in this. The hybrid forms – what Piscator did and what we wanted to do for *The Mother* in Berlin (Russian documents at the end) – are even more relevant to the definition of boundaries. The rudiments of the drama in film include the rudiments of theatre and the psychological techniques of the actors (mimicry). It is interesting to note that the theatrical director most influenced by cinema, Okhlopkov (who was himself a film actor), liquidated the picture-frame stage (*Razbeg*), which the cinema can never dispense with but which the theatre does not need. Of course I don't mean that all these things have to go into your article; I'm only giving you a few points to show you the direction I should like the discussion to take.

For *Das Wort*, I repeat, this discussion would be quite unnecessary; a few changes in the passages that would isolate us too much would be quite enough.

Cordially as ever

Svendborg, end of July 1937

334 To Lion Feuchtwanger

Dear Doctor,

Thank you very much for your invitation. I'll write to you as soon as I know the exact date of my trip to France. In the meantime I've received *Nero* and the book about Russia. I'm reading *Nero* now with great pleasure (you know how happy it makes me to see you writing satires), and I think your 'De Russia' is the best thing to have appeared on the subject in Europe. It's a long step forward to regard reason as something practical, something human that has its own morality and immorality; in so doing you bring out its experimental character, which is after all of interest to humanity but vanishes as soon as a rigid morality is imposed on it, since experimentation itself is morally dubious. I'm really glad you've written this.

The business about the German Academy prize is rather muddled. The invitation to submit entries just says 'works'; now the secretary, a Prince Löwenstein, writes that prose works are meant, as though that were self-evident. Which is most distressing. But thank you very much for answering so quickly. I could have used the money.

By the way, did I tell you that the *Dreigroschenroman* has had surprisingly good notices in England? Several of them compare it with Swift, but I don't believe it will sell at all well; apparently the English don't read Swift. True, the reviews say the book is rather nasty, and evidently the English don't like nastiness as much as the Germans do.

Cordially as ever

Svendborg, August 1937

336 To Wieland Herzfelde

Svendborg
Skovsbostrand
(Denmark)
24 August 1937

Dear Wieland,

Many thanks for your letter. I'm *very* glad the plays are coming out now and that the Malik-Verlag is publishing them.

I'll look straight away for a copy of *Die Massnahme*, which VEGAAR seems to have lost.

You're right, it would be good to have the two volumes the same size. But this is the situation: I have no set idea about the order within the volumes; you have a free hand. But when it comes to the choice of plays for the volumes, I'm not keen on seeing *Mahagonny*, which is after all awfully circus-like, cheek by jowl with *The Mother* in the second volume. I'd much rather have *Die Rundköpfe* in the second volume, but mightn't that make the second volume too thick? I could send you a short play about Spain (written for a German group in Paris), about thirty typewritten pages, that you could use to even out the volume.

If you put *Die Rundköpfe* in the second volume, where it would fit nicely, you could put *Joan* in the first, where it would fit too. And *Joan* isn't very well known.

Do write to me about it again.

The business with the novel is shrouded in deep fog, I'll have to get a statement of accounts from De Lange. Then I'll write to you at once. Universum has already informed me of your offer.

Do you still hear from Grosz now and then? What has become of those drawings you had already paid for? I've written to him about it time and again. Steff was delighted with the Sinclair books. Have you published the book about Fox? I haven't read it yet either.

I think Weiskopf's adaptations from the Czech are beautiful, except for the two ballads about the Student Vagabond, but there the original is probably at fault.

You ought to come to Denmark again. I'm deep in my *Tui* novel. Am planning a trip to Moscow in the autumn. When are you going back?

> Cordially

337 To Helene Weigel (postcard)

Dear Helli,

My cold is almost gone, and apart from the horrible picture postcard landscape it's bearable here. Feuchtwanger has been telling very amusing stories. I'll be in Paris Saturday morning. How are the rehearsals going? Write to me.

> I kiss you
> b

Send my letters to Feuchtwanger, that is, send the last batch on Thursday. How's *The Threepenny Opera* doing?

> Sanary-sur-Mer, 6 October 1937 [Postmark]

338 To the Schutzverband deutscher Schriftsteller

Dear Colleagues,

I hear there have been big discussions lately, of a kind to provoke increasing dissension among exiled writers. Some people seem to think the fight against Fascism can be carried on separately by the Communists among us. In opposition to this view, I wish to point out that the Communists among us have always made the greatest sacrifices in support of a united struggle for freedom and democracy in Germany. I do not think it is asking too much to expect all anti-fascists to take the same attitude. In this period of mounting confusion, one of an anti-fascist writer's main tasks is to sharpen people's power to distinguish the important from the unimportant. And the only important thing is to carry on an all-encompassing, indefatigable struggle against fascism on the broadest possible front.

> With comradely greetings,
> Bert Brecht

[Mid-October 1937]

339 To Helene Weigel

Dear Helli,

Everything is all right here, I think. Barbara is quite satisfied with her hotel. She had a pleasant birthday. She comes here very seldom and only for seconds at a time; too many social obligations. Steff comes every afternoon and plays billiards with me, the latest sensation. He's delighted with the Myers books, he likes the Darwin too. His visit to Copenhagen seems to have been pleasant enough, but you know, he's discreet. The garden is lovely now, yellow and transparent.

I'm sending a copy of the play to Dr Lieb in Basel. One to [E.F.] Burian in Prague, one to Wieland Herzfelde (for the Collected Plays), one to the French translator, Grünberg in Paris. I haven't received any photos from Breitenbach yet. I've been wondering if we couldn't have a German production in Copenhagen with Hodann etc., very simple, using the sets from the Danish production. It's really one of your great roles, and I'm very pleased about it.

Do write to me about the date of the Paris revival and when you'll be coming here. It would be a shame if you couldn't play in Prague. But it will take much too long unless they get started at once. And I'd like to see you again some time.

My regards to your father.

I kiss you, Helli

b

Paris was beautiful.

And do look after Hanne's grandmother. Don't forget. Should I send you another copy?

[Skovsbostrand, 26–28 October 1937]

340 To Helene Weigel

Dear Helli,

Just received your letter from Prague. I'd begun to think the Paris performance was tomorrow and I wrote to you there via Dudow. A letter full of Paris errands. The beginning of December seems a long way off, but you've got to do it. Prague is the second most important refugee centre, and your work is too good to hide. No one else has developed in exile. Only it's too bad the Paris revivals can't be done later. Why can't they, actually? That's a lot of travelling. The Czech translation is all right with me, I've already sent the play to Burian (also to Lieb in Basel). You must invite Burian to the theatre in Prague, and altogether you must have a talk with him. Don't forget that I was having that trouble with my jaws when his congress was on and that's what prevented me from going. In Zurich you must go to the bank, Crédit Suisse, and ask how much we still have on deposit there. You signed along with me at the time. In Vienna please go to Universal-Edition and see if they have any money for me. You could ask M. how we could get an enlarger for our Leica. It can be a simple one, but enlargers are very expensive in the shops. And are there still any copies of *Saint Joan* and *The Mother* at Lanyi's? The *Three Soldiers*? We really ought to buy a few. And write another letter to Prof. Dr Fritz Lieb, Basel, Aescherstrasse 25, asking him if he could speak to his friends at the Arbeiterbühne about the Spanish play.

The children are all right. I see Barbara only for seconds at a time, she is overwhelmed socially. Steff's upbringing will just have to do. Mie cooks quite nicely, but she couldn't run the whole household, so I leave the children with Mrs Andersen. If you think some other way would be better, write and tell me straight away. Steff comes in the afternoon and we play billiards, which he enjoys enormously. (You'll enjoy it too, he's already telling me how he's going to teach you to play.)

You're having to chase around an awful lot, take care you don't lose *too* much weight, especially you know where. And watch your morals.

I think fondly of Paris and am most devoted to you.

> Yours,
>
> b

Regards to your father.

> [A postscript by Stefan S. Brecht follows.]
> [Skovsbostrand, 30 October 1937]

341 To Helene Weigel

Dear Helli,

I'm sending you a poem as a little gift. Apart from the fact that it's one of the best things I've written about the art of acting, it might be useful to have it appear somewhere in Prague (with a photo) before the play opens there; it would focus the attention of the audience.*

We were rather horrified to hear that you won't be getting back much before Christmas, but of course you must play in Prague. Just don't overexert yourself and *don't smoke too much*. That's really important.

I hope to have finished the two little plays about Germany by the time you get here. Perhaps we could give them their first performance next spring in Paris. Now, after Paris, I'm eager to do that kind of thing again. Most of all for that reason. There could be no better way of developing the epic style of acting. As you see, I'm very proud of you.

Mie cooks very nicely, and the household worries along in a makeshift kind of way. The children are amusing. Steff came in this afternoon and said: 'Did you talk in your sleep? It seems to me you said: "Steff *must* go to the cinema this afternoon because his friend Kaj is going."' Except that of course he expressed himself a little more elegantly. Apart from that, he's growing and is one of the tallest boys in his class.

I don't know if I can double your ration. Maybe if you stop smoking.

> I kiss you
>
> b

Where is the key to the small cupboard? I can't find it and I've forgotten where it's kept.

Skovsbostrand, early November 1937

*I'll send it to Wieland. [Brecht's note]

342 To Helene Weigel

Dear Helli,

Norske Kreditbank Oslo is supposed to be a reliable bank. The children, I think I've told you, are still with Mrs Andersen. Mie couldn't really take care of the whole family by herself. As it is, she cooks very nicely. And the children enjoy staying with Mrs Andersen. Steff's birthday was satisfactory. At Mrs Andersen's he got food and cake, here he got your book jacket, some books (Silone's *Bread and Wine*, etc.), a memo book, 5 (five) crowns in cash, 2 small balls, etc. He ate your little box of chocolates on the spot, 'to give his weak stomach a booster'. I won part of a packet of chocolate biscuits at billiards for Barbara.

Did you get my letter asking you to find out from the Crédit Suisse in Zurich how much is left in Frau Mary Fränkel's account? I won't be able to send the poems until they're retyped.

Don't be afraid of directing in Prague. You can do it very well. Above all, make sure you keep up the pace. When a lot of breaks are necessary, things tend to drag out. Between the breaks, you need pace. And that doesn't mean noise. Write to Breitenbach (Paris 6, 70-bis rue Notre-Dame-des-Champs) and tell him to send a batch of stage photographs. Also tell him the exact date of the performance.

The little picture of Storm Petersen is for Burian in Prague.

Did you get the poem?

I kiss you

b

[Skovsbostrand], Thursday [4 November 1937]

343 To Helene Weigel

Resolution

Esteemed comrade,

The council of husbands and sons calls upon you to return *without delay* on completion of your present duties and resume your activities here. You are therefore to report as soon as possible to the undersigned.

With revolutionary greetings,
Steff
bidi

[Skovsbostrand, November 1937]

344 To Martin Domke

Skovsbostrand per Svendborg
9 November 1937

Dear Herr Domke,

Many thanks for your letters. Of course I rather miss your notes but I can imagine that you must be terribly overworked. But don't forget that there's absolutely no need for you to write your notes in classical style; quick jottings are quite enough. And, I repeat, send them only at your leisure. In the meantime, I've been studying Plutarch, Suetonius and Mommsen. Madame Tallon has written to me as follows:

'I only wanted to warn you that Banyai wants to confiscate your rights, because he claims you have received advances. He has kicked up a terrible row at the Société [des Auteurs] and with Mauprey.'

And the Société has sent the enclosed letter. I answered it as best I could and am enclosing a copy of my letter. I hope I wasn't too far wrong. In any case I'm glad you'll be there on the fourteenth, you'll be needed. On the other hand, my conscience troubles me, I'm taking up too much of your time. But this is something I can't manage by myself.

Cordially

345 To Martin Domke

Have you received the copy of my letter to the Société? I'm sending you a sheet of paper with my signature in case the letter hasn't reached you or is insufficient. It's abominable that you should be having such trouble with this business. But the eight thousand francs mean a lot to me.

And now to *Caesar*.

I've done a rough sketch of the scene. It starts with the year 691.

Caesar is involved in the conspiracy of Catiline. In Scene 2 he is praetor (692). In Scene 3 he's getting ready to leave for Spain. Plot: C. supports Catiline, the great expunger of debts. He needs more money to become praetor, and he has to become praetor to guide the investigation of the Catiline affair into the 'right channels'. Then Judge C. acquits Defendant C. Caesar also supports Pompey, now fighting in Asia, who (according to Catiline) is a second potential dictator. The more interest the Senate takes in revealing C.'s role in the Catilinian conspiracy (obviously they all know the whole story), the more C. (in 2) pins his hopes on Pompey. When contrary to all expectation Pompey discharges his army (on landing in Brindisi, autumn 92), C. is in a tight spot and escapes (Scene 3) into the Spanish governorship. Crassus pays Caesar's debts. The Second Act will again have three scenes (4, 5, and 6). 4) C. comes back from Spain, he has some money, he doesn't have to repay anything, but succeeds in borrowing twice the amount of his previous debts. Pompey's situation is bad. He no longer has any power and the Senate refuses to grant him land to distribute among his veterans. C. and Crassus decide to exploit this situation. 5) The three men meet in a steambath and form the Triumvirate. Caesar is to be made consul and then to be given Gaul. As consul he is, in return, to put through Pompey's land grants, and get Crassus control of the knights' courts, through which the provinces (including Gaul) will be subjected to the control of high finance. . . . C. quietly buys up land. 6) is the election of a Roman consul in one of the democratic clubs. C. is elected. In the Third Act Caesar puts through the land law, and it is agreed that in the ensuing years Pompey and Crassus will buy up and distribute land. This business deal hangs over C's head (he owns land) throughout the Gallic War. For now (96) he must go to Gaul, partly because his business deals during his consulate are again being investigated (his second flight). Third Act: Gaul. His profits derive chiefly from his share in the spoils of war and from kickbacks on army supplies. He also speculates on the price of slaves (he sends large numbers of them back to Rome) and of gold. According to Mommsen, the quantities of gold pouring in from Gaul cause a drop in the gold price. The war must be carried on with the utmost caution because of the requirements of the gold speculators. There must be a connection between this and the defeat at Aduatuca, where a whole legion is lost. Luca is a big question mark. Why does C. cede so much to Pompey? He has power, Pompey hasn't, he gives Pompey power. ??? By the way, do you agree that C. (apart from rake-offs) should not share directly in the gold tribute, but should make money by speculating on the price of gold, which he can manipulate? And he's so severe about the corruption of his officials! Acts IV and V take place in Gaul. (End of IV: Luca), and Act V ends with the crossing of the Rubicon. In Gaul C. is accompanied by the creditors' confidential agent, who is supposed to direct all his movements, but is occasionally hoodwinked.

Now some questions. 1) I need a business deal for Scene 1. Catiline is ruined when the Senate approves the distribution of corn which Catiline has promised. How in this situation can C. speculate and *lose*? He has to lose. (Of course he assumes that Catiline will succeed, and accordingly accepts loans which he hopes he will never have to repay). Still a risky business because the outcome of Catiline's machinations is uncertain. Logically he could speculate on a fall in the price of corn (since the free distribution of corn will, I think, bring down the price). (?) But then he'll profit if the Senate approves the corn distribution, and he mustn't profit because I need him deeply in debt (which indeed he was). He should lose as a result of the Senate's premature decision, and besides the whole thing should be simple or else it will be incomprehensible, and the scene isn't long (10 minutes).

I hope the land speculation in II and III is correct. Here I can show how democratic measures can be exploited financially.

But how do I make the Gallic War a business (the price of gold and slaves)? For France it might be best to begin with Scene 5 (Triumvirate) and then take the Gallic War as the pièce de resistance. But starting after Scene V. It's going to be a long play in any case.

What do you think of my outline?

The main political idea is that dictatorships come into being at times of violent class struggle. The dictator as the pointer of the scales. And the dependency of dictatorships on the ruling class. At first the knights are the spearhead of the bourgeoisie against the feudal Senate (the landowning and office-holding nobility). Then they go over to the side of the Senate out of fear of the plebs and because they have interests in common with the patricians. Birds of a feather flock together). C. is constantly threatening them with the plebs, whom he is constantly selling out.

For the war I still need striking evidence of the impossible social situation in Rome. And it must be explained simply and clearly, but also, of course, amusingly, why the war is intended as a solution (which of course it is not).

For the Gallic War, I need to know what sort of business was carried on between C. and the Gallic ruling class, who for one thing had been selling slaves to the Romans since time immemorial. Then they mobilise against Rome, make war and lose, whereby the lower class is directly enslaved (including those members of it who stay at home). The Roman people (lower class) have no interest in the slaves, since these have the effect of putting Latin agriculture into the hands of the big slave-owning knights. (Sicilian grain is so cheap as to defy competition.) The inflation brought about by Gallic gold tribute exactly balances out the cancellation of debts.

Please dictate a few lines about this (and possible *trouvailles* in French literature), don't worry about form, just for me.

Cordially as ever

[Skovsbostrand], 19 November 1937

346 To Lion Feuchtwanger

Dear Doctor,

Many thanks for your letter. What really can we do for poor C[arola] N[eher]? I don't know if K. will be able to do anything when he gets back, seeing that he'll be coming from abroad and will be very busy. Perhaps you should consider a telegram after all. If she has been convicted, I'm sure it hasn't been without ample evidence, but over there they don't operate on the 'one pound of crime one pound of punishment' theory, they only want to protect the Soviet Union, so couldn't they just expel a non-Russian? After all, she's somebody, a great actress. They've rightly put scientists who have committed crimes (such as Ramzin) back to work; they can't do that with N., because she can't act in Russian. But we can.

We're making small wax records now for the Freedom Radio which, so I'm told, is very important in Germany; they are to contain short scenes for actors, six minutes long. Have you anything like that?

I've been working on a play about – Julius Caesar. Do you know of any good books about him and his times? (I've got Mommsen. He's such a bourgeois). I can't get hold of Dio Cassius anywhere in German, and my Latin has got very rusty. Did you take any notes about daily life, finance, etc. when you were working on your *Josephus*? That kind of thing would come in very handy. Too bad we're living so far apart.

This would be a good thing to collaborate on, like *Edward*. I reread that recently. How does it strike you today?

Our letter to *Das Wort* hasn't been answered yet. (Fritz) Erpenbeck's mills grind slowly.

Give your wife my regards.

Cordially

brecht

Svendborg, end of November 1937

347 To Karl Korsch

Now of course there's been a holdup in our correspondence, as usual when too much or too little happens or only an average amount. In the autumn Helli and I were in Paris (where they were doing *The Threepenny Opera* in French with [Yvette] Guilbert as Mrs Peachum and altogether an excellent cast. It went very well, only I'm not getting any royalties, the German agency gobbles them up), and we put on a little Spanish play with a German troupe. Helli was better than ever, she lost nothing by the interruption, and she was glad of that. Her acting was the best and purest that has been seen in the epic theatre anywhere. She plays the part of an Andalusian fisherman's wife, and it was interesting to see how she was able to negate the usual contradiction between a realistic and a cultivated style of acting. (The little play, written just for the occasion, will be sent you in a few weeks when I receive the two volumes of collected plays that Wieland is publishing.) I've also written seven short plays set in Germany and a dozen satires for the Freedom Radio.*. Now I'm starting a play about Caesar; *Die Geschäfte des Herrn Julius Caesar* (Mr Julius Caesar's Business Deals) for Paris, where there's a possibility of a production. It's hard work and you are very much missed. I'm not trying to make it a pièce à clef, conditions were too different in the ancient world. Still, Caesar is the great prototype, and I can throw light on at least two points: how a dictator oscillates between the classes and in so doing favours the affairs of one (here the knights) and 2) that he makes war (here the Gallic War) in order to exploit his own people, not the enemy. For France this has a piquant note (the Roman Caesar with his New Imperium and his Gallic War). The trouble is this: Caesar, after all, stands for progress and it's hard to dramatise the inverted commas around 'progress'. It's hard to make it clear that this progress has nothing to do with the new dictators. Of course it's supposed to be a kind of threepenny history. Do you know of any literature? I have Plutarch, Dio, Suetonius, Sallust, Mommsen, Max Weber, and Fowler (a professor at Oxford, very weak). I should have something about class struggle and the economy.

What has become of your Marx book???? I'd be so glad to have it. I met Partos in Paris, he'd just come from Spain and was going back there, he was in a great hurry. The manuscript must be somewhere. Levi doesn't have (or know) anything either. You've been neglecting us horribly.

Have you published anything over there?

Have you been able to make contact with anyone?

Since Tretiakoff was arrested (as a Japanese spy, I believe), my literary connections with the Soviet Union have been very meagre. In the house here, under the thatched roof, you've joined our penates. You have been hung in Steff's room along with Engels and some Red Indians.

>   Cordially as ever
>   brecht

We have heard that people who had been moved from prison to a concentration camp were released if they could prove they had jobs in a country not bordering on Germany (especially America). I'm thinking of Kurt Jacob.

>   [Skovsbostrand, November 1937]

*I'm enclosing these. Please excuse the faint print. This is my next to last copy. (I give them all away for readings). [Brecht's note.]

348 To Per Knutzon

Mr Per Knutzon, Teatret Riddersalen, Copenhagen

As you know from the newspapers (and as I repeatedly informed you quite some time ago), the foreign royalties of German refugee authors are not forwarded to them. The German publishers or agencies hide behind currency control and other pretexts (confiscation of expatriate property, or some sort of fictions about the authors' alleged indebtedness, etc.).

You nevertheless made an agreement for the production of my *Threepenny Opera* with the Berlin agency Bloch Erben (through their representative in Copenhagen). You had promised to make an agreement with me, the author. Evidently someone told you that in that case you could expect the Berlin agency to sue, so you broke your promise and without informing me contracted for the work with the said agency. What you should have done is this: If you were afraid the German agency would sue, you should not, in the knowledge that a contract with the Berlin agency would deprive the author of the fruits of his labour, have contracted at all for this work.

Aware of your irregular position, you neglected until a few days before the opening, when rehearsals were already in full swing, to inform me of your intention to produce the play. You invited me neither to rehearsals, though I was in Copenhagen, nor to the opening night.

When taken to task, you admitted in the presence of witnesses that you ought never to have contracted with the German agency, and gave me your promise that you would never *under any circumstances* pay my royalties to the Copenhagen representative of the Berlin agency. Anticipating a complaint from the Berlin agency, I offered to back up with proof a statement from you that my royalties were being withheld in Berlin under futile pretexts. You said your attitude would be that you could not be expected to be party to an arrangement that would gravely injure an author who is close to you politically; that you had signed the contract because you had been led to believe quite mistakenly that the agency met its obligations just as it had done at the time when the contract between it and the author was signed, and that the author might well hold you responsible for his loss. I myself told you that of course I held no document on the strength of which I could obtain an order to pay; that a lawsuit would be my only way of definitely establishing my rights; but that since according to the terms of the contract suit could be brought only in Berlin, I could not, for reasons known to you, bring suit, that I might not be able to initiate proceedings in Copenhagen, because the court might declare itself incompetent, but that I might be able to fight the case if the proceedings were initiated by the opposing party. Since this meant a risk for you, I myself, unbidden, suggested that you should merely hand my money over to a trustee until it was made clear that you would incur no loss.

At that point I had for professional reasons to go to Paris. Taking advantage of my absence, you broke your second promise and sent the money to the Berlin agency after all. You justified yourself by saying that my lawyer had admitted to you that the papers in his possession were not sufficient ground for the Danish authorities to attach your funds. Obviously I'd have needed no promise from you if I had intended any such thing or thought it possible. If only because of the expense involved, I could not sue. What I wanted was for the opposing party to sue, for then the methods of the Third Reich would be aired in other countries. The case would never have come to trial. If it had, you might have lost it juridically, but won it morally. (The royalties would again have been yours to dispose of.)

I realise that I haven't much of a legal case against you, quite apart from the fact that I would never gratify the press with the sensation such a lawsuit would create. If it's enough for you to be technically 'in the right', there's nothing more I can say to you.

You are morally responsible for creating a precedent, on the basis of which several Scandinavian theatres are already sending my royalties off to Hitler Germany. They cite the example set by you as 'my friend'. These royalties are the only source of income I thought I could count on in exile.

[Skovsbostrand, probably end of 1937]

349 To the cast of the 1938 production of *Carrar* in Copenhagen

Dear Comrades,

I promised that after discussing the positive points in the production (your natural acting, the absence of histrionics, the great seriousness but also the humour you show and above all the dignity with which you handle the political aspect of your task) that I would say something about the negative points as well (with a view to improvement).

The most important weakness is the gaps between speeches. That is easily remedied. You need three or four runs-through (like the one before the dress rehearsal on Monday) during which we shall watch out for gaps and the prompter won't have to open his mouth.

Before the next performance you must also test to make sure you hear the prompter. At present you don't always hear him.

Before the performance you must also make sure the net doesn't hang too low in places.

The gunfire is 'unnatural'. It must be (that is, it must sound) further away, it should roll like thunder, not crackle like rifle shots.

Now to particulars:

Mrs Carrar: speaks too softly in the quiet parts, she's inaudible at the back of the house, sometimes hard to understand even in the fourth row. In two places she deviates from the tone we established ('Then you'll have to kill me' and 'I don't know what the people are saying.') The sentence 'We have to live' is lost because of her coming and going.

The worker: His tone, though only in the scene with the priest and perhaps only to counterbalance the priest's uncertainty, is too dramatic. In the dialogue with Carrar (while helping to mend the net) not quite loud enough. In rehearsal the dialogue over the card game was more humorous; the worker made it plain that the boy amused him. Takes too long to put on his knapsack at the end. Different solution needed.

Carrar is too uncertain (when the dead man is brought in).

The boy: At the beginning, when talking about Mrs Perez, he should be even more aggressive, louder. At the end, before he says: 'What, are you coming too?' he should give the workers a quick look to show that he is surprised.

The priest: Entrance should be firmer, he should speak more loudly. Let him go on buttoning the top of his cassock up wrong. (Nexö thought it was intentional and good. He said 'Of course, the man is a bachelor.') End, i.e. his exit, should be more confused.

Manuela: Even harder, less plaintive. Should talk a little faster.

Mrs Perez: Should say 'but how?' more aggressively and after a short pause during which she looks at Carrar.

The general: The second time he starts speaking the muttering should be softer; it sounds somewhat unnaturally lame.

The wounded man: Tone a little too hesitant. Could be firmer.

The mourning women: Having them start talking outside is not convincing. All must pray at once, but one more audibly than the rest. The heavy tread of the men carrying the corpse should be heard.

That's about all. Tak for gedulden.[1]

And now a question. I'd like you to talk it over at the Refugee Home (very tactfully of course) and decide whether you want to use the second performance for the Home, that is, for Refugees. It's a good thing after all that in this foreign country refugees should speak not only for

---

[1] Danish: 'Thanks for your patience.'

themselves, but for all those who are threatened by fascism. And there would be no harm in people finding out that you mean to keep doing cultural work in exile. But that's a political question, you'll have to talk it over. My opinion in any case is that your production of *Rifles* is a fine achievement by the Copenhagen refugees. As the newspapers show, it helps our cause in Denmark.

> Yours with heartfelt gratitude
> brecht

> Svendborg, February 1938

350 To the cast of the 1938 production of *Carrar* in Copenhagen

Dear Comrades,

I agree with your self-criticism. It's true, I believe, that in some spots (in his very long part) something mildly intellectualistic creeps into Kurt's diction. The more natural he is the more soldierly he will seem. The main thing is that he should be seen to observe the situation, to be surprised in the right places, etc. At the end of the play, the two men should take a little longer getting ready to leave, and Mrs Carrar should pack a little more quickly (perhaps with a somewhat changed expression). I say 'somewhat' because waiting for the bread is a realistic detail that must be fully preserved. Haste to get to the front and waiting for the bread must be balanced very sensitively.

> And now good luck
> Yours,
> Brecht

> [Skovsbostrand, February 1938]

351 To Jonny G. Rieger

> Skovsbostrand per Svendborg
> 17 February 1938

Dear Comrade R.

I believe that the editors of *Das Wort*, instead of returning a contribution because of a few objections, should suggest changes to the author if the contribution is otherwise desirable. I myself have occasionally received suggestions of this kind and taken them into consideration if they seemed reasonable. The only explanation I can think of for their changing your reminiscences of Shanghai without your consent is that the piece had already been set in type and some muddle made it impossible to use it in the number for which it was intended. Of course it's deplorable and I hope it won't happen again. I can imagine how upsetting it must be for you. I've written to the editors about this and I'm sure they will write to you.

I'm enclosing a copy of the Röhm ballad.

> With comradely greetings,
> Yours

352 To Aksel Larsen

Dear Comrade Larsen,

I regret to say that I have had no answer to my report on the astonishing behaviour in the matter of my *Threepenny Opera* of Per Knutzon and Lulu Ziegler, both of whom claim to be members of the Danish Communist Party. This has made it impossible for me to take the action it would be my right and duty to take against these people, who have done me serious harm and whose behaviour is a disgrace to the anti-fascist movement. Now the *Arbejderbladet* of 25 March announces a programme including *Señora Carrar's Rifles*, played by Mrs Lulu Ziegler. This is going too far. It pleases me not at all to have my name mentioned in the same breath as Mrs Lulu Ziegler. Far be it from me to tell you how to deal with Party members whose conduct in my opinion is politically outrageous; but you have no right to help weaken my own position vis-à-vis such people. I must ask you not to do so again under any circumstances.

> With comradely greetings

> Skovsbostrand per Svendborg
> 25 March 1938

353 To Ernestine Evans

Dear Mrs Evans,

I'd be very grateful if you could do something for *Señora Carrar's Rifles* in America. Feeling sure that you will obtain the best possible conditions, I authorise you to make contracts for the publication and production of the play.

The main point for a successful production is that Mrs Carrar be played by an outstanding actress. The part is rewarding but also difficult. In Scandinavia productions by non-professional troupes without a prominent actress in the title role have not had the minimum of success which is essential for plays on this subject. But a combination of a non-professional cast with a qualified actress is a possibility.

On Hanns Eisler's advice we are sending you two other plays, *Saint Joan of the Stockyards* and *The Round Heads and the Pointed Heads*. It would interest me very much to hear your opinion of them. True, it will undoubtedly be harder to get good translations of these plays than of *Señora Carrar's Rifles*.

May I ask you to give Jerome my best regards?

With comradely greetings

Skovsbostrand per Svendborg
(Danmark)
26 March 1938

354 To Martin Andersen-Nexö

Dear Martin Andersen-Nexö,

I'm sorry to say that a quick reading of the first two volumes has convinced me that the translation is not very good. One can't possibly fix it with a blue pencil while lying on the sofa. Many sentences are rotten to the core. Consequently we've written to the publisher that the 75 Swiss francs he offered are not enough for such a big job. Today we received a rather cool answer to the effect that the quality of the translation was your responsibility. This is most disagreeable because you have already paid for the translation in full. We've been wondering how we could help you, and if it were not that the job would undoubtedly take weeks and weeks, we would have set to work and the fee be damned. But in our position this is something we simply can't afford. (I myself am busy with a satirical novel about Julius Caesar, the prototype of all dictators. It requires a great deal of research and I have to finish it as soon as possible to get an advance.) On the other hand, you certainly can't let the books be published as they are. What's to be done? Grete says if she's given enough time she can at least eliminate the worst howlers. But that won't go very quickly, and we wonder if it might not be better for us to concentrate on the third volume. The moment a chapter is finished we'd send it to *Das Wort*. That would give *Das Wort* some backbone for at least six months.

We have already sent the first version of your fine article about *Señora Carrar's Rifles* to *Das Wort*. Yesterday we sent your revision by air mail. I like it very much.

We're enjoying the beautiful spring weather with moderation. In the garden we hear the chirping of the crickets (are they really crickets?) and the big guns of the German fleet on manoeuvres (they really are big guns). My publisher Herzfelde is in Czechoslovakia, which England doesn't want to defend, even though he is bringing out an edition of my collected plays. God is punishing him.[1]

> Cordially yours
> Bertolt Brecht

> Skovsbostrand, 25 March 1938

355 To Martin Andersen-Nexö

Many thanks for your letter. As I've told you from the start, I'd like to do all I can to help you with the translation. And I have no objection to putting my name to it, only then it would have to be: Margarete Steffin and Bertolt Brecht, because everyone knows I don't know Danish and *I* know that most of the work will actually be done by Grete.

Unfortunately there's the following to be considered: that I'm deep in a big job (I hope you don't think I'm trying to sound important); that I'm very much afraid you'll be in a great hurry after waiting so long for the first two volumes; that we'd have to give priority to the third volume which we want to publish in *Das Wort*, because no one can know how long a magazine of that sort can continue to appear in the present state of the world.

Furthermore, I shouldn't like this to cause you financial loss, in other words, I think you should first make a serious attempt to get the publisher to cover you. I'm sure you realise that I'd rather be paid by a publisher than by you.

And then, unfortunately, there's still another point. As long as our

[1] A play on the German First World War slogan: 'Gott strafe England' – May God punish England.

names were not to appear in the first two volumes, we had no reason to fear that the original translators would be especially resentful. But as things stand, we ought to come to some sort of more or less friendly understanding with them. You should let us correspond at least with Ostermoor, whom we know and who is a decent fellow. (We don't know the other translator, perhaps you could mollify him.)

You see, there's a whole mound of difficulties. A suggestion: we work on the third volume, and you try (unless the mound of difficulties strikes you as too high) to attack the above-mentioned problems connected with the first volumes.

>   With comradely regards,
>   Yours

>   Skovsbostrand per Svendborg
>   3 April 1938

356 To Erwin Piscator

Dear Pis,

In the next few days I'll be sending you several short and very short plays that I've grouped together under the title *Fear and Misery of the Third Reich*. But for a production of course we could choose a different title, such as *Deutsche Heerschau* (The German Troops March Past). This would be just the thing for America I think. Everybody is wondering how long a war Hitler could fight. And the so-called democracies are very much interested in knowing how the Nazi dictatorship affects the various social groupings. The play gives a cross section of all German society in nineteen scenes (a few more could be added). Terror and resistance everywhere. You could project some documentary material in between. The style, as I see it, should be like Goya's Civil War aquatints. I wish you would write to me about it straight away. I've been thinking a good deal about New York, I'm going to do all I can to swing a production there. Dudow wants to do a few scenes in Paris, but he hasn't got many actors at his disposal. The Zurich people, along with Weigel, could do the plays brilliantly in America.

>   Cordially as ever

Helli is very much interested in an American guest performance.

>   [Skovsbostrand, March–April 1938]

357 To Karl Korsch

Dear Korsch,

Many thanks for sending the magazine. But I'm waiting with real impatience for the *book* (in English and German). I need it.

Under the title *Fear and Misery of the Third Reich* I've written a series of (horror) scenes that we may be able to produce in Paris. Otherwise America would be the only possibility, because the fear has now gripped Europe. *Die Geschäfte des Herrn Julius Caesar* is growing slowly, much more slowly than Hitler's rearmament. After protracted research Caesar's supposedly 'positive' side, which I at first simply wanted to ignore as a prejudice, has gone up in smoke. The question 'positive for whom?' clinches it. His supposedly eternal creation lasted only a few days longer than he himself, and what Caesarism survived was what the slave economy permitted.

The shortage of proletarians in exile is becoming more acute, and the Tuis are fighting more and more bitterly for the few available specimens.

It would give me great pleasure to know what you are doing. Will the *Marx* be followed by a *Lenin*?

Helli is acting now and then in Copenhagen. The work agrees with her, she has put on at least ten pounds. Steff is making an orthodox atheist of Barbara, and the Ford is demonstrating its unswerving determination to survive us all.

In the hope that your letter will soon be followed by another.

As ever,
brecht

Skovsbostrand, April 1938

358 To Slatan Dudow

Dear Dudow,

I understand your fear that the play may be too depressing. It certainly won't cheer people up. Still, I think it shows how fragile the Third Reich is in all its parts and aspects, that it is held together by violence alone. It shows the people whom this regime wants to drive into one of the biggest and hardest wars of all time. Their resistance, yes, the increasing resistance of every section of the population is shown clearly. The farmer *feeds* his sow (while looking fearfully over his shoulder); the physicist *uses* Einstein (while loudly reviling Jewish physics); the worker throws his gas mask into the corner; the soldiers give the boy who does *not* say Heil Hitler two helpings of food; the patient (in *Occupational Disease*) reminds the surgeon of the requirements of science; the man who has been beaten sings *The International*; the judge can*not* arrive at a verdict; the woman who has received a Winter Aid package vomits up the apple; the old soldier *hangs* himself; the baker for once does *not* adulterate his bread; the sister of the man who has been killed in Spain does *not* let herself be silenced; and the Party (at the end) does *not give up the fight*. Not only do the Nazis resort to violence, they *must* resort to violence.

Actually I have only shown the points of resistance and spared the audience the infinitely depressing spectacle of the many who are still enthusiastic and the still greater number who have been neutralised.

I must confess that the argument (in connection with *Der Fehlende Mann* (*The Missing Man*)) that by his conquest of Austria Hitler increased the number of his enemies, does not sound entirely convincing to me. It should follow that if he conquered the whole world he'd have to hang himself. We don't have to call for struggle, we show the struggle. The *no* at the end does not strike me as too little.

I'll try all the same to write a positive epilogue. In the different scenes, however, one shouldn't try to do more than can be done by direction. You can't possibly put on the whole thing. The sooner you can send me your selection, the better able I'll be to help you with the transitions and write the epilogue.

I've written two scenes about the war: *Arbeitsbeschaffung* (*Job Creation*) and *In den Kasernen wird die Beschiessung von Almeria bekannt* (*The Barracks learn that Almeria has been bombarded*), which you've probably received in the meantime.

On the whole I don't think the production will depress people. No more, actually less, than a Brueghel painting or a set of Daumier drawings. Because it shows too clearly what a fragile foundation fear and misery are for a Reich, how few supporters the Nazis can really count on, how ineffectual terror is bound to be, in fact, how inevitably it must create resistance, even in sections of the population that originally welcomed it with cheers. It's generally known that even the *Brown Book* was rather more than depressing.

---

[1]Later renamed *Volksbefragung* (*Consulting the people*).

Please let me know how you feel about all this.

> Yours cordially

Don't get me wrong: I'm not trying to wish objections away. As usual, I'll do what I can if my arguments don't convince you. It goes without saying that between you and me there can be no question of resenting criticism. – What's Bressart doing? (A vital question.)

> (Skovsbostrand, April 1938)

359 To Slatan Dudow

Dear Dudow,

Your early opening date really terrifies me. Quite apart from the structure of the play, its ending and title, you don't seem to have any cast at all. Think how important and ambitious it sounds to be doing eight to ten one-acters by me. That's a big thing. In *Señora Carrar* we agreed that the play would work with Weigel for whom it was written, and written in such a way that it would only work with her. Without Weigel half the one-acters you're planning have no actor capable of sustaining them, unless Bressart and a man of Busch's quality are available. Unless each of the little plays is a gem, which is only possible with adequate actors (and plenty of time to work with them), then we are undoubtedly headed for a fiasco that will lose us all the credit we acquired with *Señora Carrar*. If you can't get the actors who are absolutely indispensable right away, I'd prefer, regardless of the disadvantages of a postponement, to wait until the autumn when, to the best of my knowledge, the German actors in Zurich will be unemployed. There you have a group of highly qualified character actors, with whom we can put on a sensational performance that will be heard about all the way to America. It's only by concentrating all our energies that we refugees can get anywhere. With your outstanding work on *Carrar*, you, Weigel and I have established a standard. After that we mustn't descend to the level of the Laterne.

If you can get the necessary actors together, I'd suggest the following order:

The Chalk Cross: (Bressart: the Brother; Busch: the SA-Man)
Charity begins at home: (Weigel: the Old Woman)
The Spy: (Bressart: the Husband)
Job Creation: (Weigel: the Woman; Busch: the Worker)

Interval

The Jewish Wife (Weigel)
Any good against Gas? (Busch)
The Missing Man (Weigel: the Woman; Busch: first Worker)
Also Busch: the Ballad.

Here I've taken the distribution of weight into account as well as such things as how long it will take Weigel and the other main actors to make up. Where *Jurisprudence* (Bressart: the Judge and possibly Weigel: the Maid) should go I haven't made up my mind. – Fürst is excellent in his line, but he can only play grotesque parts and could never do a quiet worker. I know him well. I think the date is definitely premature. Really it makes no difference whether we open at the beginning or the end of May. I'm afraid that opening too soon will create difficulties, and we both have too much at stake. You must understand how I feel. For the present, as far as I can see, you have only amateurs to work with and only three weeks in which to rehearse. In addition to the usual drawbacks of working in a foreign country. This amount of time and these actors will do for *The Jewish Wife* and possibly for *The Informer*. But now that you are no longer planning to select two to four playlets out of the whole cycle, to wit, those you are more or less able to cast and to produce in an undemanding sort of way, the whole picture changes, because a full-length play of the utmost timeliness calls for very different actors and resources. Of course it would be easier to produce three of the nineteen plays than nine. But to put it bluntly, it's all a question of casting and rehearsals.

I realise that you, involved as you are in the preliminary work, have concentrated in your letters on the urgent question of selecting plays, but you in turn must understand that once you've set so imminent a date, I'm horrified to see you without an adequate cast. And with a project that has now taken on enormous dimensions.

You mustn't suppose that I see nothing but your difficulties. To get as far as you have, you must have worked like a slave, but our interests in this matter coincide. Write to me as quickly as possible and as explicitly as possible about all these points. I'm really upset. We'll be in for a bad political lambasting and rightly so if, regardless of the difficulties we may have had to contend with, we put on something more or less embarrassing. After all, we're not showing the working-class movement and its resistance, we're criticising the Nazi system, and everything depends on the incisiveness of our criticism. This in turn depends on the incisiveness of our production, that is, the quality of the actors. Mediocre actors never communicate horror, only innocuousness. In this case feebleness resulting from insufficient artistic talent will have the effect of political feebleness. What authority can we have in exile other than that conferred by quality? We stand up and criticise the Third Reich. But nobody knows who we are, whereas the Third Reich has ten million soldiers. So the criticism has to speak for itself. We doubt the durability of the Third Reich. Then our work must show the hallmark of durability.

I see that I'm sounding rather emotional. That's because I'm upset.

Cordially yours

[Skovsbostrand] 19 April 1938

360 To Slatan Dudow

Dear Dudow,

Why do you write so vehemently? Almost like a theatre director to an author who insists on having Chaplin, Mae West, Laughton and Shirley Temple in his play? All I said in my letter was that with your casting problems still unsolved your early opening date frightened me. Take a look at my letters and I'm sure you'll see that I asked you weeks ago whether Bressart would be playing or who else. At first the choice of plays seemed the most urgent question; but really and truly, between brothers, do you think that question has been fully solved? I regret to say that even in your last letter you say nothing about my counter-proposal with regard to the choice of plays, to end with *The Missing Man* (which come to think of it might better be titled *Plebiscite*) – that, I thought, would give us our *No* at the end. And what about the title *The German March-Past*? You wrote only that I should send you an ending and title. *99%* (Important objection: it won't fit into the metre of the ballad) strikes me as a little too clever, but it's all right with me if our friends want it. Only it's rather weak and actually suggests a different sort of play. As to *Jurisprudence*, as I've said before, you shouldn't do it unless you have a real comedian. Nearly all the other plays would work without a comedian. So tell me: which plays have you chosen? And couldn't you tell me who's going to be in them? Whom have you approached? Whom are you considering if they turn you down? Is Busch for instance in Paris? Don't under any circumstances send for Weigel until you've cast the plays she won't be in. In half the plays she does not appear; so those can be rehearsed and ready to go on by the time she gets there. This is not because her time is so precious, she'd be delighted to be there from the start, but because her stay in Paris will cost money (not only what she'll need there but the extra money we shall need here if she stays away for too long).

Actually it's all very simple despite all the difficulties, which I by no means underestimate: you need only write to me as follows: I mean to put on such and such plays, I have engaged such and such actors. The rest we can decide together. If you tell me the actors' names, I may yet be able to give you suggestions as to what, given these actors, can be done with the plays.

I enclose a list of actors in connection with my suggestion (the one I made in my last letter).

Weigel says that with this order or one like it she can manage the changes of makeup and costume. (That's why I've put the interval between two plays she can appear in. It's before The Jewish Wife that she'll need the most time.

If you reread your last few letters you'll agree with me that they don't contain enough concrete answers to my questions and proposals to give me an idea of your intentions. You say I can see your ideas about the casting of the plays clearly from your letters. But how am I to see anything of the kind? You once mentioned Fürst and once Schoenlank, and that's all. Fürst is unavailable, Schoenlank (who, by the way, could not by himself sustain the plays in which Weigel is not to appear) has, as you write, 'agreed only in principle and can give you no date'. And besides, there's this to consider: Even if I, who after all can have the plays published, might be satisfied with any cast, the same cannot be said of Weigel. I can't just ship her to Paris. You must answer her last letter.

Most of all, we mustn't get caught up in an acrimonious correspondence. Why should we? After all, all these are practical questions.

In the meantime I've written six more short plays. I've stopped at twenty-five. Don't be alarmed, I'm sending them only to give you a general idea. The radio scene, to be sure, might tempt you. It would be easy to produce.

Now that the whole thing is finished, it's really representative of refugee literature. Technically interesting as well.

Yours cordially

[Skovsbostrand], 24 April 1938

361 To Martin Domke

Dear Dr Domke,

Many thanks for clearing up the *Threepenny* business in Paris. I never expected it to turn out so well. In a fortnight I hope to be able to send you the two first chapters of my short novel about Caesar. Your Carcopino has been a big help. It would be fine if you could come here for a while, in the summer let's say. Benjamin is planning to come too. We could have a pleasant time, don't you think? In the summer, believe me, it's as nice here as anywhere. There's water, woods, garden and radio. And not many people.

Once again many thanks and comradely greetings.

Svendborg, April 1938

362 To Aksel Larsen

Dear Comrade Aksel Larsen,

I take note that you've censured your member Per Knutzon for his conduct in the matter of the *Threepenny Opera* production. Since he's still a party member, I won't take legal proceedings against him. However, I do not agree with you that my accusations against him rest on rather 'flimsy' foundations. Accordingly, I can't possibly resume close personal relations with him, that is, work with him or appear in public with him, etc. By needlessly contracting with Strakosch behind my back for *The Threepenny Opera*, he enabled the fascist state to *punish* me for my antifascist opinions. *He deprived me of any possibility of using it as a basis for political action against fascism.* This, I believe, is a serious consideration. I must therefore ask you, in case you use any work of mine, not to draw him into it, because I will not have my name publicly associated with his. You can easily comply with the request and I don't think it's too much to ask. The part of your letter in which you conjecture that I might have been prejudiced against Knutzon by people I associate with would better have been left unwritten. No one has influenced me against Knutzon; after the way he has behaved there was no need to. On the contrary, members of the Danish Party (Comrade Berlau, for instance) have told me that Knutzon was useful to the party.

With Communist greetings

Svendborg
13 May 1938

364 To Ernestine Evans

Dear Comrade Evans,

Many thanks for sending me the translation of *Die Gewehre der Frau Carrar* as published in *Theater Workshop*. With a view to possible productions I have some objections to the translation. 'Rifles' sounds too old-fashioned and 'Señora' too exotic. Why not 'guns' (as the *Gewehre* [rifles] are called in the text) and 'Mrs Carrar'. 'Frau Carrar' in German has a homely character that I wouldn't like to lose. Now to details: Page 34, line 10 from the top. When José tells how his father was brought in, it says in German 'They carried him in on a *Plache*. (A *Plache* is a piece of sailcloth) and put him down on the floor'. There the actor can point to the place where his father was put down, which is important because his brother is later put down in the same place. The piece of sailcloth is graphic too, and is recognised when they bring Juan in. – When (page 40) Theresa brings in Juan's cap, she says: 'This is why they shot him.' The German says: 'Schuld war die Mütze' [The cap was to blame]. And when asked: 'How do you mean?' she answers: 'Ragged, worn-out.' In German it's a clear, short sentence: 'Sie ist schäbig' [It's shabby]. In this place such sloppy, naturalistic speech is absolutely hideous. Altogether the translation is full of such sloppiness, the kind of loose naturalism that I can't bear. But this last one must absolutely be eliminated. The same goes for the sentences with which Theresa indicates her change of heart (page 50, line 7 from top): 'The bread is ready. Ready to go, José? Take the guns!' is sloppy. The question in 'Ready to go, José?' can ruin the whole effect. Both the order of the sentences and their form must be kept in the translation. ('Take the guns. Get ready, José. The bread is ready too.') You see, I'm bringing up only the most important passages. Please have these corrected before the translation is used in a production. *In its present form, at any rate, I can authorise it neither for the stage nor for publication.*

Please don't let my criticism distress you. I'm very grateful to you for getting the little play published.

I'm sending you a sequence of twenty-seven scenes from Hitler

Germany, eight of which were performed a fortnight ago in Paris by a German company with great success. Do you think you can do anything with them? *Die Rundköpfe und die Spitzköpfe* is included in the *Collected Works*, which you have received.

Please give your husband my regards,

Yours cordially

[Skovsbostrand], 17 June 1938

P.S. Please send the fee from *Theater Workshop* to Lou Eisler.

365 To Alfred Kurella

Dear Kurella,

Many thanks for your recent letters. I'm enclosing a few lines for the 'Comment' section. We definitely owe Eisler an apology for the tone in which Lukács speaks of him in *Das Wort*.

This little incident has revived an old plan in my mind. German refugees are right in saying that fascism has driven the majority of the German 'cultural figureheads' out of the country. But they seldom give particulars. So my idea is that *Das Wort* should publish a series of well-documented monographs on significant German refugees. A series of this kind would provide a good basis for discussion and a positive, concrete indication of a certain solidarity (vis-à-vis fascism, in the cultural field). A few names: Einstein, Reinhardt, Hindemith, Eisler, Freud, Piscator, Grosz, Heartfield, Gropius, Schrödinger, Duncker, Jessner, Kortner, Bassermann, Kokoschka, Wolfgang Köhler, Fritz Lang, Klemperer. The list could be extended of course. I myself could arrange for some of the monographs.

I'll be sending my article *Volkstümlichkeit und Realismus* [The Popular and the Realistic] in the next few days.

Along with it I shall send a poem, *Der Rattenfänger* [The Pied Piper] that has been sent me from Germany.

With best regards (also to Erpenbeck)

Yours

[Skovsbostrand], 17 June 1938

366 To Willi Bredel

Dear Bredel,

Many thanks for your letter. I'm glad you're back within reach.

Unfortunately, my collaboration on *Das Wort* is becoming increasingly problematic. More and more it seems to be taking a peculiar line, turning into the organ of a strange alliance dominated by a small clique, apparently led by Lukács and Hay and committed to a very definite ideal of literary form, which leads them to combat everything that doesn't fit in with this formal ideal derived from the bourgeois novelists of the past century. As a result, the indispensable fight against formalism is itself turning into a formalism; that is, everything is judged on the basis of form (in this case an old-fashioned form). In *Internationale Literatur*, No. 7. Lukács actually strikes out at me, lumping me together with bourgeois decadence, and this at a time when God knows that questions of form should be the least of our worries. Now and again Erpenbeck asks me to take part in the debate, but it goes without saying that I have no desire to, because I regard such debates as extremely harmful and confusing at the present time, especially since they always end with good old Lukács's opinion being vaunted (at least by Lukács himself) as the one and only Marxist view. What good can come of proclaiming to the world that my picture of the Third Reich is not true to reality (for what else can it mean to say it is not realistic?) and that my convictions are not socialist? I don't know if these people are expressing the opinions and feelings of refugees in general; if not, you and the Paris comrades ought to tell the *I.L.* people so when you get a chance. *Das Wort* only sends me contributions that have already been accepted, and my objections are hardly ever taken into account. I assure you that this can't go on much longer. Yet it's really important that we should have this magazine, and it would really be a big thing if we could improve it. But how can we? I'd be grateful if you'd write to me about it.

Give Maria my regards.

Yours cordially
brecht

I'm enclosing my last letter to Erpenbeck.

[Skovsbostrand, probably July–August 1938]

367 To Alfred Döblin

Dear Döblin,

Since it makes no real difference on what day one gives thanks for gifts, it may just as well be on your birthday, one of your birthdays. Allow me, on this your birthday, to remain true to my habits and talk about myself.

I would like then to call the attention of as many persons as possible to the extraordinary zeal with which I have studied your literary works and appropriated the numerous innovations you have made in our way of seeing and depicting our environment and social life. I find it hard to see how anyone setting out to describe the movements of large bodies of people could dispense with studying your pioneering descriptive technique. You have also provided epic literature with totally novel ways of depicting the development of the individual and his position in mass processes. Your theory of the autonomy of the parts and your attitude towards the phenomenon of empathy are also, it seems to me, of great importance to epic literature. I am aware, of course, that with technical observations of this kind I am putting myself in opposition to the advocates of conventional aesthetics, but this is necessary in the interests of a literary production which aspires to achieve socially penetrating accounts of human collectivities in the present epoch. I regard your works as a treasury of enjoyment and instruction, and hope that my own work embodies some treasures of this kind. I believe I can take no worthier attitude towards you than that of an exploiter.

With warmest greetings in these most dismal of times.

Your devoted
brecht

[Skovsbostrand, August 1938]

368 To President Edvard Beneš

Fight and those who are vacillating will close ranks with you.
bertolt brecht
20 September 1938

369 To the American Guild for German Cultural Freedom

Gentlemen,

I wish to thank you once again for extending my grant. In compliance with your request that I tell you something about my work:

This summer I was engaged in completing my *Fear and Misery of the Third Reich* cycle, an attempt in twenty-seven scenes to show the reaction of almost every section of the German people to the National

Socialist dictatorship. I tried to bring out two points which I thought it vital to make known abroad: first, the enslavement, disfranchisement, paralysis of *all* sections of the population under the National Socialist dictatorship (people living in the democracies have far too little concrete knowledge of this); second, the state of mind prevailing in the army of the totalitarian state, which is a cross section of the population as a whole (to give people outside Germany an idea of the fragility of this war machine). The book will have roughly 120 printed pages and is now being published by Malik Verlag.

I have also prepared a volume of new poems under the title *Svendborg Poems*, likewise to be published by Malik Verlag. It will be a good-sized book of roughly 140 printed pages and will include the 'German Satires' that I wrote for the German Freedom Radio. At the same time, I am editing for Malik Volume IV of my *Collected Works*, which is to include my 'Collected Poems', a very time-consuming job.

At the same time, I have written a few theoretical articles, among them two, which I regard as highly important, on theatre: 'The Street Scene', a basic model for the epic theatre and 'The Theory of the Alienation Effect', in which I set forth the nature of acting in the epic theatre.

My main work at present consists in the satirical novel *Die Geschäfte des Herrn Julius Caesar*, which calls for a great deal of historical research. It deals with the founding of an imperium and the establishment of a dictatorship – on a strictly historical basis, I might add. It is not a disguised biography of Hitler or Mussolini. It will provide the modern reader, I hope, not only with valuable information about wars, democracy, etc., but also with a picture of how the persistence of slavery leads to general enslavement, i.e. of all classes of society. The book begins with the defeat of the Catilinian conspiracy and ends (after an account of the Gallic War) with the march on Rome, i.e. the crossing of the Rubicon.

Your grant has been a great help to me in doing this work, as I derive next to no income from my writings. To give you an example: Eight scenes from *Fear and Misery of the Third Reich* were played by a refugee group in Paris under the title *99%*, but they were not able to pay me any royalty. Nor have I received any fee for the first volumes of the *Collected Works*, as the publishing house is working under great difficulties. The present worsening of the political situation makes it very doubtful whether the new volumes, in which a great deal of work has been invested, will ever appear.

I am truly grateful to the American Guild for its help in furthering my work.

> Yours faithfully,
> bertolt brecht

> Skovsbostrand per Svendborg
> September 1938

370 To the American Guild for German Cultural Freedom

Gentlemen,

I am taking the liberty of entering my novel *Die Geschäfte des Herrn Julius Caesar* in your contest. Unfortunately it is not quite finished, and I am obliged to tax your patience by sending only three chapters out of six. I am, however, enclosing a synopsis of the missing chapters and hope this will enable you to form an idea of the whole.

> With best regards,
> bertolt brecht

> [Skovsbostrand], 30 September 1938

372 To Wieland Herzfelde

Dear Wieland,

Many thanks for your letter and for the cheque; the latter represents a gesture of historical magnitude, which I appreciate. It was really kind of you to think of it when you are having such a hard time.

The *Galileo* manuscript will go off to you on Monday. Of course I'll wait for you as long as I possibly can. We must stick together. Before printing the other things, do bear in mind that the Prague printer has not acknowledged receipt of the corrected proofs; in other words, the things that have already been set in type have not yet been fully corrected. Incidentally, the special edition of the poems (*Svendborg Poems*) does not strike me as all that urgent.

Please keep me informed. You can imagine how much it means to me to hear the fate of my most recent work.

I hope you're feeling better.

> Yours cordially,
> b

> [Skovsbostrand, November–December 1938]

373 To Ferdinand Reyher

Dear Reyher,

Many thanks for the books, which are indeed very interesting and for your letters. It was really refreshing to see you again.

My *Galileo* plan has worked out strangely. On my return to Svendborg I started right in and finished the play in three weeks. So instead of a film treatment I'm sending you a play. It contains a gigantic role, and if we approached a big influential actor with it, perhaps he would help bring about a production. But perhaps in America productions don't depend on actors as much as they do in Europe. I hardly dare to bother you with this, but if with no trouble to yourself you could tell me how to push the play, I'd be enormously grateful to you. True, it hasn't even been translated yet. (To tell the truth, I believe my name is known only to the Theatre Guild.)

I don't know if you can get some idea of the play's film possibilities. If you think there's a chance, I'll be glad to do a treatment. One good thing is that Galileo's main discoveries can be filmed very effectively (the moon with its mountains, the phases of Venus, the orbits of the planet Jupiter's four moons). The problem of treating the Church in a way that won't give offence would not be very hard to solve. Actually Galileo, in his eagerness to inform the world as quickly as possible of the truth he has discovered, transgresses the express prohibition of the Church to which he belongs, which would not have rejected his theory had it been represented as a mere hypothesis for scientists. The Pope can be portrayed as a tired man, too tired to oppose the belief held by all the academic scientists and theologians of his day. This interpretation would not impair the film's ethical effect.

I'm glad you have read the *Threepenny Novel* with some pleasure. My agent, who sold the book in London, is James B. Pinker & Son, Talbot House, Arundel Street, London. So far he has not put through an American edition.

You can see from the *Galileo* business what isolation we are living in on this moribund continent. Your comradely interest in Copenhagen was all it took to make me plunge straight into a rather ambitious piece of work.

I'm sorry to say that I haven't been able to find the article in which your friend's film about the test pilot was discussed. Perhaps as a slight compensation you could translate the enclosed *Kinderlied* [Children's Song] for him.

> With warm regards,
> Yours
> bertolt brecht

[Skovsbostrand], 2 December 1938

375 To Maria Osten

Dear Maria,

Your lines about Koltsov have horrified me. I hadn't heard a thing. Now I'm told that rumours have been reported in the Copenhagen papers. Please let me know at once if you hear anything more definite, or anything at all. I simply can't imagine what he may have done. I've always seen him working indefatigably for the Soviet Union. Have you any idea what he's being accused of?

Das Wort has never returned your ballads to me. Now I've complained and pressed Erpenbeck to send them back. And meanwhile the magazine is getting steadily more vapid and formless. It's an outrage what they've done to a good idea.

I've had no news at all of Wieland. What could you publish? The last book of poems? *Fear and Misery of the Third Reich?* The new play, *The Life of Galileo?* Or possibly the two plays together? (They complement each other.)

Write to me.

> Cordially, as ever

[Skovsbostrand, late 1938–early 1939]

378 To Egon Erwin Kisch

Dear Kisch,

I'm aghast at your standing up (or falling down) for that melodious old lecher. If Kerr were different, you say, he simply wouldn't be the leading critic of this bourgeois epoch. Well, mightn't that be all to the good? In our eyes, for instance. It sounds to me as if you were saying: A swinish epoch. If So-and-so were not what he is, he wouldn't have been one of the biggest swine of the epoch. But they've wronged him, you say. How? By for once not (under futile pretexts, it's true) letting him join in. Don't get me wrong, I don't claim that the Kerrs are the main enemy just now. But shouldn't we treat them with a certain reserve? I know you won't take these lines amiss. But I read what you write very carefully and approve most of it.

> Otherwise cordially
> as ever

Svendborg, January 1939

NB: As you have no doubt learnt from Kerr, I'm an assiduous plagiarist. Here's a little plagiarism of him:

> We be merry young refugees, refugees
> young refugees, young refugees
> we kin go, we kin stay, we kin do as we please
> do what we please, hooray.[1]

380 To Karl Korsch

Dear Korsch,

I've now received your Marx, and thank you very much for it. I've been reading it voraciously. It provides the necessary clarification. (And how splendid that it was produced by the most defeated of all proletariats.) It also seems to me that the extra work you put in at Svendborg was very much worthwhile. Up until then, I think, your Marxism was largely a product of the history of ideas. Now it springs from reality. Now you have the whole development *and* the break to which it led. What makes this so important is that there have been so many new eras in which everything went on as before. (Marx as the critic of the liberal era.) As if one were to compensate for the lack of new sausages by cutting the old ones into several parts.

Another good thing is that it has now become the fifth volume of the Sociologists, thus completing the series (unless you go on to write a 'Lenin'). You've left yourself time, and this time works for us.

I'm quite satisfied with your treatment of the dialectic. Alpári has published an 'Introduction to the study of *Das Kapital*' in the Basel *Rundschau*. In it he writes:

---

[1]Brecht's German is in Austrian dialect. Alfred Kerr wrote jingles in Berlin dialect.

'In *The Poverty of Philosophy* Marx cites Hegel's consecrated formula as follows: Affirmation, Negation, Negation of Negation. But stated differently, this means: Position, opposition, composition.'

The Tuis are really inexhaustible. If I could get immigration papers, I'd come to the States myself with Helli. You wouldn't happen to know how I can get an official teaching appointment? (That's the only way of avoiding the quota, which doesn't offer a chance.)

The third volume of the *Collected Works* (containing the Collected Poems and two new plays, *Fear and Misery of the Third Reich* and *The Life of Galileo*) which Wieland in Czechoslovakia had already printed has been pulped.

Thank you for sending your articles in *Living Marxism*. I definitely want everything you publish.

I'll write to you again when I've read through *Marx* again.

Cordially as ever

Svendborg, February 1939

381 To Karl Korsch,

Dear Korsch,

I've read more, so now I'm writing more. I continue to find your self-imposed restraint (in your critique of Marx) very wise. His critique (all of it grounded in the historical period) thus preserves its methodological value. The fact is that if Marx is so little known it's because so much has been written about him. It's enormously important to point up his outstanding qualities as a critic. This of course makes a fourth section necessary (for friends at least). And it would be marvellous if in this fourth section you could maintain your positive position, that is, convert your critical attitude towards the liberalistic epoch of capitalism into a critical attitude towards the present period. Such critique has not become meaningless and methodologically obsolete along with its object. Your treatment of the Soviet Union is of course alarming. But why not treat it from the standpoint of the Marxist formula? The regime, the state apparatus, the Party, its leadership if you will, are developing the country's productive forces. They are also being developed by the national form in which the Soviet Union must enter into the decisive struggle. And there you have the class character of international politics. The world civil war.

[Unfinished]

[Skovsbostrand, probably February–March 1939]

383 To Elisabeth Hauptmann

Dear Bess,

Many thanks for the translations. I'm sure they'll be a big help to the American lady. But when I look at American literature, *I wonder*.[1]

These *Mice and Men* and the novellas by [James M.] Cain, all of them guaranteed real live (hothouse) plants of amazing vitality ('You see my point')[1] – all this 'romantic realism' – is not very good soil, it seems to me. Ghastly muscle flexing.

I've finished a play, *The Life of Galileo*, maybe it could be put on somewhere. The third volume of the *Collected Works*, which Wieland had already put into page proof, seems to have come to nothing. Book-burning No. 2. It contained the 'Collected Poems' and two plays. *Fear and Misery of the Third Reich* and *The Life of Galileo*.

I should have a good agent in New York. Do you know anything about Max Lieber (or some such name)? Our old friend Ferdinand Reyher was in Copenhagen. I spoke to him, he rang me up. He was very nice and took a few things back with him. Lives in Hollywood.

[Skovsbostrand, February–March 1939]

384 To Henry Peter Matthis

Dear Mr Matthis,

Ruth Berlau has told me about your kind letter; thank you very much for it. Of course I should be glad to give a series of lectures on People's Theatre, Amateur Theatre and Experimental Theatre, especially if there is a possibility or any prospect of a possibility, of combining such lectures or discussions with practical courses. In that case my wife Helene Weigel could help me enormously. But then there's this to be said: Though it's too soon to set a date for the start of the lectures it seems advisable that my wife and I should be provided at once with entry permits, because otherwise the whole project could come to nothing. For this, I'm told, we need recommendations, preferably from

[1]English in original.

persons active in public life. I believe we'd get them if you could inform the Swedish consulate in Copenhagen what persons in Sweden want me.

Permit me to say that, at a time when medieval barriers are imposed on all attempts at free cultural exchange, I find your idea and Mr Branting's of founding this committee more than admirable.

Many thanks, and please convey my thanks to Mr Branting as well.

> Yours cordially
> bertolt brecht

> [Skovsbostrand, March 1939]

385 To Henry Peter Matthis

Dear Henry Peter Matthis

Enclosed please find copies of our passports, certified by the Swedish consulate. The consul said this was what is needed. He was very kind.

Today I applied for a new passport for my wife. We were told at the Ministry of Justice that the application would be put through as quickly as possible.

Many thanks.

> Yours cordially
> bertolt brecht

I hope the Swedish visas will be valid for as long as possible. And I hope too much delay will not be caused by the expiration of Helene's passport. The consul here thinks a visa may be issued on Helene's old passport.

> [March 1939]

386 To Henry Peter Matthis

Dear Henry Peter Matthis,

I've just been given an extension of my Danish residence permit. It's good for six months, that is, until 1 October 1939. In place of her expired passport my wife, Helene Brecht, has received an identity certificate (for refugees from Germany), No. 175, which is good until 27 September 1939 and entitles her to re-enter Denmark. The certificate is valid for all countries except Spain. It is issued by the Chief of the Danish State Police.

I believe you should inform the Swedish authorities of this. I took both papers to the Swedish consulate in Copenhagen, and they told me to tell you about them. Assuming this information to be correct, they would presumably be instructed to deliver the visas, provided our entry is approved. Consequently, they said, it was probably unnecessary to send a certified copy of our papers to Sweden.

I'd be very grateful if you would get them to issue the visas as soon as possible, so we can make our plans. The Danish police have been extraordinarily obliging, they have speeded things up and extended our residence permits by no less than six months, so that if the Swedish visas are issued in three to four months, our Danish residence permits won't expire in the meantime.

> Yours very cordially,
> bertolt brecht

> Svendborg, Skovsbostrand
> 5 April 1939

387 To Henry Peter Matthis

Dear Henry Peter Matthis

Many thanks for the *great labours* it must have cost you to get the visas so quickly. We'd been extremely depressed and worried for some weeks. According to the newspapers, Berlin has denied that German troops were being concentrated on the Danish border, etc. Everyone has been telling me that it's exceptionally difficult to get a Swedish visa. Please forgive my phone call on Saturday, I'm sure you realise how unpleasant it is to be perched on one of these little islands at a time when the slaughter seems to be on the point of breaking loose. Oh well, this year each week without a world war is an incredible stroke of luck for mankind.

> Most cordially yours and now *auf Wiedersehen*
> bertolt brecht

> Copenhagen 11 April 1939 (Tuesday)

388 To Henry Peter Matthis

Dear Henry Peter Matthis

I received the visas this afternoon, they've taken a big load off my mind. Rest assured that I fully appreciate the work you've done. I know how much trouble that sort of thing involves and how such dealings with the bureaucracy cut into productive work. Many thanks.

Now to the lecture. Branting wires that the date is set for 20 April. Don't misunderstand me: if it's absolutely necessary for you and the Committee that I should get there by the 20th, then I will. If it's not absolutely necessary, I'd much prefer to come a little later. That would enable me not only to prepare my lecture better (as you can imagine these last few weeks have been most unsettling), but also to wind up my Svendborg affairs. Thanks to the visas I shall now be able, in the event of an emergency, to leave at a moment's notice.

I shall be leaving Fyn for good after Easter. I've put my little house up for sale and of course the formalities are time-consuming. Then there's the books and furniture to be packed up, and the children's papers have to be attended to. They are being sent to Copenhagen for now, which makes at least one less Sound to cross. I'm telling you all this to show you how things stand. But I repeat: I wouldn't want to disappoint the Committee on any account. If a postponement of my lecture should be a source of trouble and inconvenience, I'll come before the 20th. But you must let me know straight away.

With warm regards to you and Georg Branting,

Yours
bertolt brecht

Please write to me care of Ruth Berlau. I get my letters more quickly that way.

[April 1939]

390 To Bruno Dressler

23 iv 1939

Dear Mr Dressler,

We have received your reader's comments on our Nexö translation. We were determined not to let his pedantic approach offend us, nor to dwell on the fact that his attitude is not one of collaboration but of blinkered determination to rule our translation out of court. Yes, these are indeed just 'random examples', but alas they are not very happy ones. Unfortunately we have not got our MSS with us, since we are in the throes of moving to Sweden, and must therefore confine ourselves to what your reader says.

It is hard to know how to comment. Take his first objection. What is wrong with a phrase like 'where it established itself in a new incarnation'? Your reader's suggestion of 'settled into a new form' is limp, lacks humour and fails to carry Nexö's meaning. If this is simply the result of his distaste for words of foreign derivation, then all I can say is that I don't share it. In my view the classic statement on this subject was made by Karl Kraus.

A further example. In place of:

'and achieved a certain relief with respect to my sometimes rather depressing (*not* "depressed") sense of responsibility'

your reader suggests:

'relief of my sometimes rather depressed sense of responsibility'.

But a sense of responsibility cannot be relieved. *I* can, however – with respect to my sense of responsibility. Your reader's suggestion is quite simply wrong.

'To impel the sack to . . .' strikes me as funnier than 'to shift the sack to . . .' *for the very reason* that 'to impel' means to exert a psychological influence.

'Appalling idleness on the part of the workers' definitely needs the words 'on the part', since this is a complaint, made from a quite specific, 'objective' standpoint, to the effect that the workers, by whom after all everything is produced, are not putting enough effort into the communal enterprise. Because, as I said, I have not got the text before me I cannot go into detail, but I am quite sure that Nexö at no point speaks of the 'appalling idleness of the workers' without saying 'on the part' – a phrase that is ideologically indispensable.

Nor can one say 'didn't want to stop shouting': it *has to be* 'didn't want to stop my shouting', no matter what your reader thinks.

I can't be bothered to explain why 'from the time when' and 'to become supreme, to become like other people' are (a) legitimate and (b) better.

As for the *corrections* on the manuscript, your reader has boobed. The changes he objects to are not ours, as he appears to think, but Nexö's. The words that strike him as 'stronger' were, in Nexö's view, too loosely expressed.

A while ago we went over these 'Memoirs' once more in view of the possibility of their serialisation. If you will send us the manuscript which you have there, then we can mark our amendments and cut down on corrections to the galleys.

When all is said and done, however, we would repeat our suggestion that the responsibility for the translation can perfectly well be left to us.

It is a pity that your reader's aggressive tone and questionable objectivity make it impossible for us to work with him. Nor, frankly, do we see any need for us to do so. In our final corrections we shall take the most profoundly pedantic requirements into account, but without necessarily having to comply with them.

Finally I would ask you not to overlook the absurdity of this whole situation. If I had to allow for views like your reader's when doing my own original work it would end up in a fine mess.

                    With best greetings,

P S. Please address any further letters to

                    Margarete Steffin,
                    Pension Westergaard,
                    Amagerbrogade 29,
                    Copenhagen

– since I shall be travelling and Mrs S. is dealing with all correspondence while I am away. If it has to do with the translation then from now on Mrs Steffin can handle any problems on her own.

4 Sweden, Finland, America
1939–1947

The Second World War

The Piscators had emigrated to New York at the end of 1938, Eisler about a year earlier (though he failed to complete all the formalities, and had to go to Mexico in 1939 and start again). Brecht's decision to follow them must already have been taken in Denmark, when Ferdinand Reyher and he discussed the prospects for a Galileo film and he then wrote his first great play specifically (so he said) with a view to New York. In March 1939 he applied for a quota visa before leaving Copenhagen, and from then on the family were, like thousands of other refugees, in the hands of those hard-pressed consular officials whom he would apostrophise in his 'Ode to a High Dignitary' (*Poems 1913–56*, pp. 356–7):

> Four times
> I succeeded in reaching your presence . . .
> Twice I have had my hair cut for your sake . . .

But unlike his friends Brecht faced two new problems. Leaving aside Ruth Berlau, who had Danish nationality and money and considerable initiative and could therefore fend for herself, papers had to be obtained not only for the four Brechts but also for Margarete Steffin, whose chronic tuberculosis barred her from being accepted on the quota. On top of that the consular machinery operated slowly, and Hitler and history were now quicker.

The story then of Brecht's last two years in Scandinavia is one of great uncertainty. On 1 September, while he was attending a Stockholm banquet in honour of Thomas Mann, the German armies rolled into Poland, next country on Hitler's plan of conquest. They were aided in this by a generally unexpected and (to anti-Nazis everywhere) deeply disconcerting German-Russian pact which allowed the Red Army to take over the Eastern half of the country, followed soon after by the three Baltic Republics to the north. Though the British and French governments rather hesitantly declared war on Germany, throughout the winter of 1939–40 their land armies remained more or less inactive while the Germans assimilated Western Poland. Stalin meanwhile launched a new and none too brilliantly conducted assault on Finland, which became the focus of many Western and Scandinavian sympathies before the fighting ended in mid-March with the loss of Karelia by the Finns.

Then came the start of the real war. In April Germany occupied Denmark and quickly conquered Norway, making it impossible for the Brechts to leave westwards as planned. Till then, it seems, Brecht had been feeling at home on the island of Lidingø outside Stockholm, living in a sculptress's house; he chaired the Swedish SDS branch and (if we can believe Peter Weiss's semi-fictional account) acted as a focus for anti-Nazi activities, not all of them legal. But a police search in mid-April helped drive the family to seek refuge in Finland, where a remarkable woman had got them official clearance from the prime minister. This was Hella Wuolijoki, an old revolutionary of the years 1905 and 1917–19, who was also a leading business woman and a successful playwright. She invited them to her country estate at Marlebäk, collaborated generously in the writing of *Puntila*, and helped them to find ways of getting out via the USSR.

The extraordinary thing was that this most difficult and dangerous time of Brecht's life should have been so outstandingly productive. The whole pattern of émigré publishing was disrupted as first Holland was overrun; then the Malik-Verlag collapsed and Muenzenberg's various enterprises lost all Communist Party support; soon Herzfelde was running a stamp shop in New York; while Muenzenberg himself, who had been interned by the French, was mysteriously murdered. The Nazis had started swallowing up the anti-Nazi theatres in 1938, and for the moment the Russians wished to know nothing more about the émigrés. Yet in the first three months of the war Brecht was able to write *Mother Courage* and the radio play *The Trial of Lucullus*, which was broadcast by the Swiss-German radio the following spring. Then, as Hitler overran Europe, he completed *The Good Person of Szechwan* (which had been started just before leaving Denmark) and wrote the *Flüchtlingsgespräche* dialogues, *Puntila* and, almost as an afterthought to take with him to America, *Arturo Ui*. Starting with *Galileo*, these big new plays, as he noted in his diary, 'try to fly apart like constellations in the new physics, as though here too some kind of dramaturgical core had exploded'. And something of their richness and force struck the world when *Mother*

Courage was performed in neutral Zurich on 19 April 1941, a month before Brecht caught the train from Helsinki for Moscow and points East.

It had taken over two years for the family's American visas to come through, including a visitor's visa for Steffin (Berlau travelled with them, but had made a separate application). Though their temporary Danish refugee documents had in the meantime expired, friends and well-wishers in the United States had been organising invitations and affidavits to get them admitted, and collecting promises of money. In New York Piscator, who had opened his Dramatic Workshop under the aegis of Alvin Johnson at the New School at the beginning of 1940, persuaded the latter to engage Brecht as a teacher at $1500 till the end of that year, then to extend this till September 1941; he also got a promise of $1000 from Sinclair Lewis's wife Dorothy Thompson. In California Fritz Lang and his friend Lily Latté collected money, as did Elisabeth Hauptmann; while William Dieterle's wife and Fritzi Massary's daughter could find $120 a month (or an average unskilled worker's wage, says James Lyon), from their European Film Fund. The newly arrived Lion Feuchtwanger also helped, while among those who provided affidavits seem to have been H. R. Hays, Dieterle and Luise Rainer. The crucial link however was the Soviet Writers' Union in Moscow, whose foreign secretary Apletin was able to organise tickets via the Trans-Siberian railway and a Swedish ship using Brecht's and Steffin's earnings from *Das Wort* and the Soviet international publishers (see Letter 420 written six months before they left Helsinki), apparently topped up from Feuchtwanger's blocked royalties.

This time, only a month before the German invasion of Russia, there was no ceremonial welcome in Leningrad or Moscow for the great anti-Nazi writer, who passed through briefly and, as Bernhard Reich remarked, 'quasi incognito'. He saw Reich, whose wife Lacis at that point had been banished to Kazakhstan, and Maria Osten in whose care he finally left the dying Steffin. To judge from a subsequent diary entry (6.9.42) his requests to Apletin (Letters 428–9) with regard to Steffin's possessions were followed, but her things went astray after arrival in the United States. A Soviet memoir of Mikhail Koltsov, whose aide Apletin had once been, suggests that Osten subsequently 'shared [his] tragic fate', but nothing is clearly known.

Once Brecht had arrived in the Los Angeles area everything changed, and it was more than a year before he began to feel even remotely at ease. Steffin's death had shaken him deeply; the decision to settle near Hollywood led him to waste time on film projects for which he was not really suited; moreover he was now living too much among great literary and musical figures and star performers – too cut off from the amateur actors and political partners who had so engaged him in Europe. Whether he would have been all that much more comfortable in New York is uncertain. Admittedly Piscator, Eisler, Grosz, Herzfelde, Aufricht, Borchardt and other friends were there, while Kurt Weill had at last conquered Broadway with *Lady in the Dark*. But Brecht's attitude to the 1935 *Mother* production had not endeared him to the American Left, and even in the East the whole climate of the New Deal had changed: the Federal Theater and the Living Newspaper were finished, destroyed largely by the opening session of the Un-American Activities Committee in the summer of 1938; the *Medicine Show* on which Eisler and Hays had collaborated in 1940 was about the last of its kind. Certainly Brecht seemed none too anxious to let Piscator set up New York productions of his works, preferring to discuss schemes with such eminent Hollywood Berliners as Bergner, Kortner, Homolka and Max Reinhardt, not all of whom were now getting jobs commensurate with their past glories. As for Hollywood's indigenous recruits from the Group Theater and other progressive outfits, Brecht found them more concerned with money than in 1935, but as old-fashioned as ever in their ideas of theatre. The exceptions were Berthold Viertel among the immigrants; Ferdinand Reyher and Mordecai Gorelik among the natives.

'For the first time in ten years', he noted in April 1942, 'I am doing no proper work.' That he managed to get out of this demoralising stagnation was due in the first place to Fritz Lang, whom he had known as director of *Metropolis* (1925) and *M* (1931), and who now asked him to write the story of *Hangmen Also Die*, and collaborate with John Wexley on its script. Some two-thirds of the year 1942 were taken up by this work, which was almost immediately followed by an enjoyable collaboration with his old mentor Feuchtwanger on *The Visions of Simone Machard*, the first and least interesting of his 'American' plays. Both operations paid off financially – the novel version of *Simone Machard* being sold to MGM for $50,000 early in 1944 – though neither was of great artistic consequence. Indeed everything that Brecht wrote for the American cinema or theatre during this six-year stay was intended to be a commercial success, though the only play of his that made it to New York was *Galileo*, which had for the most part been written earlier. At least the greater security and the change of house that resulted from Lang's film, the renewed collaboration with Eisler, together with the news of the war – Alamein and the North African campaign, the Russian successes at Stalingrad – all gave Brecht fresh hope. His opinion of Hollywood and of many other aspects of America remained scathing. But he stopped saying that he was living 'in dark times'.

By then Ruth Berlau had moved unexpectedly to New York, where she broadcast to Denmark for the Office of War Information, and there for the most part she remained based. Once *Simone Machard* had been concluded Brecht took to using her apartment at 124 East 57th Street for lengthy visits East each year from February 1943 on. 'Arizona and Texas are very reminiscent of Siberia, from the train' he noted during his first transcontinental trip. On that occasion he planned two collaborations with Kurt Weill, who was then preparing his second great Broadway success with *One Touch of Venus*, but had been drawn by Aufricht into a scheme for a Schweik musical where Lotte Lenya would at last have a part. The result when Brecht returned West at the end of May was not only the writing of *Schweik in the Second World War* but also a revised and shortened version of *The Good Person of Szechwan*, a play which Weill wanted to set as a musical or even an opera. At the same time Elisabeth Bergner and her producer husband Paul Czinner asked Brecht to make her an adaptation of *The Duchess of Malfi* for Broadway. Since this was to be in English, Eisler's friend Hoffman Hays was recruited to oversee the language and blend it with that of Webster (the dramatist).

These three projects occupied much of 1943, the year when Mussolini fell, when the German armies at Stalingrad surrendered, and Brecht's son Frank and Caspar Neher's son Georg were both killed as German soldiers on the Russian front. But the finished *Schweik* script fell foul of Piscator, who had been blithely planning a production of his own using the old 1928 adaptation (for which he counted on Brecht's help and what turned out to be Aufricht's translator). At the same time it failed to give Weill what he wanted, a Broadway-style libretto. The new *Good Person*, too, with its plot simplifications and its telling references to the drug traffic, had no more place for music than the original play. Hence by 5 December, when Brecht was in New York once more, both schemes were in Weill's opinion 'dead'. That winter only *The Duchess of Malfi* continued to tick over, though henceforward without Hays, who walked out in a fury when Czinner and Brecht told him that they had decided to bring W. H. Auden in to help.

Brecht returned to California in mid-March, and within a matter of days had made his crucial contact with Charles Laughton, at a party at Salka Viertel's house. However, before anything could develop from this he had to write and complete the version of Klabund's old Chinese story (see Note 60) which he had been commissioned to make for Luise Rainer to play on Broadway. This *Caucasian Chalk Circle*, as he called it, along with the problems of getting it adequately translated, occupied most of the rest of the year, though Rainer soon took against it and the possibility of a New York production became remote. For Brecht too the story of the play became painful, as Ruth Berlau, who had been fired from her OWI job as a Communist, arrived in Santa Monica pregnant and was taken in September to the Cedars of Lebanon hospital where their child 'Michel' was born and quickly died. Yet he remained attached enough to his play not to give up when Rainer rejected it, but to pin his hopes (in Letter 490) to a translation by Auden. By that time he had begun working with Laughton on their ambitious and long drawn-out *Galileo* scheme.

Like *Mother Courage* two years earlier, during 1943 the original versions of *The Good Person of Szechwan* and *Galileo* had their premières at the Zurich Schauspielhaus, last and most courageous of Europe's German-language anti-Nazi theatres. Since Laughton knew no German, his first introduction to Brecht's work was through a script of the *Schweik* translation. Soon however he started to become obsessed with *Galileo*, and decided with Brecht to make a new English version in which, after his many great film roles, he could return worthily to the stage. This project, on which neither time, money nor inspiration were spared, largely dominated Brecht's last two and a half years in the United States and was probably the most satisfactory experience of his whole stay there. While it was slowly coming to fruition not only did the Second World War reach its double ending – in Europe in May 1945; in the Far East in September, when the first atom bombs were dropped – but his prospects were changing in other ways too. Thus, as one of the founder members of a new Council for a Democratic Germany headed by Paul Tillich in spring 1944, he became an object of interest to the FBI, who categorised him under 'internal security', collected a mass of informers' reports and for much of 1945 bugged his telephone. At the same time he had already started thinking about returning to Germany even before he embarked on the work with Laughton; (see, for instance, Letter 506).

In the first autumn of peace Brecht, having re-established contact with his old Munich and Berlin friend Peter Suhrkamp, asked for news of Neher, Jhering, Legal – the theatre director who had played in the première of *Man equals Man* – and Burri, all of whom had, like Suhrkamp, lived in Germany through the Nazi years. He picked up the threads with Neher, (who consequently gave up his design post in Hamburg and moved to Zurich), and early in 1947 conducted a formal exchange of letters with Piscator in New York proposing a joint assault on the demoralised Berlin theatres. The deep-seated differences between the two friends, however, which seemed bearable so long as they were on opposite sides of the USA, had become all too clear just around the time of the German surrender, when a polyglot group called 'The Theater of All Nations' – a mixture of distinguished émigrés and less known Americans – was licensed, initially by Eric Bentley as translator, to mount an off-Broadway production of *The Private Life of the Master Race* (Letters 501–2), the wartime version of *Fear and Misery of the Third Reich*. Piscator started to direct this, but as soon as Brecht arrived from California he saw that their conceptions of 'epic theatre' were too incompatible for them to collaborate on a production. Piscator resigned, and Viertel took over what ended as something of a disaster.

The rest of 1945 was devoted to completing the work on *Galileo* and *The Duchess of Malfi*. That winter was a traumatic one thanks to Ruth Berlau's breakdown in New York, which took her into Amityville mental hospital and brought Brecht hurriedly over from California to be with her. Further revisions to both plays and long negotiations with possible producers for *Galileo* continued until Brecht came to New York again in September 1946 for the *Malfi* production. Although the original understanding had been that he would direct this, he was apparently regarded as something of a political liability by potential backers, so that the Czinners had unexpectedly brought George Rylands out from England as director, on the strength of his successful London production with Peggy Ashcroft and Robert Helpmann. Moreover Rylands had instantly thrown away all Brecht's work in order to return to Webster's text. Despite Brecht's angry reactions however (as in Letter 527) he seems not to have been too sorry to see the play close after a month, and thereafter to go back to the more congenial task of preparing the Hollywood *Galileo*.

While he and Laughton were trying to interest various producers and directors (including Orson Welles, Mike Todd and Harold Clurman), other operations were going steadily forward. First of all, the Brechts were once again preparing to change countries, as a number of the letters from the end of 1946 onwards confirm; secondly the House Un-American Activities Committee had started to direct its attentions to the Hollywood Left, and both Hanns and Gerhart Eisler had had preliminary hearings before it; thirdly Caspar Neher joined the directorate of the revived Salzburg Festival; and fourthly the German-speaking theatres in Europe were waking up to the works of Brecht. Thus there was a Berlin *Threepenny Opera* in July 1945; a second Zurich production of *Mother Courage*, with Neher sets; a Vienna *Good Person of Szechwan* with Paula Wessely in 1946; and in January 1947 a Basel *Fear and Misery of the Third Reich* with Neher's projections. At the Zurich Schauspielhaus Carl Zuckmayer's politically ambiguous new play *The Devil's General* was the great post-war hit.

So when at the end of July the former Living Newspaper director Joseph Losey staged *Galileo* in a small Hollywood theatre under Brecht's guidance, with Eisler's music and Laughton as a great Galileo, it was really the playwright's farewell to the United States. About six weeks after the première Brecht was summoned to appear before the House Un-American Activities Committee in Washington. This linked him to the other supposedly Communist witnesses constituting the 'Hollywood Nineteen', though in fact what interested the committee at his hearing on 30 October was not his somewhat marginal influence in the film industry so much as his connections with Gerhart Eisler, who was thought by the FBI to be a significant link in Soviet espionage regarding the A-bomb. By then Brecht's arrangements to return to Europe had already been made. Having sold his house and packed up, he left for Paris by air the next day. His wife and daughter followed by sea. His son, who had taken American citizenship, remained at Harvard. Ruth Berlau waited for *Galileo*'s New York production, then went to join them in the New Year.

392 Fredrik Martner

Dear Knud Rasmussen,
Many thanks for Waley's *Confucius*. It's really excellent. I'd just like to know whether he himself noticed and intended the criticism implied by his always substituting 'The Gentleman' for 'The Wise Man'. Probably not. Probably, by wanting to rescue Confucius for our times, he has finished him completely for our times. Of course it's a master stroke and makes the book easier to understand. A Wise Man can't very well lose his wisdom, but a 'Gentleman' can, since he is the product of a class. In German one would have to call his salient virtues '*ritterlich*' [knightly], hence aristocratic. What is significant for us is C.'s antimetaphysical attitude, his emphasis on conduct. Once again: thank you.

I hope you're not too much upset by the rejections of my work.

Remember that even *Mass und Wert*, Thomas Mann's journal in exile, rejected my Lao-tse poem. After all they're treating me as a beginner, and with some justification.

I'd be glad if you could spend your summer holiday here. The trip doesn't cost too much by boat.

> Yours cordially,
> brecht

I haven't thanked you yet for sending [your translations of] the poems (and *Galileo*). Thank you, I'm very pleased with them.

394 To Fritz Erpenbeck

Dear Comrade Erpenbeck,
I am aghast at the pay for my contributions to No. 3 of *Das Wort*, an article (on 'Rhymeless Verse'), two scenes from *Fear and Misery of the Third Reich*, and the translation of Nexö's *Recollections* by Steffin and myself – 180 crowns! The original rule was that accepted (and commissioned) contributions should in every case be paid for and if possible published. As for Nexö's *Recollections* being reprinted by *Internationale Literatur*, that is for *I.L.* to decide. I realise of course that it's hard for a magazine to serialise several epic works at once. But paying us (and presumably Nexö as well) not for a whole work but for the first measly few pages and expecting to be quit of all obligations is just about the shabbiest treatment I've had from any publication in fifteen years of literary activity. You know the difficulties we're working under in exile,

and I can't believe that you've made that really clear, because I find it impossible to believe that if properly informed any government department in the Soviet Union would behave like this about a cultural matter. Was it really necessary to follow up the crude, depressing way in which the editors were 'notified' that the magazine was being liquidated (Feuchtwanger wrote me a deeply depressed letter about it) with this disgracefully shabby financial settlement? It is your definite, unquestionable duty to keep the comrades who are responsible for such decisions accurately informed. (Did you even make it clear that *Das Wort* had *accepted* the *Recollections*?) I won't bother to ask why I was paid so much less for my last contributions than for the earlier ones, but it looks as if I'm not even to be reimbursed for the postage, typing, etc. as I was each year previously. You haven't even deigned to mention that. In short, I do not regard the matter as settled and would consider it most uncomradely of you to assume that it is settled.

With best regards,

[Lidingö], 25 July 1939

395 To [?]

Dear Comrade M.,

Since you are working on my theoretical pieces, a few observations which may save you going off at a tangent. Those that were published (originally in the *Versuche* series) were written as comments on theatrical performances and consequently in a more or less polemical vein. Since they do not contain complete definitions, they led to misunderstandings that prevent the student from working productively in the same direction. In particular, the *Notes to the Opera Mahagonny* requires a few additions if the discussion is to be fruitful. Some people have read into it the notion that I come out 'against emotion and in favour of the intellect'. This of course is not the case. I don't see how thoughts and feelings can be kept apart. Even that part of contemporary literature that seems to have been written without use of the intellect does not really differentiate between intellect and feeling. In it, the feeling component is just as putrid as the intellectual component. The idea that I mean to address myself exclusively to the intellect is held largely by persons whose intellect accepts my work (or so at least they think) but whose feeling goes on strike, i.e. the same persons who regard Communism as a cold product of the intellect, which does not 'do justice' to human feelings (that is, to the feelings of exploiters great and small). It is the same with the supposed relationship between the instructive element and the entertaining element in my notes. In reality, I have not the slightest reason to forgo either of the two elements, entertainment and instruction, which Diderot held to be the basic constituents of art. But unfortunately, the bourgeoisie does not find what teaches the proletariat and what the proletariat teaches us especially entertaining, nor does the proletariat find the entertainment to be got from bourgeois art especially instructive. Emphasis on social motivations and social characterisation in general gives the bourgeois aesthete (see *Mass und Wert*) the impression that the biological factor is being neglected, so that he expects to (and naturally does) find puppets moved by wires rather than fleshed-out characters. For he regards social conditions as wires; and only puppets, not human beings, can be moved by wires. Because they find doctrines in my work, they treat me as a 'pure doctrinaire'.

I wouldn't write you all this if my work did not indeed contain formulations that are likely to lead discussion into blind alleys. The emotion versus intellect controversy merely obscures the essential of what my works (or rather experimental studies) contribute to aesthetics: the discovery *that a phenomenon hitherto regarded as essential* i.e., *empathy, has of late been more or less banished from certain literary works.* (Which doesn't mean that feeling has been banished.)

> With comradely regards
> Yours,
> bertolt brecht

> Stockholm, July 1939

396 To Rudolf Olden

Dear Olden,

I remember receiving rather frequent communications and appeals from the PEN Club over the last few years, but I'm such a poor correspondent I don't know if I ever answered. Could you tell me if I'm a member of the PEN Club? If not, may I apply for membership herewith? And at the same time inform you of my intention to attend your congress in Stockholm this autumn? I'd appreciate a reply. Many thanks.

> With best regards,
> Yours,
> bertolt brecht

Lidingö (per Stockholm)
Lövstigan 1
[July 1939]

397 To Martin Domke

Dear Herr Domke,

Pierre Abraham has translated *Fear and Misery of the Third Reich* and at his request I have written to the Société des Auteurs authorising his translation of these short plays. Now Abraham tells me he's planning a production. I'm extremely pleased and hope that this time everything will go so smoothly that I won't have to ask for your help.

Another thing: Do you think Aufricht can repay that loan?

I'm glad to be in Sweden. From Denmark, as I gather from the papers, one can always see German warships cruising about. – I'm about to finish a parable play, *The Good Person of Szechwan* (with a big dual role for a woman), and then I'll get back to *Caesar*. Perhaps I'll be able to complete it before the next crisis. The only thing to do in this difficult and bloody peacetime is to throw oneself into work. (The Romans spoke of throwing themselves on their swords.) – I'll let you know as soon as I hear something more about *Fear and Misery*.

Yours cordially

Lidingö (Sweden)
Lövstigan 1
27 August 1939

398 To Ferdinand Reyher

Dear Reyher,

Forgive my silence, I've moved to Sweden, and that was quite a to-do. I'm now settling the *Fear and Misery* business.

As for *Galileo*, I'd be grateful if you'd let me know what changes you think necessary. Piscator has also written to me about it from New York, he seems to have all sorts of ideas on the subject. I'll let you know as soon as I know more.

With best regards,
Cordially
Brecht

The exact address is:
Lidingö (per Stockholm), Sweden

Lövstigan 1
27 August 1939

[Postscript by Grete Steffin]
Dear Mr Reyher,
Brecht tells me you think you haven't got the latest version of *Fear and Misery*. What kind of manuscript have you? Is it typed or duplicated? I doubt if you've received one of the early ones [. . .]

399 To Hans Tombrock

Dear Tombrock,
I've been thinking about your plan to do panels for community houses, always in pairs, one with a picture, one with a text. The next time we meet I'll suggest several possibilities. But now to the 'Reading Worker'.

The picture should be large, the worker larger than life. If canvas is too expensive, you'll have to take a board and work with Indian ink and a knife. But the main thing is that the worker must be imposing. He must be a big young fellow, who looks not only powerful but also menacing; it's not hard to find that type in Sweden.

One must get the impression that the only thing he still lacks is the book, nothing else; only the power to rule is lacking. There, the viewer must think, sits the true builder of Thebes of the Seven Gates, the conqueror of Asia, darkly pondering the lies about his conquests and his buildings.

For community houses it's important that the people be reminded of their strength. Precisely where cosiness runs rampant, a few vast symbols of uncosiness should be set up. The proletarian must be shown as politician, builder, and fighter, so as to provide visible support for his claim to rule.

Precisely when you turn to large formats, a switch to drawing seems advisable. The greater the aims, the more economy is in order. It's a way of mobilising your forces. That would give the panels the darkness we need ('so many reports, so many questions').

Incidentally, we would have to examine each text to make sure the translation is absolutely first class, submit each text to several Swedish poets. That's easily done.

Please ring me up. I hope moving house hasn't been too hectic for you.

As ever,
brecht

Stockholm, August 1939

400 To Fredrik Martner

Dear Crassus,

I've owed you a letter for a long time; to tell you the truth, I've been hopelessly in debt on all sides where letters are concerned. I enjoy reading the crime novels you sent me for Christmas, then take my time about thanking you, which isn't nice of me. I console myself for the disappointment I cause myself by the disappointments the world causes me and you and a few other people. It's feeble consolation.

I've resumed work on the *Caesar* novel, encouraged by the interest shown by a few proletarian readers here, to whom Grete lent half the book. But as it will take me quite a while to finish it, I'd advise you to start on *Courage*, if you can spare the time for translation. True, it doesn't seem likely that the warlike Danes will want to see such a peace-loving play. What's this, no good can come of war for the common people? And here too the prospects for the novel look bleak. What's going on here makes me think of the *Threepenny Novel*, specifically, the chapter on 'Gift Parcels'. I feel even more a foreigner than usual and I'm glad to stay at home by the fireside, as long as I have one.

Do you know anybody in Iceland? I think that might be a country for the likes of us.

Now and then I'm locked in struggle with myself: Oughtn't I to send back the *Confucius*? I know you made me a present of it, but it's really interesting and you should read it. Luckily, I've been victorious up to now and haven't sent the book back. When one considers how little moralising and how little invocation of 'higher ideals' that great moralist managed with, it gives you a clearer picture of our debased times.

With all my heart, I thank you for your many kindnesses and wish you much *happiness* for the coming year.

Auf Wiedersehen.
As ever,

b

Stockholm, beginning of January 1940

401 To Etti Santesson,

Dear Mrs Santesson,

Many thanks for your letter. It encourages me to make a rather shameless request. I've spoken to Karl Gerhardt about a review based on Aristophanes's *Pluto*. I've written a short outline, but I'm afraid he may find the German hard to read. Especially the samples of verse are difficult. Ninnan thought I might send it to you and ask if you could do a translation. It can be very cursory and approximate, the German text is itself makeshift. A rough literal translation will do for the two samples of verse. K. G. could get an idea of the rhythm and versification from the German text, his German is good enough for that. I'd be exceedingly grateful if you could do it, but of course I'll understand if you're deep in a big job and can't find time or feel you have to decline for some other reason. In that case, I wish you would give K.G. the German texts just as they are. On the other hand, if a collaboration with K.G. does materialise – theatrical affairs are so uncertain – your help would be most welcome. In that case there would be more of the present problem.

> With best regards,
> Yours,
> bertolt brecht

> Lidingö, February 1940

402 To Hella Wuolijoki

Dear friend,

It seems possible that we won't be able to stay here much longer. If we can show an invitation from you, we might get Finnish visas on the strength of it. Could you send us one? Of course it would have to be soon. We'd make use of it only if necessary.

> With best regards,
> Yours,
> bertolt brecht

> Lidingö, Lövstigan 1,
> April 1940

403 To Curt Trepte

Your two letters both came today. I fully understand your impatience to get to America. We have the same plans, but it's relatively easier for us to wait, because we can stay here for at least a month. Since as far as I know there's been no word from over there about an entry permit, I'm afraid it will be some time before we get our visas. But for you the problem of getting there seems incomparably greater. I can't conceive of Piscator's being able to do anything. He himself is a foreigner and as far as I know he has no official position. And he hasn't been there long enough to be likely to have many American friends. Furthermore, financing the trip to America represents a staggering difficulty. We'll probably have to circumnavigate the globe. If the Americans should really bring off a miracle and get (?) American visas for all the writers they mention (some are not included in the quota), there would still be the problem of getting one for you, since they after all are writers and most likely it's only for writers that anything can be done. There is certainly no point in cabling Piscator, but I'll write to him and explain your case.

Unfortunately I have no influence with the authorities here. I wouldn't know whom to appeal to. I'm sure that only a Finn can vouch for you, and that I couldn't. (But perhaps you can arrange for this through the connections you mention in your letter.) Anyway, I don't know of any lodgings for you. We ourselves are staying at a hotel. To the best of my knowledge, there is no fund to defray the expense of a stay here or of the trip to America. Of course I am in no position to judge whether the private assistance you speak of would be enough to see you through here.

Nothing in these parts looks simple to me.

My advice to you: Try to get your transit visas extended. Don't under any circumstances risk losing your Swedish residence permit and working papers. The best, of course, would be if you could get an authorisation to work here as a mason; keep trying.

Of course I'll let you know immediately if I glimpse the slightest opportunity for you anywhere.

I know that my report must come as a terrible blow to you, but I don't dare give you any illusions. I've discussed your situation with Greid, but he can't think of anything either.

I'll send you my address as soon as I've found a place to live. Until then it's Brecht, General Delivery (in case you hear anything from Mexico or the US about a visa).

> Best regards,
> brecht

[Helsinki, end of April 1940]

404 To Henry Peter Matthis

Dear H. Peter Matthis,

We've arrived safely and have been well received. Any number of people have helped us to furnish a small flat, and I've already started to work. E. Diktonius, who sends you his regards, has been especially kind. It's a big thing to find so much intellectual solidarity even (and especially) in these dark times.

I have another great favour to ask of you. Ruth writes that she would like to go to Stockholm and wants someone to ask Bolihn or Eklund of the Amateur Theatre to invite her officially to Stockholm for a directing job. Such work was actually discussed last autumn. Her address is: Royal Theatre, Copenhagen.

Could you speak to one of them and represent the matter as urgent? It would help a lot. In such an official letter it could be mentioned that R.B. would take advantage of her stay to negotiate with Radio Stockholm for the production of a radio play. Ruth does actually intend to take this matter up. She has written a play called *The Bovary Case*, and I've told Hjalmar Gullberg about it. I wouldn't bother you with this if I weren't worried about Ruth. How are you getting on? On the boat I had the feeling that I was leaving my home.

> Yours cordially,
> bertolt brecht

Helsingfors, Tölö, Walhallagatan 9
[April–May 1940]

405 To Hans Tombrock

Dear Tombrock,

I am appending three little poems that I wrote for you on the boat. My idea was that you should do drawings – or whatever brings the highest prices, possibly actual paintings, you won't get anything for drawings – and put a quatrain of this sort in the corner as in *Don Quixote*. This is the war tax you as a painter would levy. And each of these art works would be a certificate, showing that the purchaser did something for culture in dark times – when culture was going hungry. It's no disgrace for culture to say it's hungry. For *people* it is.

With this sort of thing you can approach your best customers. Write the texts *in German*, they'll understand.

I see all this as a self-portrait. Once you've sold – or rather, touted – one or two pictures, you'll know how street pedlars do it. *Don't* be cheerful about it, be gloomy, but you don't need me to tell you that.

On another picture you can put your family.

Or just yourself, pulling out your long trouser pockets to show they're empty.

I know it's hard to do anything just now, but try. Work is good medicine. I'll write soon.

As ever,
b

Helsinki, May 1940

406 To Hans Tombrock

Dear Tombrock,

Thanks for your letters. I'm looking forward to your drawings, curious to see what you've made of the subjects. In answer to my preliminary enquiries, I hear that conditions for the sale of art are not exactly favourable here. Uncertainty, rising prices, fear of possible shortages, etc. But Sweden won't be so good either, no matter how long you delay. Did the man from the Finnish People's Theatre come to see you? I ran into him yesterday. He said he had to go to Stockholm to pick up his wife who had just had a baby, and I sent him to you with greetings.

Please use all the money coming to you for things you've sent out as you see fit. You'll need it. And it probably won't come to much. Of course I'd be glad if you'd use a bigger canvas. This may sound fanatical (because canvas is so expensive these days), but work is the best of medicines, and perhaps when inflation and the 'flight to real values' set in, you'll sell big things more easily. And then there's the problem of colours that has to be solved.

In the midst of all the hardship we must get on with our work. Whether assailed by landlords or by bombers, whether it's money or paper that they won't give you, someday you'll be asked if you've solved the colour problem. In so-called historical times, i.e. times when history (or sausage) is made, there's only one thing to do: make oneself into a historical personage. I mean, when on a certain day it says in the papers that the Chinese have stormed Szechwan, you must ask yourself: What did Tombrock do that day?

I hope we'll soon be sitting together again.

> Yours cordially,
> Brecht

[Helsinki, 4 May 1940]

408 To Erwin Piscator

> Walhallagatan 9
> Helsingfors (Finland)
> 17 May 1940

Dear Pis,

You never answered our letters that I sent you (through Grete), but I hope you've received them all (including the manuscripts).

Things weren't looking so rosy any more in this part of the world, so we decided to move to Helsingfors. I've been offered a teaching post at your school, and I want to thank you and all our friends for your efforts. I hope it will get me a tourist visa. Actually we've been on the quota since March 1939, but I don't know how long we'll have to wait. (Would it be possible to find out over there?) What complicates our whole situation is that Helli and the children only have Danish refugee papers, which expire in August 1940, so I'd better do all I can to hasten our departure (whether with a tourist visa or some other way). Do you think something could be done in New York? I also hear to my dismay that one must either post a rather substantial bond or prove that one has the money. Do you know anything about that? Eisler has all our particulars (Grete's too) in case you need them.

What are you doing? Write soon again. It would be nice if we could work on something together in the foreseeable future.

> As ever,
> b

Incidentally, I've been getting letters from Trepte who is pretty desperate in Stockholm. He writes that he has cabled you and received no answer. I've tried to tell him how hard it is to do anything. But couldn't you write him a line or two?

409 To Erwin Piscator

Walhallagatan 9
Helsingfors (Finland)
27 May 1940

Dear Pis,

I'm *very* grateful to you for your efforts with the New School. We're attending to everything as energetically as possible. Quite apart from the fact that you are really helping us out of great difficulties and anxieties, I'm very much looking forward to working with you again. I'll be bringing new plays with me and, most important, an enormous desire to work. The US, I believe, is now one of the few countries where it's possible to do free literary work and to put on plays like *Fear and Misery*. – We still have one problem, a big one, that must absolutely be solved: Could the New School appeal to the American consulate in Helsingfors to give Grete a visa on the ground that she is my co-worker? Actually, she is the only person who knows her way around my thousands of manuscript pages, and without her I'd waste incredible amounts of time in working up my lectures. You could show them the *Collected Works*, where she figures as collaborator on *Die Rundköpfe und die Spitzköpfe*, *Señora Carrar*, and *Horatians and Curiatians*. She was also my collaborator on *Fear and Misery*, *Galileo* and *Mother Courage*, and you can also say that she collaborated on my theoretical works. I can't possibly leave her behind. She has been my collaborator for the past ten years and she is personally much too close to me. It goes without saying that she doesn't need an employment contract or expect a salary from the New School. If the school applies for a visa for her in Helsingfors, this will merely confirm the fact that my work (which I hope, will be done in collaboration with you) is of such a nature that I need collaborators (for demonstrations, directing, library work and secretarial work in general).

Please don't lose patience, this means a lot to me.

Yours cordially,
brecht

411 To Arnold Ljungdal

Dear Ljungdal,

Your forecast with regard to the battle of France has been confirmed. The spread of barbarism is purely a matter of technology. Our trip to America isn't getting ahead very well. The Petsamo route has now become impossible, and it takes time to work out other itineraries. But I'll keep you informed. It would be good if you could let me know the maximum amount you could spend on the trip. I don't have to assure you that I'd be more than delighted to travel with you. A book by you about my more recent production would of course be extremely welcome. I'd see that you get all the material. Nothing decent has been written about my later work, and about the earlier things there's only an essay by a Jesuit priest in the magazine *Hochland*. Without some dialectics after all one can't write about much but cookery. You could at last rid literary criticism of all the usual idiocies (e.g. the idea that an appeal to reason is a rejection of feeling, or that the epic and the dramatic are irreconcilable opposites, or that sociologically constituted characters are necessarily lacking in vitality. And it wouldn't be utterly impossible to get such a book published.

May I give you some advice about the form? I'd suggest the short glossarial chapters used by Bacon in his *Novum Organum*. Then the book wouldn't absolutely have to be completed (which in times like these is in the lap of the Gods). All the available material could be put to use and almost immediately. (Pascal's method in the *Pensées* was even freer.) Besides, we could easily correspond about it.

The Good Person of Szechwan is almost finished, or rather, completed. It uses certain techniques that are as old and as new as war itself. I'll send it to you as soon as it's copied.

Cordially as ever,

b

Helsingfors, June 1940

414 To Hans Tombrock

D.T.,

I believe your work on the *Fear and Misery* cycle has been extremely fruitful; it involved strict concentration on a closely circumscribed field with laws of its own. In each case there were similar social and artistic problems to solve, and in each case adequate material was available. In addition, you seem to have found out how much can be done with etching, that is, with a very definite technique. (It seems to me that the high points have been carried over into your painting, e.g., your treatment of the group in the etching of the unemployment office into *The Widows*). Now you are in a position to establish your painting, too, as an independent art, a technique with its own subjects, effects, field of action, etc. I'm delighted to see how well you've grasped the importance of composition in painting. And how specific social attitudes affect composition, how they directly determine the organisation of space. The lightness of the whole comes from well-balanced elements of composition and the impression of mastery from the clarity of social relations.

(A bit of advice: Do as many sketches as possible, studies in the *painterly* rendition of faces, bodies, etc. In your sketches you can achieve boldness in the use of colour. A pity I can't see your colour.)

You see, I don't make much of symbols, schematic rubbish that 'is supposed to mean something', like the wine in the Mass. How you position your people, in what attitudes towards one another, that's what matters. A compliment: You managed very well without the shoe (which incidentally would not have been a symbol). The relationships stand out clearly.

Once again, cordially,

b

[Helsinki, probably middle of 1940]

415 To the American Guild for German Cultural Freedom

Walhallagatan 20 A
Helsingfors (Finland)
1 August 1940

Dear Mr Wolf,

As I left Sweden last spring, it was only recently that I received the $180 you were kind enough to send me. I wish to thank the American Guild, the money has been a great help. I am now living with my family in Helsingfors (Finland). In March 1939 I applied for a visa to the USA and am on the waiting list. Unfortunately I don't know how long the visa will take. And it's not easy to manage here financially, because it's next to impossible at present to earn any money by literary work. (A play of mine, *Mother Courage and Her Children*, was supposed to be produced this autumn in Oslo, Stockholm and Basel, but that of course is impossible now.)

I have had to give up my work on the satirical novel *Die Geschäfte des Herrn Julius Caesar*, because it required a great deal of library work that I can't do here. In addition to *Mother Courage and Her Children*, I've written a long parable play, *The Good Person of Szechwan* and am now working on a short satirical novel on a contemporary theme. I'm convinced more than ever that this horrible interim period will soon be behind us and all my work is geared to this prospect. If the American Guild can possibly extend my *scholarship*[1], it would be a great help to me.

> With best regards,
> Yours,
> bertolt brecht

P.S. I am waiting with great concern for news of my friend L. Feucht-wanger and other colleagues, and would appreciate your telling me anything you know.

419 To Hella Wuolijoki

Dear Hella Wuolijoki,

Just so you understand that I feel a considerable responsibility for Ruth: once the Nazi machine gets to work in Copenhagen, they can hardly fail to find out about all the work she has done with us. It's not just that Helli and I lived with her in Copenhagen and she with us in Svendborg – she also directed *Señora Carrar*, placed two plays (*St Joan of the Stockyards* and a ballet) with the Royal Theatre, and, worst of all, published a limited edition of the *Svendborg Poems*, in which I say bad things about the Nazis. In addition to which she took part in innumerable anti-Nazi meetings and recited poems of mine. In my opinion she won't be able to go back until the war is over.

> Cordially with everlasting thanks,
> brecht

> [Helsinki, 1940–1941]

---

[1] 'English' in the original.

420 To Mikhail Y. Apletin

Dear friend Apletin,

Many thanks for the information. We've been waiting all summer for American visas. Now things seem to be straightening out and the question of tickets is becoming urgent. It would help us a lot if we could pay for the trip from Leningrad to Vladivostok in rubles. But in order to get visas from the American consulate, we have to show tickets to San Francisco. Would it be possible to send the Russian tickets (from Leningrad to Vladivostok) here? As I've told you, our complete ticket books must be submitted to the American consulate here. Or could Intourist in Stockholm help us in this? I hope the State Publishing House in conjunction with *Internationale Literatur* can raise the money for these five Leningrad-Vladivostok tickets; it would be a big help, because I don't see how I'm going to finance the trip.

You write that I have 750 rubles worth of convertible currency. Could you send me that in dollars (unfortunately I must show American dollars and pay for the rest of our tickets in dollars) care of the embassy here?

Steffin and I have finished our translation of Nexö's Reminiscences. I've read in Soviet periodicals that Volumes 1 and 2 have already appeared, but receipt of Volumes 3 and 4 has never been acknowledged. I'm sending you another copy (our last), would you be so kind as to give it to Mezhdunarodnaya Kniga? It was agreed between Mezhdunarodnaya Kniga and Nexö in 1939 that Steffin and I were to receive 1000 rubles in valuta, or 4000 rubles for the four volumes. Last year in Stockholm we were paid for the first volume (1000 rubles in valuta), so we still have 3000 rubles coming to us. For that we could finance the trip from Yokohama to San Francisco. Could you please ask Mezhdunarodnaya Kniga to send Steffin and me these 3000 rubles along with the 750 as soon as possible (in dollars) care of the embassy here?

I'm sure you realise how eager we are to hear from you, so much depends on what you have to tell us. I can't stay here any longer, for months we have had no answer to our application for residence permits, and if I hadn't had the prospect of American visas they wouldn't have let us into the country at all. I'm feeling more and more insecure.

Many thanks for your help.

I'm sending a story of mine, 'The Augsburg Chalk Circle' along with the two last volumes of Nexö's Reminiscences. Would you please give it to Becher? Perhaps it could be published in Russian as well.

I hope to see you on my way through and thank you in person for your kindness.

> With best regards,
> Yours,
> bertolt brecht

[Helsinki], 20 November 1940

421 To the Kurt Reiss Theatrical Agency, Basel

Helsingfors, 1 February 1941

Gentlemen,

I am enclosing Simon Parmet's music (piano arrangement) for *Mother Courage and Her Children*. Mr Parmet and I have agreed on the following points:

1) Whenever his music is used, Parmet is to receive 25 per cent of my royalties. This sum is in every case to be sent directly to Parmet. Address, Helsingfors, Tölögatan 8.

2) The theatres are entitled to use other music, which however must be approved by me. The agency is under no obligation to offer Parmet's music to the theatres.

Point 2 is necessary, because I'm not sure that Hanns Eisler has not composed music for the play. He is now in America. It is of the utmost importance for me that until further notice the agency should not inform theatres that there might be other music. As soon as other music is available, I shall so inform the agency.

Now to practical matters: Parmet will send you the instrumentation as soon as you report definite acceptance of the play. The orchestra consists of 7, possibly 8 players.

Parmet demands an advance of 300 Swiss francs against his royalties.

I am very much looking forward to a production. Please remember me to my Zurich theatre friends.

> With best regards,
> Yours

424 To Erwin Piscator

Dear Pis,

At last the consulate tells us the visas are on their way. On the other hand, the New School's employment contract will soon expire, and it would be a big help if the School could grant me an extension. I would have to produce evidence of this. Could you ask Mr Johnson? It's very important. I'm sure you realise that I have tried to leave here as soon as possible. It would be wonderful if we could actually resume our old collaboration. I've been terribly isolated here and it's very hard to do literary work under such conditions. Still, I've finished a few things, and I hope to be able to bring them to you.

What are you doing? Are you working hard? I'd be glad to hear from you.

> Cordially as ever
> b

New Address:
Repslagaregatan 13 A. 5,
Helsingfors (Finland)

[March–April 1941]

425 To Hans Tombrock

Dear Tombrock,

Just one more thing in *great* haste: On 15 April a Swedish ship left Vladivostok for America. Unfortunately, when I heard about this ship it was too late to make reservations. But now I hear that it plies regularly back and forth. Please go to Intourist straight away (they have no office here) and ask them when the next ship sails, how much it costs, its name, and so on. And if possible, make reservations for six (including a ten-year-old girl, maybe they'll let Barbara travel for half price). Then I wish you'd go to Cook's Travel Agency and ask about boat connections between San Francisco and Mexico, exact sailing times, prices, etc. It's terribly urgent. You see, they won't give me American visas unless I can tell the consul when I'm sailing, the name of the ship, and show proof that I've got reservations.

And by the way: What about Grete's little stories? Do try and sell them. But if it can't be done, please put them in an envelope and send them to Ninnan Santesson, Tegenersgatan 37 ö.g.V.[1] And if you have an unpublished story of mine, put that in too. (It's urgent.) Ninnan Santesson's sister is a translator, perhaps she can sell the things. But write to me about it in any case. Unfortunately, we have no copy of Grete's short story that was published by the *Morgenbrise*, 'The Answer', I think it was called, could you tear it out of the *Morgenbrise*? I'd appreciate it.

I wish we could finally leave (and you could come with us), but it depends on so many things. But write at once in any case.

In haste. As ever,

[Helsinki, April 1941]

426 To Hella Wuolijoki

Dear Hella,

We have just learnt to our dismay that the Japanese have stopped issuing transit visas as from today. This news hasn't been fully confirmed, but it seems likely. In any case it can happen tomorrow or the day after if it hasn't already. Please try your best to find out if it's possible to get a passage on a freighter from Murmansk or Odessa or Vladivostok. It's getting *extremely urgent*.

Cordially,
brecht

[Helsinki, April–May 1941]

427 To Mikhail Y. Apletin

Dear Comrade Apletin,

Please give the comrades at the Writers' Union my heartfelt thanks for their hospitality. These days in Moscow have been infinitely precious to me.

I am obliged to leave behind Margarete Steffin, my collaborator and friend of many years, who is gravely ill. Only your generous promise to look after her and, if she recovers, to arrange for her to continue her journey, gives me the courage to set out. Comrade Steffin is indispensable to me for my work.

And now let me thank you personally, dear Comrade Apletin, for

[1]Swedish, meaning: Across the court, 5th floor.

receiving me in Moscow, for the day at the Exhibition, for attending to my steamer tickets, and for your kindness to my sick collaborator Steffin.

> With comradely greetings,
> Yours,
> bertolt brecht

Moscow, 30 May 1941

428 To Mikhail Y. Apletin

> My temporary address:
> c/o Wilhelm Dieterle,
> 3351 North Knoll Drive,
> Hollywood, California

Dear Comrade Apletin,

A few requests concerning my collaborator Margarete Steffin:

Despite the doctors' fears I hope she will recover sufficiently from her grave illness to be able to follow us to America. I am most grateful to you for your willingness to arrange for this trip should she be able to make it. I am leaving you Steffin's travel documents (her American visa), the money she must show on landing, and her luggage.

Should Comrade Steffin die, please

1) forward her papers and the death certificate to me.

2) keep the manuscripts (sealed and unsealed), the photographs, and the letters in her possession for me.

3) send me the money I borrowed for her.

4) take the figurines, the elephants and the travelling chess set out of her luggage and keep them for me. Comrade Maria Osten can take all the other things and distribute them.

5) deposit what is left of the rubles I am leaving for Steffin in the savings account of Lion Feuchtwanger.

6) Maria Osten has promised to have a simple plaster cast of Steffin's face made in the eventuality of her death. Please keep it for me.

I know I'm giving you a lot of trouble in case all this becomes necessary – as I still can't bring myself to believe. But I know your comradely generosity and know that you understand the difficulty of our situation.

Yours cordially,

bertolt brecht

Moscow, 30 May 1941

429 To Mikhail Y. Apletin

Dear Comrade Apletin,

I hope it hasn't given you too much trouble to forward Grete's dollars. Obviously it's the fault of the bank which misunderstood the telegram from Moscow. Now I've got the 940 dollars and the authorisation to take them out of the country. For this, too, many thanks.

May I once again – for the last time – write about the matter of Grete? I take your telegram to mean that you will send me the manuscripts, the photos and the mask care of Wilhelm Dieterle, 3351 North Knoll Drive, Hollywood, California, giving the sanatorium as the return address. That is perfect. If possible, I'd also like certain of Grete's belongings that I wish to keep as mementoes, sent to the same address. These are the little elephants and other figurines and the travelling chess set in Grete's suitcase. And the personal photos which I believe she took to the nursing home with her. Maybe Lydia and Maria could pick out the things. I've written to Maria, telling her what to do with the rest.

The loss of Grete hits me very hard, but if I had to leave her, there's nowhere I'd rather have left her than in your great country. I shall never forget the comradeship and kindness that were shown to me – and to her.

And now once again, dear Comrade Apletin, I thank you from the bottom of my heart. Please remember me to Comrade Lydia, who also did so much for us, and accept a firm handshake.

Yours,
bertolt brecht

Vladivostok, 11 June 1941

As agreed, I shall write to you from the USA under the name of Karl Kinner, or just K.K.

430 To Hoffman R. Hays

Dear Hoffman Hays,

After travelling for almost three months, we've finally landed in the

States, in San Pedro as it happens. As there doesn't seem to be much point in going to New York now, I'm staying here for the present. It seems to be cheaper, and besides I have a few friends here. My main worry is where to get translations made of my plays. I've brought a few things with me, and there may be a chance for some of them here. Of course I have few illusions, I know New York from 1935, and I doubt if it's any better now. Three months ago in Helsinki I spent a long time wondering how to write you my ideas about the possibility or impossibility of producing *Courage*, but without hitting on a form in which to do so. Seen from Helsinki, it seemed as though the war would spread and change its character at any moment. It now seems to me that *Fear and Misery of the Third Reich* might almost have the best chances, 27 scenes from the years 1933 to 1939, showing life under the Nazi dictatorship, the life of the workers, petty bourgeoisie, and intellectuals, in family, school, barracks, hospital, courtroom, etc. I only have one copy left, but Elisabeth Hauptmann can probably get you another, which is in the possession of Piscator or Eisler. Her address is Colonial House, Greenwich, Conn. I'd be pleased if you'd look at the play. It's a great pity that we can't sit down together and talk. I feel here as if I were in Tahiti, surrounded by palm trees and artists, *it makes me nervous, but there you are*.[1] The worst of it is that everybody here is trying to convert himself and everybody else into a hundred per cent American in record time, it makes me feel rather seasick.

Please write to me.

> With comradely greetings,
> Yours,
> bertolt brecht

> 1954 Argyle Avenue,
> Hollywood, California
> [July–August 1941]

431 To Erwin Piscator

Dear Pis,

As you've probably heard, the ship, oddly enough, put me ashore in

---

[1]English in original.

Los Angeles, and since it's summer and it's a long way to New York and we have a few friends here, we're staying on for the time being. This is how things stand: The work at the New School would interest me very much, but I don't know whether they mean to update my contract. If so, the question is: What can I do? Purely theoretical lectures would be much harder for me than working seminars, they'd take more preparation, studies, essays, I'd have to express myself in more or less pedantic terms, etc. Besides, I doubt if the students would get much out of it. I'd much prefer to work in the borderline zone between playwriting and production, and eliminate a good part of the barrier between dramatist and director, director and actor, actor and rational human being. We have to consider the playwright's incompetence in the theatre, the actor's incompetence when it comes to writing plays, and their joint incompetence in the field of social action. So my idea is to 'direct', but not 'real' plays, to conduct a dramatic workshop, not only with students of acting but also with playwrights, student directors, etc. In this field I have some work to show, several theoretical essays and exercises for the theatre (complementary scenes of Shakespearian plays, models containing, in modern realistic form, the elements of classical scenes from *Macbeth*, *Maria Stuart*, etc.). And there's something else that might be combined with this. You know all or some of my 27 scenes from the Third Reich. They depict the behaviour of all sorts of people under the Nazi dictatorship, the breakdown of human relations under the pressure of terror. The whole was conceived as a play, with the scenes played successively, surrounded by a forest of illuminated swastika flags and a ballad inserted between the scenes. The advantage would be that the scenes could be rehearsed singly, that each would stand by itself, etc. This play would be exceedingly timely, as it shows the social background of Hitler's soldiers. It's a colossal military review, which has the additional advantage of showing what is in store for the people over here if they get a dictatorship. It would be best, I think, if my teaching activity could be invested in work on this production. Of course I'd need collaborators. You yourself would work with me, I hope. Please write to me about it.

I'm so dry and laconic because I'm in the midst of getting settled. Of course I'm dying to know what you're doing and I'm longing to see you. What are the others up to? Grosz, Borchardt, Eisler? Write to me.

As ever,
brecht

1954 Argyle Avenue,
Hollywood, Cal.
[July–August 1941]

432 To Karl Korsch

Dear Korsch,

We went further and further north, from Copenhagen to Stockholm, from Stockholm to Helsinki, now we've landed here on the last ship from Vladivostok, as chance would have it in Los Angeles, where we found many friends, so we're planning to stay for the time being. How shall we manage to meet again? Do you ever come to the Golden West? To New York? I'm eager to see what you've written in the meantime. I was unable to take your Marx monograph with me, I'd love to have another copy, galley proofs would do. Helli is well, though she has lost a little weight; Barbara is taking on human form, and Steff has become a big bruiser with well-developed muscles from carrying suitcases. We all want to see you.

With warm regards,
As ever,
Brecht

Hollywood,* 1954 Argyle Avenue

*This (unfortunately) doesn't mean that I have a job; so far it's only a sign from Providence, which made the last ship land here of all places. And please don't put off sending me your work.
[Brecht's note]

2

I was only waiting for your address before sending the enclosed letter. Pollock's card came at the same time as your letter. It would be wonderful if you could come by way of Los Angeles, because I don't know yet when I'll be going to New York. Many thanks for 'Prelude', 'The Fight for Britain', and the *Nickerson* review. I devoured them. I meet Thomas Mann only casually, and when that happens 3000 years look down on me. But I can talk to Reichenbach, next week I'll be moving into his neighbourhood (Santa Monica), though I'll see him before that. It's wonderful that Langerhans is out. A short pamphlet on those blurred slogans would certainly be possible now. I'm not being very coherent, there's too much to say. Do come by way of Los Angeles if you possibly can, it will certainly be several months before I can go east, and that's a long time, practically an era.

Please give Hanna our best regards and accept the cordial and enthusiastic greetings of the brechts.

[August 1941]

433 To Karl Korsch

Dear Korsch,

We were really depressed to hear that you couldn't come by way of Los Angeles. I'll probably have to stay here for a while to build a small financial foundation. Once that's more or less done, I'll go to New York, for a few weeks at least. I'd love to have as much as possible of what you've written. (I sorely feel the lack of your Kiepenheuer edition. I'm used to it, and I doubt if it's possible to find a copy here. I need the Marx monograph too; where was it published?) Copies of my most recent work (mostly plays) were sent to you from Finland, but probably haven't reached you. No one here has received them. Reichenbach lives nearby and we see each other now and again. I also see – with much less profit except for my 'Tui novel' – Marcuse, Horkheimer and Pollock, the last two only at parties. A film about Lourdes is being made soon; I imagine they have their eyes on the clerical roles. Even in the backwoods of Finland I never felt so out of the world as here. Enmities thrive here like oranges and are just as seedless.[1] The Jews accuse one another of anti-Semitism, the Aryan Germans accuse one another of Germanophilia. Döblin speaks of home now and then, meaning France. Leonhard Frank, who is now in a position to watch his 'good men' waging the Second World War, has declared in all seriousness that it will be necessary to wrest from the Ganghofers 'certain very important territories' they have occupied, and is writing a revolutionary boy-meets-girl story. Etc. Etc.

I wish you were coming here if only because of the Institute.

Yours ever,

b

Santa Monica, Calif., 817 25th Street [End Sept. 41]

434 To Erwin Piscator,

Dear Pis,

Our first letters must have crossed, so while answering yours I'm still waiting for your answer to mine. I'm sorry. About the play, I wish

[1]Groundless.

you'd read my last, which I think would be easier to produce. Unfortunately, I have no copy at hand, but E. Hauptmann has one. Address: Colonial House, Greenwich, Conn. The Szechwan play demands much virtuosity, it would take a lot of time, and the translation would have to be done with great care.

I'd be glad to work at the School. And a job there would make it possible for me to live in New York. But it would really have to pay enough to live on, if only modestly. Do you see a chance? I wrote saying what I could do, but I could also conduct a workshop and write a play in collaboration with the students. The younger generation don't seem to think ill of me. People like McLeish and Latouche could give the school references. You understand, Pis, I have to plan everything at once. It would be wonderful to do the Szechwan play if we're not rushed, because it will take time (to say nothing of the translation, the cuts and the music), and I don't know if the School can afford the time.

We must work out how to organise a good collaboration. It would be absurd for me to tell you to start rehearsing *The Good Person* unless I see a possibility of coming to New York, I'm sure you understand that. If there's no chance at the School, I'd much rather start by doing my best to make some money here with which to finance a stay in New York.

I'm glad you like *The Good Person*. There's nothing I'd like better than to work with you as soon as possible; the two of us could really make use of our time on Mount Ararat. I'm sure you're doing all you can to bring this about, but of course I don't know what the possibilities (or impossibilities) are. But rest assured that I too am doing my best.

As ever,
brecht

[Santa Monica, August–September 1941]

435 To Erwin Piscator

Dear Pis,

I'm glad you like *Ui*. As for *The Good Person of Szechwan*, it goes without saying that I'm grateful to you for taking it up with the [Theater] Guild. I assume that they will let me see the translation or a sample of it. But do tell them not to commission the whole translation before I've seen some of the prose and lyrics. Besides, I should know the translator's terms. You realise that I have no intention of paying 50 per cent of my royalties. But I suppose all that can be settled later. And now to *Ui*. Here again the problem is the translation. It would be best if I could be there, because the translation has to be free and I could help the translator a good deal (choosing different images, explaining the jokes, etc.). In any case, I must absolutely see a few pages before the translation is definitely commissioned. Feuchtwanger has told me about a translator who is supposed to be good and is here at the moment. I've met him and he has read the play. His name is Christopher Lazar. He says he'd need about eight weeks and his price is $500. Can the theatre afford that? The man makes a good impression, knows the German theatre and my main works and would work with me. I don't know if Hoffman Hays would be able to translate the blank verse. What do you think? Should I try to get Homolka interested in the role of Ui?

Can my presence at rehearsals be financed? It would mean the round trip and the cost of living simply in New York, so it couldn't amount to much.

Please don't lose patience with me as a correspondent, I keep having to run around looking for ways to make some money. I know how important a New York production would be and that our interests are identical.

As ever,
b

Santa Monica
817 25th Street

I've taken a passionate interest in *Troilus and Cressida* for years. It could be done with songs, and Thersites, one of the most lovable characters in world literature, could serve as a mouthpiece for all sorts of ideas. We could do an adaptation with the School group, or in some other way. But the crux is and remains: How do I get to New York? Eisler (Lou, that is) could tell you the minimum I'd need to live on, it can really be a minimum, we live simply and it wouldn't have to be in midtown.

[September 1941]

436 To Karl Korsch

Dear Comrade Korsch,

Your letter of the 14th came on the 23rd (today); not a bad record. I sent you a letter a few days ago, but I'm writing again because, now that a meeting is no longer on the cards, I want us to correspond properly. Unfortunately the copy of the book hasn't come yet, and you'll still need several months for the proofs, so perhaps it won't matter if my notes are delayed a little. In the meantime, a few very general remarks: Of course I'm in favour of numbered paragraphs, because they make it easier to quote (as your letter of the 14th shows). They chop up the text much less than the author supposes, and certainly don't suggest that something is being weighed on some sort of scales. And headings are worth their weight in gold. Your headings in *Capital*, specific concepts such as 'class', 'labour', 'productive forces', are definitely in order, but for that I need the book. I'm somewhat afraid of the preface you speak of. Of course I'd very much welcome a few words about popular Marxism with its muddy metaphysics, but the rest frightens me, because to say 'let's look and see if there isn't some coal left under the slag' would sound rather depressing, and after all you remove slag from the coal rather than the other way round. And when you speak of looking to 'see what can be taken over into science or what can be regarded as a point of departure' from the standpoint of science, what is this thing you call 'science'? And where is this 'standpoint'? Then it means adding something (after careful investigation) to something, but in our case one is adding 1000 to 1 (the 1 already being 'there' in the form of the bourgeois view of history or economic theory or political science). The danger, incidentally, of your being regarded as a guardian of the Grail, which seems to be your constant nightmare, is exceedingly slight.

I am eagerly looking forward to the book. In the USA you should have . . .[1]

[Santa Monica, 23 October 1941]

437 To Karl Korsch

Dear K.K.

Many thanks for the issues of *Living Marxism*. I read your article with the greatest interest. My first solid food for years. Of course I'm unhappy about your attitude towards the first workers' state in history, which comes through in every article. Because it's not only a workers' *state*, but also a *workers'* state. To me it seems perfectly clear that the specific (Stalinist) form of the state developed in close connection with

[1]The rest of the letter is indecipherable.

the socialisation of the economy (the Five Year Plans) and the collectivisation and industrialisation of agriculture and national defence. Doesn't it seem possible that certain basic historical tasks have imposed similar methods and institutions on the various classes? With their similar apparatuses they remain different classes, and the proletarian class nevertheless effects a far deeper transformation of the base. In any case, when the task is to centralise the economy, it becomes necessary to traverse an area showing extremely divergent tendencies. I've long wondered whether your analysis held water, and I don't believe it can be adequately substantiated. The dialectical situation (a situation charged with contradictions) calls, I believe, for dialectical (in the same sense) treatment. I see I'm expressing myself rather pompously, that's what comes of trying to condense. To put it simply: I'd expect a good deal from a historical study of the relationship between the soviets and the parties, the whole complicated process. The specific historical reasons for the defeat of the soviets would interest me enormously. It's terribly important for us, don't you agree? Apart from you, I don't know of anyone capable of looking into that. (There's a play in the back of my mind, but I don't see it clearly enough or know enough.)

I don't see Horkheimer very often, especially as Marcuse (the one from the Institute) is in New York. He used to come and see us often, he's quite approachable. But I mean to work doggedly on my plan to bring you here, you can be sure of that. Mea res agitur.

My writings will go out to you as soon as I have them here. (They were sent to New York.)

Please write to me again. The *family*[1] is well. Steff is learning to drive, but he drives too fast, and I have a hard time restraining him from treating the subjects of his school themes too sociologically. I think you'll like him on the whole. Barbara is studying *sex appeal*[1]; for reading matter she sticks to *Superman*.

Film interests me, of course and that's bad, because it's commercially too important. I have to restrain myself from treating the *boy-meets-girl*[1] theme too sociologically.

As ever,

b

[Santa Monica,], Beginning of November 1941

Regards from Helli, Steff, Barbara.

[1]English in original

438 To Berthold Viertel

Dear Viertel,

Thank you for your letters. Of course a production of *Ui* by you would interest me enormously, whether at the actors' school or somewhere else. Only I think we'd need a good Ui. Couldn't you write to Homolka? He's got the play but he isn't reading it. It wouldn't hurt him. You can judge the translation better than I. (Please find out what percentage Hays should get. I should make him an offer.) I'll have to go over the translation from the murder of Roma to the meeting with Dullfeet again very carefully. Maybe old Dogsborough's death is treated too casually.

I'm enclosing a ballad. I was planning a film and trying to put my ideas on paper, but this was the only form I could find. Do you think you could persuade Auden or Isherwood or someone to adapt it? I'd like to have it in English.

Wonderful that your poems are finally being published. Yes, our books are more easily burnt than published. I vaguely remember that you wrote a preface or afterword for them, which I must have read very quickly if at all. May I give you a bit of advice? If there is a preface, and if it contains even the slightest suggestion of a Captatio benevolentiae, anything like 'Inter exilem silent musae' or 'Don't be amazed that I'm still alive', just throw it out. Not only are we attached to our troubles; we're also entitled to them. On that score we must be adamant.

> Cordially as ever
> b

[Santa Monica, autumn 1941]

439 To Archibald MacLeish,

817 25th Street,
Santa Monica, California
December 9, 1941

Dear Mr MacLeish![1]

After my odyssey I arrived with my family in this country last summer. I have received my first papers on the strength of an immigration visa. During the first two months I have been busy settling down.

---

[1] This entire letter is English in the original.

Now that this country is at war, I am most anxious to do my bit fighting the Nazis, the world's scourge. Germany is going through the worst winter of her history. The casualty lists are just now arriving, testifying to the Nazi bankruptcy in the East at the moment when the mightiest industrial power of the world, the USA, is about to multiply its efforts to get fit for the 'rendezvous with destiny'.

Knowing Germany as I do, I feel strongly that the psychological moment has come to broadcast from here right into Germany the truth which might easily act as an incentive to revolt in the approaching hour of despair. I am aware that such an undertaking might easily act as a boomerang if not handled intelligently. I would gladly participate in any such effort. I think you know that I could be helpful.

May I ask you if there is any such undertaking being considered, and if so, where? In case there is none, would you be interested in instigating such a thing?

Realising how busy you are, I do know it is a just cause that keeps you so busy.

> Cordially yours,
> Bertolt Brecht

440 To Sam Bernstein

Dear Mr Bernstein,

Your gift gave me great pleasure. Ordinarily I make enemies for myself with my poems. It's good to know that I can also make friends.

The suit might have been made to measure for me, it needs no alteration at all. Once again many thanks for your kindness.

> Yours,
> bertolt brecht

Santa Monica, March 1942

Forgive me for writing in German. My English still leaves much to be desired.

442 To Berthold Viertel

Dear Viertel,

Thank you very much for the performance of the *Fear and Misery* scenes, which must have been excellent and also for your detailed report. It would be wonderful if photographs could be made of the second performance. (This is how Ruth used to do it: with a Leica, during the performance, from a point in the first row if possible, in such a way that each shot takes in the whole stage; this sort of film costs so little.)

Now to something else: Some time ago Max Reinhardt, who read the scenes last winter, told me he was planning to go to NY and 'look around'. [He wanted to know] how I would visualise an English-language production. I suggested a setting: A big truck placed downstage centre, full of soldiers in steel helmets, chalk-white, stiff as ramrods, four rows of them, rifles between their knees. The classical Hitler blitzkrieg vehicle. It would appear four times with a ballad (variations by Eisler on the melody of the Horst Wessel song). The rumbling of its wheels would be heard between scenes. At the same time a voice would announce the next scene. The rumbling would also be heard at menacing moments during the scenes. This truck carries the *New Order* through the world, and the scenes show where the men in it came from (*Private Life of the Master Race*).[1] Max seemed to like the idea, though he hasn't seen the whole ballad yet. Of course I don't know if he'll be able to raise the money for a production, Salka [Viertel] is more than sceptical, so probably nothing will come of an English-language production, after all your efforts. But since it's the best thing I have to contribute, I'd at least like to have the ballad stanzas well translated ('just in case'). Do you think Auden would do it? It's not a big job. Anyway, I'll send you the stanzas. (The between-scenes announcements have been translated by Ferdinand Reyher and also by Hans [Viertel], whom I'm beginning to appreciate (and whose version is much better, I think.)

I'd welcome your criticism of the ballad, as a whole and in detail. Of course I'm still cherishing the hope that even without Reinhardt we may find some way of launching the play in the heart of American New York. (But I liked the old man a lot the other day, he was fresh and simple and matter-of-fact, and I have a great weakness for his theatre mania, as you do too, I'm sure).

[1] English in original

Please thank the company in my name and again many thanks to yourself.

> as ever,
> brecht

> Hounded out by seven nations
> Saw old idiocies performed:
> Those I praise whose transmutations
> Leave their persons undeformed.
> (Dedicated to you)

[Santa Monica, late May–early June 1941]

443 To Max Reinhardt

Dear Professor,

After our encouraging talk, I did some more work on my play *Furcht und Elend des Dritten Reiches* (or *Private Life of the Master Race*) and I think I've hit on a good visual effect to go with the musical setting. The production might be centred on the classic German blitzkrieg vehicle, the armoured personnel carrier which has made its appearance from North Cape to the Mediterranean and from the English Channel to the Volga, bringing with it the *New Order* that is already established in Hitler Germany. This *truck*[1] is full of the chalk-white soldiers of Hitler's army, those slaves who bring slavery wherever they go. The truck could appear four times, in ballad style, with a song set to the distorted melody of the Horst Wessel song, a carload of twentieth century Huns. Each scene could be preceded by the roar of heavy guns and the rumbling of the truck, and a voice could introduce the scenes depicting the new order in Germany. ('And in that truck there rides a teacher / A captain now with helmet of steel / he gives his lessons to / the fishermen of Norway and the wine growers of Champagne. / For seven years ago on a certain / faded but never forgotten day / he learned in the bosom of his family / to hate informers.' – whereupon, under a big black and white sign indicating the date and the teacher's address, *The Informer* is played.) At the end, the truck is shown covered with ice in the Smolensk

---

[1]'English' in original

region; it's making no headway, for the first time it has been brought to a stop. By way of an epilogue, the actors could step up to the footlights and say to the audience (in substance): But you, when you stop this truck – and for God's sake stop it with power – don't forget that power is not enough in a world that's so cold.

I'm writing you this because you may have a chance to talk about the play in New York. One advantage is that for this sort of play no stars would be needed, but lots of faces can be shown.

With best regards,

817 25th Street, Santa Monica
[End of May 1942]

444 To Ruth Berlau,

Love,

I'm writing because I want you to have a little letter, as I'm expecting Eisler any minute and there's nothing to report. (Just one thing, so you'll know what's what in case you hear anything said about it: Max Reinhardt is trying to do something in New York and is interested in *Fear and Misery*. Stella Adler and [Harold] Clurman are trying to help him arrange for a production. I've done an outline which I'll send you when I've made a copy.) I'm looking forward to your report on the German performance. Please keep writing. I feel terribly disappointed, Ute, when days pass and nothing comes.

bertolt
dig[1]

Enclosed a letter to Max Reinhardt about the 'outline'. *Keep it*. It's a copy.

[Santa Monica, late May–early June 1941]

445 To Ruth Berlau

Dear Ruth,

Feuchtwanger says he sent you a recommendation to Huebsch; write and tell him you've received it, he's so fussy about such things. It would

[1]Evidently short for *Jeg elsker dig*. See footnote to Letter 450

be a good idea to invite Max Reinhardt to the second performance of *Fear and Misery*; I think you should go with him if possible, because he doesn't know you. You could phone him and say I asked you to. Viertel knows the name of his hotel. – I don't entirely understand the parachute scene; you didn't describe it very exactly. A *special delivery*[1] letter has come but it wasn't written *after* the first night. I don't see why you got my letters so late, but perhaps you didn't pick them up until the end of the week.

I can't write that 'Freedom Song', not if they paid me $1000. But I won't tell the woman that if she writes to me, I'll say something friendly. I'd be glad to consider doing a scene. Maybe I'll send you an outline and you can talk it over with her. What about the little radio play (*What a Nazi heard*)?

Any Animal Can Do It might be acceptable for a women's magazine, if at all.

Have you been telling me everything? (You wrote on the train that you couldn't tell me everything because I mightn't believe you.)

        bertolt

I've been working on something with [Fritz] Lang. It's too stupid that Helli has got hives or something and is lying in bed with a rash. It's the food or the climate, we eat lunch in the drugstore (which I detest). I never get to Beverly Hills. Lilli Laté sent the cable, I couldn't get away from Lang.

Do you need money? Write if you do.

        [Santa Monica, late May–early June 1942]

446 To Ruth Berlau

Dear Ruth,

You seem determined to do everything and neglect nothing to make me really bitter. Do you really want to turn our exile into an endless lovestory[1] with ups and down, reproaches, doubts, fits of despair, threats, etc. etc.? You may have gone to New York to look into the financial prospects, but why do you keep telling me that you're reluctant to come back? In one letter you tell me how happy you feel in your flat (with the implication that New York might make you forget me), in the next that you've moved because you only took the first flat for my sake

[1]'English' in original

and I haven't come as you kept hoping. (For that, as you know, I have neither the money nor the time, because I do have to make money, nor the authorisation, since I'm an enemy alien, nor a reason to give my friends here, who are just waiting for a chance to expose me as a Don Juan.) At eight a.m. I make Barbara's breakfast, at nine I'm with Lang. There I stay until six-thirty, then I go to the drugstore with Steff and Barbara, then people drop in, and not always for pleasure. In between I get one of your wicked and always barbed letters, or none at all after a depressing one. For five whole days you didn't write about the one performance I've had in the US or give the faintest hint that you were leaving town. After my wire you let another two days go by. I have the impression that when you read this you'll only be glad to know I'm thinking about you, just as you were 'glad' to get my wire. That's bad, Ruth, really bad. I don't know what to do. It's hard for me to keep from falling into a stony silence, I'm only deterred by the memory of a time when you weren't like this, when I didn't have to keep passing tests and putting up with reproaches, when you realised what I could and what I couldn't do, when you helped me and let me help you. Even then you must have seen that I was busy with matters that are not without their importance, and sometimes you still seem to see me in that light, but evidently you're no longer in the mood to look at things this way and think it's too much to your disadvantage. But you shouldn't go too far, especially now that you've gone away and we can't talk. It's a serious matter, I tell you this out of sincere friendship and because you're very dear to me: Don't make me feel utterly insecure and angry; cut out this 'all-or-nothing' nonsense, cut out everything that sounds like 'perhaps we should part'. Be serious and friendly and understanding, as you have been so often, Ruth.

bertolt

[Santa Monica, June 1942]

447 To Heinrich Mann

Dear Mr Mann,

Please forgive me if I don't come this evening. The reason is simple: reading my work to an audience makes me feel dreadfully uncomfortable. Really I've never given public readings. Besides, my wife is to read in any case, and I'm convinced that she'll read very well. What I most regret is that because I don't intend to read, even though my name is on the programme, I can't very well show my face, and this prevents me from hearing you read. If it's true, as Feuchtwanger tells me, that you may read again either at your house or his, I shall be *delighted* to attend.

Hoping you'll forgive me,
　　　　　Yours faithfully,
　　　　　bertolt brecht

　　　　　　　　　　　　　　　　Santa Monica, July 1942

448 To Karl Korsch

Dear K.K.,

I haven't written to you for so long because up to now I haven't been able to make ends meet. When we arrived here, we had very little money left, and it's only recently that I've been able to earn any by doing a script for Fritz Lang. (I don't know how it will turn out on the screen, but the script at least is nothing to be ashamed of.) My intellectual isolation here is horrendous; compared to Hollywood, Svendborg was a metropolis. You must have been in situations where you put off the most vital calls because your trousers need mending.

Brief survey: Helli is all right, I think; she is taking care of a small garden again and she has some prospect of a part. Steff is studying chemistry and driving a 1928 Ford; he has a collection of Elizabethan dramatists. Barbara is in junior high, whatever that means, and is developing a bosom.

One good thing: Eisler is here.

Your far-sighted analysis of the English mentality has been thoroughly borne out. Their nonintervention policy is a masterpiece of Tuism. Non-Aristotelian drama would have its hands full, if it had hands.

I'd so much like to read some of your work.

I've read Langerhans's book with great interest, especially now that Weil and the Institute have called it 'simply insane'. The poems are good too. But I haven't written to him either, or even thanked him, and I feel pretty badly about it. Maybe you could put in a good word for me with him. Nor have I written to Hedda, thanking her for her translation of *The Children's Crusade*, which gave me great pleasure.

Please write and at least tell me how you're doing.

As ever,

brecht

Santa Monica, Calif., 1063 26th Street
October 1942

449 To Karl Korsch

Dear K.K.

Your book has just come, and in that instant it became painfully clear to me that I hadn't posted the letter I wrote you recently, I had to find the address first. Luckily it's on your envelope though very tiny. Thank you so much for the book, it's very kind of you. I hope you believe me when I say that my silence wasn't induced by an infection with Catholicism. I regard you as my teacher; your work and your personal friendship mean a great deal to me, and everything depends on your having patience with me. We've long differed in our appraisal of the USSR, but I'm convinced that your attitude towards the USSR is not the only conclusion that can be drawn from your research. For a long time I've mentally discussed all controversial points with you before writing anything.

Once again: *Many* thanks not only for the book but also for sending it. (I presume Marcuse has told you how sorely I felt the lack of it.)

As ever,

brecht

[Santa Monica, late 1942]

450 To Ruth Berlau

Love,

Arizona, evening, deserts with grey bushes. Naturally the train is full of soldiers, they're just as we know them, no country has made itself so familiar as this one, through the cinema – and gone to such lengths in living up to its image. But a woman asks a soldier: 'Are you going beyond Los Angeles?' and he answers: '*No. That's far enough for me.*'[1] Maybe the movies don't tell the whole story.

Suddenly in the train on Sunday it occurred to me that I'd forgotten

[1] English in original.

to remind you to hide those white, grandmotherly night dresses, because of the Bachmann woman. I hope you've done so. But it was sweet of you to keep wearing them. I always see you that way. There's something of the old times in them and something of a new J.e.d.[1]

I've reread the beginning of this letter and I'm reminded of a quotation from Budzislavski that I once read in a letter from Heinrich Mann. He wrote (more or less):

'Has it ever struck you that here
the moon which in our country looks like an upright sickle
lies on its back like a boat?
Strange how *many* things
can be different in a different country.'

Are you efficient, cheerful, curious, studious, faithful, Love?
                        bertolt
                        d[2]

El Paso, Texas, 26 May 1943
[Postmark]

451 To Ruth Berlau

Love,

No, you're not getting on my nerves. – Before starting on *Schweik* I'm reworking *Simone*, because Eisler's doing music for the dreams, it's beautiful. Don't forget the *Szechwan* play completely. I'll also send the Aufricht material (records and *Schweik*) through you. By the way, has Weill got a translation of *The Children's Crusade*? Yes, I expect you here in the summer – Are you smoking too much again? Please don't. – And have your ears attended to as soon as possible.

Santa Monica, 3 June 1943
[Postmark]

452 To Ruth Berlau

Love,

Seven a.m. I've put on coffee, the radio is playing (the little leather case beside the bed). Then I'll get to *Simone* (last act).

[1] *Jeg elsker dig.* 'I love you' in Danish.
[2] Possibly short for *Jeg elsker dig.*

I forgot to take 2 songs by Dessau, *Song of a German Mother* and *Germany*. Send them. The stick hasn't come yet. I want the photos too.

Steff is on holiday and bored. Thinks the *Malfi* adaptation is 'a bit thin'. Do you think so too?

Wrote two film treatments for Lorre, who's going to try and sell them. He was crazy about *Schweik*. (Don't mention this to the Weills.) We could do with some money.

Friday, noon.

Going to see Eisler now about *Simone*, will post this. Thanks for your letter. Please write every day, Ruth, if difficult just a line.

Love,
bertolt

Santa Monica, 4 June 1943
[Postmark]

453 To Ruth Berlau

Love,

I've now received the three parcels, thanks. I've already been out with the stick, went to see Eisler and buy the *Times* with it. Anyway I got my stick back quicker than Adolf will the city where I lost it. The paper is most welcome – and not honestly come by, I hope. I'll probably use it all for *Schweik*, which just devours paper. And thanks for the copies. Do you think you could copy the *Schweik* scenes before passing them on to Weill? (But the ones that are still to come, not the short model that you already have.) And two more things: Did I forget my pipe? Could you go to 1666 Broadway or phone Circle 7-9152 and get them to send me two boxes of *El Capitan* Coronas C.O.D. (meaning cash on delivery). They're the best. But I haven't had any letters for days. The last was dated the 5th, in which you wrote that you'd received the photos (the first lot, you must have got more on Tuesday). Do I get some of them, the ones with you in them?

I'm eating my last meal, my midnight sandwich, with you. Do you mind?

Write (for one thing to tell me why you haven't written).
d.d.

bertolt

[Santa Monica] Friday, [11 June 1943]

454 To Ruth Berlau

Love,

I'd so much like you to write every day, Ruth. As I've said before, when it's hot or something I'll be satisfied with a signature.

Mr Friedman hasn't phoned.

I'll never know how your phoning could disturb me; I wasn't doing anything in particular, and I was delighted if only because there hadn't been any letters for so long. I'll phone you one of these days, OK?

If you take hot tea to work with you in a thermos flask, it may be some help against the heat. I believe the Asians do that.

Tell Aufricht everything is all right, I just want to discuss the contract with someone I haven't been able to reach yet. Now I can settle it with Weill in person. I already have about two out of three acts of *Schweik*. He should send me the story he wanted to have typed, if possible a translation as well, if he has one.

Have you read that Hella Wuolijoki has been arrested in Helsinki? Perhaps you should get Ernestine Evans, her friend (212 East 48th Street, 3D), to get after Teivola.

Eisler has read *Puntila* and is really enthusiastic. I'd never have been able to write the play without our walks in the forest.

How about your smoking?

Who says I don't miss you?

bertolt

Send the enclosed letter to Hoffman Hays; little Roth probably has his address.

In one place where I've sowed, tiny green leaves are sprouting close together. In the other, nothing, I must have done something wrong. I've watered regularly.

I'll be there at nine on Saturday night.

Santa Monica, 16 June 1943
[Postmark]

455 To Kurt Weill

Dear Weill,

I'm really sorry not to have written for so long about the contracts. At first I begrudged every single day as I was working from morning to night on *Schweik*, and contracts are such a very different department that one has to readjust completely. Now it's all done except the last scene (March to the East). I haven't sent separate scenes because they were too rough and I kept having to go back from the end to the beginning. You can expect the whole thing by the end of the week, though it's still rather rough. I've enjoyed the work a lot.

But now to the contract (for *Schweik*). What bothers me about it is, frankly, that it brands me for all time as a pure librettist, without any author's rights. (The rights which according to ¶14 you acquire after my death, are ceded by me before my death according to ¶10.) As you know, I'm quite willing to be guided by your advice in matters concerning an American production. On the strength of our recent collaboration, which I very much enjoyed, I don't believe there will be any serious differences between us. I see a great advantage in letting you conduct the negotiations, since you have experience, connections, etc., and are on the spot, and when important decisions are to be made you can always get my consent in a few hours by wire. I think you know that I also value your opinion in dramaturgical matters. Now to particulars: I believe ¶1 and ¶2 should be formulated in such a way as to make it clear that *Schweik* is our joint property, with me contributing the play and you the music. Neither the play nor the music can be used separately.

¶3 OK

¶4: In the choice of an adapter the consent of us both should be required. I'll leave the choice of an American lyric writer to you. As to the production, a veto is permissible only if the vetoer can arrange for a different production. (With regard to an American production, I'll gladly write you a separate letter giving you full powers, if you need them.) There can be no quarrel about this.

I heartily agree with the clauses about [Lotte] Lenya, but one more sentence should be added, in which you will undoubtedly concur, to wit: that you are not obliged to authorise any production without her in the part of Mrs Kopecka, owner of the Flagon, if you yourself have a prospect of a production with her in that part. No conflict is possible, since I wrote the whole part for her.

¶5 and 6 OK

¶7, 8 and 9: OK

¶10: I believe this should be omitted, since it gives me no right to deal with the adapter and, considering the difficulty of this really 'foreign' play, I shall certainly be needed.

In that case ¶11 and 12 could be slightly modified.

Please don't misunderstand these criticisms, I really think the simplest possible contract would be best, and provide the soundest basis for our collaboration. (We can easily make separate arrangements about anything you need for special negotiations, quite apart from our general contract, valid for all times and countries.) And put in a shattering ¶ requiring you to compose the music immediately. Otherwise we'll have to see what we can do about a *Czech* première.

I'll deal with the *Szechwan* contract in another letter. It's much simpler, I think.

Once again, excuse the delay, I did the play itself in an inhuman hurry and put everything else aside.

As ever

Remember me to Lenya. I keep playing her French recording to cheer me up. (Lenya has developed unbelievably.)

Dear Weill, I've just discovered what the mistake probably was: the lawyer mechanically transferred the terms of the *Szechwan* contract to *Schweik*, where there isn't any original play, etc. and the adapter doesn't need to figure so prominently. Let's just treat each of the two contracts independently.

[Santa Monica, around 23 June 1943]

456 To Ruth Berlau

Love,

Thanks for the cigars, which I'm already jauntily smoking. On Saturday night I went to the garden and put *Schweik* into Winge's hands. But then a silvery mist filled the night sky and not a constellation could be seen. Yet I knew that you too were looking up and I stood as it were beside you.

I'll send *Schweik* any day now. I've made only one carbon, and kept having to make corrections on it, so I couldn't send it. I can't wait to hear whether the play made you laugh and whether I've managed to keep the background serious enough.

I'm sending you a copy of my letter to Weill. (I've already sent Aufricht a wire.) You can show Aufricht the letter if you think he might influence Weill to draw up a more or less reasonable contract. It shouldn't really be so difficult to get a production for this play. Aufricht himself thinks he can swing it.

Why should Weill get such unreasonable rights? I'm not a librettist. It's got to be my play – which it is (not an American version as in the case of the *Szechwan* play) – and it's not just America that I have to consider. Moreover, political problems are involved in this play, I must have a say. And we don't need a translator with a big name. What for? Just a good translation. I wouldn't dream of interfering with Weill's conduct of the business end, but I must have a reasonably 'influential position', I'm not just the bottle washer. The lawyer just copied the *Szechwan* contract. But speak calmly to Aufricht, don't be aggressive.

Please don't smoke too much. And don't worry. I need you as much as you me, Ute.

                                    bertolt

                            Los Angeles, 23 June 1943
                                    [Postmark]

457 To Ruth Berlau

Love,

Did you get the air mail letter with the tiny cigars?

Your letters come rather irregularly, usually in the afternoon. Please, before you post them, write the time of posting on the envelope.

Tell Aufricht to phone Kreymborg, or better still, you ring him and tell him I'm writing a *Schweik*, no, that I've written one, and that I have the rights, etc. It's about Schweik in 1943, and does he want to translate it?

Aufricht should tell Piscator I was rather put out with him for not phoning me again after he asked me to write a revue for a pro-Jewish cause. Because I'd always made it clear that I wanted him for *Schweik*, but couldn't do anything without consulting Weill.

Yesterday I saw Cassiopeia clearly, quite high in the sky.

I hope I make some money soon.

I'm thinking of Ute.

d

bertolt

Los Angeles, 30 June 1943
[Postmark]

458 To Ruth Berlau

Love,

I'm visiting Lorre at a place called Lake Arrowhead, along with a man who wants to do a film, I don't know if anything will come of it. I'm living in a wooden bungalow under pine trees and I'm surprised that you're not here.

Now I won't get any letters from you until Tuesday (and you'll have to wait too, it's hard to get things posted here). At the end of the week I'll send you *Schweik*.

Weill and I agreed that he should draw up a normal contract for *Schweik*. I, too, would be very much in favour of trying Kreymborg; at least he's a poet. But we'd have to move quickly, after next week Aufricht won't have a book, and then it will be up to him to get a move on. The translation would be needed by the middle or, at the latest, the end of August. If not Kreymborg, then Reyher, just so we don't spend a year looking. There's always a possibility of polishing, but for polishing a good poetic translation is needed, with a rough translation it's not possible.

I've told a *producer*[1] at 'Universum'[2] our old story about the women's rights movement, the marriage strike because of the woman teacher who gets sacked[3] because she's married, you know, the business with the governor and the corset burning. He seemed very much interested. Maybe you'll make some money out of it. (Where was that funny picture of the woman with the bicycle, the cigar and the trousers?)

J. elsker dig,[4] Ruth.

bertolt

Lake Arrowhead, 3 July 1943
[Postmark]

[1] 'English' in original.
[2] No doubt Universal Pictures.
[3] Brecht's word is 'ge-fired', which is German-American.
[4] See footnote to Letter 450.

459 To Ruth Berlau

Love,

Here I am in Arrowhead, a playground of the rich; there's an artificial mountain lake with pine trees and oaks, the whole thing fenced off, because it's owned by a private company. It's as quiet as living in a forest between two sawmills, because speedboats[1] are always thundering across the lake. Lorre is living with a millionairess, the daughter of a Chicago meat king, the children bite mummy's pearls to see if they're real or prove to the guests that they are. A little girl asked me when I arrived if I was a chauffeur, then if I was an *actor,*[1] then a *writer.*[1] Already her instinct is infallible. I was obviously a menial.

We discuss the story in the morning, that's a concession to me; otherwise it's not normal to work if one goes out to work. I don't feel a single cubic metre of ground under my feet, merely Lorre's bank balance, in this polluted continent in a lost century. Of course I live too high for a classic, unless I can get paid by the hour.

I hope there'll be letters from you when I get home tomorrow (Tuesday) evening. I posted a letter up here on Saturday evening.

This story is about a museum curator in Marseilles, etc.

Are you eating properly? Not smoking too much? Taking care of your ear? Do you regard the Office[2] as a job? Are you learning to type properly? Are you waiting for me? Write, Ute.

Love
bertolt

[Lake Arrowhead, 5 July 1943]

460 To Kurt Weill

Dear Weill,

I'm about finished with *Schweik* and will send you a copy piecemeal as I receive it. I've added quite a lot at the end, to flesh out the picture; some of it is rather obscene and probably can't be used anywhere but at the Schiffbauerdamm. I'd welcome your suggestions for deletions etc. I don't think we should let ourselves be frightened into thinking it's all-

[1]English in original.
[2]The OWI. Office of War Information.

important to capture Schweik's exact way of speaking. In the bulky and widely distributed American edition of the novel there's no trace of it, but it's funny all the same. And even though the background is much more difficult (Austrian monarchy, First World War), the novel strikes the American reader as very funny and perfectly understandable. Yet there's no attempt at Americanisation. As I've already told you, I'm very much in favour of Kreymborg, he's a poet and could make the lyrics fit the music. As he has told Ruth, he understands German, he's politically OK (liberal), and will bring out the poetic man-of-the-people quality. We can always have the thing polished, at least the polisher will have an excellent translation to work on. It's simply impossible for anyone to work from a rough translation, don't you agree? Kreymborg could start *at once* and he works quickly. Please help things along. (Of course he shouldn't get more than one of us, assuming we don't need anyone else beside him.) What have you heard about *The Threepenny Opera*? Probably nothing . . . Your tobacco pouch is being sent to you. – I'm also sending you *Private Life of the Master Race*. – I'm curious to know how Lenya likes the play. Please remember me to her.

> With best regards,
> Yours

[Santa Monica, about 9 July 1943]

461 To Ruth Berlau

Dear Ruth,

It's true that Kreymborg is no humorist, but neither am I. Ask Aufricht whether he would have given my stuff to Robitschek in Berlin to use for jokes. And I also think we should have the possibility at the end of taking on someone to make the text less literary. (We could tell K. that *two* poets are too many for Broadway, he'd understand.) As for K's lack of success: In this case he's a translator-adapter, not a playwright; in other words, possible failures as a dramatist don't mean he's a poor translator. We need a *name* only if that's the only way of getting a production under way, that is, of raising money on the strength of an American author's name. It would take a year to find a successful American Broadway author, because then a rough translation would have to be done, and that would disgust any self-respecting humorist, etc. etc. K can complete the job in four weeks, a polisher would only need two weeks more, as he'd have everything he needs. And at least for the lyrics (they're not American songs after all) we're not likely to find anyone better. And another thing: If Weill were free at present, as we originally thought he'd be, *he* could work on the translation with an American who doesn't know German. But now that's impossible. On the financial side: Maybe we could offer K a third of the royalties, then he'd have as much as Weill or I. If at the end we (Weill and I) think someone else is needed, he'll have to content himself with a quarter, i.e., the same again as Weill or I, if the new man likewise demands a quarter (25 per cent). He can't expect more, since the lyrics at least would remain unchanged and the translation would be finished. But this is something Aufricht will know how to handle. I also think the time is right for this play and we should jump at it; didn't we agree that (unlike *Szechwan*) it should be done this autumn. I'm not sure about Lorre, I doubt if he'll have time in the autumn. And I wouldn't want to wait for him, as I'm against wasting time. (Back to the problems of the translation. An American with no knowledge of German or Czech has no way of knowing how Schweik talks. The American translation of the novel is *lousy*.[1] A general sense of humour isn't much help.)

You've no doubt received the one and a half acts by now. As I've told you, they've been typed without any cuts, so as to give the translator as much material as possible and examples of the tone. The vulgarities will probably have to be taken out here, but it's good for the translator to see them at least.

Many thanks for your help.

b

[Santa Monica, July 1943]

462 To Ruth Berlau

Dear Ruth,

Enclosed is the amended *Schweik* contract. Weill and I have agreed that it should be a simple collaboration contract, applying to the American production and version. Of course I'd like in addition to make another contract with Weill covering world rights, which would merely specify that Weill agrees to change the music for the German version if necessary (if he composes music for a metrically different

---

[1] English in original.

English version). We talked about this. Weill suggested the cut in ¶4 – in the event that Lenya were not available or that a production with her as Mrs Kopecka *cannot* be obtained. Weill also thought it sufficient that if offers were made for two productions the one with Lenya should be taken up, but that it would be unfair to veto any production outright – especially as a production contract with Lenya can be made at once. I am as eager as Weill to have L as Kopecka. I think Weill should set a date for completion of the music. (With regard to Kreymborg: perhaps Weill will reserve the right to draw in someone else for polishing if he thinks it necessary. I wish the translation could be begun immediately.) Weill himself wanted to change the *Szechwan* contract and send it to me, he took notes on the subject. I'm ready at any time to sign the *Schweik* contract as it is; if Weill wants any changes, he should add them and I'll respond quickly.

> d.
> Bertolt

> Los Angeles, 19 July 1943
> [Postmark]

463 To Ruth Berlau

Love,

The business about the *staging* comes in front, after the Cast of Characters. You should put the *Prologue* in the place of the old Prologue. I'm also sending a second copy.

> bertolt
> d

The contracts have been sent.

> Los Angeles, 19 July 1943
> [Postmark]

464 To Ruth Berlau

Love,

Thanks for the long letter. In the meantime you must have got another letter together with *Schweik*. Please write me all your thoughts about it (without restraint, circumlocutions, etc.), it will help me. Even about details, Ruth. I can still make use of your ideas.

How long in advance must you know when you're going to take your holiday? I'd so much like to pick a good time, Ute. (I'll write to Ute tomorrow.)

Could you ask Laurin (one of the Czechs) where I can get hold of Czech folk songs in English translation? I'd use a few in *Schweik*. (Has Bartók published any?) And another question: Have the Czechs in the USA (Chicago) invented a variant of English similar to their variant of German? If so, Kreymborg could benefit by it.

You must have received the contracts by now. Another copy of *Schweik* has gone out to you by regular mail.

Weill was going to send a new draft contract for *Szechwan*.

Have you heard anything about [Elisabeth] Bergner's première? (H. Hays has finally written to say that he has sent Czinner the new adaptation.)

        Love.
        bertolt

Be sure to sell them Kreymborg. That's the most urgent.

Santa Monica, 23 July 1943
[Postmark]

465 To Ruth Berlau

Love,

The solution with Kreymborg seems excellent. I'll borrow the advance from Lorre (I'd prefer to send the $150 direct to K, I mean, if you haven't given it to him already, I'll send it to you). As for Aufricht, the play is now my sole property, neither he nor Weill has any right to it, please get him to confirm this in writing (since he was unable to keep his promise to pay me $500 and the American author $500 as soon as an American was found). Even so I'll try to draw him in if a production should come about. Weill has written to me that some American writers had told him the play was too un-American for Broadway, etc. etc.; however, he thinks only Aufricht could swing an experimental production but doesn't seem to believe in the play. In other words, Weill would apparently let us use his name, that is, Aufricht can say he's going to write the music in the event of a production. What does Aufricht say about this? What's holding him back? If he can't start, I have to know soon, because then I'll try something else. But most of all I need the agreement with the Czechs, Aufricht must send me that at once, I can't do anything without it. The best would be for you to go with him to see Laurin and the lawyer. Promise them a copy.

Your wire was phoned to me this morning, but it hasn't yet been delivered. I assume that it acknowledges my letter. Right?

I'll write to Kreymborg tomorrow.

Another thing: Lilli Laté, Lang's secretary, has arranged with the San Francisco Museum for a showing of George Grosz's paintings. It was nice of her, because he'd get the pictures sent for nothing, (and he wanted to show here anyway), she did it at my suggestion. And now there's no answer. As I didn't know Grosz's address, Laté wrote to Wieland. Could you inquire? Laté doesn't stand to make anything by this, she did it as a favour. If Grosz no longer wants to show out here (and let the San Francisco Museum pay for shipping his pictures), he need only write a few friendly words. But that he should really do.

I'll write you a letter for Czinner tomorrow; I haven't got his address.

It's so good when you write at length, Ruth.

I close in haste and take my letter to the box.

J E D[1]
bertolt

[Santa Monica], Thursday evening [11 August 1943]

466 To Ruth Berlau

Love,

I didn't write yesterday because I was working with Hans Viertel on a treatment for Lorre. And then all of a sudden it was too late. It's really idiotic for you to be stuck in the New York heat when you're needed here, Ute. Of course what you're doing about the autumn possibilities is fine. (I hope to be able to send Lorre's cheque tomorrow.)

What is your exact objection to the last sentence of the text for Tillich? Of course the whole thing is wishy-washy twaddle, but even as it is nobody wants to touch it, it's incredible how cowardly people can be. Write to me about it.

[1] See Note to Letter 450.

Thank you, Ute, for your good, long answer to my question about whether everything is all right.

This is Sunday afternoon. Eisler is coming later to play chess. I still have a bad taste in my mouth from last night, there was a party for Döblin (he's sixty-five) and at the end he made a speech telling us we should all get religion.

I'd rather make some money and come and see you.

bertolt

Santa Monica, 16 August 1943
[Postmark]

467 To Ruth Berlau,

Love,

This house is much better than the one in 25th Street. It's old, forty years old, built in the days when Hollywood didn't exist, and the garden is pleasant too, neither as small nor as pretty as the other; in it one can even recognise the work of human hands, carried on over many years. But everything here is pervaded by the indescribable ugliness of the lie traffic. Even the fig trees sometimes look as if they had just told and sold some really contemptible lies. The early morning hours are almost the only time when I can write anything halfway decent. There's a morning mist, as the sea isn't very far away, only twenty-seven streets. I don't mean that the mist hides the area, which isn't unpleasant; no, I'm thinking of the mist itself, which reminds me of other places. So don't be impatient if you don't get the Moldau song for a few days, I'll work on it in the mornings.

The ugliness of the stories I'm involved with – when I think of your face, they get even uglier. I see you examining them for some human trait, an acceptable sentence, anything. Not a trace.

That in running away from Hitler we've had to hide in this shithouse – must mean something.

I'm proud of the Danes, even in Svendborg there's been fighting. This name on our little book[1] has very much gained in value. At any rate those friendly people have opened their little Second Front. I only hope they're not expecting help . . .

jed[2]
bertolt

Santa Monica, 31 August 1943
[Postmark]

¹*The Svendborg Poems.*
²See Note to Letter 450.

468 To Ruth Berlau

Dear Ruth,

I wanted to write to you immediately after our phone call Monday evening, but I've waited until this morning, Tuesday. I hoped my anger would have evaporated; it hasn't entirely. I got Helli to write at once to Karin, telling her to come. I didn't say she has a chance here for a story about Tycho Brahe; in my opinion she has none, she's not a child, it would be an expense for her and a gruelling trip, and I simply don't dare deceive her. I didn't understand what you said about Liesel Neumann; to the best of my knowledge she hasn't been here for some time, and if there's something she shouldn't do, I don't see how I can tell her or why I should or what I have to do with her anyway. After that, all you had to say was that you didn't know why I didn't jump at the idea of your bringing Karin here. This has been going on for months, and your main idea seems to be 'that I don't want you to come'. Your tone is hateful and ironic. This petit bourgeois theme that I don't love you enough, the stupidest and most contemptible of all possible themes, because it's so overworked and out-of-date and so unanswerable between two people, has become your standby. In case you've forgotten, I never wanted you to leave here. When you went to Washington you promised to come back. As I didn't realise until later, you had no intention of coming back. But I did realise that you had been unhappy here, that you were not satisfied with the amount of time I had, etc. and I hoped to be able to get to New York as often as possible, or even for good, in other words, act according to your wishes. We had no way of knowing that our time together would be under such a shadow, and I did what I could to dispel the shadow. Once again I arranged for my work and activities to centre on New York. Then came your financial difficulties, at a time when financial difficulties were beginning for me here too. The solution lay chiefly in New York and chiefly in your hands. I never got any letter from Aufricht or Weill or Bergner. Nothing was done except what you did. Financial considerations and the realisation of our plans made it necessary to abandon the idea of your holiday here. We never got the $500 I expected from Aufricht, you'd have been able to live on that. Bergner is supposed to pay $500 on November 1st, but that's a long way off. I doubt if it's any easier to find a job for you here than in New York. And supposing my trip to New York should materialise after all, then you'd be here and I there, and besides you wouldn't be able to help me make one of my projects work. Even so, I've written to you from the start that if you have to you should come here without hesitation.

If you'd think it over for five minutes, you'd understand the whole situation. But you prefer to keep humiliating me by saying that I prefer to perpetuate a petit bourgeois idyll here and that I'm afraid of your upsetting my domestic happiness. On the other hand, even a total stranger could see in five minutes that I'm not exactly that type.

I no longer know what to do or what advice to give you, Ruth, for I do know what your shift from love to hate, from friendship to enmity has already cost us.

                        bertolt

                                    Santa Monica, 7 September 1943
                                                    [Postmark]

469 To Ruth Berlau

Love,

I've received *Schweik*. I'm glad we finally have a translation. Of course it has as many mistakes in it as a dog has fleas, but that's natural, it's dialect, not ordinary German. By tomorrow – I've already started – I'll have corrected the first act, that is, taken out the mistakes, and then I'll be able to send Kreymborg my notes. It would be good if Hauptmann would go through it with him, because you may not know every construction or every (South German or Prague) expression. Could you arrange that? We shouldn't let the translation out of our hands yet, Ruth. It has to be corrected first. Some parts would be very hard to read because of the mistakes. But on the whole I have the impression that Kreymborg has found a good tone and shown that he can do it. The mistakes are easy to correct, the tone wouldn't be.

Thank you for arranging matters again. If you phone at five in the morning, it's two here, I think, and that night I was out late with Eisler or Kortner, that's all.

Please write regularly, I'll start writing to you again every day, Ute. And always tell me whether everything is all right. I'll get to New York yet, Ute.

> bertolt
> d.

> Los Angeles, 14 September 1943
> [Postmark]

470 To Alfred Kreymborg

Dear Alfred Kreymborg,

I'm very happy about your translation; the tone seems perfect, simple and powerful. I can imagine that it must have given you a lot of work.

May I correct a few mistakes straight away? The play is written in dialect, and certain expressions and constructions are not immediately intelligible even to Germans, especially North Germans. (On the stage of course it's all perfectly clear to a German audience.) I'm amazed how well you've managed. But perhaps a few passages can do with a little polishing. So I'm enclosing a list for Scene 1. (I.o. means instead of.) It would be wonderful if we could work together on *Schweik* in a theatre.

> Yours very cordially,
> bertolt brecht

I'm also looking forward to *The Children's Crusade*.

> [Santa Monica, beginning to middle of September 1943]

471 To Alfred Kreymborg

Dear Alfred Kreymborg,

Many thanks for *Schweik*; it has given me great pleasure to read it in English. It's a splendid achievement, doing a poetic translation in so short a time. The dialect in which the play is written must have made the work still harder. Ruth Berlau writes that she'll be glad to help you correct the inevitable mistakes. Please send me the corrections as soon as they're done, I want to show them to Lorre here, and perhaps I can contribute an idea or two. (We mustn't show the play to outsiders before it's corrected.)

And thank you too for *The Children's Crusade*. It really reads very well. I'd be so glad to talk with you about it. Do you think any of the big magazines might take it? Perhaps this autumn?

Yours very cordially,
bertolt brecht

[Santa Monica, September 1943]

472 To Ruth Berlau

Love,

Point by point:

1) the most important: Are you able to do enough for your anaemia? Please, Ruth. Do all you can. You *must* be healthy. And write to me about it, regularly and in detail.

2) Lorre thought *The Children's Crusade* was very well translated. The mistakes can be corrected. The one in the funeral scene is important. Of course the socialist can't possibly talk *'about his future birth'*.[1] He talks 'about the future of the living'. (This means neither more nor less than the future of those who, precisely like the little Jew, have not died. Everything religious must be thrown out, everything mystical must go.) And then the *vision* (*'and when I close my eyes I see'*[1]) is not quite clear, it's not quite clear that in the clouds I see other visionary processions above the procession of children which has been described. Kreymborg could bring that out a lot better. The last stanza is also misleading. Since the peasants read the dog's message, 4 (by now it's been four) years have passed. And the dog was already half starved. In other words, it's terribly urgent. The children are starving. Now to the new stanzas you've sent me. The first is better in Kreymborg's original, it seems to me. So is the second. About the third, I'm not sure. Nor about the fourth. The new fifth one strikes me as better. The sixth is definitely a lot better. Likewise the eighth (about the little mother). Who wrote the new ones? If it's not K himself, you must be careful about proposing them. (Perhaps you could give Weill the good new ones and he can say he did them. Do you think that would be all right?) I really think K's work is good. His working so quickly means a lot to us. The mistakes can be corrected. We shouldn't hold it against him that the meaning is often obscure in his first translation; lyric poetry is usually obscure and no one complains. Everything can be corrected, it's

[1]English in original.

much easier than striking the right tone, and K did that, in *Schweik* as well. I can easily fix the *Schweik* poems with him once I'm on the spot.

3) *Schweik* (without Weill). Eisler is ready to do the music; he has already done part of it, because he has done the *Kälbermarsch* and the *German Miserere* – for recordings. No problem there. The question is: how badly do we need Weill to get a production. I have nothing against Mostel. That would solve many problems. An American (and especially a comedian) would have a much surer judgement about what the public here would and would not understand. He'd be more productive. Less timid. Has he read the play? Can you find out what sort of production it would be? (In principle I have no ojection to Piscator's directing, but I must have the last word in the direction, that is, I would very officially have to be co-director). I'd been thinking along those lines myself. Is it perfectly clear that Aufricht has no further claim of any kind, since he could not keep his promise to produce the play (and to pay me $500 immediately, and the translator as well)? Get him to give you something to that effect in writing. On the other hand I'd have no objection to his working with us. Could you go with him to see the Czechs and tell them about the difficulties? And assure them that I alone hold the rights now?

The position with Lorre is this: He advanced me the money for the translation. (I'll send you the $100.) So my only possibility was to say to him: I have such and such an opportunity, can you too offer a production? He knows that I need the money badly. The more practically and realistically you can work out a production with Mostel, the more easily I can sell it to Lorre – or drive him to make a counterproposal.

Addendum to 2): In the stanza with 'Frie . . .' could we say something like: 'and on the side of the tank / only half the word "Friede"'[1] was written?

It's true that you're clever about my affairs. It would be best if you handled all my affairs. When I come again (or you come here) I'll bring everything with me.

(I ought to have realised that you'd already be correcting the mistakes in *Schweik* and wouldn't need Hauptmann in spite of the Prague dialect. Besides I'd rather have it this way, because I can't offer Hauptmann anything, and she isn't rich either.)

I'll send you the *Szechwan* contract tomorrow for French.

When you write about things like *Schweik* or *The Children's Crusade*,

---

[1]Peace.

you're as friendly and as wise and as close to me as if you were wearing the long white thing.

> d
> bertolt

Dear Ute, with me it's the same as with you. I turn all my thoughts to finding the best possible way of coming to you as quickly as possible.

> bertolt

Pencil won't last on the stone. But I'll write it again for you.
Ink won't take either, and the stone is too hard for a knife.
But what's on it means something Ute.

> Santa Monica, 18 September 1943
> [Postmark]

473 To Ruth Berlau

Dear Ruth,

I'm in despair about the *Schweik* translation, which I've now worked through with Steff. Naturally we haven't noted all the places where it's muddy or feeble, all the mistakes, only the most important, and there are an enormous lot of them. Even when corrected as scrupulously as possible, it will still be a rough translation and unplayable. We'll never get a production on the strength of it. Lorre and the Americans he's shown it to are greatly disappointed. What should we do?

I know you did all you could, and I'm terribly grateful to you, Ruth. But now you must absolutely help me to get a presentable version.

> Your most affectionate
> brecht

> [Santa Monica, September 1943]

474 To Ruth Berlau

Love,

Please write and tell me what our commitment to Kreymborg actually amounts to. If his translation is unacceptable, can we reject it? I mean, can we treat it as a rough translation and let someone else adapt it? I'm enclosing a short sample of an attempt by Gorelik (on the basis of K's translation and with my help). K's is so terribly slipshod. But it's good we have it, at least as a rough translation. Write to me about it, and also tell me if K is working on the corrections. I send them regularly, but I keep having to wait for Steff.

Why don't you write? Please write.

bertolt

Santa Monica, 25 September 1943
[Postmark]

475 To Ruth Berlau

Love,

I really don't see how I can do these *Schweik* corrections here. For the first scene I had Hans Viertel, but now he's too busy. (Gorelik and I have translated the love scene together, I'll send it tomorrow.) Of course I'll try to keep on with the corrections, but don't you think it would save an awful lot of time if we could get Hauptmann to help? (But I must say her letter to you is a big disappointment to me.) After all, it's not a first *draft*,[1] there shouldn't be any substantive mistakes. A lack of sparkle and elegance would be acceptable. It's too bad you've given him the $100, I hope he's still working, otherwise he's just a crook. You're quite right. It's dreadfully sloppy and irresponsible.

And *The Children's Crusade*, too. Once my suspicions were aroused, I went over it with Gorelik and Viertel. It's not publishable in its present form, far from it. At the most two or three stanzas, in all the others there are glaring mistakes or horrible rhymes, and all so heavy. You've made some improvements, but you're right, by no means enough. What shall we do, Ruth? Joe Fields is supposed to be good (though no longer young). A good comedian, some say. It would be a pity to lose Mostel. Is that final? He might have been the best of all. Maybe it's all the travelling that puts him off.

Please tell me about your anaemia. You *must* get well. You probably haven't got enough to eat.

I wish I could go to New York tomorrow.

(to be with you)
bertolt

Santa Monica, 27 September 1943
[Postmark]

[1]English in original.

476 To Ruth Berlau

Wednesday

Love,

I left Los Angeles at 7.15 Monday on the Scout. Here in Texas the train is already five hours late. Tomorrow, Thursday, I'll probably miss the two-thirty train out of Chicago. If so, I'll arrive on one of the next trains and take a cab to 57th Street. I have a key. I can't wait.

Love bertolt

Newton/Amarillo, 17 November 1943
[Postmark]

477 To Thomas Mann

Dear Thomas Mann,

You know how much importance I attach to attempts to foster unity among German anti-Nazis in exile, in view of the fact that the dissension between the two big working-class parties under the Republic was largely reponsible for Hitler's seizure of power. Knowing how much you can contribute to such unity, I feel obliged to tell you of the consternation you aroused in all the people I spoke to after the meeting by saying quite plainly that you doubted whether there is any appreciable difference between the Hitler regime and its following on the one hand and the democratic elements in Germany on the other. The representatives of the old working-class parties and Paul Tillich, the latter clearly on the strength of a profoundly religious feeling, feel that they have neither the right nor the duty to sit in judgement on the German people and that their place is rather on the bench of the accused. The crimes of Hitler Germany are patent. We exiles were the first to call attention to them and to summon a long incredulous or indifferent world to combat them. And it is also we who know of these monsters' crimes against their own people, and our people's resistance to the regime. Germany's conduct of the war shows with terrible clarity that the physical terror to which the regime has subjected the people has left them with hideous moral and intellectual deformities. And yet by 1942 more than three hundred thousand people in Germany had sacrificed their lives in largely invisible struggles against the regime, while at the beginning of the war no less than two hundred thousand active anti-

Nazis were being held in Hitler's concentration camps. Even today the anti-Nazi forces in Germany are tying down more than fifty divisions of Hitler's élite troops, the so-called SS. This is no small contribution to the defeat of Hitler. It seems to me that we who can contribute so much less bear a heavy responsibility towards those fighters. Accordingly, esteemed Mr Mann, all our friends are sincerely afraid that you, who more than any of us have the ear of the American people, may cause them to doubt the existence of democratic forces in Germany more than they do already; for the future, not only of Germany but of all Europe, depends on whether or not these forces are helped to win out. I am writing this letter because I am sincerely convinced that it would be of the utmost importance if you could reassure our friends as to your attitude in this most important of all questions.

> Yours,
> Bertolt Brecht

> New York City
> 124 East 57th Street
> 1 December 1943

478 To Wystan Hugh Auden

Dear Auden,

Last summer I wrote an adaptation of Webster's *Duchess of Malfi* for Elisabeth Bergner and wish to ask you whether you would be interested in a collaboration. I dealt very gently with Webster's text, but was obliged to insert a few new scenes and lines. These exist in English, but I believe they should be improved, and I have told Miss Bergner that no one could do this as well as you. The question for now is whether this would interest you and whether you could find time. I believe you could easily agree with Miss Bergner on terms. And with me as well.

Please write to me about it. As you can imagine, it would give me great satisfaction to be able to work with you.

> Yours very cordially,

> [Early December 1943]

479 To Ferdinand Reyher

Dear F.R.,

Of course I've again neglected to write, my old failing. I'll be in New York for a few weeks and I've been trying to work out a way of seeing you. I'm enclosing *Schweik*, which I wrote last summer. There is a rough translation, but it has none of the charm which, I hope, the original possesses. Do you think the play might interest you? Certain things would have to be changed for a production here, I know that. The main thing is to find the right tone. *If* you're interested, you might try a scene and see how it works out. It's a matter of luck, I think. The central figure is classical and definitely belongs on the stage. Weill was going to do the music, but now he doubts whether a good adaptation and translation is even possible. If I could show him a single scene, I'm sure he'd bite again, and with his name it would be easier to get a production. Please write to me about it.

Don't you ever get to New York? It would be wonderful.

How's the leg? A leg should only be broken once. There, too, moderation is in order. In Germany, which you're invited to visit, there will be many rough spots in the roads and for some time it will be necessary to walk properly.

As ever,
brecht

124 East 57th Street,
NYC [early February 1944]

Your *US* story is beautiful. And so useful. If only I could think of things like that.

480 To Heinrich Mann

Dear Mr Mann,

I'm writing on behalf of a Committee to establish a Council for German Democracy, to which Tillich, Bärwald (Professor of Catholic Theology, Centre Party), Lips, Budzislawski, Grzesinski, Hertz, Hagen, Boenheim, Walcher, Glaser, Maria Juchacz (a Social Democrat), Bärensprung, and Hirschfeld belong. As you see, all the old working-class parties are represented as well as the Centre and the religious socialists. We would like you to become a member of the leading committee. In my opinion it is a serious attempt to unify the German democratic forces in exile. The attitude of the State Department – as Thomas Mann has no doubt informed you – was rather cool at first but has now become quite friendly. I'd have been glad to report to you personally, but I can't leave here until the twenty-second, and the commission is eager to have your consent before that. I am enclosing a statement of the projected Council's basic principles.

With best regards,
Yours faithfully,
bertolt brecht

[13] March 1944

Tillich, Kantorowicz, Budzislawski and Lips have asked me to give you their regards.

481 To Karl Korsch

Dear KK,

On my return yesterday from New York, where I was sadly disappointed to hear that you have gone off to the South, I found your letter. At least I'm answering it promptly if not at as much length as I would wish. The main question of course is when do you have your holiday and might you 'drop in' (and not just between planes). I'll talk to Florence Homolka tomorrow. Steff is studying chemistry here at UCLA, but I'm not sure they won't ship him off to the army all the same. He opened your letter straight away and appropriated it, I only got it on loan. His reading courses are still going on, so it seems your teaching is still with him. Barbara is going to High School. She has written three poems, they're humorous, which cushioned the shock. I had money trouble for a good six months (now I've drawn a number in the Hollywood lottery that should last me about two years) and am trying my hand at commissioned adaptations (*The Duchess of Malfi* for Bergner and a new version of *The Chalk Circle*, that I'm still working on). I've also written a *Schweik* play. The Council for German Democracy owes its existence to mild alarm over certain imperialistic tendencies and has no connection with the committees in Mexico, London and Moscow. Its chairman is Paul Tillich and its leading committee includes representatives of the old working-class parties (Schreiner of *The German-American*, Walcher, Hagen, Hertz and Grzesinski), members of the Centre Party (such as Bärwald, the professor of Catholic theology) and men like Budzislawski, Lips, Pollock, and Heinrich Mann. It's against either eastern or western orientation of a democratic Germany, against partitioning, against intervention in the event that Germany liberates itself from Hitler and the classes behind him and against Pan-Germanism. What can come of it? An attack or two on the Ludwigs, Vansittarts and Ehrenburgs. In short, the Committee is an amusing cross-section. Characteristic of the development here, not of that in Germany. I'll have to discuss the practical question you ask (about your next year) with Steff, who knows these institutions. The monocle they're giving you here didn't do Karl Marx any harm; at least he had time to write books.

Obviously questions are a good thing if in answering one is allowed to forget them and if one can answer them in writing. I can only assure you that I feel the loss of every word you don't write down (*and that's a fact*)[1] It doesn't seem likely that the AMG we can expect in Germany will be made up of girls from your college.

Please forgive this hasty letter. It's only two months to the first of June, and I'd be so glad to see you here during the summer, regardless of what the winter may bring. (Not that I wouldn't like to have you nearby in winter as well.)

As ever,
bb

[Santa Monica, late March 1944]

482 To Paul Tillich

Dear Mr Tillich,

All the men I was asked to contact struck me as extremely interesting. It's just that everything takes time here, partly because of the long distances (and the petrol shortage) and partly because people are so busy. So far the following have accepted: Heinrich Mann, Fritz Kortner, Lion Feuchtwanger, Elisabeth Bergner, Paul Czinner, Professor Leopold Jessner, Berthold Viertel. Döblin, Horkheimer, and F. Lang asked for more discussion. Reichenbach wants to consult the officers of his university, but he personally is absolutely in favour. He'll be going on a

[1] English in original.

lecture tour in the next few weeks and then he'll speak to Einstein and others, who, he believes, will join, but will want to be informed through personal contact. Bruno Frank is very ill and can't be disturbed. Dieterle is busy with a film, I hope to see him in the next few days. (And through him is the best way to approach Bassermann.) I hope you people in New York aren't getting impatient, the interest here could not be greater, but each one of these VIPs is a small committee in himself, they all have to clarify their ideas and make up their minds, which as you know takes time, but they'll get there in the end. But what matters most, it seems to me, is the mere fact that we exist, and that's worth spending time on. I realise, though, that from the standpoint of the Protestants, who are the most important people to be reached, it is essential that the Council be set up quickly. But we already have a good many names and very good ones. (As I see it, just about all the names on the West Coast list will be available next week.)

What strikes me as most important now is a regularly issued circular letter to keep the members posted on the activities of the Committee.

There's a particular interest here in supplying German POWs with anti-Nazi literature, and in possible broadcasts beamed to Germany.

But everything, I believe, depends on steadying our pace, on normalising the infant organisation's breathing, which is bound to be rather spasmodic, and its reactions to outside impressions.

I look back with real pleasure on our discussions in New York. I took a most pleasant feeling 'home' with me.

> Yours cordially,
> bertolt brecht

> April 1944
> Santa Monica, California
> 1063–26th Street

483 To Ruth Berlau

Love,

Just to show you how lucky it is that you had a second translation of *Schweik* made: I gave it to Laughton yesterday, he read it last night, and he seems, so far at least, to be sincerely enthusiastic. Perhaps something will come of it.

Please write. Even if I am a poor correspondent. I'm always deep in some play. Wearing your coolie jacket. I'll send more material tomorrow.

Write.

D
bertolt

This is Sunday. Naturally Winge is here.

[Santa Monica, 2 April 1944]

484 To Ruth Berlau

Love,

The idea of making a novel out of *The Children's Crusade* strikes me as glorious. But you must be very free.

The cigars have come, I'm smoking one right now. And, love, I could use two more boxes.

Thanks for the detective story.

And even more for the keys.

How's the typing?

Tell Wieland when you get a chance that I like Weiskopf's *Anecdotes* a lot, an excellent choice for his first volume.

Here are some new scenes. Please always write to me about them. It's very important for me.

ddd
bertolt

Santa Monica, 5 April 1944
[Postmark]

485 To Ruth Berlau

Love,

I want you to insert the enclosed page in the scene where Katya[1] knocks down the Ironshirt, on the page beginning: 'In the peasant's house the peasant woman is bending over the basket', after the line: 'They'll be coming out from behind the trees, I shouldn't have . . .', then the page goes on up to: 'But if they ask for it' inclusive. Then

[1]Grusha in the final version.

comes a new page up to: 'He can't do that to me' and the last three lines of the new page take the place of the three top lines of the next old page, which continues with 'Knocking at the door . . .'.

Paste it up and bear in mind, Ute, that this is art and that I'll check up on you.

Ask Bergner what has become of the last page. Hays too. Love, you simply shouldn't have to worry about money for next year. Just take care of your health. (Dentist too, if you please.) I think you're beautiful.

Did I leave the *Threepenny* translator's attempts to translate *Schweik* there? If so, send them. Laughton would like to see them. Yesterday he read two acts of your translation to Eisler and me and Winge. He says 98 per cent of the play comes through and the translation is much better than we thought. Actually we laughed like mad, he understood *all* the jokes[1]! See?

And I'm sure I left the beginning of a poem there. The one about the Germans. Did I?

Write.

Tomorrow you'll get more C[aucasian] C[halk Circle].

> bertolt
> epep[2]

Santa Monica, 18 April 1944
[Postmark]

486 To Ruth Berlau

Love,

Your present has just come, I haven't been so pleased for a long time. I immediately spent a whole hour cutting three more black sheets to size and pasting up Persian and Chinese reproductions showing scenes like in the play. And now, Love, I can't wait to show them to you.

Here is more of the third act. The singer's style is rather different in this act. (We need variety.) How do you like it? I've heard some Arabic and Chinese records of epic singing, and much as the music varies they all suit the Singer's texts.

Most important: Could you give special attention to the last scene I'm sending (after that there's only the scene by the brook – incidentally,

---

[1]English in the original.
[2]epep: 'et prope et procul' – 'both near and far'.

have you got any notes on that?) You might even do a new outline of it, either making or not making use of the present version. I'd have liked to write this scene with you. It's a hard one to do. Please try. I mean, if it comes easy to you, otherwise some criticism will do.)

The *Galileo* business seems to be coming along. Not bad, eh? (For the autumn.)

j.e.d.[1]
bertolt
(Thank you)

A copy of *The Threepenny Opera* has come from Weill. I'm sorry I haven't sent you the money yet. I haven't been able to get to the bank.

Santa Monica, 20 April 1944
[Postmark]

487 To Ruth Berlau

Love,

Karin is nice and she's easy to have around but she works too hard. Those films with six carbons and a bound copy, all for $80. (Though I tell her she can stay here for years.) And last week she got me to drive her in to Hollywood at half past nine in the morning. A warehouse was auctioning off goods the storage hadn't been paid on. Including a lot of unopened crates and trunks. She had read in the paper that years ago someone had found a pile of gold in just such a crate. Karin sat there from ten to two, and nothing could stop her from bidding a total of $50 for some unopened cardboard boxes and trunks in a frenetic contest with other golddiggers.[2] The stuff arrived two days later. In the meantime Karin and Barbara, who should have known better long ago, were having the most sordid dreams of untold millions. The unopened boxes contained old kitchenware, a gramophone without a sound box, men's underwear, a broken clock, toothless combs, much mended children's shoes, door mats, calendars, and a douche bag without a tube. I was more depressed over the poverty of the people who had bothered to save this rubbish than Karin over her punctured dream of millions.

Ruth, Love. I'm delighted with your notes on *The Chalk Circle*.

[1]See note on Letter 450.
[2]English in original.

(You don't seem happy about the new scene with the peasant. Even if I tried to reinstate a certain friendliness?)

Is it bad of me to write about nothing but *The Chalk Circle*? I enjoy it, and then you're so very much with me.

Love,
bertolt

Santa Monica, 30 April 1944
[Postmark]

488 To Ruth Berlau

Love,

Please write and tell me if the two cheques are all right (and keep some sort of receipt or something for my tax return; it's for six months' collaboration. I'm a little late with the *CC*, because I still have to plan the fourth act. (And in the third act Eisler wants to combine the marriage and resurrection scenes. What do you think?)

Jeg elsker dig.

bertolt

Santa Monica, 2 May 1944
[Postmark]

489 To Ruth Berlau

Love,

I was playing chess with Homolka, we'd been to see *Memphis Belle* (you've got to see it), when Eisler phoned that the landings had begun. I thought it was late in New York, so I phoned because I wanted to tell you. – My only reason for not writing was that I was driving myself to finish the fifth act of the *CC*, I'm supposed to deliver it on the fifth or seventh. You must tell French that I've delivered the whole play to Rainer as agreed and wired Leventhal promising him a copy for 15 June. Perhaps the rough translation should be done by the woman who translated *The Threepenny Opera*. (But I'm not giving any percentages and Leventhal has to pay for it, as agreed.) I haven't written to Leventhal because I heard Rainer was coming here, and because Isherwood hasn't got time to do the adaptation. Now I'm suggesting Auden. (I only saw Rainer once, she's still going on about how disappointed she is that the play wasn't finished months ago. I already find her repulsive, and it's all right with me if she turns the play down.) Please get me an extension of the *Schweik* contract, so as to make it definitive for Europe and good for at least two years here. And in my name alone. That's important. – I got one more shipment of cigars, but that was a long time ago, and they're gone. Please send more. Or rather, ask when they sent the last lot. Thanks for the newspaper. Everything is all right, Ute. Write.

bertolt

When is your birthday?

[Santa Monica, 7–8 June 1944]

490 To James Stern

Dear Mr Stern,

I've received your lightning translation and it looks quite successful to me. (However, I've done a new version in the meantime and I'm sending it. I still hope we can arrange with French or the producer[1] for you to make the changes.) Unfortunately, I've heard nothing, nothing, nothing from French or Rainer about the project. Not even whether they are really trying to fix anything up with Auden. I wired about it, and I enclose the answer. Is that true?

I find it most unpleasant that they don't really seem to be trying to engage Auden. It means an awful lot to me. (I'd much rather have an imaginative free adaptation by him than a Broadway production.)

With most sincere thanks,

Yours,
bertolt brecht

Incidentally, I haven't got the end of your translation, I only have up to p. 114 inclusive. What about Auden's address?

b

Santa Monica, 13 December 1944
[Postmark]

[1]English in original.

491 To Leo Kerz

Dear Kerz,

Thank you for the letter, which gave me great pleasure. As I said in my wire, what I'd like best would be a production of the *Szechwan* play with a Negro cast (it could be set in Jamaica). Weill has no further connection with the play. Unfortunately there is no translation. The best would be if you could get W. H. Auden interested. He has just adapted the *Chalk Circle*. His friend Stern supplied him with a rough translation, which seems to be good. Especially if we are planning a Negro production, we need a first-class literary translation. (Stern, incidentally, works very quickly, and Auden is also said to work quickly.)

                    Yours cordially

                                                    Santa Monica, Calif.
                                                    1063–26th Street
                                                    January 1945

492 To Wystan Hugh Auden

Dear Auden[1]

I am very pleased to have your collaboration for *The Circle of Chalk* (by the way, do You think the title reads well in English?) and I am eager to read Your adaptation. If You do (or have done?,) the lyrics first, Eisler would like to get them as soon as possible. Perhaps Mr Stern told You that I made some changes – I send them to You.

                    Herzlich Ihr

                                                    Santa Monica, 1063–26th Street,
                                                    January 1945

493 To Karl Korsch

Dear KK

You know that my not-writing is only an old ingrained vice; really, you are observing the 'eye for an eye' rule too pedantically. I'm sending a little enclosure. Severe criticism desired. And, a tooth for a tooth, could I have some of what you've written in the meantime?

[1] This whole letter, except the last two words, was written in English.

Steff has been sent to the University of California on detached service. They want him to learn Japanese.

There's always a room for you.

As ever,

bb

Santa Monica, 1063–26th Street
[February 1945]

494 To Karl Korsch

Dear KK,

Thanks for your long and as usual meaty letter. In the last few weeks I have cursed these American distances, as I've let myself in for a laborious task, in which your help is absolutely indispensable. I am trying my hand at a didactic poem in the venerable metre of Lucretius's *De Rerum natura* about, let's say, the unnatural nature of bourgeois society. The core of it is the [Communist] *Manifesto*, which takes up the two middle cantos. A first canto is to deal with the difficulty of understanding the nature of society. A last one with the monstrous growth of barbarism. I'm sending you the second canto, which I wrote first, containing the first chapter of the *Manifesto*. My first canto will contain a cursory summary of the third chapter of the *Manifesto*, the critique of contemporary socialist literature. For the third canto (second chapter of the *Manifesto*) I'm trying to get hold of Engels's draft in catechism form and I would also like to have your *Kernpunkte* (Central Points). (If you send it to me Ruth will guarantee that you'll get it back in a few days, she'll photograph it for me.) I've numbered the lines so you can criticise it in a letter. Everything can be changed of course, and inserts are possible. Cuts desired, possible changes in wording, etc. etc. I imagine that the whole undertaking may strike you as aesthetically dubious, so you may not even want to bother with this page (actually I'd be grateful for criticism even then, even a question mark next to a lame or dull passage would be worth its weight in gold), but even if you regard the project as aesthetically sterile or unsuccessful, I wish you would straighten out the theoretical part a bit. Citing the number of the verse, you could make corrections or at least give me some clarification. I've changed a few things in the *Manifesto* as gently as possible, substituted insecurity resulting from chronic unemployment for the pauperisation theory, etc. Do you think that is all right? Otherwise, I've stuck pretty slavishly to the classical texts, and I think this is right, but perhaps I should express myself a little more freely. I believe the canto reads well; Weigel and Kortner think so. Please don't imagine I'm going to involve you in an endless task. I'm sure I can make good use of a few quickly dashed-off notes.

Now I'm going into the second chapter of the *Manifesto*. So now the classical authors will be answering questions. Should I smuggle in some new questions? It would be good if I could weave in some exposition (such as the account of unemployment in the canto I'm sending). Can you think of something?

(For my final canto, I found a magazine article drawing a comparison between street fighting and jungle fighting: that kind of thing is splendid.)

I hope you're not groaning too much, but you know, you'll be a teacher as long as you live, *so take it easy*.[1]

As ever,

b

Regards from all.

[Santa Monica, late March–early April 1945]

495 To Berthold Viertel

(Dear B V)

I haven't given anyone rights to *Private Life of the Masterrace* [sic]. I like your general idea, I'll think about it. But I'm still racking my brains trying to decide whether a production now would really be a good thing. Any reference to the 'sound core' of the German people, who are still displaying a very crude shell, takes on a very special meaning in the USA. It's not true that once the Nazi cancer is removed the healthy, valuable, 'authentic' German will be restored to life. You can't say: 'So and so is healthy except that he's got cancer'. The theory of the sound core would imply that the Western democracies should establish in Germany a 'healthy' decent, unaggressive, contemplative capitalism, free from crises (with book clubs, a law prohibiting uniforms, plenty of open-air activities, etc.) Ridiculous. But in reality, still from

[1] English in original.

the American point of view, the only way of suppressing Nazism is to suppress the German bourgeoisie, and naturally the proletariat will have to pay the bill. Please don't pass these rather radical ideas on to the Council [for German Democracy] (*it might not get my point*);[1] but I'd be glad to hear your opinion on the matter. I'm not saying that one shouldn't try to talk the Council out of its *tabula rasa* idea, which will be premature for quite some time; but the performance or nonperformance of these scenes does not strike me as the best occasion for such a debate. The Council's task, I think, is to convince people *over here* of the full extent of German imperialism, which goes far beyond the ranks of the Nazis. The best way to defend the innocent is to attack the guilty. The innocent, after all, have done less to help the peoples attacked by Hitler than the guilty to harm them; they are now regarded as accomplices because they were unable to help themselves. If people were to take a more lenient attitude towards the accomplices it would only be in the hope of stretching this category to include those of the guilty who backed the wrong horse. In short, we must do nothing to obstruct the total repression of the German bourgeoisie (including the physicists, teachers, and judges of *Fear and Misery*). Proletariats *must* help themselves.

Do write and tell me what you think about this.

Cordially,

b

Of course you can tell Elisabeth about my misgivings.

[Santa Monica, February–March 1945]

496 To Berthold Viertel

Dear BV

In discussing my last letter to you with a few friends, I discovered that it does not fully bring out the *tactical* character of my suggestion that here and at the present moment the *tabula-rasa* demand should be raised with great circumspection. The difference consists in whether one says 'Hitler and Germany are not the same thing, get rid of Nazism and the German people remain' or 'Nazism is essentially a principle and an apparatus for repression outside and inside Germany, and has deep

[1] English in original.

roots in the economic structure of Germany.' The first formulation ignores the fact that Germany before Hitler carried on an uncompromising class struggle, showed no sign of political balance, and under the rule of the Junkers and industrialists was characterised by the incurable pauperisation of the petite bourgeoisie, peasantry and proletariat. The reduction of Germany industry, contemplated for example by Morgenthau, had been accomplished in time of the deepest peace, when seven million workers were unemployed. This did not make Germany an agrarian state; on the contrary, the peasants were bankrupt. Etc. Etc. With such a conception, I feel certain, no state can be built, not even a German state. But in all our utterances, we should keep it in mind. De Gaulle's grab for the Rhineland is a grab for the throat of the French people. The East-Elbian farm worker will probably get land from the victorious Poles. *They* will settle him there after a thousand years of mere 'presence'. Here and in the USSR people are growing impatient with too much patience, and we too should adopt this attitude. It is one of the nobler impulses. The secret thought 'just leave it all to us' should not stop us from representing the fight against Nazism as an immensely *difficult* problem, which can no more be solved without force than by force alone. The important psychological fact is that the Allies did not go to war to save the German people but to destroy the imperialistic Nazis. Our task is to transform the second objective into the first.

Forgive the doctrinaire tone, which you really did nothing to provoke; I brought it on myself by my previous letter.

As ever,

b

Santa Monica, March 1945

497 To Naomi Replansky

Santa Monica, California
March 1945

Dear Naomi Replansky,

I have reread your poems and they impressed me even more than the first time. Curiously sophisticated Volkslieder. They have the youth, the verve, and the sensitive vigour of your great cities, virtues one expects of the contemporary American literature (but doesn't often meet).

In my opinion the publisher of this collection will one day be proud of it. Some of these poems I will translate into German; at least I will attempt it.

> Cordially yours,
> Bertolt Brecht
> [This whole letter written in English]

497x To H. R. Hays

. . . Thank you so much for the arrangement with your publisher for the edition of my poems, the specification of exclusive rights for two years is *fair*.[1] As to the choice: please write me which volumes of poems you have. I'll put together a group of unpublished poems for you. The second step is that we exchange proposals as to what seems best. Naturally much depends upon what pleases you and what you are at home with. There are some, of course, which seem important to me, so I should like to get up a list which you can then add to. I should like to have the opportunity to write to you this or that about the translations: I know one cannot 'correct' translations, nevertheless in the verses there are implications which may escape the most ingenious student of language and, above all, there are political implications which here and there we must discuss (lack of clarity in my writing, misconceptions, etc). I would at any time answer quickly – in the heat of actual work I can completely overcome my letter-writing-phobia. Again *many* thanks for your trouble.

> [March 1945]

498 To Ruth Berlau

> Monday morning

Love,

I was worried only because at about a quarter to one New York said your number didn't answer. I was afraid you were ill. When you said everything was all right, everything was all right.

You straightened that out with one bold stroke.

Important: Get yourself examined straight away for your fatigue (blood test). Now of all times nothing must be neglected. I need you in good health, Ruth.

How can we get those improvements out of Auden? We absolutely need them. By the same post I'm sending an old copy of the first version, but not transcribing the changes because it would take too

[1] In English.

long. Perhaps, if necessary, you can do it with Stern.

The verses under 'The Pokerfaced Girl':

> I hear the lords of Downing Street accuse you
> Saying you stuck it out, so it's your fault.
> They may be right, but how can *they* now choose to
> Condemn the people's strange reluctance to revolt?

I agree that we can't afford a cheap, slipshod production of *Master Race*. Bentley has the right to refuse his translation; but no one but me can give out production rights.

About the Council. Heinrich Mann must be highlighted. That will mean a lot to some of the people we'll be dealing with in Berlin. I'm sure of it. And in Paris as well he is just about the most important name on our list. It's important to realise these things now.

But don't run around too much. Take care of yourself, be cheerful. And eat properly.

bertolt

About *Master Race*:

Be diplomatic. I simply insist on a *very* good cast,[1] etc. I can only approve an excellent production.

[Santa Monica, March–April 1945]

499 To Ruth Berlau

Love,

Thank you for sending *The Chalk Circle* so quickly. I've skimmed through the translation. Some of the poems seem beautiful. All the poetry hasn't been done with the same care, and worse, Auden hasn't changed one word of the prose. I don't think it will do. It's Viertel who knows Stern best. He must go into action before they both fly off to England. Of course great tact will be needed. Especially as the reworked version hasn't been translated. (I haven't been able yet to correct a copy of the old *Chalk Circle*, it's a big job, how can we do it?) Have you given Viertel Auden's version to read?

I'm sending notes on the first two acts. Viertel might make use of them (with caution).

As you'll see, Auden has only worked on the poetry. The prose is by

[1] English in original.

Stern. Try and find out what people think of it. If he possibly can, Auden should look through the prose. It's a few days' work.

About our phone call: I wrote to you first thing Monday morning; everything was all right, Ute. It's just that I was still nervous on the phone, because of worry that you might be ill. Thanks for the explanation in your letter.

I must close now. Laughton is coming over to work on *Galileo*. (How would Elsa Lanchester be for Grusha? That too would have to be broached very tactfully.) Love,

bertolt

(Don't show Stern my notes in their present form. He might feel insulted.)

[Santa Monica, March/April 1945]

500 To Ruth Berlau

Love,

Here's the poem. But are you really sure it's all right with Viertel? It's a pity Auden hasn't done the whole translation. Couldn't we get him to do it? And his going away is practically a catastrophe. I'm so glad you're taking care of these things, Ruth. By the way, I miss you.

bertolt

The worst thing about Roosevelt's death is that it makes Churchill the leader of the western democracies.

Please write and tell me what our friends say – and not just about R's death.

Whom have you been seeing?

Please give Piscator the enclosed letter. Tell him of course I can't accept a job, but would accept an invitation that would get me a visa and transportation for a short tour of inspection.

[Santa Monica, April 1945]

501 To Ruth Berlau

Love,

After Mamoulian we could ask van Druten or Kazan. I'm sending a copy of the new signed contract, so you can show it to somebody and ask if it's all right (Reyher perhaps). If so, I'll send more copies. I've written to Bentley that I would not oppose a *good* production but that he has no production rights whatever. *I* authorised Schnitzler's San Francisco production and merely told him he should ask Bentley's permission to use his translation. Furthermore: Bentley can have (not as he supposes 50 per cent of my royalty, but like Auden) 33 per cent. I'll give Hauptmann 17 per cent; she was a big help and got nothing for her pains. I've written that to Bentley and I'd like you to tell Hauptmann. Another thing about the *Chalk Circle* contract: It has Auden down as adapter, but so far he has worked only on the poetry. How is that? Stern did his rough translation in a few days, and that's how it looks – absolutely useless. Yesterday we took Mrs Steuermann to see *A Tree Grows in Brooklyn*, you should see it too (directed by Kazan), Barbara was with us. Please take all these dry-as-dust lines as lines of love.

Have you been to see the doctor?

I'll send money next week.

I'm working again on *Galileo*, the *Manifesto*, and the Gorelik play.

> bertolt
> epep[1]

[Santa Monica, April–May 1945]

502 To Erwin Piscator

Dear Pis,

The disgusting part of it is that we just haven't time to think our theoretical differences through. Of course it's quite possible that the present balladesque framework isn't enough by itself. You just have to believe that, even if I were convinced, it's too late for me to make an artistically radical change (and the one you suggest would be radical, it would have to be studied carefully and then completely worked out). I'm very grateful to you for helping us to go on by letting us have your people and otherwise facilitating our work. That alone should dispel the impression (which some people might welcome) that we have become bitter enemies.

> As ever,
> brecht

[Santa Monica], Saturday 2 June 1945

[1] See note to letter 485.

502a To Berthold Viertel

July 1945

Dear BV

As we were still working yesterday afternoon, I was unable to drop in. In brief: 1) Please don't let E. Bergner draw you into conversation about the *Duchess [of Malfi]*. The slightest hint could lead to a demand for a complete reworking, hence a postponement ad calendas graecas. The play is finished. Of course I'd be grateful to you if you could convince her of my general competence and my feeling both for the Elizabethans (here you might mention my adaptation of Marlowe (*The Life of Edward II*) and for Elisabeth [Bergner]. (I have already written parts to order for actors, Steinrück, Homolka, Neher, Weigel.) 2) Important: the general's Salzburg Festival. I've spoken to Zuckmayer about it. Mention Kortner and Weigel, also Hanna Hofer and Liesel. Homolka should also be mentioned. And Lorre as Schweyk. I've spoken to Kortner about a new version of *Faust* (Part I and Part II in one evening). Klemperer would be glad to do *The Magic Flute*. 3) I wish I could have a few copies of the Austrian newspaper with your article and also the English article (for Laughton). 4) Keep pruning your poems. The best thing about them, apart from their richness, is their fragmentary quality.

And thank you again for your quick and wholehearted help, taking no account of your own interests, in the *Master Race* business.

As ever,
brecht

1063 26th Street,
Santa Monica
California

503 To Ruth Berlau

Love,

I'm writing this in my quiet compartment. Send the letter to Viertel. And send me a long letter from Piscator that I received a few days before leaving for Vermont and only half read. It's a criticism of the *Master Race* production. And could you phone Greisle? And apologise for me for not calling him. If the phone number isn't in your little book, get it from Steuermann. Please read the letters to Viertel and Bergner carefully so as to be informed about the projects. Also write to me about the *Duchess*. – I think it would be a *very* good idea for you to copy the sailor[1] stories.

They'd be good for Europe (e.g. the Aurora-Verlag.).

> Love,
> bertolt

[Santa Monica, July 1945]

504 To Ruth Berlau

Love,

I haven't had a letter for days, not since you went to Karin's.

?

I've also waited to write, partly because I've been working with Laughton the whole time, and talking English all day is so tiring.

Thanks for the photographs of the production. They're very good, some of them really beautiful. But the best are the ones where one sees the whole stage.

Reynal and Hitchcock have written that they want to give me a contract. That's wonderful, of course. Please write and tell them I'll be writing at the beginning of next week. I'll also have to correspond with Bentley.

(For that you'll have to tell me how much my royalty from the *Master Race* came to.)

On Churchill's fall – Laughton said straight away: now I can play *Galileo* in London.

But of course everything will be very difficult in Germany. When I think of it, I'm glad I'll have you, Ruth.

It's pretty boring here.

> bertolt

Do also send *The Chalk Circle* (the English).

505 To Paul Tillich

Dear Mr Tillich

The Potsdam Declaration will probably throw the Committee into

[1] English in original

something of a crisis – our nationalistic wing will have convulsions. A few of them have always hoped that we could quickly win the war Hitler lost. It strikes me as essential that on the contrary we should decide quickly and clearly to treat the new situation as a basis for the reconstruction of Germany. To me it seems definitely positive that Germany is going to be treated as an economic unit, since in due course this will lead to its being treated as a political unit. Anyway, to have a democratic administration built from the bottom up is better than establishing a central government, which in the present state of things could not have accomplished much. Besides, it seems to me that the occupation period has been made surprisingly short. I have the impression that the Allies plan to evacuate Germany some time after 1948 on the condition that democratic, anti-imperialist institutions have developed sufficient strength in the meantime. We can't help seeing that at present Germany is nothing but a subjugated capitalist state. Apart from a socialist solution, which cannot be dictated as a condition for a peace treaty, the only way to destroy the industrialists is to destroy industry. This would inevitably cause untold suffering among the workers, but I have always thought the old Social Democratic doctrine that the workers can only prosper if the employers prosper extremely dangerous. Really democratic institutions can accomplish a good deal. I still can't bring myself to see the Berlin metal workers as shepherds. I don't believe the Silesian workers will be worse off in a new democratic Poland than in a subjugated capitalistic Germany.

[The rest of the letter is missing]
[Santa Monica, August 1945]

506 To Ruth Berlau

Love,

I also tried to call you on the day of the Japanese capitulation. Waiting time seven to eight hours. It would have been morning in New York.

Laughton worked on *Galileo* until Friday night; his film starts on Saturday morning. But we've finished.

Now I could use the little Korsch-Engels book, as I want to go on with the poem.

Do you remember the people we met at Hella [Wuolijoki]'s? They asked me if I intended to go back to Berlin. I said it would probably take some time, but that then I would want to. They agreed and said they would help me.

You know, whatever happens, I won't make any plans without you.

I'm still hoping to do something with *Galileo* in New York, it would be important for several reasons. (If only we could do something with the *Chalk Circle* as well.) Why is French still holding back Leventhal's money?

Get well quickly. *Please* don't go out too soon!!!

> bertolt
> epep[1] Love

[Santa Monica, August 1945]

507 To Ruth Berlau

Love,

Could you work out in what concentration camps the other scenes in *Fear and Misery* take place? For Scene 4 take one that hasn't been used yet (Dachau, Oranienburg, Buchenwald, etc.).

Two young people who have been here will probably go to see you, Germans; you can give the young man (rather talkative) Sternberg's address and the girl some information about photography courses. They don't seem to be poor, so don't put yourself out too much for them. Maybe you can put them to some use, but do it circumspectly if at all.

I'll send you the English *Galileo* next week. It's been a lot of work. Now I'm back with the didactic poem.

If Dorothy's secretary doesn't throw up his job soon, he'll be a big drag on the Council, don't you agree?

> Love, I miss you very much
> bertolt

I'm waiting for letters.

Santa Monica, 12 September 1945
[Postmark]

[1]See note to letter 485.

508 To Ruth Berlau

Love,
It wasn't only about Döblin that I phoned; I could just as well have
written. But it was a good pretext. How long were you away? Where?
Was it nice?

The business with *The Threepenny Opera* is all right (You know, it ran
for years in Moscow); they were right to suppress it, I'd never have
allowed it myself. If there is *one* situation it's not suited to, this is it.
Galileo is on the playbill of the Deutsches Theater. I'll try to stop that
too, until I'm there myself (with you). I'm working hard with Reyher
on a treatment for Lorre. Maybe I can sell it.

Please write to me.

If I could only convince you that I'm all right.

> Love,
> bertolt

Just as you say, I'd like the contract with the publisher to be worded
in such a way that I won't have to pay out anything now. First of all we
should sign up Auden for *The Chalk Circle*.

> Love

[Santa Monica, September–October 1945]

509 To Peter Suhrkamp

Dear Suhrkamp,
Your letter was the first to reach me from Germany, and you were
one of the last people I saw in Germany – it was from your flat that I
went to the station the day after the Reichstag fire; I've never forgotten
your help in getting away.

We spent five years in Denmark, a year in Sweden, a year in Finland
waiting for visas, and now we've been almost four years in the USA,
in California. Of course I've written a good deal, and I hope we'll be
able to work on some of it together. (By the way: please tell anyone you
can that I implore them not to produce any of my longer plays, old or
new, without consulting me. They all need changes.)

I haven't been able to find out anything about Caspar Neher. I only hope
he has kept clear of stupid politics, because I'm counting heavily on him.
The fact is I can scarcely conceive of producing anything without his sets.

I'm sure you'll be able to give Jhering my regards.

And Legal, who after all owed his dismissal from the Staatstheater to his production of *Mann ist Mann*.

What has become of Hesse-Burri? And Dr Mullereisert?

You probably aren't able to correspond.

We've been worried about you and our other friends and hope to send you parcels as soon as it's allowed. Auf Wiedersehen.

> Yours,
> Brecht

October 1945
Address: BB, 1063-26th Street, Santa Monica, California, USA

Perhaps the American theatre officer will accept communications for me. (Mr Edward Hogan, APO.)

Heinrich Mann, Feuchtwanger, Leonard Frank, Kortner and Eisler are still living here.

Döblin is going to France – he's a French citizen.

510 To Donald Ogden Stewart

Dear DOS

It seems to me that the magnitude of your subject (The Intellectuals and Bourgeois Society) admits of (and demands) a certain crudeness of treatment. If we want 'neutralised bourgeois intellectuals' we must realise (and say) that the neutrality we have in mind will be an unstable condition – even DDT is effective only for a limited time. We tend to overestimate the 'pangs of conscience'; when the chips are down, most people would rather suffer pangs of conscience than be gobbled up by the sharks of society. The best radicals are not troubled by conscience; they possess, or are possessed by, a remarkable feeling for productive solutions to social problems, the kind of solutions that will benefit large numbers of people: they usually fight for compromises and keep within the limits of their class. In this connection , it is not without interest to compare Ibsen's dramatic work with Chekhov's. Ibsen saw solutions within the prevailing system; Chekhov saw none. The Scandinavian bourgeoisie had several decades longer to live than the Russian. Your professor is kept in line not only by threats, but also by a share in the spoils. Within the existing system it may be possible to solve the problem of his attitude to the Negroes, but never the problem of his attitude towards his assistants and colleagues (or for that matter his boss). (With regard to this last relationship: The scientific institutes might be nationalised as they are in Europe, with the professors enjoying life tenure, etc. but competition among scientists, the unproductive competition among sellers of the commodity science, will persist and the nationalised institutes will still be subservient to the bourgeois state.) There's something particularly funny about the guilty conscience of nuclear physicists; this species sees any form of regulation (compared with which, as they see it, the Holy Inquisition was a babe in arms) as a threat not so much to their jobs as to their actual work. The uranium curtain is descending on all science. In future they will be permitted neither to write letters nor to travel. If one scientist wants to condemn another to living conditions which up until now were known only to prison inmates, he will only have to bruit it about that his colleague has made a discovery in the field of nuclear physics. Compared to this, the possibility that our planet may tomorrow be blown sky-high is of merely journalistic interest to these gentlemen. In short, it's not the period most conducive to hope. The public will certainly not be galvanised into action by comforting references to 'the human decency which after all continues to exist'. It was easy to pour water in our wine; it will become difficult to pour the wine out of the water.

I am jotting down these few reflections because your idea of a comedy in which bourgeois astronomers discover a nova in the sky, and then conjecture that similar progress in physics and similar conditions must exist on this star, strikes me as most useful.

[Probably autumn 1945]

511 To Peter Suhrkamp

Dear Suhrkamp,

Enclosed is a power of attorney. I have put in restrictions to make it easier for you to say no, as I can well imagine how necessary that will be in many cases. The reconstruction of the German theatre cannot be improvised. Besides, you are well aware that even before Hitler I found it necessary, in view of the experimental nature of my plays, to take an active part in their first productions. As for Galileo, the only available version, the one that has been played in Switzerland, must not under any circumstances be produced, because I've completely reworked the play in collaboration with Charles Laughton, and there are still no copies of the German version. Seen from here, the most suitable of my plays would seem to be *Mother Courage and her Children*. But I wrote the leading part for Weigel, who in various productions in exile has developed a very special style for it. So any theatre that is interested in a production should arrange for a guest performance by Weigel. Of course I want to help your publishing house as much as I can. The easiest, I think, would be Songs and Poems. They are all available, and I'll send you things whenever I get a chance. Today I'm enclosing *The Children's Crusade*. Please accept it as a small personal gift (It seems to me that Ernst Busch and Kate Kühl might be able to use such songs.)

Please let me know at once if there is any way of sending you food.

You can imagine how glad I'd be to work with you again.

> Cordially, and Auf Wiedersehen,
> Yours,
> brecht

[Late 1945-early 1946]

512 To Elisabeth Bergner

Dear Elisabeth

Let me tell you briefly how far Auden and I got in two conversations.

In discussing Antonio, the main difficulty was that Auden regards the play as pure decadence and Malfi's 'affair' with Antonio as something she does out of devilment, to pit her will against her brother's, etc. In this case, Antonio can perfectly well be a kind of gigolo, silk stockings and bombast are not inappropriate, and he can also be cowardly and self-seeking. Tentative agreement: On the ground that it does not appear in the text, I retained the conception (deeply engrained in Auden) that Malfi is led by her 'perversity' to enter into such a marriage, and suggested that her marriage to a commoner (perfectly normal behaviour as we had it) should be regarded as an adventure, which then turns out to be fatal. In this way Antonio can become so much more powerful, more rational, and in his way more significant, and the family, which with the gigolo conception would be almost incomprehensible, would recover its pure and poetic normality. However, it is not necessary to keep the additions we made to the courtship scene; in this scene a few small changes will do.)

We thought of combining the first two scenes into one. This would involve keeping Auden's new lines, but putting different interpretations on the brothers' motives for forbidding the marriage, the cardinal's being shown as more or less financial, the duke's as mysterious.

Bosola becomes a *librarian, a frustrated scholar*.[1]

The midwife, stepping forward after the love scene and attracting Bosola's notice, is reinstated.

The short Antonio-Delio dialogue amidst the tumult is deleted, some of it is given to Cariola. (Delio can't be sent to the cardinal by Antonio, unless, as in Webster, the story of his mission is told.)

Something else we'll have to discuss is whether Ferdinand should get the letter with the news before, as I believe, or after being taken prisoner.

In the scene where Ferdinand surprises Malfi in her bedroom, Antonio should be more forceful and insist on his right to defend his wife.

In the excommunication scene, only the cardinal's first sentences should be in Latin; the third section, where the Church forbids all Christians to help Malfi, etc. stays in English.

That's as far as we've got. The discussion is interesting, Auden is very friendly and open.

Let me know if you have any objections; I have hopes that the love tragedy, really one of the most beautiful in all literature, will gradually crystallise out.

Up to now I've seen Ruth only once. Yesterday, for the first time, they gave me a more optimistic report, I may be able to see her again in a few days. I'm very grateful to you.

Yours cordially

New York
16 February 1946

513 To Eric Bentley

Dear Bentley,

I don't think there's any need of new examples to show you what a poor correspondent I am. This insight is one of the main reasons why I need expert help in bringing out the English edition of my plays. I proposed Elisabeth Hauptmann, who edited my *Versuche* in Germany, knows my work in detail, and most important, will be able to judge

[1] English in original.

every play's chances of being produced. This is how I envisage the work process:

1) *Selection of plays for the various volumes and choice of translators or adapters*: EH will let you know which plays I wish to see published first for the simple reason that they have a chance of being produced. (For Vol. 1 we must think first of *Galileo* and *The Chalk Circle*, because for them I have contracts with theatres.) Translators must as far as possible be chosen with an eye to the theatre. (Laughton is going to play Galileo in a version done by him in collaboration with me. Auden and Stern are translating *The Chalk Circle*. There I must be in a position to use my theatrical connections. So the last word must rest with me.)

2) All dealings with translators and adapters in connection with the published edition will be up to you. Also all business with the publishing house. You would also represent the edition vis-à-vis the press and critics.

3) Corrections. Since the translations must be revised with a view to production, further work by EH (if possible in collaboration with me) is necessary. (Example: In translating two poems from different acts of the *Chalk Circle*, Auden used different metres as he had no way of knowing that one and the same metre was needed if only for musical reasons. EH would have pointed this out to you. EH will forward corrections and suggestions from the author to *you*; thus there will be no interference with your dealings with the translators.

So as to avoid unnecessary delay (in case I cannot be reached or once again fail to answer) I will give EH *plein pouvoir*. This will enable her to write to you immediately.

You mustn't suppose that all this (it means a lot to me) is a mere question of jurisdiction. It's just that I see no other way of organising a close collaboration between us over a period of years. After all, I'm not dead like Ibsen or Sophocles, and the theatre, as you understand so well, is a living organism, subject to constant changes.

Yours cordially

514 To Casper Neher

Dear Cas,

I got your address from Kasack after asking around for months. Obviously the main thing now is survival. The best thing would be if we could start collaborating again as soon as possible. I've received inquiries for plays from Berlin (Deutsches Theater) and Heidelberg (Hartung), and in every case I'm going to insist on your doing the sets. In addition I'm negotiating for the production of two plays in New York (one with Charles Laughton) and I hope to find an official way of getting at least sketches from you, which would of course be paid for. Perhaps the British Embassy can help with this, I'll get someone to inquire in New York.

[April 1946]

[A handwritten postscript by Helene Weigel follows]

515 To Elisabeth Hauptmann

Dear Bess,

I've written to Czinner about your money; it can only be an oversight and it's most annoying; but I'm sure no disparagement of your work is intended; that would be an offence to me as well. There's no reason why you shouldn't give Czinner's secretary, Mrs Roth, another ring, you wouldn't be asking for a present, only for what's owing to you. I was more than pleased with your work and I'm well aware that even when the remainder is paid you won't have received your due. If my own finances were even in slightly better shape, I could manage these things a lot better, I realise that I'm deeply indebted to you.

Re the contents of the first volume: Actually only *Galileo* is ready. I'm sending Bentley a copy. Only you can decide whether *The Threepenny Opera* is ready for the printer. You must absolutely get the publishing house to help you with copying the corrections. (Hays has only given them one copy.)

Stern should get the $75 from Leventhal, the producer, not from me: it was from him that he got his first payment. The French agency should attend to that, Stern should phone them.

Maybe the prose of *The Chalk Circle* should be given to a young translator, Gerhard Nellhaus (75 Homestead Street, Roxbury 21, Mass). Bentley seems to have promised him translations. He has read the play in German. Perhaps he could do a sample (not from the Prologue). He should also see the rough translation.

Courage in Hays's translation also needs a lot of work; will he do it? There are many things that he didn't understand. And now, after the disaster with the poems!

And I need the translation of *Joan* so badly. I want Laughton to read it.

Czinner promised to get a few more copies of *The Chalk Circle* out of Leventhal. Mrs Roth should have them by now. I need one to enter corrections in that I did in New York.

Thank you for your work, Bess.

As ever,

b

Does our contract say how the money is to be divided with Bentley? Has he signed my statement of work procedure? I insist on credit for you; even if you don't want it, I want you to have it. Your name is (and will be) better than his.

[Santa Monica]
28 May 1946 [Dating: E Hauptmann]

516 To Ferdinand Reyher

Dear R,

Looking through my notes to your *Galileo* corrections for Laughton (he is awaiting them with great interest) I find that the notes to Scene 1 (One) seem to be in your copy. Could you send me this first scene? – Helli sends regards. She and Steff enjoyed your book *very much*, they'll write to you about it. This last trip was very interesting, it changed my picture [of New York] considerably. Helli thinks Maria knows about Reuss. So please phone her.

Again *many* thanks for all your work and Auf Wiedersehen here.

Remember[1] *Hotch Potch*.

[Santa Monica, May 1946]

517 To Berthold Viertel

Dear Viertel,

I don't know what (if any) progress has been made on that little handbook of exiles' literature. More and more I think it could be a masterpiece. The criticism of our achievement could outdo our achieve-

[1] English in original.

ment. The decline (continued vegetative existence, regrouping) of bourgeois literature is becoming evident, what with the increasing contradiction between the superstructural and substructural existence of the writers. The heritage ends up on the black market. Perhaps we should set up models for ways of dealing with these things.

Have you seen Orson Welles's revue? Wilson, his manager, will probably get you tickets if you mention me – I don't know if you know Welles.

Could you ask Auden for his adaptation of *The Children's Crusade?* You could intimate that you're writing something about it. And Laughton is waiting impatiently for an English version (for the radio and recordings). I mustn't press Auden, though; he told me straight away that he couldn't do anything before July. But tell him please that Laughton admires his ballad in *The Chalk Circle* enormously. He knows the difficulties.

What's your play about the Jewish family doing, that little gold mine. And the book? Altogether, *what's cooking?*[1]

Another thing: How is Hauptmann's health? If I weren't so really short just now, I'd treat her to a thorough checkup. I'm awfully glad she's able to do my work again. She's irreplaceable.

Don't eat any sweets.

As ever,
brecht

June 1946
Santa Monica

Regards to Wieland and Butsch.

518 To George Pfanzelt

Dear George,

I don't know what has happened but I have a feeling that you're still around. We've been in California for five years, and I hope to see Europe again at the end of the year. I haven't heard from Otto for a long time, and I have no address. How is Hartmann getting along? Do you think my house in Utting still belongs to me? If so – I didn't sell it – you can move in. I've gone on writing plays. ('The leopard can't . . .')

[1]English in original.

but no more about America, which is very badly characterised in my earlier plays. Charles Laughton, whom you may have seen in the film *The Private Life of Henry VIII*, is going to act in my play *Galileo* in New York next autumn. That's enough about art and business. Helli is keeping house, Steff, my boy, is studying chemistry, Barbara is in secondary school.

If you know an American soldier, he can cable me your address. (He might be more impressed if you ask him to send your address to your friend Peter Lorre, almost every American knows him.)

I hope to see you soon.

bidi

My address:
1063 26th Street
Santa Monica, California, USA
Lorre's address:
Peter Lorre,
1670 Mandeville Canyon,
Los Angeles 24
California
[Santa Monica, about the middle of 1946]

519 To Ferdinand Reyher

Dear Reyher,

The notes with your objections and improvements flung me into more work with Laughton, which we didn't finish until today. As soon as copies are made, the first one will go out to you. L ponders every suggested comma; he was very much inspired and his respect for you grew steadily. He's a great worker, and he appreciated your help, which really proved to be splendid. In the meantime we've signed up with Mike Todd for the production. '*That's protection*', said L. '*That's what you need.*'[1] We still have no director. Kazan wanted to do the play and spoke quite sensibly about it (what I liked best, of course, was when he said he didn't know how to handle that sort of play) but he can't do it before November because of a film engagement. Do you know Vincent Sherman?

Do you think Virginia Farmer could control her primadonna instincts;

[1]English in original

we'd want her mostly for the organisational end.

But I hope this letter finds you hard at work (on *Hotch Potch* or the novel about the photographer); in that case I'll gladly dispense with an answer.

If not, there's something else: a German by the name of Schüfftan, who is now doing independent productions, is interested in *The King's Bread*. Have you got a copy? I can't find one. Lorre isn't getting anywhere with *Macbeth*, they probably don't want to give him the title role. I'd feel guilty about drawing you into this if it hadn't turned out to be rather interesting; as it is, I'm sure something will come of it eventually. Schüfftan (he started out as a great camera man and the inventor of a few technical mirror processes, etc., then did some good things in Paris. He's a nice man, a real clown) will look you up, I hope. How is your health? Seriously, you should go to Switzerland or Denmark with us in the spring. Chess and *Hotch Potch* and the *American Histories* (each only 40 minutes long, but quite a few of them). It's cruelly boring here, I hope you'll come here in the autumn at least. My *Galileo* rehearsals will probably be in September. If I make some money, I'll buy a new car (Chevrolet); then we could do the East-West tour again.

Regards to your daughter. Thanks again for the notes.

Cordially, as ever

b

520 To Elisabeth Hauptmann

Dear Bess,

I've been wondering what sort of *Introduction* the collected plays should have if the reader is to adopt a productive approach. (And I'm assuming that Bentley is planning to write as an explicator, not as a critic.)

I think he should make it clear that the plays were written at a time of wars and revolutions. (In this sense it's a transitional period, but not in the sense that the gentle reader, sated with Ibsen and waiting for an Ibsen No. 2, may leaf through B. in the meantime.) Literature doesn't necessarily disintegrate at the same time as the social order; a part of it contributes to the disintegration of the social order. American readers may be interested in the fact that I also write poetry and epics and theoretical works. In all these areas one can find old things that haven't been seen for a long time, and some new ones which I hope will be seen for a long time to come (in the work of other authors).

The traditional element should be examined first.* Here we have the great themes, the great stories (inventions) and the great individuals (poets), and perhaps Bentley should describe this new portrait gallery: Kragler, Garga, Galy Gay, Begbick, Uriah, Callas, Judith, Dark, Mauler, Galileo, Courage, Puntila, Matti, Simone, Schweyk, Grusha, Azdak, Shen-Teh, Baal, Macheath, Peachum, Polly. As examples of themes: *The Good Person of Szechwan* (the fatal effects of bourgeois ethics under bourgeois conditions); *The Caucasian Chalk Circle* (Property and Justice); Galileo (Science and Society).

Then come the new elements (that will create tradition). Here you have two experiments of a realistic nature. (It must definitely be brought out that I am a realist and nothing else; obviously there's nothing unrealistic about the poetic element.) 1) My realistic attitude towards my theme (which is treated as a social theme). 2) My realistic attitude towards my audience (addressing it as a representative of society, in conflict with society).

My 'doctrinaire' attitude, supposedly outweighing the entertainment factor, will have to be dealt with, because others have so frequently remarked on it and criticised it. The criticism is largely a consequence of class divisions in the audience. People seldom feel entertained when their interests are attacked. In the days of the great bourgeois classics no one sensed any contradiction between the entertainment and didactic aspects, though both were certainly present. Even my method (dialectical materialism) is hard for the bourgeois part of my audience to accept.

It's too bad Bentley can't come here this summer. However, I'll put together a small collection of my theoretical writings for him. (Who, incidentally, is going to translate the 'Notes to *The Threepenny Opera*'? That's something Bentley should do, and put off writing his Introduction until he's done it.)

All in all, I'm glad to have Bentley in charge of the edition and hope he'll take advantage of this unique opportunity to do a piece of scholarly, i.e. careful, work. Otherwise there's nothing much being done but feature articles.

[Santa Monica, July-August 1946]

*Cf. the efforts of Picasso and Stravinsky to come to terms with classical forms.

521 To Eric Bentley

Dear Bentley,

It's quite legitimate your asking me to take your book as a starting point; I'm reading it slowly and with real pleasure. Your opening thesis that all recent literature is dominated by naturalism is illuminating, and I believe I see why you don't speak of 'realism'; for many people this would have removed the shock effect. Actually the new theatre opens up a view of human society as natural history, between which and the poetic or artistic view there is no contradiction. Just leave me a little time for my reading; such matters should not be disposed of in haste. (And by the way, your wife should translate your book into German straight away; I'm sure it will be easy to find a publisher for it, as soon as they start publishing again over there.)

The selection for the first volume is good, I believe. Only I'd like to read the translation of *Joan*; and perhaps *Señora Carrar's Rifles*, the little Spanish play, should be included; not because it's very important but because there should be something contemporary in the first volume. It has been done into English, I think, though perhaps not very well. Laughton has begun to translate the *Chalk Circle*. (Azdak is a perfect part for him). As the second volume would be a good place for *The Visions of Simone Machard* (a play about the fall of France) I'd like to send it to you as soon as I've revised it. Perhaps you'd be interested in translating it.

In the meantime best regards and thank you for the book.

> Yours,
> brecht

Galileo goes out to you next week. The latest version has just been finished.

> [Santa Monica, July–August 1946]

522 To Eric Bentley

Dear E B

What makes writing for or about the theatre so difficult at the present time is the mixed smell of corpses and prosperity in the air; the most recent product of the bourgeoisie was fascism, and it has been defeated, or rather to judge by recent reports, it has not been defeated and is reappearing in the form of 'Neo-fascism'. And the 'new era' seems to be the era when the earth will parade as a nova. Thus the period of decline becomes a 'period of transition', which means a second rate period. Consequently freshness in the arts has to spring from the individual, and one must be careful not to remove it from the refrigerator. Thus the People's Theatre of the dialecticians takes on a Utopian quality, and we've had Utopias before, they're old stuff. What I like about your method is that you always start from scratch. Only it's important that we should stand by our own times, interpret their 'transitional character' as their potential greatness, and refrain from flirtation with the so-called periods of 'fulfilment' (pipe dreams about the good old days).

It is quite right, I believe, to regard bourgeois naturalism (with its social reformism) as a prelude to the new theatre; but to arrive at a 'great' period of the theatre, we must go back a lot further than Ibsen, namely, to the revolutionary period of the bourgeoisie. Quite apart from the poetic element, the reflection of reality in Ibsen is very muddy if you compare it with Shakespeare. And what monotony and rigidity of form. And when he pictures reality in order to influence reality, he does it in such a way that reality becomes an utter illusion (elimination of the 'fourth wall').

In all this, I am not claiming the predicate 'great' for any particular theatre; I am only attacking the usual neutralising treatment, towards which you yourself are not always severe enough. I am referring to the reassuring observation that these are temporary, tentative, noncommittal endeavours, in a word, experiments, whereas in reality we are faced with a tendency to establish the experimental as a definitive function of the theatre. (Thus F. Bacon's experiments were not the crucial factor; crucial was his definitive introduction of experimentation into the sciences.) The very divergent forms of theatre are certainly not attempts to arrive at a definitive form; the one thing that should be definitive is diversity of form. And the introduction of experiment into drama is not just a matter of form. Actually the audience should be transformed into social experimenters, and critique of the reality shown should be tapped as a main source of artistic enjoyment.

I don't know if you mean to raise all these questions; if so, we should talk about it. I'm sending you an outline that might, I believe, be useful; but it's only a suggestion.

I'm also sending *Galileo*. I only got the copy yesterday, as the whole thing had to be reworked. I'd like to keep *Joan* for another few days. Hauptmann will be here at the end of August; that will make everything easier.

> Yours cordially,
> brecht

> August 1946
> Santa Monica

> (Enclosures)

Possible points:

That the plays were written in times of revolution and world war. In periods when social orders are disintegrating literature does not necessarily disintegrate. Some literature is one of the factors of disintegration.

1) Continuation of *tradition*. (Significant themes, rich plots, great 'roles'). Analysis of the themes. The disastrous character of bourgeois morality under bourgeois conditions in *The Good Person of Szechwan*. Productivity as the foundation of a new morality in *The Caucasian Chalk Circle*. Truth as a commodity in *Galileo*. Goodness without understanding in *St Joan of the Stockyards*. Etc.

Analysis of the plots.

Analysis of the roles. Baal, Galy Gay, Callas, Jane Dark, Mauler, Galileo, Courage, Simone, Schweyk, Grusha, Azdak, Shen-Teh, Peachum, Polly etc.

(Compare the strivings of Picasso and Stravinsky to come to terms with classical forms.)

2) The new dialectical realism.

a) Realistic attitude towards the theme.

b) Realistic attitude towards the public.

We must explode the myth that in this sort of drama the 'doctrinaire' overshadows the 'entertaining'. This impression comes from a class conflict in the audience. (Classes whose interests are under attack seldom feel entertained!) The bourgeois classics and the works of antiquity have both – instruction and entertainment – and no contradiction is felt.

Question: Will you translate the 'Notes' on the *Threepenny Opera*?

Incidentally: It may interest you to know that the notices I've received from Vienna, where *The Good Person of Szechwan* was played last summer, are absolutely idiotic; the poor fools take everything symbolically, they interpret a conflict between Shen-Teh and Shui-Ta as an eternal, universally human conflict, etc. The difference between a symbol and a parable should be made clear once and for all. In a parable a passing historical situation (i.e. one that should be made to pass) is depicted realistically. The rending in two of Shen-Teh is a monstrous crime of bourgeois society.

523 To George Pfanzelt

Dear George

I've heard from my brother and from Otto that you're alive. We've been in California for five years and are well. Santa Monica like Hollywood is part of the city of Los Angeles (City of the Angels), and to tell the truth this is exactly how I always imagined the angels. Otto tells me your house is in ruins, and I imagine that a walk down the Lech will be rather depressing. But now at least there's a possibility of our seeing each other again. Though it's not all that simple from here. We've tried now and again to send packages by a roundabout route; I assume that none has reached you, because the return address was on them and you would have written. I have to send this letter (and another package, this time by a rather more reliable route) to your old address, in the hope that it will be delivered to you in Haunstetten[?]. Cas has written to me from Hamburg. I know that Hartmann is dead. Write to me. If the (C A R E) package* reaches you, we'll send them regularly. (Let me know if there's anything special you need.)

I'm glad the world still has you in it. Regards to your wife.

Bertolt Brecht
1063 – 26th Street,
Santa Monica, California,
U S A
4 August 1946

*Sent to your old address, Klauke Strasse 20. [Brecht's note]

524 To Ferdinand Reyher

[Santa Monica], August 1946

Dear Reyher,

Thanks for the letters. I've taken care of the *Norman* business. The translation was so bad that I sent it to Bentley to correct and notified Norman. Now to Clurman. It's a ticklish affair. He's a Stanislavsky man. And in all the many things he said to me (on the phone) and wrote there was never the slightest mention of co-operation in the theatre. He doesn't seem, for instance, to have heard that I've directed more than he has and that there is in my work a new dramatic style, which he can't fathom by listening to his own heartbeat. In other words, the first thing he should be made to understand is that half his activity should consist in learning, in tactfully assisting for a time. And how can we get him to stop psychologising, since this *approach*[1] won't work with my plays (Laughton agrees). If he could understand and appreciate this methodological consideration, he would be a distinct possibility, because he's an intelligent critic and is interested in theory. Could you find out how he feels about it? (Does he know that I keep a close watch on groupings and movements, etc.? For Chekhov he has the printed stage directions. His job would be to teach the actors an unfamiliar acting method.) In short, if he wants to study and produce while studying, this is his chance. We do not need a 'basic artistic concept', a 'directing personality', or a 'creative centre'.

I'm sending you the latest version today; a little worried of course.

As ever,

b

526 To Ferdinand Reyher

Dear Reyher,

Many thanks for the letter, from which I gather that you've survived the invasion. Steff will probably show you New York, so you'll have something to tell people about when you get back to Büdingen. (And by the way, things are beginning to look as if it might be a good idea to look around for some ruins to hide under; science is just making too much progress.)

Your criticism of the last version of *Galileo* seems justified. In fact, I've started entering your corrections in a fresh copy for the printer, I'll struggle through it again with the help of the director (it will probably be Joe Losey). It worries me that you don't seem to like the change in

---

[1]Englsh in original

the sunspot scene; it's the only big one, I think. But I won't bother you any more with this if I can possibly avoid it.

I'd very much like to start on the short stories about American history that we talked about. This continent is becoming more important every day (and amusement harder to come by).

Yours cordially,

b

I'm enclosing something for Steff.

[Santa Monica, August 1946]

527 To Paul Czinner

Dear Dr Czinner,

A few points concerning absolutely necessary changes:

1) The lights must be much brighter, since the long speeches in verse are almost impossible to understand.

2) The actors must be regrouped in such a way that they won't have to say speeches which are hard to understand (and which they do not enunciate perfectly) with their backs to the audience.

3) The adaptation supplied by Auden and myself must absolutely be reinstated. I mean it, no cuts must be made without our consent. Nor should additions from Webster's original play be made without consulting us (since the adaptation consists partly of carefully considered cuts, which were discussed with Elisabeth Bergner and approved by her).

4) Ferdinand is miscast, as Elisabeth agrees. Furthermore, the director misinterprets the role, as you and Elisabeth herself have said; and to such an extent that the meaning of the whole play is drastically obscured and distorted. You must find another Ferdinand.

5) Nearly all the scenes must be reworked (from the standpoint of direction) so as to make the story intelligible to the audience. I suggest that you put in a different director. The present director has paid no attention to the adaptation and seems in general to be incapable of directing in such a way that the audience can follow the plot. (The London critics, I hear, also complained of the 'obscure plot', when he directed Webster's original.)

Please let me know by Monday 30 September what you plan to do about these points.

Yours,

Bertolt Brecht

Boston, 26 September 1946

528 To Stefan S. Brecht

Dear Steff,

Thanks for the Luther quotations, which well demonstrate the pathetic nature of the early bourgeois opposition (and remind one of the Social Democratism and Fabianism of the proletarian opposition.) I think you are right in saying that I should have defined Galileo's progressiveness more closely. But he is not 'for the peasants' when he contradicts the physicist-monk and the landowner, he is against the subhuman conditions to which they are reduced. (In the last – I hope – version I have secured the end of the eighth scene against misinterpretations.) Actually G does not simply advocate the free practice of his profession (which he recognises as a link in the ideological chain which holds down the peasants and the bourgeoisie, and which it is up to him to saw through). He saws rather cautiously. First, in Padua, he doesn't so much as mention Copernicus; then he finds proofs and decides to make a career with them, goes to Florence, grovels before the prince and submits his proofs to the papal astronomer. His proofs are acknowledged but he is forbidden to draw inferences from them. For almost ten years he complies and is again silent. Then he relies on the liberal Pope (not on the people or the bourgeoisie) and when the Pope leaves him in the lurch he submits totally and publicly. While imprisoned, he collaborates shamelessly (in the play) and allows his main work to be stolen from him – meanwhile suffering violent stomach cramps. I really believe that the 'attractive' quality which irritates you is his vitality.

[September–October 1946]

529 To Caspar Neher

Dear Cas,

I'm glad you're in Switzerland; it's so important now to survive (completely) and that means food, heating and medicine. Even the Man of Water and Fire needs them. Now and then.

For Georg too, we can do more outside Germany. I've spoken to Weill about it. Your presence in Germany can do no good at all.*

The theatre here (the whole continent has only a single street with theatres on it, Broadway) is the most cold-blooded merchandising of evening entertainment, a branch of the narcotics trade operated by gamblers. No idea can be expected from here, at the most dollars. (But that's not so easy, money doesn't just stink, it thinks too.)

It would be best if we could work together for a few years in northern Italy or Switzerland, concentrating on theory and occasionally working up a play for Germany. If we make your sets obligatory, like music, it will mean more money for you. It would be nice if the Theater am Schiffbauerdamm in Berlin, for instance, were available to us again. Geis would have to manage it, I think. (Which reminds me: what has become of Hesse-Burri?) At the moment, though, I'm lacking a passport and a few visas.

I don't think I have any illusions about the extent of the destruction. But some useful things can be done straight away, and for other work we'd only need a minimum of practice.

Have you read *The Caucasian Chalk Circle*?

You don't seem to have received some letters (and parcels) I sent to Hamburg.

I fervently hope you can stay in Switzerland.

Yours cordially

b

[New York, end of October 1946]

*To judge by everything I can find out here, it's likely to be years before we hear anything from the East. That's bad Cas, but it's best to be prepared for the worst. [Brecht's note]

530 To Caspar Neher

Dear Cas,

I posted a letter to Zurich today and now I'm sending this one in the hope that at least one of them will reach you. If you possibly can, I think you should stay in Zurich, because the search for Georg can be conducted more easily from outside Germany (and, especially important, in Switzerland you won't be likely to get involved in certain political quarrels – which would only interfere with your search and detract from our work).

Do you remember the big panels you made for me (with Indian ink and a knife) ('Baal with the two coats' and 'Leprous old age instructed by youth')? They're in Sweden. Couldn't you make another? And start by sending me a photograph of it? I need something of the sort.

As ever,

b

In New York at the moment. Back to Santa Monica soon.

1 November 1946

531 To Caspar Neher

Dear Cas,

Thanks for your letter which I found here on my return from New York, the one from Zurich too. You don't seem to have received any of the parcels I sent you, or got other people to send by various routes. From now on I'm going to ask my publishers in Basel (Reiss-Verlag) to try something. I want them to send you *Galileo* too. I'll write to you later on about the style of the production. At first I tried in every possible way to get them to bring you over to do the sets, but apparently it can't be done. The trouble is I'm really worried about your survival, Cas. If you could get to Zurich for just one theatrical season. I've written to Suhrkamp in Berlin that every theatre wanting to produce anything of mine must commission the sets from you (he has a sort of power of attorney for me). I'm convinced that we'll build up a theatre again; really no one but you and me can do it. The only trouble is that everything has to be organised. At the moment I'm working on a possibility of getting to northern Italy, where a big publishing house is bringing out an edition of my collected plays (in Italian); perhaps we could stay there together for a while and forge plans. Of course you could bring Erika [Neher] along as your assistant if that's the only way of getting visas. (I have a strangely vivid memory of Positano.) Write and tell me what you can do, what you want me to do, etc.* (Incidentally, my country house in Utting on the Ammersee still belongs to me as far as I know; I can send you an authorisation to move in any time you like if you have anything to do in Munich.) I can't help wondering how many more times you'll be a sergeant-major and how many times after that we'll start putting on plays again. This time I've had the opportunity (that I didn't exactly ask for) to visit many countries, and I can inform you that I have nowhere found anyone capable of doing the sets for my plays (or others) – which I hope will give you some little satisfaction. I also take the liberty of reminding you or your *Hydatopyranthropos* (*Man of Water and Fire*), major nisi Himalaya / tamen Monte blanco, semper aequam servens mentem.

As ever,

b

Santa Monica, Calif.
1063 – 26th Street,
USA

*I could probably get you an official invitation from a theatre in Milan. If you . . .
Weill has got rich on Broadway, I've sent him your address.
He has much better connections than I have.
Helli is well and sends her *best* regards.
If you pass through Augsburg, go and see George Pfanzelt (Klaukestrasse).
Don't mention the northern Italy plan to anyone. [Brecht's note]

[December 1946]

532 To Caspar Neher

Dear Cas,

It's no wonder that in starting to rebuild they're trying to make everything as hideous as before. And not just in the theatre. But as they persevere, so will we. They will rebuild the old abscesses, but there will also be other building. The Nazis carried their tragic fate down with them; now the Parisians are fishing it out of their sewers and calling it existentialism. Here they're doing a bit of surrealism before establishing realism, i.e. as an ersatz. The same old black market opium is being served up in the theatres everywhere. We'll put on our own show and among other things make very sure we enjoy ourselves. Dieterle has given me a good account of the ruins, and my guess is that he missed some of the foulest smells. I have never regarded Nazism as an excrescence but always as a consequence of perfectly normal development. The pus stinks of course, but as long as the boil is closed, the flesh over it looks flourishing. The two of us might do something splendid with the Aristophanic revue form, with lyrics, etc. Then there are the small forms we attempted in *Die Massnahme* and the little revue (with Busch and Weigel). In the parables (such as *Chalk Circle, Szechwan, Spitzköpfe und Rundköpfe*) I'd like to go far in the direction of virtuosity. Dessau's music for *Mother Courage* is really brilliant, such a play must be produced in the noblest Asian style, delicately etched as though on gold plates. For *Galileo*, too, I've thought of a stage like an exhibition stand. (Let's say, upstage to the right and left tall, thin brass surveyor's instruments, in the background prospectuses with reproductions of old prints, the action being plastic and gestic, with drawable scenes; Scene I, for instance, broken up into five subscenes: 1. 'The boy Andrea Sarti, later Galileo's favourite student, gets himself a free lesson from the great Galileo by the little trick of showing interest.' 2. 'While his pupil rubs his back, Galileo proclaims the dawn of a new era.' 3. 'Lack of funds forces the great physicist to take on a rich student rather than an intelligent one.' 4. 'Galileo demands leisure in which to demonstrate his hypotheses; the university authorities demand inventions that will make a profit.' 5. 'To get money, Galileo constructs his telescope according to a traveller's description of a new Dutch instrument.') We could do that very nicely with Homolka, I think.

I am working on getting to Switzerland about June, I've had offers from Berlin to use the Theater am Schiffbauerdamm for certain things – this last, Cas, must be kept strictly between ourselves. I haven't come to any decision about it, in any case I'd need certain actors from here and from Switzerland etc. I hope it will be possible in the meantime for a company to give guest performances all over Germany, during the next season, that is. The main thing is for us to keep in touch and make plans. I fervently hope the Reiss agency will do all it can to enable you to stay in Switzerland till I get there. Couldn't [Lazar] Wechsler help you to make some money in the cinema? I'm planning to work with him and I'll write to him about it.

> As ever,
> b

> Santa Monica
> December 1946

534 To Erwin Piscator

Dear Pis,

I'd be interested in knowing how you feel about theatrical operations in Berlin. Of course everything one hears from there sounds depressing, it's not just the buildings that are badly damaged. I'm always being asked to authorise the production of plays, but so far I haven't authorised any. They can't be cast; what I hear about the prevailing style is revolting and in the theatre bad is not better than nothing. Besides, muddling along is hard on the mud. I'd have to be there. But whenever I've spoken of a visit, I've raised the question of a visit by you as well, as I find it hard to conceive of a successful campaign against provincialism, empty emotionalism etc., and for a great, politically mature theatre without you. My idea is not that we should start a theatre together, though as before, you can always count on me to help with projects of interest to us both (i.e. most projects). We should at least operate from two different points. But do you want to? If so, we should work out a plan and send it over.

Cordially as ever,
brecht

Santa Monica, 1063 – 26th Street
February 1947
My new address

535 To Erwin Piscator

Dear Pis,

Let me go on record as saying that of all the people who have been active in the theatre in the last twenty years, no one has been as close to me as you. But I believe, and in this I see no contradiction, that we need *two* theatres. The reason is not only that we must occupy at least two points in order to establish the ideas that we both hold; for a part of my work I must develop a very definite directing style which differs from yours. This is my only reservation, and I think it is a productive one. You of all people can't believe in a mechanical distinction between playwrights and directors. Nevertheless we work along the same lines (and face the same resistances). Actually, I'm working just now on an idea that we would best carry out together. A kind of Aristophanic revue, showing the war god returning from a war that has gone wrong to a ruined country. He is lame, half blind and prepared for any concession if only his presence in the lowest of hovels is tolerated. (A part for Bois, for instance.) The war god and the goddess of commerce (and industry) are bound together by an old, indestructible love, as powerful as that between Tristan and Isolde. In other words, the goddess despite all the sorry experience she has had with the war god, is sexually dependant on to him etc. etc.

Scenes of action: The black market, etc. – The main thing, it seems to me, is that we should work towards getting them to bring back exiled actors (Weigel, Kortner, Lorre, Homolka, Bois, even though some of them would be interested only in guest performances for the present.) What would you like best to start with? We should suggest concrete things that can be done if enough refugees are invited (Rewalt, Roth, Neumann, Donath, Haas etc.) Please write to me about it.

[Santa Monica] March 1947.

536 To Ferdinand Reyher

Dear Reyher,

Once again many thanks for your quick help in the Lorre business. It's not only that I like him, I also need him badly in Germany, if I'm going to get my theatre together again. Writing plays has become a complicated, many-sided profession; now I'm trying to disentangle, Lorre's muddled affairs. Obviously he's fallen into the hands of a racket. Just like Laughton, Lorre is living in shamefaced poverty with four horses and several Japanese gardeners in a $50,000 villa.

We've applied for exit and re-entry permits; Helli and Barbara already have positive answers, but the photos on my application weren't big enough; I hope that's the only trouble.

I'm no longer sure about the food situation in northern Italy, maybe Italian Switzerland would be better (the Lugano region). I'm making enquiries. I still hope you'll be coming with us.

Could you send me that Reuss article, so we can translate it for Berlin? Laughton will have finished filming by the middle of April. What will happen then is uncertain. Perhaps you could ring Losey (in Ruth's flat), he knows more than I do.

How's the novel going? Aren't there any *bottle necks*[1] [sic] for me?

> Cordially as ever
>
> b

> Santa Monica
> March 1947

[1]English in original

537 To Ferdinand Reyher

Dear Reyher,

It's absurd that the gentlemen of the medical racket[1] still haven't discovered the cause of those damn nosebleeds. You really should have a general checkup[1] at the Medical Centre. So far we've got our exit[1] and re-entry permits.[1] I'll keep you informed. I've never heard anything about Columbia being interested, there seems to be some mistake. Of course we'd sell if at all possible; we'd made up our minds to it. [Lewis] Milestone showed some interest but met with opposition from his box office.[1] He's still interested but at the moment he's cutting his latest film in New York. I hope you're getting a rest, you were running round too much. In Switzerland (or Italy, I haven't had any reliable reports) we'll see that you get proper care.

As ever,

b

If you can, you should see Malraux's *Man's Hope* film. And Chaplin's latest picture, which should be called *The Provider*.

539 To George Grosz

Dear George,

I'm sending you a poem that might be publishable in Germany. It would be wonderful if you could do a few drawings for it. I think I can get the book printed here (with drawings) though crudely, and send the little book over to you as a present. That of course would only be a makeshift solution; later on Wieland could put out a decent edition. We really should do something for the old land of culture.

Cordially,

brecht

If you think it would be better, we could bring the little book out anonymously.

[Spring 1947]

[1]English in original

540 To George Pfanzelt

Dear George,

Thanks for the letter. It's as if the (let's hope un-) holy family were there before our eyes. Helli will send the balls for Junior as soon as she puts another parcel together. Helli would like to know whether there was any women's clothing in the parcel. (We hear from Berlin that lots of things are stolen from the parcels, that good stuff (it goes without saying that the things we send are whole and absolutely clean) is fished out and rags put in.) I gather from your letter that at least the Lech is still there. So there's still enough left for a third World War. Here everything can be had except the little dollars without which nothing can be had. Hollywood, now undoubtedly the cultural centre of four-fifths of the world, is only fifteen kilometres away, you can smell it from here.

We hope to get to Switzerland at the beginning of September. Then it will be easier to communicate and perhaps a game of chess can be arranged.

As ever,
b

[A postscript by Helene Weigel follows]

[Santa Monica, summer 1947]

541 To Herta Hanisch

Dear Mrs Hanisch,

In the summer of 1940 Grete accompanied us from Stockholm to Helsinki (Finland), as it was feared that Hitler would invade Sweden. At the approach of winter the situation in Finland as well became menacing, we didn't know what to do, because Grete did not, like us (Helli and the children and me), have a Mexican visa. So we tried to get American visas; that too was difficult for Grete, as she could not meet the health requirements for an immigration visa and they had just about stopped giving out tourist visas. There were more and more motorised divisions in the country, Helsinki was full of German 'tourists'. Finally, on 12 May, we obtained a tourist visa for Grete. We left the next day and on

15 or 16 May we were in Moscow, where we had to wait for boat tickets to America. By the time we got the tickets, Grete had had to be taken to a nursing home. The state of her health had been good in Sweden; the cavities in her lungs were beginning to calcify; we had moved to a wooded island near Stockholm, where the air was good, and she had good food. Then in Finland, the food got very bad, there was hardly any fat, no fruit, etc., and the excitement (over the visas and not being able to get away) exhausted Grete completely. In Moscow we tried to change our boat tickets, but the later boats were full. As a special favour, the authorities got us a ticket for Grete on a ship that would be leaving about six weeks later. Grete was glad to be able to stay in Moscow and rest up for the boat trip. She was quite calm and confident, for now she had a visa, a boat ticket, and the prospect of a cure in a Moscow sanatorium where she had a room to herself and the best doctors in Moscow. Helli, the children and I left for Vladivostok on 30 May. On the Trans-Siberian express I received a telegram on 4 June with the news that Grete was dead. Another wire from her friend Maria said: 'Grete did not want to die, she thought only of living. Asked for books. Thought of you. She longed to get well and follow you. After the next night she ate breakfast calmly, read your telegram with care, and asked for champagne. A little while later she felt sick and trembled, but thought it would pass. Just then the doctor came in. At the next moment she said the word Doctor three times. Died calmly. In the post mortem the doctor found both lungs in the last stages.'

Grete was the noblest person imaginable, a great woman and for me a teacher.

I wrote to you from Vladivostok, but ten days after we sailed Hitler invaded the USSR and my letter can't have reached you. Immediately after the end of the war we tried to get your address. I wrote again to Herta Hanisch, Gartenbausiedlung bei Berlin, Block 22, Parz 3. We also sent two parcels. I don't know why we were unable to reach you, and I didn't have your mother's address. Please give Mrs Steffin the enclosed letter.

I hope we'll be able to see you soon, our travel plans are uncertain. We're very glad to know you've come through.

> Cordially and in comradeship,
> Yours,
> bertolt brecht

[Santa Monica, June–July 1947]

542 To Johanna Steffin

Dear Mrs Steffin,

I've written to Herta about Grete, because I haven't got your address. Grete knew that her illness was brought on by political conditions, that in more peaceful times, or if she herself had not been involved in the struggle, she would have had a good chance of getting well. But to the end she remained confident that one day she would return to Berlin with us, and even in the last days in Moscow she spoke a good deal of you, her sister, your husband, the boy and her father. In her quiet, sensible way she sacrificed herself as bravely and unselfishly for the cause as if she had fought in street battles. She is irreplaceable.

There's one thing that may comfort you: she never thought she was going to die, and up to the end she was treated with the greatest respect; she was sent to the best nursing home in Moscow, and had the best doctors, she had the visa that would have enabled her to follow us, and even her boat ticket.

In comradeship your
berthold[!] brecht

[Santa Monica, June–July 1947]

543 To Ferdinand Reyher

Dear Reyher,

So you've got back ahead of us. We were going to sail in mid-September but we didn't get our French transit visas and we couldn't sell the house. The house is sold now and we're definitely going to sail from New York in the middle of October. We're going first to Zurich, then to Basel. I'm definitely counting on your staying in the same place as we do in Switzerland or northern Italy. *Galileo* has a chance of going on Broadway, but I'm not waiting. The stage and the production reminded me very much of the Schiffbauerdamm-Theater in Berlin, as did the intellectuals in the audience.

Ruth photographed and filmed everything, so they can manage in New York without me. There's a good chance that Rod Geiger, who had a hand in *Open City* and *Paisa*, will make a picture of *Galileo* in Italy with Laughton and other English actors in the summer of 1948. You and I would then, beginning in March, do a script, living in northern

Italy, where Geiger has lire, but he'd have to, and would, pay us partly in dollars. In other words, I'm counting on your doing it with me. Laughton is all for it, even his agent is for it. Helli wouldn't want to spend the winter too far from a city, preferably Zurich or Basel. But perhaps Lucerne (in Italian Switzerland) [*sic*] would be *all right*.[1] A month or two in Berlin would be welcome, I'd put on *Mother Courage*. How are you doing? If *Galileo* hits Broadway or a film is made of it, I'll take a car to Europe. Could you find out what kind would be best? I suppose it shouldn't burn too much petrol. But Nashes are hard to repair. How about a Chevrolet? I hope you're being careful in the Wild West of Europe.

As ever,
brecht

[Santa Monica, September 1947]

544 To Charles Laughton

Dear Charles

You wanted Czinner's address: 1545 Broadway (Circle 5–7620–1). Private telephone: Butterfield 8–8966. In order to keep me busy now I am translating back *Galileo* into German, a 'helluva job'! It is especially hard to remember that sort of twilight (lack of clarity) which my poor country is so fond of.

Sincerely yours
and with my best wishes to Elsa
b

1063 – 26th Street
Santa Monica, Calif.
[August–October 1947]

545 To Emil Hesse-Burri

End of September 1947
Santa Monica, Calif.

Dear Hesse,

Thanks for your letter. We're planning to go to Switzerland at the

[1]English in original.

end of October. Then it will be easier to communicate. Of course I'm interested in your plan to do a *Szechwan* film. We might also see whether a film could be made of *Mother Courage and her Children.* As I say, when I'm in Switzerland we can be in closer contact about all this. Just to let you know that I understood your situation: in a book of plays which appeared somewhere around 1938 and was pulped soon afterward by the Nazis, I faithfully mentioned your collaboration, but changed your name to H. Emmel because of the Nazis.

> Hoping to see you soon,
> Yours cordially,
> brecht

Regards from Helli
Regards to Geis

546 To George Pfanzelt

> End of September 1947
> Santa Monica

Dear George,

Now it looks as if we'd be going to Switzerland at the end of October. I fervently hope this means we'll be seeing each other soon. Of course we're doing our best to get someone to keep sending you parcels after we leave here. According to everything I hear from Germany, the food situation must be horrible. Please, George, don't hesitate to wire me if you're in urgent need of anything. I must say that you are a prime attraction for me in the old latitudes.

> As ever,
> bidi

Letters will reach me in Switzerland care of Theaterverlag Reiss A.G., Basel, Bäumleingasse 4

5 Zurich and East Berlin
1947–1956

Last years in a divided Europe

Landing on his own in Paris on 1 November 1947, Brecht found himself spending four days in a city where he was virtually unknown. Existentialism had replaced the Popular Front culture of ten years earlier; the exiles had gone; the epic theatre (which had made little enough impression even then) had been overtaken by the new theatres of Cruelty and the Absurd. But his German contemporary and comrade the novelist Anna Seghers was there. She had just spent some six months on both sides of the sector boundary in Berlin and could recommend him to be cautious in his approach to that city of mutual suspicion and tale-bearing. This he intended to do by first spending a year in Switzerland, where three of his biggest plays had been premièred during the war and his earliest and most essential collaborator Caspar Neher was now waiting to swap the ideas and experiences which the two men had accumulated during nearly fifteen years of separation. Neher had not only watched the decline of the German theatre under the Nazis, and knew what needed to be done to 'cleanse the Augean stable of confusions' (as he put it), but he had also become involved with the Austrian composer Gottfried von Einem in the post-war revival of the Salzburg Festival. In Zurich in a month of stimulating and wide-ranging daily discussions he and Brecht made a number of plans.

First and foremost, in the short term they would do an experimental production of Hölderlin's *Antigone* in which Helene Weigel, arriving in mid-November, would try a major role for the first time for ten years. They for their part would see how well they still got on as joint directors, with Brecht as adaptor of Hölderlin's translation and Neher designing costumes and stage. This had only five performances, four of them remote from Zurich; but for the participants it was a crucial test, and one without which Brecht might well have hesitated to take *Mother Courage* to Berlin a year later. After that there would be *Puntila*, the fourth of the Zurich Schauspielhaus's Brecht premières, which Brecht this time would direct himself (though the fact was not made public since he had no permit to work). Neher was too busy to execute designs for it, though he did some inspired and imaginative drawings; but following *Antigone* he worked very promisingly with Brecht on the scheme for a post-war 'Aristophanic revue' which the latter had proposed before leaving America (Letters 532 and 535) and which now half-surfaced under the title *Ares's Chariot*. After *Puntila*, while Neher went off to Salzburg, Brecht concentrated on distilling his theatrical principles in the form of the *Short Organum*: another prelude to his impending plunge back into the German theatre. And all the while he was seeing old and new friends and negotiating for performances of his earlier plays.

Barely noticed in Switzerland, Brecht's fiftieth birthday in February 1948 was celebrated in the Soviet sector of Berlin by a production of *Fear and Misery* at the Deutsches Theater under the Intendant Wolfgang Langhoff, and also by an article by the cultural affairs officer Colonel Alexander Dymschitz. This was part of a move to bring back Brecht that had been launched originally by Herbert Jhering, Legal and Felsenstein (all of whom had remained in Nazi Germany) somewhat against the ideas of most of the returned exiles from the USSR, but in line both with Brecht's own wishes and with his expectation of being able once more to use the Theater am Schiffbauerdamm. So he could now plan to produce *Mother Courage* with Weigel and (as co-director) Erich Engel under the wing of Langhoff's theatre and using his actors, as soon as he could get his travel papers sorted out. At the same time, whatever this might lead to in Berlin or the Soviet Zone of Germany, he could pursue Neher's and Von Einem's invitation to go along with their Salzburg plans as the Festival's 'house' playwright every summer, starting with the idea of a *Salzburg Dance of Death*.

Salzburg was in the American Zone of Austria, and Brecht's temporary US papers had expired and would not be renewed. He could not now enter the American Zone of Germany – which is one reason why he had to get his old colleague Jacob Geis to supervise his affairs there – nor stop off in Salzburg without special permission; and without proper documents it would be impossible for him to work both there and in the Russian sector of Berlin where the Deutsches Theater and the Schiffbauerdamm were located. As an insurance against similar restrictions Neher, whose wife (like Weigel) was Austrian, had towards the end of 1948 taken Austrian nationality; and he and Von Einem together suggested that Brecht should do likewise so as to be able to work either side of the rapidly hardening demarcation lines. Accordingly Brecht applied in the following spring, giving Von Einem's as his future Salzburg address; and was granted his citizenship in April 1950. Unfortunately the *Dance of Death* remained, like *Ares's Chariot* with its Neher visualisations, a brilliant fragment. For a year later a virulent attack was launched by the Austrian press against Brecht's naturalisation and against Von Einem for sponsoring it, with the result that the latter was gradually squeezed out of the counsels of the Salzburg Festival. With that, Brecht's chance of having a role in Salzburg had gone.

But the Berlin *Mother Courage* was an historic success, whose effects set the parameters of Brecht's work for the rest of his life. For, thanks to Langhoff (who had acted in the original Zurich production of 1941 but was no adept of Brechtian theory) and to the support of Becher's Communist Kulturbund and the Russians, the Brechts were now able to set up their own Berlin Ensemble under the wing of Reinhardt's old theatre, and its composition and repertoire were thereafter (from Letter 575 on) their most demanding concern. Helene Weigel became its able and strong-willed Intendant, giving great performances as Courage and Pelagea Vlassova. Brecht was director of its artistic policy and (with or without Engel) of its most famous productions; Dessau and Eisler were its composers; Neher (who had missed designing *Mother Courage* supposedly because of permit problems: see Letters 572 and 576) was for three years its exemplary designer. Part of the intention from the first was to stage Brecht's post-1937 plays, which were as yet unknown in any part of Germany. Otherwise he would be more active as a director and mentor than as a creative writer. He worked on *The Days of the Commune* (based on Nordahl Grieg's *The Defeat*) when he returned alone to Zurich to recruit actors, collect his daughter and settle his affairs there (including the establishment of a Swiss Franc account, for which see Letter 589). But this was with the needs of the new company in mind.

The Ensemble opened its career in November 1949 with the Brecht-Engel production of *Puntila*, which once more featured Leonard Steckel (a former Piscator actor from Zurich) as Puntila but this time had music by Dessau and sets by Neher, who had meantime moved back into his old flat in West Berlin. The main aim, as conceived in 1947 if not earlier, was to re-establish a standard and a style for the German theatre, using a modified version of Brecht's methods and a repertoire which would include such further modern playwrights as Gorky, Lorca, O'Casey and maybe Odets, as well as adaptable German classics to be directed with the additional aid of Viertel and perhaps Ernst Legal. Weigel and Brecht accordingly recruited some of the ablest survivors of the old German 'Left' theatre – Therese Giehse from Zurich, for instance, and Ernst Busch and the agitprop actor Ernst Geschonneck from Berlin – and hoped to attract such returning Hollywood exiles as Lorre, Homolka and Fritz Kortner (who was offered the lead in *Galileo*). Elisabeth Bergner too was invited (Letter 784) to play Shen Teh/Shui Ta in *The Good Person of Szechwan* as late as 1955.

With these they mingled much younger performers whether from Germany or from Switzerland, some of them virtual beginners, and also a growing number of embryo directors and dramaturgs. Increasingly these younger members of the company became the centre of Brecht's attention, and as the Ensemble got more established he began to give his young assistants tasks of their own, starting with Egon Monk's direction of *Urfaust* in Potsdam in 1952. Elisabeth Hauptmann arrived back from the United States in 1949 and was instantly swept into full-time work as dramaturg, translator and supervisor of the publication of all Brecht's works, which (after various false starts) was undertaken by their old friend Peter Suhrkamp. And then there was the continuing problem of Ruth Berlau, who returned at the beginning of that same year hoping to be quite equally at the centre of Brecht's affairs. From then on most of his many letters to her (of which we only print a part) seem designed to pacify her and get her to concentrate on her contribution as a photographer, particularly in connection with the 'model' books in which he wished her to record his productions, as she began systematically to do with that of *Antigone*. There is nothing in his published correspondence about his various relationships with new women members of the ensemble.

Over all this, from the Brechts' first venture to Berlin up to the Berliner Ensemble of 1956 (and later), hang the major political developments of that time. Captured in the first place by the Russians, Berlin had been divided into sectors in the summer of 1945 as part of the four-power occupation of Germany. When after three years there seemed no prospect of a permanent treaty, a radical and economically 'miraculous' currency reform was introduced in the three Western Zones and in the corresponding sectors of Berlin. The USSR, fearing that its restorative effects would be felt in the Eastern sector too and thereby upset their policies for the whole Soviet-occupied Zone, cut the Western land communications (which had been guaranteed by no agreement) with Berlin. This happened in June 1948, just when the Brechts were planning their Berlin trip, and for eleven months the three Western sectors of the city had to be maintained by air (since the USSR *had* guaranteed the Western air corridors) while checkpoints were set up by the Russians to keep the strong new currency out of their sector. Later in 1949, following the failure of the intended blockade, two separate German states were created, each under its own constitution and government: the Federal Republic (FRG) in the West, composed of the American, British and French occupation Zones, and the smaller and, in many respects, poorer Communist-led Democratic Republic (GDR) in the Soviet-occupied East. Berlin became a four-power enclave inside the latter, with an internal frontier that developed into an Iron Curtain of its own, largely cutting Brecht's theatre off from Neher and others who had to choose which side of this to work.

Once the airlift was over Brecht found travel less difficult (witness his visits to Salzburg and Munich in the summer of 1949) and, with Wilhelm Pieck's appointment as president of the new GDR (Letter 618) occurring just before *Puntila* opened in Berlin, the Ensemble could make its bow as a state company under its Ministry of Education. From then on the Brechts were not merely members of the establishment, writing diplomatic letters to ministers and making the occasional public statement, but also genuinely committed to that republic's future and particularly to its younger generation. For another two years or so Brecht tried at times to write 'positively', i.e. in a constructive rather than critical sense, contributing a pacific Laureate-like poem 'To my countrymen' on Pieck's accession, for instance, as well as the 'Reconstruction', 'Future' and 'Peace' songs and the anti-FRG *Herrnburger Bericht* which Monk staged for the 1951 World Youth Festival. His 'Children's Anthem' of 1950 to Eisler's music was a 'counter-song' to 'Deutschland über Alles' (though it was Becher who wrote the new national anthem). Moreover, as a founding member of the new German Academy of Arts in East Berlin he took an active part in its work, particularly where any form of education or apprenticeship was concerned. (See Letters 665–667, with their emphasis on the need to tell the new generation how to detect kitsch.) He was also moved to defend an exhibition of Barlach's sculptures which it held in the winter of 1951/52 and which the Party paper criticised as negative and formalistic.

Brecht's 'positive' stance became shaken however by the Party's increasingly uncomprehending attitude to his own work, whose innate pacifism was found to be inconsistent with the GDR's defence policy, its formal originality unwelcome and its attitude of criticism potentially subversive. Thus *The Days of the Commune*, with which he had hoped to launch the Ensemble, was indefinitely postponed because of its defeatist attitude to the historic events of 1870–71; *Lucullus*, which Dessau had made into an opera, was compulsorily withdrawn for revision after a trial performance in March 1951, mainly because of the modern idiom of the music, but also for its blanket condemnation of war. Even *Mother Courage* was seen by Fritz Erpenbeck – last encountered at the deathbed of *Das Wort* – as a product of 'decadence'. The *Herrnburger Bericht*, with its deliberately simpler Dessau settings, was given five performances, then (said Brecht's diary for 17 August) 'suppressed'; Monk's *Urfaust* was thought to be an insult to the 'cultural heritage'. By March 1953 Brecht could note in his diary that 'our performances in Berlin now attract virtually no response'.

One persistent factor in Brecht's growing unpopularity with right-thinking critics and officials was his 'negative' (or pessimistic) view of Germany history: his emphasis on what Marx termed the 'German Misere' typified by the Thirty Years War, to whose divisive effects he attributed the delayed unification of the country and the cringing attitude adopted by its teachers and public servants, particularly towards the military, right up to his own time. This was the underlying theme of his adaptation of *The Tutor* in 1950, and it surfaced in the Academy's debates of spring 1953 about *Urfaust* and the libretto for Eisler's intended Faust opera, both of which offended the new Communist patriotism. Another factor adduced by some of his theatrical colleagues – with Erpenbeck prominent – was the incompatibility of his methods as defined in the *Short Organum* with the officially propagated naturalism of Stanislavsky. Together they became the main pretexts for complaint by the Party's art medics, and when in April the Academy organised a big Stanislavsky conference Brecht made matters no better by sending his wife to represent the Ensemble, and himself appearing in the background or not at all.

During this time the whole Communist movement, along with the Soviet government's control of it, was radically affected first by Mao Tse-tung's victory in China at the start of 1949, and then in spring 1953 by Stalin's death. Despite his Communist convictions Brecht had few illusions about his countrymen or about the popularity of the Party's policies. He saw the working class as flaccid and demoralised after its support of Hitler, found the GDR People's Chamber to be a 'giant façade' (Letter 767 to the Deputy Premier), thought free elections would bring back a Nazi majority, and felt that 'socialism to order is better than no socialism at all'. 'This country still gives me the creeps', he wrote in one of his rare diary entries after 1953. That was the year when the East Berlin workers rose against their government's demands and were joined in violent demonstrations by a variegated mob from West Berlin on 17 June: the dangerous and sinister moment described by Brecht to Suhrkamp in Letter 728. At his new country home at Buckow two months later he noted that that day's events had 'alienated his whole existence', forcing him to look at everything afresh (a process vividly distilled for us in the elegies which he wrote there) because for the first time 'the class' had at last shown its presence, in however 'depraved' a form.

Yet his instant reaction, unlike that of many of his more conformist colleagues, had been to assure the Party that, whatever its past mistakes, he was on its side. And this is the attitude which emerges from Letters 725–727, and whose open adoption earned him the apparent right to be listened to when he made the immediately following suggestions about cultural policy (and wider matters: 730, 732–3 etc., and the immediately preceding suggestion too, the very opportune 724). The result was a new boost to his status and to that of his theatre, if also to the efforts of his enemies in the West. Within the GDR, and by osmosis elsewhere in the Soviet bloc, it certainly strengthened his argument against the bureaucratic enforcement of the ideas of Socialist Realism still being promoted by the writings of Georg Lukács and the supporters of Stanislavsky, and backed by the posthumous authority of the now defunct Stalin. The bureaucrats in question were obscure communists who had been put to run the various dictatorial 'commissions' for the various arts set up under the Education Minister Paul Wandel; they seem to have been at their worst in the visual arts, where their horror of 'formalism' had lasting effects (see Letter 756). Brecht, who believed that creative artists were open to political arguments but must in the end be left to choose their own forms, now launched a campaign via the Academy and an important article in the Party paper on 12 August (*Brecht on Theatre*, pp. 266–70) which led to the replacement of the commissions by a new Ministry of Culture at the end of 1953.

Its minister was Brecht's old sparring partner Johannes R. Becher, whom he had addressed with the familiar 'du' since 1937 but never rated very highly as a poet; and with his appointment the formalism issue was soon shelved. Publicly at least the two Bavarians were allies, and early in 1955 Brecht and his young assistant Manfred Wekwerth directed Becher's Second World War play *Winterschlacht* (which the Czech avant-gardist E. F. Burian should have directed for them), while Becher got Brecht a permit to buy a new BMW car. By that time the Ensemble had at last moved into the Theater am Schiffbauerdamm, the 890-seat nineteenth-century theatre where Brecht had had his great success under Aufricht's management some 27 years earlier. Brecht himself had directed the première of *The Caucasian Chalk Circle*, the most complex of his still (professionally) unperformed plays, become a vice-president of the Academy and been awarded a Stalin Prize by the Russians, as had Becher and Anna Seghers before him. *Mother Courage* had been a formidable success at the First Paris International Theatre Festival, and this success was repeated with *The Caucasian Chalk Circle* the following year. Admittedly neither of his long drawn-out film schemes turned out well, for the DEFA *Courage* (subject of several increasingly frosty letters) was broken off, while Cavalcanti's Austrian *Puntila* proved something of a travesty (Letter 790, written a month before the première, could never correct its basic faults).

Probably the most gratifying development for Brecht towards the end of this last phase was the launching as directors of his younger disciples. For Käthe Rülicke, Benno Besson, Manfred Wekwerth, Peter Palitzsch, Carl Weber and Angelika Hurwicz all had their first productions staged at the Schiffbauerdamm during 1954 and 1955 – a good omen for both East and West German theatre in the decades after his death. He himself at last began preparing and, at the end of the latter year, rehearsing his long-delayed *Galileo* production with Engel as co-director and Ernst Busch as final choice for the lead. Work was interrupted in the spring of 1956 by a virus infection which struck him not long after the 20th Party Congress in the USSR had unleashed Khrushchev's appalling revelations about the past, and he went off to hospital with a determination to study all the relevant material about Stalin's crimes. To another young protégé, the writer Peter Hacks, he said that the exposure of these would be the task for the next generation of dramatists. Back at Buckow in convalescence that summer, he worked with Wekwerth and Besson on the eventual production of *Days of the Commune* in a provincial theatre, and even came to rehearsals of *The Caucasian Chalk Circle* to help tighten up that play for the Ensemble's impending London season. A fortnight before this opened, with lasting effects on the English theatre, he died of a heart attack.

547 To Wilhelm Dieterle and family

October 1947

Dear Dieterles,

This is the second day and we're still eating your meats, sugar and cake, the homemade black bread and the butter from your cows – a motorised orgy.

The trains are no longer full, the big boom is over. The shops in the stations show the high cost of living. The people lose *all wars*.

> Yours,
> the brechts

548 To Ruth Berlau

[Paris] Monday 3 November [1947]

Love,

While changing money at the Paris airport, I spied Ella Winter and [Donald] Ogden Stewart beside me, they had flown over from London. They got me a room in a hotel around the corner and treated me to a few meals that I couldn't have paid for. And we're expecting Anna Seghers to come from Berlin to visit her children here. So I won't be leaving until tomorrow, Seghers will be able to tell me about Berlin, she's going back there in four weeks, – I've arranged with Ella Winter that you are to go and see her (after the tenth, then they'll be back in New York). Tell her you can try to sell the articles she wrote about America (written for *The Manchester Guardian*) in Switzerland and Scandinavia. They are useful people, personally and in general. Address: Ella Winter, 8 East 10th Street, New York 3. – Neher is in Zurich, what do you think of that? – For Switzerland travellers' cheques are better than dollars. – Paris is expensive. And cold.

Tuesday

I'm writing in a café to keep warm. A. Seghers has just been telling me about Berlin. Definitely, one must have a place to live outside Germany. I'm going to Zurich tomorrow morning. I'll write to you from there and tell you what to do on your way through France. – Please take care of yourself, Ute.

Love,

bertolt

Judging by everything Seghers says, you'll be very much needed in Berlin.

549 To Ruth Berlau

Address;

Hotel Urban, Stadelhoferstrasse 41

Zurich

Love,

Here are two letters, to Joe Losey and to Laughton. I haven't got their addresses. (Laughton, I *think*, is in Algonquin.)

I'm in the train on my way to Zurich. It's raining. The old continent is shabby and impoverished, but I think you'll like it, as I do. We'll be able to work.

About Berlin: I gather from what Anna Seghers told me that it's very important for us to build up a strong group. It's impossible to exist there alone or practically alone. I'm glad you're 'up to snuff' again. I'm going to need you quite a lot.

I hope there will be letters from you in Zurich. Is your forehead smooth?

Love,

bertolt

5 [November] 1947

550 To the National Theatre in Prague

Dear Mr Goetz,

I was glad to hear from Mr Lotar that the National Theatre is planning to put on *The Visions of Simone Machard*. Wishing the play to be as effective as possible, I have one great request to make. The part of Simone should really be played by a child, because otherwise her childlike quality becomes childish. I know, of course, that this is not the usual practice of theatres, but in writing the play I intended precisely to improve on this practice. And indeed, in a recent production of *Galileo* in Los Angeles, I did very well with nine-to-twelve year-olds. The tragic element in the play is that this child takes patriotism seriously (whereas her teachers, the adults, are found wanting).

> With best regards,
> Yours,
> Bertolt Brecht

> Zurich, middle of November 1947

551 To Hanns Eisler

Dear Eisler,

In Paris I met Anna Seghers who had come from Berlin for a few weeks to visit her children. Berlin seems to be getting like Shanghai. (Big difference apparently between the fly-by-nights and the responsible people). By the way, I see from some newspaper cuttings that certain journalists thought I behaved arrogantly in Washington; the truth is that I simply had to obey my six lawyers, who advised me to tell the truth and *nothing* else. Not being a citizen either, I could no more refuse to testify that you could. But now to practical matters: Prague wants to produce *The Visions of Simone Machard* in the summer (or spring). Please send me your music straight away (you had some things for the Angel). It's very important. Perhaps you can rehearse the music there. Will you be able to get to New York for *Galileo*?

It's very expensive here. Lodgings hard to find.

Write to me, or get Lou to write.

> As ever,
> b

Best regards to Gerda; she should write to me too.

Zurich, Schauspielhaus [November 1947]
Letter put aside, as I have no address.

552 To Ruth Berlau

I haven't received all the notices. *PM* is missing, also *Daily News* and *Daily Worker*.* And of course the magazines, *New Masses, New Republic Nation, Time*).

It would be good to have a recording of the long speech in Scene 13. If Laughton has left, perhaps Winge could attend to it.

For my digest of the notices; to show how risky it would have been to move the play to Broadway, I need to know from Hambleton what the *initial costs*[1] came to and also how much it took to cover the weekly operating costs. And write me the price of a pound of bread and a pound of butter.

If you see Laughton, tell him I wrote him a letter. From the notices (and your report) I gather that the performance must have been excellent, containing all the elements of the original production. Atkinson's review struck me as the only nasty one. It may have prevented a Broadway run and thereby a genuine consultation of the broad public, but after this demonstration of the new theatre to the specialists I doubt if the serious drama in the States will ever be the same again. With this negative balance sheet we must and can content ourselves – in 1947.

On the whole Laughton accomplished his self-imposed task masterfully; his performance was in every respect exemplary; he is now *the* pillar on which the English-speaking theatre rests. I am proud of our work together and I hope he is too.

[Zurich, mid December 1947]

*Just received *PM* from you. Thanks.[Brecht's note]

553 To Stefan S. Brecht

Dear Steff,

I'm sending you an adaptation of *Antigone* that I've done for Helli. We're giving a kind of preview[2] for Berlin in Chur, two hours from Zurich. I've used Hölderlin's (relatively faithful) translation from the Greek; there's something Hegelian about it that you'll recognise and a Swabian popular gest that you probably won't. (The 'popular grammar' extends even to the ultra-sophisticated choruses.) It's my second attempt,

[1] English in original
[2] English in original

following *Edward*, to develop a heightened stage language from classical elements. The reason for the changes, which obliged me to write whole new sections, is that I wanted to get rid of the Greek *moira* (destiny); in other words, I try to uncover the underlying popular legend. You'll be better able to judge this experiment when you see what has been done with the choruses. – A piece of good news from Sweden: apparently the books are still there: (*Neue Zeit*, Karl Marx, Ilich, [i.e., Lenin], Machiavelli, Montaigne, Aristotle, Hegel, etc.) – If *Galileo* is done in New York, I'd like you to see it again and write to me about it. And please make sure that Korsch gets tickets. Just speak to Hambleton or Laughton. – And about the car, you should correspond with E. Hauptmann (c/o Lorre) directly. She wanted to sell the Buick and send you the money, but it seems she can't get very much for it.

Cordially,
b

December 1947
Zurich

554 To Ruth Berlau

Love,

It will take a lot of work, but the cast doesn't seem bad. To most people's surprise, the outlook is fairly promising. We still have no Creon. We'll probably have to come to a decision about it tomorrow. I hope you've got *Antigone* from Erika Neher. Have you heard from Hanne?

If you want to phone me, I'll be at the hotel after seven o'clock on Monday (and Tuesday) evening (Tel. 23556)

bertolt

I'd love to hear your voice.
Love

[Mid-January 1948]

555 To Ruth Berlau

Dear Ruth,

There must be beautiful Swiss peasant masks, something like the Chinese, in the Schweizerisches Landesmuseum (Zurich). Maybe you could get permission to photograph them? Or at least the best ones? (It would be a kind of chronicle, but we could use it for the files.) The rehearsals are going well. I was disappointed when you didn't phone last night. Also, I was told you hadn't been at the theatre.

bertolt

[January-February 1948]

556 To Hans Curjel

Dear Doctor,

It is now becoming clear that the *Antigone* production will be of some interest after all. There will be plenty that's new and challenging for theatre people as well as for would-be spectators. It's true that apart from certain problems that have been fully solved (stage set, props, costumes, grouping) the epic element still has to be looked for; but once looked for, at least it can be found. It's the same with Weigel as with Laughton; the epic way of playing can hold its own against dramatic surroundings, but can't take the offensive against them, and there's no middle ground for the epic actor to fall back on – one thoughtless move and the curve is bent out of shape, irreparably for that night, or until there has been another rehearsal. Gaugler is a discovery, especially for mime. I wish you could have been there last night, but if you had been nothing could have stopped the actors from 'acting', and that would have jelled them in an unfinished state. I'm definitely counting on you for Sunday.

Chur, Saturday 7 February 1948

557 To Caspar Neher

Dear Cas,

The two Friday rehearsals went normally; in the evening the audience surprised us and themselves with real applause. Your *Antigone* stage (including costumes and props) is exemplary, and must be kept, all the more so as it can absorb all sorts of variations. And in my opinion your solution of the chorus problem is among your lasting contributions. I'm glad we've been able to do this thing.

Next Thursday we're going to put black laurel wreaths on the horses' skulls as well.

Chur 7 February 1948

558 To Karl Korsch

Dear K K,

I've given the book to a few people but I haven't any good news yet, Switzerland is a small country, the subject is strange, and they like books that are easy to understand. But I'm still talking about it. We haven't got to Berlin yet, though we've made a few attempts; now we have to get Swiss travel papers, as the others are no longer valid, and I wouldn't want to settle permanently in Germany just now. In the meantime I've put on *Antigone* in Chur with Helli, in my adaptation (from Hölderlin's translation). It's being sent to you as soon as I have copies. Do you see Steff? What's the unholy family doing? How's your work coming along? Sometimes I wish you kept a diary with lots of entries in the Baconian style, about everything that interests you at the moment, altogether unmethodical, I mean unsystematic. Such scientific aphorisms could be used singly, in various combinations and for various purposes, they would all be finished at any time; instead of modifying one of them, you could make a new one, etc. – That would be epic science, so to speak.

Please write to us.

As ever,
b b

Feldmeilen bei Zurich,
Bünishoferstrasse 14,
April 1948

559 To the American Academy of Arts and Letters

April 5, 1948

The American Academy of Arts and Letters
To the Chairman of the Committee on Grants
Dear Sir,

I thank you for the honor that you have accorded to me. In a time like this such an award is especially encouraging. Unfortunately, I will be unable to attend the annual ceremonial as I am at present living in Switzerland. I am, however, enclosing the material which your assistant wished.

Sincerely yours,
Bertolt Brecht

Feldmeilen bei Zurich, Switzerland
Bünishofer Str. 14
(bei Mertens)

560 To Ferdinand Reyher

Dear Reyher,

This year seems to be just the same as last; at that time we were waiting for a chance to leave for Europe, now we're waiting for a chance to get to Berlin. And in the meantime all our threads are breaking off. What's the photographer novel doing? I often think of it. It's such an excellent idea. Couldn't you send me a few pages, in case you've started. I haven't been able to do any real work here. With Helli in Chur I did a new adaptation of *Antigone*, an attempt along the lines we discussed, to see what we can do for the old plays and what they can do for us. Helli was extraordinary and I had Caspar Neher again for the set. Otherwise we carry on the exhausting occupation of exiles: waiting. By the way, an astonishing olive branch has come from the States: The American Academy of Arts and Letters, 633 West 155th Street, New York, has granted me an award of $1000. Do you know who they are? Evidently there's more than one State Department in the States. I also owe you many thanks for the help you gave T. E. Hambleton; he's a very decent fellow, a rare commodity; I wish he'd go to Rome and try to get a *Galileo* film under way; then we could write the script in Italy and have lots of fun. I miss the chess too.

As ever
b

Feldmeilen bei Zürich
Bünishoferstrasse 14
April 1948

At the moment I'm thinking of settling in Austria, somewhere near Salzburg, so as to have a base to come back to (and to get away from). We hope to have a room for you.

561 To Gottfried von Einem

Dear von Einem,

Forgive my silence, I hoped to have my papers to order any minute, so as to be more or less free in my movements. I'm still determined to come if the business can be attended to in Salzburg. I think we could work well there.

Yours cordially,
brecht

Zurich, 23 May 1948

562 To Max Frisch

Dear Frisch,

I've been thinking more about your new play (which just to myself I still call *Berlin Theme*) quite apart from the housing blocks it leads through, which are so very different from the ones in Zurich. At the moment I'm working on a *Short Organum for the Theatre* and I won't really be interrupting my train of thought if I put down my reaction to your play. It's not a criticism of the subject or of the poetic intention, or of the execution except in one respect, to wit, that you seem to expect considerably less of the theatre than did earlier playwrights with your talent. I probably wouldn't make this point if I didn't think it could be made about some of my own plays. Sometimes one is led by 'outward' circumstances to write a tolerable, rather than an excellent play on a certain subject. To put it baldly: I have the impression that you simply declined to analyse the reasons why this subject (treated as you planned from the start) struck you as so fruitful. As you treated it, it presents highly significant aspects; but it seems to me that for these you did not choose the adequate form, Grand Form, as it were. By this, of course, I don't mean verse etc., but just a form that would bring out the great aspects. In the form you chose, which undoubtedly yielded a certain beauty, these aspects are only hinted at, as though you hoped to open them up in this way, but in my opinion this sort of hope is encouraged by a society that does not want a deeper, much less a more general understanding of social phenomena, and wishes the social mechanisms to be barely 'touched on', not vigorously attacked. They do not – any more than burglars – like to see arguments driven home with a club. But the history of great drama shows that in aesthetic productions a club is a legitimate instrument. From a classical point of view, you are dealing with the Judith theme. The new turn you give it is that the raped woman falls in love with the rapist, after which she can't help regarding him as her 'rightful owner', so that she can no longer do justice to the demands of the lover, who represents a higher morality. These aspects, so it seems to me at least, are touched on in your play, but not brought out. They are political. I hope you take this complaint lightly, as we who are involved with art must all learn to do. In rehearsing the play, which I look forward with real interest to doing with you, we may be able to discuss such general aesthetic matters in greater detail.

Yours very cordially

Zurich, July 1948

564 To Jacob Geis

Dear Geis,

I hear the Munich Radio has shown an interest in my play *Mr Puntila and his Man Matti* by raising the question of its authorship. My friend, the prominent Finnish writer Hella Wuolijoki (from whom, I might add, I have received a letter of congratulation about the opening in Zurich) told me when I was in Finland about the model for Puntila, who to the best of my knowledge was still living. She herself was planning a play and a film about him, but as I wished to treat the material on my own, to which she consented, I let myself be guided not by her project but by her stories. That is why the Zurich posters and programme carried the note: 'After the tales of Hella Wuolijoki'. Would you please so inform the Desch agency.

Yours cordially
brecht

[Feldmeilen, 28 August 1948]

566 To Hanne Hiob

Dear Hanne,

Please write and let me know the results of the examination, it's very important, omit nothing. And tell me what *I* can do. (I understand medicine, so ask the doctor to give you a medical report for me.) It's disgusting that I've had to wait so long for the papers, they've just come, so I'll be getting to Berlin that much later than I had planned. It won't be until October. Then I'll look around on your behalf. Perhaps I can get you straight to Berlin, provided of course that the state of your health permits. And if you're not having *Threepenny Opera* rehearsals. Apropos of *The Threepenny Opera*, you may have the impression that I wasn't doing enough about it. But now I've asked Ruth to tell the theatre people they'd be doing me a great favour by giving you a good part (Lucy or Jenny, whichever you please). But I didn't want to exert undue pressure 1) because I didn't know whether I myself would be present at the rehearsals, 2) because it would be bad for you at the theatre if they found out that pressure had been exerted, 3) because I haven't seen you act, so I have no way of knowing what progress you've made. (For that reason I'd have been glad if you could have stayed here and played in *Puntila*.) But now I hear that Schweikart has promised to look after you, so I think it will be all right. On the whole, Hanne, I regret to say that my chances in Germany (in its present state) cannot be rated too low.

Please write to me, especially about your health.

[Feldmeilen, September 1948]

567 To Caspar Neher

Dear Cas,

At last I have Swiss travel papers and am able to plan. How to explain my silence I don't really know, I can only say that I stalled and procrastinated from day to day in the hope that I'd be able to tell you something definite in a day or two, and then the question arose: what justification could I offer for not writing at least that, etc. etc.? Now I'll just take up where I left off, hoping you're not too angry to read my letter. This summer was miserable. In the first place, with all this waiting I couldn't really get down to work; in the second place I wanted to do the *Ares* and needed you for it, in the third place we need sketches for *Courage*; in the fourth place staying here costs francs, etc. etc. So now I'm going to Berlin with Helli via Prague (and if I get a permit[1] via Munich). I hope you've been able to do the *Threepenny* sketches for Munich. However, I only want a production with Albers.

[1]English in original.

But what about *Courage*? How can we do designs? Should I try to come to Salzburg after all? I ought to be in Berlin at the beginning of October. What do you suggest? Could you come to Berlin for a few weeks this winter? Anyway, I've written that they should make out an entry permit via Prague for you as they did for me. Have you got Austrian papers? Or what?

As ever,

b

[Feldmeilen, September 1948]

568 To André Simone

Dear A.S.,

As I'm stateless and my American identification papers have not been renewed in Switzerland, I've been obliged to wait in Zurich for Swiss travel papers. Now at last I can go to Berlin as planned. I have a Soviet permit for Berlin and I've applied in Berne for a Czech transit visa. I'd like to go in the middle of October. But I haven't got much money here. Could you try to get Helli and me plane tickets from Zurich to Prague, but arrange for me to pay you in Prague out of advances on royalties? A Prague theatre was considering a production of *The Visions of Simone Machard*, a play I wrote with Feuchtwanger in the USA. Another theatre is supposed to have expressed interest in *Galileo*, which Laughton played in America. I also think I have a little money on deposit in Prague to pay for my trip through. I have royalties waiting for me in Berlin. Is it shameless of me to bother you like this? Mightn't you get me an answer through your embassy in Berlin?

In any case we're looking forward to seeing you again. I'm hoping to direct *Courage* at the Deutsches Theater in Berlin.

Feldmeilen bei Zurich
Bünishoferstrasse 14,
September 1948

570 To Kurt Weill

Dear Weill,

I've done a version of *The Threepenny Opera* which can pass legally as a new version; in other words, we don't have to bother any more with the Bloch-Erben agency. I've already arranged with Hans Albers for a tour through West Germany, starting next spring. The actual changes are slight. The cripple scenes are minimised, they can't possibly be played in Germany at the present time. The ballades are unchanged except for a few words, but additional stanzas have been supplied, some of which Lenya has already sung. This version has been accepted by the Kammerspiele in Munich, which shows you that it's politically unobjectionable for West Germany. A copy is being sent you, but it will reach you later than this letter. Please send your agreement here by return of post, preferably to me care of Suhrkamp Verlag. I'll also notify Universal Edition.

We're working here on an important project for a theatre; it's to open in the summer 1949. (Probably the Schiffbauerdamm-Theater.) Of course I'll need Lenya. So I'll keep you informed. Living conditions here are not at all bad for artists, the picture the newspapers have painted of Berlin is altogether ridiculous. I'm living at the Adlon, eating as usual, keeping reasonably warm, etc. Of course we theatre people have a good many privileges.

Are you really bringing *Lady in the Dark* here?

> Yours cordially,
> brecht

> Berlin NW 7, 6 December 1948
> Schumannstrasse 13–13a
> Deutsches Theater

571 To Berthold Viertel

Dear B V,

I'm now in the midst of *Courage*, I've got Bildt, Hinz and a few young actors, and Engel is helping me. The project for next year that we talked about in Zurich is making good progress. But I want you to tell me as soon as possible what your plans are at the moment. As to *this* season: Should I approach the Deutsches Theater or the Hebbel Theater about the *possibility* of a play under your direction? I suggested to Ingenohl that he make you an offer for Strindberg's *Dream Play*, assuring him that you were very much interested in a directing job in Berlin. He said that in view of the food problem etc. he was always hesitant about inviting artists from abroad. I put his mind at rest by pointing out that you as a writer could eat as I do at the Kulturbund or the Möwe. We ourselves have all sorts of privileges and eat very well. We are comfortably lodged at the Adlon. As for housing, we can help you of course, through the Deutsches Theater even if you are working at the Hebbel-Theater. Please write to me at once, also if possible about *Courage* in Vienna. And another thing: Peter Huchel wants your Brecht article, published in *Twice a Year* (Dorothy Norman) for his new journal *Sinn und Form* [Meaning and Form], which will be very representative.

As ever,
brecht

Berlin NW 7, December 1948
Schumannstrasse 13–13a
Deutsches Theater

572 To Caspar Neher

Berlin NW 7, 29 December 1948
Schumannstrasse 13–13a
Deutsches Theater

Dear Cas,

No one here understands how it could happen that, as you say in your telegram, there was no visa waiting for you in Vienna. We inquired any number of times, and were always told that there was a visa waiting for you in Vienna. Otherwise I certainly wouldn't have sent you on a wild goose chase to Vienna, and I'm well aware that you have suffered a good deal of annoyance and expense. Until your wire came we went on hoping and kept everything open, so now the production will certainly not be anything like what it should have been. According to the competent office here, there is a visa waiting and after my phone call I really felt relieved. It's disgusting. But believe me, I left no stone unturned.

I'll be back in the middle of February and then I'll have all sorts of things to tell you. Please don't make any definite arrangements yet for next season. There are interesting projects afoot. Thanks to the many privileges enjoyed by artists, life here is almost normal, and the cultural climate is incomparable.

As ever,
b

573 To Paul Dessau

Dear Dessau,

I'm writing you this partly to get a certain item straight in my own mind. It seems that in the present ruined state of the theatre our 'Song of the Hours' can't be done. You yourself had doubts, before I had mine. The text is good, and the music, I think, is full of meaning, in fact it is one of your best pieces, but even if the actor didn't lack the hardness and subtlety, even if the general artistic standard of the production were higher and it were possible to use the new alienation technique, we'd still be forced to doubt whether the audience would accept it – Cf. the misgivings of Jhering and Engel – even though Kuckhahn, who is younger, is in favour of using it. In some of the plays you have 'rescued' a good deal by quick accommodation to the available means, and even created new beauty – I admire this more than you may think – but in the present case even that wouldn't help. So we shall probably have to put the song aside, but whenever the play is revived a discussion of whether or not the 'Song of the Hours' can be performed will be a clear indication of how high or low theatrical standards are at that time.

Happy New Year.

As ever,

b

Berlin 1 January 1949

574 To Gustaf Gründgens

Berlin NW 7, 18 January 1949

Dear Mr Gründgens,

You asked me in 1932 for permission to produce *Saint Joan of the Stockyards*. My answer is yes.[1]

Yours,

bertolt brecht

---

[1]Gründgens replied by wire: 'Your letter scared me to death, but delighted at your remembering. Please send book at once . . .'

575 To Leonard Steckel

Berlin NW 7, 24 January 1949
Schumannstrasse 13–13a
Deutsches Theater

Dear Steckel,

Next year we shall be doing guest performances of modern plays at the Schiffbauerdamm-Theater. The Ensemble won't be bad at all, and Engel (as well as Viertel, I hope, and you, I hope) will direct. We want to start with the *Zhelesnova* play, and for that we need you and Therese badly. We could do *Puntila* too.

Helli guarantees food and lodging for you and J. There won't be any trouble about that. The audience, especially the working class audience (we work in close collaboration with the unions and the Youth Organisation), is magnificent, as the reception of *Courage* shows. This is a place where the tradition of the Zurich exiles can really be carried on. So at least for the next few months of the season please steer clear of other commitments. Until I get to Zurich, which will be at the end of February.

As ever,
brecht

576 To Caspar Neher

Berlin NW 7, 28 January 1949
Schumannstrasse 13–13a
Deutsches Theater

Dear Cas,

Our theatre project seems to be shaping up. We're getting the Schiffbauerdamm-Theater for the coming season. We mean to organise an ensemble and put on three or four plays (O'Casey, Lorca, Odets, Gorky, etc.) Engel is going to work with us and likewise, I hope, Viertel, and there will be guest performers as well. You wouldn't have to be here for the whole season unless you wanted to be, but of course you'd have to be some of the time. Your food and lodging would of course be taken care of, your fare as well, and you'd also get some (not much) hard currency to cover possible expenses abroad. Erika should come with you of course. Thanks to the many privileges accorded to theatre people, we're as comfortable here as in Zurich, but the work is much less exhausting. We'd also be able to work for ourselves, very comfortably in fact. So don't, whatever you do, commit yourself to anything for next season before I get back (end of February). In the summer I want to do the *Tales of Hoffmann* film with Engel, in colour if possible. In March and April we (you and I) will have to get it into scenario form, and then if you could come to Berlin in June or July (for eight or ten days), I could get you about 800 francs for it, but I'll also have some francs for you for your April and May work (in Zurich).

The *Courage* set was no good. We waited for you till the last moment and then had to improvise. We should definitely work out new designs for other productions in Germany. Helli was a big success. All in all, the west sectors gave us as good a press as the east sector. In theatre, it's still possible to work both in the east sector and the west sectors. So next season you could probably do something at the Hebbel Theater too, if you feel like it.

As ever,

b

577 To Berthold Viertel

Berlin NW7, 25 January 1949
Schumannstrasse 13–13a,
Deutsches Theater

We've submitted a theatre project here and it has been accepted. We're getting the Schiffbauerdamm-Theater, organising an ensemble, and producing some four plays (O'Casey, Lorca, Odets, and Gorky). Engel would direct one, Legal may do another, and you should direct at least two. Your position would be that of chief director or – if you prefer – simply director, in either case with a formal contract. Actually, you'd be helping Helli, who is artistic director. Meals, housing, etc. are no problem. We're also planning guest performances with Giehse, Steckel, Gold, etc. There would be no problem about your directing at the Hebbel-Theater as well; in the theatrical field one can work in all the sectors at once. You need no *facilities*.[1] And no one will object to your working here (think of Klemperer). In addition, the DEFA wants

[1]English in original.

you for a film, and for the following season they're planning to open the Volksbühne. So you *must* come (with Liesl of course). We've applied for a Russian permit,[1] a Czech transit visa will be given you automatically.

It would be a big thing if you could come now – for a few weeks at least – to give Helli a hand. If Giehse is still in Vienna, please tell her I wrote to her directly in Zurich and that Helli and I are absolutely counting on opening the theatre with her as Zheleznova. And please ask Paryla in confidence if he'd come here at least as a guest; and ask any good actor you'd like to see here. The audience here (on the opening night of *Courage* we played to an audience of workers) is as good as ever.

> Yours cordially,
> brecht

578 To Kurt Weill

> Berlin NW 7, 28 January 1949
> Schumannstrasse 13–13a
> Deutsches Theater

Dear Weill,

Many thanks for your quick answer. I made the changes for very simple reasons. Mr Peachum's phony cripples wouldn't go down in Germany just now, there are too many authentic (war) cripples or relatives of cripples in the audience. Something had to be found to take their place. Luckily it was possible to keep the changes so slight that they didn't affect the character of the play. Here, as in the added verses of the songs, the changes were only temporary, valid only for the present period (and not to be published).

Your objections to the monotony of the two stanzas I thought of adding to the 'Ballade of Good Living' strike me as well founded, and I also mean to revise the end of the last ballade so as to make it fit the music. I haven't heard anything about *The Threepenny Opera* being prohibited in Munich. Somebody is just trying to sabotage it, I imagine.

I think I'm coming to an amicable agreement with Bloch-Erben. They will relinquish their right to represent us. But before the agreement becomes final, I'll send you the wording in case you want to make

[1] English in original.

suggestions. In the interim, in connection with the Albers guest tour I'd like us to be represented by Jacob Geis, who would send your royalties to Universal-Edition (if that's all right with you). He is absolutely reliable. Of course these are provisional measures; for a final settlement we shall just have to get together. Believe me that I shall do nothing contrary to your interests, nothing whatever, and shall always ask your opinion, if only because I'm still hoping for further collaboration with you. I'd be very glad if you would give your consent soon to the Albers guest tour, so that Albers can get started.

With best regards to you and Lenya (who should really make up her mind to give a guest performance here)

Yours,
brecht

NB: If you wish, Geis could probably convert your royalties into some sort of commodity. What do you think?

579 To Erwin Piscator

Berlin NW 7, February 1949
Schumannstrasse 13–13a,
Deutsches Theater

Dear Pis,

I've been in Berlin for three months now, I've directed *Courage* (in collaboration with Engel), I've looked round and my findings are as follows:

It is extremely necessary and quite possible to get the theatre here going again. The audience, i.e. the working class audience, is excellent. There aren't many actors left. And hardly any directors. So in the autumn we're going to organise an ensemble and produce some four modern plays. To this end I hope to bring in a few good guest performers from Switzerland (Steckel, Giehse, Kalser, etc.). In addition, we'll take the best of what there is here, which isn't bad. (All, it goes without saying, miles above the New York level).

Now my main question: would you take on a play? You really must come and look round. The Volksbühne, which is counting on you as director, won't be ready until the season of 1950–51, but we'll have its subscribers (so far about fifty thousand of them) in the Schiffbauerdamm-Theater as well. And the best way for you to look round would be to start working straight away. As a play, I'd suggest an O'Casey or a Lorca or best of all *The Defeat* by Nordahl Grieg, a play about the Paris Commune. The best thing would be for you to go to Switzerland, I can get you a formal invitation from the Züricher Schauspielhaus. From there there are several easy ways of getting to Berlin. I don't know if you can pay for the trip yourself. There would be advantages, you'd be independent. But if you can't I'll see what I can do with the theatre here.

You mustn't be discouraged by the example of Kortner, who hasn't started acting yet. He asked too many questions, took noncommital and unofficial answers too seriously, and insisted on American *facilities*.[1] Klemperer, who's an American citizen resident in Budapest, is a director at the Komische Oper in the East Sector and no one has raised the slightest objection.

My première of *Courage* was attended by theatre officers from all sectors. People come to see it from all sectors and in all of them the press was positive (all over Germany for that matter). You must absolutely come and not too late. Now is the right time, I think.

Food and housing are no problem here for our sort of people. You'd be just as well off as I am. And you'd really be welcomed with enthusiasm. You're badly needed. I myself am going back to Zurich next week. I have to renew my papers, but that will only take a few weeks. Then I'm coming back to Berlin. (Helli is staying here to play Courage.) Write to me in Zurich.

I think you should decide on the spur of the moment (such decisions can only be made on the spur of the moment) to come here for eight to ten weeks, let's say in September at the latest.

As ever

b

580 To Johannes R. Becher

Dear Becher,

Before leaving, I wish to thank the Kulturbund for its extraordinary hospitality. It would be next to impossible for a man on his own to gain a foothold in this destroyed city; it would scarcely be possible for him to organise his work. In addition, I owe the Kulturbund thanks for its

[1] English in original.

comradely help and any number of personal favours. One in particular: without the unstinting support of the Kulturbund the field of activity that is now being created in the theatre could not have been created. Once again my heartfelt thanks. And Auf Wiedersehen.

Yours,
bertolt brecht

Berlin, 20 February 1949

582 To Helene Weigel

Dear Helli,

The trip went well, and most important, quickly. I was able to fly from Prague to Zurich (with an advance on the *Kalendergeschichten*). I arrived here yesterday, Thursday. Barbara has recovered [. . .]¹ I've found a room, very small but independent. Cas has already been to see me – he's here, not in Salzburg. Prepared to come to Berlin on 1 September for at least eight weeks. I'll speak to Therese [Giehse], Steckel and Seyferth today. There's a wonderful marionette theatre in Prague, they'd be willing to come to Berlin (just the thing for the Kammerspiele). The Theatre of Satire could probably bring its panto-mimes to the Kammerspiele in October or at some time when the Kammerspiele has a gap, because in October they could only rehearse for four weeks (if we rehearse the Gorky play in November). So a little later. Give Engel *The Visions of Simone Machard*, Jette Ziegler could play Simone. (She did the child in the Nexö film and she's magnificent.) That's just an idea, I've just read *The Defeat*, don't show it to anyone else, it's astonishingly bad, but I think it can be changed, I've taken lots of notes. Anyway, I now understand Engel's horror. Still, the play has good roles and they could be made better. I'll cut out the petit bourgeois nonsense and put some life into it, while sticking to the historical facts.

Friday: Spoke to Therese, who sends her best regards. She's willing to come (from 1 November to 1 February), but she'll have to discuss the dates with Hirschfeld. She's also willing to travel out of Berlin.

Saturday: Spoke to Steckel. He wants to come too. It's important for him to keep up his household in Zurich. Says he needs $300. Sounds like a lot to me, but maybe we'll have to pay it. Will bargain. (Therese probably won't need more than $100.) As Steckel wants to go on working here, I spoke to Hirschfeld about dates. He thinks they won't

¹The deleted passage deals with the state of her health.

let him go for more than four months: beyond that they'll get difficult and possibly start looking for another director. That leaves the following possibility:

He starts on 1 February, rehearses *Puntila* until 15 March and plays it until 1 June (we'll give the Gorky to somebody else).

We'll have to arrange things so that *Puntila* more or less finishes its run and ends late enough so we can take it up again next season. Ten weeks would come to about twenty performances in Berlin and a maximum of twenty elsewhere.

The schedule would then be as follows:

1 Sept. – 1 Nov. Rehearsal at the DT [Deutsches Theater] *Fall of the Commune.*

1 Nov. – 1 Jan. Rehearsal at the DT [Deutsches Theater] *Fall of the Commune.*

1 Nov. – 1 Dec. Rehearsal at the KS [Kammerspiele] Gorky.

1 Dec. – 1 Jan. Rehearsal at the KS [Kammerspiele] Gorky.

1 Jan. – 1 Feb. Commune play and Gorky on the road.

1 Feb. – 15 March Rehearsals at the DT *Puntila.*

15 March – 1 May *Puntila*

1 May – 15 May (–)

Then Steckel could take over the Gorky on 15 Feb., and it would continue without Giehse.

Spoke to Seyferth. He could come for four months (1 Sept. – 1 Jan.). That is, he could play Thiers and the brother in the Gorky.

Of course he's an unreliable character, I'll have to check with the Munich Kammerspiele.

I think we should stick to the order: Commune play or other alternative – Gorky – *Puntila*, because beginning with *Puntila* would mean chopping it in mid-season.

I hope I can rework the Commune play; in its present form it's impossible. Viertel should do the Gorky. Therese would like that very much.

I hope to hear soon that the foreign currency can be approved.

The *Courage* production has caused a sensation even here, where most people have read only the West Zone papers. Everyone says your success has been enormous. People are taking a real interest in the new company, all the more so as the theatre here is falling apart. Giehse's and Steckel's commitment is wearing thin, Knuth is in Munich most of the time, Seyferth is leaving for good. No director. Main actor Quad-flieg.

Let's hope the Ensemble gets good ones.

And take care of yourself. Please no business appointments on acting days. And hurry up and get a car.

Your work takes too much out of you.

I'll be back as soon as possible.

> I kiss you
> b

Regards to Engel

[Zurich, end of February 1949]

583 To Helene Weigel

Zurich, Hottingerstrasse 25

Dear Helli,

Had a letter from Kasprowiak. Thanks. Working on the Commune play. I need Teege, Kahler, Hurwicz and Schäfer for it. Spoke to Gaugler, who first has to wind up his toy business. (Incidentally, I also need the young man in the eighth scene of *Courage*, the one with Mrs Reich, whom I also need.) Spoke to Lutz, she wants to come, I'll need contract forms from the Deutsches Theater if we have none of our own. I hope things will work out, because I'm getting people here to commit themselves. Otto is coming on 1 Nov. for *Zheleznova*; I need Viertel for that too. I've wired him. Can Cas get a permit[1] for May? To Berne? He's an Austrian. (Passport No. III P – 4012/48; Rudolf Neher, born 11 April, 1897, home address Salzburg, issued on 1 December 1948 in Salzburg.

Have a room near the theatre.

Applied for new papers for Barbara and me. Gitermann thinks everything will be all right.

I'm fairly confident about guest performances. Steckel is coming on 1 Feb. for *Puntila*, then if necessary he can take over *Zheleznova*. I've assigned Seyferth the following parts: Brother in *Zheleznova* and Thiers. Engel should enclose a note for him encouraging him to come.

Perhaps we could mention the following as corresponding members:

[1]English in original.

Viertel (Burgtheater Vienna – haven't got his agreement yet), Hirschfeld (Schauspielhaus Zurich, wants to work with us); Otto, Zurich; Neher, Salzburg. We ought to have someone in Munich and Hamburg. But please no announcement yet.

Take care of yourself, and don't overdo it.

I kiss you, Helli,
b

3 March 1949

584 To Helene Weigel

Der Helli,

Today, Friday, am taking Barbara to Basel for the carnival high jinks. She's been having a great time wearing an Empire costume at innumerable balls. This seems to attenuate her intolerable boredom, induced by laziness. I'm fervently hoping that the business with the papers here will soon be settled. Gitermann is optimistic and helpful.

I've wired Viertel about directing *Zheleznova*, starting 1 Nov. He'll probably come here to talk it over.

Would Engel be interested in Büchner's *Danton's Death* (in case we have trouble with *The Defeat*)? It would have to be supplemented: Danton actually betrays the Revolution, because he associates with aristocrats, protects them, admires them, lets them admire him, and in general behaves like a prima donna etc. So he's to blame for the necessary terror (necessary against him), which then devours Robespierre. Seyferth would be good for Robespierre if we could get Dahlke for Danton (and if he filled the bill).

Title for *The Defeat*: *The Days of the Commune* or *At the Time of the Commune*.

Take care of yourself. I kiss you.

b

Did S get my letters?

[Zurich, 6 March 1949]

585 To Helene Weigel

Dear Helli,

Viertel has wired from Vienna that he's keeping November open for the Gorky with Therese. Now it's important that Engel should keep himself free from 1 Sept. to 1 Nov. Tell him I've unearthed an old French play that can be used with some reworking. Cas also thinks he would be interested. We could show off our young actors in it (Trowe, Hurwicz, Kahler, Schäfer, Teege). I'll send an outline of the first few scenes soon. I'm rather worried at not receiving the definite approval of the DWK: the people here are beginning to count on Berlin, they're making arrangements and relying on me. Also it looks bad that you're not even living at the Möwe and have no office. And the fact that A.D., as Kasprowiak writes, has given a farewell party, sounds discouraging. Who's going to help us now? What about visas for Cas (and for me and Barbara)? It is awfully boring here after Berlin. Has Weisenborn written to the French theatre officer? *About my permit?*[1] For the Commune play we'd need at least fifteen male actors, so at least for five months at the start we should take people like that actor from the Russian POW camp, whom Jhering showed us. Go and see what's available from cabaret. And by all means send me contract forms, from the Deutsches Theater if necessary, for Lutz and Gaugler, also for Steckel and Giehse. This letter is rather muddled, forgive me, I'd like to know how you are, please write to me or call me (328890). Just ask G.S. to let me know through his office when you mean to call, then I'll be at home. I'll be glad to get back.

and I kiss you, Helli,

b

[Zurich, beginning of March 1949]

586 To Erwin Piscator

Dear Pis,

I'm back in Zurich from Berlin where I directed *Courage* (in collaboration with Erich Engel). I'm glad to say it was quite a success, presswise in the East and West sectors as well as the East and West Zones; The Deutsches Theater is regularly sold out when it's playing. (Weigel in particular has been a big success), and for the first time the cultural affairs officers of the occupying powers attended the opening night.

[1]English in original.

Inside Berlin there's unrestricted freedom of movement and it's perfectly peaceful. At the Deutsches Theater the artists have enormous privileges in respect of food supply. No one goes hungry, far from it. We're living at the Adlon but we can get a flat or house at any time. Working conditions are excellent, we rehearse for eight weeks. Now we're building up an Ensemble of our own, independent of the DT, but we play there and at the Kammerspiele, three plays a season. First the Commune play. Rehearsals begin on 1 September, the opening should be on 1 November. The Ensemble will be pretty good. Then comes Gorky's *Zheleznova* (with Giehse as guest performer) at the Kammerspiele and then my *Puntila* at the DT. The Commune play started out as *The Defeat* by Nordahl Grieg, a Norwegian. But now I'm going to rework it myself, though perhaps not officially, with ballads by Pottier (in Weinert's translation) between scenes. Busch will be in it. Could you direct it? I could first get you a directing job at the Zurich Schauspielhaus; it would be after your Berlin guest appearance and still be the official purpose of your trip. Your trip to Berlin would have to be organised here in Zurich, but that's no problem. Giehse is English, I'm stateless, Steckel has Swiss identity papers.

It would be a chance for you to look round and take a look at the work situation. Weigel is the artistic director of the new Ensemble. We couldn't make a better start than with a play directed by you. The time is right, you shouldn't wait too long, now everything is fluid, and the direction of the flow will be determined by the talents at work. You'd be welcomed with open arms and everyone would understand if you were somewhat noncommittal at first, a bit cautious about setting foot in the china shop. I myself have never made any official statement, just done my work.

Write to me immediately, the theatre has to open on 1 September and I have to know whether you can come.

As ever

b

Zurich, Hottingerstrasse 25
or Züricher Schauspielhaus
March 1949

587 To Erich Weinert

Dear Erich Weinert,

I'm in Zurich for a short time, back from Berlin. Everyone there wanted to know how you're getting on, I must be able to tell them when I get back. I myself want to know, I missed you very much in Berlin. And now to something specific: In the autumn we're putting on a play about the Paris Commune at the Deutsches Theater, and for that we need your translation of Pottier's poems. A few appeared in *Internationale Literatur*, have you still got them? Of course you'd get royalties. And would you be willing to do a few more?

Yours cordially,

brecht

Zurich, Schauspielhaus
[Probably March 1949]

Best regards to Kurt Kläber and wife.

588 To Berthold Viertel

Dear Viertel,

Your letter putting the date (1 Nov.) in doubt has rather upset me because I don't see how we can shift those few dates without throwing everything off. We and our (independent) Ensemble use the stage and workshops of the Deutsches Theater, and we have a tight rehearsal schedule. We've got the Deutsches Theater for rehearsals from 1 Sept. to 1 Nov., and then the Kammerspiele from 1 Nov. to 1 Dec., then the Deutsches Theater again from 15 February to 1 April. From 1 January to 10 February we'll be doing guest performances in Dresden, Leipzig etc. We can have Giehse from 1 Nov. to 1 February (perhaps only until 1 January). Steckel for *Puntila* from 15 February. We're not sure yet which play we'll do first, but the date has been set. For that Engel would be available. The Gorky project with Giehse has been the most definite from the start, that's why I picked it for you, especially as you might not be able to stay the whole time. Having you as director was a great and irreplaceable attraction for Giehse. So you *must* do it, it's vitally important to the project. Partly because the main argument against the whole expensive undertaking was that no one would show up, and what then? Yes, that's the crux: What then? A good deal is still in flux, but other things are taking definite shape. Theatres are becoming outposts and front-line positions. Rifts are deepening, scepticism is turning to suspicion, prejudices are crystallising; mediocrities getting big jobs and forming tenacious cliques, etc. The audience is magnificent, we first played *Courage* to the Henningsdorf workers (steel mills), the young people have an inner strength, which makes our work pleasant. We're getting a lot of money to bring first-rate people here; one of our main arguments was that the Volksbühne that's now being organised will have neither an ensemble nor a director. So this is really a cry of distress. Believe me, it's really important to build up a production *group*. We must show that such a project can be realised. And time is running out.

So I hope your Vienna affairs will arrange themselves in a way favourable to us all, or that you will force matters; it's not like me to give that sort of advice, but I'm doing it this once because so much is at stake.

> Cordially yours,
> b

My papers are still in a muddle and I don't know if I can get to Salzburg.

I feel I should add to my explanation of why I attach so much importance to your working with us and to the date. I've just read your letter of 5 March through again. You definitely wrote: 'Dear B., accept gladly. I don't know the play, but Therese has told me a lot about it, and doing it with her is such an alluring prospect. So in making my final arrangements with the Burgtheater, probably before the end of this month, I shall keep the period from November to roughly the middle of December open and not start the two plays I have agreed to direct for the Burgtheater until after New Year's 1950. I showed your telegram to Gielen immediately and told him I was going to accept your offer. At the moment he . . .' You haven't forgotten that?

Regards to Lisl, who'll be coming with you, I hope.

[Zurich, March–April 1949]

589 To Helene Weigel

Wimmer writes from Munich that she'd come for the Gorky play (for the part of Vassa's daughter-in-law). All right? She has a name in Berlin.

Dear Helli, thanks for the double letter. I'm delighted about the house. So is Barbara; she was overjoyed with the coat, and the cold weather has given her a chance to exhibit it everywhere, which was good propaganda [. . .]

A problem. I ought to have a fund of francs here for phone calls, telegrams etc. I can't pay for these things. And Bertha has to pay here for train tickets. And we should have money in the bank in Prague as soon as possible, so people on their way through, including myself, can get crowns. It's important. One has to spend the night, buy train tickets, etc. I'm working steadily. I'm on the last act of *The Days of the Commune*, Cas has already done sketches. He could get the costumes ready in May, it will be an enormous job, so he should start very soon. And he can't be in Berlin until the beginning of September. Can you take on Kuba as dramaturg to give him a steady job? – I'm awaiting the letter you sent via Basel. – Something has to be arranged to get Eisler to come to Berlin (through DEFA, the Dudow film? or a call from us), I need him for the Commune music, because songs like 'All of us or none' and 'Resolution' will be used in it, and he'll have to do all the rest as well. He's already working on this. Don't overtax yourself.

> I kiss you
> b

Bernhard R would be a big help. He's a dramaturg, director and theatre historian, and he speaks the language.

[Zurich, April 1949]

590 To Helene Weigel

Dear Helli,

I'm expecting the papers with the visas back from Berne any day; then we'll leave immediately. I'll have to spend three days in Salzburg, that's all. I have the following contracts:

Giehse 1 Nov. – 31 January;
Lutz the whole season;
Gaugler beginning 1 January (earlier if necessary, that is, if we do *The Days of the Commune* first)
Teo Otto November (after that available to the Deutsches Theater)
Neher 1 Sept. – 31 Oct. and 1 February – 31 March;

Besson: whole season.

Seyferth is keeping four months open for us; after that it depends on the part.

Steckel, beginning 5 Oct. for *Puntila* (or 1 February for *Puntila*), but he won't sign without a guarantee of three hundred a month, which I haven't given him; his offer is binding until 15 June.

We could have Fueter beginning 1 February. No contract yet.

Viertel has accepted for Nov.

We've bought the small stuff here, I hope Barbara got the right things. She can't wait to get to Berlin. It drives her to despair when the papers drag on and on. She's well and plump. Has gobbled up a small fortune.

> I kiss you
> b

Teo Otto, who has to go to Berlin for ten days to see Tschesno, will probably travel with us.

[Zurich, April 1949]

591 To Helene Weigel

Dear Helli,

Today, Wednesday, after all sorts of difficulties, Bern has finally sent a re-entry visa, though only for me, nothing for Barbara. In the meantime, I had taken steps, through von Einem in Salzburg, towards getting an Austrian passport. It would be valid for you and Barbara and would at least be a paper to travel with. The prospects are not bad, and I should try to keep the line open to as many German-language theatres as possible. Then we could work wherever we pleased. Well, I still need a *permit*[1] for Barbara and the one Bern has granted *me* for Munich. If Barbara doesn't get one, I'll go ahead and meet her in Salzburg. I hope the Russian permits[1] are in Bern too, so far we haven't been able to find out. The Commune play is in good shape, I've polished it a bit more and haven't sent it off yet. But now I think it would be better to start with *Puntila*, which is much less *controversial*[1]; besides, the Commune play is an enormous *production*[1] and if we put it in third place, we could work on it all through the season. What about Busch? (Should I try to

[1]English in original.

get Paryla interested?) I have to make sure Steckel can come at the
beginning of September, I'll find out in the next few days. (He can
definitely come in February.) I think we could also get Seyferth for
Puntila, and I believe Engel would be glad to have him. (In my opinion,
Steckel would be better.) Please ask Engel and let me know what you
think. Otherwise Seyferth would come in February, then it would be
for the Commune play in the dual role of Thiers and Bismarck. – The
information about the actors is being sent you. – Also the figures on
travel costs. – It's possible that the heavy luggage can be brought only
as far as the Czech-German border. Can we get someone to pick it up
there? – If we went straight from Munich to Hof, could a car meet us at
the eastern border? I'll also get some money in Munich for the house.
Barbara is dying to get to Berlin, she has been terribly worried about
being stuck here for too long. I don't see any point in trying to arrange
guest appearances for the Ensemble in advance, it seems unwise to risk
rejections. What is Budzislawski's exact address? – (And Lorre's?) –
Some letters from Kasprowiak have just come, posted during the
stampless period. Tell her everything is *all right*[1]. Of course you can't
tell her anything definite about which play is to be done first, until
you've read the Commune play. But you know the subject, and of
course I've stuck scrupulously to the truth, which as we know is not to
everyone's liking. Hirschfeld has read it; he spoke of it with great
enthusiasm, but advised me to run it third, and possibly with an
Ensemble augmented by the Deutsches Theater.

> I kiss you
> b

[Zurich] 21 April 1949

592 To Helene Weigel

Dear Helli,

Steckel has just told me he can't be in Berlin before 3 October – in
case we want to do *Puntila* first. Of course we could start preliminary
rehearsals before that (and train an understudy at the same time). Write
and tell me what you think. I'm still waiting for Barbara's permit for
Munich, but I won't wait too long. If she doesn't get one, I'll go ahead
to Munich for a week and meet her in Salzburg. The play goes off to

you on Monday. But before you give it to anyone, it needs to be copied (above all don't let Engel see it in its present patched-up condition).

I kiss you

b

[Zurich, April–May 1949]

593 To Helene Weigel

Dear Helli,

We have crates, we'll be able to pack early next week at Barbara's in Feldmeilen, then the stuff goes to the *Sanitaire*, but I'll leave the blankets out. All this will take a certain amount of running around. So will our papers. I'll have to see about them again. The extension was only until 6 October, a very unfortunate date, in the middle of rehearsals. And so far they don't want to give us re-entry visas. The play is finished in rough draft, time enough to polish it in Berlin. I'll send it off at the beginning of the week, to be retyped by Kasprowiak: don't show it to Engel until you have a clean copy, that's important I think. I'll have to go over it again for the language, and scenes 7–11 need more dash (and documentation). – It's been a lot of work. – It's important that there should be a small fund here when I leave, so the actors can buy their tickets here and have a little money for the trip. In Prague, too, we have to arrange for their lodgings and tickets, otherwise they'll need too many [Swiss] francs that they haven't got, and we want the engagement to look respectable. It wouldn't be right to reimburse them in Berlin and it wouldn't help. About the house you should speak to Suhrkamp and Wendt; if we can raise the money it would be good to buy the house. *Courage* in itself should bring in enough, plus the other plays. Somebody will just have to advance the money. If only I weren't detained here; so far I haven't wasted any time, I've been able to do the play, I had Cas here for it, now we're working on the sets, which will be beautiful, I think. Oh yes, another thing: Hauptmann should ask old Duncker for literature, he's the one who compiled the 1871 Book. What I especially need is *Documents historiques contemporains* (Collection de la Reine de France): *Les 31 séances officielles de la Commune* (1871).

b

Zurich, April–May 1949

594 To Helene Weigel

Dear Helli,

Well, here's the play, I hope you like it, Engel too. The songs at the end and in between are missing. If we do it in February, we can open with *Puntila*, Steckel can be in Berlin on 5 October. The Commune play is a training play for the Ensemble, a lot of actors can be trained in small but well-rounded roles, and if we do it in February we can bring in actors from the DT for a sort of joint production, but in the style of the NBE – February would be better than September for Gaugler, and he would be good as the snooping officer in Scene 12 or as Rigault.

I've been negotiating with Munich for a guest appearance of the whole *Mother Courage* production (Kammerspiele). – Did you get the receipts from the Sanitaire? – What is this story Kasprowiak tells me about *Puntila* and the Hebbel-Theater? Obviously we and no one else are doing *Puntila*. Find out if Desch has some new breach of contract up his sleeve. He has no right whatever to dispose of the play in Berlin without consulting me.

> i.k.y.–
> b

Please don't show anyone the manuscript (the original). It's very important.

595 To Ilse Kasprowiak

Tuesday

Dear K,

We (Barbara and I) have received notice of the visas from Berne; in other words they're there, and we've sent our passports. So we have hopes of finally being able to leave next week. However, we have to stop in Salzburg for three days. It would be good if there were some Czech crowns for us in Prague. One isn't allowed to take an unlimited amount of crowns from here to there, and the exchange rate in Prague is terrible. We shall go and see Eisnerova. (Still no visas for Neher or Berlau.)

Ruth Berlau is going via Munich. But you must have a room ready for her in Berlin. Also please ask Tschesno about the room in the publishing house.

Too bad the play hasn't arrived. We sent it by air mail to the British Press Centre. I've got one copy left. Perhaps you could enquire at the Press Centre. And if it has come wire me.

We're having terrible problems with the luggage. We need an authorisation to take it out of the country. Each piece must be listed, etc. The money has gone off to Sweden, so now perhaps the things from there will be sent too. Enclosed the information about the actors I'm expecting, for their visas.

> Regards,
> brecht

[Zurich, May 1949]

596 To Elisabeth Hauptmann

Dear Bess,

About Eulenspiegel:

Material about the Peasant War; look especially for a phase when it seems to be, or really is, going well for the peasants.

I want to show how the peasants are in too much of a hurry to think they've won, they go home to their harvests, fight among themselves, relapse into old servitudes, etc.

What did those knights who sided with the peasants do about their own peasants (as regards their corvée)?

Why did they side with the peasants?

At what point did they leave the peasants in the lurch?

What was the attitude of the burghers?

Was there a big meeting of the appropriators of the peasants' land?
    To decide how the campaign was to be carried on?

Was there much starvation?

What were the peasants' main mistakes?

Was there guerrilla warfare?

Was there clandestine resistance?

Sabotage on the farms? Punishment for it?

Were there sons of peasants fighting for the enemies of the peasants?

Did the universities take a hand? Who were the students? What did
    they study? Who were the judges? On what basis did they judge?

Do we have any contemporary satires (about the priests, the *jus
    primae noctis*, the overlords of the towns, the robber barons, etc.)?

Luther's writings against the peasants.

What was the reaction to them?

About the Commune:
Documentation of mistakes.
The different tendencies among the Communards.
Were any big businesses threatened?
What about war profits?
What connections were there between Paris businessmen and the victorious Germans?
Food prices. Black market
Bureaucracy in the Commune.
Did the courts sabotage the Commune?
What about the students?
Jokes and anecdotes.
The journalists.
Attitude of the Goncourts. Of Zola.
Is there anything by Maupassant? Baudelaire?
Attitude and role of England.
Did the Church agitate (against the Commune)? What was the attitude of the lower clergy?
Were some of them favourable?
Were there shifts of mood?
Songs in the cabarets?

> Yours cordially
> b

[Spring 1949]

597 To Gottfried von Einem

Dear von Einem,

I'm sitting here with Cas, we've been talking about the Festival, and it looks as if it may come off. Now I can think of an equivalent, worth more to me than any advance; that would be a haven, in other words, a passport. Of course, it should be managed without publicity if at all possible. And perhaps something of this sort would be best: Helli after all is a native Austrian (Viennese) and like me she has been stateless since 1933. At present there is no German government. Could she get an Austrian passport? And could I get one simply as her husband? You understand, I don't know the legal position. However, a passport would be of the greatest importance to me. I can't settle in one part of Germany and be dead for the other part. Perhaps you can help me.

> Yours cordially,
> brecht

The Swiss are giving us trouble again. So *again* I'm unable to get away from here.

[A postscript by Caspar Neher follows]
April 1949, Zurich

598 To Gottfried von Einem

[Zurich, 22] April 1949

Dear von Einem,
    Here are the two letters. I'm very grateful to you for your quick and efficient help. Yesterday I finally received a re-entry visa valid for another six months, that is, until September 1949, but after great difficulties and probably for the last time. As far as the Landeshauptmann is concerned, I feel that you represent me better than I could myself. Don't you think it best that we shouldn't meet? About the Burgtheater, it would be good if Viertel directed a play, and he could tell us which one. As to the choral text, I'll think it over. The best might be a simple news item about an actual incident in which someone behaved creditably – it still happens now and then. I hope to see you soon in Berlin.

> Yours very cordially
> brecht

    About *The Trial*: I'm just glad I was able to get my little ideas in (after being so annoyed at the Gide adaptation in Paris). A share in the royalties is out of the question of course; I'm constantly getting such advice in connection with my own work.

599 To Gottfried von Einem

Dear von Einem,
    Curjel has just been here, and I've written the two letters in all haste. I'm enclosing my birth certificate and proof of my expatriation. We were married in Berlin, and copies of marriage certificates are no longer obtainable, the registry office in Charlottenburg was destroyed. I'll come as soon as I can, I'll travel direct (cutting out Munich) via Salzburg and Prague. We just phoned the Austrians and were told that

stateless persons are no longer allowed to stop over in Austria, not even for the two days permitted last year. So unless you find some solution, I won't be able to get out of the train. I'll wire you the date of my arrival, I'll be travelling with my daughter Barbara; but I must first get the Czechoslovakian and Russian visas (for the East Zone) put into my passport; they are allegedly ready. As things stand, I can't just set out, because I have permission for only a single re-entry into Switzerland. But I'm hurrying as much as I can, because of Salzburg and because I must really get to Berlin. Please let me know if there's anything I can do about stopping on the way through. (Here they tell me petitions take at least six weeks to get through and then the answer is negative.) We can attend to everything else when we meet in Salzburg, if we do. Otherwise, I'll write to you about it. (Try and find a news item that appeals to you, then I might help you with the stylisation.)

> Cordially and with sincere thanks,
> Yours,
> b

References?

Albert Einstein, Princeton
Oskar Wälterlin, Director of the Zurich Schauspielhaus
Horwitz, Director of the Basel Stadttheater

[Zurich, April–May 1949]

600 To Gottfried von Einem

Dear von Einem,

On 4 May I applied at the Consulate General here in Zurich for a five-day entry and exit visa in May and June (for myself and on separate forms for my daughter Barbara Brecht who is accompanying me to Berlin.) You have my personal details. (Once again: Identity card No. 9180, issued in Berne on 30 August 1948 by the Chief of the Police Department, valid until 1 October 1949. I was born on 10.2.98 in Augsburg. I am stateless. I intend to enter by way of the Swiss-Austrian border and to leave by way of the Austrian-Czechoslovakian border.) If you can't get the stopover for my daughter, she'll have to travel later, which would be rather inconvenient.

I hope we can discuss those literary matters when we meet. I have no choral text at hand; the best would be for you to find a news item that appeals to you and I'll help you reformulate it. But I'll be looking for one too.

I would rather not submit a summary of the festival play (*Salzburg Dance of Death*) in writing, for several reasons. Better if you tell the interested parties what we discussed (The Emperor's pact with Death, Death undertakes to limit the victims of the next war, to spare the Emperor and his nearest and dearest, provided they make the sign agreed upon. But Death is overworked and forgets the sign. Moral: You can't do business with Death) *in what you consider the most effective way.* (I'm awkward in these things.) Now I have everything except the *Russian* visa! So I don't know when I'll be leaving. It's disgusting.

> Yours very cordially,
> brecht

[Zurich, May 1949]

603 To Ferdinand Reyher

Dear Reyher,

It's fair enough, but none the less beastly that because of my not writing I never got any news. What are you doing? What about *Hodge Podge*, the fragment? If you send it to me, I'll arrange to have it translated, and then we wouldn't be dependent on Wilder. And the thing with the photographer? And when are you coming to Berlin, where a room is ready for you in Helli's house in Weissensee. Another thing: We're putting together an Ensemble of actors and we need plays, one about *American politics,*[1] even in a light vein. Isn't there a fairly recent play about the White House, a comedy (by Behrman or somebody like that), dealing with a presidential election? Couldn't you send me something of the kind? Or *Pin[s] and Needle[s]*? There must be things which if suitably adapted or directed would enlighten people here (I mean in Berlin). You might send a few plays or just one to BB, Suhrkamp Verlag, Zehlendorf-West, Forststrasse 27, American Sector. But most of all a letter.

I've been in Zurich for two months and am going back to Berlin the day after tomorrow for the summer and autumn.

> As ever,
> b

[Zurich], 21 May 1949

[1] English in original

606 To Peter Huchel

Dear Peter Huchel,

I want to thank you for the excellent special issue, it's really the first publication that brings me together with the Germans, apart from my own efforts. A kind of petition for admittance to literature.

But I've also read the first three issues and I admire your witty and methodical contribution to building and rebuilding. Your view that this building must be done *on a large scale*, in accordance with a *broad* plan and through a general development of productivity in the material as well as the formal sense, is always clearly and refreshingly apparent.

What a good idea to present Lorca and Mayakovsky together – their progress from the folk song to the song for a whole population. I'd welcome more of Bloch's notes on Hegel.

Congratulations.

Yours,
brecht

[Berlin], 1 July 1949

Please give my regards to Hermlin, whose poems I liked very much.

607 To Arnold Zweig

Dear Zweig,

Rudi Engel tells me that Wandel expects you to invite me to the conference that has been convened to set up an Academy of the Arts. Unfortunately I don't know much about it, because I have never been asked to attend conferences (I should really feel offended), but this Academy, I hear, will pay salaries, procure flats, and even enable certain members to obtain grants for young artists and writers, and I've been hearing a good deal lately about real need among the young people. So there would really be some point in this Academy, especially if it doesn't turn out to be a showpiece like the Weimar Academy. So I am entirely at your disposal.

Cordially, your old
brecht

[Berlin, June 1949]

608 To Arnold Zweig

Dear Zweig,

Thank you for the poem. Naturally it's easy to write poetry when your health is good.

I've written to Wandel that I'll attend the meetings as soon as I'm out of hospital. In the meantime a few notes:

1) It would be good if the members could each choose two or three advanced students. But these students would have to get scholarships to enable them to live.

2) And the *new* arts are important. The *poster* (and photomontage) Johnny Heartfield (London).

Photography, I think your suggestion of Lerski is brilliant. For stage design there's Caspar Neher.

For the cinema Erich Engel.

In short, we should get the most modern people for the modern arts.

>   Yours cordially,
>   brecht

>   [Berlin, June/July 1949]

610 To Ferdinand Reyher

>   Berlin NW 7, 7 July 1949
>   Luisenstrasse 18
>   Tel: 421968

Dear Reyher,

As I've often told Bentley, I don't want any more little experimental productions in New York. I've had too much of that. Moreover, the lead in *The Good Person of Szechwan* has to be played by a top-flight actress. Nowadays a good person can be played only by an actress with plenty of imagination; good intentions aren't enough.

Bentley did excellent spadework by getting me access to the university theatres and I'm sure he will be more at home in that considerably purer atmosphere than in the hopeless atmosphere of Broadway. Please talk him out of his plan. Two years of crisis, and the soil may (not necessarily) be more favourable to such things.

Your decision to come in February was greeted with joy. Room ready as usual.

Yours very cordially,

b

N B In my opinion Bentley has a good deal to learn before he can direct such difficult plays. Better send him here for the purpose.

b

N B Dear Reyher, thanks for all the greetings, though I'm grieved at the way you neglect your correspondence with my daughter.

But now I have a favour to ask. Liebling-Wood has sent me the enclosed cheques. I'm returning them to you, because I'd like Steff to receive this sum from Liebling-Wood. Help! Steff's address: S.S. Brecht, 1118 4th Street, Santa Monica, California.

612 To Ruth Berlau

Love,

I rode through to Freilassing (on the border) so I only saw Munich for half an hour towards evening, half demolished and full of purchasables.

I hope you too have arrived safely. I'm dying to hear how the rehearsals etc. are going. (Most important, be friendly, go *slow*, don't forget that they have to keep up, remember the little animal that was always standing on my desk in Skovsbostrand.) Write to me *express*. (Address: Brecht, c/o Föttinger, Freilassing, Münchener Strasse 22).

And the forehead is smooth.

Love,

bertolt

Most important: Do you know how long you'll stay?

Freilassing, 29 August 1949
[Postmark]

614 To Gottfried von Einem

Dear von Einem,

I have no official function or duties in Berlin and receive no salary. The reason for the absurd rumour that I'm directing the Deutsches

Theater in Berlin in Langhoff's place must be that, because of the acute shortage of theatres in Berlin, the Berliner Ensemble, which is producing my play *Mr Puntila and his Man Matti*, is using the stage of the Deutsches Theater. Another reason may be that Leonard Steckel, who created the part of Puntila in Zurich under my direction, is playing the part in Berlin at my request. All this doesn't make me a theatre director. I still intend to regard Salzburg as my permanent residence and build up a sphere of artistic activity in Austria. At the moment I'm working on a carnival play for the Salzburg Festival.

> Yours cordially,
> Bertolt Brecht

Berlin, 12 October 1949

615 To Albert Schreiner

Dear Comrade Schreiner,

I've written a play about the Commune that we (the Berliner Ensemble) may produce in the spring. I'd welcome some advice from you, so I'm sending the play. Of course it's an enormous (and risky) undertaking to squeeze all that into three stage-hours. I used what material I could get hold of in Zurich: Lissagaray, Duncker's collection of documents, what I could find in the usual authorities, and the minutes of the thirty-one sessions of the Commune.

I don't know if you can afford the time to look the play over for historical accuracy, but I'd be satisfied with a few brief hints in connection with the political aspects.

It's a pity we don't see more of each other, but last summer when I might have had a little free time, I was ill.

> Yours cordially,
> brecht

Berlin-Weissensee, Berliner Allee 190
October 1949

The manuscript is going off to you by the same post.

616 To Eric Bentley

Dear Bentley,

You're right. Section 68 of the *Short Organum* needs a footnote and a correction.

Correction: 'and in a barbaric bloodbath butchers his uncle, his mother and himself' must be changed to 'and in a barbaric bloodbath puts his uncle, his mother and himself to death.'

Footnote:

'We regard Act IV, Scene 4 ("A plain in Denmark"), in which we encounter Hamlet for the last time before his return "in the flesh" and he speaks the long monologue in which he entrusts his father to Fortinbras's army, as the turning point. ("O, from this time forth, my thoughts be bloody or be nothing worth.") True, the letter to Horatio in the scene after next announces that Hamlet has nevertheless boarded ship for England, but here there is no room for acting and the account he gives Horatio of the King's plot against him (V, 2) does not supply the actor with a moment in which to take a decision.'

This interpretation of Hamlet is only an example of *interpretation*. In other words, shifts of accent, transpositions, possible cuts and even (not in this case) occasional additions are needed.

At present, incidentally, the *Short Organum* is read mostly by students. However, my idea that theatres should use our models is still under discussion. You know the *Antigone* model and now Suhrkamp is publishing the *Courage* model. And I've also written an article about 'Building up a part', i.e. Laughton's Galileo.

I'd be glad if you could come here again this winter. Unfortunately we can't get anything done in the Golden West.

Yours cordially

617 To Eric Bentley

Dear Bentley,

Re *Hamlet* and *Organum*, I think I have kept within the limits of interpretation. Few textual changes are needed. It is true that after the heating of his reason and his blood, after his 'storing up (of) warlike spirit' during his meeting with Fortinbras, it still takes the discovery that his own life is threatened to bring on Hamlet's final offensive. But this discovery is only spoken of; after the monologue (in praise of action) the actor has nothing more that he can show on stage. Thus it is quite as a matter of course that this monologue becomes the centre of gravity. (And the rest can definitely stand). In short (to put it somewhat more pointedly): It can be argued that *without* the meeting with Fortinbras Hamlet's subsequent discovery of the king's plot would not in itself induce him to clean out the Augean stable. – I agree to that, because your criticism strikes me as important. Could you look into it again? I'd appreciate it.

As for your suggestion that I should add irony towards the East to my irony towards the West, do you think it's possible to be objective without taking sides?

Now to *The Days of the Commune*: It's probably true that the play can't be accepted unless one accepts the Marxist point of view. But to take a classical example: To accept *Hamlet* or *Troilus and Cressida* mustn't one accept the attitudes of Montaigne or Bacon? Anyway, Hirschfeld's interpretation is wrong. What the play can show is only that the proletariat cannot counter the force of its adversaries unless it is prepared to use force. I've made no attempt to bring out parallels between Paris in 1871 and Berlin in 1949, not those that would have simplified the play.

You know, you're about the only person with whom I discuss such things, and to whom I write about them (though too little). After all you've done for me, a harsh word on your part about one of my plays can't possibly lead to *estrangement*[1] on my part; you have every right to criticise.

Please don't be embittered by my hesitation to let you produce my plays in the commercial theatre. The question is not whether I regard you as a 'Westerner' or not. (What a term!) In view of your really extraordinary* advocacy of my theory, your directing would have every reason to be representative and exemplary, but since theory and practice are two different things and I have never seen any of your directing, since moreover my own experiments are still in their infancy, I'd rather have you first practise here with us for a while. If you see any chance of that, I'll do all I can to help you.

In the meantime, no bitterness, if you please.

Anyway, I prefer university productions to commercial ventures.

As ever,

Brecht

Berlin 12 November 1949

*We are now trying to sell a few of your articles to the *Neue Rundschau* or *Sinn und Form*; they are excellent. [Brecht's note]

[1]English in original.

618 To Wilhelm Pieck

Dear Comrade Wilhelm Pieck,

May I, to express my pleasure at your accession to office, send you a little poem, which might far more aptly be spoken by you than by its author?

> With warm regards from Helli and myself,
> bertolt brecht

> Berlin, 2 November 1949

619 To Erich Engel

Dear Engel,

Forgive my impatience in our conversation about dialectics; 'swearing like a trooper' seems to be inevitable in that context. It also seems to indicate that thought-forms are life-forms in the present case, of classes. Actually it amounts to a kind of social or cultural earthquake; not a move from place to place, but a fall, where the essential is to land on one's feet and not on one's head. To put it simply, the proletariat regard dialectics as the last word of the bourgeoisie (who naturally do not regard it as their last word) and set out to transform it, just as they transform industrial production. This is an enormous undertaking and our attitude towards it should be adequate. Materialistic dialectic is in its infancy, but what Marx and Engels said of the Commune applies to it: It is a manifestation of the proletariat in its infancy, but the infancy of a giant. My suggestion that this way of thinking should be studied as a way of life means only that dialectics must not be derived from the traditional way of thinking or refuted on that basis, any more than the new way of life can be derived [from the older way of life]; a leap is necessary, or a tumble (which may turn out well). For people like you and me it is wiser to understand dialectics on the basis of its political adaptability, in other words, to derive the new concepts from actions. (To transform one quality into another is to castrate the principle of transformation; it then becomes a truism, i.e. an irrelevant, ineffectual truth. Perhaps what is needed is a conceivable and anticipated event, in the course of which, massive changes engender a new quality, which is of a very specific nature, whereas the quality from which it sprang was not specific in this respect, but indeterminate, *unworkable*, so that it might best be designated as no quality at all.) Here concepts should not be regarded as fixed possessions; we take the liberty, as it were, of adding to the old ones. A kind of expropriation. Please take this digression as a sort of penance, which I have imposed on myself for my vehemence.

Stemmle's enthusiasm and the colour-film experiments will undoubtedly cause no end of trouble in your absence, but I'm glad you're finally getting some rest, all the more so as I am largely to blame for delaying your holiday. I'm deeply grateful to you for disregarding your exhaustion and helping to get the Ensemble on its feet.

Yours very cordially,

Berlin, November 1949

620 To Hanns Eisler

Dear Eisler,

Here is the *Koloman Wallisch Cantata*. It goes without saying that you will cut and transpose as you see fit; if you have to put in anything new, formulate it yourself and let me work it over if possible. I'm curious to know what you do with the long ballad. I imagine you'll use several melodies and won't make the accompaniment too naive. *But it's up to you.*[1]

I've done *Puntila* here and I think you would have been amused. The type is still running around loose in various parts of the world, but in the play he makes the impression of a prehistoric fly encapsulated in amber.

If you have a copy, please send me the *Weissbrot-Kantate*, I'd like to put it into a matinée so the people here get to hear something of yours.

What's your brother up to?

As ever,

b

[Berlin, November–December 1949]

621 To Paul Wandel

Dear Comrade Wandel,

You were called away just as you were saying something about plans

[1]English in original.

for the Academy and I was on the point of contradicting you. I'll have to retrieve myself now, because one has no right to sidestep contradiction. You argued against master classes on the grounds that they turned out epigones. And that doesn't strike me as quite right. One of Stanislavsky's students was Vakhtangov, who developed an entirely different sort of theatre; and one of Schönberg's students is Eisler. Actually, what's taught is not style but technique; in other words, a standard is passed on. One function of the Academy would be to enable gifted persons to study (and in a measure to produce), by giving them a sum of money in the form of a scholarship. The students must be left free to take advice or not. I'd have been very glad at one time to submit my projects to Hauptmann or Kaiser or Wedekind, and above all, to get a scholarship. (I don't believe the originality of my plays would have suffered.) But in any case our Academy should be productive and not just representative. (The literary section might, for instance, help to vet school anthologies or help with translations of foreign literature.) Otherwise we'll get an Academy where rhetoric flourishes and the plaster crumbles.

With comradely regards,

[Berlin, December '49]

624 To the Dresden Staatstheater

I have prepared models for the performance of my plays and offered to help theatres make use of them. For two reasons. 1) The way to produce these plays effectively is at present not very well known; they must therefore be protected against bungling. 2) I have tried to provide theatres with something new. (Exposition and theory don't seem to be enough; practical application is needed.)

The Dresden contract for *Puntila* was made with the Volksbühne, and though the Volksbühne has applied to me for a director who collaborated in drawing up the model in Berlin, the Staatstheater has not renewed this request. Under these circumstances, I no longer wish to insist on this contract and suggest that you drop the production of *Puntila*. Moreover, I have asked the director, Mr Kuckhahn, not to insist on the contract but in my interest to go to Dresden, see if he can interest you in letting him direct the play and also find out what guarantee there is that the play can be produced appropriately without the use of the model, or using the model but with a different director. Please don't think me unfriendly – plays of mine have too often been mangled by excellent but not specifically informed directors. Perhaps it is a weakness of the plays that they require such unusual measures.

With best regards

[Berlin, late 1949 early 1950]

625 To Hermann Duncker

Dear Hermann Duncker,

I've written a play about the Commune and used your collection of documents, which is marvellous. Of course I have no way of knowing whether you can spare the time to look through the play, and how your eyes are – the copy is not especially good, but it's the best we've been able to get.

There are probably dreadful mistakes. It was very difficult to bring out the errors of the Commune and its greatness at the same time. I badly need your advice. If you prefer, I can get one of our young actors to read you the play.

Yours cordially,
brecht

Berlin-Weissensee, Berliner Allee 190

The manuscript is going off to you by the same post.

[1949]

626 To the South German Radio, Stuttgart

Gentlemen,

If you wish to broadcast *Lindbergh's Flight* as part of a historical survey, I must ask you to add a prologue and to make a few slight changes in the text. Lindbergh is known to have had close ties with the Nazis; his enthusiastic report on the unconquerable German air force had a paralysing effect in several countries. L also played a sinister role as a fascist in the USA. The title of my radio play must therefore be changed to *The Ocean Flight*, the prologue must be spoken and the name of Lindbergh expunged.

1) in 1 (Appeal to all) 'Captain Lindbergh's Ocean Flight' is replaced by 'The First Flight Across the Ocean'

2) in 3 (Introduction of the Flier, The Take-off) 'My name is Charles Lindbergh' is replaced by 'My name doesn't matter'

3) in 10 (All through the flight the people said . . .) 'of Captain Lindbergh will succeed' is replaced by 'of Captain Soandso will succeed'

4) in 16 (Arrival of the Flier . . .) 'I am Lindbergh. Please carry me' is replaced by 'I am Soandso. Please carry me.'

If this version is acceptable to you, I have no objection to your broadcasting the play. The changes may detract slightly from the poetry, but the removal of the name will be instructive.

> With best regards,
> Yours
> bertolt brecht

Berlin 2 January 1950

N B If the titles are read, it must always be 'The Flier'.

628 To Berthold Viertel

Dear Viertel,

We hear that the Russians – I use the plural because we don't know any individuals – are enthusiastic about your production and go so far as to say it's better than any production of Gorky that can be seen in Moscow; which is considerable praise. It seems to be holding up, or even to have become more impressive.

You've left a very effective visiting card.

My adaptation of *The Tutor* [by Jakob Lenz] is finished, Gaugler has arrived from Switzerland. Lorre may come in March. Your emulation of Arnold Winkelried paved the way for him (even within Kortner's realm some stronger voices are being heard).

Thank you for returning Neher so promptly. He has started work on *The Tutor*.

How is *Richard* coming along? I hope you'll take a rest after that.

> With regards from all,
> As ever,
> b

Berlin, 17 January 1950

629 To Max Frisch.

Dear Mr Frisch,

Thank you for the package. To tell the truth, it's rather alarming to sit for one's portrait particularly when the portraitist is not merely tolerated but respected. But then I read with amusement your charming and friendly sketch of the strange bird of passage – a man with whom I myself am slightly acquainted. It made me curious to read the whole book.

Zurich has had great success in Berlin with Giehse and Steckel. It would be splendid if you could manage to come some time.

I'm also looking forward to your new play.

Yours cordially,
brecht

632 To Stefan S. Brecht

Dear Steff,

I've read your observations about *The Tutor* with great interest, it is a highly moral play without trumpets. I hope you like my adaptation, which is being sent to you. We have now got more or less used to Berlin, at least to the changes that are going on everywhere. Helli has done an enormous amount of work since she first drove on to the German stage in Courage's covered waggon, but it has not gone unnoticed. I wish you could come here at least for a visit in the spring. If only I had the $! (But I send you what comes in and as you see it's pitifully little.) Many thanks for the books, and for your letters as well.

Yours

Berlin-Weissensee, Mid-February 1950

633 To Peter Suhrkamp

Dear Suhrkamp,

About the *Mother Courage* model book, I think I've found a form that's not too pedantic. It won't consist of explanations of the pictures; the text and the illustrations will separately record and comment on the production. The text will concentrate on the principles of direction rather than the 'moves downstage left' etc. At the same time, we'll make new photographs of detail, as you suggested. The ones done by the publishing house are excellent, really beautiful, not to be compared with the *Antigone* illustrations.

But how are you? Are you really getting some rest? Are you able to keep the doctors away? Perhaps you should write a little, I don't mean letters.

As ever,
brecht

Our guest appearance in Braunschweig and Cologne was an amazing success (even in the Catholic and Social Democratic papers).

[Berlin], February 1950 [Dating: Suhrkamp secretariat]

634 To Ferdinand Reyher,

Dear Reyher,

Helli, Barbara and I are waiting eagerly for you to get here. In June you'll still be able to see a few plays. *Courage* with Helli, *Puntila* with Steckel, and *The Tutor*. Fine if you could bring a few plays with you. If you should need a recommendation for your visa to Berlin, give the title of the play you want to offer Barlog, who directs the Steglitz Schlosspark Theater in the West Sector. Then he'll write to you. (Actually you don't need the visa straight away, you can get it in Germany.) Another thing; if you see Homolka, ask him if he'd be willing to act in Berlin. He could appear in the West Sector, but of course I'd rather have him in the Berliner Ensemble, which gives guest performances at the Deutsches Theater (and is directed by Helli). Viertel, who is also an American citizen, has directed for us and will again. And then there's another actor, Rewalt, whom Piscator knows. We'd take him on straight away if he'd come. We're all curious about Piscator's intentions. Do speak to him. He should at least pay a visit to the scene of his triumph. And not wait for offers, things are moving too fast here. He's very much needed.

But most important, manage to get some time off, so you won't have to go back for at least a year.

As ever,
b

[Berlin, February 1950]

635 To Fritz Kortner

Dear Kortner,

Please forgive me for not coming backstage: I am simply no longer capable of enjoying – and commending – an artistic performance when the statement does not strike me as being worth formulating or the pretext as justifying the production. Of course I was all the more exasperated because I knew that you and I are in complete agreement about this. We may have to take conditions into account, but we really mustn't let them dictate to us. Scrupulously setting all tact aside, I propose that you do *Galileo*, next season at the latest.

> In cordial irritation
> Your old

> Berlin, February 1950

636 To Gottfried von Einem

Dear von Einem,

Cas tells me there's a document you still need and that you had written to me about it. But I've received no such letter from you, so I don't know what it's about. Believe me, I'm as much interested as ever, possibly more. So much depends on it for my artistic work (and collaboration), there are so many countries, among them perhaps West Germany, where it may become impossible to travel without a passport. Cas has just gone to Vienna to help Viertel at the Burgtheater with *Richard III*. He says if there's anything he can do there about the passport, you need only phone Schuh.

> Cordially and expectantly yours,
> bertolt brecht

> [Berlin], 2 May 1950

637 To Ruth Berlau

1 Again there is the *third thing*, and again the personal and private recede into the background. The *third thing* is socialism, the essential is what we can do concretely for socialism at this stage and in these years.

2 The judgements 'good' and 'bad' are transposed into the judgements 'useful' and 'not useful', and even so these judgements are applied more often to actions than to persons.

3 Since we look to the future and not to the past, we remember the good and forget the bad in the past; in other words: We forget the good we ourselves have done and remember the good others have done. In future there will no longer be tributes (which are owed) but gifts (which are gladly given); conditions will no longer be stipulated; there will only be requests. No one will owe anyone anything; everyone will owe everything to the *third thing*.

4 Let's pretend we have only just met and try to be nice to each other.

[Berlin], 10 March 1950
[Dating; Ruth Berlau]

638 To Hans Mayer

[Berlin], 25 March 1950

Dear Hans Mayer,

I'm glad you are going to address the secondary schoolteachers on the subject of Lenz and *The Tutor*. May I suggest a few points, it may help us if you touch on them.

This marks the abdication of German classicism, that more or less voluntary masquerade of the bourgeois caryatids, who turn to pillars of salt at the sight of the revolutionary Sodom. The significant beginnings of realism must be re-established. The banishment of Lenz from the history of literature must be exposed. The theatre must go back to that point in order to go forward, in order to achieve a realistic style for the treatment of major themes, for the grand style has come down to us only in connection with idealistic themes. The problem of teachers as such in *The Tutor* must be regarded as an aspect of the German Misère, and perhaps it is necessary to explain the castration episode. Obviously this story is not purely symbolic; indeed, the self-emasculation of the intellectuals, virtually all of whom, as a caste so to speak, were driven into the teaching profession at about that time, is presented quite realistically (the play is based on a gruesome incident that actually took place in East Prussia) through a flesh and blood example. In other words, the physical castration not only *signifies* intellectual self-emasculation, but is represented as a grotesque way out of Läuffer's social situation. The play is a true *comedy*, and it is characteristic that the classical authors totally neglected this realistic genre. (*The Broken Jug* may be an exception, but it is also Kleist's most realistic work and interestingly enough it too, like *The Tutor*, is a parable.)

Forgive me for bringing up these points; they have come up in occasional discussions about the stageworthiness of the play and may show you what a minefield it all is.

Yours cordially,
brecht

639 To Ruth Berlau

Love,

The Tutor has been getting an amazingly good press (East and West), and has particularly impressed such actors as Bildt or Hinz or Wäscher. Anyway, it went well.

The photos I've received up to now show what *might* be done, i.e. with the light as it is. But they're strangely unpoetic, and almost all lack your special, individual eye. Photography simply isn't a mechanical business. Today I finally got your letter – I went to Charitéstrasse every day for it – and it makes me happy. Don't overtax yourself, that's the main thing.

My 'holiday' is as follows: preparing for the technical rehearsal of *Days of the Commune*. Writing the *Tutor* model book. A review of the *Puntila* reviews for the *Versuche*. Also we're threatened with recasting problems in *Courage* (Hinz's part). And now Engel wants us to start planning the film. You'll have to help. Suhrkamp is back in Frankfurt, worried sick about the lawsuit. I didn't even see him.

Write.

It's a little boring here. That ought to give you some satisfaction.

Love,
bertolt

Berlin, 19 April 1950
[Postmark]

640 To Peter Suhrkamp

Dear Suhrkamp,

It goes without saying that whatever happens I'd like to be published by the house you direct.

Yours very cordially,
bertolt brecht

Berlin, 21 May 1950

642 To Caspar Neher

Dear Cas,

I now have the paper, that is the document, but before I can get a passport I need a birth certificate, etc., so I can't come. It's too bad; as things are, we can't work together on anything of any length. The situation of the Ensemble is as follows: I'd like to start work on *Galileo* about 10 October (with Steckel as Galileo). I suggest that we do it together again; it's simply the best way. The première could be on 1 December, it really can't be earlier. Or much later either, because then Viertel will be here with Giehse. (And I can't get into the theatre before 10 October.) So could you postpone your holiday until after 1 December or to be on the safe side let's say 10 December? And don't completely forget *Lucullus* at the Staatsoper, you wangled[1] that yourself (and it was on your advice that Legal engaged the conductor from Göttingen); I'm sure Legal hasn't discussed a contract with you, they just assume that everything will be all right. – Wagner-Régeny has probably written to you that Felsenstein wants to do *Der Darmwäscher*. That's good news. I'm especially fond of that opera. Please apologise to Gottfried (von Einem) for me, it's hard working on the *Totentanz* without at least a few talks with you. And there's nothing more I can do about the passport, the Augsburgers are in no hurry to send my birth certificate. Also I had to have the Steyr overhauled, it took five weeks!) When are you coming here? How are you? (I hope you won't have to travel too much next season.)

As ever,
b

Regards to Erika and Gottfried

[Berlin, middle of 1950]

---

[1]Brecht's word is the German-American '*gemanaged*'.

644 To Berthold Viertel

Dear Viertel,

I'd like to get back to the idea of staging *Der Biberpelz* [The Beaver Coat] and *Rote Hahn* [Red Rooster] (the two plays shortened and woven together, in one evening). We could get permission from the Hauptmann Estate. Giehse could create a tremendous character, I mean, combine the two given characters into one; who would forsake her [proletarian] class to become a criminal – it's forsaking one's class that doesn't pay. It wouldn't even need very big changes. The weak repetition of the Wehrhahn investigation in *The Beaver Coat* would be dropped and the repetition taken from *Red Rooster* would bring out a development of the principle. What you are planning to do with *Die Ratten* [The Rats] could be done even more splendidly in this case. The setting for the first part [*The Beaver Coat*] could be a May Day, for the second a Navy Day (preparation for the big conflagration). Why apply a historical perspective to his weaknesses in these plays rather than letting them benefit by it. Nowhere better than at the Berliner Ensemble can you implement your great project of bringing the [German literary] heritage to the new public. I know how much importance you attach to *The Rats*, but after all you, like the undersigned, are one of those men who are able to cope with temptations. (A man shows he can cope with temptations by succumbing to them.) If we weigh the plays with (passionate) coolness, we must conclude, I believe, that *The Beaver Coat – Red Rooster* is the more galvanising play, it presents a mistake (rather than a miscarriage). Wolffen, despite her great vitality and wisdom, is on the wrong track. Of course it's up to you. Both plays are being worked on.

As ever,

b

Berlin, End of August 1950

I'm going to Munich tomorrow to do *Courage* at the Kammerspiele with Giehse. Could you come by way of Munich? When?

645 To DEFA

Dear friends,

I've spoken to Engel and Burri and come to the conclusion that the continuation of our work on the *Courage* film could be organised as follows: Engel will be back in Berlin at the end of December provided that DEFA renews its contract with him and that work can begin. Burri could be in Berlin by the end of November and start work, so we'd have a rough draft by the time Engel joins us. I think Burri could speed up his work on the script, he knows the style from previous experience and has plenty of technical know-how. And we'd have Neher too. Engel wants him very much, also in connection with writing the screen play. Engel, so he tells me, would consider Burri's collaboration a decisive factor. So I presume we could start shooting in February or March. But you must tell me straight away how much you can offer Burri.

Since my return here, I see even more clearly how important a great poetic peace film like *Courage* would be. You needn't worry about its being too passive. It has to be a stirring warning, and the figure of mute Kattrin can be a poetic means of creating enthusiasm for the fight against war if we do a decent script. Necessary as semi-documentary films are and excellent as they can be, we also need imaginative films that grip the broad masses from a different angle.

Do let me know soon.

> With best regards,
> Yours,
> Brecht

Munich, Kammerspiele, Herrnstrasse, 6 September 1950

646 To Gottfried von Einem

Dear von Einem,

I didn't get to Munich until late Sunday, so I missed your mother, which I very much regret. Please give her my best regards. I have my citizenship papers. I haven't got the passport yet, but it will be sent here as soon as it arrives. I'm infinitely grateful to you and your mother. When I get my passport, I'll come to Salzburg one Sunday and greet you as a fellow countryman. Then we'll be able to make plans for the Salzburg Festival, Cas was still here when I arrived, and I've arranged to work with him in December. I hope my cardinal sin No. 11 – failure to answer letters – hasn't soured you to the point of writing me off.

> As ever,
> b

Munich, Kammerspiele Maximilianstrasse
14 September 1950 [Dating von Einem]

647 To Elisabeth Hauptmann

Dear Bess,

Thanks for your letter. Rehearsals are going well. Giehse is wonderful, a tough businesswoman. Bentley has come to work as an assistant, likewise an Austrian. And some Dutchmen and an Italian will come for the last rehearsals. They're all crying out for study material. Burri is all right now, he's making money in films, though not terribly much. The cost of living has gone up quite a lot. Geis and Burri were with me at Lorre's in Garmisch, and now I'm discussing *The Overcoat* with him (Geis). L has just been down with jaundice, but he was as lively as ever and made a great impression on Geis and Burri. – Could you get hold of a copy of *Simone* somewhere? I need it badly. – I've written to Suhrkamp about Hamburg. Keep your fingers crossed because I've wired authorising the production on condition that they use Neher's sets.

I'll arrive 9 October
As ever,
b

Could you send my war poem? 'You who live on in cities that have died' – air mail.

649 To Berthold Viertel

Berlin, November 1950

Dear B V,

A few words about our method of adapting *The Beaver Coat* and *Red Rooster*. We've decided to trust Hauptmann's powers of observation implicitly (that is, we've studied the significance of every slightest detail and preserved it if possible), but to put less trust in his knowledge of what is historically essential. Accordingly, we had to bring in the working-class movement (Social Democracy), which Hauptmann almost entirely overlooks. Of course we've kept Dr Fleischer, the representative of the liberal bourgeoisie, but contrasted his liberalism with the more radical demands of the working-class movement, i.e. we made it [his liberalism] look slightly comical. In *Red Rooster* we substituted a Social Democratic worker for Rauchhaupt, chiefly so as to confront Wolffen with a conscious representative of her own class. The dialogue between the two in the last act seems to have turned out pretty well, largely because this man, being the father of the scapegoat Gustav von der Wolffen, has also suffered personal injury. The two plays are kept neatly separate (outwardly by the long interval); we give *The Beaver Coat* two, *Red Rooster* three acts. Comedy is followed by tragi-comedy. Amusing thievery is followed by crime. *Red Rooster* shows the bitter end of Wolffen's individualistic struggle for existence. Both plays preserve their essence (perhaps the comedy is somewhat intensified in the first, the tragedy in the second), but they can no longer be performed singly. *Red Rooster* includes only characters who in Hauptmann as well figure also in *The Beaver Coat*, but one is dropped, Dr Boxer. Rauchhaupt's character is changed, and he is renamed Rauert. We have been very much amused by the accuracy of Hauptmann's observation and our young collaborators' respect for him has increased steadily. At present we are still trying to get stylistic balance by slightly shortening Hauptmann's text and somewhat broadening the language of our version. (Luckily most of our collaborators are Berliners and one is a Silesian.)

We are looking forward to your keen-eyed judgement.

As ever,

b

651 To Gottfried von Einem

Dear von Einem,

My work on the *Salzburger Totentanz* hasn't really been getting ahead because Cas, as a result of his guest commitments, is never here for very long. Also, I've discovered that a sub-plot (in addition to the Emperor-Death plot) is needed – something closer to humankind. I've now sketched it in. When the Emperor gives up the crusade and returns to Salzburg, the Sultan's army does not pursue him, because it too has been wiped out. The Great Death is followed by the Plague. The sub-plot takes pace in the family of the merchant Frühwirt. The Widow Frühwirt has heard that a strange disease is raging in Hungary and that the peasants are selling their cattle for a song so as to be able to leave the country. She sends her brother-in-law to Hungary to buy cattle cheap. The brother-in-law is infected with the disease, realises that he has been sent to do business with Death, and hurries home, bringing the plague into the Frühwirt household. It is carnival time. The servant girl, an old maid, who has been working for the widow Frühwirt for many years, escapes death by finding the strength to disobey her mistress and go to the carnival. It has taken me some time to work this out, but it will prove worth while. How is your opera coming along? I'm looking forward to it. Don't waste too much time organising and working for other people instead of composing your music.

But it's the same with me. Trying to build up a new theatre leaves me no time to write for it.

Yours cordially,
b

Berlin, 7 January 1951

652 To Walter Ulbricht

[Berlin], 12 March 1951

Dear Comrade Ulbricht

Formal objections have been raised to the production of the opera *The Trial of Lucullus*, the libretto of which is by me − because of the music. It seems to be seriously endangered. The opera is a unique condemnation of wars of conquest, and given the shameless way in which West Germany is mustering former generals with a view to a new invasion, such a work, in which an ancient conqueror is condemned by the court of posterity, is worth producing in a city like Berlin, whence its influence will radiate powerfully to the West. I do not advocate indifference to the question of form. I believe that we must strive especially for *intelligibility*. The text of this opera was written in 1937, the music in 1944. Thus it can scarcely be regarded as *the* work providing the long-awaited model of a *form*. I do not know whether the music is easily understandable, but the *opera*, its message and its content are easy to understand, and in my opinion we should let ourselves be guided by *content* until the difficult problems of form have been solved. After all, it is only on the basis of content that artists can solve the problem of form.

May I ask you to help me?

With socialist greetings,
Yours

653 To Paul Wandel, Minister for People's Education

Berlin, 19 March, 1951

Dear Comrade Wandel,

We are deeply grateful to you for [authorising] the performance of *Lucullus* before an audience of the most progressive elements of our young republic. Such performances can indeed help to clarify the problems of a new art.

It goes without saying that the applause, obviously inspired by the work's message of peace and by its exemplary production, does not blind us to the seriousness of the objections that have been raised to the musical idiom. On the other hand, I hope that the many things which you and a number of comrades found disturbing won't lead you to overlook the considerable beauty of the music, the composer's ability to establish a progressive content and make it intelligible, and also his passionate devotion to our people's desire for peace.

Your generosity in putting the magnificent resources of the State Opera at our disposal and your engagement of a world-famous conductor will go far towards giving the artists a clear understanding of their inspiring, but by no means easy task.

Again many thanks. With socialist greetings,

Yours

654 To Walter Ulbricht

Berlin, 19 March 1951

Dear Comrade Ulbricht,

I wish to thank you and the comrades for making possible the production of Dessau's opera. In doing so you have demonstrated the republic's great comradely understanding for the difficulties besetting artists in the present phase of reconstruction. A production of this kind shows artists – and the most progressive element in the public – the way that art and the public should take. We attribute the applause on the one hand to the exemplary production, on the other hand to the peace-promoting tendency of the work. Believe me that Dessau takes the objections that have been raised to the musical idiom very seriously. I myself am profoundly convinced that the qualities which may make the music difficult for the new public are in the last analysis superficial, and that the composer with his great talent and his devotion to this public will undoubtedly be able to rid himself of these qualities.

His aim is an intelligible, realistic people's opera, which will generate new socialist impulses.

Thanking you again, with socialist greetings,

Yours

655 To Anton Ackermann

Dear Comrade Ackermann,

I've spent Easter morning studying the objections that have been raised to the opera *Lucullus*, and have begun at once to rework the text in such a way as to render even a *mistaken* opinion that the work embodies pacifist tendencies impossible. Indeed, I owe you thanks for insisting that *activity* must be mobilised against wars of conquest. This, I see, can be done by the addition of two new scenes. And the question of who had sent Lucullus to Asia should also be answered. (Of course it's not 'Rome', but the silver trusts which existed in Rome, the tax farmers and the slave traders).

I believe I can prove that the subject is *not* badly chosen and that it can serve as a means of treating these important points.

As for the music, I can't say that I agree with you. For one thing you do not put forward any arguments as you do in connection with the text, but merely express a general condemnation which gives the composer nothing to go by. It is not true that Dessau is an advocate of formalism, and he denies that his music is formalistic. He may be mistaken, but then he should be shown. Otherwise he is dealing with a mere expression of taste. At least – and this is something very, very unusual in the literature of opera – he has wholly subordinated his music to the text, hence to the content, and he has not dispensed with melodies. His melodies may not immediately appeal to everyone's ears, but he is willing to do a good deal of improving; moreover some of the music, you will have to admit, is unquestionably of great beauty, and speaks directly to the soul. Comrade Lauter admitted that the music at the Tuesday rehearsal (where everything was unfinished) and at the Saturday performance were as different as night and day. (Another reason for his impression is that he was hearing the music for the *second* time.) As I say, a good deal can still be done. The main thing is that our artists are prepared to make changes and that they support you wholeheartedly in your struggle for a great new art.

With socialist greetings and special thanks for your suggestions.

> Yours,
> brecht

[Berlin, 25 March 1951]

657 To Wilhelm Pieck

Berlin, 6 April 1951

Dear Comrade Pieck,

I wish to thank you and the other comrades once again for the suggestions concerning *Lucullus* put forward at our conference of 24 March. I hope that the work I immediately did on the text will have eliminated some potential misunderstandings. I also believe that the poetic quality of the work has been greatly improved. Moreover the addition of three new arias with positive content (and Dessau's planned changes in one of the existing ones) will bring about a shift of emphasis which along with the projected optimistic finale will make a big difference.

Dessau has rejected an offer from the Cologne Opera to perform the work at the June Festival, because there was reason to suspect that the Cologne people could misguidedly make so hasty a production the occasion for a demonstration. He informs me that he has not yet finished reworking the music.

> Thanking you again,
> Yours
> bertolt brecht

Enclosures:
Reworked passages

660 To Fritz Kortner

[Berlin] 5 May 1951

Dear Kortner,

I don't know your present situation, but I'd like to ask you if you see any possibility of playing the part of Galileo in our Ensemble in the autumn. Neher would do the sets and we are having no difficulties with the casting. I think we must do everything in our power to oppose the rift in the cultural sphere. Please talk to Engel about it. Maybe he could direct the play.

Yours

661 To Wolfgang Völker

Berlin, 5 May 1951

Dear Mr Völker,
The *Lucullus* business has finally been settled. It will be performed here at the beginning of the next season in the repertory of the Staatsoper.

I've done a slight addition to the scene with the king and put in a new 'Song of the Legionaries' towards the end. As soon as Dessau has composed the music for it, you can get it along with the other material from Scherchen, who is our agent empowered to conclude contracts. I think you will like the changes, which are not very substantial. Scherchen seems to like them a lot, and I'm looking forward to your direction.

With best regards,
Yours

665 To the Ministry for People's Education of the German Democratic Republic/Paul Wandel

Berlin, 14 May 1951

Dear Comrade Wandel,
Some time ago I offered to conduct a class in directing, dramaturgy and theatre criticism. Once again herewith the details:
1. The class should be organised as a master class of the Academy, Dramatic Arts Section.
2. Admission Requirements:
    a) School-leaving exam from a Workers' and Peasants' Faculty or from a Secondary School.
    This can be dispensed with in special cases. The applicant must then take an appropriate course in social science during the school term.
    b) The applicant must submit a short study of a play of his choice or of a performance given in the GDR.

3. The Ministry should enable such pupils to attend the university as guest auditors.

4. The Academy of Arts should enable the pupils to attend rehearsals of representative Berlin theatres.

5. The pupils will participate in the regular activities of the assistant directors and dramaturgs of the Berliner Ensemble. They will attend conferences with stage designers, mask makers, costumiers and stage technicians, in addition to rehearsals. They will take notes on production problems. At a certain point in their training they will direct amateur groups in factories on their own.

6. They will take part in the work of adapting plays. (So far *The Tutor* by Lenz, and *The Beaver Coat* and *Red Rooster* by Gerhart Hauptmann have been adapted by the Berliner Ensemble. Shakespeare's *Coriolanus* is in course of adaptation.)

7. The training is to take two to three years and should enable the pupil to become a dramaturg, a director, or theatre critic.

8. Maximum number of students: 6

(Bertolt Brecht)

666 To the German Central Institute for Pedagogy

Berlin, 28 May 1951

Dear Mr Sothmann,

In your material for the study of literature I deplore the lack of repellent examples. Neither political nor aesthetic judgements can be formed on the basis of good examples alone. Why not cite Ganghofer's prose as a contrast to Tolstoy's? Where is *Der Trompeter an der Katzbach*, that fine example of mindless chauvinism?

That's one point. Another is that good (and once again also bad) examples of slogans should be studied in the schools. The pupils should be taught how to think up slogans and formulate them.

And then there are no examples of curricula vitae, reports and speeches. This is especially important as young people must learn not only to read, but also to write, not least as a way of learning how to read.

Thank you for sending me the syllabus.

Yours,

667 To the German Academy of Arts

Berlin, 20 June 1951

To the German Academy of Arts,
Berlin NW 7

Would you please inform the Ministry of People's Education of the impression I carried away from two discussions with students at the University of Berlin (Workers' and Peasants' Faculty)?

These students show a shattering ignorance in the aesthetic field. Evidently too little attention is paid to aesthetic analysis as compared with sociological analysis, the importance of which must not of course be underestimated. Perhaps the Ministry should organise a discussion between the professors of literature at the university and members of the Academy.

bertolt brecht

668 To Berthold Viertel

Dear B.V.,

All of us here are quite put out that you haven't directed any play for us this year. We've done only *The Mother* and *Beaver Coat* and *Red Rooster* (and are rehearsing a new production of *Courage* with Busch as the cook and Geschonneck as the chaplain and Lutz as Yvette). As you're doing *The Broken Jug* in Salzburg, couldn't you direct it here in October? I'm sure Geschonneck would make a good Adam. But Homolka too, would be welcome. (Do you know his address?) What would you say to *The Chalk Circle* with Homolka, here or somewhere else? Or *Galileo?* The Ensemble has rather improved thanks to a few good men, and we have a new rehearsal studio, it's a pleasure to rehearse. There's been something of a to-do about *Lucullus*, allegedly the music was hard to understand, but now it's going on in September, and all in all the controversy was refreshing and instructive. I continue to believe that in these years the arts must provide avenues of communication. Come for a few weeks.

As ever,
b

[Berlin, June–July 1951]

669 To Hanns Eisler

Dear Eisler,

Of course I will protect your opera from any possible harm. The studio production in Potsdam is so unimportant for Berlin (anyway it's the *Urfaust* [Goethe's first version] they're doing) that I didn't even mention it to you, I didn't connect it in any way with your opera plans. In June I think it was, we promised our malcontents to let them do something. We got in touch with Potsdam and among other things they had *Faust* on the playbill (for next Easter). We could have cast that, but we wanted the *Urfaust*, which is only half as long. Monk will probably direct it. Really, you can let the young people do that, it will be a decent performance, pure Goethe of course, and no programme. No application of your ideas, good as they are, really inspired, you can see the whole thing for yourself when it's ready. You can't call that competition, I'd feel ridiculous calling the young people off again on such grounds. As for your opera, which will really be an important production, you can be sure I'll see that you get all possible help; from Neher if you can use him, and from every one of my actors. I repeat, the studio production is really nothing to go to court about, and if you like I'll hide my light under five bushels, you yourself can decide about *publicity* or *unpublicly*[1]. And it's a long way to Easter.

As ever,
b

[Berlin, July–August 1951]

[1] English in original.

672 To Gottfried von Einem

Dear von Einem,

Cas tells me, and I'm sorry to say I see it in the papers as well, that you've got into trouble over your helpfulness to me. Do write at once and tell me if you need any sort of statement or letter from me. Should I send you a few pages of the *Salzburger Totentanz*, the synopsis is finished? I don't see how they can find fault with you as an artist for helping a fellow artist – why, I had no papers whatever at the time.

As ever

Berlin, 18 October 1951

679 To Peter Suhrkamp

Dear Suhrkamp,

It's a shame that you haven't been able to come here for so long, and I'm rather worried by what you tell me about your health. I can't do the translation of Eliot's poems, for one thing because they would demand a great deal of work, and I already have too much. Besides, they're very hard for a non-Englishman to understand. When will you be coming here?

Yours very cordially,

Berlin, 2 January 1952

682 To three Young Pioneers of the Gottleuba Primary School

Berlin, 15 January 1952

Dear Gerhild, Utta and Margitta,

How I chose my profession? First I wrote songs and accompanied them on the guitar for friends, to amuse them and myself. I started writing plays when other people's struck me as wrong. Of course I couldn't tell you now whether or not I was right. I said to myself: No, people don't behave towards each other the way they do in this play; they behave entirely differently, and I'll try to show it. Besides, I made money by this, and of course I liked that, so one thing led to another. One fine day it turned out that I'd become a writer. I've told you this in a rather jocose way, but why not?

Whatever our profession, we must fight for peace.

Yours

684 To Günther Strupp

Dear Mr Strupp,

The main reason why the propaganda here is so feeble is that it doesn't begin to show the depth of the changes that are taking place here. Western counterpropaganda also neglects to do so for obvious reasons, since the changes in question – expulsion of the Prussian junkers, distribution of the land, ending of the bourgeois monopoly on education, schooling of the proletarian youth – would have been sure to fire West Germans with enthusiasm.

As things stand, it's only the GDR's art and philosophy that attract attention in the West; but the fact is that it is impossible to understand such phenomena as the formalism-realism controversy, let alone judge them without a knowledge of those great changes. If only because of the economic and political upheavals, no one in his right mind can expect the new system to function without errors and slip-ups in the cultural field. Nevertheless, many thanks for your letter and your essay, which I have forwarded.

> Yours

[Berlin], 18 January 1952

688 To Sepp Schwab/(DEFA)

Dear Comrade Schwab,

Politically speaking, the new screenplay by Burri and Staudte strikes me as a distinct improvement. A few slight changes can easily be made before the script goes to the studio. (For instance, I'd suggest moving the first scenes to North Germany, so as so establish the Babylonian confusion of languages on German territory.) Also a few passages could be formulated more poetically (as in Burri's original version). I expect to go over the dialogue again with Burri.

In any case I'm glad we now have a screenplay that suits the director and is undoubtedly more up to date politically. I congratulate DEFA on the work they have done so far on *Mother Courage*, and hope for a satisfactory conclusion.

[Berlin] 25 February 1952

693 To Friedrich Wolf

[Berlin], 14 March 1952

Dear Wolf,

I've received your suggestion for improving the courses at the Academy and am wholly in agreement. The one thing I miss is a recommendation that examples of kitsch and bad style (bad poetry, barbarisms, etc.) be included in anthologies. Couldn't we add that?

> Yours cordially,
> brecht

695 To Hermann Scherchen

[Berlin], 14 March 1952

Dear Scherchen,

Many thanks for your letter and the Frankfurt production which I hear nothing but good of. Considering the general cowardice, I'm curious to know whether the opera will continue to be played in our fatherland.

Yours

696 To Neues Deutschland

[Berlin], 14 March 1952

Dear Comrades,

I'm on the best of terms with Hella Wuolijoki. She has been in Berlin, where she attended a performance of *Puntila*, saw the poster and programme, and spoke enthusiastically of the performance. After the Munich production, in 1947 I believe, I sent her the press release which tells exactly how the play came to be written and gives an account of my collaboration with Hella Wuolijoki. I've asked Desch Verlag in Munich for a copy of this press release, and as soon as I get it I'll send it to you. Hella Wuolijoki's play is not at all the same work; it is a different dramatisation of the same real-life happenings.

With best regards

697 To Dolf Sternberger

Dear Mr Sternberger,

Before the Second World War, when I wrote *The Trial of Lucullus*, it seemed superfluous to add any condemnation of the aggressor. Now, after the War, I believe it to be necessary, and I can only wonder at my past confidence in people's good judgement. Your criticism in poetic form appeals to me because of the poetic form, but to your version I would add yet another condemnation, a condemnation of those jurors who approve of war because of its economic advantages.

And please believe me: it is not true that I am opposed to wars of aggression merely because the government of the GDR is opposed to wars of aggression. But one of the reasons why I am in favour of the GDR is its opposition to such things.

Yours

Berlin, March 1952

698 To Sepp Schwab/DEFA

Dear Comrade Schwab,

I'm sorry, I can't come to the meeting after all, as I have to go to the Second Clinic for Internal Medicine at the Charité for an unpleasant stomach examination that can't be put off any longer.

I too think it wouldn't be a bad idea to have certain characters in the *Courage* film played by actors of like nationality; of course it could only be the minor roles, because as we decided in our discussion, the Courage family and Yvette have to be German. As for the cook, we should first do test shots of Busch, who is just about unequalled as an actor and is a past master of the Dutch accent.

Please give Staudte my best; we're working hard on the final version and doing all we can not to lose any of his improvements.

And please apologise for me to the Commission.

Yours

'Berlin, 8 May 1952

699 To Peter Suhrkamp

Berlin-Weissensee
14 June 1952

Dear Suhrkamp,

The disagreement over the Hesse books makes me rather unhappy. For your sake and for Hesse's. Wendt and Janka of the Aufbau-Verlag are also sincerely dismayed that the negotiations should have taken such an unpleasant turn. I'm assured that efforts are still being made to arrive at a solution satisfactory to you. Considerable sums are on hand here for both publisher and author and Janka assures us that they can be collected in cash at any time.

Perhaps if Hesse knew how large the printings here are and how enthusiastically his books are received, he wouldn't blame the GDR for the deplorable fact that GDR money is so grossly undervalued in the West. And I think you'll agree that Germany will not have suffered a real cultural rift when business dealings become difficult or fall through, but when great literary works can no longer be read in one part of Germany.

With regards to Hermann Hesse,

Yours cordially

701 To Elisabeth Hauptmann

Dear Bess,

The first volume seems to be in good shape. The missing stanzas of the Hymn were probably left out on purpose, I don't remember.

Please leave the contract as it is, even if you don't want the money, though I don't see why. I'll take it for the time being. I insist on the contract. The rift [between the Germanies] will be bridged some day and then we'll need the contract the way it is. I discussed it thoroughly with Suhrkamp at the time; having you in the contract is more useful to the publisher and to me than to you; for you it just means a lot of work.

Do you know if there is a good edition of Horace? Could you enquire? Second hand will do. Would you like to come out here when you've finished with the proofs?

[Buckow], July 1952

703 To Friedrich Wolf

Dear Friedrich Wolf,

I must apologise to you for spelling your name wrong in the *Theaterarbeit* book. The printers must have declared their independence at the last minute. After getting myself into the bad books of the FDJ (by spelling Honecker's name in a telegram with two 'g's instead of 'ck', I have to be doubly careful. I really must try to keep a few friends.

Yours cordially,

brecht

704 To Paul Fabig

Dear Fabig,

I don't believe *Socrates Wounded* could have the right effect just now without a whole sheaf of footnotes.

The only one of my works suitable for amateur dramatic groups at the present time is *Señora Carrar's Rifles*. What we need is a collection of anecdotes contributed by many persons, out of which short plays could be made. A people's art requires the collaboration of the people.

> With best regards,
> Yours

[Buckow], 1 August 1952

706 To Hanns Eisler

Dear Hanns,

I too think that you now have *Faust* under control. I hope we'll be able to have our housewarming in August and start adding the finishing touches.

As far as Siemens-Plania is concerned, I think we should wait; they misunderstood the whole thing just as we expected. We'll have to take it up again with the politicians in September.

It would be very nice if you could come, for one thing because we could look at the Garbe material together. And we could also discuss the music of the Strittmatter comedy.

> Yours cordially,
> b

Is Fischer coming back to Berlin?

[Buckow], 1 August 1952

709 To Helmut Holzhauer,

I hear that my play *The Mother*, an original composition after themes from Gorky, is not to be included in the repertory of the Berliner

Ensemble's guest tour of Poland. But – with Weigel and Busch in it – it is one of the Ensemble's finest productions, a positive socialist counterpart to *Mother Courage*. A few objections with regard to details have been taken into consideration; changes are being made. Gorky himself read and approved it. At first sight, because of its musical elements, it may seem influenced by agitprop theatre, but in reality it is constructed along classical German lines (from *Götz*[1] to *Wozzek*[2]). For these reasons I ask you not to omit the play from the Polish tour until the matter has been discussed at a meeting.

> With socialist greetings,
> bertolt brecht

NB I believe our Polish friends will appreciate the production and realise that the play was written in 1930.

710 To Carl Orff

Dear Orff,

When Emil Burri was here he promised to ask you if you would be interested in writing music for my play *The Caucasian Chalk Circle*.

I don't know if he got round to it. How do you feel about this? I'd be delighted.

> With best regards,
> Yours

> Berlin, 20 October 1952

711 To Carl Orff

> [Berlin], 15 November 1952

Dear Orff,

When I got your letter I tried again to see if I couldn't come to Frankfurt after all. But it was impossible, because that Sunday night Helene Weigel is appearing in the première of one of my plays and

---

[1] Goethe's *Gotz von Berlichingen*.
[2] Georg Büchner's tragedy *Woyzeck*.

the following Sunday we are putting on a play by Anna Seghers, rather sooner than planned, since the Ensemble is going on tour in Poland in December.

If there is the slightest possibility of your doing music for *The Chalk Circle*, I shall at least write you a letter with my ideas and try to come to Munich as soon as possible.

Yours cordially

712 To Egon Rentzsch/Central Committee of the Socialist Unity Party

Dear Comrade Rentzsch,

I have read the report on literature and art of the 19th Party Congress of the CPSU with great interest.

Time and again I have been impressed by the efforts of the Soviet Union to promote and create an educational literature in which Soviet life is depicted in a productively critical way and models are put forward. Especially worthy of our attention, it seems to me, are the call for quality and specialised training and the criticism of superficial, schematic treatment of important themes.

It is imperative, I believe, that these questions should be discussed in depth.

With socialist greetings

Please do not publicise these remarks. As soon as I can, I shall write about them at length.

716 To Emil Burri

[Berlin], 17 January 1953

Dear Burri,

Many thanks for your letter. I must also apologise for taking so long to write. The *Courage* business is in a hopeless state of doldrums, I've lost all desire to do anything more about it. And it's really one of the most magnificent film scripts I know of.

Käutner has not been here. I would be very much interested in a film version if you did the scenario. Give Geis my regards.

Yours cordially

b

718 To Hans Mayer

[Berlin], 22 February 1953

Dear H M,

Another word about the 'negativism' that certain people – I don't know if you are one of them – attribute to Eisler's *Faust*. Surely a justified desire for positive heroes (models) mustn't lead us to reject the portrayal of great figures like Faust, whose influence can be just as positive in the social sense. Literature shows that tragedy can perform some of the functions of comedy, a certain social clarification, I mean.

You said that every new portrayal of Faust would inevitably detract from Goethe's, simply because Goethe's Faust is so deeply graven in the popular consciousness that any new portrayal is bound to be considered in relation to Goethe's. How then do you feel about the works of Euripides, who reinterpreted the characters of Aeschylus and Sophocles, for the most part very critically?

> Yours cordially,
> brecht

Do please send me your essay about *Theaterarbeit*.

721 To Wolfgang Langhoff/Deutsches Theater

Dear Langhoff,

We have been wondering for some time what to do with our *Urfaust* production, originally conceived for Potsdam. Couldn't we simply put it on at the Deutsches Theater, possibly as a studio production (it's being done by the young people). It would be a new departure, and not a bad one, for a theatre to put on the whole *Faust* and the *Urfaust* at the same time. One advantage would be that we'd have no further need of the workshops, either for the sets or the costumes.* I'd be sincerely grateful to you if we could do it.

In the meantime, best wishes for your recovery. And I'm looking forward to [*Faust*] Part II.

[Berlin, April 1953]

---

*And we'd only need the stage for a short time. [Brecht's note]

724 To Otto Grotewohl

[Buckow], 15 June 1953

Dear Comrade Grotewohl,

When the Volksbühne building is ready, the Schiffbauerdamm-Theater will be vacant. This is the theatre where I worked before emigrating, where for one thing I staged *The Threepenny Opera*. Ever since the Berliner Ensemble was founded, we have been promised this theatre once the Volksbühne building is finished. Since then we have been enjoying the hospitality of the Deutsches Theater, and it has often been difficult for both parties to work productively. Now, given the general need for economic stringency, Helene Weigel and I find it increasingly distressing that the Ensemble should be regarded as an economic luxury though it could very well fill a house on its own. (We could probably keep Curt Bois busy; he is our only great popular comedian, and we may well lose him if we can't give him enough to do.) If a building should be needed for new purposes – the papers speak of a plan to open a Theatre of Satire – the old Admiralspalast, now occupied by the State Opera, will soon be available; it is very large and suitable for musical productions.

You have probably heard that the wildest rumours have been circulating in West Germany about friction between the government of the German Democratic Republic and myself. If the Berliner Ensemble, which is known far beyond the borders of Germany, were to take over the Theater am Schiffbauerdamm, my solidarity with our republic would be evident to all.

But what concerns Helene Weigel and myself most of all is that the Ensemble, which caters for the best part of our youth, should be enabled to carry on its fruitful work.

> With socialist greetings,
> Yours,
> bertolt brecht

725 To Walter Ulbricht

Berlin, 17 June 1953

Dear Comrade Ulbricht,

History will pay its respects to the patience of the Socialist Unity Party of Germany.

The great debate with the masses about the tempo of socialist construction will have the effect of testing and safeguarding the achievements of socialism.

At this moment I feel I must assure you of my allegiance to the Socialist Unity Party of Germany.

Yours,

726 To Otto Grotewohl

Dear Comrade Grotewohl,
What can we at the Academy of Arts and the Berliner Ensemble do?
Will you speak on the radio? That would be a good thing. We would be glad to provide songs and recitations by Ernst Busch and other artists as an introduction and in conclusion.

[Berlin], 17 June 1953

727 To Johannes R. Becher / Academy of Arts

Berlin Weissensee,
Berliner Allee 190
23 June 1953

Dear Becher,
Perhaps we should suggest to our members ways of keeping the masses better supplied with newspapers, magazines, films etc. We might suggest to Rodenberg, for instance, that the DEFA consider programmes with two films, one of which could be purely entertainment and the other one of our educational films. This is no time to be prodigal with our reserves of kitsch while withdrawing our educational films from circulation.

Yours

728 To Peter Suhrkamp

Berlin-Weissensee,
Berliner Allee 190
1 July 1953

Dear Suhrkamp,
You ask about my attitude towards the events of 16 and 17 June. Was it a popular uprising, an attempt 'to win freedom', as the overwhelming

majority of the West German press claims? Was I indifferent, not to say hostile, to a popular uprising, was I against freedom, when on 17 June in a letter to the Socialist Unity Party, the last sentence of which was published, I expressed my readiness to contribute in my own way (in artistic form) to the absolutely indispensable debate between the workers and the government? For three decades I have tried in my writings to champion the cause of the workers. But in the night of 16 June and the morning of 17 June, I saw the stirring demonstrations of the workers degenerate into something very far from an attempt to win freedom. The workers had reason to be embittered. The unfortunate, unintelligent measures taken by the government in an attempt to precipitate the development of heavy industry in the GDR outraged peasants, artisans, tradesmen, workers and intellectuals alike. Last year's drought-induced crop failure and this year's flight of hundreds of thousands of peasants from the land endangered the food supply of all sections of the population. Such measures as the withdrawal of ration cards from small tradesmen were a threat to their barest existence. Other measures such as the counting of sick leave against convalescent leave, the suppression of special train fares for workers, and the general stepping up of norms at a time when the cost of living remained unchanged or had actually gone up, drove the workers, whose unions functioned poorly, into the streets and caused them to forget the undoubtedly great advantages that the expulsion of the junkers, the socialisation of Hitler's war industry, planned production and the smashing of the bourgeois monopoly of education had won them. Yet even in the early hours of 17 June the streets displayed a grotesque mixture of workers not only with all sorts of déclassé youth, who poured through the Brandenburg Gate, across the Potsdamer Platz, and in columns across the Warschauer Brücke, but also with gross, brutish figures from the Nazi era, the local product, who hadn't been seen gathered into bands for years, *but who had been here the whole time*. The slogans changed quickly. 'Down with the government' was followed by 'Hang them'; the gutter took over. Towards noon, when demonstrations were turning to riots throughout the GDR, in Leipzig, Halle and Dresden, *fire* made its appearance once again. From Unter den Linden one could see the clouds of smoke rising from the Columbus House at the Potsdamer Platz sector boundary, just as on a fateful day long ago one could see clouds of smoke rising from the Reichstag building. Now as then, that fire was not caused by workers; fire is not the weapon of people who build. After that – here and in other cities – bookshops were stormed, books thrown out and burned, and the volumes of Marx and Engels that went up in flames were no more hostile to the workers than were the red flags that were publicly torn to shreds. (Look at the photographs published in the West-German press; you won't need a magnifying glass to see who was tearing those flags.) In the provinces 'liberation' went on. But when the prisons were stormed, strange prisoners emerged from the 'Bastilles'; in Halle the onetime commandant of Ravensbrück concentration camp, Erna Dorn. She made incendiary speeches in the marketplace. In some places there were assaults on Jews, not many, as there aren't many Jews left. And all day long RIAS suspended its regular programmes, broadcast incendiary speeches, with refined voices mouthing the word 'freedom'. Everywhere those elements were at work, who think day and night of the welfare of the workers and the 'common people' and who promise those high living standards which in the end turn out to be dying standards. There seemed to be ringleaders who were ready to lead the workers directly to the freedom of the munitions factories. For several hours, until the occupation forces stepped in, Berlin was on the brink of a third World War.

Dear Suhrkamp, let us nourish no illusions. Not only in the West, but also here in East Germany, such 'elements' are again at work. On that tragic June 17 I heard 'Deutschland über Alles' resounding from middle-class voices and the workers in the roadway drowning it out with the Internationale. But in their confusion and helplessness, they couldn't quite carry it off.

The Socialist Unity Party has made mistakes which were extremely serious for a socialist party and which antagonised some workers, including old socialists. I am not a party member. But I respect many of its historical achievements, and I felt at one with it – not because of its mistakes but because of its good qualities – when it was attacked by fascist, warmongering rabble. In the struggle against war and fascism I have always supported it and still support it.

730 To Otto Grotewohl

12 July 1953

Dear Comrade Grotewohl,
    Everywhere the New Policy is obstructed by the rigidity of the

administration. Wouldn't it be possible to promote all the many changes that are going on and encourage a certain enthusiasm? In radio programmes, for instance, in DEFA films, etc., right down to the herring fisheries. (I hear that the Baltic fishermen are missing the herring shoals because they are forced to observe sailing schedules that the herring haven't been told about.) Why not consider Wolfgang Harich's suggestion of setting up small roving committees, to go everywhere introducing the new style? Of course their composition would have to be quite unorthodox, people with sound common sense, natural socialists. Forgive my directness and brevity, I know how little time you have.

>With socialist greetings,
>Yours,
>bertolt brecht

731 To Helene Weigel

Dear Helli,

Hill has found me a flat – a painter moved out of his studio, and Ulrich seized it – it was already disposed of and what's more to a private firm. (Such things have to be handled with kid gloves these days.) Chausseestrasse, in the second street from the square you cross on the way to the Academy. Block at the back (like the front block very old, two storeys, dates from the eighteen thirties, consequently congenial, modest, built for unpretentious people), one enormous room with a large window, one medium-sized room and one small (not very small) one. Small kitchen, a shower will have to be put in, gas and electricity already installed. Toilet on the stairs. Garage downstairs, goes with the flat. Behind the back block a small garden which, let's hope, belongs to it, with an unimpressive tree. Windows look out on cemetery, all very green and spacious. I'm not far from Friedrichstrasseneck and the rehearsal studio; the corner of Chausseestrasse and Friedrichstrasse is lively, full of people. The place comes vacant on 1 August.

About the programme for 53–54: First *Katzgraben*, then *Don Juan*. Then (perhaps) some one-act comedies, the young people would like that. Beginning 1 December, *Chalk Circle* (or *Coriolanus*). Beginning 1 February, *Among Thieves and Robbers* [*Des Heisse Herz*] by Ostrovski (or the alternative if Therese comes). Then *Coriolanus* (or *Chalk Circle*).

I hope the weather you're having isn't too bad and that the police are putting their feet up.

Do take care of yourself, don't swim too much, it's fatiguing in salt water and one doesn't notice it until weeks later.

Frau Mutter isn't a bad cook.

Yours,

b

[Middle of 1953]

732 To Paul Wandel

Dear Comrade Wandel,

Like a lot of other people, I believe that the Arts Commission should be ruthlessly and sweepingly dissolved. Reasons:

1) Some such measure was what mainly moved the members of the Academy of Arts, absolutely all of whom had been deeply worried by the sudden evidence of bitter dissatisfaction, to put forward constructive proposals for the improvement of artistic production. If the commission were now upheld, anyone who in the hope of avoiding a breakup had proclaimed the imminence of a new, productive atmosphere, would look like a gullible fool to his colleagues.

2) As the deliberations of the Academy show, the Arts Commission has not succeeded in making a single friend among artists – not even among those belonging to the Socialist Unity Party. It has even managed to bring the most progressive principles into something close to disrepute.

3) If it were upheld, now that it has made itself disliked by all and moreover been publicly discredited, it would function even more poorly than hitherto, because for want of any authority it would have to make even more use of coercion.

4) Such administrative tasks as it performs could be handled by a Ministry of Culture, and the Cultural Section of the Socialist Unity Party could exert a far more authoritative influence in artistic matters.

5) A reorganisation of this sort would quite naturally bring artists into contact with non-artists, something that can do a world of good.

6) Confirmation of the Arts Commission would be interpreted not as firmness but as obstinacy, as inflexible opposition to reason. Indeed, what point can there be in prolonging a creeping malaise, a feeling, ruinous to all creativeness, of being at the mercy of an all-powerful institution that is unable to make its demands understood? What we

need now is simply to leave artists free to produce; they can do so much if left alone (and intelligently guided).

> In real alarm

> [August 1953]

736 To Hans J. Leupold

> [Buckow], 20 August 1953

Dear Hans J. Leupold,

The stage designers of the Paris and Copenhagen refugee productions of *Señora Carrar's Rifles* were inexpensive, but they were far from devoid of ideas. The whitewashed walls and the immense dark fishing nets over them were beautiful and they helped the play. Of course those sets had nothing to do with Dadaism, nor for that matter with Proletkult, to which I have no objection, far from it. Stage sets shouldn't evoke an illusion, they should fire the imagination, and those sets did.

> With best regards,
> Yours

Please forgive me for taking so long to answer.

738 To Hans Otto Münsterer

> Buckow, 29 August 1953

Dear Münsterer,

Walter Nubel writes from the USA that you might be able to send him a proof sheet of the *Augsburg Sonnets*. I wish you could, because I can't lay hands on the copy you sent me. He would also like to have a photocopy of the *Pocket Devotions* made at his expense, and it would be very kind of you if you could get this for him. He has an almost complete collection of my work, such as I haven't had for a long time. What with the giant strides of our physics in developing means of destruction, it might not be a bad idea to preserve, here and there on the earth's surface, a specimen of something that took so much effort to produce.

> With best regards,
> Yours,
> b

739 To Renata Mertens-Bertozzi

Dear Reni,

Too much is happening here (in a screwy rather than significant sense) for me to go deeply into aesthetics. So read the following critically: To begin with, the potential beauty of art never lies in the object. (The beauties of the object require a process of transformation, as though they were not there to begin with, I mean in proportion to the scope of the work.) In the course of perceiving certain artistic beauties, you can utterly cancel them out if you feel that the asocial impulses determining that art form are utterly hideous. As for activation and its contrary (passivation?), obviously their social value varies with the situation; in art these contraries are not absolute; that's where art is so wise.

I know this isn't much, but it looks as if one can't supply much of anything from here. Thanks for your letters (your wires never came) and for everything else.

Regards to Hans and the others.

[Autumn 1953?]

740 To Comrade Wenk

Dear Comrade Wenk,

I agree that any article on cultural policy needs to be written in such a way that our new worker and peasant intellectuals can understand it. But it is not enough simply to 'use the language of the workers', since this is too impoverished. The language of the workers will get richer, the more the workers come to influence those various sectors which sometimes make use of other expressions. This is not just a matter of words of foreign origin. Not long ago actors working on a new play which dealt with rural development asked that some of the technical expressions should be rephrased so as to make them instantly intelligible to a city audience. The playwright said no. He thought it was high time the city audience learnt the language spoken in villages. That I should have forced you to turn to *Duden* and *Liebknecht* does not strike me as all that bad. At least you have learnt a few more words of foreign derivation.

And you will also have noticed that words of foreign derivation are not so easy to replace: they nearly always have some quality that would disappear if they were translated. (The word 'feature' is an incomplete substitute for the word 'quality' – the latter carries an extra overtone of 'value'.) All the same, the learning process should not be made too difficult. The sentence cited by you is certainly too awkward, and your letter will force me to revise my way of expressing things. (Or should I say 'look into' it? The word 'revise' is better, because of its suggestion of Gogol's *Revisor* and an audit.)

I fail to understand your criticism of my syntax. In the sentence about the Academy the comma after 'decisive' is a misprint. If you substitute a full stop, all will be well. As for the two sentences in para. 5, there is nothing wrong with them, I can assure you.

On the other hand your letter does make me realise that my article was altogether too tightly written (note that I've begun avoiding the word 'compressed'). Written at greater length it would certainly have been more provoking.

With thanks for your letter,
Yours

Berlin, Sept. 53

742 To Ruth Berlau

Thanks for your letter. I'm glad *Courage* is going well and that you had a good reception. Scandinavia is getting to be very important. The weather here has been sunny, rain would be better for work, but it's going well, and most important, quickly, I've got to about the middle of the rough draft. I've apportioned my time exactly, I've only got a few weeks, so I have to write a definite amount each day.

Now about the *Courage* film. Simple accommodations at the guest house in Neu-Babelsberg. Payment in hard currency possible. Could they both come here if invited? The quickest would be if they laid out the money for the trip, as it's hard to send money. Of course they'd be fully reimbursed. We'd discuss debates, etc. when they get here. (It couldn't be before December, because Helli isn't available until then.) I won't send the copy of *Turandot* until more of it is finished; I need your impression of a whole section. Please keep on writing.

And don't overexert yourself, do your best to keep comfortable. And please don't forget the pills. They make a big difference, I've seen that.

d
bertolt
epep[1]

[Buckow, August 1953]

743 To Ruth Berlau

Dear Ruth,

Thanks for your letters and for writing *often*. The business with *Courage* is bad, and now the whole thing is being forgotten. It's good you've got an actress who has done operetta, in operetta one has to be clear. Don't forget *Courage*'s toughness. And apart from that make changes wherever you see fit. What pleases me most is the cheerful tone of your letters. You'll never be ill again if you can get your forehead smooth. And be productive.

Palitzsch is already in Malmö. Your efforts for him were successful. For *Turandot* I still have two and a half scenes to write out of eleven. But it's still rough. I've been writing against the clock, so to speak.

We're getting the Schiffbauerdamm-Theater at the beginning of January. That will give us more elbow room. And we'll be able to rehearse all sorts of things on the side.

When I'm finished with T – incidentally no one has seen it yet, I'll need the copy until then, so as to enter changes – I'll try to write something for the programme. The Penguins haven't come yet, I'm looking forward to them. (I know Berkeley's *Chocolates* and Carr's *The Emperor's Box*, but not the others.)

The Walchers are still in the tower, they come here in the afternoon. Yesterday Strittmatter was here and Hans Garbe. But I keep strictly to myself in the morning.

I hope you're having a pleasant time, and if you need anything in the vestimentary line, buy it.

d bertolt

[Buckow, September 1953]

744 To Ruth Berlau

Dear Ruth,

I was very glad when you phoned last night; your call came after a long gruelling day, full of conferences and confusion. – Your voice was

[1]See footnote to letter 485.

lovely. – I'll send you your copy of *Turandot* as soon as it's typed. Though it still needs polishing, which makes a big difference. But you can see the broad lines. We'll be moving to the Schiffbauerdamm-Theater in January. I'll get my flat at the beginning (?) of October. In September, I mean to spend as much time as possible in Buckow. I've written a few pages of a short chronicle about *Courage*, I'm still putting the finishing touches to it, perhaps it could be published in Denmark. The crime novel has come, thanks, it's new to me. Be firm with Martens, he must give you the money.
    Write.

>   Love,
>   bertolt

Did you get my birthday telegram?
I'm completely out of envelopes.

>   [September 1953]

746 To Peter Suhrkamp

>   Berlin NW 7, Luisenstrasse 18
>   17 September 1953

Dear Suhrkamp,
    If I direct *The Chalk Circle* here, I don't think I'll make any more changes than were in the second edition of *Courage* as compared to the first. I'm sure such changes as you fear will not be necessary, unless you can suggest some. Of course I'm going to stage the Prologue; after all it's printed in *Sinn und Form*. (In Göteborg, Sweden, where the play was first produced, the Prologue was omitted and they probably won't use it in Frankfurt either.)
    [. . .]
I'm looking forward to your visit to Berlin.

>   Yours cordially
>   for Brecht, who was called away after dictating the
>   above.
>   Elisabeth Hauptmann

749 To Pablo Picasso

Berlin N W 7, Luisenstrasse 18
13 November 1953

Dear Comrade Picasso,

I am the director of a theatre in East Berlin, the Berliner Ensemble, I wish to ask your permission to use your magnificent poster design for the [–] for publicity purposes, especially at the university in West Berlin. I must confess to you that we have been using your dove as our curtain emblem ever since the theatre was founded. With heartfelt admiration for all your beautiful and useful work.

With socialist greetings,
Yours

750 To Johannes R. Becher

[Berlin], 11 December 1953

Dear Becher,

I too believe the Academy of Arts should take the initiative, if possible before the Berlin Conference, in setting up a committee of humanistic writers and intellectuals. Judging by the West German reaction to my Open Letter of two years ago, I'd say that in addition to addressing an appeal to the West Germans we should go ahead and set a good example. In the past they said: Why don't you go ahead? But that was only a demagogic attempt to get a conference under way; they'd no doubt be quite content to discuss postage stamps or beer mats. So we should simply set up a provisional committee with full powers in the GDR and call on the West Germans to help establish a full committee, empowered to operate throughout Germany.

Yours,
Brecht

751 To Walter Ulbricht

Dear Comrade Ulbricht,

It has given me special pleasure to read your appeal for the founding of an all-German Committee to supervise the world of letters. Such a committee could work against the cultural partitioning of Germany and at the same time provide an opportunity to discuss humanistic principles with West German writers and intellectuals. This of course would require a certain sureness on our side of the discussion. I must own that I am alarmed to see how little progress we have made in acquainting our writers, artists and intellectuals with the world of socialist ideas; I mean those who were not already socialists in 1945. Can they be expected to represent these ideas when collaborating with West German colleagues? That is why I think it vital that the project of establishing a ministry of culture should no longer be postponed; any delay would lose too much of the impetus already manifested by the new policy.

A bureaucratic spirit [.] in the cultural sphere has done much to prevent us from winning important artists over to Marxism and the GDR.

Forgive me this little importunity, to which I have been prompted by my devotion to the common cause.

> Yours,

> Berlin 12 December 1953

752 To Leo Kerz

> Berlin NW 7,
> Luisenstrasse 18
> 18 January 1954

Dear Mr Kerz,

I am sure the action of *Mann ist Mann* could take place in Korea. Do you know the later form of the play? I sent it to you.

> Sincerely

753 To Johannes R. Becher

Dear Becher,

I hope the hollow pathos and general coldness of the Leipzig performance didn't ruin your evening. Such treatment certainly does not befit the great poetic work you threw into the breach against Hitler's offensive of 1941. Our theatres still have a lot to learn, and I don't mean just in the technical sense. – When I read the play on the trip back, I saw all the things those wretched people had omitted, the fresh dramatic beauties and nearly all the poetic stage directions. Helli and I have decided to give the play to our young people to work through in depth and see if they are up to such a task. Something, it seems to me, must absolutely be done. People who served in the Nazi army have seen or read the play and – from our driver Lindemann to our dramaturg Palitzsch – think you set the clock ahead too much. Your impatience led you to give your characters insights that were not to ripen until much later. This gives the play passion, but it disturbs eyewitnesses and there are lots of them in the theatre. I would therefore suggest preceding future performances by a prologue in which this is set out. We can talk it over.

> Cordially

> [Berlin], 2 February 1954.

754 To Peter Suhrkamp

> [Berlin], 8 March 1954
> [Postmark]

Dear Suhrkamp,

I'm now living in Chausseestrasse, next to the 'French' graveyard, where Huguenot generals and Hegel and Fichte are buried; all my windows look out on the cemetery grounds. It's not without its cheerful side. I have three rooms on the first floor of the back building, which like the front building is said to be about a hundred and fifty years old. The rooms are high and so are the windows, which have pleasant proportions. The largest room is about nine metres square, so I can put in several desks for different jobs. Actually the whole place is well-proportioned, it's really a good idea to live in houses and with furniture that are at least a hundred and twenty years old, let's say, in early capitalist surroundings until later socialist surroundings are available. Now that I live so much nearer to the theatre, I've got my young people on my hands more than ever, they come in droves, but to tell the truth I like it.

With which I close, this letter is meant as entertainment (?)

> As ever,
> b

756 To the German Academy of Arts/Otto Nagel

> Berlin 6 April 1954

Dear Comrade Nagel,

I gather from our stage designer Karl von Appen that the students at the Dresden Academy of Fine Arts are forbidden to look at or discuss the works of artists ranging from Picasso back to the Impressionists (inclusive). What's more, they can't get books about these painters from the library. The justification seems to be that they must first understand Socialist Realism before being exposed to contemporary art of any kind.

Von Appen asks me if this regulation is a matter of principle. I think it would be a good idea for you to find out and for us to hold a discussion at the Academy about this astonishing pedagogy. As the director of a theatre for one thing, I am interested in seeing a younger generation of stage designers who are properly educated and well informed.

> Most cordially
> Yours

759 To Joris Ivens

Berlin, 7 May 1954

Dear Joris,

I now have all the stanzas, at least in rough draft, except the Volga stanza. (I'll send you the last stanza on Monday, slightly modified.)

But I have a suggestion. Couldn't Kirsanov write the Volga stanza, which I'd then translate into German. That would be a pleasant bit of collaboration.

> With best regards

760 To Anton Ackermann / Ministry of Culture of the GDR

Berlin, 21 May 1954

Dear Comrade Ackermann,

I hear that we are hesitant about acquiring the Italian film *Miracle in Milan* for the GDR. I think it would be a great pity not to bring this film with its trenchant social criticism to the GDR. I'm sure the mystical ending won't infect anyone with superstition, since here in the GDR everyone knows it doesn't take miracles to do away with intolerable conditions.

> Regards

761 To Hans Henny Jahnn

[Berlin], May 1954

Dear Hans Henny Jahnn,

Perhaps no one told you but I once directed rehearsals of your excellent play *Pastor Ephraim Magnus*. It was in Berlin in the early twenties and I did it for only a few days. The dying man's heartrending plaint rings in my ears to this day; it is one of the most magnificent monologues in German literature. And today I can't get hold of the book – a disgrace. Well, we met in Danish exile, and we shall even meet here in Germany. And I'm glad the world had you, and still has you, in it.

762 To Peter Suhrkamp

Dear Suhrkamp,

[Elisabeth] Hauptmann will see to it that the *Elegies* are printed more closely, I agree with you. I don't quite understand your objection to the Prologue, that was the part of the play I wrote first, in the States. The problem of the parable-like play has to be derived from the needs of a real situation, and I think this is done in a light, amusing way. Without the Prologue there's no way of knowing why the play is no longer 'the Chinese Chalk Circle' (with the old verdict) or why it's called 'Caucasian'. I started by writing the short story (published in *Tales from the Calendar*) first. But for purposes of dramatisation, it needs an explanatory historical background.

As for your feelings about doctors, you're right: the patient has to be up on his high horse.

As ever

[Berlin], May 1954

767 To Otto Grotewohl

Dear Comrade Grotewohl,

While spending my holiday in the country, I am able to make certain observations and would like to inform you of my conclusions. Enclosed please find some notes on the People's Chamber.

Since its sessions are more or less closed, it strikes the population as a gigantic façade. (An impression which RIAS of course does its best to substantiate.) Couldn't we breathe some life into the People's Chamber?

> With socialist greetings,
> Yours
> bertolt brecht

Buckow, 19 July 1954

768 To Hanns Eisler

Dear Eisler,

The question is bound to come up: Will you be doing the music for *Die Winterschlacht* [*The Winter Battle*]? Of course Becher would like you to. It would be a big thing for the Ensemble. You wouldn't have to make any concessions. You could compose a short overture exactly as you want it. You see, I'm listing the advantages like a good huckster. On the other hand I don't want to drive you into a piece of work that will distract you from other work. (But to put it objectively: it would scarcely prevent you from discussing an opera libretto.) This enquiry is written without Becher's knowledge. Let me know what you think and I'll back you up.

I miss our chess and talks. I hope you'll be over soon.

> As ever,
> b

Die Winterschlacht is going into rehearsal at the beginning of October. We've made considerable cuts, so – providing that Becher accepts them – there will be room for music.

[July 1954]

771 To Emil František Burian

Dear Comrade Burian,

We're all delighted that you're coming. The production of *Winterschlacht* will be politically important, not only because it marks the beginning of productive collaboration between our peoples in the arts, but also because the play is being done at a time when the West-German bourgeoisie is staking everything on rearmament aimed at aggression against us and the Soviet Union – to which end they are bound to resort increasingly to former Nazis.

I am especially pleased that our actors will have an opportunity to learn from you.

Most cordially

[Berlin], 20 September 1954

772 To Vladimir Pozner

Berlin, 6 October 1954

Dear Pozner,

I don't really understand the letter from the dramaturg's office of Wien-Film about the *Puntila* script. Of course you have made certain changes in the play – which are absolutely necessary if a film is to be made of it. The character of Matti strikes me as quite right in your script. Just so long as the acting is right. Making Matti stage the marriage test in the presence of his mother seems an especially good idea.

Cordially,
Bertolt Brecht

773 To Emil František Burian

Dear Comrade Burian,

Of course I don't wish to interfere in any way with your directing. The following is only by way of information.

I believe that for our audience the final flight of the Wehrmacht is of the utmost importance, because the army of 400,000 men, which Adenauer is preparing to mobilise, is being mobilised exclusively for war in the East. One can still hear voices saying things like: 'If it's against the Russians, I'll shoulder my rifle again.' It's good for our public to see the Wehrmacht getting bogged down (in the material as well as the moral sense) in the Russian campaign. That will serve as a warning. It will frighten some and fortify others. A judgement on the whole adventure. Eisler was particularly enthusiastic about this scene and began straight away to write music for it.

Yours very cordially
brecht

[Berlin, October–November 1954]

774 To Emil František Burian

Dear Comrade Burian,

The Ensemble deeply regrets not being able to give a great likeminded artist the opportunity to direct a play. We were very much looking forward to this collaboration which the friendship between our countries makes possible and we sincerely hope that it may yet come to pass, and the sooner the better. We must create more favourable conditions for this collaboration. Our present arrangements were unfortunate: everything was wrecked by our inability to carry on the work in the way you wanted during your absence. Next time we must come to a detailed and comprehensive agreement before starting to work. Becher's fine play raises difficult questions for the theatre, especially for the German theatre. In our divided country, the process of getting at the truth about Hitler's wars is still artificially hampered by the apologists of capitalism. The theatres of the German Democratic Republic can and must do everything in their power to further this process. In our theatre a great deal of work is needed to get the new insights across the footlights and understandably, in view of your extensive activity in your own theatre, you didn't have the requisite number of working hours to give us. Moreover, our Ensemble is young and needs a lot more training. Given the work tempo dictated by our merciless schedule, we couldn't hope to do justice to your intentions and our duties.

Please don't let yourself be discouraged. Only recently, when we came to you with our troubles, we conceived a great liking for your comradely warmth and your mature political thinking.

Yours,

Berlin, December 1954

776 To Ernst Schumacher and family

Dear Schumachers,

Every evening I drink the Paulaner with emotion, and as you know there is a state of mind that goes with it. These orgies, which I try to keep within limits, are a reminder that I am living in exile, though quite voluntarily.

What are the book and its author doing? Is it coming out? Is he getting in? If the book's to get published, I gather, several forests will need to believe in it.

Thanks again
Yours b

[Berlin, December 1954]

778 To the International Stalin Prize Committee/Dimitri V Skobeltsyn

Berlin, 4 January [1955]

Dear Mr Skobeltsyn,

My heartfelt thanks to you and the International Stalin Prize Committee for awarding me the Stalin Peace Prize. I believe it to be the highest and most desirable of all prizes awarded today.

As soon as I get a better view of my schedule – I am the director of a theatre in the German Democratic Republic – I shall let you know when I can come to Moscow.

780 To Wolfgang Harich / Aufbau-Verlag

Berlin, 5 January 1955

Dear Harich,

It is too much for me now in the midst of rehearsals to state my position on Lukacs. (I can and will send him a telegram of congratulations.) From the standpoint of the history of philosophy I find Lukács's works interesting, especially those dealing with literature written before 1900. I must add, however, that they have few pointers to offer writers and have even done damage where their technical recommendations have been put into practice. But for want of time and interest I cannot formulate all this properly now. So please excuse me from contributing to your short volume.

With best regards

782 To Otto Grotewohl

Berlin, 20 February 1955

Dear Comrade Grotewohl,

Six months ago the Academy of Arts approved a project, submitted by me, for an association of dramatists. Particularly promising playwrights were to be enabled to work here with the Berliner Ensemble for a year to two; also some well-known writers. I would supervise their productions and try to give them the right kind of outlook. As you no doubt know, our dramatists are working harder than ever to create a seriously Marxist drama on a basis of dialectical materialism, and I think it important that we should train outstanding talents in this direction. Furthermore, the presence of such a study centre at the Academy of Arts would undoubtedly benefit the reputation of the German Democratic Republic abroad. Nothing of the kind exists anywhere.

So far two talented young writers have applied, Dr Peter Hacks of Munich, now residing at Goethestrasse 10, Dachau, who has already been awarded a drama prize by the city of Munich, and the Dutchman Lucebert, Berger Weg 8 in Bergen, North Holland, who has been awarded several prizes in Amsterdam and is thought to be the most gifted of Dutch writers.

Funds have already been put at our disposal, but your help is still needed to provide the young men with entry-permits and accommodation.

I should be very grateful for your help in this matter.

With thanks and kind regards

784 To Elisabeth Bergner

Berlin, 1 February 1955

Dear Elisabeth,

I'm sending you both *Mother Courage* and *The Good Person of Szechwan*. These issues of *Versuche* contain the latest versions. *The Good Person* strikes me as the more suitable for London. You yourself could play both parts, but perhaps Shen Teh would suit you better to begin with. I myself have not yet directed the Szechwan play. However, for the Frankfurt production, which incidentally was a big success, I arranged a few groupings, planned the dual role with the actress, and discussed the style of her musical recitation with her. Teo Otto of Zurich did the sets – light, elegant and beautiful. The photographs in *Versuche* are not very helpful, because they don't show the exquisite colours. Bentley has done English translations of both plays, which in my opinion are rather academic; but I'm sure you can do something about that. (Neither Bentley nor anyone else has exclusive English-language production rights.)

I shall be in Berlin for the next three months and I'd be delighted if you came for a visit. You'd be able to see both *Mother Courage* and *The Chalk Circle*, which may also interest you – though the music and verse add to the difficulties of translation.

Of course you could play *The Good Person* here at the Schiff. We would set aside a convenient time for you. *How is that?*[1]

With best regards. Also from Ruth and Helli.

785 To Geneviève Serreau

[Berlin], 9 February 1955

Dear Mrs Serreau,

Unfortunately there are two politically unpleasant mistakes in your Preface.

p 6: 'Le pacte germano-soviétique, alors en vigueur, lui interdit l'accès de l'URSS.' That is absolutely misleading. At the time, a number of refugee writers condemned the pact that enabled the Soviet Union to stay out of the war (which began as a purely imperialistic war) for another few years. I was not one of those writers. I thought the pact was good policy. Except that while the pact was in force it was a little harder for the Soviet Union to publish poems and plays specifically calling for war against Hitler. This no doubt is what you meant by your sentence. My relations with the Soviet Union were normal and friendly at the time, and I travelled round the Soviet Union, helpfully guided by the Writers' Association.

p 6: 'En 1948 il retourne en Allemagne, dans la zone soviétique de Berlin, après avoir attendu de longs mois à Zurich l'autorisation de rentrer chez lui.'

This looks as if I had difficulty with the Soviet authorities. Obviously this was not the case. My only difficulty was that after the Americans cancelled my identity card I could not travel through American-occupied southern Germany and had to arrange a complicated detour via Austria etc.

In the bibliography I find Lüthy's totally corrupt article cited as a source. It appeared in *Der Monat*, an American magazine published in the American zone of Germany. You probably saw it in French translation. But it gives me no pleasure to see this gentleman mentioned as an authority on me.

Please do your best to have these mistakes deleted from the Preface. I know that distance makes for such problems. But please in future get my approval before publishing programmatic articles of this kind.

[1]English in original

The book itself, incidentally, looks very nice. Many thanks.

> Yours,
> B

PS Please get them to send me a few more copies.

790 To Wien-Film AG

Dear friends,

The scenario in its present form doesn't look right to me. Superficially it seems on the whole to follow the line that Volodya and I decided on, but in the execution the story of Puntila seems to have slipped into a *genre* that makes it more ridiculous than amusing. It has become a refined drawing-room comedy, in which the crude jokes seem out of place and almost vulgar. The Puntila stories as told me in Finland by Hella Wuolijoki were authentic folk tales, and that is how they should be told in the film, 'from below', as coming from the people. If that is done, such characters as Matti and Eva will automatically be right. As the scenario stands, Matti is too flabby and nondescript; it doesn't come out that despite, and because of, his menial position he is always, in every speech, opposed to his master. Eva, who must be every inch Puntila's daughter doesn't love him for his muscles – he needn't have any – but because he's a real man, a man of humour, dignity, etc. Of course Matti needn't believe for one moment that Eva would be the right wife for him or that Puntila would really let him have her. His test is merely his way of carrying Puntila's drunken ideas *ad absurdum*. It must remain a game, otherwise Matti will look like a fool.

When I say that the Puntila stories must be folk tales, I am also saying that they must not be naturalistic. The common people don't tell naturalistic stories. And the same goes for the costumes, the buildings and the colours (which in my opinion should be intense, bright and unbroken).

Knowing that the studio can't wait long, we have already outlined a new scenario. Like a true comrade, Volodya set bravely to work. We're sending you about half immediately, the rest will be along in a few days. But as far as I'm concerned, this scenario is the final version. Of course it can be cut, but nothing can be added. Once again: it's not a matter of personal style – that can vary – but of genre. Of course Cavalcanti, who has been incredibly comradely and patient, can and

should make the film entirely in his own style. Dear comrades, I don't
enjoy having to create difficulties. I couldn't possibly have signed my
name to the present scenario, I wouldn't even have allowed the names
of Puntila and Matti to be used in a film made in the wrong genre, a film
that would not have told the folk tales of Puntila and Matti. On the
other hand, I'm convinced that, if done according to the new scenario,
the film will be really good and useful. Ruth's suggestion, which I am
enclosing, may be a real help.

With best regards

Berlin, 20 February 1955

792 To Harry Buckwitz

Berlin, 1 March 1955

Dear Buckwitz,

I want to tell you about my experience with the *Chalk Circle* music,
but I'd rather you didn't quote me to Dessau because – I believe – it is
not necessary and most probably would only upset him.

If the music is difficult for the audience, I think it's chiefly because
it's difficult for the musicians and singers, and this is often noticeable. It
never has the precise casualness of light-hearted incidental music without
which everything seems so deadly serious. It might gain a good deal by
being wisely reduced and simplified. Music should help and not need to
be helped. And yet I think it's a really important and pioneering bit of
work. It's only a question of time before it gets the right effect.
Pioneering just happens to be an activity that calls for wisdom.

We'll recast Reichel here as soon as we can. We haven't definitely
engaged anyone for the music rehearsals, and I wouldn't want to spend
the Ensemble's money for work done outside the Ensemble. But Reichel
is unusually musical.

Of course I'll be grateful if you give the Landestheater Schleswig
[Schleswig Provincial Theatre] your directing script and possibly our
costumes as well. A mask and also a description of the process are going
off to you.

Please give [Teo] Otto my regards.

Yours cordially

793 To Paul Dessau

[Berlin], 2 March 1955

Dear Dessau,

I deeply regret our quarrel about the *Chalk Circle* rehearsals and want to apologise for my vehemence. You exasperated me by saying we hadn't done enough for the music. Actually we spent so much on the music rehearsals we didn't know how to justify it to the finance office. We took woman singers because we couldn't find any men, and if we haven't got a conductor it's because there's none to be found. You couldn't bring yourself to help us; you should have. Here in our theatre no artist can expect to have everything he needs for his art handed him on a silver plate. We simply felt deserted. Now, with no one to watch over it, the music is rapidly degenerating. It seems strained and therefore strains the listener. Consequently I think we should experiment with simplifications and reductions. Please go over the music again with Iva Besson – or do you prefer someone else? – and tell her what you mean to do about Frankfurt.

796 To Ernst Schumacher

Berlin, 12 April 1955

Dear Schumacher,

I took a look at your book over Easter and found it extremely interesting, useful, informative, etc. Here just a few trifling remarks: The word 'concrete' is used too often and in too many senses to have any precise historical meaning (e.g. p. 21).

You've gone too far in drawing Strindberg into a system. What about the *Comrades* stories, what about the great novels? You can find lots of realism there.

Perhaps you should treat my story 'Bargan gives up' [*Short Stories 1921–1946*, p. 3] more dialectically. Escapism – yes, if you will, but something more. Why not treat it in connection with *Puntila*?

Also, you might omit a few value judgements and leave a few questions open. That always helps. Why put everything under one head, even the best of heads?

Forgive me if this sounds ill-tempered, but I always get irritated when I read something, good or bad, about my early works. All the same, even this cursory reading – I have to return the proofs soon – gave me a good laugh (and not at you).

I was able to correct the one Christmas poem from memory. Now I'll try to put a little pressure on the publishers to bring the book out quickly. Thanks, and also for the Paulaner.

Yours

797 To the Nordmark-Landestheater / Horst Gnekow

Berlin, 8 April 1955

Dear Dr Gnekow,

From reviews of the Wuppertal performances of *The Good Person of Szechwan* I gather that the tobacco factory scene with the 'Elephant Song' in it is hard to play. In this case it's necessary to sacrifice a revolutionary effect to the somewhat bitter truth. It's true that the tobacco workers sing the song to make fun of the overseer, but the crux of the scene is that the overseer cleverly gets the workers to work faster by speeding up the tempo of the song. In the end the singers are practically panting, while the overseer sits back in his comfortable chair and laughs. The scene shows the weakness rather than the strength of their resistance and therefore should strike the audience as tragic.

Forgive me for writing you this when you may already have planned the scene this way without being told.

With regards and best wishes

800 To Ruth Berlau

Dear Ruth,

The production doesn't seem bad. Reichel is very interesting as Grusha, and Teo Otto's sets are splendid. Azdak is rather primitive, but effective in a hulking sort of way. But the scene changes take much too long, so I'll have to stay here tomorrow after all and won't be able to leave for Munich until tomorrow evening. I'll be back in Berlin on Thursday morning.

I hope you've been able to work a little and that conditions are not too bad. There's already a lot of green here and I wonder if you too have been seeing green.

Auf Wiedersehen
b

Once again I see how important model books are.

Frankfurt am Main, 24 April 1955
[Postmark]

801 To Ruth Berlau

Dear Ruth,

Palitzsch is just back from Frankfurt. He says it's a great success. The whole series (Cologne, Wuppertal, Frankfurt, Kiel, Munich) is important, because afterwards, whatever new things are put on, these will leave a memory. For Munich (*Szechwan*) I've suggested Hanne [Hiob] in case Wilhelmi is ill. I ran through a couple of scenes with Hanne, she's amazing. Just the way she laughs over them shows talent. The *Trumpets* rehearsals aren't going badly, but it's hard to give them pace. [Friedrich] Gnass can't learn his lines. They're starting to paint your flat on Monday, I hope it will be bright and pleasant. I haven't seen anything from the photolab lately. But my Paris publisher is here and doesn't seem entirely averse to publishing the model books. I'll keep you posted. – In the mornings I work on a few notes to the *Organum* from a dialectical point of view. – And collect material about Einstein.

brecht

[Berlin], 7 May 1955
[Dating: Ruth Berlau]

804 To the German Academy of Arts

To the German Academy of Arts, Attention R. Engel

In the event of my death I do not wish to lie in state or to be publicly exhibited anywhere. No speeches are to be made over my grave. I would like to be buried in the graveyard next to the house where I live, in Chausseestrasse.

Bertolt Brecht

Berlin, 15 May 1955

808 To Bernhard Reich

Dear Reich,

I was delighted to hear from you and Asja [Lacis]. After all there has been an enormous war, and ten years have gone by since last we met. I've often asked about you. We could make good use of you in the Berliner Ensemble at the Schiffbauerdamm. Couldn't you come and direct at least one play? You could teach our young actors a thing or two, it wouldn't hurt them. And how do you expect us to put on plays like *Die Reiterarmee* [*The First Cavalry Army* by Vishnievski] etc.? I'm sure you're all booked up, but if it's at all possible for you and Asja to come, let me know straight away what arrangements I should make. The people here are very friendly to us and I'm pretty sure they'll make such wishes come true if they possibly can. I shall be here in Moscow with Helli until about Friday of next week; the Peace Prize is being awarded on Wednesday. I hope there will be more letters from you.

Yours cordially

[Moscow, 19 May 1955]

809 To Nikolai P. Okhlopkov

Moscow, 21 May 1955
Hotel Sovietski, Room 305

Dear Comrade Okhlopkov,

It really grieves me not to have been able to show my plays in the Soviet Union up to now.

Some of them, it's true, have been translated into Russian and are to appear in book form. But to get the theatres to produce them, I'd have to show my way of staging them. It's really too bad that my plays and productions should be accessible only to western audiences.

It is my greatest wish to bring my theatre – the Berliner Ensemble – to Moscow. Can you help me?

Yours cordially

814 To Vassili Osipovich Toporkov

Berlin, 8 June 1955

Dear Comrade Toporkov,

It still grieves me that I did not get a chance to talk with you at the Club. I have heard your acting praised so highly and your book *Stanislavsky in Rehearsal* is a standard work, which I ordered from the Theatre Institute before it was even off the press. It is my best source of information on Stanislavsky's way of working. I hear you've expressed interest in the role of Galileo. The play is now being translated and I'm sure you can get a copy either from Comrade Fradkin of the Writers' Union or from the Foreign Workers' Publishing House.

Yours cordially,

815 To Joan Littlewood

Dear Miss Littlewood,

Our production contract was contingent on your playing the part of Courage, and I can't change that under any circumstances. I regret that the presence of my associate at rehearsals should annoy you. I respect individual working methods, but I don't believe you should reject technical advice in connection with new-style plays. If art is to keep pace with the times, artists must take cognizance of new methods and then use them confidently, in their own way. Forgive this lecture, which seems to have been necessary in the interest of my play. It bores me no less than it does you.

With best wishes for your work,
Yours

816 To Henri Magnan

Dear Henri Magnan,

Alienation effects have long been known in the theatre and in other arts. The fact is that we always get an alienation effect when art does not sustain the illusion that the viewer is face to face with nature itself. In the theatre, for instance, the objective world is alienated by the convention of versification or by a highly personal style or by abrupt shifts between verse and prose or between the serious and the comic. I myself make use of alienation effects (including the old ones mentioned above) to show that the nature of human society is not all that natural ('Naturally, my friend, that's nature') that is to say, not as self-evident or unquestionable as one might think. Science has long treated 'natural phenomena' (such as great plagues, meteorological monstrosities, the night, etc.) as engendered by nature, but by no means natural. Art is still powerless in the face of human nature and hence of social catastrophes of an individual or general kind (such as the will to power, love, war, etc.). It takes a defeatist view of human nature. In a few theoretical essays I have tried to show why an alienation technique – though not necessarily mine – is needed in dramatic art.

Paris, 26 June 1955

819 To Ernst Bloch

Dear Bloch,

I've mislaid a short article that I wrote for your birthday; so I've prepared an outline for you and am now offering you my work rather than its result. Still, the poem puts a kind of date on your birthday.

With all best wishes

Buckow, 6 July 1955

821 To Wolfgang Staudte

Dear Staudte,

Last night for the first time I saw Blier in the film, and I believe a few changes must be made in the script for him, because I doubt if he'd do very well as the corpulent Don Juan of the scenario as it stands. I'm enclosing a few suggestions of what could be done. I worked them out with Wekwerth, who will be able to give you the details.

[Berlin, July–August 1955]
[Enclosures]

The Cook 1

If Blier is to be effective as the Cook, it should be made clear that the Cook is a good man in good times and a bad man in bad times, generous when he has money, anxious and ruthless when broke. War makes people bad.

His good nature can be shown in his bargaining for the horse. His offer to marry Courage if she abandons her daughter shows a man hardened by war and poverty.

The political discussion between Courage, Chaplain and Cook gives
the Cook his true stature and should be reinstated.
The Cook 2
Scenes 35–38 should be revised in the interest of the Cook. The Cook
must be magnanimous, and I don't think he should have had dealings
with Yvette. There's no point in her singing her song to him.

822 To Hans Schweikart

Dear Hans Schweikart,
Everyone who has seen the production of *The Good Person* tells me
how fine it is. This only convinces me that I was right in suggesting that
you do it in Berlin. The Berlin public knows my plays only as directed
by me, and I don't think that is a good thing. These productions
provide no basis for judging the *general* stageworthiness of my plays.
And the actors of the Berliner Ensemble would also learn a great deal
from seeing the Munich production with its interesting direction and
great actors. We would do our best to arrange dates that would enable
them to attend. In exchange, I'd send the Ensemble to Munich, preferably with a play not by me – to show that our methods are not
confined to my own plays. The financial question would have to be
settled between theatres; that's not my province.
I'm delighted to learn that an important authority in Munich has
already agreed to such a visit. It would be wonderful if it came about.
The Ensemble is very much excited at the prospect.

> Yours cordially

> Berlin, 7 August 1955

823 To Albert Wilkening/DEFA

> Berlin, 13 August 1955

Dear Dr Wilkening,
Re costumes: I believe that Prof Kilger, who designed the costumes
that Staudte is using for the main characters, should also be consulted
about the other costumes – for the sake of harmony.
Once again I wish to say that if I rejected the designs, which were not
shown to me until 5 August, it was not just on grounds of taste, though
this had something to do with it. The costumes strike me as unrealistic

and not at all in the spirit of the play. As for the question of colour, black-and-white or a special tint, we came to the following agreement, if I am not mistaken: As Staudte stipulated, he is shooting the film in colour, but I reserve the right to make the final decision in this matter at some time that you will indicate, but no later than on completion of shooting.

No other solution was really possible, because Staudte insisted on a film which all of us, including him, are bound to regard as experimental, since neither you nor I have been convinced by the attempts made so far.

Rest assured that I appreciate your helpful attitude in this matter.

With kind regards.

826 To Ruth Berlau

Dear Ruth,

Don't imagine that I take the publication of the first model book lightly. Please write the twenty lines you have in mind. But they really shouldn't contain anything too personal. After all it's a manual, a book for directors to work with. The drier, more matter-of-fact, more sensible it is, the better – you know that. Some of the ideas in your first letter would do better for an article like the one in *Theaterarbeit*. Once the book is out, you can say anything you like in a magazine. I don't believe anyone will speak of you as chiefly a photographer. You've taken pictures because you wanted to record performances and communicate what you saw. From this standpoint, from the standpoint of the theatre, no one has done better work, and it will always be difficult to make such photographs because one must always, as you have done, photograph from the standpoint of the director and the playwright. Anyone looking at the book sees that at a glance. It's obvious to me that such books will not immediately be appreciated at their true worth. *So what?*[1]

b

On p. 9 of the old edition there's something about the use of the bridge verses. Should that be changed?

[Berlin], 30 August 1955
[Dating: Ruth Berlau]

[1]English in original

828 To Wolfgang Staudte

Dear Staudte,

I think we should stand firmly by our decision not to quarrel. Apparently a harmless telephone conversation between Wekwerth and me has been reported to you in a maliciously distorted version. You had told Wekwerth that if any of the costumes struck him as unrealistic he should see Kilger. When he couldn't reach Kilger, he asked me to get hold of him – which I did. After all, Wekwerth isn't a spy, not least because I'm not a hostile power.

The postsynchronisation is a serious problem. Helli will be very much against it, so it shouldn't be used except when absolutely necessary.

[Berlin, August–September 1955]

829 To Hans Rodenberg/DEFA

Berlin, 5 September 1955

Dear Hans Rodenberg,

I am beginning to feel more and more strongly that preparations for the *Mother Courage and Her Children* film have been made with unbelievable irresponsibility.

In the matter of costumes, I asked you as early as last spring to make use of the preparatory work for the theatrical production. This was done at the last moment, only a few days before shooting started, when the costumes were already finished. Up to 5 August I hadn't even been shown the sketches. And you yourself agreed with me at the time that they could not be used.

The contract stipulated that the main roles should be cast in consultation with me. Only a few days before shooting started I was shown some photographs that didn't look promising to me, of possible Kattrins. Mrs Roth, whom Helene Weigel had singled out for her looks, was engaged at such short notice that I had no opportunity to judge her artistic abilities. Months ago an actor was chosen for the part of the Cook; I still know nothing about him and I found out his name by pure chance only a few days before shooting started. (When I pointed this out to Mr Teichmann, he had the effrontery to insist that I had been informed of this engagement.)

For lack of time we've had to settle the question of colour or black-and-white in such a way that I might later be blamed for the expense involved in a colour film.

Even the usual makeup tests for Frau Weigel, who after all is playing the lead and has never acted in films, were dropped. To this day, she has not been shown any rushes that would enable her to appraise her acting.

When my assistant Wekwerth informed me that costumes were being used which Mr Kilger, on whose collaboration I had insisted, had not yet been able to check, Mr Teichmann called him a spy. He was barred from the studio, though he had been hired by agreement between the DEFA management and myself, and not by Mr Teichmann.

And now a new question arises which in my opinion puts the whole picture seriously in doubt. Namely, the problem of postsynchronisation. Helen Weigel has said from the start that she would not be able to speak the lines for scenes that had already been shot. I'm told that it's not customary in serious films except in very special cases. In a film like *Courage* it strikes me as totally impossible, and it looks as if the choice of studio, if nothing else, might make it necessary to postsynch important parts of the film. Furthermore, a good part of the film is to be shot on location, and that will probably necessitate further postsynching.

I was not able to meet Messrs Staudte and Teichmann on Sunday for a discussion of this serious problem. Mr Teichmann kept me waiting on Sunday morning, as he didn't think it necessary to let me know that a conference could not take place. Up until now, Monday morning, I have had no explanation from Mr Teichmann. I would at least like to prevent good artistic work and enormous sums of money from being wasted, but I don't know how. Please help.

831 To the Members of the Berliner Ensemble [Notice for bulletin board]

Berlin, 27 September 1955

To the Members of the Berliner Ensemble

I have the impression – and not for the first time – that the Ensemble is misjudging the work of our young directors. There is no need to underestimate my contribution to their productions, but neither should too much be made of it. Not only have our young directors learned their so-called trade here with us; in addition, they are learning a very special kind of theatre, which is still in the process of development and gives me too plenty of difficulties. Thus every production is still an experiment and will, I hope, continue to be one. I will *not* let a reactionary attitude on the part of the actors deter me from participating in the experiments of anyone in the Berliner Ensemble. And none of the younger directors should be made to pay for this attitude of mine.

brecht

832 To Lion Feuchtwanger

Berlin, 28 September 1955

Dear Doctor,

The English Stage Society [sic] is opening its own theatre this season. They have engaged George Devine as their chief director and among other things they are interested in *Galileo*. First of all, I urgently want to know whether Laughton might be interested in playing Galileo in London. He seems very hard to approach at the moment, because, so I hear, everything is filtered by an extremely energetic manager and friend of Laughton's. Could you call Charles on the phone, give him my regards and ask him? During their guest performances in Berlin, I spoke to Peggy Ashcroft, John Gielgud and George Devine, who really seemed taken with the Berliner Ensemble and want to help bring it to England. Since Paris there's no real danger in staging a play of mine in Western Europe.[1]

How are you? How about a visit, to see the *Chalk Circle*, for instance?

Yours cordially

833 To Therese Giehse

Dear Therese,

I couldn't advise you to take on the role of Courage in the DEFA film. On my advice Helli reluctantly gave up the part because, from the standpoint of art as well as health, working conditions had become intolerable. Staudte, the director, had planned a supercolossal production and to make matters worse his preparations for it were quite

[1]Reference to the Berliner Ensemble's guest appearances in Paris 1954 (*Mother Courage*) and 1955 (*The Caucasian Chalk Circle*).

inadequate – all summer, until ten days before shooting started, he was busy with a film in Holland. The colour experiments agreed to at my demand were not made, the costumes might have been done for a musical, the supercolossal sets had been put in the biggest studio, where even the most intimate scenes would probably have had to be postsynchronised because that studio has an echo. The schedules for the foreigners, perfectly good actors actually, were so tight that the necessity of having new costumes made and the illness of the woman playing Kattrin threw everything out. The work got more and more slipshod and Helli was expected to be on call for a practically unlimited number of hours. At that point I stepped in, all the more resolutely as several good people of our generation had recently died of heart trouble (Fr[iedrich] Wolf, [Franz Carl] Weiskopf) or had fallen gravely ill (Becher, Bredel, Fürnberg, Ackermann). This point of view met with the full understanding of the government. They were ready to accept a considerable financial loss rather than countenance the systematic wrecking of indispensable people. Now we must try to replace the 'usual' routine, which according to Mr Staudte 'seems unreasonable only to people outside the cinema', by artistically (and otherwise) healthy working conditions.

Thank you for your staunchness.

> Yours
> b

When will you be in London?

Berlin, 5 October 1955
[Postmark]

837 To Ruth Berlau

Dear Ruth,

Thanks for the phone call.

There's been a slight calm in the theatre since Palitzsch tried his hand with the Chinese farce *Der Tag des grossen Gelehrten Wu* [*The Great Scholar Wu's Day*]. Now Angelika [Hurwicz] is rehearsing Ostrovski's *Stepdaughter*, and I don't have to go yet.

Just now I'm having an article typed (I'll send you a copy), in which I describe the first scene of *Coriolanus* and its dialectical structure and go on to explain how it can be brought off on the stage, that is, what sort of inventions and so on are needed. The article is something like 'Die Strassenszene' ['The Street Scene'] and will interest you.

I'm glad you've got a place to live and only wish you could find out whether the money from Sweden has come. If it hasn't, give me a ring.

Thanks for the little pewter jug.

> epep
> bertolt

[Berlin] Wednesday [November/December 1955]

838 To Ruth Berlau

Dear Ruth,

Thanks for the letter and the print.

Here it's getting grey and colder. I'm helping a little with Angelika's directing of the Ostrovski. These plays seem easy but they're difficult and now and then the plot seeps away like a river in the desert. Hanns [Eisler] often comes over in the evening, he has been composing a lot and is 'in good shape'. I can't really get started on *Galileo*, I still tire very quickly.

Busch is eager to do it.

If you think it will pick you up to stay in a *pension* for a few weeks, you should do it, Ruth.

I'm looking forward to the crime novels.

> bertolt
> epep

[Berlin, November–December 1955]

840 To Ruth Berlau

Dear Ruth,

One day is like the next, and it's always hard to write. Especially as I'm waiting to hear from you. I've had a *Galileo* rehearsal with Busch. It's interesting. I only rehearse for two hours from ten to twelve. For the *Galileo* film we'll have to get an older projector; otherwise it jerks like the old Chaplin films, and it's so important. The little colour photos in the cardboard holders are a wonderful help for the costumes.

One of these days I want to write and tell you how I feel about the future and what in my opinion you should do. For that I need time to think. Perhaps during the Christmas holidays. First you should arrange everything so that you feel good and settle down a bit. That's important for here too.

bertolt

epep

Now I'm rushing to the rehearsal.
We're doing our best to get the list.

Berlin, 14 December 1955
[Postmark]

841 To the GOKS, Tbilisi

Berlin, 21 December 1955

Dear Comrades,

Dr Hugo Huppert has asked for my opinion about the time and place of action of my play *The Caucasian Chalk Circle*, as you are to do costume sketches for a group in Strasbourg.

I've heard that similar events occurred in feudal Georgia. But it would be quite sufficient to use motifs from old Georgian and Persian pictures for the sets and costumes. Any naturalistic historical costume would be dreadful.

With socialist greetings
Yours

842 To Wolf von Beneckendorff

Berlin, 27 December 1955

Dear Beneckendorff,

I find your interest in the role of the Cardinal Inquisitor quite understandable and it's a very special consideration that leads me to choose a different type of actor for it. It would be different if we saw the Inquisitor as embodying the hide-bound, haughty conservatism of the church bureaucracy, if we wished to present the Cardinal Inquisitor to the audience as a bureaucrat systematically opposed to all progressive thinking; we have chosen, however, to regard the Cardinal Inquisitor as a modern, adroit Jesuit, capable of holding his own on any level of conversation, still young, and thanks to his considerable abilities, likely to make a brilliant career for himself, an almost Stendhalian figure, not without 'sex appeal'.

I hope I have made it clear that this consideration implies no under-estimation of your abilities.

> Yours,
> Brecht

846 To Ruth Berlau

Dear Ruth,

I am slowly getting ahead with *Galileo*. I believe Cas has some good ideas for the sets. Busch is treating the stage hands to copious lectures on astronomy etc.

My heart is gradually picking up. They're giving me digitalis.

Angelika has directed Ostrovski's *Stepdaughter*. She got on well with the actors and it was a good production.

Next week they're doing the *Szechwan* play in Rostock. With Besson directing and Reichel as Shen-Teh. That's about all.

I'd welcome a letter from you about our friends in Copenhagen and your daily activities. Are we being virtuously sober?

That's important. One word from you and I'll feel better.

Are you getting the newspaper and the magazines? And what else?

> bertolt
> j e d[1]

> Berlin, 31 December 1955
> [Postmark]

848x To Ruth Berlau

Dear Ruth,

Before you come back to Berlin we must be quite clear about how things must be. The last seven years have been bad for both of us, and with my health as it is now I couldn't stand a repetition. Please don't fly off the handle again when I say that you were regarding Berlin as your meal ticket and looking at everything on the basis of outdated claims. You wanted the ENSEMBLE to pay you a salary, regardless of whether

[1] See note to Letter 250

you worked or not, and me to pay all your bills, regardless of how much you attacked and slandered me. All the women around here work for a living, they do so quietly and without special privileges: Hilde Eisler just like Hauptmann, Gloger just like Barbara. If you are not prepared to accept that and adjust your needs to your income, you cannot live here and maintain your self-respect. It's still the old story of 'from each according to his contribution', and not according to his needs. I myself have not turned into a pensioner living on the proceeds of my past activities. I go to work every day, as you know, and I am not going to have you living on income from royalties. We are not two playwrights who have collaborated in writing plays. If you gave me advice, I also gave you advice, and though I made more use of your advice than you of mine, the fact remains that your share of say, PUNTILA would be infinitesimal, less than one per cent. That is the truth and we have to accept it. Still, your criticism of plays while they were being written was useful, as were some of your suggestions at rehearsal, and your invention of the Model Books did a good deal to make my works accessible to study. You were responsible for the publication of the *Svendborg Poems*, the *Antigone Model* and the *War Epigrams*. And for a long while you were a friendly and in many ways stimulating helper.

Quite apart from our friendship, it is only natural that I should help you in any way I can. It is only that I can't for ever remain your outstanding debtor. It takes away all the pleasure there is in giving pleasure. When you left here, you meant (a) to try and give up drinking along with the aggressive behaviour to which it leads; (b) to take a detached look at Berlin (so as to arrive at a more realistic attitude); (c) to get back on your feet in Denmark (not so much in the economic sense as by getting in touch with old friends and taking up new projects). Our most recent telephone conversations, in which you announced your return, showed a great change in your attitude, a dreadful relapse which told me that (a) had not been entirely successful, with the result that (b) hadn't either; moreover it seems that you have again been alienating people. Scherfig told me how friendly you were for a long time while you were not drinking or drinking very little, and just like you used to be. What happened? You *must* lick it, Ruth. It is better for you to have your lapses there than here, but you must not give up the struggle, not for one instant. Only Shen Teh can return, never Shui Ta. Fix up a room for yourself, buy furniture, you can always let it when you come here.

But this time you must treat Berlin as an unfamiliar country, like a visitor trying it out. Wouldn't that be sensible?

20 Jan 1956
[Incomplete]

849 To Friedrich Siems

Berlin, 24 January 1956

Dear Mr Siems,

I'm delighted that you're going to put on *Galileo* in Nuremberg. I myself am now directing it for the Berliner Ensemble. I have now translated the inter-scene verses for the boy singers, and Eisler's music sounds glorious. How soon do you need it?

852 To Rudolf Engel/German Academy of Arts

Berlin, 4 February 1956

Dear Engel,

Hermlin, Wiens and Seeger have met with me to discuss publication of a small volume of Nazim Hikmet's poems. Max Schröder and Ernst Fischer have translated some of his poems and I will try my hand at a few myself.

Hikmet has a contract with *Volk und Welt* but we thought it would be good to have a small volume appear under the aegis of the Academy of Arts. Such publications are so likely to get buried in our country. Could you – I myself have to leave town – take the matter up with the Creative Writing Section?

853 To Peter Huchel/*Sinn und Form*

Berlin, 4 February 1956

Dear Huchel,

You know I think highly of Laxness. I regard him as a great writer and a special friend, but I don't see how we can publish his play, because everything we do in our theatre is interpreted as a lesson, as the expression of a point of view, and the reader here would think he is being told to regard the artistic career as immoral, more so for example than that of a housewife – however unsatisfactory the latter may be from an intellectual point of view.

I don't believe Laxness would regard such an attitude on our part as hostile. You might tell him that this is how the Presidium of the Academy of Arts seemed to feel about it.

Cordially

855 To Peter Suhrkamp

Dear P S,

I don't believe your selection from the *Poems* should appear in the *Bibliothek*. It was all right for *Devotions*, because that was a reprint. But the first edition of my *Poems* in West Germany shouldn't look as if I were a foreigner. If it's not possible to bring the *Poems* out in an adequate way – as a single volume, in the same format as the *Early Plays* – then we might just as well accept this as a historical reality and simply not publish them.

Yours cordially,
b

Milano, 9 February 1956

856 To Ruth Berlau

Dear Ruth,

The performance – brilliant in conception and detail and very aggressive – went on from nine-thirty to two in the morning. Because of a flu epidemic the actors weren't quite ready, they hadn't had a complete run-through, so they were amazed at the length. But it seems to have been a big success, and my impression was one of remarkable freshness. Strehler, who is probably the best director in Europe, set the action in 1914 and Teo Otto made marvellous sets (a garage instead of a stable, etc.) This is a splendid idea and after the third World War it could be updated to 19... I do wish, Ruth, that everything could again be as it was between us, on a new basis, since we're not as young as we used to be, especially me. Then it would be good to have you with me somewhere.

bertolt
epep[1]

Milano, 11 February 1956

[1]See footnote to letter 485.

857 To the Piccolo Teatro, Milan

Berlin, 27 February 1956

To the Members of the Piccolo Teatro

Let me again thank you and your great director for your excellent performance of my *Threepenny Opera*. Passion and coolness, ease and precision distinguish this production from many that I have seen. You have given the work a true rebirth.

I also wish to thank all the members who contributed to this great event with their unstinting work on the programme and on the little exhibition in the foyer.

I would consider it a pleasure and an honour if your theatre were to produce *The Threepenny Opera* at the Schiffbauerdamm-Theater in Berlin, where it first opened.

860 To Paul Wandel

Dear Comrade Wandel,

At the Second Party Congress Hanns Eisler and I suggested that cultural and political centres be established in the big factories. Our suggestion was not taken up. I should nevertheless like to make it again at the Third Party Congress. Can I discuss the matter with you? Could you arrange to come and see me one evening next week?

With best regards

862 To Fritz Selbmann

Berlin, 28 March 1956

Dear Comrade Selbmann,

Is there any chance of my getting a look at material about the economic development of the GDR? For my literary work I am interested in data about dismantling, reparations, increase in the productivity of labour, increase in real wages etc. To the best of my knowledge, such data are kept under lock and key. Can you help me get at them?

Yours with thanks.

865 To Paul Patera

Dear Mr Patera,

Die Massnahme was not written for an audience but exclusively for the instruction of the performers. In my experience, public performances of it inspire nothing but moral qualms, usually of the cheapest sort. Accordingly, I have not let anyone perform the play for a long time. My short play *The Exception and the Rule* is better suited to productions by nonprofessional groups.

                    With best regards

866 To Boris Pasternak

Dear Comrade Pasternak,

Someone has just sent me an anthology including some twenty of my poems. The selection is bad and the translations are bad. I don't know whether it would interest you to translate the poems I am enclosing, but I believe they might be useful if published now. In any case I should be very grateful to you.

                    As ever

868 To Lion Feuchtwanger

                                        [Berlin], 3 May 1956

Dear Doctor,

This will be brief because at the moment I'm lying in the Charité recovering from the after-effects of flu.

The most important thing about a production of *Simone* is that the title role must not under any circumstances be played by a young actress (not even if she looks like a child), but only by an eleven-year-old girl who looks like a child. I think you agree with me about this. And really we mustn't be in too much of a hurry. There's a vague plan of doing the play first in the GDR and then in Paris, directed jointly by Besson, our best director, and the Paris director [Jean-Marie] Serreau. But Eisler must first finish his music for the mimed scenes.

What about your *trip* to Europe?

                    As ever,

PS: Your letter has just come. As ever, it's endocarditis, but benign, and it seems to be subsiding.

869 To Boris Pasternak

Berlin, 9 May 1956

Dear Comrade Pasternak,

I've decided to ask you once again to translate a few short pieces, knowing that the mere request may come as a nuisance. But I should like to publish a few of my Lenin poems in the USSR in the best possible translation. I've never attempted anything of the kind before. It goes without saying that I'll understand if you have neither the time nor the inclination.

Yours cordially,
bertolt brecht

871 To Johannes R. Becher

Dear Becher,

It's customary for people to wish themselves something on the birthdays of our friends and one or two comrades. So on your birthday I wish myself the long life of your health and revolutionary humour. The era of collectivism has become largely an era of monologue; therefore I also wish myself many more conversations with you.

Yours very cordially
brecht

Berlin, 22 May 1956

N B. I wish *you* good weather and fresh vegetables for the current week.

872 To The German Academy of Arts

Berlin, 29 May 1956

To The Academy of Arts
Creative Writing Section
Berlin N W 4
Robert-Koch-Platz 7

I regret to say that illness prevents me from attending the sessions at which the awarding of the National Prize is being discussed. I do not believe that prizes have to be awarded at any price.

In the literary field I find [Willi B.] Bredel's *Gastmahl im Dattel-garten* [*Banquet in a Date Grove*] remarkable both in content and in form. Also Maurer's poems recently published by Insel-Verlag. Maurer has also published articles that our young poets will find instructive; he is an interesting figure of all-German stature.

Strittmatter speaks well of Benno Voelkner, an elderly Mecklenburg farm worker. He has now written his third novel, but I myself haven't read him.

876 To Bernhard Reich

Berlin, 16 June 1956

Dear Reich,

Many thanks for flinging yourself into the fray. It's a good idea to publish *The Good Person* in *Inostrannaya Literatura*, if only because the Berliner Ensemble may take the play to Moscow. I've written to the editors about it, and also asked them to submit the translation to you.

As for a preface to the *Collected Plays*, I'll think it over. I always need lots of time to make that sort of thing short enough, and besides I'm not well. It's important that you should come here. Buckow in Prussian Switzerland is peaceful and boring enough for work.

> Cordially

877 To Bernhard Reich

Dear Reich,

I can't tell you how glad I am that you're helping with the transla-tion.

Judging by what you say, *Mamasha Courage* is definitely right for *Mother Courage*. (I hope you got my wire about it.)

About *Galileo*: 'It seems to me that in this respect the pursuit of science requires special courage.' All I meant was that scientific work requires special courage. I'll send you some more notes on *Galileo*.

I'm trying to write a short preface.

If you ever see the actress Ranevskaya, please ask her why she never played Courage under Savadski's direction. A great shame.

When are you coming to Berlin or to Buckow in 'Prussian Switzer-land'? Of course it's important to me that you should keep an eye on the editions, but I'd like you to come here all the same, if only for a short time to begin with.

　With many thanks,
　　　　　　　　Cordially

878 To Nina Polyakova

　　　　　　　　　　　　　　　　Berlin, 24 July 1956

Dear Comrade Polyakova,

　May I briefly explain our objections to your courageous introduction to my plays? It's not the first time that someone, with nothing to go by but my own observations, explanations, etc., has presented an incomplete picture of my plays and the way in which they should be performed. Evidently one has to have seen a few of the plays on the stage. That is why it is so important that opportunities should finally be created for interested persons like yourself to come to Berlin and study the productions of the Berliner Ensemble. If I can help you in this, I shall be glad to do so.

　　　　　　　　With best regards

879 To Peter Suhrkamp

　　　　　　　　　　　　　　　Buckow, 25 July 1956

Dear Suhrkamp,

　I'm better now, but I'd like to go to Schmitt's in Munich for the last weeks in August and the first two weeks in September for the follow-up treatment. Couldn't you come with me? His opinions and methods of treatment are unconventional, but I think he should be listened to when conventional medicine has failed. I have definite knowledge of excellent cures accomplished in his place, and we could have a good time in Munich.

　Now to *Simone*. I think it presents a truthful picture, so it can't do any harm except perhaps to the truth-teller. Just put it with the others. I don't think we should have any qualms about publishing it.

　About Schmitt's clinic, I'm awaiting your agreement so I can reserve a room for you.

　　　　　　　　As ever

882 To the Members of the Berliner Ensemble [Notice on Bulletin Board]

For our London season we must bear two things in mind. First, as most of the audience won't know German, we shall be offering them a mere pantomime, a kind of silent film on the stage. (In Paris we had an international festival audience – and we played for only a few days.) Second, the English have long dreaded German art (literature, painting and music) as sure to be dreadfully ponderous, slow, involved and pedestrian.

So our playing must be quick, light and strong. By quickness I don't mean a frantic rush; playing quickly is not enough, we must think quickly as well. We must keep the pace of our runs-through, but enriched with a gentle strength and our own enjoyment. The speeches should not be offered hesitantly, as though offering one's last pair of boots, but must be batted back and forth like pingpong balls. The audience should be made to see that a collective of many artists (an ensemble) is engaged in a common effort to bring stories, ideas and feats of skill to the audience.

Good work!

brecht

[Berlin], 5 August 1956

884 To Paul Dessau

Berlin, 8 August 1956

Dear Paul,

When I began to feel a little better, I tried several times to phone you, but you were always away. Brugsch was always enthusiastic about the state of my health, but actually a five-minute conversation was too much for me. I'm still not very well, but I hope to see you soon.

As ever
brecht

886 To the Iskusstvo Publishing House, Moscow

Berlin, 9 August 1956

Dear Comrades,

I've seriously tried to write a preface for the Soviet edition of my plays. It's the only thing I've tried to write this summer, but I haven't succeeded. At the moment I'm just too exhausted. Forgive me. A suggestion: Use my poem 'To the actors' instead of a preface.

With socialist greetings

887 To Theodor Brugsch

Berlin, 13 August 1956

Dear Professor Brugsch,

None of the gains brought about by your treatment has been lost, but there has been no recovery. We consulted your assistant, Prof Hennemann, and he too, though with some reservations, agreed that I should go to Schmitt's clinic as soon as possible.

Schmitt will keep you informed and I hope to be with you soon again.

With many thanks,

Yours cordially

Editorial Notes

Notes on individual letters

Our numbering corresponds to that of Günter Glaeser's German editions, with two modifications. (1) An asterisk is placed *before* the number of any letter which has been omitted from this volume; and a short resumé or description then follows as a note. (2) One or more x's are placed *after* a number to indicate a letter's omission from the German edition. A given item can of course fall into both categories.

1 and 2 To the Reitter family   July 1913
Written from Bad Steben. Hermann Reitter, an engineer at the Haindl works, was married to Brecht's maternal aunt Amalie Brezing. Their sons Fritz and Richard were contemporaries of the young Brechts.
    Das Konzert: play by Hermann Bahr.

3 To Caspar Neher   10 Nov. 1914
Constantin Meunier: Belgian sculptor and painter, specialised in figures of industrial workers.
    Franz Defregger: Munich genre painter.
    Leo Putz: Munich Impressionist painter.

4 To Heinz Hagg: a school friend.   Early Jan. 1917
'Sylvester' is New Year's Eve.

5 To Max Hohenester: a school friend.   8 June 1917
Paula = Paula ('Bi') Banholzer.
    Pfanzelt: Georg ('Orge') P., Augsburg friend figuring in Brecht's early diaries and poems.
    Wolfzahn: meadows on Augsburg outskirts.
    'Vulture Tree': 'Das Lied vom Geierbaum', poem by Brecht.
    Wolfshöhle: The wolf's lair.

6 To Caspar Neher   c.20 June 1917
7 Ditto   Early Sep. 1917
Plärrer: twice-yearly Augsburg fair.
    Sophie = Sophie Renner.
    'New Life': at Munich university, where Brecht registered on 2 October 1917.
    Müller-Otto = Otto Müllereisert, a lifelong friend.

8 Ditto   Sep. 1917
Rosa Maria = Marie Rose Aman, an Augsburg schoolgirl. There is a photograph of her in Werner Frisch/K. W. Obermeier: *Brecht in Augsburg*, East Berlin 1975.

9 Ditto   Sep. 1917

Wiedemanns: Ludwig W., a school contemporary, had joined the navy.

Alexander and his Soldiers. Three or four pages of notes survive in the Brecht Archive.

10, 11, 12 Ditto   c.Oct. 1917, 26 Oct. 1917, 8 Nov. 1917

13 Ditto   23 Nov. 1917

Neuhausen: Munich suburb on the way to Nymphenburg.

Kutscher: Artur Kutscher, professor of theatre at Munich university, friend and biographer of Wedekind. His reminiscences, *Der Theaterprofessor*, were published in Munich in 1960.

The Kunstverein: a Munich exhibiting society.

14 To Heinz Hagg – school friend   23 Nov. 1917

15 To Neher   18 Dec. 1917

Brecht's poem about Rosmarie 'Remembering Marie A.' (*Poems 1913–1956*, p. 35) was written some two and a half years later.

16 Ditto   29 Dec. 1917

Fritz Gehweyer: a school friend who had left to go to the Munich Academy.

17, 18 Ditto   30 Dec. 1917, Early Feb. 1918

19 Ditto   27 Feb. 1918

Im Zwinger: in the dog kennel. i.e. Brecht's attic room.

20 Ditto   March 1918

Lech: the river at Augsburg, flows into the Danube.

21 Ditto   Mid-March 1918

Ludwig and Rudolf Prestel were school friends of Brecht's, as were Georg Geyer and Otto Bezold ('Bez.').

22 Ditto   10 April 1918

The *Neueste Nachrichten*: the Augsburg daily paper.

23 Ditto   13 April 1918

'A child that I saw there', from 'Fairground Song' in *Poems 1913–1956*, pp. 10–11.

24 Ditto   April 1918

George = Pfanzelt.

25 Ditto   End April 1918

Auer Dult/Munich suburban carnival.

26 To Hans-Otto Münsterer   May 1918

Münsterer, a slightly younger Augsburg friend, wrote the important short book *Bert Brecht. Erinnerungen aus den Jahren 1917–1922*, Verlag der Arche, Zurich 1963.

27 To Münsterer   May 1918

Wedekind's *Samson*: the performance was on 6 May 1918. By 'SPCA' Brecht means the censorship.

28, 29, 30 To Neher   May 1918

31 To Paula Banholzer   May 1918

Ehrenberg: Carl Ehrenberg, conductor at the Augsburg Stadtheater.
Palestrina: opera by Hans Pfitzner. It had had its première at the Munich
Prinzregenten-Theater on 12 June 1917.

32 To Neher   May 1918
Hodler: the Swiss painter Ferdinand Hodler died on 19 May 1918.
Swimming in the Lech: see the twin poems 'Of climbing in trees' and 'Of
swimming in lakes and rivers' in *Poems 1913–1956*, pp. 29–30.

33 Ditto   18 June 1918
'Strindhills and Wedebabies' are facetious diminutives of the names Strindberg
and Wedekind – 'berg' being a mountain and 'kind' a child.

34, 35 Ditto   Mid-June 1918, Early July 1918
36 Ditto   22 July 1918
Glaspalast: hall (destroyed by fire in early 1930s) where the main Munich art
exhibition was held each year. The Nazis replaced it with the still extant House
of (German) Art.
Paula Banholzer's baby was born on 30 July 1919 and christened Frank
Walter Otto – after Frank Wedekind, Brecht's brother Walter and Otto
Müllereisert.

37 To Paula Banholzer   10-12 Aug. 1918
Fritz = Fritz Gehweyer (according to *Brecht in Augsburg*), who was killed soon
after returning to the front.
Hartmann = Rudolf H., a school friend.
Oskar: not identified.
Fräulein Wiktor: not identified.

38 To Neher   26 Aug. 1918
39 To Münsterer   Aug. 1918
Corpse-Kutscher: 'hearse driver', a play on Artur Kutscher's name. He was
professor of modern literature at Munich University and Brecht had attended
his theatre seminar.

*40 To Heinz Hagg   4 March 1919
Hoping for another outing next Sunday. Can he bring his sister, Bi's sister
Blanka and a girl called Grass?

41 To Jacob Geis   28 April 1919
Geis: a lifelong friend of Brecht's, at that time dramaturg at the Bavarian State
Theatres, where the actor Albert Steinrück was briefly the director of plays
before the overthrow of the Munich revolutionary government.
Ur-Baal: the original version of *Baal* (presumably that of 1918).
For Johst see letter 43.

42 To Neher   May 1919
Ma = Neher's sister Marianne.

43 To Hanns Johst   Dec.-Jan. 1919
Johst: Expressionist playwright and friend of Kutscher's, whose *Der Einsame*, a
play about Grabbe, had had a dual première at the Düsseldorf Schauspielhaus
and the Munich Kammerspiele, both on 2 November 1917. Brecht had already
visited him in the summer of 1918 to talk about *Baal*, which had been prompted

by Johst's play. In 1932 he emerged as the principal Nazi playwright, and under the Third Reich was the first president of the Chamber of Writers.

Bötticher: Hermann, B., whose play *Friedrich der Grosse* had been published by S. Fischer in 1917. His *Die Liebe Gottes* had its première at the Düsseldorf Schauspielhaus on 13 April 1920.

44 Ditto   Jan.-Feb. 1920

45 Ditto (46 in Aufbau edition)   21 Feb. 1920
Frank Warschauer: poet, journalist and film critic, who entertained Brecht in Baden-Baden in September 1920 and lodged him in Berlin that winter. A nephew of the popular historian Emil Ludwig. In the 1930s he emigrated to England, where he became a London schoolmaster.

46 To Neher (45 in Aufbau edition)   Feb. 1920
Pasetti: Leo P. was head of design at the Bavarian State Theatres till 1937.

47 Ditto   Feb. 1920
Wegener: Paul W., 1874–1948, a leading actor of the German theatre and silent cinema, known elsewhere mainly for his performance in *The Golem* and his portrayal in Emil Nolde's watercolours.

Müller: the publisher Georg Müller, since merged with Albert Langen in the Langen-Müller Verlag. He had agreed to publish *Baal*, but subsequently backed off.

48 To Jacob Geis   29 Feb. 1920
*49 To Dora Mannheim   Mid March 1920
Flirtatious letter to a friend met in Berlin, who had given him F. T. Vischer's book *Auch Einer* (Stuttgart 1918). He reports that on getting back to Munich he went to see Karl Valentin's cabaret and laughed himself silly.

*50 Ditto   24 March 1920
He has not heard from her.

*51 To Hans-Otto Münsterer   24 March 1920
On M's father's death.

*52 To Dora Mannheim   End March 1920
Thanking for her photo. He will send one of himself when he has one with an irritated expression.

*53 Ditto   Mid-April 1920
Will not be back in Munich till early May. He encloses a story.

*54 Ditto   End April 1920
Recalling 'three minutes when I liked you better than ever before'. This appears to have been when they went to Rosa Valetti's 'Grössenwahn' cabaret in the Café des Westens. (Valetti would play Mrs Peachum in *The Threepenny Opera* in 1928.)

*55 Ditto   May 1920
Brecht's mother had died on 1 May.

56 To Münsterer   Early May 1920
Hedda = Hedda Kuhn, a Berlin friend, addressed in Brecht's poems as 'He'.

57 Ditto   ? Summer 1920
Embahuba Tree: probably a creation.

58 To Neher   7 July 1920

R. J. Becher: Johannes R. Becher, a rhapsodic Expressionist poet who in the mid-1920s became an important Communist cultural functionary and ended in the 1950s as East German Minister of Culture. Prior to that decade Brecht was generally critical of his poems.

*59 To Dora Mannheim   Dec. 1920
When is she coming to Augsburg?

59a To Marianne Zoff   19 Sep. 1921
She became Brecht's first wife. He first mentioned her in his diaries on 9 February 1921, a year or more after the Augsburg theatre had first engaged her for the opera. Here he addresses her intimately as 'du'.

Lawsuits: brought by the Augsburg actress Vera Eberle as a result of Brecht's reviews in the left Socialist *Augsburger Volkswille*; the result was a public apology by Brecht and a fine of 150 Marks for insulting her lawyer. By that time the paper had been suppressed.

Recht: a previous lover of Marianne Zoff's.

60 To Paula Banholzer   Early Dec. 1921
Merkur: the Munich magazine *Der neue Merkur*, whose September issue published Brecht's story 'Bargan gives up' (*Stories*, p. 3).

Klabund: pseudonym of the poet Alfred Henschke, adapter of the Chinese play *The Chalk Circle* and short-lived husband of the actress Carola Neher (unrelated to the designer). Brecht knew him from Munich.

Matray and Sterna: Ernst M. and Katta S.

Granach: the actor Alexander Granach, 1890–1945.

Paula Banholzer does not figure again in this correspondence till 1935 (letter 254).

61 To Neher   Dec. 1921
Tilla = presumably Tilla Durieux 1880–1971, a leading Reinhardt actress who married the art dealer Paul Cassirer and was painted by Renoir. 'A really great actress' noted Brecht in his diary after seeing her in Ibsen's *When We Dead Awaken* in December 1921.

'Garga': i.e. *In the Jungle*.

Gurlitt: Berlin art gallery.

Kaiserisms: i.e. echoes of Georg Kaiser, the Expressionist playwright.

Fräulein Roecker: The Brecht family housekeeper.

Lilli: probably Neher's sister Ellen.

Port: not identified.

v.d.Sch.: possibly 'von den Schiffschaukeln' = of the swingboats.

62 Ditto   Winter 1921-2
Otto = Otto Müllereisert.

Orge = Georg Pfanzelt.

Jessner: Leopold Jessner, Intendant of the (Prussian) State Theatre, Berlin since 1919.

*63 To Hans Otto Münsterer   Dec.-Jan. 1921-2
Has he any cabaret material that Brecht could try to place for him in Berlin?

64 To Arnolt Bronnen   May 1922
Bronnen, real name Bronner, was an Austrian Expressionist playwright whom

Brecht met in Berlin. Both in some measure protégés of the *Berlin Börsen-Courier* critic Herbert Jhering, they struck up a friendship and a self-promotional alliance which lasted till the mid-1920s. Thereafter Bronnen, with such works as the nationalist *Rheinische Rebellen,* moved to the Right while Brecht went the other way.

The Second Flood: prize-winning film treatment by Bronnen and Brecht, subsequently published in the *Berliner Börsen-Courier* under the title *Robinsonade auf Asuncion* and supposedly filmed as *Isle of Tears.*

Kasack: Hermann K., then a reader for the Gustav Kiepenheuer Verlag.

Dr Lipmann: Heinz Lipmann, dramaturg at the Prussian State Theatre.

Jacob: Heinrich Eduard Jacob, author and editor, subsequently Vienna correspondent of the *Berliner Tageblatt.* Emigrated to the United States in 1934, after release from Buchenwald concentration camp.

65 Ditto   May-June 1922
Kyser: Hans Kyser, subsequently author of the nationalist play *Es brennt an der Grenze,* (1931).

Stefan Grossmann: editor of *Das Tagebuch,* and promoter of the film competition.

*66 Ditto   ?Early June 1922
Brecht has arrived in Munich and seen machine-guns in the streets. Should he find Bronnen a flat?

*67 To Trude Hesterberg   Sep. 1922
Hesterberg (who would play Widow Begbick in the 1931 Berlin *Mahagonny*) was running the 'Wilde Bühne' cabaret in Berlin, where Brecht had sung his songs. He asks her to spare Annemarie Hase, one of her performers, for the first production of *Drums in the Night.*

68 To Bronnen   Sep. 1922
Servaes: family of Frank Servaes, a conservative theatre critic who had made a flat available to Bronnen. His daughter Dagny became a leading Reinhardt actress in Berlin and Vienna.

Biti (or Bidi): nickname for Brecht.

Feilchenfeldt: Walther F., a reader for Paul Cassirer. With Grete Ring he took over Cassirer's business following the latter's suicide in 1926.

Gerda = the actress Gerda Müller, 1894–1951, later married to Hermann Scherchen the conductor.

69 To the Lessing-Theater   22 Sep. 1922
The theatre was then licensed to Victor Barnowsky, who had Julius Berstl as one of his dramaturgs.

70 To Herbert Jhering   22 Sep. 1922
See Note 64. Jhering would be Brecht's principal critical supporter in Germany up till 1933 and again from 1948 on. Under the Third Reich he did not emigrate but continued working as a critic until banned by the Propaganda Ministry. After 1945 he would become involved with the playwright Freidrich Wolf and others in a scheme to reestablish the Volksbühne (or People's Stage) movement in Berlin, with its theatre in the Soviet sector.

71 To Bronnen   3 Oct. 1922
Klöpfer = the actor Eugen K., 1886–1950, whom Brecht wanted to play Baal at the Deutsches Theater.

George: the actor Heinrich G., 1893–1946.

Viertel: the director Berthold Viertel, also a poet and later a film director, portrayed as 'Bergmann' in Christopher Isherwood's novel *Prater Violet*.

72 Ditto   22 Oct. 1922

Hannibal: unfinished project of which one scene was published in the *Berliner Börsen-Courier* on 13 November 1922.

Kragler: leading character in *Drums in the Night*.

Verrat: earlier name for Bronnen's play *Anarchie in Sillian*. This was staged by Heinz Hilpert for the 'Junge Bühne' on 6 April 1924 and later transferred to another theatre.

73 To Jhering   Mid-Oct. 1922

74 Ditto   Oct. 1922

Reich: Bernhard Reich, an assistant director at the Deutsches Theater who became a lifelong friend of Brecht's. With his wife Asya Lacis he was working at the Munich Kammerspiele in 1923/24 and later emigrated to the USSR.

75 To Alexander Granach   Christmas 1922

Granach: mentioned in Letter 60. He played Kragler in the short Berlin run of *Drums in the Night* which opened at the Deutsches Theater on 20 December.

76 To Bronnen   12 Jan. 1923

Gerda = Gerda Müller. In the event neither she, Steinrück nor Blandine Ebinger (Mrs Friedrich Holländer) were in the production.

Reigbert: Otto Reigbert, Falckenberg's chief designer, had made the designs for *Drums in the Night*. But *In the Jungle* was designed by Neher.

77 Ditto   Jan. 1923

Grossmann: see Letter 65.

Oswald: Richard Oswald, 1880–1963, a film producer who had Brecht and Bronnen under contract.

78 Ditto   ?Feb. 1923

Die Excesse: play by Bronnen, staged by Hilpert for the 'Junge Bühne' on 7 June 1925, then transferred to another theatre. Gerda Müller, 'our big sister', played in it.

Penthesilea: by Kleist, a German classic.

Film: presumably one of the shorts starring the Munich comic Karl Valentin, of which *Mysterien eines Frisiersalons* is known to have involved Erich Engel, Brecht, Blandine Ebinger et al.

'Nur wer die Sehnsucht kennt': first line of a poem by Goethe – 'Only the lovelorn/Know what I suffer' – set by Schubert.

79 To Jhering   Feb. 1923

Films: as above.

Leibelt: Hans L., Faber: Erwin F.: two actors at the Kammerspiele.

Holländer: Felix H. uncle of the composer Friedrich H., and temporary Intendant of the Deutsches Theater.

'The dead soldier' alludes presumably to Brecht's ballad included in *Drums in the Night*.

80 Ditto   27 March 1923

'The Ballad of Mazeppa'. German text in German Collected Works, 233

81 To Bronnen   March 1923
Aschinger: a Berlin restaurant.
 Gleisdreieck: station on the Berlin S-Bahn.
 UFA: principal German film company.
 Wannsee: a Berlin lake.
 Monopteros: pseudo-classical temple in the Englischer Garten, Munich.
 Augustenstrasse: where the Kammerspiele then was.
 Olympia: play by Ernst Weiss, staged by Karlheinz Martin for the 'Junge
Bühne' at the Renaissance-Theater on 18 March 1923.
 'Clown Gottes': not identified.
 Romanisches Café: fashionable with Berlin intellectuals.

82 To Barrett O.Clark   26 April 1923
Brecht was appointed assistant dramaturg in October 1922 on Feuchtwanger's
recommendation.
 Barrett Clark, an editor of *Drama* Magazine, worked for Samuel French
agency, New York, from 1918-36.

83 To Bronnen   4 May 1923

84 To Jhering   5 May 1923

85 To Bronnen   19 May 1923

86 Ditto   July 1923
Gösta: Brecht was adapting Ellyn Karin's dramatisation of the novel by Selma
Lagerlöf, but evidently got no further than the first two acts. The prologue to his
version was published in *Das Kunstblatt* (Potsdam) for January 1924, pp. 7–12

87 Ditto   ?end July 1923
Mahagonny: Brecht's 'Mahagonny Songs' (in his first book of poems) were
written with Elisabeth Hauptmann in 1924. Despite their American dress he
used the words as a symbol: perhaps for Berlin (as its use here suggests) or less
probably (as suggested by Bronnen in his memoirs) for the Nazis and separatists
in Bavaria.
 Brecht and Bronnen had been making an adaptation of Hans Henny Jahnn's
play *Pastor Ephraim Magnus* for a new Berlin company called 'Das Theater'.
Bronnen directed, and it opened at the Schwechtensaal in the Lützowstrasse on
24 August 1923. See Notes, 761, 812.

87a To Marianne and Hanne Brecht   Sep.-Oct. 1923
Pichling: near Linz in Austria, home of Marianne Brecht's parents the Zoffs.
Hanne: today an actress under the name Hanne Hiob, she was born on 12
March 1923.

88 To Jhering   17 Oct. 1923

89 To Granach   ?Autumn 1923
Edward the Second: Granach was associated with a short-lived group called 'Das
Schauspielertheater', who performed Marlowe's play in A. R. Meyer's
translation under Karlheinz Martin in Berlin on 2 November 1923. The Brecht-
Feuchtwanger version (based on Meyer's) was not seen there till Fehling's
Staatstheater production a year later.

89a To Viertel   Oct.-Nov. 1923
The Emperor Jones: by Eugene O'Neill.

90 To Helene Weigel   End of year 1924
Brecht met Weigel, here addressed as 'du', in Berlin in the autumn of 1923. The
two plays of which he writes were probably *In the Jungle* and *Edward the Second*.

91, 92 To Jhering   Feb.-Mar. 1924

93 To Helene Weigel   ?First half 1924

94 Ditto   ?First half 1924
Little Peter = their expected child.

95 Ditto   18 June 1924
Esther = Esther Warschauer.
  Spichernstrasse: Weigel's studio apartment, taken over by Brecht in February
1925 when she took a similar apartment at 52, Babelsbergerstrasse.

96 To Weigel   June-July 1924
'Yes, we have no bananas' was a popular dance tune. Brecht quotes it in
English.
  The *Song of Songs*. The passage cited starts 'My beloved spoke' and includes
the references to the voice of the turtle and to the little foxes.

97 To Weigel   Aug.-Se p. 1924
Kastanienallee. Close to his Augsburg home. The play referred to appears to be
Galgei, first version of *Man equals Man*.
  Staatstheater. The Prussian State Theatre in Berlin would perform the
Brecht/Feuchtwanger version of *Edward II*, directed by Jürgen Fehling, on 4
December 1924.
  Jungle was performed at the Deutsches Theater on 29 October 1924 in a
production by Neher with Neher's sets. Franziska Kinz played Jane.

98 To Jhering   ?1925
Wallenstein: Schiller's Thirty Years War play, which in some ways anticipates
Mother Courage, was performed at the Staatstheater on 10 and 11 October 1924 in
Jessner's production with an outstanding cast that included Kortner, Granach
and Agnes Straub.
  Piloty: Karl P., 1826–1886, was a gaudy Munich painter of historical scenes.
  Rheinische Rebellen: a Nationalist-Expressionist play by Bronnen, which Jessner
directed at the same theatre in mid-May 1925.

99 To Weigel   June 1925
Orge = Georg Pfanzelt.

100 To Weigel   June 1925
Hanne. See Letter 87a.
  Wozzek (sic). Weigel played Marie in the Munich Kammerspiele production of
Büchner's *Woyzeck*, which opened on 16 June 1925.
  Ullstein. Big newspaper and publishing combine, owners of Propyläen and
Arkadia, Brecht's book and playscript publishers in replacement of
Kiepenheuer.
  Step = Stefan Sebastian, Brecht's son.

101 To Lutz Weltmann   Aug.-Sep. 1925
Weltmann was then a dramaturg for Viktor Barnowsky (see Letter 69) and had
asked Brecht for a contribution on the theme 'Problems of the modern theatre'.
This appeared in a symposium called *Zwischenakt* in September 1926.

101a To Marianne Brecht   Oct. 1925
Otto = O. Müllereisert.

101b Ditto   Jan. 1926
Baal. The 'Junge Bühne' performance was actually a week later. Presumably
Brecht had hoped that Berthold Viertel (see Letter 71) would direct it.

*102 To Martin Elsner   March 1926
Elsner, a Chemnitz journalist had written to Brecht about the latter's visit to see
Dresden with Döblin and Bronnen. Brecht tells him the incident was private.

103 To Fritz Kortner   Early April 1926

104 To Leopold Jessner   10 April 1926
Both letters arise from Jessner's production of Hebbel's classic play *Herodes und
Mariamne* which had its première at the Staatstheater on 26 March 1926. Kortner
played Herod, Weigel Salome, the sets were by Traugott Müller. Along with
others such as Bergner, Bronnen, Kortner, Viertel and Jessner himself Brecht
had been asked to contribute to an enquiry in the *Vossische Zeitung* on the theme
'Is the drama dying?' His contribution, printed on 4 April, picked on this
production as a 'plaster relief', an example of 'the trivial stuttered stuff [that] can
no longer satisfy us'. It is included in the section entitled 'Materialwert' in his
Schriften zum Theater.
    Drums in the Night. The revival did not take place.

*105 To Ernst Hardt   12 May 1926
Hardt, originally a writer, was then Intendant of the Cologne Schauspielhaus,
where he was staging *Edward the Second*, with Lothar Müthel as Edward, and
Gerhard Bienert as Gaveston. Brecht writes that 'enormous cuts' were essential
and that he would like to come if someone would pay the trip. (He got a free flight.)

106 To Jessner   Mid-May 1926
The dating is uncertain. *Man equals Man* was first performed in Berlin at the
Volksbühne on 4 January 1928 under Engel's direction. It had 44 performances
there.

107 To Jessner   nd
Dating again uncertain. There were many campaigns against the Jewish-born
Jessner, who was a member of the SPD. Eventually he resigned his
Intendantship in 1930, though he continued to direct at the Staatstheater. Ernst
Legal (who had played Galy Gay at Darmstadt) provisionally took over the
Intendant's role. It was he who agreed to stage *Man equals Man* there in winter
1930–31, but resigned as director in favour of Brecht.

108 To Jhering   End May–July 1926
Ernst Hardt, having been held to be a failure as city theatre Intendant in
Cologne, was made (on Konrad Adenauer's recommendation) the first head of
the WDR, or West German Radio, from 3 July 1927. As such he directed the
Baden-Baden première of Brecht's *Lindberghflug* in 1929. He was sacked when
the Nazis came to power.
    Lothar Müthel became a Nazi in 1932–33, played leading roles at the
Staatstheater and was Intendant of the Vienna Burgtheater after the Anschluss
of 1938.

109, 110 Ditto   Early June 1926

***111** To Emil Faktor   21 July 1926
Telling the editor of the *Berliner Börsen-Courier* that he was sending a copy of the
article he had been asked to write for Shaw's sixtieth birthday. It appeared both
there and in the Vienna *Neue Freie Presse*, and can be found in translation as
'Three Cheers for Shaw' in *Brecht on Theatre* pp. 10–13.

112 To Willy Haas   2 Aug. 1926
Haas was editing *Die literarische Welt*. (Brecht has got the title wrong.)
Thomas and Klaus were Thomas Mann and his writer son (the subsequent
author of *Mephisto*), who had published a pair of articles in the Ullstein
magazine *Uhu* for August 1926 under the titles 'The New Children' and 'The
New Parents' respectively. Brecht's derisive article actually appeared in Stefan
Grossmann's *Das Tagebuch*.

***113** To Herbert Jhering   Sept. 1926
When is Jh. coming to Darmstadt, where B. was rehearsing *Man equals Man*?

***114** To Berthold Viertel   c. Autumn 1926
What news of *Man equals Man* in Düsseldorf (where Viertel was working at the
Schauspielhaus and had apparently hoped to direct the play)?

***115** To Alfred Kantorowicz   21 Dec. 1926
About a poem falsely published under Brecht's name by K., who had written a
review of *Man equals Man* to which B. took exception.

***116** To Helene Weigel   31 Dec. 1926
New Year wishes.

117, 118 To Emil Hesse-Burri   April 1927
Burri, who had known Feuchtwanger in Munich, became part of the 'Brecht
collective' in the late 1920s, working on *Man equals Man*, *The Breadshop*, *Saint
Joan of the Stockyards* and other projects. A former sparring partner of the boxer
Paul Samson-Körner, he introduced that distinguished middleweight to Brecht.
Later he went over to the cinema.

His *Amerikanische Jugend* was renamed *Tim O'Mara* and staged by the 'Junge
Bühne' on 15 May 1927 in the Theater in der Königgrätzerstrasse. Lothar
Müthel directed.

The 'Junge Bühne', as can be seen from Brecht's letters to Bronnen, was of
importance to both men between 1921 and the *Baal* production of 1926. It was a
club directed by Moritz Seeler which gave single matinée performances of new
plays in various Berlin theatres, mostly with the support of major directors and
actors. What so turned Brecht against it is not clear, though by 1927 it appears
to have reached the end of its useful life.

119 To Jhering   13 April 1927
Jhering had been the club's chief supporter among the Berlin critics.

***120** To Prince Heinrich XLV of Reuss   June–July 1927
A message for the twenty-fifth anniversary of the Reuss theatre in Gera, of
which the prince was Intendant.

***121** To Dr Hüttner   1 July 1927

Refers to a project for a 'Ruhr Epic 'in the form of a 'scenic oratorio' which the enterprising Rudolf Schulz-Dornburg of the refurbished Essen theatres wanted to commission from Brecht, Weill and the film-maker Carl Koch. Neher had joined him as his resident designer in September 1927. The likely costs, particularly of the film material, prevented the project from being pursued further.

122 To Helene Weigel   July 1927
The 'big success' was the Baden-Baden festival production of *The Little Mahagonny* with Lotte Lenya et al.

123 To Felix Gasbarra   Early Aug. 1927
Gasbarra had been appointed by the KPD as Piscator's literary collaborator or dramaturg for an agitational revue which the latter staged for the party's electoral campaign in winter 1924–25. When Piscator left the Volksbühne to set up his own company in 1927 Gasbarra organised a 'dramaturgical collective' of Brecht, Döblin, Toller and half a dozen other writers, with Wilhelm Herzog, the editor of the anti-war magazine *Das Forum* (1914–1929) initially as its nominal head. Its work for the opening season was planned that summer at a villa on the Wannsee in S W Berlin. It seems to have been Gasbarra who wrote most of the statements on behalf of the successive Piscator companies until Piscator left for the USSR in April 1931. In exile he showed himself critical of Brecht and worked for the Italian radio's German service in the Second World War. He subsequently edited the West German edition of Piscator's book *The Political Theatre*.

   Brecht's work as a member of the collective appears to have focused on three of the first company's productions (1927–28): *Rasputin*, *Konjunktur* (where Gasbarra wrote 'Seashells from Margate' for Weill to set) and above all, *Schweik* with the George Grosz drawings and film. He dropped out before the next season.

124 To Erwin Piscator   Early Aug. 1927
The 'Red Club': There had been a 'Red Group' of artists in 1924 and 1925, with Piscator, Grosz and Rudolf Schlichter (another ex-Dadaist) among its members. Brecht had not belonged to it, and it was now beyond revival, since the new 'proletarian' cultural groupings had taken over. Neither Weill nor Jhering were known as adherents of such bodies.

   Fritz Sternberg, a sociologist whom he had recently met through Schlichter, was regarded by Brecht as his first (Marxist) teacher. He later emigrated to the US.

125 To Herbert Jhering   6 Aug. 1927

126 To Helene Weigel   Aug.–Sep. 1927
Steuer and Kanter: not identified. Weigel was rehearsing for the opening of Molière's *Georges Dandin* at the Volksbühne on 1 September.

   Fatzer: Brecht's unfinished play set in Germany after 1918. The 'pornographic sonnets' were to have been printed in Augsburg in 1927 and privately published. The exact scope of the series is still debated, but two examples are included in *Poems 1913–1956*, p. 161, while twelve more were included in the *Gedichte aus dem Nachlass*, pp. 192–199 under the heading 'Augsburger Sonette'. Letter 738 also refers.

Hesse: Emil Burri.

German versions of Joseph Hergesheimer's *Tampico* and Jack London's *Martin Eden* were published in 1927, which also saw the start of an official Soviet *Illustrated History of the Russian Revolution* in German, published in parts by Willi Muenzenberg's Neuer Deutsche Verlag in Berlin.

Koch: the film director Carl Koch, who was then collaborating with Brecht and Weill on a project for an oratorio or pageant on Ruhr industry for the Essen opera house. See Note 121.

127 To Piscator   nd (1927)
Upton Sinclair's play *Singing Jailbirds* was performed by Piscator's Studio under Ernst Lönner at the Lessing-Theater. It opened on 1 March 1928. There is no trace of the translation which Brecht was supposed to make for it.

The Weavers and *Driver Henschel* are plays of the 1890s by Gerhart Hauptmann. They are regarded as classics of socialist naturalism.

128 To Hardt   18 Oct. 1927
For Hardt see Note 108. Alfred Braun of the Berlin 'Funkstunde' had directed a radio production of *Man equals Man* in March, and now sent Brecht a review of Hardt's Cologne radio production on 30 June. He too was sacked by the Nazis, but returned as head of Radio Free Berlin in 1954.

The plan for a radio play about the Flood was not executed. Its ideas were absorbed in the libretto for *Rise and Fall of the City of Mahagonny*.

129 To Edith Jacobsohn, Verlag Williams & Co   16 Dec. 1927
Edith J. was the widow of Siegfried Jacobsohn, founder of the magazine *Die Weltbühne* and himself an outstanding theatre critic during the first two decades of the century. Williams & Co, her publishing firm, was best known for the children's books of Erich Kästner, another *Weltbühne* contributor, and his illustrator Walter Trier. In the emigration it became the Swiss-based Atrium Verlag, with Kurt Maschler as its principal director.

The poet Else Lasker-Schüler had been married to Herwarth Walden, editor of *Der Sturm*. In 1920 Brecht heard her give a reading in Munich and found her poems 'exaggerated and unhealthy, but extremely beautiful in parts'.

130 To Finance Office Wilmersdorf-Nord   16 Dec. 1927
Publishers' advances: Brecht's former contract with Kiepenheuer Verlag specified a monthly advance of 500 Marks. In 1926 this obligation was taken over by Ullstein.

*131 To Erich Engel?   Spring 1928
Incomplete and largely impenetrable philosophical rumination.

132, 133 Ditto   Late 1920s
The dating and context of these two letters are uncertain. In the professional theatre of the 1920s Brecht was seldom able to direct, so he laid considerable store by his relationship with Engel, whose work came closer to his own ideas than did that of any other director. This relationship originated in Munich, where Engel staged the première of *In the Jungle* in 1923, and was resumed when, along with Caspar Neher, both men were promptly engaged by the Deutsches Theater in Berlin. Engel however, like Neher with whom he collaborated off

and on throughout his life, would direct classics and well-made box-office hits as well as the works (not exclusively Brecht's own) that interested Brecht; and as a result the Brecht-Engel collaboration was more fitful. After the winter of 1924–25, when Brecht was unofficially involved in the Engel-Neher *Coriolanus*, there was a three year gap before Engel (again with Neher) staged the first Berlin production of *Man equals Man* at the Volksbühne (5 January 1928). Later that year he directed the immensely successful *Threepenny Opera*, then was commissioned by the same management to repeat the process with *Happy End* a year later at the same theatre. Though there were other plays which Brecht might have wanted or expected Engel to direct, and even written about in much the same terms as Letter 133, it seems that this last is the likeliest subject of that letter; it was certainly not a formally very venturesome work, nor was it properly completed, and the result was not merely a failure but also a break in their working relations that lasted until after Brecht's return from exile. Neher too did little with Engel between *Happy End* and their resumed collaboration at the (Nazi-controlled) Deutsches Theater in 1937.

*134 To Rudolf Schulz-Dornburg   4 May 1928
Further to Letter 121. Brecht, Weill and Koch had applied to the city for compensation following the collapse of the 'Ruhr-Epic' project, and would hold Schulz-Dornburg responsible if he failed to support their claim.

135 To Ferdinand Reyher   9 May 1928
Reyher was an American playwright and script writer of German descent. James Lyon (whose study *Brecht's American Cicerone* prints both sides of the correspondence) suggests that Brecht met him through the publisher Ernst Rowohlt in the winter of 1927/28. His boxing play *Don't Bet on Fights* was translated by Elisabeth Hauptmann and staged at the Staatstheater on 31 December 1929 under the title *Harte Bandagen*. Lotte Lenya, Paul Bildt and Gustav Knuth (not Kortner) were in the cast; the director was Jessner. It was severely criticised by Jhering, who took it as evidence that Jessner was finished as a theatre Intendant.

The *Beggar's Opera*: *The Threepenny Opera*, which had not yet acquired that title. It was to work on this that Brecht was going to Le Lavandou near Marseilles.

136 To the *Literarische Welt*   6 June 1928
This answer to a characteristic editorial appeal for birthday testimonials was printed in the issue of 13 June. Stefan George, a gifted linguist and friend of Mallarmé, was the outstanding German aesthete of the early years of the century.

137 To Reyher   19 July 1928
Mr Rowohlt: Ernst Rowohlt, the publisher. But there is no record of his having shown interest in the play.

138 To Helene Weigel   July 1928
Utting is in Bavaria on the Ammersee, roughly equidistant from Munich and Augsburg. Brecht bought a house there in 1932. The Heidelberg production of *Jungle* opened on 14 July. *Kalkutta 4 Mai* by Feuchtwanger, directed by Engel with sets by Neher, had opened at the Staatstheater in Berlin on 12 June. Brecht

helped with its revision, and his Kipling-inspired 'Ballad of the Soldier' was included, in a setting by Hanns Eisler. Rudolf Forster played the lead.

Gottron: a Berlin dermatologist.

*139 To Bernard von Brentano   July 1928
Supporting him against an adverse criticism by Thomas Mann.

140 Ditto   Sep.–Oct 1928
Brentano (1901–1964) was at this time on the board of *Die neue Bücherschau*, the left-wing rival to *Die literarische Welt*. Within a few months its chief KPD representatives, Egon Erwin Kisch and Johannes R.Becher, had left to found *Die Linkskurve*, official organ of the new BPRS or League of Proletarian-Revolutionary Writers. Brecht's sceptical inquiries concern the latter, whose inaugural congress was held that October. Brentano could attend this as a correspondent of the *Frankfurter Zeitung*.

Peter Suhrkamp, later to become Brecht's publisher, was then working for the Ullstein papers in Berlin.

141 To Piscator   Sep.–Oct. 1928
The Red General: *Der rote General* by Hermann Ungar opened on 15 September at the Theater in der Königgrätzerstrasse in a production by Engel and sets by Neher.

Kaufmann: Walter Mehring's *The Merchant of Berlin*, which became the sole production of Piscator's short lived second company in September 1929. It had music by Eisler and spectacular scenic and film effects by Moholy-Nagy.

Shanghai film: *A Shanghai Document* by Yakov Blyokh (director) and V. Stepanov (photography) produced by Soyuzkino in 1928.

142 To Helene Weigel   Sep.–Oct. 1928
For *Fatzer* see Note 126.

*143 To Ullstein-Verlag/Emil Herz   12 Oct. 1928
Brecht is inquiring about a story of his which had been accepted and paid for but not yet published.

144 To Alfred Döblin   Oct. 1928
Brecht was a long-standing admirer of the novels of Alfred Döblin, of which the best known outside Germany is *Berlin Alexanderplatz* (1929). *Wang-lun* and *Wallenstein* had appeared respectively in 1915 and 1920. He was a Berlin doctor, collaborator on Herwarth Walden's *Der Sturm* and perhaps the most important Expressionist prose writer before 1914.

The initial reference is to *Anarchie im Drama* by Bernhard Diebold, chief theatre critic of the *Frankfurter Zeitung*.

The weekly evening meetings had been held in Brecht's flat, with Piscator and Fritz Sternberg among the other participants.

145 To Jhering   Oct. 1928
Drums in the Night appears not to have been staged since its Berlin failure at the Deutsches Theater in December 1922. Between 18–24 November Brecht, Piscator and Fritz Sternberg discussed how it could be adapted for a new production; a report of their discussion is in the former's *Schriften zum Theater*. However, no further work was done on this project, and the letter referred to in the postscript has not survived.

146 To Elisabeth Hauptmann   Mid-year 1929
This appears to be the original 'story' for *Happy End*, the would-be successor
to *The Threepenny Opera*, which was put together in the summer of 1929 much as
its predecessor had been a year earlier. That is to say there would be a basic
script written by Hauptmann, for which Brecht would write songs to be set by
Weill. The result would be put on by E. J. Aufricht in his Theater am
Schiffbauerdamm as the season's opening production, with Engel as director,
Neher as designer and Theo Mackeben as musical director, all as before. In the
event the show was a failure for which Brecht was quick to disclaim
responsibility, but this letter makes his involvement plain.
     In the play, whose authorship was ascribed to an imaginary 'Dorothy Lane',
Dick becomes Bill Cracker, Bess is Lilian Holiday, the 'Song of the Brandy
Peddler' is sung (from the 'Postille' or *Devotions* – Brecht's first collection of
poems) to a Weill setting.
     The reference to Massary remains obscure. Fritzi Massary, wife of the actor Max
Pallenberg, was a star of the pre-Nazi musical comedy and revue stage. At the
end of the 1920s she became recognised also as a straight actress, but is not
known to have had any dealings with Brecht or his works.

*147 To Bernard von Brentano
Hoping to see him in Bavaria and talk about starting a magazine.

148 To Hardt   July 1929
See letters 108 and 128. The public rehearsal of Brecht and Weill's
'Radiolehrstück' *Lindbergh's Flight* was held at the Baden-Baden music festival on
27 July. The photograph in *Brecht on Theatre* corresponds to Brecht's
specification. Hardt directed. The radio broadcast took place next day, with
Hermann Scherchen conducting. Certain musical numbers contributed by Paul
Hindemith were later omitted, but can be found in the complete edition of his
works.

149 To Gerhart Hauptmann   27 July 1929
Henri Guilbeaux, former editor of *L'Assiette au beurre*, had been condemned to
death in absence by a French military court. He spent most of the First World
War in Switzerland, where he worked closely with the artist Frans Masereel,
then went to Russia with Lenin, whose biography he wrote. He was subsequently
amnestied and returned to France.
     The 'experiment' was the *Lehrstück* or *Baden-Baden Cantata* which was directed
by Hardt and Brecht and conducted by Scherchen, with Josef Witt, Gerda
Müller and Theo Lingen among the performers.

*150 To Burri   Nov. 1929
Brecht had hoped he would come to Bavaria. Refers to 'my recent setback', i.e.
the failure of *Happy End*.

151 Ditto   ??Winter 1929/30
The three projects on which Burri was to collaborate were all left unfinished.
The most important was *Joe P. Fleischhacker from Chicago*, an epic play about the
Chicago wheat market based on Frank Norris's novel *The Pit*. It was listed as
Weizen (Wheat) on the forthcoming programme of Piscator's company

The reference to Aufricht suggests that Burri was working at the Theater am Schiffbauerdamm.

*152 To René Schwachhofer   April 1930
Thanking S. for dedicating two poems and sending them to him.

153 To Hanns Eisler   June–July 1930
Eisler succeeded Weill as Brecht's principal musical collaborator with the political Lehrstück *Die Massnahme*, on which they began working early in 1930.

   At the time of writing Brecht was probably in Le Lavandou again. Schmitt was presumably Johann Ludwig S., a Munich doctor favoured by the Brechts. The triumph with the 'Neue Musik' lay in the rejection of *Die Massnahme* by the Berlin festival of that name, whose principal animator was Hindemith. There was a legend that Brecht disguised his light reading (e.g. the popular thrillers of Edgar Wallace) under a Marxist dust-jacket.

*154 To Brentano   21 July 1930
A card giving his address and hoping Brentano will visit him.

155 Ditto   ?Autumn 1930
Brecht, Jhering and Walter Benjamin were planning a Marxist review to be called *Crisis and Criticism* which Rowohlt would publish: a rival to the Proletarian-Revolutionary Writers' *Die Linkskurve*. Franz Hessel was a Rowohlt editor. Benjamin withdrew from the editorship in February 1931, and the review never came out.

   The lawsuit was presumably that brought by Brecht and Weill against Nero-Film for the changes made to *The Threepenny Opera* in Pabst's film version. It was heard at the end of 1930.

156 To Georg Lukács (incomplete draft)   Winter 1930–31
At the time when this letter was supposedly written Lukács was still working at the Moscow Marx-Engels-Lenin Institute. He was sent to Berlin by the Comintern in summer 1931 'to take part in the guidance of proletarian-revolutionary writers', e.g. through his contributions to *Die Linkskurve* criticising such figures as Brecht, Piscator, Willi Bredel and Ernst Ottwalt. It is not known what form of magazine he had proposed to the Brecht-Benjamin-Brentano group.

157 To Karl Klammer   16 Feb. 1931
Under the name 'K. L. Ammer' the Austrian Klammer had republished his translations from Villon. These had been used by Brecht in 1928, with some modifications, for a number of the *Threepenny Opera* songs, leading Alfred Kerr and other critics to accuse him of plagiarism. In expiation Brecht paid Klammer a small royalty and wrote a sonnet (see *Poems 1913–1956* p. 180) to introduce the book.

158 To Helene Weigel   May 1931
Hesse = Burri. The Soviet playwright and documentary writer Sergei Tretiakoff met the Brechts in Berlin at the beginning of 1931. Barbara, their daughter, had been born the previous October.

   Dudow's film = *Kuhle Wampe*, written by Ottwalt and Brecht and first shown in May 1932 in Moscow.

159 To the Proletarian Theatre, Vienna   Aug.–Sep. 1932

This refers to a single performance on 20 September 1932 of the Brecht/Eisler *Die Massnahme* (see note on Letter 152) directed by Hans Vogel and conducted by Alex Sjegoff. The line references are to the German 'Versuche' edition published by Kiepenheuer in 1931.

160 To Hanns Eisler   Summer–autumn 1932
Brecht bought the house at Utting (subject of the poem on p. 220 of *Poems 1913–1956*) in August or September 1932. Nothing is known of the film project.

Grete is Margarete Steffin, the Communist daughter of a Berlin working-class family who played the servant girl in the first production of Brecht/Eisler's *The Mother* in January 1932 and thereafter was part of the Brecht circle as collaborator, typist, lover and political conscience until her death from tuberculosis in Moscow in 1941.

Measure for Measure. Started in November 1931, the adaptation was made by Ludwig Berger to direct for the Berlin Volksbühne, but was abandoned by them as the political climate worsened. The left-wing splinter group called 'Die junge Volksbühne' and chaired by Hans Rodenberg appeared briefly willing to step into the breach. Eventually the play was swallowed up in *The Round Heads and the Pointed Heads*.

161To Helene Weigel   c. 1932
Like the two following letters, this evidently refers to the start of Brecht's close relationship with Margarete Steffin, for whom during 1932 he organised an operation by the Berlin surgeon Friedrich Sauerbruch and a stay at a Crimea sanatorium.

162 Ditto   Winter 1932–33
Uhu was an Ullstein magazine. The balled was 'Zehr und Petschek' (*GW Gedichte*, pp. 383–5), said to be based on a true story. Its traditional prototype 'Henry slept beside his Newly-wedded' was later included in *Schweik in the Second World War*, where it is printed as an appendix. Otto was clearly Teo Otto, chief designer at the Kroll Opera and later at the Zurich Schauspielhaus; Wolfgang Roth was then his assistant. The *Illustrierte Rote Post* was a Communist magazine published by Willi Muenzenberg. The song is in *GW Gedichte*, pp. 374–6 under the title 'Der Führer hat gesagt'; it is not among those set by Eisler.

163 Ditto   Winter 1932–33
*164 To [?]   Early Feb. 1933
Acceptance in principle of an invitation to give a reading in Vienna.

165 To Thomas Mann   End March 1933
Thomas Mann's statement in support of socialism was printed in the *Frankfurter Zeitung* of 20 February 1933, three weeks after Hitler had been appointed Chancellor. It had been read out by Adolf Grimme, the former Prussian Minister of Culture, to a meeting in the old Kroll Opera entitled 'The Free World'.

*166 To Brentano   27 March 1933
A card to recommend the hotel where he is staying.

167 To Helene Weigel   March–April 1933
Weigel had remained in Vienna while Brecht looked for a temporary home in Switzerland. Kurt Kläber was a Communist novelist, author of *Die Passagiere der Dritten Klasse* and a leading figure in the BPRS or League of Proletarian-

Revolutionary Writers. The Brechts stayed with him at Carona near Lugano.

Anna Seghers's best-known novel is *The Seventh Cross*, Alfred Döblin's is *Berlin Alexanderplatz*; both were friends of the Brechts from Berlin. Which Mann is referred to is not clear.

Erwin Ratz was a Schönberg pupil at the same time as Eisler, and edited the piano score of *Die Massnahme* and other works. The texts of the two Eisler songs mentioned are in *Poems 1913–1956*, pp. 122 and 186. The *Arbeiterzeitung* is the Austrian Socialist daily.

168 Ditto   March–April 1933
Schmidt: J. L. Schmidt-Radvanyi, a Hungarian sociologist, had directed the MASch or Marxist Workers' School in Berlin. He was married to Anna Seghers.

Höllering: presumably the lawyer Georg Höllering, one of the producers of *Kuhle Wampe*, later a founder of the Academy Cinema in London.

Alexander: Elias Alexander, owner of the London agency European Books Ltd.

Korsch: Karl Korsch, Marxist philosopher, Minister for Justice in the Thuringian provincial government before 1924, expelled from the KPD in 1926, Reichstag deputy till 1928. Brecht attended his discussion groups and his course on Marxism-Leninism at the MASch. His edition of Marx's *Capital* appeared in 1932.

169 To Margot von Brentano   April 1933
For Brentano see note on Letter 140. Ottwalt was a former Nationalist who joined the Communists and worked with Brecht on the script of *Kuhle Wampe*. A documentary writer, he went to the USSR in 1934, was arrested and sent to a northern camp where he died in 1943.

Job in Paris: Brecht wrote the song texts for Lenya to sing in Kurt Weill's ballet *The Seven Deadly Sins*, which Kochno and Balanchine had devised for Les Ballets 1933. Neher came from Germany to design the sets. The first performance was at the Théâtre des Champs Elysées on 7 June 1933.

Neurath's book: Otto Neurath: *Empirische Soziologie*. Springer, Vienna 1931.

'The firm' or 'the club'. In refugee circles the Communist Party was often referred to thus.

170 To Sergei M. Tretiakoff   April 1933
For Tretiakoff see Letter 158. The Richter here mentioned was probably the film-maker Hans Richter, a friend of Tretiakoff's whose unfinished film *Metall* was produced partly in the USSR.

171, 172 To Helene Weigel   May–10 June 1933
The subject is *The Seven Deadly Sins*. Following the Paris première on 7 June 1933 the same company performed at the Savoy Theatre, London. Weigel, the two children and their Augsburg housekeeper Marie Hold were staying at Thurø in Denmark at the invitation of the writer Karin Michaelis. Brecht joined them from Paris in late June. The Ottwalts arrived in July.

173 To Johannes R. Becher   28 June 1933
The former Expressionist poet Becher (1891–1958) became the KPD's leading literary functionary in the mid-1920s, and thereafter edited *Die Linkskurve*, organised the BPRS with Kläber, and represented the Germans at the Kharkov International Revolutionary Writers' Conference of 1929. After at

first basing himself on Paris he moved to the USSR at the end of 1935, and became editor of the German version of *International Literature*. He returned to Berlin ten years later as principal director of cultural life in East Germany.

Theatre Olympiad: amateur theatre festival held by the International Organisation of Workers' Theatres in Moscow in June 1933.

'authoritative friends': these may not have been the ones the dutiful Becher would have picked. Radek (long responsible for German affairs to the Comintern), Koltsov (Pravda journalist, magazine publisher and head of the Writers' Union foreign bureau) and Tretiakoff (former *LEF* editor, official of VOKS and the Writers' Union) were all arrested and executed during the purges of the later 1930s. S. S. Dinamov was the chief editor of *International Literature*.

Trude and Otto were probably Trude Richter, a BPRS member who had remained working underground in Berlin, and Otto Bihalji-Merin, the Yugoslav art critic also known as Peter Thoene. Richter went to the USSR in 1934, was arrested and remained in prison or exile till 1959.

174 To Felix Bloch Successors   End June 1933

Fritz Wreede owned this Berlin theatre agency, with which Brecht had two contracts: one for *The Threepenny Opera* (26 April 1928) and a second for all plays he might write between 17 May 1929 and 1 July 1936. In return it would pay him a monthly advance. The two plays handed in were *Saint Joan of the Stockyards* and *The Round Heads and the Pointed Heads* neither of which could be produced. Elisabeth Hauptmann had a separate contract for *Happy End* (11 May 1929).

After Hitler's accession to power the agency stopped paying Brecht's advance, and he cancelled his contracts in 1949. See Letters 146, 344, 348 and the post-war correspondence with Weill.

175 To Karl Kraus   Early July 1933

This is Brecht's first known letter to the Austrian writer and polemicist, whom he had come to know in 1928. It was evidently never posted. The newspaper cutting tells of 'the Hermit of Gloggnitz,' a man some tourists found living in a cave. Unemployment and poverty had made him misanthropic.

176 Ditto   ?Mid-'30s 1933

Dating uncertain. Kraus's one-man magazine *Die Fackel* ceased appearing in 1936. Brecht used the Chinese story as the basis of a short story of 1926 and the later poem 'Legend of the origin of the book Tao-Tê-Ching' (*Poems 1913–1956*, pp. 314–316).

177 To Tretiakoff   11 July 1933

Tretiakoff replied that he had already returned *Mann ist Mann* and that *St Joan* would go into rehearsal in Moscow in September. Carola Neher was in Moscow (she was with a Soviet engineer called Becker), and he was about to meet Piscator and the director Nikolai Okhlopkov to discuss various projects. He reported progress with his translations of *St Joan, The Mother* and *Die Massnahme*. (These were published together as *Epic Dramas* in 1934.)

Slatan = S. Dudow, director of *Die Massnahme* and *Kuhle Wampe*, who was a Bulgarian subject. The 'Lullabies' (*Poems 1913–1956* pp. 188–191) did not appear in *International Literature* after all.

178 To the International Association of Revolutionary Writers   13 July 1933

Forwarding the 'Lullabies', which should be printed with Eisler's music.

Payment for them to be made to Margarete Steffin in Paris.

The Association, headed by Béla Illés, was a sister body to Piscator's MORT, and published the magazine *International Literature*, whose German version would later be edited by Becher.

179 To Otto Neurath   ?Summer 1933
See the reference to his book in Letter 169. A pioneer of visual statistics and founder of the Isotype institute in Vienna, he had been economics adviser to the Munich Soviet of 1919. For Brecht's 'representation of sentences in a new encyclopedia' see *Brecht on Theatre*, p. 106 and the section 'Über eingreifendes Denken' in *GW Schriften zur Politik und Gesellschaft*. The Association was not formed.

180 To Hermann Kesten   20 July 1933
Kesten had been literary adviser to the Kiepenheuer Verlag from 1927 till March 1933. Till 1940 he ran the German section of the Dutch publishers Allert de Lange, with whom Brecht was engaged in negotiating a contract for *The Threepenny Novel*. Fritz Landshoff, who had been Kiepenheuer's partner till 1933, had now founded the exiled Querido Verlag in Holland to publish German books. Kiepenheuer himself remained in Germany, where his firm was now under Nazi control. He gave Brecht the rights to the banned *Versuche* series, but neither they nor the early poems were republished.

181 To Johannes R. Becher   ?July–Aug. 1933
B. could be Bihalj-Merin.

Neue Deutsche Blätter was published monthly, nominally by a notional Faust-Verlag, actually by the Malik-Verlag, the leading German Communist literary publishers, now established in Prague. It existed from September 1933 to August 1935, after which it was effectively succeeded by the Moscow *Das Wort*. Editors were Wieland Herzfelde, Oskar Maria Graf, Jan Petersen (still living underground in Berlin) and, for a time, Anna Seghers.

Grete = Steffin. Anna = Seghers. Ottwalt's pamphlet: nothing known.

*182 To Brentano   Aug. 1933
Exchanging news and recommending Denmark, where Ernst Ottwalt was proposing to stay. B. wants to read Silone's book on Fascism (*Der Faschismus*, Zurich 1934).

183 To Helene Weigel   11 Sept. 1933
Lio = Lion Feuchtwanger, who was living at Sanary on the Mediterranean. This became a centre for such exiled writers as Thomas Mann, Franz Werfel, Toller, Kesten, Alfred Kerr and Friedrich Wolf.

The second volume of *Versuche*: Brecht's personal bound copy, which included the proofs of *The Pointed Heads and the Round Heads*. He needed these in connection with the planned Paris production (which did not materalise).

184 Ditto   Sept. 1933
Weigel was to visit Moscow in late September in connection with a radio programme. Illés was Béla Illés, secretary of the International Organisation of Revolutionary Writers there.

The Reichs = Bernhard Reich and Asya Lacis, Munich and Berlin friends (see letter 74) who had been working in Soviet theatre and film since 1926. Reich became Piscator's deputy at the International Organisation of Revolutionary

Theatres and in the German-language theatre at Engels. They were arrested in 1937/38, deported to Kazakhstan and 'rehabilitated' again in the 1950s.

Ottwalt = Ernst O, real name Ernst Gottwalt Nicolas, was a former nationalist who became well known on the far left because of his documentary novels and reportage, despite some severe criticism by Georg Lukács for his neglect of more traditional forms. He collaborated with Brecht on the script of *Kuhle Wampe*. See Note 305 about his later experiences.

Martha = Martha Franke, Weigel's maid. The Professor was the Brechts' name for Karl Korsch.

185 To Bernard von Brentano   Sept. 1933
Büchergilde = the Büchergilde Gutenberg, a book club founded in 1924 by the German printers' trade union, whose director Erich Knauf was arrested and killed by the Nazis. The Swiss branch continued its policy of publishing works of a broadly socialist/humanist leaning, notably the novels of B. Traven. The Büchergilde still exists, producing books of high quality.

Hartung: Gustav Hartung, one of the leading directors of the Weimar period, left Germany to work at the Zurich Schauspielhaus and subsequently in Basel. Gasbarra (see Letter 123 and note) appears to have been instrumental in getting the play turned down.

186 To Gérard de Lange   9 Oct. 1933
He was the owner of the firm of Allert de Lange, whose newly-founded German section was to publish *The Threepenny Novel*. The firm had written on 25 August to announce that they would publish nothing directed against the government of the Third Reich.

187 To (?)   Autumn 1933
It is suggested that the addressee was Karl Jaray, a friend of Herr K(raus). On 9 August Brecht had bought the house at Skovsbostrand on the Danish island of Fünen (or Fyn) where the family was to live for the next five and a half years. Svendborg, which gave its name to the poems he wrote there, was the nearest town.

188 To Helene Weigel   Oct. 1933
Weigel was in Moscow, where she was taken ill and was unable to perform on the radio as planned.

Borchardt = Hans Borchardt, a teacher who had collaborated with Brecht, Burri and Hauptmann on *Saint Joan of the Stockyards*, then went to the USSR to teach in Minsk. A good friend also of George Grosz, he was arrested in the purges but allowed to leave the country thanks to Feuchtwanger's intervention.

The 'small but important job' was reputedly in connection with the *Brown Book on the Reichstag Fire and Hitler's Terror*, whose first volume Willi Muenzenberg of the Comintern and the International Workers' Aid (IAH) was about to publish from Paris. Supervised by Otto Katz, Piscator's former business manager, this appeared in the course of the Reichstag Fire Trial (21 September–23 December 1933), supporting in great detail the Communist view that Goering had himself organised the burning of the Reichstag, using the pathetic Marinus van der Lubbe as a tool. Brecht's contribution (some of his suggestions are in *GW Schriften zur Politik und Literatur*) is thought to bear on the second volume on the Leipzig Fire Trial, entitled *Dimitroff contra Goering* and published in spring

1934. Many other writers, including Arthur Koestler, worked on these extremely influential books, which also dealt with the Nazi anti-Jewish campaign and the book-burning in Berlin, giving a list of forty-five concentration camps and a chronology of about a thousand political murders up to the end of March 1934.

189 Ditto   Oct.–Nov. 1933

190 Ditto   Nov. 1933
Weigel returned from Moscow to Svendborg in November. In Paris Aufricht was planning a production of *The Mother* which did not materialise. No details are known about the *Medea* idea.

191 Ditto   Dec. 1933
Walter's father: Brecht's father, from Augsburg. He is said to have helped find the money for the Svendborg house.

192 To Hermann Kesten   Dec. 1933
This appears not to have been sent.

   Kesten and Brecht had met on 14 December at the former's Paris hotel, where the latter allegedly agreed to give Allert de Lange first refusal of his next novel (a 'China novel', presumably the so-called *Tui-Roman*) if they matched the terms already offered by Muenzenberg's Editions du Carrefour. Kesten sent Brecht a note of the conversation, which claimed that he had gone on to propose a pact by which both men would 'agree to speak of one another's works with respect, though also with ideological reservations'. Following another meeting the argument lapsed.

193 To Tretiakoff   ?Dec. 1933
The volume of poems was *Lieder Gedichte Chöre*, Editions du Carrefour, Paris, 1934: a collection of old and new poems with some settings by Eisler. Eisler during 1933 had written the music for Trivas's *Dans les rues*, Ivens's documentary *Zuiderzee* and Jacques Feyder's *Le Grand jeu*.

   An Archive for the Study of Fascism was subsequently set up in Paris by Muenzenberg, supposedly with assistance from the French authorities.

194 To Walter Benjamin   12 Dec. 1933
Maria Lazar was a sister of Helene Weigel's friend Auguste Lazar, a French writer. Benjamin was having his library sent from Germany to Svendborg, where he himself arrived the following June.

195 To Karl Korsch   End Dec.1933
Bauer: Otto Bauer, a leading Austrian Social Democrat and political theorist.

*196 To Brentano   End Dec. 1933
In response to a pamphlet by B. which he had sent to Brecht. Suggesting also that he come to Skovsbostrand and take the house next door.

197 To 'K'.   Winter 1933–34
Though there was more than one 'K' involved in the preparation of the *Brown Book*, it is suggested that Otto Katz is the likeliest addressee here. 'Bü' is Wilhelm Bünger, the judge presiding over the Leipzig Fire Trial. The third Brown Book was published in 1935 under the title *Das braune Netz* and devoted to Nazi agents and propaganda abroad.

198 To Ernst Ottwalt   Late 1933–early 1934

Brecht arrived back in Denmark from Paris with Margarete Steffin around 20 December. It is uncertain which of his poems is meant.

Ottwalt's 'other novel' was *Erwachen und Gleichschaltung der Stadt Billingen*, of which extracts appeared in the first two issues of *Neue Deutsche Blätter*.

The anti-fascist institute was then being planned by Kurt Kläber, Otto Bihalj-Merin and the *Deutsche Volkszeitung* editor Lex Ende.

'Johnny' might be the photomonteur John Heartfield, who was then in Prague and involved in the production of *NDB*.

199 To Allert de Lange Verlag   25 Jan. 1934
For Dr Landshoff see Note 180.

200 To Karl Korsch   Jan. 1934
Neues Vorwärt:, émigré Austrian Socialist paper, published from Karlsbad. Otto Bauer was a leader of the party, Karl Kautsky its principal theoretician and an old opponent of Lenin's. By the previous winter's 'exercises' Brecht means Korsch's lectures on 'Living and dead elements in Marxism'.

Neue Zeit: a Berlin SPD weekly, founded in 1883. Brecht had the complete set.

201 To Bernard von Brentano   Jan. 1934
Schwerdt: not known.

Uncle Joe and 150,000,000 eyes: Stalin and the approximate population of the USSR. 'Over there' then meant Russia; (it now means the other half of Germany).

Slatan = Dudow.

Kesser: Hermann K., a German journalist and playwright. He took Swiss nationality in 1934 and would spend World War II in the United States.

Fyn: the Danish island on which Svendborg lies.

202 To Kurt Kläber   Jan. 1934
Lisa Tetzner = Mrs Kläber

Institute: the Institute (or Archive) for the Study of Fascism referred to in Letter 198 was set up by Muenzenberg with official French support: not at all what Kläber had wished.

Boniface: an eighth century martyr. The allusion is to Pastor Niemöller and the Protestant opposition to Nazi paganism.

ECCI: the Comintern Executive, which met in Moscow in December 1933.

SPÖ = the Austrian Socialist Party.

*203 To Alfred Döblin?   End Jan. 1934
Refers to his family Christmas duties 'as a good communist'.

*203x To Walter Benjamin   6 Feb. 1934
Letter dated 'Skovsbostrand 6 February 1934' to say that Brecht has sold Benjamin's pieces to 'a very good trade union paper here'. Brecht himself is 'doing a little work on the side on a novel about three old men in Berlin'. It is not clear what this refers to.

204 To Walter Benjamin   Early 1934
The letter appears to refer to a questionnaire sent by the Writers' Union in Germany.

Maulerism. Pierpont Mauler is the millionaire figure in *Saint Joan of the Stockyards*.

*205 To Ernst Schön   Mid-March 1934
Saying Schön can have work by him if he thinks it useable in England, where
S. worked for the BBC. A lifelong friend of Benjamin, he had been artistic
director of Frankfurt radio before 1933.

206 To Karl Korsch   April-May 1934
Refers to Korsch's book *Marxismus und Philosophie*. Brecht was then working
with Eisler on *The Round Heads and the Pointed Heads*.

207 To Korsch   May–June 1934
Madame Lou = The second Mrs Eisler.
    Henry VIII = Charles Laughton.
    Paul Partos: a philosopher, friend of Korsch. Apparently he had sent Korsch
a letter through Brecht, but Brecht had left it lying on his desk.
    Lima, Czuch: allusions to *The Round Heads and the Pointed Heads*, where these
terms signify Germany and the Nazis.

208 To Eisler   30 April 1934
Per Knutzon was to direct the play, which Otto Gelsted was translating.

209 To Per Knutzon   May 1934
R = Rothenburg, a lawyer representing the project's backers. He expected the
censor to ban the play and thought that wealthy Jews would not support it.
    Ferdinand Bruckner's *Die Rassen* was performed by the Zurich Schauspiel-
haus in 1933.
    Feuchtwanger's immensely successful novel *Jew Süss* was published in 1917,
his play *Vasantasena* in 1923.

210 To Benjamin   ?Spring 1934
His article on 'the present social position of the French writer' appeared in the
Zeitschrift für Sozialforschung (Paris) no. 3, 1934.

211 To George Grosz   May 1934
The 'Society for Moderate Progress' etc: a title originally devised by Jaroslav
Hašek, here refers to the SPD The 'Society of Friends' etc: refers to the KPD.
    Hans (or Hermann) Borchardt, a mutual friend from Berlin, had helped on *Saint
Joan of the Stockyards*. He taught at Minsk University in the USSR from 1934–36.

212 To Allert de Lange Verlag   23 June 1934
Dated from Svendborg hospital (Sygehus). This presumably is the illness that
stopped Brecht attending the First Soviet Writers' Congress that year.

213 To Lion Feuchtwanger   June–July 1934
A formal tribute for Feuchtwanger's fiftieth anniversary on 7 July 1934. Though
now best remembered for his historical novels, Feuchtwanger was held to have
been an exponent of 'asphalt literature' – i.e. writing on urban, city themes – by
critics in the Weimar Republic. His most recent novel, *The Oppermans* (autumn
1933), had by then sold 257,000 copies in all languages.
    'Blubo' = 'Blut und Boden', the Nazi concept of Blood and Soil.

214 To Bernard von Brentano   June–July 1934
Ernst Ottwalt's book *Deutschland erwache!* (1932) along with Silone's *Faschismus*
(mentioned in Letters 182 and 201 and published in German by Europa-Verlag,

Zurich in 1934) was one of the earliest serious Communist studies of Fascism. Within the Communist Party it had been criticised for its refusal to identify fascism with social-democracy.

Though the KPD were just beginning to abandon their doctrine of 'social-fascism' their change of line seems not yet to have penetrated to Brentano's Moscow critic Frank Leschnitzer (nor perhaps to Brecht). Ottwalt himself was in Prague, charged by that Party with liaison with their underground members in Berlin. The Prague gossip was that he had been quoting from Brentano's letters to Brecht.

RGO was the Revolutionary (or Red) Trade Union Opposition set up by the KPD in the late 1920s to split the predominantly Socialist trade unions.

215 To Brentano   July 1934
Refers to Hitler's massacre of Ernst Röhm and other SA leaders on 30 June 1934. After Hindenburg's death on 2 August Hitler succeeded to the Presidency and became 'Führer and Reich Chancellor' and commander of the armed forces.

The *Rundschau*: a Comintern organ published from Basel 1932–39. The 'Runa' was its cyclostyled daily news service edited by Theo Pinkus from Zurich.

Friedrich Pollock was a leading member of the (Frankfurt) Institute for Social Research.

216 To Korsch   Mid-year 1934
Appears not to have been sent off.

217 To Allert de Lange Verlag   20 July 1934
The original edition of the *Threepenny Novel*, printed in Holland, is set in a bold, rather squat, seriffed type on nearly square pages. Brecht's suggestions were not followed.

218 Ditto   23 July 1934
Elias Alexander ran a London agency called European Books Ltd. Bernard Grasset was among the French publishers interested, but no French edition appeared.

219, 220 Ditto   23 July, 3 Aug. 1934
Again the publishers did not in fact follow Brecht's suggestions. The paragraphs remain (inexcusably) un-indented, and the italics, though bold, are not in a larger size.

221 Ditto   15 Aug. 1934
They did however italicise the numerals in the italic text. The abbreviations were normally printed, in full, and the unwanted full stops removed.

222 Ditto   18 Aug. 1934
Lord Bloomsbury's name was spelled like the district (and/or the Group).

223 Ditto   23 Aug. 1934
The title was printed as requested, but the suggested note was omitted.

224, 225 Ditto   26 Aug., 1 Sep. 1934
The italic setting is the same throughout.

226 To George Grosz   2 Sep. 1934
Three Soldiers: this was the long 'children's book' by Brecht published as vol. 6 of the *Versuche* in 1932, with pen illustrations by Grosz.

'Big Chinese painting': Benjamin in his *Versuche über Brecht* reported Brecht's description of such a painting belonging to Karin Michaelis which he thought could serve as model for 'a sequence of picture stories from the new Germany. Photograph for Grosz. Portraying The Life of Hitler. The Reichstag Fire and Trial. The Thirtieth of July'. See letter 233 for his impression of another Chinese painting.

*226x. To Margarete Steffin   11 Sept 34
She was on the way to Leningrad, for convalescence in the USSR.

*226xx. To Margarete Steffin   20 Sept 34
B. wishes he could have given her the *Threepenny Novel*.

227 To Helene Weigel   Sep. 1934
Per = Per Knutzon.
    Mari = Mari Hold, the Brechts' housekeeper.
    Cases: of spinal meningitis, around Svendborg.

228 To Gustav Kiepenheuer   26 Sep. 1934
In a letter of 3 October from Germany Brecht's former publisher replied that their old contract was annulled.

229 To Helene Weigel   13 Oct. 1934
Brecht was in London (his first visit) from October to December working on a film script about Ignaz Semmelweis and the conquest of puerperal fever, with Piscator's former dramaturg Leo Lania. Eisler was also there, writing the music to Ottwalt's radio play *Kalifornische Legende* and Karl Grune's film *Abdul the Damned*, which starred Fritz Kortner. With Brecht he wrote the United Front Song, the Saar Song (for the Saar plebiscite of 13 January, 1935, a triumph for the Nazis) and the song 'All of Us or None', the first two being at the request of the International Music Bureau in Moscow. Among the plays which Brecht saw after sending this card was the Group Theatre production of *Sweeney Agonistes* that December.

*229x To Margarete Steffin   21 Oct 34
The *Threepenny Novel* is supposed to appear in Amsterdam, but he has not yet had a copy. Willi (? Muenzenberg) is publishing the 'Saar Song' in an edition of 10,000 copies.

*229xx To Margarete Steffin   22 Oct 34
Can she see how things are going at the State Publishing House? She has his full authority.

230 To Weigel   7 Nov. 1934
The poem was the 'Dankgedicht an Mari Hold' written for the latter's wedding.

231 Ditto   Nov. 1934
Helene Weigel was travelling to Vienna via Zurich, where Felix Gasbarra (by his own account) had discouraged the Schauspielhaus company from staging the première of *The Round Heads and the Pointed Heads*, for which Eisler had given them an option.

    Kraus: Karl Kraus had criticised the rising of the Austrian Socialists in February 1934 – last gasp of Austrian democracy – which led Brecht to attack him in a poem. Karl Jaray was a friend and collaborator of his; Richard Lanyi was the Vienna bookseller who published his magazine *Die Fackel*.

Frank: Brecht's son by Bi Banholzer, was then living with Helene Weigel's sister in Vienna.

George: the actor Heinrich George, subject of a polemical open letter from Brecht, had become a Nazi. Hans Dammert had been charged with publicising the letter.

*232 To Alexander Moritz Frey   8 Nov. 1934
Thanking him for a print of Jack the Ripper and a letter praising Brecht's novel, which Frey would review in *Neue Deutsche Blätter*, Prague, vol. 2 no. 3 (January 1935).

233 To Stefan S. Brecht   27 Nov. 1934
The card was a reproduction of a Ming Dynasty drawing 'The Hundred Children (A Puppet Show)' in the British Museum.

234 To Princess Elisabeth Bibesco   Late 1934
Daughter of Herbert and Margot Asquith, and married to a Rumanian prince, Elisabeth Bibesco was in touch with Ernst Toller and others about the case of Carl von Ossietzky, the former editor of *Die Weltbühne*, who was then in a concentration camp. He was awarded the Nobel Peace Prize for 1936, and killed by the Nazis in 1938. Brecht's poem 'On the death of a fighter for peace' is in *Poems 1913–1956*, p. 305.

235 To Margot von Brentano   Dec. 1934
Mrs Brentano had sent Brecht the Basel *National-Zeitung*'s review of his novel and asked for the address of Margaret Mynatt, a leading English Communist and friend of Elisabeth Hauptmann, who looked after the London affairs of the Malik-Verlag.

236 To Johannes R. Becher   End Dec. 1934
Becher had written from Paris on 21 December 1934 to tell Brecht of a plan to hold an International Writers' Congress there, arising out of the Soviet Writers' Congress. The Stalin-Wells conversation had appeared in *The New Statesman* on 27 October (Brecht kept the cutting).

Brecht's article was the long essay 'Five Difficulties in Writing the Truth', which was summarised in the *Pariser Tageblatt* of 12 December. In his letter Becher had approved of it. Becher's Moscow address would presumably still have been the offices of MORP, the International League of Revolutionary Writers, since he did not definitively move 'over there' till the end of 1935.

*236x To Steffin   28 Dec. 1934
All quiet at Skovsbostrand. He has written to Piscator. Is she getting the *Threepenny Novel* advance?

*236xx Ditto   1 Jan. 1935
Has heard nothing from Tretiakoff, Piscator or Koltsov.

237 To Bernhard Reich   Winter 1934–5
Apparently not finished or sent. Reich had written from Moscow on 2 November to report that Piscator was now president of the International League of Revolutionary Theatres (MORT). Carola Neher was in Moscow with her Soviet husband Becker. It is not known what poem Brecht intended to send her.

238 To Paul Hindemith   Winter 1934–5

Hindemith (1895–1963) had been the moving spirit of the Baden-Baden music festivals, for which he composed the first *Lehrstück* (called by Brecht *Badener Lehrstück vom Einverständnis*) and part of its companion piece *Lindberghflug* in 1929. He also made a choral version of Brecht's poem 'Concerning Spring' the same year. For the following festival however he rejected the Brecht/Eisler 'Lehrstück' *Die Massnahme*, and thereafter the two men ceased to collaborate.

The present somewhat two-edgedly polemical letter appears to have been neither sent nor (at the time) published. It was occasioned by the German controversy over Hindemith's suite from his new opera *Mathis der Maler*, which Wilhelm Furtwängler performed with the Berlin Philharmonic on 12 March 1934. This led to the conductor's resignation on 4 December from all his official posts, amid accusations by Goebbels and Rosenberg that Hindemith was profaning German Music.

239 To Johannes R. Becher   Early 1935
The journalist Alfred Kantorowicz, a KPD member since 1931, was then secretary of the exiled SDS (or Schutzverband deutscher Schriftsteller) in Paris; he later went to Spain. Becher replied that he himself disagreed with the review; that *Unsere Zeit* (which was edited by Alexander Abusch and published by Muenzenberg) would print a second review; and that Kantorowicz himself would write to Brecht. The second review appeared more than a year later.

*240 To Brentano   Early Jan. 1935
Complains about Kantorowicz's article, invites him to Denmark in the summer (cheaper than Switzerland) and asks how was Herzfelde.

241 Ditto   Jan. 1935
Dühring: refers to Engels's *Anti-Dühring*, of whose German text Brecht had a copy published in Moscow in 1934.

242 Ditto   ?1935
Martov, leader of the Mensheviks at the time of the split in the Russian Social-Democratic party in 1903, wrote a History of Russian Social-Democracy whose German edition appeared in 1926.

243 To Reich   18 Jan. 1935
See letter 184. According to Reich's memoirs the magazine, originally intended as a weekly, was to have been edited by him at the MORT offices in Moscow and published from Zurich. It appears to have been distinct from *The International Theatre*, which was published from Moscow with S.S. Podolsky as editor. Two issues were prepared but never printed. Apparently Brecht was the only outside contributor to send an article – the 'Open Letter to the actor Heinrich George' in *GW Schriften zum Theater*, pp. 229–234.

Hans Otto, a young actor at the Staatstheater, had been arrested for his work for the Red actors' union and beaten to death by the Nazis on 24 November 1933. The article reproached George, now a convert to Nazism, with his failure to intervene.

244 To Feuchtwanger   18 Jan. 1935
Feuchtwanger had written on 29 December 1934 inviting Brecht to Sanary-sur-Mer. The novel was part two of his *Josephus* trilogy.

Hermann the Cheruskian: the hero of Kleist's play *Die Hermannsschlacht*.

Leopold Schwarzschild: editor of *Das neue Tage-Buch* (Paris and Amsterdam 1 July 1933–11 May 1940); he emigrated to the US.

The Weill-Reinhardt-Werfel collaboration was the financially disastrous pageant *The Eternal Road* which opened in New York some two years later.

Arnold Zweig had written about Brecht.

245 To George Grosz   Jan. 1935
Grosz had written on 10 October 1934 to say that he was keen to illustrate the plays. He said he would make a special price of $300–400 per play, and asked Brecht to send any ideas. Later he changed his mind.

246 To Robert Storm Petersen   Jan. 1935
Storm Petersen was a Danish cartoonist. The 'short characterisation of Mr Peachum' enclosed was that which Brecht wrote for the notes to *The Threepenny Opera* in 1930. See Methuen edition, page 91.

247 To Walter Benjamin   6 Feb. 1935
This was a postscript to a letter from Helene Weigel. Benjamin had written on 9 Jan and 3 Feb 1935 saying that Max Horkheimer of the former Frankfurt Institute for Social Research was trying to get him (Benjamin) an American grant. He himself would publish a review of the *Threepenny Novel* in the Institute's journal. It had originally been intended for Klaus Mann's Amsterdam-based magazine *Die Sammlung* (which did indeed come to an end in August 1935).

*247x To Margarete Steffin   17 Feb. 1935
A message for Ottwalt. B. has been working on the *Tui-Roman*, and would like to read her something from it.

*247xx To Margarete Steffin   2 March 1935
George Grosz wants to hold an exhibition. Can she say if there is an English translation of Stanislavsky, and if not can she translate some selections for B. from the Russian?

*248 To Götz Mayer   Feb. 1935
Recipient not identified. He had asked about rights to Brecht's poem 'Die Drei Soldaten' in connection with a magazine planned by Clara Malraux. Brecht would be glad to contribute.

*249 To Steen Hasselbalch   Feb. 1935
Recipient was publishing *Threepenny Novel* in Danish, and Brecht thanks for proof of Storm Petersen's jacket drawing.

*249x To Steffin
B. expects his visa (for the USSR) in a week. He will bring the verses for *Internationale Literatur* with him.

250 To Helene Weigel   March 1935
This was the beginning of Brecht's two-month visit to Moscow at the invitation of MORT. Tretiakoff was at that time responsible for the foreign relations of the newly-formed Union of Soviet Writers.

A year earlier the 'Deutsches Theater Kolonne Links' had been set up in Moscow on the basis of the agitprop group of that name, strengthened by new recruits from Gustav von Wangenheim's 'Truppe 1931' with Wangenheim himself as overall director. The aim had been to open this as a fully professional Moscow 'Deutsches Theater' at the beginning of 1935, drawing in Carola Neher and other star actors; however, the changed Soviet policy about the recruiting of German workers meant that there was no adequate audience in the capital, so that the company could only work as a travelling theatre for German-speaking minorities in the Ukraine and the Volga Republic. Wangenheim thereupon resigned, to concentrate on film work.

K = Karl Korsch, presumably not a welcome name to the Soviet censors.

'Oskawa': see Brecht's poem of 1935 'How the ship "Oskawa" was broken up by her own crew'. The book was Louis Adamic's *Dynamite. The Story of Class Violence in America* (New York, 1931).

251 To Weigel   March-April 1935
Film about Dimitrov. This was *Kämpfer* (Fighters; Russian title *Borzy*) directed by Wangenheim for Mezhrabpom-Film, with Granach, Lotte Loebinger, Bruno Schmidtsdorf, Heinz Greif and other Germans including Fritz Erpenbeck and the young Konrad Wolf. The political instigator seems to have been Dimitrov's then secretary Alfred Kurella. Ivens is not known to have been involved. The film was not released till 1938.

Neher's child: Georg Becker, subsequently a musicologist, now reported to be working in the German Federal Republic. *Me-Ti*: Alfred Forke's translation of the aphorisms of Mo-Tse, which Helene Weigel had taken to be bound.

252 Ditto   April 1935
Wangenheim's behaviour. Unknown.

The German-Russian city: presumably the Ukrainian city of Dniepropetrovsk, headquarters of the new travelling theatre under Maxim Vallentin and the actor Curt Trepte. The other project mentioned by Brecht was probably Piscator's scheme to develop the academic German State Theatre at Engels in the Volga Republic, which had been founded in 1929 or 1930 with local amateur actors. He took this up in earnest with the local government in the summer of 1935.

Royal Theatre: in Copenhagen.

Marianne: Brecht's first wife. Ruth: Berlau (first mention).

*253 To Egon Erwin Kisch   April 1935
Message for publication in the Moscow *Deutsche Zentralzeitung* on the eminent journalist's fiftieth birthday. See Note 378.

254 To Paula Grosz, née Banholzer   29 May 1935
Details of the life of Frank Banholzer have never been made public. According to Werner Mittenzwei's *Das Leben des Bertolt Brecht* his stepfather would not have him, and he lived with his maternal grandmother. The German edition mentions letters from him to Brecht.

255 To Mikhail Koltsov   May-June 1935
Koltsov, head of the foreign bureau of the Soviet Writers' Union, was much involved in preparations for the Paris writers' congress 'in defence of culture' that summer. He lived with Maria Osten (real name Gresshöner), who had been an editorial assistant in the Malik-Verlag in pre-Nazi Berlin. *Den' Mira* ('Day of the World') was an anthology edited by Koltsov and Gorky and published by

Jourgaz, the publishing house over which Koltsov presided. It included Brecht's story 'The Soldier of La Ciotat'.

256 To Alfred Döblin   Early June 1935
Döblin's *Berlin Alexanderplatz* appeared in Berlin 1929, his *Drei Sprünge des Wang-lun* in 1915. The 'new novel' was *Pardon wird nicht gegeben*. His son Peter studied printing with the printers of Brecht's *Versuche*; hence 'my typesetter'.
     Fritz Sternberg's book was *Der Faschismus an der Macht*, Amsterdam 1935.

*256x To Steffin   5 June 1935
B. has not got the Russian address of Reich, MORT etc.

257 To Thorkild Roose   12 June 1935
Roose was principal director at the Copenhagen Royal Theatre, which had made a contract to stage *Saint Joan of the Stockyards*. This was not honoured in Brecht's lifetime.

258 To Benjamin   13 June 1935
The First Writers' Congress for the Defence of Culture was held in the Palais de la Mutualité from 21 to 25 June 1935.

259 To Korsch   June-July 1935
The 'definitor'. Rudolph Carnap, according to a note by Korsch.
     'P' = Paul Partos.
     The 'other animal' by Hobbes is thought to be *Behemoth or The Long Parliament*.
     'Tui' (or Tellect-Ual-In'): Brecht's mocking term for an intellectual. He worked on the proposed novel between 1935–1943, but it remained a fragment.

260 To Brecht's father   Mid-1935?
Apparently the draft of a letter designed to dissociate the family (who had remained in Germany) from Brecht's anti-Nazi views.

*261 To Ernst Bloch   July 1935
Refers somewhat facetiously to Brecht's meeting with the Marxist philosopher at the First Writers' Congress (see note 258)

262 To Ernst Bloch   c. 1935?
'Neue Sachlichkeit' or New Matter-of-Factness was the name given (from 1925 on) to the coolly 'objective' movement in the arts which succeeded Expressionism.
     'Winter Aid', 'People's Community' (Volksgemeinschaft) and 'Strength through Joy' (Kraft durch Freude) were Nazi slogans and/or institutions, notably after 1933.

263 To George Grosz   ?July 1935
Brecht addresses Grosz as 'du'. The argument between Gide and Barbusse would be used in the *Tui-Roman*.

264 To Becher   July 1935
Written after the Paris congress. 'H' stands for 'Hans'.
     Rundschau: a Comintern journal published from Basel from July 1932 to October 1939.

265 To Alfred Döblin   31 July 1935
Korsch had apparently been suspected of being a Nazi agent following the suicide of a friend called Dora Fabian. The 'jacket designer' was Peter Döblin.

266 To Wieland Herzfelde   July-Aug. 1935

It was only in exile that Herzfelde and his Malik-Verlag became Brecht's
publishers. He had written on 24 July to ask Brecht's views on the three works
mentioned. 'HK' has not been identified, but the others were Willi Bredel's *Die
Prüfung* (which he published the same year) and the concentration camp novel
Die Moorsoldaten by the actor Wolfgang Langhoff, who had been released by the
Nazis in 1934 and joined the Zurich Schauspielhaus company.

Böff (or 'Boeuf'): old nickname for George Grosz.

267, 268 To Hanns Eisler   29 Aug., Sep. 1935

During Brecht's Moscow visit Eisler had been lecturing and performing in the
United States, whence he returned in May. From 8 to 10 June he was at the First
Workers' Musical Olympiade in Strasbourg – evidently a MORT operation –
after which he spent some weeks in Moscow before joining Brecht in August.
He may well have brought the 'Lehrstück' commission back from Russia with
him. He then spent the first half of September in Prague for the ISCM festival,
mainly on behalf of MORT's International Music Bureau (of which he had just
been made president). He was due to catch a liner back to the US from Le
Havre on 25 September. In the event he let the project drop. Brecht and
Margarete Steffin had meantime written the brief text.

269 To Grosz   Early Sep. 1935

Grosz had visited Brecht in Denmark the same summer, shortly before Eisler's
arrival. See his letter to Piscator of 23 August, which reports Brecht living 'very
agreeably' and appearing much impressed by his Moscow visit.

'Party Congress of Freedom': i.e. the Nuremberg Rally.

270 To Erwin Piscator   25 Sep. 1935

BK – Béla Kun, the Hungarian revolutionary and Comintern member. Brecht
met him during his Moscow visit (see Reich: *Im Wettlauf mit der Zeit*, pp. 370–
1), and later told Walter Benjamin that Kun 'was his greatest admirer in Russia'
(Benjamin: *Understanding Brecht*, p. 117, diary entry for 21 July 1938). Piscator's
letter had asked for a message for Kun's fiftieth birthday. Kun would later be
arrested and shot.

In the same letter Piscator had reported that the Moscow Jewish Theatre under
Mikhoels was considering a production of *The Round Heads and the Pointed Heads*.
This never materialised.

Film: various projects had been discussed, including a *Schweik* film. Ernst
Held was a Moscow German critic and board member of MORT.

271 To Fritz Sternberg   ?Sep.-Oct. 1935

The book appears to have been Sternberg's *Der Faschismus an der Macht*
(Amsterdam, 1935). Erna = Erna van Pustau, Sternberg's companion.

272 To Paul Peters   End Aug 1935

Peters wrote an American adaptation of *The Mother*, of which the opening will
be found reproduced in the notes to that play. The intention was to use it for the
New York production by the Communist-led Theatre Union group, which had
performed Friedrich Wolf's *The Sailors of Cattaro* in a run of 96 performances
starting on 10 December 1934. The twenty-three-year old Victor Wolfson
would direct, with Mordecai Gorelik as designer and the eighteen-year old

Jerome Moross as musical director. On the theatre's board were Manuel Gomez (who had originally proposed that the group do 'Gorky's *Mother* in the Eisler operetta'), Albert Maltz and George Sklar (co-author with Peters of the play *Stevedore*). See Lee Baxandall's account in Erica Munk's symposium *Brecht* (Bantam Books, New York 1972) and the special Brecht issue of *The Drama Review*, vol. 12, no. 1, 1967.

273 To V. J. Jerome   Early Sep. 1935
The writer Victor Jerry Jerome: a writer and head of the agitprop section of the American Communist Party.

274 To Peters   3 Oct. 1935
See Note 272 above. Manuel Gomez had been sent over to Europe to 'win Brecht over to our point of view as regards the Peters version'. (See Gomez's statements to Lee Baxandall.) The page references given by Brecht are to the 'Versuche' edition of 1932. There is no 'railway scene' in any of Brecht's texts.

275 To Helene Weige   Oct. 1935
In the final cast the mother was Helen Henry.
   K K = Karl Korsch, then working on his *Karl Marx* (London, 1938).
   Elisabeth Hauptmann, who had taken a job at a girls' school in St Louis near her married sister, was hoping to visit Hans Borchardt in Minsk, but the news of his deportation from the USSR evidently made her cancel her trip (see Letter 309).

276 To Weigel   Oct.-Nov. 1935
Hanne = Brecht's daughter by his first wife. She visited him several times in Denmark.

277 To Theatre Union   9 Nov. 1935
The pianists, according to Baxandall (see Note 272), were Jerome Moross and Alex North. Eisler had made the arrangement of his score, adding a tenth number, 'Der zerrissene Rock'. 'Mrs Cook' appears to have been Helen Henry's married name.

278, 279, 280 Ditto   9, 15, 17 Nov. 1935
281 Ditto   21 Nov. 1935
The première had taken place on 19 November at the Civic Repertory Theatre. Hauptmann and Lou (the second Mrs) Eisler attended, Brecht and Eisler not. On 22 November the theatre replied saying that Equity rules forbade more than one weekly rehearsal after the première of a play.

282 To Erwin Piscator   8 Dec. 1935
'The Club' = the Communist Party.
   Andrew Kertesz; a former Hungarian (hence 'son of the Puszta'), New York agent for Piscator and Friedrich Wolf.
   Franz Hoellering: an exiled German writer, former editor of the *Arbeiter-Illustrierte-Zeitung* and the sports magazine *Arena* to which Brecht had contributed in Berlin.
   'The A. T.': Piscator's adaptation of Theodore Dreiser's novel *An American Tragedy* was made around 1931–32 and first staged in spring 1935 at the Hedgerow Theatre, Moylan, Pennsylvania. The Shuberts bought it for the

Group Theater, who produced it at the Ethel Barrymore Theatre, New York City on 13 March 1936 under the direction of Lee Strasberg.

Greenburger: Sanford J. Greenburger - agent for Jakob Wassermann and other authors.

Mezhrabpom Film: a Soviet film company owned by the International Workers' Aid or IAH. It employed a number of German film-makers and administrators, and was dissolved in June 1936.

Brecht's article 'The German Drama, pre-Hitler' appeared in The New York Times (section 9, pp. 1 and 3,) on 24 November 1935. A version is included in Brecht on Theatre.

283 To Stefan S. Brecht   Dec.1935

284 To Weigel   Dec.1935
'Negotiations': Eisler had already been trying to interest unidentified managements in The Round Heads and the Pointed Heads before Brecht's arrival, and Brecht was also hoping that Simon and Schuster would take the Threepenny Novel. It was eventually published by Hillman and Curl, New York, in 1938, the year following its appearance in London.

Uncle Otto: not identified.

285 To Maxim Gorky   18 Dec. 1935

286 To Weigel   Dec.-Jan. 1935-6
Weill's first American concert, with Lenya and a chorus, took place in New York on 10 December.

287 To Lee Strasberg   27 Jan. 1936
Letter written in English. The 'group' was presumably the Group Theater, which Strasberg was then directing. Nothing is known of their work with Brecht on Die Massnahme (The Decision or The Measures Taken).

288 To Victor J. Jerome   Feb. 1936
See Notes 272, 273.

Eva Goldbeck (d. 1936) the wife of Marc Blitzstein, author and composer of The Cradle Will Rock. She was translating Brecht's 'Five Difficulties in Writing the Truth' for the Communist weekly The New Masses.

Clifford Odets's play Paradise Lost was staged by Harold Clurman with the Group at the Longacre Theatre, New York, on 9 December. Brecht is thought to have written the poem 'Letter to the Playwright Odets' (Poems 1913–1956, p. 260) soon after having seen it.

Nat Turner: Brecht and Jerome had discussed the linguistic problems of writing a play about this nineteenth-century leader of a slave revolt. According to Lyon (Bertolt Brecht in America, pp. 15–16) Brecht wanted the slaves to speak standard English where Jerome wanted dialect.

289 To Walter Benjamin   1935-6?
The 'son' is presumably Stefan Brecht.

Benjamin paid three visits to Denmark: June-October 1934, August-September 1936 and July-October 1938.

*289x To Steffin   21 Feb 1936
Grosz has written to B. about Borchardt (see Note 307).

*289xx Ditto   5 Mar 1936
B. has got Steffin's elephant in London – one of those he used to send her from

foreign cities. Is optimistic about *Das Wort* (see Note 298). Has written to
Tretiakoff, who is involved with Ernst Busch's Soviet tour.

290 To Benjamin   April-May 1936
Benjamin's article 'Probleme der Sprachsoziologie' appeared in the *Zeitschrift für
Sozialforschung* (Paris), 1935, vol. 4, no. 2. pp. 248–268.

'Narcotics trade': refers to a job of spring-summer 1936 in London which Fritz
Kortner got Brecht in connection with the dialogue for a *Pagliacci* film for
which Eisler arranged the music. Richard Tauber starred and Brecht was paid
off.

'The small hand press': nothing further is known of this plan.

Bernard von Brentano's novel *Theoodor Chindler* was published by Oprecht,
Zurich, in 1936. The other writers mentioned are Ernst Glaeser, Erik Reger,
Joseph Roth and Hermann Kesten.

291 To Becher   29 May 1936
The galley proofs in question were those of a Soviet edition of *Die Massnahme*
which the Foreign Workers' Publishing House VEGAAR planned to bring out
under licence from Wieland Herzfelde's Malik-Verlag. But this never appeared.
Brecht's Moscow editor Erich Wendt was arrested in September 1936 and the
firm dissolved in 1938.

*292 To Arnold Zweig   30 May 1936
Thanking him for a copy of his novel *Erziehung vor Verdun* (published by
Querido, Amsterdam 1935) and suggesting a joint trip to Moscow in the
autumn. Zweig was living in Haifa.

293 To Piscator   May 1936
Mordecai (or 'Max') Gorelik spent two weeks visiting Brecht in Denmark in
connection with his book *New Theatres for Old* (French, New York 1940) for
which he had a Guggenheim fellowship. He wrote to Brecht from Stockholm
on 1 June 1936 to complain about his difficulties with the Soviet authorities.
Piscator was then still in Moscow in charge of MORT. On 18 July Gorelik
wrote again to tell Brecht that he had got his visa and would travel to Moscow
on 17 August.

294 To the International Association of Writers for the Defence of Culture
                                                               21 June 1936
For Brecht's earlier proposals for a new encyclopaedia in the tradition of the
Enlightenment see Letter 236. A not dissimilar idea seems to have been put
forward by Malraux to the London Congress (though the fragmentary poem
'Inselbriefe I' which Brecht wrote about it suggests that Malraux was primarily
concerned with history) and partly materialised many years later as the
Encyclopédie de la Pléiade.

295, 296 To Piscator   June, July 1936
148, Abbey Road: Brecht is writing from the address of André van Gyseghem, a
leading director at Unity Theatre.

The Volga-German (or Engels) plan. See Note 252. Piscator hoped to attract
major anti-Nazi actors (such as Carola Neher and Alexander Granach) to the
German-language theatre at Engels, where he wished to stage *The Round Heads and
the Pointed Heads* and wanted Brecht himself to be dramaturg. Instead Brecht

here proposes Slatan Dudow, the Bulgarian co-director of *Kuhle Wampe* and the 1930 *Die Massnahme*, who was working with an émigré cabaret group in Paris. Helene Weigel thereafter did make tentative arrangements with Piscator to visit Engels, but cried off in August when it appeared that the whole plan was collapsing in the new climate of the purges.

Adam Scharrer; an émigré novelist resident near Engels, was involved in a film which Mezhrabpom had planned to make there, involving also Piscator and Julius Hay. It was not made. Grete: Margarete Steffin had gone to a Soviet sanatorium in January, returning to Denmark in May.

Reich: see note 184. From July 1936 he was effectively in charge of what was left of the project.

297 To Otto Bork   20 July 1936
Bork (real name Otto Unger) was a director of VEGAAR until (according to Pike, p. 324) he was arrested in November 1937. The proposed editions of the plays (see Letter 301) and the poems fell through. *The Threepenny Novel* had appeared from Moscow in German in 1935; it was reviewed in the *Deutsche Zentral-Zeitung* by the Austrian-born Soviet poet Hugo Huppert. A Russian translation was published by Gosizdat in 1937.

297x To W. H. Auden   Aug. 1936
Some two years earlier Benjamin had told Brecht that he felt it particularly important that *The Round Heads and the Pointed Heads* should be performed in London.

298 To Piscator   12 Oct 1936
The Moscow German-language magazine *Das Wort* was set up by Koltsov, Becher, Maria Osten and Herzfelde during the first half of 1936 as a successor to Herzfelde's *Neue Deutsche Blätter*, whose last issue appeared in August 1935. *Das Wort*'s first number, edited by Feuchtwanger, Brecht and the Communist novelist Willi Bredel, came out on 21 July 1936. Bredel, till he left for the Spanish Civil War, was the only editor to be based in Moscow. After he had gone the actor Fritz Erpenbeck effectively took over.

For the Copenhagen production of *The Round Heads and the Pointed Heads* see the next letter.

299 To Per Knutzon   Nov. 1936
Knutzon directed and played the Viceroy in the first production of *The Round Heads and the Pointed Heads* at the Copenhagen Riddersalen Theatre on 4 November 1936. Brecht's play was given in Danish, with Hanns Eisler's songs accompanied on two pianos. Knutzon's wife Lulu Ziegler played the prostitute Nanna.

*300 To Ebbe Neergard   Nov. 1936
Answering some criticisms of that play.

301 To Otto Bork   30 Nov. 1936
See Note 297. *The Round Heads and the Pointed Heads* appeared in volume 2 of the incomplete Malik edition of Brecht's *Gesammelte Werke* in 1938. It had no epilogue.

302 To Benjamin   Early Dec. 1936
Benjamin's first 'Paris Letter' was printed in *Das Wort*, vol. 1, no. 5 (Moscow,
November 1936). A second was accepted by Bredel but did not appear. Nor did
his classic essay on 'The Work of Art in the Era of its Technical Reproducibility',
despite Brecht's editorial recommendation and his expectation that it would.

Gide's book was *Return from the USSR*, which Gallimard published in Paris
in 1936; a German-language edition followed from Zurich in 1937. The first
great 'show trial' of Stalin's enemies, beginning with Zinoviev, Kamenev and
other 'rightists', had been held in August 1936. The *Pravda* article was dated 3
December. Brecht's much more reasoned criticism 'Kraft und Schwäche der
Utopie' is in *GW 19*, pp. 434–438. It was not published in his lifetime.

303 To Korsch   ?1936
Günter Glaeser thinks this was a note handed personally to Korsch in Denmark
by Brecht. It refers to *Karl Marx* (see Note 275). The German text of this work,
as read by Brecht, no longer exists, though a version has been reconstructed.

304 To Korsch   Winter 1936-7
Korsch had emigrated to the US in December 1936. The book of 'maxims'
relates to *Me-ti*, Brecht's collection of coded aphorisms setting out many of his
own criticisms of Stalin's USSR. For a view of these see *Brecht in Context*,
pp. 190–192.

Nausicaa. Possibly Brecht means Odysseus's wife Penelope.

WD = Walter Dubislav, a 'neo-positivist' philosopher. Nothing by him
appeared in *Das Wort*. Barbara = one of Korsch's daughters.

305 To Brentano   Early Feb. 1937
Ernst Ottwalt, Brecht's collaborator on *Kuhle Wampe*, had adapted his 'Ballade
vom Reichstagsbrand' for performance in Moscow by Kolonne Links in February
1934. He also wrote an excellent radio play *Californian Ballad* which Eisler set to
music around the same time. Having settled in the USSR after the Soviet
Writers' Congress of 1934, he was arrested with his wife Waltraut Nicolas on
6/7 November 1936, charged with 'anti-Soviet agitation' and sentenced to five
years' imprisonment. David Pike terms him 'semi-alcoholic'. He died in one of
the northern camps in 1943. His widow was handed over to the Germans in
1941, but survived.

*306 To Arnold Zweig   18 Feb 1937
Covers much the same ground as Letter 292, which Brecht feared might have
gone astray.

307 To George Grosz   Feb. 1937
Grosz had written to Brecht on 12 February 1936 to say that their mutual Berlin
Jewish friend Hermann ('Hans') Borchardt had been deported from the USSR
to Nazi Germany without explanation. Once there he was put in Dachau
concentration camp, where he lost a finger. He was released after a few months,
and by August 1937 had arrived in the US.

Felix Weil and Friedrich Pollock were wealthy patrons of the (former)

Frankfurt Institute for Social Research. Weil had also supported Piscator's theatre and the Malik-Verlag before 1933.

Otto Ruehle's life of Marx had been named by Brecht as one of the best books of 1928. He died in Mexico City in 1943.

*308 To Max Warburg   3 March 1937
W. had told Brecht that Borchardt was in Dachau, to which B. answers that he has little information, but has been told that a private invitation to Denmark (as suggested by W.) would not be enough to get him released.

309 To [?]   ?March 1937
Kawenauer: appears to be an error for Siegfried Kawerau, a Berlin historian.

310 To Max Gorelik   Early March 1937
Gorelik had become an editor of the new American theatre magazine *Theater Workshop* (New York) which included I. Rapaport's article on the Stanislavsky Method in its October 1936 issue.

TRAM was the semi-agitprop Theatre of Working Youth, whose Leningrad branch was dissolved in February 1936.

Nikolai Okhlopkov, known for his productions in the round, lost his Realistic Theatre, which was dissolved in 1937.

P. M. Kerzhentsev's *Pravda* attack on Meyerhold, under the title 'An Alien Theatre', appeared on 19 December that year as a prelude to the dissolution of his theatre as 'anti-national' in January 1938.

The 'Society' was Brecht's projected 'Diderot Society' for theatrical research, in connection with which he circularised a number of like-minded colleagues around this time. Gorelik and he had already discussed it during the former's visit to Denmark. It also tied in with MORT's earlier ideas for a serious theatre magazine to be published from Zurich, which had been frustrated by MORT's liquidation and Piscator's decision not to return to Moscow in autumn 1936. Brecht's own 'article on stage construction' was never completed; the sections 'Über den Bühnenbau der nichtaristotelischen Dramatik' in *GW 15*, pp. 441ff. appear to relate to it.

Letter to the *Times*: Gorelik had written to the *New York Times* disagreeing with Ernst Toller's criticisms of the epic theatre. His letter appeared on 7 February 1937.

311 To *Theater Workshop* (New York)   Mid-1937
Fragment of a statement evidently designed to accompany Gorelik's summary of the notes to *The Threepenny Opera*, which appeared in the magazine's third number, April–July 1937.

312 To Reich   2 March 1937
A Russian edition of *The Round Heads and the Pointed Heads*, translated by Valentin Stenic and Semyon Kirsanov was published by Gosizdat, Moscow in 1936. It also appeared the same year in the August number of *International'naya Literatura*.

Julius Hay, the Hungarian communist playwright, had made his reputation in Berlin between 1930–33. He was invited to the USSR by MORT in 1935 and became involved in Mezhrabpom's plan for a film about the Volga Republic. In

1936 he wrote his best-known play *Haben* about Hungarian village life. Reich had criticised him in an article 'Zur Methodik der deutschen antifaschistischen Dramatik' in the January issue of *Das Wort* (vol. 2, no. 1). By 'these people' Brecht means Hay, Lukács and Andor Gábor.

Hanns Eisler was in Denmark with Brecht for much of the first half of 1937, writing, among much else, the *Lenin Requiem*, the choral variations *Gegen den Krieg*, part of the *Deutsche Symphonie* and several songs to Brecht's texts; also seven cantatas to Silone's.

313 To Julius Hay   March 1937
Hay had written an article in answer to Reich's, but Brecht vetoed it for *Das Wort*. Feuchtwanger however wrote the magazine a laudatory review of *Haben* (vol. 2, no. 7), while Becher published the text of the play in *Internationale Literatur*. The 'Trojan Horse' technique had been proposed by Dimitrov at the Comintern's Seventh World Congress in 1935 as a key to the new Popular Front against Fascism.

Wangenheim: see Note 250.

314 To Becher   2 March 1937
Becher as editor of the Moscow *Internationale Literatur* was always close to what Brecht called 'the Hungarian clique'. Brecht did write a short critique of *Haben* (*GW 15*, pp. 325–6), but it was never published in his lifetime.

315 To Piscator   ?March 1937
Mexico: Piscator, now temporarily settled in Paris after the dissolution of MORT, was trying to get a footing in Mexican film and theatre affairs.

Brecht's 'film plot': almost certainly 'Die Judith von Saint Denis' (*Texte für Filme II*, 1969, pp. 366–8).

'Auntie Voss': the conservative Berlin *Vossische Zeitung*.

The rag: *Das Wort*. Most Soviet publishers paid their foreign authors in blocked roubles rather than hard currency (or 'valuta').

316 To Piscator   16 March 1937
See note 310. This is the 'Diderot Society' scheme, as discussed with Gorelik. Piscator wrote affirmatively on 31 March.

317 To Jean Renoir   17 March 1937
Brecht knew Renoir through his friend Carl Koch. A meeting of the three near Paris provided the idea for his short story 'A question of taste' (*Short Stories 1921–1946*, pp. 183ff) in 1940. It appears that this letter was given to Walter Benjamin to post, who forgot it.

318 To Gorelik   19 March 1937
The 'prospectus' included with this letter (German text in *GW 15*, pp. 305–309) was translated by Gorelik, who wanted the name to be changed to 'Society for Theatrical Research', but was not published till 1961. Of the further names listed, Léon Moussinac was a French film critic who headed the École des Arts Décoratifs after the Second World War; Rupert Doone at the (London) Group Theatre directed the plays of Auden and Isherwood. E. F. Burian, a former composer, headed the Prague experimental theatre D38 till he was sent to Mauthausen concentration camp by the Nazis; after the War he headed the

Czech Army theatre. Per Lindberg was a left-wing Swedish director, Archibald MacLeish the American playwright and poet, who had admired *Mother* and met Brecht in New York. For Knutzon and Okhlopkov see Notes 208 and 310; for Tretiakoff Notes 173 and 177.

Others whom Brecht thought of approaching included Dudow, Eisenstein, Nordahl Grieg the Norwegian playwright, Georg Hoellering, Carl Koch, Kortner and Per Lagerquist.

*319 To James B. Pinker   19 March 1937
To the same effect as the next letter. Pinker was agent for the book.

320 To Robert Hale & Co   March 1937
Robert Hale published the book under the title *A Penny for the Poor*, in a translation by Desmond Vesey with the poems translated by Christopher Isherwood. Vesey had written on 12 March asking Brecht to confirm that no cuts had been made. It was later republished by Grove Press and Granada under the title *Threepenny Novel*, as which it also appeared as a Penguin Modern Classic.

*321 To Brentano   March 1937
Apologising for the review of his novel *Theodor Chindler* in the first issue of *Das Wort*, and wishing that he and Armin Kesser would nonetheless become contributors.

322 To Piscator   4 April 1937
Piscator had written to tell Brecht of his plan to film *Schweik*, for whose rights he had been negotiating in Paris since November. Leo Lania and Henri Jeanson had already been engaged to work on the script. The film was not made, but Brecht's comments on the treatment (in Letter 324) show that the intention was to bring the Good Soldier up to date.

323 To Piscator   21 April 1937
Piscator's outline was never, it seems, fleshed out, and remains unpublished.

Sandor Bartos had made an animated film of the Belgian engraver Frans Masereel's woodcut sequence *Story Without Words*.

F. Olivier-Brachfeld: Piscator's secretary in Paris. The *New York Times* article is evidently the one referred to in Letter 282.

'Potato Jones': an obstinate merchant navy skipper who was a minor popular hero of the Spanish Civil War.

324 To Piscator   June 1937
Jacob Tiedtke: was a Berlin actor.

The Marshal: presumably Hermann Goering. The Palazzo Venezia: Mussolini's residence in Rome.

325 To Benjamin   April-May 1937
The novelist Anna Seghers had settled in Paris, but moved on to Mexico after the fall of France in 1940. She returned to East Germany in 1947.

The 'Laterne' cabaret opened in the Caveau Desmoulins, Paris in April 1934. Its members – among them Steffi Spira, Günther Ruschin and Marianne Oswald – had come to France with Wangenheim's Truppe 1931 and remained behind when the bulk of that group went (at Piscator's invitation) to Moscow. The organiser was Alphonse Kahn, the artistic director Hans Altmann. Heinz

Lohmar was the designer. After some initial difficulties the cabaret reopened in the Salle Duncan in January 1936. Then following the outbreak of General Franco's rebellion against the Spanish Popular Front government, Slatan Dudow asked Brecht to write a Spanish Civil War play which would be performed by Helene Weigel and some of the 'Laterne' actors.

For Benjamin's 'Paris Letters' see Note 302.

326 To Benjamin   c. Mid-1937
Fuchs: Eduard Fuchs, author of standard works on Daumier and on caricature.

327 To Feuchtwanger   May 1937
'Over there' = in the USSR, where he was preparing his book *Moscow 1937* – designed evidently as a counter to Gide's.

Maria = Maria Osten. Feuchtwanger wrote on 30 May that he had not received any letter.

Success: Feuchtwanger's best novel (English translation, London and New York 1930) which deals with events in Bavaria around 1923 and includes a character based on Brecht.

Carola Neher, the Polly of the *Threepenny Opera* film, had married a Soviet engineer named Becker and emigrated to the USSR, where they had both been arrested in the purges – she apparently in August 1936. She was sentenced to ten years' imprisonment for spying. In his reply (see Pike, pp. 356–7 and footnote 184) Feuchtwanger wrote that she 'was in jail while I was in Moscow. She is said to have been involved in a treason[able] conspiracy of her husband's. I don't have any details.'

328 To Feuchtwanger   June 1937
Feuchtwanger was received by Stalin. Both this and the previous letter read as if Brecht expected them to be read by the Soviet police.

The second half of the letter refers to Feuchtwanger's enthusiastic article about Julius Hay's play *Haben* (see Notes 312, 313).

329 To Martin Andersen-Nexö   5 July 1937
Nexö, the author of a classic early twentieth-century Danish socialist novel, *Pelle the Conqueror*, appears to have been a good friend of Brecht, who dedicated his poem 'Literature will be scrutinised' to him for his seventieth birthday in 1939 (*Poems 1913–1956*, p. 344).

The second International Writers' Congress for the Defence of Culture opened in Spain on 4 July 1937, then moved to Paris where Brecht addressed it on the 17th.

330 To Hermann Borchardt   ? Mid-1937
Out – of Dachau, Nazi Germany and Europe. See Note 307. The novel may have been *Suum quique*, of which an extract had appeared in *Neue Deutsche Blätter* (Prague) vol. 1 no. 5.

331 Ditto   ?early-mid '40s
Date uncertain.

332 To Slatan Dudow   July 1937
Aufricht, the Berlin impresario of *The Threepenny Opera* and *Happy End*, had emigrated to France, where he mounted a Paris production of the former in a

version by André Mauprey and Ninon Tallon at the Théâtre de l Étoile. He invited Brecht and Weigel to come for four weeks, the opening being scheduled for 28 September during the Exposition Universelle.

The 'Spanish play' = *Señora Carrar's Rifles*, the work referred to in Letter 325, which opened on 16 October.

Katz: Otto Katz, former manager of the first Piscator company, who worked in Willi Muenzenberg's Paris HQ.

The 'series of short plays' would turn into *Fear and Misery of the Third Reich*, part of which Dudow would stage, again with Weigel, the following year.

The 'satires' = the 'German Satires', (*Poems 1913–1956*, pp. 295–300).

The 'speech' to the Congress mentioned in Note 329 is in *GW 18*, pp. 247–250.

'Grenzbestimmungen' ('Demarcations') must have been an article which Dudow was writing for the proposed Diderot Society. The theoretical articles by Lukács, Mikhail Lifschitz and others which had led to the formal restriction of the concept of Socialist Realism had already been published in the magazine *Literaturny Kritik*.

333 To Dudow   End July 1937
Eddington's *The Nature of the Physical World* appeared in a German translation in 1931. A copy in Brecht's library is dated 'brecht 31' and contains many annotations by him.

Okhlopkov staged *Razbeg* in the round at his Realistic Theatre in Moscow in winter 1931/32.

334 To Feuchtwanger   Aug. 1937
Feuchtwanger had asked Brecht to visit him at Sanary-sur-mer. His novel *Der falsche Nero* was published by Querido, Amsterdam in 1936. The 'German Academy' referred to was the American Guild for German Cultural Freedom, which had been founded by Hubertus Prinz zu Löwenstein, an associate of the former conservative Chancellor Heinrich Brüning (then a guest of Harvard University). This Guild appears to have made Brecht a grant in the first part of 1938, which was subsequently prolonged.

*335 To Prince Hubertus zu Löwenstein (American Guild for German Cultural Freedom)   Aug. 1937
Objecting to the exclusion of poetry from a competition held by the Guild.

336 To Wieland Herzfelde   24 Aug. 1937
Herzfelde had written on 21 August 1937 to tell Brecht that VEGAAR in Moscow had abandoned their intention to co-publish Brecht's works. The first two volumes of these appeared in March 1938 and were printed in Czechoslovakia (where Herzfelde was based) though the place of publication was given as London WC 1 (i.e. the Communist Party's Central Books c/o Margaret Mynatt). They contained *Die Massnahme*, *Señora Carrar's Rifles* and *The Round Heads and the Pointed Heads* (in vol. 2) and *St Joan of the Stockyards* (in vol. 1), but not *Mahagonny*. Herzfelde hoped to include the *Threepenny Novel* in the edition if he could get the rights. Universum was Muenzenberg's book club, which also wanted to get the book for its members.

George Grosz had illustrated Brecht's 'children's poem' 'Die Drei Soldaten' in the Versuche edition (1932), and was asked by him in the summer of 1934 if he would also illustrate the plays. He agreed, was paid an advance by Herzfelde and completed a number of drawings which Brecht saw and approved, presumably during his 1935 visit to New York. In July 1936 he told Herzfelde he felt he must withdraw, because 'I just can't any longer make the necessary contact with B's writing'; then a week later he apologised and promised not to let him down. But on 11 September 1937 Herzfelde wrote back to Brecht saying that Grosz had finally cried off.

Upton Sinclair Presents William Fox appeared in Los Angeles in 1933 and was published in the Malik-Verlag in 1936. F. C. Weiskopf's Czechoslovak poetry anthology *Das Herz – ein Schild* included the 'bitter ballads' of Robert David (Malik, London 1937).

*336x To Steffin   21 Sep 37
Mentions contributions by Benjamin and [Nordahl] Grieg, presumably for *Das Wort*. Brecht was then in Paris for *The Threepenny Opera*.

337 To Weigel   6 Oct. 1937
Aufricht's Paris production of *The Threepenny Opera* had some fifty performances in all.

338 To the Schutzverband deutscher Schriftsteller   Mid-Oct 1937
The SDS, or German Writers' Defence League, had been founded in 1908, and at the time of its dissolution by the Nazis was chaired by Arnold Zweig. In 1933 exiled members of the Berlin branch re-established the SDS in Paris, with Rudolf Leonhard as chairman and David Luschnat as secretary; branches in London, Prague, Brussels and other capitals followed. The fact that Communist writers were now prominent in the organisation led to the establishment of a rival 'Bund freie Presse und Literatur' under Leopold Schwarzschild and Konrad Heiden. Brecht's message was directed to the SDS's second Annual General Meeting at the Café Méphisto on 18 October.

*338x To *Das Wort*   18 Oct. 1937
Joint letter with Feuchtwanger dated 18 October 1937, copy in TsGALI, Moscow, See Note 346 below.

339, 340 To Helene Weigel   26–30 Oct. 1937
Weigel was visiting Vienna and Prague after the short Paris run of *Señora Carrar's Rifles*, the play referred to. She did not perform in the Prague production (12 February 1938, with Charlotte Küter and Erwin Geschonneck) and there was no Paris revival.

'The Myers books' = presumably the two volumes of Gustavus Myers's *The History of the Great American Fortunes*, a work that had helped inspire the *Threepenny Novel*.

Hodann: Traute Hodann, wife of the socialist doctor Max Hodann who fought in Spain and later worked for the British Legation in Stockholm. They were friends of Ruth Berlau, who directed the Danish-language Copenhagen production on 19 December 1937, with Dagmar Andreasen as Carrar, followed by a German-language production with Weigel on 14 February 1938.

'Hanne's grandmother' the mother of Brecht's first wife Marianne (who could be 'M' in letter 340). Mrs Andersen was the Brechts' housekeeper, Mie her niece.

341 Ditto   Early Nov. 1937
The poem appended was 'Die Schauspielerin im Exil' (*GW*9, p. 781).

The two little plays about Germany formed part of *Fear and Misery of the Third Reich*.

342 Ditto   4 Nov. 1937
Mary Fränkel. Not identified.

Robert Storm Petersen was a Danish comic draughtsman.

343 Ditto   Nov 1937

344 To Martin Domke   9 Nov 1937
Domke was a German refugee lawyer in Paris. The 'notes' he had been sending Brecht were material for the Julius Caesar play project of which fragments survive in the Brecht Archive. Later it became an incomplete novel. He also represented Brecht in legal matters connected with *The Threepenny Opera*.

Ninon Tallon made the rough translation of *The Threepenny Opera* for André Mauprey. A niece of Edouard Herriot, she directed the Théâtre Pigalle. Tommy Banyai held the French performing rights.

The Société des Auteurs collects authors' and composers' royalties for them. Brecht, on Domke's advice, had formally made over his rights to Fritz Lieb, a theologian friend of Walter Benjamin in Paris. This seems to have been in the hope of circumventing the Berlin agents Felix Bloch Successors, who were trying to deduct advances paid on other plays (see Note 174).

345 Ditto   19 Nov. 1937
The year 691. Brecht is using the Roman system of dating 'from the founding of the city'. But he soon starts omitting the initial '6'.

346 To Feuchtwanger   End Nov. 1937
CN = Carola Neher (see Note 327). The case against her was that she allegedly carried messages for Erich Wollenberg, a German supporter of Trotsky.

K = Mikhail Koltsov, returned from Spain at the end of 1938 and was promptly arrested; he never reappeared.

Neher's husband was shot in 1937 according to David Pike; she herself, reputedly, on 28 June 1942.

Ramzin: a Soviet engineer, was accused of economic sabotage in the Shakhty case in 1928.

The German Freedom Radio was a 'black' transmitter supposedly inside Nazi Germany. In fact however it was run from Paris (by Gerhart Eisler and others) transmitting mainly from Barcelona. Brecht wrote his 'German Satires' for it (see Note 332). It is not known which 'short scenes' are referred to, but some of those in *Fear and Misery of the Third Reich* would surely have qualified.

The joint 'letter to *Das Wort*' is presumed missing by the Brecht Archive, but is clearly that seen by David Pike in the Moscow literary archives TsGALI (*German Writers in Soviet Exile,* p. 220) and dated 18 October 1937. In this the two editors proposed that the magazine should appear every two months, with more pages and longer articles – which would give them a better chance of judging contributions before publication – and that there should be a West European editorial office with its own permanent editor. For this they had in mind Koltsov's wife Maria Osten. Apparently if these changes were not made they threatened to resign.

After getting Koltsov's views Fritz Erpenbeck replied on 30 December that Osten would be the Paris editor as requested and that the number of pages would go up by a third, but that publication would still be monthly.

347 To Karl Korsch   Nov. 1937

Fowler, the Oxford classicist, was William Ward Fowler, author of *Julius Caesar and the Foundation of the Roman Imperial System* (New York and London 1892).

Herbert Levi was a doctor, friend of Korsch. Kurt Jacob: not known.

Sergei Tretiakoff had been arrested in July 1937.

348 To Per Knutzon   ? End 1937

Knutzon was the director of the Copenhagen production of *The Round Heads and the Pointed Heads* in November 1936. On 17 September 1937 he staged *The Threepenny Opera*, once again in the Riddersalen Theatre, Copenhagen, with his wife Lulu Ziegler in the part of Polly, but without ensuring that the royalties would go to Brecht rather than to the agents back in Nazi Germany.

See Note 174 for 'the author's alleged indebtedness'.

349 To the cast of the 1938 production of *Carrar* in Copenhagen   Feb. 1938

This was the German-language performance of 14 February 1938, directed by Ruth Berlau, with Weigel as Carrar. A second performance was given at the Odd-Fellow-Palaet on 6 March. The 'Home' referred to by Brecht was the 'Emigranthjemmet'.

350 Ditto   Feb. 1938

Kurt = Kurt Krauter, the actor playing Pedro.

351 To Jonny G. Rieger   17 Feb. 1938

Rieger's real name was Wolf Harten. His books *Feuer im Osten* and *Fahr zur Hölle, Jonny* were published by the Büchergilde Gutenberg in Switzerland. His article 'Ecke Hongkong-Road' appeared in *Das Wort* vol. 3, no. 1 (January 1938); his book on Shanghai was published in Swedish the same year. He is said to have been caught in Denmark by the German occupation in 1940, and conscripted into the German army. His fate is uncertain.

The Röhm ballad was Brecht's 'Ballade vom 30 Juni' (also called 'Ballade vom armen Stabschef'), which is in *GW 9*, p. 520. Ernst Röhm, chief of staff of the SA, was among those killed in Hitler's purge of that body on 30 June 1934.

352 To Axel Larsen   25 March 1938

Larsen was chairman of the Danish Communist Party. Brecht's 'report' has not been made public; presumably it repeated the gist of Letter 348. Larsen however replied on 7 April that it was open to Brecht to sue Bloch's representatives, and appears to have dismissed the whole matter as a triviality based on gossip.

353 To Ernestine Evans   26 March 1938

Jerome: V. J. Jerome, recipient of Letter 269. Mrs Evans was a friend of Hella Wuolijoki, with whom Brecht would write *Puntila* in Finland.

354, 355 To Martin Andersen-Nexö   25 March, 3 April 1938

For Nexö see Note 329. His memoirs had been translated by Alfred Ostermoor and Alfred Bertolt with a view to publication by the Büchergilde Gutenberg in Zurich. Margarete Steffin and Brecht (though the latter knew no Danish) made a new translation which appeared under the title *Eine Kindheit* from

Mezhdunarodnaya Kniga in Moscow in 1940 and subsequently from another Zurich firm called 'Kultur und Volk'.

Nexö had reviewed Ruth Berlau's *Carrar* production in the Copenhagen *Arbejderbladet* on 18 February, and this was the basis for his article in *Das Wort* vol. 3, no. 3.

356 To Erwin Piscator   March–April 1938
The title eventually chosen for US production was *The Private Life of the Master Race*, a wartime version of the play in seventeen scenes. The nineteen-scene script dates from March–April 1938 (Steffin's dating); then during April Brecht wrote six more scenes. Later the title 'The German march-past' became used for the introductory verses only.

Goya: Brecht is referring to *The Disasters of the War*.

'The Zurich people' = the actors of the Zurich Schauspielhaus, most durable of the anti-Nazi German-language theatres.

357 To Karl Korsch   April 1938
The magazine is thought to have been *Living Marxism*, to which Korsch contributed.

Brecht had abandoned the scheme for a Caesar play in favour of a novel. Under the title *The Business Affairs of Mr Julius Caesar* its unfinished torso is in *GW 14*, pp. 1169–1379.

'Tuis' is Brecht's term for inverted intellectuals, a category that did not entirely exclude Marxists.

358 To Slatan Dudow   April 1938
Further to Letters 332 and 333. The play is *Fear and Misery of the Third Reich*. The war, the Spanish civil war.

Felix Bressart: an actor who Brecht had hoped would be in the cast. Later, in Hollywood, he played in the film of Anna Seghers's *The Seventh Cross*.

359 Ditto   19 April 1938
For the 'Laterne' cabaret in Paris, see Note 325.

Ernst Busch: the Communist actor-singer who performed in *Kuhle Wampe* and *The Mother* (1932) and toured the USSR and republican Spain with Eisler's militant songs. He was not available.

Fürst: possibly Manfred F., who was involved in plans to set up a permanent German theatre in Paris. He was not available either.

360 Ditto   24 April 1938
This letter may not have been sent off. Erich Schoenlank was one of the actors.

The play as given finally consisted of eight scenes only, under the title *99%. Scenes from the Third Reich*, including 'Jurisprudence' but omitting 'Consulting the People' which Brecht had put at the end. Weigel played in 'Charity begins at home', 'The Jewish Wife' and 'Job creation'. She was not happy about Dudow's direction, which she found too authoritarian. Among the other actors were Günter Ruschin and Steffi Spira, Nora Reissmann, Josef Leininger, Erich Berg, Friedel Ferrari, Ludwig Turek the proletarian novelist and the 'Laterne's' organiser Hans Altmann. Heinz Lohmar and Sylta Busse were the designers. Paul Dessau (under the pseudonym Peter Sturm) composed the linking ballad, which he reputedly sang himself, though the programme gives the singer as Fritz Seiffert. The première was on 21 May 1938.

361 To Martin Domke   April 1938
Domke had given Brecht volume 2 of Jérôme Carcopino's *Histoire Romaine: La République Romaine de 133 à 44 avant J-C.*, Paris 1936.

Walter Benjamin arrived in Skovsbostrand, where he took a room close to Brecht's house, on 22 June 1938. He stayed till October, working on his study of Baudelaire.

362 To Aksel Larsen   13 May 1938
Continuing the argument about Brecht's *Threepenny Opera* royalties from Letters 348 and 352. Strakosch: the Danish agent for Bloch-Erben.

*363 To the American Guild for German Cultural Freedom   28 May 1938
Thanking them for a grant, reporting work on the 'satirical novel' *The Business Dealings of Mr Julius Caesar*, and complaining about Bloch-Erben's confiscation of his *Threepenny Opera* royalties.

364 To Ernestine Evans   17 June 1938
Follows Letter 353. The translation in the April–June 1938 number of *Theater Workshop* was by Keene Wallis.

365 To Alfred Kurella   17 June 1938
Kurella was an art student in Munich before the First World War, after which he was involved in the leadership of the Communist Youth International. A Soviet citizen (according to David Pike), he was a member of the 'October' group of artists in 1928, then spent the years 1929–32 in Berlin as a KPD cultural spokesman. From 1932–34 he was in France as secretary to Henri Barbusse and editor of Barbusse's review *Monde* before returning to Moscow as secretary to Dimitrov at the Comintern. At the time of Brecht's letter he was standing in for Erpenbeck as Moscow editor of *Das Wort*.

Georg Lukács had attacked Eisler in contemptuous terms in an article called 'Es geht um den Realismus' which summed up the so-called 'Expressionism debate' in *Das Wort*, vol. 3 no. 6. Brecht had been against its publication, and now wrote 'A slight correction' (text in *GW 19*, pp. 337–8) in defence of his friend. Pike (*German Writers in Soviet Exile*, pp. 293–5) shows how Kurella and Erpenbeck, possibly in concert with Walter Ulbricht, decided tacitly to ignore Brecht's objections.

It is not clear if Brecht actually sent his article on 'The Popular and the Realistic' (*Brecht on Theatre*, pp. 107–112), but it certainly never appeared in *Das Wort*. The Poem 'Der Rattenfänger' could be his own poem 'Der Rattenfänger von Hameln' (*GW 9*, pp. 802–3).

366 To Willi Bredel   ? July-Aug. 1938
Bredel, the former 'worker-correspondent' and 'proletarian novelist' who was nominally *Das Wort*'s senior Moscow editor, had been with the International Brigades in Spain, but arrived in Paris in June 1938. The 'Paris comrades' would be the KPD's foreign bureau in that city. The 'Moscow Hungarian clique' (see Note 314) were favoured by Johannes R. Becher as editor of the

German edition of *Internationale Literatur*, where he published Lukács's article on Marx and 'ideological decline' in the July issue.
Maria = Maria Osten.

367 To Alfred Döblin   Aug. 1938
Döblin, the Berlin doctor-novelist who wrote the 'epic' work *Berlin Alexanderplatz* in 1929, was sixty on 10 August 1938; he was twenty years older than Brecht. In 1933 he emigrated to France and became a French subject. A convert to Catholicism, he spent the years 1940–45 in the United States before returning to Germany with the French occupation forces. Brecht sent this letter to one of the organisers of a literary reception for Döblin in Paris, who forgot to give it to him.

368 To Professor Edvard Beneš   20 Sep. 1938
To the president of Czechoslovakia on the occasion of the Munich Agreement of 20 September 1938, when Britain and France allowed Nazi Germany to take over the Sudeten (German-speaking) areas of his country.

369 To the American Guild for German Cultural Freedom   Sep. 1938
See Note 334. Brecht had applied to the Guild for a literary prize in August 1937. The grant which he was subsequently paid would have expired in September 1938, but was renewed for at least two further periods of six months. During that time it was raised to $60 a month.

A full text of *Fear and Misery of the Third Reich* was announced by Malik for volume 3 of their Brecht edition, but not published till 1945, when Herzfelde's Aurora-Verlag (successor to Malik) brought it out in New York. It only included 24 scenes; the remainder will be found in the Methuen *Collected Plays* vol. 4 iii.

The *Svendborg Poems* were published by Malik from London in 1939 (but apparently only distributed later). Volumes 3 and 4 of their edition were typeset but never appeared, since the Czech printers were overrun by the Nazis when Prague was occupied in March 1939. Proofs were sent to Brecht and are now in the Brecht Archive.

'The Street Scene' is in *Brecht on Theatre*, pp. 121–8. 'The Theory of the Alienation Effect' embraces the 'Short Description of a Technique of Acting' and its Appendix, ibid., pp. 136–47.

370 Ditto   30 Sep. 1938
It appears that no award in this 'contest' was made till 1 January 1940, and then not to Brecht. The published text of his unfinished Caesar novel is divided into 'Books' rather than chapters. Three are coherent, the fourth partly in note form. Books V ('re the Gallic War') and VI have not been published at all, and are limited to brief fragments.

*371 Ditto   Nov. 1938
Addressed to Prince zu Löwenstein, saying the finished portion of the novel has been sent off, and he would be grateful if the grant could be extended.

372 To Wieland Herzfelde   Nov.-Dec. 1938
The cheque was presumably for the first two volumes of Collected Works, of which 2000 copies had been published from London in March 1938. According to the *Arbeitsjournal* (Working Diary) which Brecht began keeping that summer,

he finished his play *Life of Galileo* on 23 November of that year. For the
Svendborg Poems see Note 369 above.

373 To Ferdinand Reyher   2 Dec. 1938
Reyher, for whose earlier contacts with Brecht see Note 135, reappeared during
a visit to Copenhagen (28 October to 4 November) when he met Brecht a
number of times. He was then on his way back from visiting Germany with
'Spig' Wead, an aviator friend who was interested in the Luftwaffe. Learning
that Brecht was thinking of following the examples of Eisler and Piscator, i.e.
getting a quota visa for the United States, Reyher offered to take Brecht's idea
for a Galileo treatment back with him and try to sell it to Hollywood. Brecht
continued to talk about the film possibilities of the subject, but never wrote the
treatment. Instead he sent the first script of the play.

   Wead had written a film about flying. The poem which Brecht sent him could
have been 'Mein Bruder war ein Flieger' (*GW 9*, p. 647) or the children's poem
'The Tailor of Ulm' (*Poems 1913–1956*, p. 243). It is not known if Reyher
translated either.

*374 To Mr Schneider   22 Dec. 1938
About a possible production at S's theatre (unidentified, but evidently in the US)
of *The Round Heads and the Pointed Heads*. Brecht says Eisler (38, Barrow Street, New
York City) is empowered to act for him, and he recommends Gorelik for the sets.

375 To Maria Osten   Winter 38/39
For Koltsov see Notes 255 and 298; for his arrest Note 346. For Brecht's own
Arbeitsjournal entry of January 1939, which called him 'my last Russian link
with [the USSR]' see *Brecht in Context* p. 189; it summarises the fate of his other
Soviet friends and contacts.

*376 To Fredrik Martner   6 Jan. 1939
About a possible Danish translation by M. of *Galileo*.

*377 To Fritz Kortner   Jan. 1939
To reassure K. (now living in the US) that Brecht had never spoken ill of him.

378 To Egon Erwin Kisch   Jan. 1939
Kisch was the great German-language reporter from Prague, who had made his
name before 1914 by exposing the spying activities of the Austrian Colonel
Redl, and in 1919 was one of the Vienna Red Guard. He had recently become
famous in Australia for swimming ashore when refused permission to land, then
passing a language test in Gaelic to prove his right to enter that country.

   Alfred Kerr, Brecht's 'melodious old lecher', was the doyen of the Berlin theatre
critics before 1933 and showed little appreciation of Brecht, whose
unacknowledged borrowings from Rimbaud and from Klammer's translation of
Villon he had brought to light. As a Jew and a Socialist he was unacceptable to
the Nazis, and Kisch had written in the *Neue Weltbühne* 1939, no. 2, to defend
him against one of his denigrators. From 1936 till his death in 1948 he lived
in England, where he was a founder (with Kokoschka and others) of the
émigrés' 'Free German League of Culture' and worked in the wartime BBC.

*379 To Prinz Hubertus zu Löwenstein (American Guild for German Cultural
Freedom)

Answer to a request for a manuscript for a planned auction.

380 To Karl Korsch   Feb. 1939
Korsch's *Karl Marx* was published in London by Chapman and Hall in 1938, in
New York by Wiley in 1939. It was the fifth in the series 'Modern Sociologists'.

Gyula Alpári was editor of the Comintern's review *Rundschau über Politik,
Wirtschaft und Arbeiterbewegung*, which was published from Basel.

The U.S. immigration quota for Austrians and Germans was set at 27,230
admissions per year.

*380x To Kurt Weill   4 Feb. 1939
Weill had written on 9 February 1939 complaining about the failure of the
agents Bloch-Erben in Berlin to pay him his royalties on *Threepenny Opera*
productions in Paris, Stockholm and other cities. If Brecht agrees he will get a
US lawyer to cancel the contract with them. (Cf. Letters 348 and 352.) This
short letter of agreement dated 23 March incidentally mentions work on *The
Good Person of Szechwan*, the parable which B. says he described to W. in New
York (i.e. in 1935).

381 To Korsch   ? Feb.-March 1939
Left unfinished and not sent.

*382 To Heinrich Mann   3 March 1939
Congratulating the elder Mann on his book of essays published under the title
Mut (Courage) in Paris in 1939. B. hopes he will write more like the one called
'Die Rede' which adopts the internal monologue form.

383 To Elisabeth Hauptmann   Feb.-March 1939
The translations and the American lady remain a mystery. For an extract from
Brecht's *Arbeitsjournal* entry of 5 March 1939, giving his views on American
literature, see *Brecht in Context*, p. 33.

Maxim Lieber was Anna Seghers's American agent. He is not mentioned
again in Brecht's letters or journal.

384–8 To Henry Peter Matthis   March-April 1939
Matthis was an author involved in the Swedish association of amateur theatres.
With Georg Branting, a leading Social-Democrat politician, and four others he
had set up a 'Brecht Committee' to get the family out of their increasingly
precarious situation in Denmark. That country was about to sign a non-
aggression pact with Hitler – something that the other three Scandinavian
governments were refusing to do.

Thanks to Matthis's invitation and his activities on their behalf Brecht and
Helene Weigel would arrive in Stockholm on 23 April 1939. On 4 May he
would give his lecture 'On Experimental Theatre' (*Brecht on Theatre*, pp. 130–
135) which was the formal justification for their trip.

*389 To the American Guild for German Cultural Freedom   April 1939
Addressed to Prince zu Löwenstein, and thanking for the extension of his grant
for another six months.

390 To Bruno Dressler   23 April 1939
Dressler, who had been one of the founders of the Büchergilde Gutenberg, a
remarkable Trade-Union-sponsored book club in the Weimar Republic, set up a

similar club in Switzerland in association with the Oprecht family. Brecht's and
Steffin's Nexö translation however (for which see Notes 354–5) eventually
appeared in a series called 'Erbe and Gegenwart' under the imprint of 'Kultur
und Volk', Zurich. This seems to have been the same as the Mundus-Verlag
which Dressler ran from Basel.

*391 To Fredrik Martner   May 1939
To thank him for various translations into Danish and announce the family's
safe arrival on Lidingö island, five km from Stockholm.

392 Ditto   June 1939
Martner and 'Crassus' were pseudonyms of the Danish journalist Knud
Rasmussen, whom Brecht knew through Karin Michaelis. He had made
translations of some of Brecht's short stories.

The Confucius is *The Analects of Confucius*. Translated and annotated by Arthur
Waley, Allen and Unwin, London 1938. The book was sent him by Martner on
23 May 1939, and was still in his library when he died. The 'Lao-tse' poem
rejected by *Mass und Wert* is his 'Legendary Origin of the book Tao-Tê-Ching'
(*Poems 1913–1956*, pp. 314–16).

*393 To the American Guild for German Cultural Freedom   June 1939
Addressed to Prince zu Löwenstein, to whom he is sending the *Svendborg Poems*,
just published, which bear a note acknowledging the Guild's patronage.

394 To Fritz Erpenbeck   25 July 1939
For Erpenbeck's role at *Das Wort* see Notes 298 and 365. Following Koltsov's
arrest in mid-December the magazine was in the hands of Mezhdunarodnaya
Kniga, who notified the editors on 29 March that it (and its hard currency fund)
would be merged with the German edition of Becher's magazine *Internationale
Literatur* (Deutsche Blätter). Koltsov was not mentioned, and the pretext given
was that the Nazi occupation of Austria and German-speaking Czechoslovakia
had made further publication uneconomic. No March issue appeared, but
contributors were assured that accepted contributions would be paid for.

According to David Pike, Bredel and Feuchtwanger reacted almost as angrily as
Brecht, while Becher later complained that *Das Wort*'s hard currency fund had
never been handed over. Erpenbeck replied to Brecht on 8 August that technical
matters, including contributors' payments, were not his responsibility and that
he was sending the present letter on to Mezhdunarodnaya Kniga. There is no
answer from them in Brecht's papers.

395 To [?]   July 1939
It is not clear to whom this letter was addressed. The 'Notes to the Opera
Mahagonny', containing the famous tables contrasting 'epic' and 'dramatic'
aspects of theatre and opera, can be found in *Brecht on Theatre*, pp. 33–42. This
appears to be the first instance of Brecht seeking to qualify his statements there.

Mass und Wert, published every two months from Zurich by Oprecht, was the
most ostensibly 'distinguished' of the exiles' reviews. It lasted for three years
from September 1937, when the opening number was introduced by an essay
from Thomas Mann. What Brecht is referring to is the July-August issue (no. 6)
of 1939, which devoted two unsigned articles to his conception of theatre, the

one ('Was ist episches Theater?') by Walter Benjamin, the other less favourable ('Grenzen des Brecht-Theaters') supposedly by the editor Ferdinand Lion.

396 To Rudolf Olden July 1939

Olden, an outstanding liberal journalist and former editor of the *Frankfurter Zeitung*, was secretary of the German exiled PEN which had been set up at the end of 1933. Brecht, who had been elected in 1935 on the initiative of Heinrich Mann and Becher, was suspended because he never answered letters. Olden replied that he was now back on the society's books. Its Stockholm congress however was never held, and Olden went down on the torpedoed liner *Arandora Star* in the Second World War.

397 To Martin Domke 27 Aug. 1939

Domke had written from Paris to ask if Brecht had authorised the proposed Abraham production. Abraham, editor of the French review *Europe*, was the brother of the dramatist Jean-Richard Bloch. Having performed various scenes from his own translation of *Fear and Misery of the Third Reich* with his amateur group 'Les Comédiens d'Anjou', Abraham was now preparing to stage nine of them in sets by Frans Masereel at the Théâtre Hébertot in Paris on 15 September 1939.

Aufricht loan. Aufricht at this time was apparently planning a *Happy End* film to be directed by René Clair. This did not come off.

398 To Ferdinand Reyher 27 Aug. 1939

Further to Letter 373. Reyher had written on 13 June from Hollywood to say he had finished his adaptation of *Fear and Misery of the Third Reich*, which he thought of renaming *The Devil's Opera*. A Dramatists' Guild contract for this was being sent to Brecht for signature. Since Reyher also said that he had eliminated all 'propaganda' from the play and tried to make it one 'whose story will hang together' Brecht's non-committal answer is understandable.

399 To Hans Tombrock Aug. 1939

Tombrock was a little known self-taught artist, a miner's son who had belonged to Gregor Gog's Communist league of tramps. The 'Reading Worker' was his illustration for the poem 'Questions from a worker who reads' (*Poems 1913–1956*, p. 252), which starts 'Who built Thebes of the seven gates?' and ends 'So many reports./ So many questions'. Translated by Johannes Edfelt, poem and illustration constituted two panels for the Gävle People's House.

See the section (IV) devoted to Tombrock in the catalogue *Bilder und Graphiken zu Werken von Bertolt Brecht*, Neue Münchner Galerie, Munich n.d. (?1964), which lists some fifty works by him relating to Brecht.

400 To Fredrick Martner

For Martner/Rasmussen/Crassus and his loan of Waley's *Analects of Confucius*, see Note 392.

Courage: ten days after the German attack on Poland Brecht noted in his journal that his work on the *Good Person of Szechwan* had got stuck. He must have begun concentrating on *Mother Courage* soon after, actually writing the first complete script between 27 September and 3 November. *Lucullus* immediately followed, being written between 5–11 November (according to Margarete Steffin, who helped on both works).

'Comforts for the Soldiers' is the title of one section of chapter 9 of the *Threepenny Novel* (Granada, London 1981) pp. 176–9, where Polly joins a committee of ladies sending clothes, cigarettes and 'little notes of encouragement, all tied up in pink and mauve ribbons' to the troops fighting the Boer War.

401 To Etti Santesson   Feb. 1940
Etti Santesson was a Swedish writer, and her sister Ninnan the sculptress who put her house on Lidingø island at Brecht's disposal.

Karl Gerhardt was a Stockholm impresario. There are a few sketches for a revue by Brecht based on Aristophanes's *Pluto*. The scheme was not pursued.

402 To Hella Wuolijoki   April 1940
Wuoljoki, a supporter of the Bolsheviks in 1917 who had written a number of plays, notably the *Women of Niiskavuori* sequence, was recommended to Brecht by Ruth Berlau (who had played in them in Denmark) and by the Swedish deputy Georg Branting. She got Finland's premier to agree to the Brechts' admission, and was their principal hostess in that country. Her story and play about 'Puntilla' [sic] were the basis for the play which she and Brecht submitted for a competition in autumn 1940. Its German version, normally credited to Brecht alone, is the *Puntila* which had its première in Zurich in 1948 and is now a standard work.

403 To Curt Trepte   End April 1940
Originally an actor with Wangenheim's 'Truppe 1931', Trepte had emigrated with it to Paris, then gone with other members to the USSR where they helped form the 'Deutsches Gebietstheater Dniepropetrovsk' which toured the Ukraine. He moved to Sweden at the end of 1937, after MORT had closed and its German-language enterprises come under suspicion. There he directed Swedish amateur actors in several performances of *Señora Carrar's Rifles* and helped set up the Stockholm 'Freie Bühne' with the support of Hermann Greid and the Austrian Socialist Bruno Kreisky. Trepte was later a well-known actor in the GDR.

404 To H. Peter Matthis   April-May 1940
Elmer Diktonius. A Finnish-Swedish poet of Brecht's generation, sometimes called 'the Finnish Horace'. The Brechts had spent their first week at a Helsinki hotel, then took a flat in the Tölö district for a month. Berlau had remained in Denmark.

Ossian Eklund had played in Brecht's one-acter *How Much is your Iron?* in Stockholm.

Hjalmar Gullberg. A Swedish poet.

405, 406, To Hans Tombrock   May 1940
Tombrock made etchings incorporating all three poems. Two are reproduced in the catalogue mentioned in Note 399, and show the artist himself. The texts of the poems are also in *GW 9*, pp. 753–4.

*407 To Tombrock   May 1940
Thanking for letters and photographs of T's work. Suggests T. should try seeing landscapes from the air and study photos taken from above.

408 To Piscator   17 May 1940
'Your school': the New School, New York, of which Piscator's new Dramatic
Workshop formed part. The invitation came by telegram on 17 April, a
confirmatory letter is dated 2 May.

409 To Piscator   27 May 1940
Grete is of course Steffin.

*410 To Alvin S. Johnson   June 1940
A letter of thanks to the director of the New School.

411 To Arnold Ljungdal   June 1940
Ljungdal, a good friend of the refugees from Hitler, was a Swedish critic and
librarian. The Norwegian Arctic port of Petsamo was now controlled by the
Germans.

Just the essay on Brecht's poems in *Hochland* (Munich), 29, no. 5 (February 1932)
was by Karl Thieme, who headed it 'The Devil's Prayer Book'.

Some seven or eight years later Brecht would be using the *Novum Organum* as a
formal model for his own principal theoretical work.

*412, *413 To Tombrock   June 1940
Encouraging letters, commenting on his etchings and his first oil painting.

414 To Tombrock   ?Mid-1940
Tombrock had made a series of eight chalk drawings based on *Fear and Misery of
the Third Reich*. The painting showed 'The Osseg Widows' of Brecht's 1934
'Ballade von den Osseger Witwen' from the *Svendborg Poems* (*GW* 9, pp. 643–4).

415 To the American Guild for German Cultural Freedom   1 Aug. 1940
Mother Courage: though none of these productions took place, the Zurich
Schauspielhaus would stage the world première the following spring.

The satirical novel may have been the *Flüchtlingsgespräche* dialogues, which
Brecht originally thought of writing in novel form.

Feuchtwanger was then in French internment at Les Milles near Aix-en-
Provence. He and his wife got away that summer and, with the Heinrich Manns
and the Werfels, crossed the Pyrenees, reached Lisbon and took ship for the
United States. Brecht's diary for 27 August records hearing of their safe arrival
in Lisbon.

*415x To Lion Feuchtwanger   6 Nov. 1940
Dated 6 November 1940. Brecht is enormously relieved to hear that F. got
away. They are trying to go to the US: can F. help, via Dorothy Thompson and
Ernestine Evans? Margarete Steffin is not on the waiting list for an immigrant
visa, so can he mention her too?

This was accompanied (or maybe followed) by a letter to Feuchtwanger from
Elisabeth Hauptmann in Hollywood to say that Brecht needs affidavits, for
which Clifford Odets and Fritz Lang are to be approached.

Feuchtwanger replied to Brecht from New York on 2 December, saying that
the Mexican consul in Helsinki has been instructed to give him a Mexican visa.
He himself says Brecht can make free use of Feuchtwanger's accounts in Russia,

both at the bank and with the State Publishing House. If there is trouble about
Brecht's (extended) family he must not hesitate to travel alone and hope to
extricate them later. A postscript adds that a 'money man' [evidently William
Dieterle] has offered to pay his travel costs via the official Emergency Rescue
Committee. (William Dieterle the Hollywood producer was the most influential
of all Brecht's US sponsors. He had been an actor in Max Reinhardt's Berlin
theatres in the 1920s.)

A subsequent letter to Feuchtwanger from Elisabeth Hauptmann (dated
Hollywood, 7 January 1941) suggests that objections have been raised by
Thomas Mann, one of the advisers to the Committee. She reminds F. how he
helped Brecht and her to pay their rent fifteen years earlier.

All printed in the Brecht Centre's *notate*, East Berlin 1984, no. 3, pp. 11–12.

*416 To Tombrock   End 1940
Welcoming his intention of paying a visit to Helsinki.

*417 Ditto   Winter 1940-1
The opening of this letter shows that Brecht was responding to the artist's
request for information about Galileo's character and appearance. Brecht's
answer is given in the notes to our edition of *Galileo*, pp. 119–20.

*418 Ditto   Winter 1940-1
Suggestions by Brecht for paintings satirising Hitler's regime.

419 To Hella Wuolijoki   Winter 1940-1
Hella Wuolijoki (see Note 402) had invited the Brechts to stay in an annex to
her country house at Marlebäck, and was reputedly not pleased at the idea of
Ruth Berlau coming too. In the event Berlau followed and is said to have
pitched a tent in the neighbourhood, though by her own account (in *Brechts Lai-
tu*, p. 129) she stayed in the main house.

The ballet was *The Seven Deadly Sins*, which was taken off at the king's request
after two performances. The production of *Saint Joan of the Stockyards* never took
place. The *Svendborg Poems* appeared under the imprint of the Malik-Verlag.

420 To Mikhail Y. Apletin   20 Nov. 1940
Apletin worked in the Foreign Relations department of the Union of Soviet
Writers, which effectively replaced the International Organisation of
Revolutionary Writers after its dissolution at the end of 1935. He was associated
there with Koltsov, and may well have had some previous contact with Brecht.

The State Publishing House, through its 'Chudozhestvennaya Literatura'
section, had published translations of the *Threepenny Novel* and *The Round Heads
and the Pointed Heads*. Since the closing of *Das Wort* the German edition of
Internationale Literatur, edited by Becher, had published 'The Heretic's Coat'
from the *Short Stories*, scene 6 of *Mother Courage*, and *The Trial of Lucullus*.

'The Augsburg Chalk Circle' (*Short Stories 1921–1946*, pp. 188–200) would
appear in its January 1941 issue.

About payments for the Andersen-Nexö translation see Letter 394.

*420x To Feuchtwanger   2 Dec. 1940
Cable of 2 December addressed to Hotel St Moritz, Central Park South, New
York, saying visa is 'at last attainable' if he can get a 'good' affidavit.

421 To the Kurt Reiss Agency   1 Feb. 1941
The Finn Simon Parmet had started writing music for the play's planned
première at the Helsinki Swedish theatre, which however was cancelled – in
deference, apparently, to the Germans. He composed three numbers and met
Brecht in Helsinki that winter to discuss orchestration (see diary entry for 2
February 1941). Hanns Eisler, who had set the 'Song of the Girl and the
Soldier' at least ten years before the play was written, never composed anything
specifically for it, though at one point it seems that he meant to. Eventually the
Zurich Schauspielhaus production – which the agency must have been in the
process of contracting for – used a new score by that theatre's regular composer
Paul Burkhard, and incorporated the Eisler song.

*421x To H. R. Hays   3 March 1941
Asking for an affidavit for the U S consulate in Helsinki.

*422 To Tombrock   March 1941
A short note on his *Galileo* drawings.

*423 Ditto   March 1941
Thanks for the *Galileo* etchings. Suggests a series on *Mother Courage*, for which
he himself would write 'a kind of novella'.

424 To Erwin Piscator   March-April 1941
Mr Johnson: Alvin Johnson, head of the New School.

*424x To Lion Feuchtwanger   8 April 1941
Dated 8 April 1941. Telling him that the family now have their Mexican visas,
that they are quite certain of getting their US immigration visas and hope that
Steffin will be given a tourist visa as the result of a cable of recommendation
from Dieterle. She still has to get Dieterle and Luise Rainer to certify that her
US expenses will be covered and that she will return to Europe. Brecht himself
will not wait for these matters but wants to leave at the first opportunity.
However, the routes via Petsamo and Japan are now barred, and travelling via
Baku, Basra and Bombay would involve sending all their passports to London
for the necessary transit visas. But they have been promised [not specified by
whom] that a route will be found, and are expecting to be away within a
fortnight. A postscript says he has worked quite well but they all look forward
to going: 'this continent had better be left to itself for a while'. (Printed in the
Brecht Centre's *notate*, East Berlin, May 1984, no. 3, p. 13.)

*424xx To Wetcheek [Feuchtwanger's old nom-de-plume]   April 1941
A cable to say Steffin's visa depends on Dieterle and Rainer cabling Washington
to the above effect. Washington must then cable Helsinki. (Reproduced in same
issue of *notate*.)

425 To Tombrock   April 1941
This must have been written between 15 April and 3 May, when the U S
consulate in Helsinki finally issued Brecht a quota immigration visa, with visas
for his family, followed on 12 May by the tourist visa for Steffin. Berlau, with
her valid Danish passport, was now going to travel as the sixth member of the
party.
    'Die Antwort' is not listed among Steffin's (mostly unpublished) writings in

volume 4 of the Brecht-Archive catalogue, (items 19729 to 19827). The *Morgenbrise* was presumably an émigré periodical in Sweden. For an account of Steffin, her work for Brecht and her own writings, see pp. 482–506 of *Kunst und Literatur im antifaschistischen Exil*, vol. 5, Reclam, Leipzig 1980.

426 To Hella Wuolijoki   April-May 1941
Last of Brecht's letters from Finland. His party left for Leningrad and Moscow on 16 May.

427 To Apletin   30 May 1941
Written on the last day of the Brechts' stay in Moscow, where they had been waiting for the steamer tickets to come through. Bernhard Reich saw them in the Metropol hotel, and they were also in touch with Maria Osten. Asya Lacis had been deported to Kazakhstan; according to Werner Mittenzwei, Reich himself had been temporarily released.

428 Ditto   30 May 1941
Given to Apletin at the station just before the departure of the Trans-Siberian express. Steffin had collapsed and been taken to a sanatorium under the Central Tuberculosis Institute. Brecht, according to his diary (entry for 13 July), had tried in vain to change the family's tickets and catch a later ship.

The elephants. Alluded to in 'The Nineteenth Sonnet' (*Poems 1913–1956*, p. 275) and the twenty-first sonnet (*GW 605*). They were small figures which Brecht used to send her from various cities. See Note 289xx.

429 Ditto   11 June 1941
Brecht and Steffin exchanged telegrams daily during the family's ten-day journey to the Far Eastern port of Vladivostok. On 4 June a telegram signed by Apletin and Alexander Fadeyev (then chairman of the Union of Soviet Writers) reported that she had died that morning. It was given to Brecht at Ulan Ude, just East of Lake Baikal. (See his *Arbeitsjournal* for 13 July, a summary which he wrote at sea.)

On 9 June Brecht telegraphed Apletin at VOKS (Society for Cultural Relations) to say the dollars had arrived but not the permission to export them. Comrade Lydia: unidentified, but presumably an aide of Apletin's.

430 To Hoffman R. Hays   July-Aug. 1941
Hays was a New York playwright, anthropologist and poet who had written *Ballad of Davy Crockett* for the Federal Theater and collaborated with Oscar Saul and Hanns Eisler on the *Medecine Show*, which Jules Dassin staged on Broadway on 12 April 1940. He translated a number of plays and poems by Brecht, starting with *Mother Courage* for the 1941 issue of *New Directions*, and worked with him in the US on the *Duchess of Malfi* project.

San Pedro is the harbour for Los Angeles, where the Brechts' ship had docked on 21 July. Elisabeth Hauptmann had rented the flat for them in Argyle Avenue, Westwood. After having taught for some years in schools in St Louis (where her married sister had lived since before 1933), she was then living on the East Coast with the exiled Social-Democratic lawyer Horst Bärensprung.

431 To Erwin Piscator   July-Aug. 1941
Resuming the correspondence from letters 408, 409 etc. The 'Shakespearian

scenes' written for Naima Wifstrand's acting class in Stockholm are in volume 6
of the Random House *Collected Plays* and will be in volume 5iii of the
Methuen edition. Piscator's only production in New York so far was the *King
Lear* with which his Dramatic Workshop had inaugurated its Studio Theater in
the New School.

432 To Karl Korsch   Aug. 1941
Pollock. The sociologist Friedrich Pollock was a leading member of the
Frankfurt Institute for Social Research who had settled in Los Angeles.

Korsch had told Brecht that he would be staying in Seattle with Hanna
Kosterlitz. His articles 'Prelude to Hitler' and 'The Fight for Britain' had been
published in *Living Marxism*. Thomas Mann and Hans Reichenbach were his
referees for a teaching job in Minneapolis. The writer Hans Langerhans had
been released from French internment.

433 Ditto   End Sep. 1941
Hans Reichenbach: a physicist, had been joint editor with Rudolf Carnap of the
pre-Nazi magazine *Erkenntnis*.

Herbert Marcuse and Max Horkheimer: old members of the Institute for Social
Research, like Pollock and Adorno.

'Film about Lourdes': presumably *The Song of Bernadette*, based on Franz Werfel's
novel about that shrine. It sold over 400,000 copies in the US by October 1942.

For Döblin see Note 367. MGM engaged him as a script writer, but let him go
after a year. He remained in California as a freelance writer. Leonhard Frank's
very successful book of World War I stories was called *Der Mensch ist gut* – Man
is Good.

Ludwig Ganghofer was a widely read German popular novelist of
Victorian/Edwardian times much despised by Brecht.

434 To Piscator   Aug.-Sep. 1941
Archibald MacLeish had been one of the playwrights considered by Brecht for
his 'Diderot Society' plan of 1937.

John LaTouche had met Brecht in 1935. He was one of the lyric writers for the
Federal Theater's most ambitious production, *Sing for Your Supper*, which
opened at the Adelphi Theatre, New York in March 1939. His 'The Ballad of
Uncle Sam' to music by Earl Robinson was later renamed 'Ballad for Americans'
and became widely known.

Hays made a translation of *Arturo Ui* for Piscator (now in the Brecht Archive),
but the project never got further, thanks to the withdrawal of its potential CIO
union backers. LaTouche was said to be keen to translate *The Good Person of
Szechwan*, but seems not to have started work on it.

This letter is dated after the Brechts' move out to Santa Monica, a pleasant
coastal suburb of Los Angeles where they lived initially in a small house on 25th
Street. Ruth Berlau lodged nearby.

435 Ditto   Sep. 1941
Oskar Homolka, who had worked with Brecht in the 1920s on *Edward II* and
the Berlin *Baal*, emigrated at first to England, then to Hollywood.

Christopher Lazar. There is no record of his having translated anything by
Brecht.

*435x To Kurt Weill   nd
An undated letter from 817 25th Street to report arrival and intention to stay for
some months. Did Weill receive the copy of *The Good Person of Szechwan* from
Finland? Any prospects for *The Threepenny Opera*? B. would like to do it with
Negro actors, whom he thinks better suited to that work than 'Americans'.

436 To Karl Korsch   23 Oct. 1941
The illegible conclusion is not more than a line long.

437 Ditto   Early Nov. 1941
Brecht here uses the term 'soviet' in its proper sense to mean the committees or
councils that made the 1917 revolution, *not* (as in current 'Western' usage) a
citizen of the USSR.

   Marcuse: besides Herbert, the philosopher, who is here referred to, there was
also Ludwig the journalist and biographer (1894–1971), who had emigrated to
Los Angeles in 1938 and become a professor at the University of Southern
California; he was not connected with the Frankfurt Institute. Brecht knew
them both.

438 To Berthold Viertel   Autumn 1941
Viertel (1885–1953) was the Viennese theatre and film director who figures
under the name 'Bergmann' in Isherwood's short novel *Prater Violet*. He was
also a fine but not very productive poet. Though his career in the German-
language theatre began before the First World War, his best-known achievement
was probably his organisation and direction of a Berlin company called 'Die
Truppe' in 1923–24 (when Brecht's impresario Aufricht was one of his actors).
He was in Hollywood between 1928 and 1931, and finally emigrated to the US
in 1939, when he at first settled in New York. His former wife Salka, a script
writer for Greta Garbo, lived in Santa Monica and knew both Isherwood and
Brecht.

   Ui: following Piscator's idea of an off-Broadway production to be sponsored by
the unions, Viertel had evidently proposed staging the play with the Dramatic
Workshop.

   The 'ballad' was evidently 'The Children's Crusade' (*Poems 1913–1956*, pp. 368–
73, in Hays's translation). Hedda Korsch made a first translation in November
1941, and another by Alfred Kreymborg followed.

   A book of Viertel's poems was published by Barthold Fles, New York, during
that year under the title *Fürchte dich nicht*. 'Captatio benevolentiae' means in
effect an appeal for indulgence; 'inter exilem silent musae' is a quasi-Ciceronian
phrase for 'in times of exile the muses are silent'.

439 To Archibald MacLeish   9 Dec. 1941
James Lyon suggests that Brecht may have met MacLeish in December 1935,
when the latter took part in a debate on 'Poetry and Music in the Labor Theater'
organised by Theatre Union in support of their *Mother* production. He had been
appointed by Roosevelt to the Library of Congress, where he got posts for such
exiled writers as Thomas Mann and Kurt Pinthus. There was however no reply
to Brecht's letter.

*439x To H. R. Hays   ? Jan. 1941
For Hays see Note 430. In his essay 'The Story of Selected Poems' (Brecht: *Poems*

1913–1956 p. 517) he reports receiving this letter in January 1942 in response to one or more letters of complaint to Brecht. He cites it as follows:

> I don't quite know how to explain why I have not written you long before this, expatriation, the loss of my closest collaborator, the unaccustomed windlessness and isolation from world affairs that I have fallen into here, all this cripples me to such a degree that actually in 6 months I have only written a couple of letters to Hauptmann, Eisler and Piscator, and not more than 2 or 3 poems. I don't even get around to thanking those who helped me to get here, which lies heavily upon my conscience. I don't know whether you can pardon my neglect of you, no matter how much I should like you to. Unfortunately I must in this case once more beg you to help me, that is, now work out some kind of system for our collaboration, which for me is extraordinarily important. You have done so much for me. We must go through everything. Can you clarify this complex of questions for me? I know this is asking a lot but I do hope that you will not consider my peculiar behaviour as mere ingratitude and temperament. Please, write soon about what I should do.

*439xx To Weill   ? Feb. 1942
Apologising for delay in writing. Clarence Muse, who was planning to start a National Negro Theatre with the help of Paul Robeson, has made an adaptation of *The Threepenny Opera*, set in Washington during a presidential Inauguration. Muse wants to launch it in Los Angeles with Katharine Dunham as Polly, and to rearrange Weill's music. He will send Brecht a contract relating only to Negro theatres.

A handwritten postscript thanks Weill for the money he had sent (evidently to help the Brechts leave Finland) and blames his failure to thank him earlier on the confusion and the last illness of Steffin.

440 To Sam Bernstein   March 1942
Bernstein, a Los Angeles tailor, saw Brecht with Alexander Granach at the Soto Jewish Center in that city around New Year, 1942, when a poet was performing Yiddish versions of two recent Brecht poems. He was moved to send Brecht his own wedding suit: an incident mentioned in the poem 'Überall Freunde' (*GW 10*, p. 844).

*440a To Manfred George   March 1942
Sending Letter 441 for publication in the New York magazine *Aufbau*.

*441 To Karin Michaelis   March 1942
An open letter of good wishes for her 70th birthday.

*441x To Kurt Weill   Early March 1942
Has heard of Weill's telegraphed objections to the *Threepenny Opera* project (Note *439xx above) and repeats his own enthusiasm for it. If it fails, it will never get to New York; if it succeeds, then why should it not run there as well as any other production? Brecht is doing no proper work, and this could make all the difference to his US prospects.

A handwritten postscript says he is enclosing a song for broadcasting to Germany which he hopes W. may compose for Lenya. (This must have been 'And what did the mail bring the soldier's wife?', later included in *Schweik*.)

This letter evidently crossed Weill's (of 9 March), which says that W. has been discussing an American adaptation of *The Threepenny Opera* with Hecht (a great friend) and MacArthur, which would be a far better prospect for Brecht. No successful New York show has ever been launched from California; he himself worked on a scheme for a black TPO some years back; and he is sure that Muse's production would set back the Hecht/MacArthur scheme by ten years.

On 13 March Weill wrote a friendly answer to Brecht, thanking him for the song and saying he would set it. About the TPO: they did not, he suggested, want any repetition of what had happened in New York in 1933 (where the work had failed dismally) or more recently in Paris. So he himself must check the translation, particularly of the songs, and then, after speaking to Robeson, he would discuss matters with a producer who knew Robeson and had long admired the work. Meanwhile Muse must be patient.

*441xx To Kurt Weill   16 March 1942
A note forwarding another song to go with 'And what did the mail bring the soldier's wife', written with Lenya's unforgettable performance of 'Nanna's Song' in mind. (It may have been 'Deutschland' – *GW 8*, p. 843.)

*441xxx To Kurt Weill   28 March 1942
Dated 28.3.42. To say that what he has seen of Muse's version is original and understandable, quick but relaxed. The company are reading all kinds of duplicity and prejudice into Weill's reservations, and are already thinking of adapting the *Beggar's Opera* instead. Can he cable to put them at ease?

After hearing also from Muse, Weill replied on 7 April to Brecht in English (for Muse's benefit) to say that he would let his music be used for performance in California only, on the basis of a Dramatists' Guild contract to be negotiated through his agents, and for at least 3.33% of the gross box-office receipts. But the music publisher will insist on seeing the 'lyrics' first, and it seems odd that Brecht won't send any samples of the translation.

He is being amenable because of Brecht's high expectations and the genuine enthusiasm shown by Muse.

*441xxxx To Kurt Weill   20 April 1942
To clear Weill's mind of any suspicion that B. had embarked on the whole plan with Muse before ever consulting Weill. In fact Muse had heard about the play, and came to see Brecht about it, who let him see a rough translation made back in Berlin. This Muse began adapting in a way that impressed Brecht, though he refused to let Brecht keep the specimen song translation as he was not yet satisfied with it. Robeson saw the material and offered to put up the money, upon which Brecht told Muse that he would first need Weill's agreement. There had been no collaboration and no promise of a contract, and he had found it impossible to get the material as W. had asked. But B. would like to resume his own collaboration with Weill and to write off all past misunderstandings and half-quarrels. So far he has lost none of his friends.

Weill replied on 26 April, saying that he was glad of Brecht's explanation, keen to avoid misunderstandings and hoping for a chance to collaborate once more. But the contract submitted by Muse takes no account of his expressed conditions or the rules of the Dramatists' Guild, guarantees nothing and offers himself and

Brecht 4% between them – calculated, however, not on the takings but on the adaptor's royalty of 5% – and amounting in other words to about one twentieth of W's stipulated minimum. This is just impossible.

442 To Viertel   May–June 1942
In New York Viertel had held a staged reading (in German) at the Fraternal Clubhouse of four scenes from *Fear and Misery of the Third Reich* for the 'Tribüne' German-Austrian writers' group on 28 May 1942. A fifth ('The Box') was added in a repeat performance on 14 June. This group led by Friedrich George Alexan is said to have organised thirty such events between 1941 and 1945.

For Brecht's discussion with Reinhardt and his conception of the 'Private Life' version of the play, with the soldiers in an armoured troop-carrier, see the *Arbeitsjournal* entry for 20 May. Eisler only wrote his music for it three years later.

The concluding epigram, written evidently in gratitude, is in *Poems 1913–1956*, p. 383.

443 To Max Reinhardt   End May 1942
The great Reinhardt, for whom Brecht had worked briefly as a trainee director in 1924–25, lost his Berlin theatres when Hitler came to power, then had to leave Salzburg and Vienna too on their annexation by Germany in 1938.

Despite his successful tours in the US before that date, and his direction of the 1935 Warner Brothers *Midsummer Night's Dream* film in Hollywood, once he arrived there as an exile he tended to be treated as commercially unacceptable by the American screen and stage. Even the acting school which he established in Hollywood was never a success. He would die in New York aged seventy on 31 October 1943, some eighteen months before Brecht's play had its English-language première there, with Viertel again as its director.

444 To Ruth Berlau   May–June 1942
Early in May 1942 Berlau went off to Washington to speak at a women's congress (so she later called it, though Klaus Völker speaks rather of a meeting of Danish emigrés). Once there she made contact with the Danish embassy and decided to accept the offer of a job in the Office of War Information (OWI) in New York, broadcasting to Denmark.

Fear and Misery: Brecht wanted her to report on the second New York reading on 14 June.

445 Ditto   May–June 1942
Ben Huebsch was the head of Viking Press in New York.

The 'parachute scene': in *The White Silk Heaven*, one of Berlau's radio plays.

Any Animal Can Do It: the title of a Danish book of stories (Copenhagen 1940) which she had written under the name Maria Sten.

'Freedom Song': presumably needed by the OWI.

What a Nazi heard: nothing known. Brecht had started working with Lang on the film *Hangmen Also Die*.

Lilli Laté: Lang's secretary.

446 Ditto   June 1942

According to Hans-Joachim Bunge, her editor and quasi-biographer, Berlau
had found the ambiguities of her relationship with Brecht unbearable and
intended from the first to remain in the East. She shared a third-floor flat with a
woman OWI colleague at 124 57th Street.

447 To Heinrich Mann   July 1942

Long respected by the German Left, Heinrich Mann was Thomas's elder
brother. Both were among the Hollywood exiles.

448 To Karl Korsch   Oct. 1942

Non-intervention was the policy of the Chamberlain government during the
Spanish Civil War.

   Langerhans's book. He had written a little-known *Sociology of the Concentration
Camp*, which may be what is referred to.

   Weil: Felix Weil, chief patron of the Frankfurt Institute for Social Research.

   This is the first of the published letters to be dated from the larger and more
agreeable house into which the Brechts moved on 12 August 1942. It is
briefly described in the *Arbeitsjournal* for that day.

449 Ditto   Late 1942

Korsch had sent Brecht a copy of the English edition of his book on Marx, the
American edition having gone out of print.

450 To Ruth Berlau   26 May 1943

Isa Bachmann was Berlau's flatmate and OWI superior. When Brecht arrived
on his first New York visit on 12 February 1943 she tactfully went to stay with a
friend. He remained for some three months. This letter was posted on the
journey back.

   Budzislawski: the journalist Hermann Budzislawski took over the editorship of
Die neue Weltbühne in Prague in 1934 and held it for five years till the paper
closed in Paris on the outbreak of war. He was interned by the French but
managed to escape to New York in 1940. There he became secretary to Dorothy
Thompson (see her article 'How I was duped by a communist' in the *Saturday
Evening Post*, 1949), took part with Brecht and others in setting up a Council for
a Democratic Germany in 1944 and, according to James Lyon, coached Brecht
for his Un-American Activities Committee hearing in 1947.

451 Ditto   3 June 1943

Simone: the main work with Feuchtwanger on their play *The Visions of Simone
Machard* had been completed before Brecht went to New York. In May Eisler
started writing the music.

   Aufricht had reached New York from Spain in June 1941, after having spent
the first year of the war in French internment. He ran a radio programme called
'We Fight Back' for the OSS, with distinguished émigré speakers (including
Weill) and a play series *The Schulzes in Yorkville* by P. M. Lampel. He proposed
to Brecht and Weill that they make a Schweik musical, and by the end of May
Brecht had begun writing the text. For the events leading to its collapse see the
introduction to *Schweik in the Second World War* in volume 7i of the Methuen
edition. There seems to be no trace of the records which Aufricht apparently
made of Lenya's songs.

452, 453 Ditto   4 June 1943
Paul Dessau had come to the US as a music teacher in 1939, and impressed
Brecht by his setting and impromptu performance of a song from *Saint Joan of
the Stockyards* at one of the 'Brecht evenings' held during the poet's New York
visit.

'Song of a German Mother' was sung by Lenya for an OWI broadcast which
Brecht says (*Arbeitsjournal* entry for March–May 1943) was 'sabotaged by the
German desk'.

'Germany' was a setting of 'O Germany, pale mother' (*Poems 1913–1956*,
pp. 218–220). Dessau moved to California that autumn.

Malfi: commissioned by Elisabeth Bergner. Brecht and Hays (see Notes 430,
434) worked on the adaptation during the former's New York visit, and a first
script was completed and copyrighted during 1943. It can be found in vol. 7 of
the Methuen edition.

Peter Lorre had been recommended to Aufricht by Brecht around 1928/29 as a
promising actor, and played in *Happy End*, the 1931 *Man equals Man* and
Marieluise Fleisser's *Manoeuvres in Ingolstadt*. His reputation as a film actor was
made however as the murderer in Fritz Lang's *M*, and although he never
reached the same peak again he was in steady demand in Hollywood. Brecht
envisaged him as Schweik and visited him some weeks later (see Letter 458)
with a film project called *Crouching Venus*. (This is presumably the story about a
museum curator in Marseilles, which is not in the collected *Texte für Filme*.)

454 Ditto   11, 16 June 1943
'The story': see volume 7 in the Methuen edition, pp. 279–288. This preliminary
outline was datelined 'New City, May 1943' when Brecht stayed there for a
week as the Weills' guest.

Hella Wuolijoki (see Notes 402, 419) was arrested in 1942, during Finland's
wartime alliance with the Nazis, when she helped a parachuted Soviet agent,
daughter of an old friend.

Teivola: not known, a Finnish name.

Wolfgang Roth, not a tall man, had worked in pre-Hitler Berlin on the staging
of *Die Massnahme* and the Piscator §*218*, then emigrated to Zurich and thence to
New York, where he would die in 1989.

455 To Kurt Weill   c. 23 June 1943
Szechwan: Brecht's outline story, evidently made for Weill, is in volume 6i of
the Methuen edition, pp. 121–6. For the 'Santa Monica 1943' version which
followed it, see ibid. pp. 132–47. This project too collapsed or was indefinitely
postponed, though it appears that Weill never entirely lost interest.

Lenya's French recording: Decca issued a record of six Weill songs in 1943,
sung by Lenya and including 'Complainte de la Seine', text by Maurice Magre.
It was on the basis of this that Brecht wrote the 'Song of the Moldau' in *Schweik*,
which was eventually set by Eisler.

456 To Berlau   23 June 1943
Winge: Hans (John) Winge, an Austrian script writer then working in
Hollywood. After 1945 he would work for Wien-Film in Vienna.

The lawyer: Weill's New York lawyers were Maurice J. and Herbert A. Speiser.

457 Ditto   30 June 1943

Alfred Kreymborg was an American left-wing writer and contributor to the 30s
magazine *New Theatre*, whose play *America America* had attracted attention
before World War 2. The contract for him to translate *Schweik in the Second
World War* was signed on 12 August.

Piscator. Nothing is known about the 'revue' scheme. But Brecht and he had
been discussing a revival (by the Theater Guild) of their 1928 *Schweik* adaptation,
which Piscator asked Kreymborg to translate. It seems that Brecht showed him
the new version, which he hoped Piscator would stage, and the latter certainly
wrote (undated) comments on it. So it came as a nasty shock when Piscator
learned from Kreymborg that not only his translator but also the rights had
been captured from under his nose by his old rival Aufricht, and that the
intention was now to engage an American director. The ensuing confusion was
probably one of Weill's reasons for abandoning the project.

*457x Ditto   2 July 1943

458 Ditto   3 July 1943

The visit to Lorre: see Note 452. The 'man' was the producer Ernest Pascal.
Nothing is known about the 'women's rights' film story. The funny picture
seems to have been of Berlau setting out to cycle from Copenhagen to Moscow
and back in 1930. (There is one on p. 30 of Hans Bunge's book, but it shows her
in a skirt and not smoking.)

459 Ditto   5 July 1943

460 To Weill   c. 9 July 1943

The 'American edition' of Hašek's *Schweik* novel used Paul Selver's (shortened
and bowdlerised) translation which had appeared in England.

Schiffbauerdamm: the reference to Aufricht's old Berlin theatre, where *The
Threepenny Opera*, *Happy End* and *Manoeuvres in Ingolstadt* were all performed
before 1933, shows Brecht's continued identification with it.

461 To Berlau   July 1943

Enclosed with 457x as 'possibly to be shown to Aufricht'.

Kurt Robitschek ran the Kabarett der Komiker in pre-Hitler Berlin.

'Translation of the novel': contrast with Brecht's view in Letter 461. In fact
Selver knew Czech and Brecht did not. On the language of the play see pp. 292–
3 of volume 7 in the Methuen edition.

462 Ditto   19 July 1943

463 Ditto   9 July 1943

'Staging': presumably the note appended to the play and printed on p. 289 of
volume 7 in the Methuen edition.

464 Ditto   23 July 1943

Laurin has not been identified.

Bartók was then living in New York. One of his *Five Slovak Folksongs for Male
Chorus* was reputedly made use of by Brecht in *The Caucasian Chalk Circle*.

Bergner's première: Presumably an opening date for *The Duchess of Malfi*, which
he was hoping to direct. Paul Czinner was Elisabeth Bergner's husband.

465 Ditto   12 Aug. 1943
The lawyer: the Hašek rights were with Dr Jan Löwenbach, formerly of
Prague, from whom Aufricht obtained them.

   Grosz: there is no mention of any San Francisco show either in Hans Hess's
monograph or in the artist's own letters.

466 Ditto   16 Aug. 1943
Hans Viertel was a son of Berthold and Salka Viertel, and helped Brecht with
English translations. Paul Tillich, a Protestant theologian (and friend of Auden),
was one of the group working to set up a US equivalent to the Moscow Free
German Committee founded under KPD leadership and the presidency of
Erich Weinert in the summer of 1943. Brecht took part in preliminary talks in
California and in the work of the ensuing Council for a Democratic Germany.
The former were supported by Thomas Mann, the latter not.

467 Ditto   31 Aug. 1943
This letter appears to have been mis-dated, since the Brechts moved into their
26th Street house in 1942, not 1943. The sentiments expressed were still valid a
year later.

468 Ditto   7 Sep. 1943
Karin = Karin Michaelis, one of the most prolific and successful Danish writers,
who had lodged the Brechts when they first came to Denmark as refugees. She
had arrived by 28 October.

   Elisabeth (Liesel) Neumann was a Viennese actress who took part in various
New York émigré productions, including the 1945 *Private Life of the Master
Race*. She became Berthold Viertel's second wife.

469 Ditto   14 Sep. 1943

470 To Alfred Kreymborg   mid-Sep. 1943
Probably not sent. Brecht got the translation on 4 September.

471 Ditto   Sep. 1943
Doubtless sent in lieu of Letter 470.

472 To Berlau   18 Sep. 1943
Kreymborg's translation of 'Children's Crusade' is in the Brecht Archive. *Poems
1913–1956* uses the Hays version from *Selected Poems*, which is more accurate.

   Mostel: Zero Mostel, an outstanding New York comic actor.

   French: Samuel French, theatrical publishers and agents.

473 Ditto   Sep. 1943

474 Ditto   25 Sep. 1943
Gorelik: Max Gorelik the designer, author of *New Theatres for Old*, (see Note
293), was living in California.

475 Ditto   27 Sep. 1943

476 Ditto   17 Sep. 1943
Brecht arrived in New York again on 19 November for a four-month visit, and
once more settled in Berlau's 57th Street apartment.

*476x To Weill   ?
An undated note from 124 East 57th Street to say B. will confirm in the next

few days whether 'we' have the *Schweik* rights from the Czechs (i.e. from Hašek's heirs). Zero Mostel will be away for two months. Has Weill written to (Ben) Hecht? Can they sign an agreement for *Szechwan* so that B. can get a rough translation made, probably by Hans Viertel?

Weill was still in Los Angeles at the Twentieth Century-Fox studios, whence he wrote on 30 January to say that an announcement by Leo Kerz had put potential helpers like Moss Hart off the *Szechwan* project. A letter from Brecht (not located) had denied any involvement with Kerz (recipient of Letter 491 some months later), and Weill and his lawyer were working out a scheme which would help B. financially and keep the project warm. (Brecht's note therefore may have been written between November and the New Year.)

477 To Thomas Mann   1 Dec. 1943

Mann and his brother Heinrich had taken part with Brecht, Viertel, Feuchtwanger, Ludwig Marcuse, the physicist Reichenbach and the writer Bruno Frank in a meeting at the Viertels' house on 1 August and drawn up a short declaration differentiating between the Nazi regime and the German people. The next day Mann withdrew his signature in order not to embarrass the Allies. Later Brecht heard that he had been saying that 'left-wingers like Brecht were acting on orders from Moscow to get him [Mann] to declare that a distinction should be made between Hitler and Germany' (*Arbeitsjournal* entry for 7 September 1943). It remains unclear what meeting (presumably in New York) Brecht is here referring to.

Mann replied on 10 December citing a speech at Columbia University where he had adduced some of the same arguments as Brecht while arguing that the organisation of a common German movement against Hitler would be seen as an attempt to shield Germany from the consequences of Hitler's crimes.

It was only when Brecht returned to Germany that he realised how far the supposed working-class resistance to Hitler was wishful thinking. The figures quoted by him appear to be myth.

478 To W. H. Auden   Early Dec. 1943

Written in English, probably Brecht's own, with corrections in a strange hand.

According to H. R. Hays, when work was resumed on the Malfi project Paul Czinner announced that it now needed a 'British' poet, and named Auden. Hays thereupon withdrew. Brecht's letter, it will be noticed, makes no mention of Hays's substantial contribution; nor does the account given in Elisabeth Bergner's memoirs.

479 To Ferdinand Reyher   Early Feb. 1944

For Reyher see Notes 135, 373. Brecht had been seeing him in California, e.g. at Christmas 1942. It seems that he did not like *Schweik in the Second World War* and made no attempt to translate it. His US story has not been identified.

480 To Heinrich Mann   13 March 1943

The telegraphic answer on 17 March was 'Agreed'. The Council was launched on 2 May. For its inaugural statement published the following day, together with the names of many supporters and American well-wishers, see *Exil in den USA*, vol. 3 (1983) in the Reclam *Kunst und Literatur im antifaschistischen Exil* series, pp. 637–44. Among the supporters were Elisabeth Bergner, the former head of the Marxist Workers' School Hermann Duncker, Homolka, Kortner, the anthropologist Julius Lips, Lorre, Piscator, Fritz Sternberg, Jakob Walcher and Otto Zoff; among the well-wishers Ben Huebsch, Alvin Johnson of the New School, the theologian Reinhold Niebuhr and Dorothy Thompson.

Hermann Budzislawski (see Note 450) and Elisabeth Hauptmann worked in the secretariat.

This was after Brecht's return to Santa Monica on 22 March.

481 To Karl Korsch End March 1944
UCLA: the Los Angeles campus of the University of California.

'Hollywood lottery': MGM had contracted to film *Simone Machard*, or more precisely the novel which Feuchtwanger had based on it. Brecht's share (which may have included Ruth Berlau's) was $20,000. The film was never made.

Chalk Circle: this had been commissioned for Luise Rainer by a backer called Jules Leventhal during Brecht's stay in New York. It was originally to be based on Klabund's *Chalk Circle* play.

'Ludwigs, Vansittarts and Ehrenburgs': During the Second World War Emil Ludwig in the USA, Lord Vansittart in the U K and Ilya Ehrenburg in the USSR were particularly sweeping in their condemnation of the German people as a whole.

AMG = Allied Military Government, as at first instituted in former enemy countries.

482 To Paul Tillich April 1944
Bassermann: Albert Bassermann, holder of the Iffland Ring as the finest German actor of his time (until he laid it on Moissi's coffin in 1935, allegedly in order to stop it going to a Nazi), had emigrated on account of his Jewish wife, but had difficulty in finding adequate parts.

483 To Berlau 2 April 1944
Laughton. Brecht had met the great English actor at a party at Salka Viertel's soon after his return from New York.

484 Ditto 5 April 1944
Wieland Herzfelde, who had been running a stamp dealer's shop in New York, had started a new publishing business at the end of 1943 in succession to the Malik-Verlag. This was called Aurora and was jointly sponsored by Brecht, Viertel, Oskar Maria Graf, Döblin, Feuchtwanger, Heinrich Mann, the Marxist philosopher Ernst Bloch, the playwright Ferdinand Bruckner (who taught in Piscator's school), the Austrian poet Ernst Waldinger and the Czech-German Communist writer F. C. Weiskopf. Weiskopf's contribution *Die Unbesiegbaren* was a selection of reports on episodes from Nazi Germany. Herzfelde's list also included the first publication of Brecht's *Furcht und Elend*, Anna Seghers's *Ausflug der toten Mädchen* (one of her finest stories) and another book of Viertel's poems.

The 'new scenes' were from scene 3 ('The Flight into the Northern Mountains') of *The Caucasian Chalk Circle*.

485 Ditto 18 April 1944
The references are again to scene 3, pp. 176–7 in the Methuen edition. But

Bergner's 'last page' refers to the *Duchess of Malfi* script. The *Threepenny* translator was Elinor Rice, who had contracted on 19 February to translate that work.

'Your translation' of *Schweik* must be that by Kreymborg, with amendments by Berlau; she kept a script, of which photocopies are in the Brecht Archive. There was then no other complete American version.

'Poem about the Germans': may refer to 'To the German soldiers in the East' (*Poems 1913–1956*, pp. 373–7, written on 9 January 1942).

486 Ditto   20 April 1944
'Pasting up'. There are some fifteen such reproductions in the Brecht Archive. The early scripts too are prefaced by Brueghel's *Dulle Griet*, the scrawny woman striding through a warlike landscape.

'Epic singing': Eisler thought this an impossible aim. Eventually Dessau would compose the music.

The *Galileo* business. In New York Brecht had talked to Jed Harris, producer of Wilder's *Our Town*, who was interested in the idea of staging the play. This was before Laughton's involvement.

487 Ditto   30 April 1944
Karin = Michaelis, then a lady of seventy-four.

488 Ditto   2 May 1944

489 Ditto   7–8 June 1944
Memphis Belle: A film by William Wyler, made in 1944.

'The landings' were those of the Anglo-American-Canadian armies in Normandy. See *Arbeitsjournal* entry for 6 June 1944.

Leventhal: see Note 481. The 'rough translation' was done by Auden's friends the Sterns, who in the event did most of the final translation too, leaving Auden to translate the verse. For Isherwood's prior refusal see Brecht's *Arbeitsjournal* entry for 17 May. See also the chapter 'The Case of Auden' in *Brecht on Context*.

*489x Ditto   Sep. 1944
A note to her at the Cedars of Lebanon Hospital in Los Angeles, where she gave premature birth to Brecht's short-lived child Michel on 3 September 1944. Cited by Lyon, p. 224. See also her own *Brechts Lai-tu*, pp. 200–201. She subsequently stayed in the Viertels' house.

490 To James Stern   13 Dec. 1944
The telegraphic answer from French reads: 'mailing today copy rough translation brecht play. also we are now in process of drawing contract with auden for a finished version. regards samuel french.'

491 To Leo Kerz   Jan 1944
Kerz was a German designer and director who had reputedly had some contacts with both Brecht and Piscator before 1933. According to Bruce Medford's article in *Gestus*, Dover, vol. II no. 4, pp. 257–64, he was active in South Africa, where he worked with the Bantu People's theatre of Johannesburg and staged *The Threepenny Opera* at the Pioneer Theatre in what appears to have been the Vesey/Isherwood translation. He came to the New School to join Piscator in 1942, and made designs for the latter's frustrated *Schweik* project for the Theater Guild (see Note 457). Early in 1944 he had told Weill that he wished to produce

The Good Person of Szechwan – not clear which version – in New York. Nothing came of this scheme, but in 1959 he set up a production company which had a certain success with an Ionesco musical on Broadway in 1961, though its Brecht plans remained unfulfilled. Kerz designed the Piscator production of *The Private Life of the Master Race* in 1945, and in 1962 would work with him in West Berlin on Hochhuth's *Der Stellvertreter*. He died in 1976.

492 To W. H. Auden   Jan. 1945
Written in English.

493 To Korsch   Feb. 1945
Stefan Brecht had been called up by the US Army on 26 September. The 'little enclosure' appears to have consisted of some poems drawn from the *Kriegsfibel* wartime 'photoepigrams' (of which Brecht had written sixty by 20 June according to his *Arbeitsjournal*) and the 'Studien' set of literary sonnets (of which those on Villon, Shakespeare, Dante, Lenz and Kant can be found in *Poems, 1913–1956*).

494 Ditto   March–April 1945
The project for a 'Didactic Poem on Human Nature' in Lucretian hexameters, with two cantos devoted to a versified version of Marx's *Communist Manifesto*, was never completed. No full English translation has yet appeared.

Central Points: Korsch's *Kernpunkte der materialistischen Geschichtsauffassung* was published (Berlin and Leipzig) in 1922.

'Engels's draft' was his *Grundsätze des Kommunismus*, of which Brecht had a photocopy at the end of his life.

495 To Berthold Viertel   Feb.-March 1945
Viertel's conception for the staging of this play is in his *Schriften zum Theater* (Henschel, East Berlin 1970, pp. 216–21). It was overtaken by Piscator's project.

'Elisabeth' = the actress Elisabeth Neumann (see Note 468).

496 Ditto   March 1945
Henry Morgenthau, a Democrat banker and close adviser of Roosevelt's, was the main proponent of a plan to eliminate German heavy industry after the imminent defeat of the Nazis, and to split the country into a number of small, primarily agrarian states.

497 To Naomi Replansky   March 1945
Replansky is a poet and New York social worker who became a friend of the Brechts in Santa Monica. The letter was a recommendation for a literary award, written in English. Some of her translations of Brecht poems can be found on pp. 55, 231, 275 and 381 of *Poems 1913–1956*. She also translated the *Kriegsfibel*.

'Volkslieder': Folk songs.

497x To H. R. Hays   March 1945
Dated March 1945 by Hays, who included it in his essay 'The Story of Selected Poems' for *Poems 1913–1956*.

498 To Berlau   March-April 1945
'Pokerfaced girl' (phrase in English). The poem is No. 67 of the *Kriegsfibel* epigrams (see Note 493) and accompanies a photograph of a grim- (rather than poker-) faced German girl seated with bulging rucksack and other baggage on the edge of a devastated street in Cologne. In the book she has no title.

Eric Bentley had got to know Viertel when he was directing scenes from *The Private Life* in 1942, and had been given a script to read. With some encouragement from Berlau he made a translation of this and gave it a staged reading at Black Mountain College. Hays, who had been commissioned to translate the play for a production at Piscator's Dramatic Workshop in spring 1943, then refused to go on. The plan for a Piscator production was resumed in spring 1945, with the results described in *Theatre of Erwin Piscator*, pp. 162–3 and the introduction to volume 4iii of the Methuen edition.

499 Ditto   March–April 1945
James Stern was assisted by his German-born wife Tania.

Elsa Lanchester was Mrs Laughton. The idea of her as Grusha is an interesting fantasy in view of her dislike of Brecht and resentment of his friendship with her husband, who was now working regularly with him on the translation and adaptation of *Life of Galileo*.

The present Auden-Stern translation of *The Caucasian Chalk Circle* (in volume 7 of the Methuen edition) is a revision made at the end of the 1950s. See *Brecht in Context*, pp. 66–9.

500 Ditto   April 1945
The poem was 'I, the survivor' (*Poems 1913–1956*, p. 392). Günter Glaeser's suggestion that it was written for Viertel's sixtieth birthday conflicts with Salka Viertel's recollection of finding it pushed under her door following a conversation about one's guilt at surviving.

Franklin D. Roosevelt, United States president in the New Deal and the Second World War, died on 12 April 1945 aged sixty-three.

The letter to Piscator has not survived but clearly refers to his *Private Life* project.

501 Ditto   April–May 1945
Rouben Mamoulian was a leading film and theatre director, as was Alfred Kazan.

Jan van Druten was the playwright who wrote *A Tree Grows in Brooklyn* – Brecht's reference here is to the film – and adapted Isherwood's Berlin stories to make *I Was a Camera* and ultimately *Cabaret*. Brecht appears to have considered these people in connection with *The Caucasian Chalk Circle*, for which a Broadway production was under contract.

Bentley's production rights. With reference to *The Private Life of the Master Race*. Henry Schnitzler, son of the playwright, was directing a student production at the Wheeler Auditorium, University of California Berkeley campus. This was to open on 7 June, five days before the New York production.

Elisabeth Hauptmann went over the translation with Bentley, who says that she wrote the last third of the 'Peat-bog soldiers' scene (scene 4 in the full *Fear and Misery* text).

Eduard Steuermann, a pianist of the Schönberg circle, was Salka Viertel's brother. He was the teacher of Alfred Brendel.

Gorelik play: briefly described in *Arbeitsjournal* entry for 2 April 1945.

502 To Piscator   2 June 1945
See Note 498. Brecht disagreed with Piscator's direction and with the new

framework which he had devised, and Viertel took over a fortnight before the opening. This was on 12 June at City College, New York, some five weeks after the German surrender had put an end to the war in Europe. The play had lost its topicality.

502a To Viertel ? July 1945

Ad calendas graecas = indefinitely.

'Parts to order': not clear which he is referring to. Albert Steinrück, who died in 1929, is not known to have performed in any Brecht play, though Brecht greatly admired him. Homolka was Mortimer in *Edward II* and Baal in the 1926 version of that play. Polly in *The Threepenny Opera* was intended for Carola Neher, who played her in the second cast and in the film.

Salzburg Festival. This was being revived under the auspices of the US Military Government. Under the Four-Power arrangements made in London, the US occupation zones of Germany (including all Bavaria) and of Austria (Upper Austria and Land Salzburg) were contiguous. Brecht's interest in the Festival can be seen to antedate his renewed collaboration with Caspar Neher.

The playwright Carl Zuckmayer was still in the US, running a goat farm in Vermont. Johanna Hofer was the actress wife of Fritz Kortner.

Liesel = Elisabeth Neumann, later Mrs Viertel. Viertel's article on Brecht appeared in *Austro-American Tribune*, New York, vol. 3 no. 12. His 'English article' was in the double issue of Dorothy Norman's *Twice a Year* for 1948. Called 'Bertold Brecht and Writing the Truth' it accompanied a translation of 'Writing the Truth: Five Difficulties' and five Brecht poems translated by Replansky.

503 To Berlau July 1945

After visiting Bergner and Czinner in Vermont to work on the *Duchess of Malfi* project, Brecht arrived back in Santa Monica on 18 July. (See *Arbeitsjournal* entry June to mid-July for a summary of his activities in the East.) The letter from Piscator, written on 15 June, is cited in *Brecht in Context*, p. 101.

Greisle: Felix Greisle, a member of Schönberg's family, worked for the Edward B. Marx Music Corporation in New York.

The 'sailor stories' may refer to those told in the bars in Nyhavn near Copenhagen, which Brecht and Berlau used to visit before the war.

504 Ditto July-Aug. 1945

Churchill's fall followed the General Election of 26 June. If the photographs were of the *Private Life* production they have not subsequently been seen.

By a contract of 18 April Reynal and Hitchcock had already accepted the bilingual *Selected Poems*, with translations by H. R. Hays, which they finally published in 1947; but their general project for a set of translations of the plays under Bentley's editorship came to nothing.

505 To Paul Tillich Aug. 1945

The Potsdam Agreement between Britain, the US and the USSR was signed on 2 August.

506 To Berlau Aug. 1945

Japan surrendered on 14 August, five days after the dropping of the second atomic bomb on Nagasaki.

The 'poem' is the didactic one 'on Human Nature'.

Leventhal's money must have been his advance on *The Caucasian Chalk Circle*.

'The people' met in Finland: presumably responsible Communists, whether German or Soviet we do not know.

507 Ditto   12 Sep. 1945

The scene is now Esterwegen camp. 'Dorothy's secretary' was Budzislawski (see Note 450). For the Council see Note 480.

508 Ditto   Sep.-Oct. 1945

The Threepenny Opera had of course not been performed in Germany since 1933. Brecht and Berlau now heard that an attempt to revive it in Berlin had been stopped by the Russians. Actually however it was performed at the Hebbel Theater (the former Theater in der Königgrätzer Strasse) on 15 August 1945 under Karlheinz Martin, an old socialist director, with his wife Roma Bahn in her original part as Polly.

Galileo was not performed in Germany at this time, though Herbert Jhering asked to see a script in his new capacity as head dramaturg of the Deutsches Theater.

A number of Brecht's unrealised film projects were conceived with Lorre in mind. (Two are cited in Note 519.) The publishers' contract will have been that with Reynal and Hitchcock in connection with the publication of the plays (see Note 504).

509 To Peter Suhrkamp   Oct. 1945

Suhrkamp, who had remained in Germany under Hitler, had been a progressive school teacher, then a dramaturg in Munich in the early 1920s, (when he first met Brecht), then an editor for the Ullstein magazine *Uhu*. He appears to have collaborated on the notes to *Lindbergh's Flight* in 1929–30. Under Hitler he became the head of the Samuel Fischer Verlag, whose Jewish founders and owners had been dispossessed. After the return of Gottfried Bermann-Fischer, who had run the exiled branch of the firm from Stockholm with such authors as Thomas Mann, Jakob Wassermann and Stefan Zweig, Suhrkamp started his own imprint for those authors who wished to remain with him, among these being Brecht.

Ernst Legal, who produced the 1931 *Man equals Man* when temporary Intendant of the Prussian State theatres, had also acted Galy Gay at Darmstadt in 1926. He could only find employment under the Nazis as an actor. He was now again Intendant of the State Opera in Berlin, which was temporarily housed in a revue theatre, the Admiralspalast.

Emil Hesse-Burri (see Note 117). He too had stayed in Germany and worked as a script writer in Munich.

Brecht's Augsburg friend Müllereisert was a doctor in Berlin.

Edward Hogan was part of the Berlin US military government.

APO = Army Post Office.

By 'parcels' Brecht means food parcels, which he and Weigel were sending to a number of old friends.

*509x To US Military Government, Berlin   14 Oct. 1945

On 14 October, objecting to any performances of his plays except under his own supervision. Lyon cites Edward Hogan's reply on 1 November, saying that *The Threepenny Opera* had caused no controversy and that Martin's theatre was 'the cleanest in Berlin' (politically speaking).

Lyon refers to a further exchange of letters during November–January, during which Brecht asked to be allowed to come and supervise. He was referred to the State Department.

*509xx To Karlheinz Martin   14 Oct. 1945
Same day, to the same effect. Mentioned by Lyon, p. 311.

510 To Donald Ogden Stewart   ? Autumn 1945
Stewart, winner of an Oscar for his script of *The Philadelphia Story*, was one of the same generation of American humorists as James Thurber and Robert Benchley. He and his Australian wife Ella Winter, previously married to Lincoln Steffens and one-time secretary to Justice Frankfurter of Roosevelt's Supreme Court, were neighbours of the Viertels in Santa Monica till they fell foul of the Un-American Activities inquiry and emigrated to England. They were among the Brechts' few intimate non-German friends in California. Stewart had sent Brecht his play *How I Wonder* and asked him to comment. Raymond Massey would star in it in New York in 1947.

511 To Suhrkamp   Winter 45/46
In response to Letter 509 Suhrkamp had asked for a power of attorney. For the first ('Danish') version of *Galileo* see the Editorial Note in the Methuen edition, pp. 166–93. It was staged by Leonard Steckel at the Zurich Schauspielhaus on 9 September 1943. The 'American' version was completed by 2 December 1945, when Laughton read it to the Brechts and their circle.

The reference to 'various productions' cannot apply to *Mother Courage* since no such productions are know to have taken place. Nor was the title role originally intended to be played by Weigel, though its Schweikian aspects were certainly well suited to her.

Ernst Busch. See Note 359. (He would play the Cook in the 1951 production of *Mother Courage*, with Weigel.)

Kate Kühl was the Berlin cabaret singer who had sung the early version of 'Surabaya Johnny' in 1927. She played in Karlheinz Martin's *Threepenny Opera* production in 1945.

*511x To Ferdinand Reyher   Nov.-Dec. 1945
Thanking him for his help when Berlau in New York had attacked Ida Bachmann and a doctor summoned by her. Also enclosing a letter for Berlau. Undated. According to James Lyon (who prints it in his *Brecht's American Cicerone*, p. 183) the attack occurred on 27 December 1945 and was reported to Brecht by Fritz Sternberg. Reyher next day brought another doctor and a policeman who escorted her to Bellevue Hospital. On 31 December she was transferred to Amityville Hospital on Long Island, where she was given electric shock treatment.

*511xx Ditto   Early Jan. 1946
Note printed in Lyon's *Cicerone*, p. 184.

512 To Elisabeth Bergner   16 Feb. 1945

On the alterations to *The Duchess of Malfi*, both before and after Auden's involvement, see A. R. Braunmüller's Editorial Notes in volume 7 of the Methuen and Random House editions.

The last paragraph relates to Ruth Berlau's breakdown and her ensuing removal to Amityville. Lyon reports that Brecht had arrived from California on 10 February and gone to visit her with Bergner and Paul Czinner, who were paying for her medical treatment. Bergner, wrote Berlau later in *Brechts Lai-tu* (p. 175) 'helped me more than anybody'. During March she was released into Brecht's care and allowed to return to the 57th Street apartment. In May he took her back to California in Laughton's car. According to Lyon, Czinner subsequently deducted the amount of the doctors' bills from sums due to Brecht from the receipts for *The Duchess of Malfi*.

513 To Eric Bentley   27 Feb. 1946
For the plans for a Brecht edition see Note 504. Brecht signed a contract for the plays with Reynal and Hitchcock during February 1946, Hauptmann's involvement presumably being due to Berlau's illness. Bentley (*The Brecht Commentaries*, p. 286) says he himself 'jibbed at' the idea of collaborating with her. The following year however the firm was taken over by Harcourt, Brace, who were apparently not interested in publishing Brecht – particularly, we may assume, since he had by then returned to Europe.

514 To Caspar Neher   April 1946
Seemingly their first contact since Brecht went into exile in 1933.

Kasack: Hermann Kasack, a friend of Suhrkamp's, had been an editor for Gustav Kiepenheuer, who published Brecht's *Versuche*.

Hartung: Gustav Hartung, a leading director before 1933, particularly of Expressionist plays, had spent his exile in Switzerland, where he worked for the Zurich Schauspielhaus and the Basel Stadttheater.

Neher was then in Hamburg, but left to work in Zurich for three years.

515 To Elisabeth Hauptmann   28 May 1946
Czinner paid her for her work – presumably on *The Duchess of Malfi* – within a fortnight of this letter. *The Threepenny Opera* was to go into the planned edition in Desmond Vesey's pre-war translation, revised by Bentley.

Gerhard Nellhaus, then a Harvard student, did a number of translations; he was to become a (medical) doctor. The 'disaster with the poems' is thought to relate to a number of publications in magazines before *Selected Poems* had appeared.

516 To Reyher   May 1946
Brecht and Reyher had worked on the *Galileo* translation in New York in April–May 1946. His book *I Heard Them Sing* had recently been published by Little, Brown in Boston.

Maria = Maria Czamska was a German actress living in New York.

Leo Reuss had played the Sergeant in Fleisser's *Manoeuvres in Ingolstadt* in 1929. In Hollywood he acted under the name Lionel Royce.

Hotch Potch is the title of an unidentified project of Reyher's to which Brecht refers several times in their correspondence. (For Reyher's side of this see Lyon: *Bertolt Brecht's American Cicerone*.)

517 To Viertel   June 1946
The 'handbook' was probably Weiskopf's *Unter fremden Himmeln*, which was
eventually published in East Berlin in 1948.
    Welles's 'revue' was a musical by Cole Porter called *Around the World*; Richard
A. Wilson was his co-producer.
    Auden never seems to have done the translation of 'The Children's Crusade'.
    Viertel's play about a Jewish family *The Way Home* had been given a public
reading in New York by Homolka, Elisabeth Neumann and others under the
auspices of the 'Tribune'. His book of poems *Der Lebenslauf* was published by
Herzfelde's Aurora-Verlag that year.
    Wieland = Herzfelde.
    'Butsch' = Budzislawski.

518 To George Pfanzelt   Mid-year 1946
First post-war contact with one of Brecht's earliest Augsburg friends, the 'Orge'
of his youthful poems and dedicatee of *Baal*. Pfanzelt was a librarian in
Augsburg. Otto Müllereisert and Rudolf Hartmann had formed part of the
same group.

519 To Reyher   July 1946
Mike Todd. A Hollywood film producer and husband of Elizabeth Taylor. He
dropped out when Brecht and Laughton rejected his idea of using bits of old
Renaissance-style film sets for *Galileo*.
    Virginia Farmer had been co-director of the Federal Theater Project in Los
Angeles. Vincent Sherman, director of the film *It Can't Happen Here*, had also
worked for the FTP.
    Reyher's 'novel about the photographer' was never finished.
    The King's Bread: fragments are in the Brecht Archive.
    The Brecht/Reyher/Lorre film story 'Lady Macbeth of the Yards' (also known
as 'All Our Yesterdays') is in *Texte für Filme 2* (Suhrkamp edition), pp. 438–75.

520 To Hauptmann   July–Aug. 1946
The 'new gallery'. Kragler in *Drums in the Night*; Garga in *Jungle*; Galy Gay,
Begbick and Uriah in *Man equals Man*; Callas in *The Round Heads*; Joan Dark and
Mauler in *St Joan of the Stockyards*; etc. Note that Pelagea Vlassova in *The Mother*
is omitted, as is Jenny in *The Threepenny Opera*. Baal too is omitted here, but
included in the list appended to the following letter.

521 To Bentley   July–Aug. 1946
Eric Bentley's influential *The Playwright as Thinker* was published by Reynal and
Hitchcock in 1946. His wife was Maja Apelman. In later editions he changed
'naturalism' to 'realism'. See Brecht's *Arbeitsjournal* entry for 30 March 1947 for
an attempt to clarify the distinction between the two concepts.

522 Ditto   Aug. 1946
The Good Person of Szechwan, directed by Rudolf Steinböck with Paula Wessely as
Shen Teh/Shui Ta, opened at the Theater in der Josefstadt, Vienna on 29 March
1946. Brecht got the date wrong, and was altogether displeased at this unlicensed
production starring leading actors of the Third Reich.

523 To Pfanzelt   4 Aug. 1946
   CARE: an American aid organisation through which food parcels could be
sent to civilian families in Europe.

524 To Reyher   Aug. 1946
In answer to R's letters of 23 and 24 July 1946. The second of these mentioned
that R. had run into Dorothy Norman, who was concerned about Brecht's
objections to the translations of his essay (see Note 502a). He had also just seen
Harold Clurman, who had read *Galileo*, recommended it to Tyrone Guthrie for
England and felt that he himself was the right man to direct it in the US (with
Kazan as the best alternative). Reyher advised Brecht to talk to Clurman: he had
worked with the Group Theater and the Theater Guild, had long experience of
Broadway, was a friend of Eisler's and had produced the Paul Green/Kurt Weill
play *Johnny Johnson* for the Group.

*524x Ditto   ?
Forwarding comments on Reyher's novel about the photographer (see Letter
519). A postscript asks if Alfred Lunt would make a possible director, or was he
too old-fashioned or reactionary?

*525 Ditto   Aug. 1946
Joking response to a newspaper cutting from Reyher about the disappearance of
valuable works of art – including possibly the Hesse crown jewels – from
American-occupied Büdingen, this being the village where Reyher's mother
lived. A postscript asks what about Michael Gordon as director?

526 Ditto   Aug. 1946
Reyher had written to report the arrival of Stefan Brecht, to whom Maria
Czamska would lend her apartment. He disliked the revisions to the latest script
of *Galileo*, and felt 'the presence of another influence'. Nothing is known of the
'short stories about American history' project.

527 To Paul Czinner   26 Sep. 1946
Brecht arrived from California via New York, and saw the second out-of-town
production at the Shubert Theater in Boston on 25 September 1946. It is not
clear if he was aware that George Rylands, the Cambridge scholar who had
been brought in as director, had reinstated Webster's original text in defiance of
the Dramatists' Guild contract which Czinner had signed with Brecht and
Auden six days earlier.
   His requested changes were not made, and by the time of the New York
opening (15 October at the Ethel Barrymore Theater) he had removed his name
from the billing. He was however allowed to make some directorial changes
once Rylands had returned to England. The play closed on 16 October.
Ferdinand was played by Donald Eccles.

528 To Stefan S. Brecht   Sep./Oct. 1946
Brecht's son had written to say that he found Galileo's sympathy for the
peasants historically improbable. He should not be presented as likeable.

529 To Caspar Neher   End Oct. 1946
Neher was now, with Teo Otto, chief designer at the Zurich Schauspielhaus.
Brecht needed him for the production of his unperformed plays.

A drawing by Neher of Brecht sitting cross-legged in a bowler hat, a rosary round his wrists and the Himalaya behind him, was included in his first book of poems in 1927 under the title 'The WaterFire Man'.

Georg: Neher's son, born three weeks before Stefan Brecht, had been missing in Russia since 8 April 1943.

Jacob Geis, who directed the Darmstadt *Man equals Man* in 1926 and the Theater am Schiffbauerdamm's *Manoeuvres in Ingolstadt* in 1929, subsequently went into script-writing and film production. He had remained in Germany.

530 Ditto   1 Nov. 1946
The 'big panels' have not been located.

*530x To Horst Bärensprung   8 Nov. 1946
A letter of 8 November 1946 explaining Brecht's contracts with Bloch-Erben, Berlin, for *The Threepenny Opera*. Brecht will not make a new contract unless the other party agrees that Bloch had no right to withhold Brecht's earnings during the 1930s (or since). For Bärensprung see Note 430. This letter is printed in Siegfried Unseld: *The Author and His Publisher*, University of Chicago Press 1980, pp. 288–9.

531 To Neher   Dec. 1946
The Italian publishing house was Einaudi of Turin. Their contract with Brecht was however only signed on 12 April 1949. Brecht had joined the Nehers at Positano on the Sorrento Peninsula in summer 1924.

'Hyd[a]topyranthropos' was Neher's handwritten title to the WaterFire Man drawing. The Latin continuation means 'greater, if not than the Himalaya, at least than Mont Blanc, always keeping a level head'.

532 Ditto   Dec. 1946
The 'Aristophanic revue' scheme became the *Ares's Chariot* project on which Brecht and Neher worked in Zurich. The 'little revue' was the Junge Volksbühne's *Wir sind ja sooo zufrieden* of 18 November 1931, to which Brecht, Eisler, Weill, Lenya, Weigel and Busch all contributed. Among the Brecht items, it seems, were 'The ballad of §218' and the 'Song of the SA man' (*Poems 1913–1956*, pp. 186 and 191).

Dessau composed some of the *Mother Courage* songs in California in 1946.

'Offers from Berlin': there is no known record of these, and it is not clear who put them forward. The Theater am Schiffbauerdamm was in the Soviet sector of the city, where the military government, represented by Colonel Sergei Tulpanov and Lt-Col. Alexander Dymschitz, were in close touch with the newly formed Free German League of Culture headed by Johannes R. Becher.

Lazar Wechsler was the head of Praesens-Film, the Zurich-based production firm who had helped to complete *Kuhle Wampe* in 1931–32.

*533 To George Pfanzelt   Dec. 1946
Thanking him for letters, inquiring what he needs, asking for his size in shoes and giving news of Brecht's own family.

534 To Piscator   Feb. 1946
535 Ditto   March 1947
The 'Aristophanic revue'. See Note 532.

Curt Bois was a notable comic from the Berlin cabaret before 1933, played in Gottfried Reinhardt's *Polonaise* at the Alvin Theatre, New York through the winter of 1945/46, and had been in some demand in Hollywood as a supporting actor. Brecht had a high regard for him.

Lothar Rewalt and Hugo and Dolly Haas had acted for Piscator's Studio Theatre at the New School.

Ludwig Roth and Elisabeth Neumann were in *The Private Life of the Master Race*.

Ludwig Donath performed in New York for Ernst Lothar's Austrian Stage.

Piscator replied on 29 March in similarly warm terms, but was more hesitant about the atmosphere in Berlin. He had already been in touch with the Communist playwright Friedrich Wolf, who wanted him to direct a play for the Volksbühne there.

536 To Reyher   March 1947
Lorre, a morphine addict, had been arrested in New York for possessing drugs. On hearing this, Brecht telephoned Reyher from California to ask for his help. Reyher's letter of roughly a week later is printed in Lyon's *Brecht's American Cicerone*, p. 198.

537 Ditto   March–April 1947
The permits were for travel to Switzerland. Columbia Pictures had allegedly shown an interest in the Brecht/Reyher/Lorre story 'Lady Macbeth of the Yards'. 'The Provider' was Brecht's suggested title for Chaplin's *Monsieur Verdoux*.

Reyher's reply from New York, strongly recommending Joseph Losey's work after having seen his production of *The Great Campaign* for the Experimental Theater, is printed in *Brecht's American Cicerone*, pp. 200–202.

*538 To Heinz Kuckhah
Kuckhahn, whom Brecht had met during the making of *Kuhle Wampe*, had evidently written from Germany about his difficulties. Brecht sent a C A R E food parcel and subsequently made him an assistant at the Berliner Ensemble.

539 To George Grosz   Spring 1947
The poem is surely 'The Anachronistic Procession, or Freedom and Democracy' (*Poems 1913–1956*, pp. 409–414) which Brecht, according to his *Arbeitsjournal* entry, finished on 20 March 1947. Grosz replied at length on 30 March, turning the idea sardonically down. His letter is printed in his *Briefe 1913–1959*.

540 To Pfanzelt   Summer 1947

*540x To Fritz Kortner   June 1947
From Santa Monica in June 1947 to explain a telephone conversation where he had criticised Kortner's refusal to play the Pope in the forthcoming *Galileo* on the pretext that the part was too small. Brecht argued that it was the only part other than the title role that 'requires a great actor', that 'this production is my one theatrical operation in the States' and promised to publicise the fact that Kortner would be playing the title role in Berlin. (To appear in *Fritz Kortner. Schauspieler und Regisseur*, published by Hentrich, West Berlin, under the editorship of Klaus Völker.)

541 To Herta Hanisch   June/July 1947
She was Margarete Steffin's sister. Maria was Maria Osten. See Notes 428 and
429.

542 To Johanna Steffin   June/July 1947
Margarete's mother.

543 To Reyher   Sep. 1947
Reyher was then in Paris.

   Galileo had opened at the Coronet Theatre in Beverly Hills (Los Angeles) on
30 July 1947. The theatre was managed by Norman Lloyd and John Houseman.
T. Edward Hambleton was the main backer. Losey directed. Ruth Berlau
photographed the production, her pictures later being published in the folder
Aufbau einer Rolle, Henschel-Verlag, East Berlin 1956. Brecht's account of the
preparatory work, along with the text of the Laughton version, is included in
the notes to volume 5i of the Methuen edition. The audience included Chaplin
and Stravinsky.

   Open City and *Paisa* were made by Roberto Rosselini in 1945, and were
landmarks of the Italian neo-realist, anti-Fascist cinema. The scheme for a
Galileo film to be produced by Geiger never materialised.

544 To Charles Laughton   Aug.-Oct. 1947
Written in English from Santa Monica.

   Elsa = Elsa Lanchester, Laughton's wife.

545 To Emil Hesse-Burri   End Sep. 1947
For Burri see Notes 117 and 509. He was one of the old associates with whom
Brecht had particularly wanted to make touch. In the 1937 Malik edition of his
plays Brecht had named 'H. Emmel' with 'R. Kass' (i.e. Neher) as collaborating
on *Man equals Man*.

546 To Pfanzelt   End Sep. 1947
Written before Brecht's examination of 30 October by the House Un-American
Activities Committee in Washington. There appears to be no allusion to this
interesting event in his published correspondence. The Brechts flew to Europe
the following day, leaving their son to pursue his studies at Harvard.

547 To William Dieterle and family   Oct. 1947
Written on notepaper of the Union Pacific Railroad, probably on the way to
Washington via New York.

548 To Ruth Berlau   3 Nov. 1947
Donald Ogden Stewart (see Note 510) and his wife Ella Winter, would become
exiles in Hampstead, London in the McCarthy years.

   Anna Seghers. See Notes 167–8 and 325. Her *The Seventh Cross* had been
successfully filmed by Fred Zinnemann (with Helene Weigel in a very small
part). Its successor, the novel *Die Toten bleiben jung*, would be published in 1949.
She became a vice-president of Becher's Kulturbund and later a member of the
East German Academy.

549 Ditto   5 Nov. 1947
Erroneously dated 5 October by Brecht. The 'smooth forehead' or 'brow

without a frown' refers back to the poem called 'Ruth' which Brecht had sent
her in September 1943 (*Poems 1913–1956*, pp. 382–3) It became his codeword for
her in her calmer moods.

550 To the National Theatre in Prague   Mid-Nov. 1947
The proposed production, which Brecht had been told of by the Kurt Reiss
agency in Basel, never materialised.

551 To Hanns Eisler   Nov. 1947
Eisler had not been allowed to leave the United States freely, though he had
written on 24 November of the previous year to tell Becher that he would
like to come to Berlin. He was now under threat of deportation, and a
'solidarity concert' was arranged for him in the Coronet Theater, Los Angeles
on 14 December. Among his supporters were Leonard Bernstein and
Stravinsky.

   Early in 1948 his brother Gerhart was rearrested and went on hunger strike.
He himself was eventually deported to Prague on 26 March.

   Lou = the second Mrs Eisler.

   Gerda = the photographer Gerda Goedhart, Ruth Berlau's friend.

552 To Berlau   Mid-Dec. 1947
Galileo opened in New York at the Maxine Elliott Theater on 7 December.
Laughton made a private recording of parts of scene 13 for Brecht. Hambleton
was the producer. Berlau took photographs. Brooks Atkinson wrote an
unfavourable review in the *New York Times*. The play had only a short run.

553 To Stefan S. Brecht   Dec. 1947
Chur is a town in Eastern Switzerland. The municipal theatre was directed
by Hans Curjel, originally an art historian, who had become musical director at
the Düsseldorf Schauspielhaus in the mid-1920s and helped Brecht stage the
'Little' *Mahagonny* at Baden-Baden in 1927. He was then a dramaturg at
Klemperer's Kroll Opera, and in 1930 became its deputy director. Emigrating
to Zurich, he directed the Corso Theatre there before moving to Chur.

   After talking with Brecht and Neher he offered them his help in preparing
for the Berlin *Courage* production with Weigel. Brecht saw his own motive
for adapting *Antigone* as 'my return to the German language area' (*Arbeitsjournal* entry for 16 December 1947). Ruth Berlau's photographic record of the
production is in Brecht/Neher: *Antigonemodell 1948*, Gebr. Weiss, Berlin 1949.

   Edward: Marlowe's *Edward the Second*, which Brecht and Feuchtwanger had
adapted for production at the Munich Kammerspiele in 1924.

554 To Berlau   End Jan. 1948
Hans Gaugler, one of the theatre's young actors, stood in at rehearsals while a
Creon was sought in Zurich and elsewhere. Eventually Brecht so liked his
interpretation that he gave him the part and subsequently brought him to play
the lead in Lenz's *The Tutor* with the Berliner Ensemble.

   Erika Neher was the designer's wife.

   Hanne Hiob was Brecht's elder daughter.

   Ruth Berlau arrived in Zurich from New York on 22 January 1948, six days
after rehearsals had started in Chur.

555 Ditto   Jan.–Feb. 1948

556 To Hans Curjel   7 Feb. 1948
See Note 553. 'Sunday' would be Sunday 15 February, the day of the opening.

557 To Neher   7 Feb. 1948
The acting area was bounded by four tall poles topped by (real) horses' skulls.
Behind it was a semicircle of benches on which any actors not immediately
involved remained sitting, backed by dark red rough canvas screens. In the
copy received by Neher Brecht concluded 'all the best to Erika. Yours, b.'

558 To Korsch   April 1948
The book appears still to have been Korsch's *Karl Marx* (London 1938).
Korsch replied on 12 May that he had decided not to publish it (i.e. presumably
the German text) and wished the manuscript to be retitled *Svendborger Marx*.

559 To the American Academy of Arts and Letters   5 April 1948
Brecht had been given a grant of $1000 'for creative work in literature'. His
letter is written in English.

Mertens: Hans and Renata Mertens had been put on to Brecht by the young
Benno Besson, then an assistant at the Zurich Schauspielhaus. It was they who
had suggested that the Brechts move out to Feldmeilen to a house belonging to
Mertens's father.

560 To Ferdinand Reyher   April 1948
For the 'photographer novel' see Letter 519 and its note.

Galileo film. Brecht had begun discussing this with a producer called Rod
Geiger the previous year, who wrote on 24 May to suggest making it in north
Italy with Herbert Marshall as director. Marshall had been an assistant to
Eisenstein in the mid-1930s and was associated with Unity Theatre in London.
Later he spent many years as a professor at Southern Illinois University,
Carbondale.

561 To Gottfried von Einem   23 May 1948
In the summer of 1947 Neher had designed the Salzburg première of von
Einem's opera *Danton's Death*, which Oskar Fritz Schuh from the Vienna Opera
directed. Henceforward the three men took a leading part in the planning of the
annual Salzburg Festival, in which they were supported by the head of the
Federal Theatre Administration Egon Hilbert. Von Einem came to see Brecht
at Feldmeilen, along with Neher and proposed that Brecht too should become
involved. It seems that Brecht not only agreed to make his plays available to the
Festival, but also specifically to write a new open-air Salzburg *Dance of Death*.

'Papers': Brecht had submitted his US identity and travel documents to the
Consulate in Zurich for renewal. They were reputedly sent on from there to
Chicago and never returned.

*561x To Neher   nd
Puntila went off 'painlessly', but the Schauspielhaus's plans for the 47/48 season
are a let-down. B. has heard that the Munich Kammerspiele has designs by N.
for *The Threepenny Opera*. This would make a revival possible if the right actors
were available. Meantime he would be glad to take up N's invitation, presumably
to Salzburg.

562 To Max Frisch   July 1948

Frisch, a Swiss writer and architect then aged thirty-seven, had met Brecht at a party given by the Schauspielhaus director Kurt Hirschfeld four days after the playwright's arrival from America. The two men got on well, and Frisch attended readings from the *Short Organum* given by Brecht in the Feldmeilen house. Its text, which was 'more or less finished' on 18 August 1948, is in *Brecht on Theatre*, pp. 179–205.

Frisch's own 'new play' would be staged by Kurt Horwitz at the Schauspielhaus on 8 January 1949 under the title *Als der Krieg zu Ende war* ('When the War was over'). Later, internationally known plays by him include *The Fire Raisers* and *Andorra*. He is also an important novelist.

*563 To an unidentified General   ?

This long, apparently unfinished and unsent letter, starting 'Dear General', is written in German and designed for the US military government authorities either in Berlin or in Munich. In it Brecht takes their failure to answer his request (made to one of the Theater Officers) to visit Berlin as an indication that anti-Nazis are being handicapped because of their 'social opinions'. But 'at least 30 divisions of civilian fighters fell in the struggle against Hitler'. And 'in this continent where you have been sent, writers are not regarded as employees of the entertainment business'.

564 To Jacob Geis   28 Aug. 1948

Geis, whom Brecht addresses here with the familiar 'du', was a dramaturg in the Munich theatres in 1919. He supported the production of *In the Jungle* in 1923 and himself directed the premières of *Man equals Man* at Darmstadt in 1926 and *Manoeuvres in Ingolstadt* (jointly with Brecht) at the Schiffbauerdamm in 1929. He then became a director and dramaturg first at Kassel, then at Frankfurt. After 1933 he stayed in Germany and worked in films. Brecht drew him into his plan for a Munich *Threepenny Opera* with Hans Albers as Macheath.

Puntila: for Hella Wuolijoki, for the 'model' for the Puntila figure and the use made by Brecht of her play and stories, see volume 6iii of the Methuen *Collected Plays*. Kurt Desch, the Munich publisher, had been handling the rights to Brecht's play.

*565 Ditto   Sep. 1948

Congratulating Geis on his play *Die Brüder Allemann* ('The Brothers Allemann'), which was performed at the Munich Kammerspiele in 1948. A further letter warned him against the Zurich audience and its lack of understanding.

566 To Hanne Hiob   Sep. 1948

'Papers': these were from the Foreigners' section of the Zurich police, permitting the Brechts to leave Switzerland and return. They were issued on 15 September 1948 and would be valid for six months.

Schweikart: Hans S. was Intendant of the Munich Kammerspiele from 1947 to 1963.

567 To Neher   Sep. 1948

Ares: the *Ares's Chariot* revue scheme, for which Neher that year did some of his best post-war drawings. See Letter 535.

Courage: presumably Brecht wanted something quite different from the designs which Neher had provided for Lindtberg's second Schauspielhaus production in spring 1946. These were of a remarkable gaiety.

568 To André Simone   Sep. 1948
This was a pseudonym of Otto Katz, a lifelong fixer who had been Piscator's business manager in 1927–29 and was sent to Moscow in 1931 to work for Mezhrabpomfilm. He left there in 1933 to join Muenzenberg's office in Paris, where he was involved in the production of the Brown Books (see Note 332) and in raising money abroad for the illegal KPD, then went via the USA to Mexico and helped edit the magazine *Freies Deutschland* to which Seghers, Kisch, Alexander Abusch and other émigré Communists contributed. In 1946 he was invited back to his native Czechoslovakia (a country he had not lived in since 1922) whose Communist government executed him following the Slansky trial of 1952. Arthur Koestler and Claude Cockburn were among those who found him a dubious, if entertaining figure, but he appears to be gratefully remembered in the GDR.

*569 To Peter Suhrkamp   Sep. 1948
About the planned publication of Brecht's *Versuche* vols. 9 to 14. Brecht wanted Suhrkamp (who had been running the S. Fischer Verlag under the Nazis) to undertake this for Germany, while Emil Oprecht took charge of the distribution in Switzerland and other German-speaking areas. In the event Oprecht dropped out and the East German Aufbau-Verlag came in, but the project began in 1949 with *Mother Courage* as suggested here.

570 To Kurt Weill   6 Dec. 1948
Looks forward to Letter 578. Universal-Edition were (and are) publishers of *The Threepenny Opera* and other Weill works. For the two men's views about Bloch-Erben see Letters 174, 348, 352 and 380.

The Adlon was commonly reckoned the best hotel in Berlin before 1945, but when Brecht arrived there it had been largely destroyed by the bombing.

Lady in the Dark, a musical with lyrics by Ira Gershwin and Gertrude Lawrence as its star, had been Weill's first great Broadway hit in 1941.

Weill's reply on 20 December says he understands that the Munich production altered and added to his music, and has asked the US Theatre Officer to stop it. He cannot believe that this is the new version of which B. speaks, but must in any case see the new text. Then a month later he gets it and writes that he cannot see the point of the changes, which only weaken the play with their ephemeral attempts at topicality.

571 To Berthold Viertel   14 Dec. 1948
The 'project' was the Brechts' scheme for a Berlin ensemble.

Paul Bildt and Werner Hinz, who played Cook and Chaplain respectively in the 1949 *Mother Courage*, were Deutsches Theater actors who had remained in Germany under the Nazis. Brecht thought Bildt the best of the German actors, but neither he nor Hinz joined the new Ensemble.

Oscar Ingenohl was the Intendant of the Hebbel-Theater in the US sector. It had had a distinguished record under the Weimar Republic as the Theater in der Königgrätzer Strasse.

The Kulturbund, or Free German League of Culture, had been set up by Johannes R. Becher on his return to Berlin from Moscow in 1945. It was not intended as an entirely Communist body, but in 1947 the three Western powers forbade it to operate in their sectors.

The Möwe was an artists' club in the Soviet sector.

Mother Courage was performed in the Vienna Scala by the Zurich company on 2 December 1948. This was Lindtberg's revised production of 1946, which used Neher's sets.

The poet Peter Huchel edited the (Eastern) Academy of Arts journal *Sinn und Form*, which would become Brecht's main literary outlet in the GDR.

572 To Neher   29 Dec. 1948
Neher had been needed for the Berlin *Mother Courage* production, whose set was eventually designed by Heinrich Kilger of the Deutsches Theater on the basis of Teo Otto's Zurich sets of 1941.

573 To Paul Dessau   21 Jan. 1949
Dessau wrote most of his *Mother Courage* settings in California in 1946. Brecht however added the 'Song of the Hours' for the Chaplain to sing in the Berlin production, and Dessau set it after his return from America in 1948. Evidently it was cut at rehearsal, to be introduced only in the revised production of 1951 when Erwin Geschonneck took over the Chaplain's part from Hinz.

For Kuckhahn see Note 538.

574 To Gustaf Gründgens   18 Jan. 1949
Gründgens had directed the Staatstheater under Goering, after starting his career in the late 1920s as a reputed man of the left and a friend of the murdered Communist actor Hans Otto (see Note 243). History says nothing about what happened in 1932, when more than one *Saint Joan* project fell through thanks to the mounting reaction in the arts. Brecht, who had no use for the 'Goering-theatre', none the less respected Gründgens both as an actor-director and for his action in getting a lawyer to represent Ernst Busch when he was tried for High Treason in 1944. This saved Busch's life.

In 1949 he was General-Intendant of the Düsseldorf City Theatres, where he agreed to give what would still have been the world première of Brecht's important play. The plan fell through because Fritz Kortner turned down the part of Mauler. Gründgens would realise it at the Hamburg Schauspielhaus ten years later.

575 To Leonard Steckel   24 Jan. 1949
Steckel, a pre-1933 member of Piscator's companies, was with the Zurich Schauspielhaus, for whom he had directed *The Good Person of Szechwan* and *Galileo* and played both Galileo and Puntila.

The Schiffbauerdamm-Theater would in the event be occupied by the East Berlin Volksbühne under Fritz Wisten for another six years. Gorky's *Vassa Zhelesnova* was accordingly played at the Deutsches Theater under Viertel's direction, with Therese Giehse (also from the Zurich Schauspielhaus) in the lead. Steckel again played Puntila as suggested. In January 1952 Curt Bois would take over from him.

J. = Jo Mihaly, Steckel's wife.

Helene Weigel was responsible for such matters as Intendant of the new Ensemble.

576 To Neher   25 Jan. 1949
The Tales of Hoffmann: Brecht had made some notes for a film version in the spring of 1947, before leaving California, and appears to have submitted the project to Lewis Milestone. Nothing came of it in Germany either.

577 To Viertel   25 Jan. 1949
Ernst Legal, who was acting Intendant of the Staatstheater at the time of Brecht's *Man equals Man* in 1931, was another actor who had remained in Nazi Germany, though he was no longer trusted to direct a theatre. After 1945 he became Intendant of the State Opera (whose bombed remnants were in the Soviet sector) in its temporary home, the Admiralspalast.

Klemperer, a US citizen, was based in Hungary from late 1947 to the summer of 1950. In January 1949 he conducted *Carmen* for Walter Felsenstein at the East Berlin Komische Oper.

DEFA = the East German Film Corporation and successor to UFA
Liesl = Elisabeth Neumann-Viertel.

Karl Paryla, another of the Zurich actors, would move to the Vienna Scala and make a great reputation in that city.

578 To Weill   28 Jan. 1949
For Weill's 'quick answer' see Note 570. On 14 February Weill replied that since the new text was only temporary he would sanction its use for the Munich production with Albers, then consult again once Brecht himself had seen it.

Meantime Universal-Edition's Munich representative had told him that changes in the music were planned and a local 'Jazz Arranger' was to re-orchestrate the whole score. Accordingly he had cabled forbidding any such measures, and asked the US Theater Officer to prevent them. He would like to hear from Geis.

The Threepenny Opera directed by Harry Buckwitz eventually opened at the Munich Kammerspiele on 27 April 1949. Hans Albers played Macheath, Trude Hesterberg Mrs Peachum, Erni Wilhelmi Lucy; the sets were by Neher. There was no ensuing tour.

579 To Piscator   9 Feb. 1949
The plan for Piscator to take over the Volksbühne, whose old theatre on the Bülowplatz had been bombed out, dates from spring 1947 if not earlier, and was first mooted by Jhering and Friedrich Wolf. Brecht's suggestion that he stop off on the way in Zurich to direct *The Defeat* was new. This was the Norwegian work that impelled Brecht to write his own Paris Commune play. Piscator however stuck it out in New York till 1951, when he returned to West Germany rather than East.

580 To Becher   20 Feb. 1949
The Kulturbund (see Note 571) had met the Brechts on their arrival in Berlin and supported their proposal to form the Berliner Ensemble. Becher and his deputy Alexander Abusch put them also on a good footing with the Soviet cultural officer Alexander Dymschitz.

*581 To Reyher   21 Feb. 1949
Asking R. if he can come to Berlin 'for quite a while', perhaps for a magazine.
B. was off to Zurich to renew his papers but would be back there in April.
(Printed in Lyon: *Bertolt Brecht's American Cicerone*, p. 209.)

582 To Helene Weigel   End Feb. 1949
The *Kalendergeschichten* (or *Tales from the Calendar*) was the first book of Brecht's
short stories, published by Gebrüder Weiss in Berlin in 1948. Negotiations for a
Czech edition fell through.

   Seyferth: Wilfred S., a German actor who had joined the Schauspielhaus
company, as were Gustav Knuth and Willi Quadflieg.

   Hirschfeld: besides directing plays, Kurt H. was deputy director of the
company.

   The Defeat see Note 579.

583 Ditto   3 March 1949
Ilse Kasprowiak was Brecht's secretary at the Berliner Ensemble.

   Lutz: Regine Lutz, a young actress with the Schauspielhaus company, had done
well as Lisu the milkmaid in their *Puntila* production. She was with the
Ensemble for a number of years.

   Otto: Teo Otto.

   Gitermann: Valentin Giterman, a member of the Swiss parliament.

584 Ditto   6 March 1949
Elements of the Basel carnival were absorbed in the work on the *Salzburg Dance
of Death*. Nothing came of the *Danton's Death* suggestion.

   Dahlke: Paul D. The 'S' of the postscript (like the G.S. of the following letter) is
thought to be Gody Suter, who seems to have helped the Brechts with long-
distance telephone calls to and from Berlin, where he was correspondent of the
Zurich *Tagesanzeiger*.

585 Ditto   Early March 1949
French play: it is not clear what this might be, unless Brecht means the Belgian
Charles de Coster's novel *Till Eulenspiegel*, which he and Günter Weisenborn
had been considering as a film project for Hans Albers (see also Letter 596).

   DWK = Deutsche Wirtschaftskommission, the economic authority for the
Soviet Zone, who had to approve all hard currency expenditure.

   A.D. = Lt-Col. Alexander Dymschitz, a relative of Alexei Tolstoy.

586 To Piscator   March 1949
This is in effect a repetition of Letter 579, which Brecht had written from Berlin
the previous month, though it says nothing about the Volksbühne and
concentrates instead on *The Days of the Commune*. Piscator in his reply however
was hesitant, saying that he had had no official approach about the former. He
later noted his suspicion that enemies in the East Berlin theatre were opposed to
his coming back. Mittenzwei (vol. 2, pp. 361–2) quotes relevant letters from
him to Wilhelm and Arthur Pieck.

   Pottier: Eugène Pottier, the author of the 'Internationale'.

   Weinert: the German Communist poet and cabaret artist Erich W.

   The 'Jacques Delorne' sometimes cited by Brecht as the play's 'official' author was an invention. In the course of the year Neher produced a large number of fine designs and sketches for it.

Giehse, like her friend Erika Mann (the nominal Mrs Auden) had married a British husband in the 1930s.

587 To Erich Weinert   c. March 1949
Weinert, then in his fifties, had returned from emigration in the USSR and was now in Switzerland convalescing after TB. For Kurt Kläber see Note 167.

588 To Viertel   March–April 1949
In the event the Ensemble opened on 8 November with *Puntila*, directed by Brecht and Engel, sets by Neher, with both Steckel and Giehse in the cast.

Joseph Gielen, after directing the Dresden Opera, was now director of the Burgtheater in Vienna.

589 To Weigel   April 1949
The beginning of this letter is missing.

Wimmer: Maria W., a leading West German actress.

'The house': Berliner Allee 190, in North-West Berlin (Soviet sector).

Bertha = Mrs Teo Otto.

Kuba = the poet and singer Kurt Barthel, who had been in emigration in Britain. He did not become a member of the Ensemble, though at one point he would be briefly cast as the ballad-singer in *Galileo*.

Eisler, still based in Vienna, was writing music for a film by Dudow to be made by the East German State Film Corporation DEFA.

For the German-Soviet director Bernhard Reich see Letter 312 and earlier references. Brecht had last seen him on the way through Moscow in 1941, when it appears that he had been temporarily released from Stalinist internment. When Brecht wrote, he had not yet been officially 'rehabilitated'.

590 Ditto   April 1949
'Visas': to leave Switzerland for Berlin via the US Zone. Valid one way, and dated 20 April.

Besson: the Swiss Benno Besson was with the Ensemble as actor and director till the 1960s. The *Trumpets and Drums* production seen during the Ensemble's first London season was his work. Bilingual in French and German, he became the East Berlin Volksbühne's leading director.

Fueter, another Zurich actor, was not engaged.

Michael Tschesno-Hell was an East Berlin writer and critic who headed the 'Volk und Welt' publishing house there.

591 Ditto (592 in Aufbau edition)   21 April 1949
'Keeping the line open': the Soviet blockade of West Berlin was still in force, so that its only links with the Western Zones were by air. Hof is on the autobahn between Nuremberg and Leipzig near the crossing point in the Soviet Zone; it is also close to the Czech frontier.

Budzislawski: see Note 450. After leaving the US he settled in the Soviet Zone, where he became professor of journalism at Leipzig University.

592 Ditto (593 in Aufbau edition)   April–May 1949
'The play.' i.e. *Days of the Commune*.

593 Ditto (594 in Aufbau edition)   April–May 1949
The Sanitaire: A Zurich fumigation plant.

Wendt: Erich Wendt, former German director of the Vegaar (or Foreign
Workers' Publishing House) in Moscow, then for a time under Soviet arrest,
had returned to become head of the Aufbau-Verlag, set up in the first place by
the Kulturbund and subsequently the GDR's main literary publishing house.
From now on it took over the East German publication of Brecht's works
under licence from Suhrkamp-Verlag.

Duncker: Hermann Duncker, a Marxist publicist who taught at the MASch
(or Marxist Workers' School) before Hitler and now became head of the East
German trade union school at Bernau. His documentary compilation *Pariser
Kommune 1871* was published by Neuer Deutscher Volksverlag, Berlin in
1931.

594 Ditto (595 in Aufbau edition)   April–May 1949
NBE = New Berliner Ensemble, which was officially established on 15 May,
following a letter from Walter Ulbricht, the Socialist Unity Party secretary, to
the head of the German Economic Commission (for the Soviet zone). The
company would become operative on 1 September. The adjective 'New'
disappeared almost at once.

Desch: see Note 564. He could only dispose of the rights outside Berlin.

595 To Ilse Kasprowiak (596 in Aufbau edition)   May 1949

596 To Elisabeth Hauptmann (597 in Aufbau edition)   Spring 1949
Hauptmann had returned from the US not long before and was put on the
board of the new Ensemble as a dramaturg. She was also in editorial charge of
the publication of Brecht's works.

597 To von Einem (591 in Aufbau edition)   April 1949
Brecht made his formal application for citizenship on 20 April. The Berlin
blockade was lifted on 12 May.

*597x, xx To Landeshauptmann Rehrl, Salzburg, and Felix Hurdes, Austrian
Minister of Education   April 1949
These letters are treated as confidential by the Austrian archives, and are
presumably those forwarded with 598. A draft for one of them in Kurt Palm's
book (p. 70) shows Brecht wishing not to be repatriated to Germany but to
work in the right atmosphere as a creative writer ('Dichter') serving no specific
political ideology. It is dated 20 April.

A Landeshauptmann is an Austrian *Land* (or provincial) premier, in this case
of Land Salzburg which with Upper Austria constituted the American Zone.

598 To von Einem   22 April 1949
Von Einem was working on an opera version of Kafka's *The Trial*, which was
eventually staged in Salzburg four years later, and also at the Vienna State
Opera. Brecht had seen Gide's dramatisation on his way through Paris in 1947,
and had not thought much of it. As the 'choral text' which Von Einem also
wished to set, Brecht sent him the 'Song of the Hours' (see Note 573). Von
Einem's setting would be performed first by the Hamburg Radio orchestra in
1959.

599, 600 Ditto   April–May 1949
Brecht did not manage to stop in Salzburg, which he finally visited in August
after the end of the Berlin theatre season.

   Of his three referees, Kurt Horwitz had performed in the 1922 première of
Drums in the Night at the Munich Kammerspiele, and would later become
Intendant of that theatre.

*601 Ditto (604 in Aufbau edition)   27 May 1949
With extra verses and refrains for the 'Song of the Hours', and the suggestion
that 'the whole thing needs to be a wild piece'.

*602 To Kurt Hirschfeld (601 in Aufbau edition)   Spring 1949
With suggestions (not to be communicated to the author) for dramaturgical
improvements to Friedrich Dürrenmatt's play *Romulus the Great*, which the
Schauspielhaus were planning to play in Germany and possibly the US.

603 To Ferdinand Reyher (602 in Aufbau edition)   21 May 1949
Written to Brecht's 'American Cicerone' while waiting to leave Zurich. The
Berlin blockade had just ended. The American plays mentioned are clearly the
George Kaufman-Morrie Ryskind political musical *Of Thee I Sing* (London
1933; music by George Gershwin) and Harold Rome's revue *Pins and Needles* for
the Union of Ladies' Garment Workers, which contained such numbers as 'Sing
me a Song of Social Significance' and 'One Big Union for Two'.

   Wilder: Thorton W's *Our Town* and *The Skin of Our Teeth* were much performed
in West Germany after World War 2.

*604 Ditto (603 in Aufbau edition)   End May 1949
To much the same effect as the preceding letter, but ending with a request to
look after Kurt Hirschfeld when he came to New York.

*604x To Weill   9 June 1949
Letter dated 9 June following up a cable saying 'Am joining your action against
Kammerspiele' to explain that on getting W's letter of 14 February (Note 578)
B. too had written insisting that W's music and orchestrations must not be
touched, and that the theatre would not get his agreement to the proposed
Albers tour without this proviso. All this had nothing to do with his alterations
to the text.

*604xx Ditto   10 June 1949
Dated the next day and written from Suhrkamp-Verlag in West Berlin to
propose that Suhrkamp should take over the TPO rights from Bloch-Erben
and make a contract for Weill with Universal-Edition.

*604xxx Ditto   23 June 1949
Dated 23 June, in answer to Weill's letter of the 14th. This had reported that
W's musical demands had been ignored by the Kammerspiele, and also enclosed
cables sent to Bloch-Erben and Universal-Edition, the second of these calling
for future performances to be stopped until the legal position with regard to the
'new version' (Letter 570) had been clarified. For in W's view the whole case
against Bloch-Erben might be weakened by it, and he noted that his request to
Brecht for more information about its handling had still not been met.

   Brecht tells him that he will do nothing more about the Munich affair pending the result of W's measures, and meanwhile he again recommends breaking with Bloch and moving to Suhrkamp.

*605 To George Pfanzelt   Mid-1949
Pfanzelt had evidently transmitted a request from the Augsburg theatre to stage one of Brecht's plays. Brecht agrees, suggesting that they write to Suhrkamp about the rights, and apologising for his silence. (He called on Pfanzelt in Augsburg that September.)

606 To Peter Huchel   1 July 1949
See Note 571. Huchel in 1949 published a special number of *Sinn und Form* devoted to Brecht. Ernst Bloch had been one of the founders of the New York Aurora-Verlag in 1943 (see Note 484) but returned to the Soviet Zone in 1949 to take up the chair of Philosophy at Leipzig University. After having been removed from this post in 1957 he was given a professorship at Tübingen in the Federal Republic.

607 To Arnold Zweig   June 1949
Born in 1887 and best known for his World War I novel *The Case of Sergeant Grischa* (1927), Zweig was a highly prolific writer who emigrated to Palestine in the 1930s and was at once a Zionist, a Socialist and a friend of Freud's. In 1948 he returned to East Berlin where he became the first President of the new Academy of Arts in the summer of 1949. Rudolf Engel was its Director.

   By 'the Weimar Academy' Brecht probably means the pre-Hitler Prussian Academy.

608 Ditto   June–July 1949
Paul Wandel, the Zonal education chairman, appointed Brecht a member of the Academy's organising committee at the end of June 1949. Brecht was then in hospital with a kidney infection. The committee held its first meeting on 4 July.

   Wieland Herzfelde's brother John Heartfield returned from London (where he took refuge when the Nazis entered Prague) in September 1950. He was not immediately appreciated in his old home, and Brecht helped him to re-establish himself by getting him to design stage settings and posters for the Ensemble.

   Lerski: Helmut L., the photographer and film cameraman.

*609 To Hans Albers   July 1949
From hospital, congratulating Albers on the success of the Munich *Threepenny Opera*, though he has been told that the production should have been tougher and more disquieting. The Zurich Schauspielhaus wants to do its own production in the autumn, with Steckel (apparently) as director, and Brecht would like Albers to play Macheath there too. A touring production might then eventuate.

*609x To Weill   17 July 1949
Also from hospital (Hedwigskrankenhaus), and dated 17 July, to say that Bloch-Erben have dissolved the *TPO* agreement, and that he would like to take it up with Suhrkamp and has written to Universal-Edition about this. He imagines W. will agree (and makes no reference to the new approach to Albers).

   Weill, having written six days earlier to say he was taking steps to get the Bloch agreement dissolved, after which they could negotiate with Suhrkamp – a letter which may not yet have reached Brecht – was amazed to hear this news, and to get it first not from Brecht but in the form of a letter from Bloch-Erben. Telling Brecht so, he said he had instructed Universal-Edition not to allow further performances of his music until he signed the new agreement. (And certainly the Albers tour plan came to nothing.)

That was in a letter dated 5 August, which ended by reporting that Eric Bentley had asked for the rights for a New York production, to be directed by himself with a group called the 'Interplayers'. Weill 'naturally' refused, though he felt they might give a good performance of *Szechwan*. He had also had talks with 'a great English star' with a view to an American *TPO* production.

610 To Reyher   7 July 1949
Reyher, who still had authority from Brecht to license *The Good Person of Szechwan* outside New York, had now forwarded a plan for a New York production by Bentley and the 'Interplayers'. Following Brecht's refusal, Bentley abandoned this till after Brecht's death, when he directed the play with Uta Hagen as Shen Teh. In the summer of 1950 he would come to Germany to be Brecht's assistant on the Munich *Mother Courage* production.

Liebling-Wood was a New York agency.

*611 To the Wuppertal City Theatres   26 Aug. 1949
Asking that Ruth Berlau, 'who has worked with me for many years and is an excellent director' be allowed to establish the blocking (or 'groupings') for their *Mother Courage* production before they rehearse further. It opened on 1 October and was directed by Willi Rohde.

612 To Berlau   29 Aug. 1949
From Freilassing, a Bavarian village just outside Salzburg, on the way to see the Nehers about the *Dance of Death* and other projects. According to Berlau the 'little animal' was a silently nodding donkey.

*613 To Walter Oberer, Zurich Schauspielhaus   6 Sep. 1949
Oberer was the theatre's administrator. Brecht fears that the 'revue' (presumably *Ares's Chariot*) no longer figures in its plans, in which case no matter. He has seen Albers, who would be willing to perform in a *Threepenny Opera* directed by Lindtberg or Steckel. The Munich production was evidently not good enough to tour. Suhrkamp's theatre department is now handling the performing rights to this work.

614 To von Einem   12 Oct. 1949
Written five days after the establishment of the new German Democratic Republic, presumably for Von Einem to show to opponents of Brecht's proposed naturalisation. (The Western Zones had already been constituted as the Federal Republic, with its capital at Bonn, immediately after the ending of the Berlin blockade in May.)

615 To Albert Schreiner   Oct. 1949
Schreiner, a Marxist historian, had been on the Council for a Democratic Germany in the US with Brecht.

Lissagaray: Prosper L., whose contemporary history of the Commune was published in German translation in 1877. For Duncker see Note 593.

616 To Eric Bentley   31 Oct. 1949
Bentley had written on 18 October to criticise Brecht's misreading of *Hamlet*. Brecht's somewhat circuitous self-justification never resulted in any correction

of the *Organum*'s published text, which remains unamended to this day.

The illustrated 'model books' here referred to have not been published as such in English, but significant parts of their texts are in *Brecht on Theatre*, pp. 209–222 (*Antigone* and *Mother Courage*) and 163–68 ('Building up a Part: Laughton's *Galileo*'). See also Brecht's notes in our edition of *Mother Courage* (Brecht: *Collected Plays* vol. 5ii, London 1980).

617 Ditto   12 Nov. 1949
Bentley had said in reply that Brecht's interpretation of Shakespeare was about as true to the original as was his *Threepenny Opera* to John Gay. He had not thought highly of *The Days of the Commune*, but cited the view of Kurt Hirschfeld that it was intended to refer to the Berlin blockade.

618 To Wilhelm Pieck   2 Nov. 1949
Pieck, leader of the KPD in succession to Ernst Thälmann, became the first President of the new GDR. He had attended the 'Brecht evenings' on 26 April and 12 May 1935 in Moscow (where he was a member of the Comintern) and more recently, with Otto Grotewohl, had first proposed the formation of the Berliner Ensemble to the East German Politboro. He was the father of Arthur Pieck who had been a close colleague of Piscator in the workers' theatre movement both in pre-Hitler Germany and in the Moscow offices of MORT.

The poem 'To my countrymen' can be found in *Poems 1913–1956*, p. 417.

619 To Erich Engel   Nov. 1949
Brecht and Engel had been working together not only on the *Puntila* production, with which the Ensemble opened in November, but also on the project for a *Mother Courage* film to be made by the official East German DEFA with Engel as director and Neher as designer/visualiser. The first treatments were by R. A. Stemmle. Where and why they were arguing about dialectics is not clear, but both liked to be thought of as philosophers.

620 To Hanns Eisler   Nov.–Dec. 1949
Koloman Wallisch, subject of a remarkable piece of reportage by Anna Seghers in the mid-1930s, was an Austrian Socialist leader in Bruck an der Mur, Styria, who was caught in the mountains and hanged by Dollfuss's forces during the fighting of February 1934. Brecht and Eisler are thought to have planned the cantata in the US around 1945, and the text (which somewhat recalls their first Lehrstück *Die Massnahme*) is published in *Gedichte aus dem Nachlass*, pp. 385–95. No music however has been found.

Eisler's *Weissbrot-Kantate* of 1937, Op. 60 no. 2, is to a text by Silone. His brother was the former Comintern official Gerhart Eisler, who had escaped from the US that May and later because the GDR Information Minister.

621 To Paul Wandel   Dec. 1949
Wandel was now the GDR Minister for Education, and generally responsible for cultural matters. He replied to Brecht saying that while he was in favour of master classes he was primarily concerned about the development of a stimulating climate of ideas for their students.

*622 To Weigel   Dec. 1949
New Year greetings.

*623 To Henry Peter Matthis   Dec. 1949
Matthis was the Swedish writer addressed in letters 384–8, who had now
undertaken to get Brecht's books and manuscripts sent to him from Sweden,
where he had left them in 1940. Brecht was suggesting that the Soviet Consulate
might be of use.

624 To the Dresden Staatstheater   Winter 49/50
The Volksbühne referred to is the Dresden branch.

For Heinz Kuckhahn see Note 358. In the event he did direct the play, which
opened on 23 February.

625 To Hermann Duncker   1949
See Note 594.

626 To the South German Radio, Stuttgart   2 Jan. 1950
In reply to a request of 19 December 1949. *Lindbergh's Flight* was a 'radio
Lehrstück' first performed at the Baden-Baden music festival in 1929, with
music by Weill (and initially also Hindemith). Its theme was the young American
airman's first solo crossing of the Atlantic. Three years later the Lindberghs'
baby was kidnapped and murdered, just before Hitler came to power. Thereafter
he lost much sympathy because of his favourable attitude to the new German
regime and its Luftwaffe.

*627 To Martin Hellberg   9 Jan. 1950
Hellberg was General-Intendant in Dresden. Brecht wrote to reinforce his
insistence (in Letter 624) that *Puntila* must be directed by Kuckhahn.

628 To Viertel   17 Jan 1950
Viertel's production of *Vassa Zhelesnova* with Giehse and the Berliner Ensemble
opened on 23 December 1949. *The Tutor* would follow, as a replacement for *The
Days of the Commune*, whose production was being delayed on political grounds.

Winkelried was a hero of the Swiss War of Independence against Austria, who
seized the enemy spears at the battle of Sempach and turned them against
himself.

Viertel was now directing *Richard II* for the Burgtheater.

629 To Max Frisch   23 Jan. 1950
Frisch (see Note 562) had sent Brecht passages from his diary about their
meetings in Zurich which he would publish in the course of 1950 as *Tagebuch
1946 bis 1949*.

*630, *631 To Hans Tombrock   Jan.–Feb. 1950
Suggestions much as before (in various letters between numbers 399 and 425)
for the stories and themes of T's pictures.

632 To Stefan S. Brecht   Mid-Feb. 1950
Brecht's son had remained in the U S, where he was studying at Harvard and
completing a dissertation on Hegel.

633 To Peter Suhrkamp   Feb. 1950
The new 'model books' (see Note 616) were designed by Peter Palitzsch, who
had been recruited from Dresden as a dramaturg and graphic designer, and

published by Henschel-Verlag in East Berlin. It would still be some years before they appeared.

Guest appearances. Of the BE with the *Mother Courage* production.

634 To Ferdinand Reyher   Feb. 1950
James Lyon reports that as a result of this letter Reyher went to see Piscator in New York on 6 March 1950. Piscator evidently had abandoned hope (see Note 586), and Fritz Wisten (a former concentration camp inmate then directing the Theater am Schiffbauerdamm) became Intendant of the East Berlin Volksbühne that June.

635 To Fritz Kortner   Feb. 1950
Kortner's production of Strindberg's *The Father* had opened on 1 February at the Hebbel-Theater, with himself playing the lead. He never performed with the Berliner Ensemble, in *Galileo* or anything else.

636 To von Einem   2 March 1950
It was *Richard II*, not *III* that Viertel was directing (Brecht's mistake).

Schuh: Oskar Fritz Schuh, a German director who had worked in Vienna throughout the 1940s and done some fine opera productions. He was closely associated with Von Einem and Neher at Salzburg.

637 To Berlau   10 March 1950
In one of the songs in Brecht's and Eisler's *The Mother* Pelagea Vlassova sings of the 'Third Thing' that binds her to her son Pavel where other parents and children drift apart.

638 To Hans Mayer   25 March 1950
Mayer was another notable Marxist critic in the lineage of Lukács and Bloch, but better disposed to Brecht than the former. He was for some years a professor of literature at Leipzig University before moving to Hannover in the Federal Republic.

Lenz, a contemporary of Goethe, was long one of the interesting outcasts of German literature. Brecht and his young colleagues adapted his rambling play *The Tutor* to fill the gap left by the postponement of *The Days of the Commune*. Neher was co-director and designed costumes and sets. It opened on 15 April 1950, but its pessimistic attitude to German history (the conformist 'misère' of a country of small states) did not please some GDR critics.

639 To Berlau   19 April 1950
'*Tutor*' model book': no such thing was published, so presumably Brecht was speaking of the one-off albums made for the instruction of producers elsewhere. Suhrkamp's lawsuit had been brought by the heirs of S. Fischer, whose publishing firm he had managed under the Third Reich. At the end of April it was agreed that Suhrkamp should leave and set up his own firm, and that authors who had leased him their rights in 1936 or later should choose whether to go with him or stay with the Fischers. Brecht's response is given in the following letter.

640 To Suhrkamp   21 May 1950
*640x ?To the central committee of the Socialist Unity Party   nd
On 26 April 1950 the Party's cultural adviser Stefan Heymann (who had been

home affairs editor on the *Rote Fahne* before 1933) wrote to Brecht with objections to some of the *Kriegsfibel* epigrams. B's undated reply, cited in Christiane Bohnert: *Brechts Lyrik im Kontext*, Athenäum-Verlag, Königstein 1982, pp. 307–8, shows the failure of such officials to appreciate his use of irony. The effect was to make him drop his plan to publish the cycle for four years.

*641 To Wieland Herzfelde   May 1950
This is the 'Letter to the editor of the selection *A Hundred Poems*' included in the notes to *Poems 1913–1956*, pp. 462–3. The last sentence, omitted in Elisabeth Hauptmann's transcription, tells Herzfelde that 'The method of selection you've adopted at the outset is brilliant'.

642 To Neher   Mid-1950
Brecht was granted Austrian citizenship on 12 April 1950, but got his passport only on 3 November. The *Galileo* plan fell through, to be replaced by *The Mother*, for which preparations would begin on 11 October. Neher did the sets, with projections by Heartfield and his brother.

The conductor for *Lucullus* the following year would be Hermann Scherchen. For Legal see Note 577.

Neher wrote a number of librettos for the East German composer Rudolf Wagner-Régeny, and was still working on *Der Darmwäscher* ('The Offal-cleaner', later known as 'Persian Legend'), with some slight assistance from Brecht.

In August Brecht would use his Steyr car (of Austrian manufacture) to go on holiday at Ahrenshoop on Rügen Island in the Baltic, which had been allotted to the Kulturbund in 1946 as a resort for the intelligentsia. 'A completely Nazi area', he called it. He subsequently drove with Ruth Berlau to Munich, where he remained throughout September and the first week of October.

*643 To Rudolf Wagner-Régeny   Spring–Summer 1950
Detailed suggestions for Act 4 of *Der Darmwäscher*. Why not insert his (W-R's) setting of 'Lasst euch nicht verführen', the early poem which Weill had set in scene 11 (the hurricane) of *Mahagonny*? (This was done.)

644 To Viertel   End Aug. 1950
The Hauptmann conflation was directed not by Viertel but by Egon Monk – then one of Brecht's young assistants – and opened at the Deutsches Theater Kammerspiele on 27 March 1951, with Giehse as Mrs Wolffen. An illustrated account is given in *Theaterarbeit*. The Hauptmann Estate objected to the adaptation, and it was taken off after fourteen performances.

Brecht directed the Munich Kammerspiele's *Mother Courage*, which opened on 8 October, using Teo Otto's sets and following the Berlin 'model'. Besides Giehse in her original (1941) part, the cast included Erni Wilhelmi (as Kattrin), Hans-Christian Blech and Friedrich Domin. Berlau, Monk and Eric Bentley assisted Brecht. Neher wrote (on 16 September) regretting not being involved.

645 To the DEFA   6 Sep. 1950
Burri, to whom Brecht had written about the possibility even before leaving the US (Letter 545), had succeeded Stemmle as script writer. Sepp Schwab (an old Munich Communist who had run the German section of the Soviet Radio and

was now head of the GDR Film Committee) and Albert Wilkening answered on 13 October that no decisions could be taken till they knew how Brecht meant the story to end. The question for them was 'can a film for peace be effective only in a pacifist sense, or can it contribute to the active struggle against war'?

646 To von Einem   14 Sep. 1950
Von Einem's mother was thought to carry some weight in Salzburg. About three weeks later he was in Munich, where Brecht and he agreed a Salzburg production of the (as yet unperformed) *Caucasian Chalk Circle* with Käthe Gold and Homolka under the direction of Viertel. It never took place.

647 To Elisabeth Hauptmann   Sep. 1950
The Austrian assistant was Harald Benesch from the Vienna Scala.

  The Overcoat was a film story after Gogol which Brecht and Hauptmann had written in California for Peter Lorre. It was never made.

  The proposed Hamburg production was of *The Threepenny Opera*.

***647x** To Reyher   Oct.–Nov. 1950
Apologising for having been absent so much of the time when R. paid his long-anticipated visit to Berlin at the end of August 1950. This fiasco is described by Lyon in *Brecht's American Cicerone*, pp. 142–9. The letter is on p. 217 of the same.

***648** To Viertel   Nov. 1950
Trying to persuade him to direct the Gerhart Hauptmann programme (Note 644) and mentioning the Ensemble's new rehearsal stage in the Reinhardtstrasse. 'It is important not to give up our cultural collaboration, particularly now – and probably for a long while to come.'

649 Ditto   Nov. 1950
The adaptation was a collective one involving Brecht, Wolfgang Böttcher, the actor Ernst Kahler and four of the young assistants: Hubalek, Monk, Palitzsch and Vera Skupina.

***650** To the director of 'Golden fliesst der Stahl'   11 Dec. 1950
Congratulating the amateur actors of a play by Karl Grünberg, which Brecht and other members of the Ensemble had seen at the House of the Press.

651 To von Einem   7 Jan. 1951
Neher and Brecht had been occupied with the work on *The Mother*, which would open five days later on 12 January 1951 (when Brecht wrote the letter that follows).

652 To Walter Ulbricht   9 Jan. 1951
Ulbricht, originally a carpenter from Saxony, had been Pieck's second in the Moscow emigration and was now the secretary of the Socialist Unity (i.e. Communist) Party for the GDR. A man of narrow views, he had been a rigid supporter of Stalin's line for many years.

  Brecht now appealed to him in connection with Paul Dessau's opera version of *Lucullus*. This work of uncompromisingly modern music had been accepted by Ernst Legal at the State Opera with the support of Paul Wandel as Minister of Education. Following the first chorus rehearsals in January however the Ministry had asked to look at the score once again, found that it did not conform to the official standards of Socialist Realism (which followed Stalin's lieutenant A. A. Zhdanov in rejecting all innovatory works as 'formalistic') and decided that the production must be cancelled.

Despite Brecht's emphasis on the 'content' of such an anti-militaristic, anti-rearmament work, and on its topicality in 1951, the official objections were predominantly formal ones. The upshot was a single performance five days after Brecht had written this letter, before an invited audience whose reactions would be studied.

653 To Paul Wandel   19 March 1951
The invitation performance took place on 17 March.

654 To Ulbricht   19 March 1951
The terms 'realistic' and 'people's opera' conform with Zhdanov's terminology. But it was no use pretending. According to Werner Mittenzwei none of the party leaders was so vehemently hostile to the music as Ulbricht, who felt that the modern movement in general ran counter to 'the efforts of the best elements among the workers to work themselves up to a degree of art appreciation that could understand and honour classic beauty. This is where his efforts at compromise and political reconciliation stopped short.' (*Das Leben des Bertolt Brecht*, vol. 2, p. 433.)

655 To Anton Ackermann   25 March 1951
Ackermann was a top functionary of the Party secretariat with a special interest in film and other cultural matters. Together with Pieck, Hans Lauter, Grotewohl, Wandel and the party paper's editor Wilhelm Girnus, he had met Brecht and Dessau on 24 March to discuss the results of the test performance.

The same points about passive (or pacifist) and active (or militant) resistance to aggressive war were made as in connection with the *Mother Courage* film (Note 645). However, according to Dessau, Brecht did not speak.

Hans Lauter was head of the cultural section in the Central Committee. A week earlier at its Fifth Meeting that committee had adopted a resolution on the 'Struggle against Formalism in Literature and Art, and for a Progressive German Culture' which specified the *Lucullus* music as 'formalistic'.

*656 To Becher   March 1951
A flattering letter after having found *Verbrüderung*, an early (1916) book of Becher's poems in a provincial second-hand bookshop. Becher is not known to have taken up a position with respect to *Lucullus*.

657 To Wilhelm Pieck   6 April 1951
Brecht's textual changes are relatively insignificant. They can be followed in the notes to Brecht's *Collected Plays* volume 5 in the Random House edition. He sent further copies of them to Ackermann, Grotewohl, Kurt Bork of the Education Ministry and Herrnstadt of the Party paper.

*657x To Hermann Scherchen   ? April 1951
Married to the actress Gerda Müller, Scherchen (1891–1966) was a leading conductor of modern music who had emigrated to Switzerland in 1933. He conducted the *Lucullus* test performance, which he termed the greatest success he had ever experienced with a modern work.

Brecht here tells him that the opera cannot be performed in West Germany until the revisions have been made, since Dessau, while not accepting the charge of 'formalism', does not want to be involved in any performances that might be used as propaganda against the GDR. He himself would likewise find this 'absolutely horrible'. See Lucchesi and Shull (1988). p. 722

*658 To Leonard Steckel   April 1951
Asking him to play Galileo in the coming season with the Ensemble. (By then he had ceased to perform with them.)

*659 To Suhrkamp   16 April 1951
Asking for addresses to which he might send his poem 'To my countrymen' (Letter 618) in order to 'avoid taking part in the frightful splitting of our country, at least so far as the theatre is concerned'. Suhrkamp replied to Elisabeth Hauptmann on 27 April that 'I like the poem. But I don't like it being distributed as propaganda'.

*659x To Hermann Scherchen   22 April 1951
Summarising changes to the *Lucullus* libretto. (BBA 586/13).

660 To Fritz Kortner   5 May 1951
Sequel to Letter *658. Kortner did not accept either.

661 To Wolfgang Völker   5 May 1951
Völker directed both the test production for the State Opera and the revised and retitled version that finally went into the repertoire on 12 October. He had applied on 23 April for the material with a view to staging it in Hamburg.

*662 To Hildegard Steinmetz   5 May 1951
Thanking her for prints of her photographs of the Munich *Mother Courage* (including a striking picture of Eilif's sword dance which was included in *Theaterarbeit*).

*663 To Jacob Geis   5 May 1951
Mainly personal, and praising Burri as 'an exceptional talent and remarkably unsullied' (presumably by the Nazi years).

*664 To Therese Giehse   9 May 1951
Thanking her for a card and telling her that *Lucullus* would be done 'in a normal public way at the State Opera, which is really very sensible'.

665 To the Ministry for People's Education of the German Democratic Republic/Paul Wandel   24 May 1951
This is a development of Letter 621. 'Workers' and Peasants' faculties' were now part of the GDR educational pattern, as they had been in that of revolutionary Russia. Brecht's study of *Coriolanus* with his young assistants started that spring.

Wandel, who had been personally committed to *Lucullus* (and to Dessau's work in general), would be relieved of his responsibility for the arts in August. Two new bodies were founded outside his ministry: the State Commission for Art Affairs and the Office for Literature and Publishing. They were subsequently much criticised by Brecht and others.

666 To the German Central Institute for Pedagogy   28 May 1951
Brecht had been sent examples of the proposed teaching material and asked to comment. Ludwig Ganghofer was a popular novelist of the late nineteenth century, ridiculed incidentally in Hašek's *Adventures of the Good Soldier Švejk*.

'Der Trompeter an der Katzbach' (The Bugler beside the Stream) is cited critically in Brecht's essay 'Where I have learned' (*Poems 1913–1956*, pp. 474–5) in which he says that it 'was in all the school anthologies when I was young'.

667 To the German Academy of Arts   20 June 1951

668 To Viertel   June–July 1951
A letter from Viertel to Helene Weigel dated 20 June says that he will talk about the *Chalk Circle*, which he greatly loves, to Hilbert and Gielen (of the Austrian Federal Theatre administration and the Burgtheater respectively). 'You know how interested I was and am in everything the BE does. But I must pursue my own path.'

669 To Eisler   July–Aug. 1951
Eisler was evidently nervous that an *Urfaust* production by Egon Monk with Berliner Ensemble actors at Potsdam might spoil the prospects – commercial or political, it is not clear which – for his planned Faust opera. The production actually opened on 23 April 1952.

*670 Ditto   Aug. 1951
Brecht has been reading a report of Zhdanov's 1948 encounter with the Soviet composers, where Z. told them to avoid the false, ugly, alien formalism of Shostakovitch and Prokofiev and seek a 'deep organic connection with the People and its folk songs' instead. (see Alexander Werth; *Musical Uproar in Moscow*, London 1949). Brecht cites some early German folk poetry which Eisler could take into his libretto as a way of 'introducing a degree of warmth into the story'.

*671 Ditto   31 Aug. 1951
Thanking Eisler for sending an essay by Karl Schönewolf on his music for *The Mother*, which was to be included in *Theaterarbeit*.

672 To von Einem   18 Aug. 1951
As a result of the Austrian press campaign against the granting of citizenship to Brecht, von Einem had been forced to resign from the Salzburg Festival Board.

  The Dance of Death project seems not to have progressed beyond this point. We are left with some fifty disjointed pages of typescript, of which the more coherent parts occupy pp. 2993–2999 of *GW7*.

*673 To Rüdiger Syberberg   Oct./Nov. 1951
Syberberg and the better-known Ernst Penzoldt had both replied to Brecht's 'Open Letter to German Artists and Writers' of 26 September 1951 – the often-quoted one that refers to the destruction of Carthage in three wars.

*674 To Otto Ernst Tickardt/Theatre of the City of Greiz   20 Nov. 1951
Congratulating them on their *Antigone* production, and enclosing a new prologue for it. This consists of 25 lines of free verse to be spoken by Tiresias in place of the original 'Vorspiel' set in Berlin at the end of World War 2.

*675 To H. O. Münsterer   22 Nov. 1951
A reply to his early Augsburg friend, who had differed from him about the exact wording of the round 'A dog went to the kitchen' and the historical personality of Lucullus.

*676 To Willi Bredel   22 Nov. 1951
Turning down a request to write a postscript to a book of Kuba (Kurt Barthel)'s poems which his old colleague on *Das Wort* was editing.

*677 To Albert Bussmann/Landestheater Eisenach   Early 1952
To complain about the sacking of the director who was due to stage *The Mother*,
because his production of a Sternheim play had apparently been too stylised.
(He was reinstated for Brecht's play.)

*678 To Marieluise Fleisser   2 Jan. 1952
Sending her a short story by Jacob Geis which Brecht thought she might make
into a good play. She wrote back on 23 February 1952 turning it down.

679 To Suhrkamp   2 Jan. 1952
Suhrkamp had asked Brecht to translate two poems from *Old Possum's Book of
Practical Cats*.

*680 To the Aufbau-Verlag   2 Jan. 1952
To thank Erich Wendt and Walter Janka for the care taken over his *Hundert
Gedichte* (selection of a Hundred Poems, edited by Wieland Herzfelde). This was
Brecht's first GDR book of poems, and the one for which Heartfield designed the
jacket showing a Chinese tea-root lion. See *Poems 1913–1956*, p. 431 and the
corresponding note.

*681 To the German Academy of Arts/Rudolf Engel   29 Nov. 1951
Engel was secretary of the Academy. Cf. Note 666. The proposed curricula of
the Central Institute for Pedagogy had been submitted to Friedrich Wolf for
vetting by the Academy, and Wolf had asked Brecht to help.

He accordingly suggests a 'basic school course' which would include poems by
Rückert, Goethe ('der neue Amadis'), Karl Kraus (epilogue to *The Last Days of
Mankind*), Hölderlin and Gerhart Hauptmann – all of whom had been neglected in
the proposed curricula – as well as his own 'Legend of the origin of the book Tao-
Tê-Ching' and 'The Tailor of Ulm' (*Poems 1913–1956*, pp. 314 and 243).

The Communist Manifesto, he says, *must* be included in the German course, and
he notes that Flaubert, Stendhal and Maupassant do not figure at all. Likewise
Homer, Virgil and Lucretius are missing. Under the heading *Kitsch* he regrets
that there are no examples of bad writing: 'neither political nor aesthetic
discrimination can be taught entirely on the basis of what is *good*'. So why not
contrast Tolstoy's prose, say, with Ludwig Ganghofer's? Moreover, there should
be examples of 'CVs, reports and speeches' as well as slogans good and bad.

682 To three Young Pioneers of the Gottleuba Primary School   15 Jan. 1952

*683 To Peter Hacks   15 Jan. 1952
Hacks, who was then living in Munich, had written to Brecht for advice about
his writing and asked if he should come over to the GDR. This he did, and
wrote some interesting, amusing and often controversial plays. He also translated
The Playboy of the Western World for the Berliner Ensemble to stage in 1956 under
the joint direction of Palitzsch and Wekwerth.

684 To Günther Strupp   18 Jan. 1952
The Augsburg artist was another who wrote as a result of Brecht's 'Open
Letter' (referred to in Note 673).

*685 To Paul Schurek   5 Feb. 1952
Schurek, author of the play *Kamerad Kasper* (1932) for whose Volksbühne
production in April 1932 Brecht had contributed some songs set by Eisler, and

of a number of plays performed under the Nazis, had written criticising Brecht's
'Open Letter' for wishing to restrict freedom of speech, which he saw as
indivisible, by denying it to war propaganda.

*686 To Alfred Schulz   5 Feb. 1952
(He being another who commented on the 'Open Letter').

*687 To Alois Grill   5 Feb. 1952
Ditto.

688 To Sepp Schwab   25 Feb. 1952
For Schwab see Note 645. The new script was the second version. A third was
approved both by Brecht and by DEFA on 19 June 1952. After that Engel
made way for Wolfgang Staudte. The conclusion was *not* 'satisfactory'.

*689 To Leon Schiller   March 1952
A formal letter thanking the Polish director for his hospitality to the Brechts
when they visited Warsaw as guests of the Writers' Union in February 1952.

*690 To Karl Köther/Landestheater Eisenach   5 March 1952
Köther was Intendant of the theatre to which Brecht had already written (Letter
677). He now sent him some notes on Kaspar Königshof's production, which
had opened on 1 March.

*691 To Louis Fürnberg   14 March 1952
About the Hašek rights in Brecht's play *Schweik in the Second World War*: where
should they be sent? (They were 20 per cent of Brecht's share.) The poet Fürnberg
had been born a Czech, and was now the GDR Ambassador in Prague.

*692 To Joachim Bodag   14 March 1952
Bodag had written to Brecht about verse rhythms, and this was a curt answer.

693 To Friedrich Wolf   ?
Though Brecht addresses his Communist fellow-playwright as 'Du' they were
never close friends. For their partnership in the matter of school curricula see
Letter 681 and its note.

*694 To Konrad Schrader   ?
Brecht's correspondent had seen a provincial production of *Puntila* and written
to ask various questions. Brecht replied that 'Puntila-ism' had still not been
overcome, that he saw scene 8 ('Tales from Finland') as a 'principal scene', that
Berlin audiences had not found the play hard to understand, that they tended to
agree with Matti's 'Questions from a worker who reads' approach, and finally
that one play was not enough to instigate 'a new humanism'.

695 To Hermann Scherchen   14 March 1952
Scherchen had written to tell Brecht that the Frankfurt Opera production of
Lucullus was a success, with 26 curtain calls on the opening night (30 January
1952).

696 To *Neues Deutschland*   14 March 1952
The Party paper had forwarded Brecht a letter from a Finnish journalist,
Friedrich Ege, asking why their review of *Puntila* had not mentioned Hella
Wuolijoki as co-author and offering to write them an article on this point.

Most of what Brecht says is true; moreover Wuolijoki had apparently tried to
get a performance at the Helsinki National Theatre under his direction. However

the relationship of his play to their collaborative Finnish version is closer than his
final sentence would suggest.

*696x To Reyher   Spring 1952
Commenting on a request to R. from Berlau, who wanted him to get some
photos for her in New York and reminded him of a debt which had in fact been
paid. Would he please ignore this misunderstanding and forget it? (Reyher had
stopped communicating after his unhappy Berlin visit in 1950.)

697 To Dolf Sternberger   March 1952
Sternberger was a West German writer who had sent Brecht an article of his
(from *Die Gegenwart*, Frankfurt, 1 March 1952) in which he proposed a fourth
version of *Lucullus*.

698 To Sepp Schwab/DEFA   8 May 1952
Further to Letter 688. Engel had now dropped out and been succeeded by
Wolfgang Staudte, one of the most successful of the new DEFA directors. A plan
emerged for a Franco-GDR co-production, with Simone Signoret as Yvette.
Busch, whose introduction of a Dutch accent in the revised Ensemble production
of 1951 was not entirely to the play's advantage, would not have a part.

699 To Suhrkamp   14 June 1952
Hermann Hesse was one of the former Fischer authors who had opted to go to
the new Suhrkamp-Verlag. Aufbau, who were then publishing the GDR
Brecht edition under licence, seem to have assumed that they could do the same
for Hesse, and published two of his novels without waiting for Suhrkamp's
agreement. But the GDR Mark, nominally at parity with that of the Federal
Republic, was worth only about a quarter as much on the free (or black) market.

*700 To Helmut Holtzhauer (State Commission for Art Affairs)16 July 1952
Criticising the new Commission for not allowing for adequate time in the scenic
workshops, particularly in view of a proposal by Brecht and Eisler to the
Second Party Congress for special factory performances. Holtzhauer, the
Commission chairman, had hitherto been Minister for Popular Education in the
Saxon provincial government. He later became director of the national literary
archives in Weimar and president of the Goethe Society.

701 To Elisabeth Hauptmann   July 1952
Refers to the two volumes of *Frühe Stücke* with which the first collected
Suhrkamp edition would start the following year. The Aufbau equivalent
would follow, with some changes and corrections and a new foreword to
volume 1. The 'Hymn' is that at the beginning of *Baal*.

The contract of 1 February 1949, which provided for Hauptmann as chief
editor, licensed Brecht's publication rights to Suhrkamp for all Germany, but
allowed Suhrkamp to sub-license in cases where his own edition could not be
distributed (i.e. in the GDR).

This is the first of the Letters to be written from the Brechts' country
establishment at Buckow in 'Prussian Switzerland' East of Berlin.

At the end of 1953, following nearly half a year's illness in and out of hospital,
Hauptmann would write to Brecht in a mixture of German and English to say
that she was earning too little and getting no recognition.

*702 To Wolf   1 Aug.
Promising to send him the Ensemble's album *Theaterarbeit*, and asking for
Wolf's collected plays as soon as possible. Also complaining that Wolf has spelt
Bertolt with a 'd'.

703 Ditto   Autumn 1952
F D J = the Free German Youth, a Party organisation then chaired by Erich
Honecker. He would become Ulbricht's successor as Party secretary, finally
resigning on 18 October 1989.

704 To Paul Fabig   1 Aug 1952
Fabig, who had been a stage manager at the first night of *Drums in the Night* at
the Munich Kammerspiele in 1922, had asked leave to adapt *Socrates Wounded* for
amateur actors. This short story by Brecht is about the good sense of the
philosopher in running away from a battle.

*705 To Burri   1 Aug 1952
Thanks for contacting Carl Orff (whom Brecht wanted to write the *Caucasian
Chalk Circle* music). 'If Orff shows the faintest interest I'll write to him at once . . .'.

706 To Eisler   1 Aug. 1952
The Siemens-Plania works in Lichtenberg (an eastern suburb) had asked to
sponsor Brecht's and Eisler's plan for factory performances, thinking apparently
that they meant to encourage amateur groups.

   The 'Garbe' plan was for a didactic play based on the experiences of a much-
publicised furnace worker of that name at the Lichtenberg works who had
completed a difficult repair job in half the allotted time.

   Erwin Strittmatter was a young East German writer whose play *Katzgraben* was
the first real GDR drama to be tackled by the Ensemble. Brecht spent much
time on its revision and production, because he liked the author's humour,
powers of observation and interest in language. It would open on 23 May 1953.

*707 To Becher   Summer–Autumn 1952
Forwarding an analysis of Becher's poem 'Deutschland' for a World Youth
Movement anthology to be called *Freundschaft-Druzhba-Amitié* and published in
1953.

*708 To Hans Gaugler   Sep. 1952
Telling him of next season's plans for the Berliner Ensemble and regretting that
he should 'hesitate'. (Gaugler had left the company for good.)

709 To Helmut Holtzhauer (State Commission for Art Affairs)   4 Oct. 1952
The play was after all performed in Cracow, Lodz and Warsaw during the
Ensemble's 1952 Polish tour. The agitprop forms of the Weimar period were
still frowned on as 'formalist'.

709x To Adolf Fritz Guhl   11 Oct. 1952
Guhl (1917–77), who was musical director of the Berliner Ensemble till 1953,
had resented Brecht's criticisms of the playing of the Eisler music at a
rehearsal of *The Mother*. Letter in Lucchesi/Shull, p. 246.

710 To Carl Orff   20 Oct. 1952
See Note 705. Orff replied that he hoped to see Brecht at the opening of *The
Good Person of Szechwan* in Frankfurt. But he had little free time.

711 Ditto   15 Nov. 1952
The plays referred to were *Señora Carrar's Rifles* and the stage adaptation (by
Brecht and Besson) of Anna Seghers's radio documentary *The Trial of Jeanne
d'Arc at Rouen in 1431*.

712 To Egon Rentzsch/CC of the Socialist Unity Party   27 Nov 1952
Answer to the Central Committee's request for comments on the Soviet party
congress (the last to be held in Stalin's lifetime).

*713 To Leopold Infeld   1 Dec. 1952
Thanking the Polish physicist for his book *Whom the Gods Love* about the short-
lived nineteenth-century mathematician Evariste Galois.

*714 To Helene Weigel   15 Dec. 1952
Weigel had gone on the Polish tour with the company, and Brecht is reassuring
her that all is well, notably as regards the latest script of *Katzgraben*.

*715 to Albert Einstein   Early Jan. 1953
A telegram asking him to do something for Ethel and Julius Rosenberg (about
to be executed for alleged atomic espionage). It ends 'they are innocent'. Similar
telegrams went to Arthur Miller and Hemingway.

716 To Burri   17 Jan. 1953
Brecht had met the West German director Helmut Käutner, who was interested
in making the *Courage* film. Geis apparently favoured his involvement.

*717 To Erwin Geschonneck   28 Jan. 1953
Trying to persuade him to stay with the Berliner Ensemble, for whom he had
played Matti in *Puntila* and the Chaplain in *Mother Courage*. Brecht felt that,
thanks to his unprofessional background (in agitprop and the exiled groups) he
needed to attend to his technique if he was not to decline. He should therefore
sign his new contract and trust Langhoff to give him a big part at the Deutsches
Theater over and above his Ensemble work.

   Geschonneck was much in demand for the films, but he prolonged his
association with the Ensemble, his last part being the Governor in *The Caucasian
Chalk Circle*, which opened on 7 October 1954.

718 To Hans Mayer   22 Feb. 1953
For Mayer see Note 638. Brecht is following up a conversation. By the end of
1952 an article in praise of Eisler's libretto by the Austrian Communist Ernst
Fischer had appeared in *Sinn und Form*, interpreting his Faust character as 'a
central figure of the German Misere . . . the German Humanist as a renegade'.

   Even so intelligent a critic as Mayer appears to have been upset by this slur on
the 'cultural heritage'.

*719 To Annemarie Auer/German Academy of Arts   3 March 1953
About a story that had been submitted to him for an opinion.

*720 To Herbert Klecha   4 March 1953
He had asked Brecht to look at a play he had written. Brecht advised him to
start by writing short stories.

721 To Wolfgang Langhoff, Deutsches Theater   April 1953
The Deutsches Theater were currently performing *Faust* Part One. Langhoff
turned Brecht's idea down on 26 April.

*722 To Li Weinert   April 1953
Short letter of sympathy to the widow of Erich Weinert, who had died on 20
April. (See Notes 586, 587).

*723 To Kurt Desch   May 1953
Short letter of good wishes to the Munich publisher on his fiftieth birthday
(2 June 1953).

724 To Otto Grotewohl   15 June 1953
On Brecht's expectation of using E. J. Aufricht's former theatre (which he had
sometimes treated as his own) see Letters 529, 532, 575 and the relevant notes.

In view of what was about to happen this letter seems a remarkably intelligent
piece of anticipation. A letter from the premier's secretariat on 22 July would
give the government's agreement in principle, as soon as Wisten's Volksbühne
could move into its new building.

725 To Walter Ulbricht   17 July 1953
Addressed to the Party secretary, this was Brecht's reaction to the attempted rising
of 17 June 1953. *Neues Deutschland*, and consequently also the Western media,
cited the last sentence alone, omitting Brecht's emphasis on popular consultation.
See also the poems written around this time (e.g. *Poems 1913–1956*, pp. 435–6).

726 To Grotewohl   17 June 1953
This and the foregoing letter were dictated by Brecht to his young assistant Isot
Kilian around 8 a.m. on 17 June, and handed personally to the premier's secretary.

*726x To V. S. Semyonov   c. 17 June 1953
According to Werner Mittenzwei's *Das Leben des Bertolt Brecht*, vol. 2 (where
there is a chapter on these events, pp. 482–510) Brecht wrote on the same
occasion to the Soviet ambassador. He also telephoned Rudolf Engel at the
Academy, where (according to the recollections of Alexander Abusch) he and
Eisler attended a meeting that afternoon and proposed that members should
join in a series of short broadcast statements.

There are no entries for this crucial year in Brecht's *Arbeitsjournal* (as
published) between 4 March and 20 August.

727 To Becher   23 June 1953
Hans Rodenberg, a member of the Moscow emigration (and a Soviet citizen)
who had been the organiser of the 'Junge Volksbühne' before 1933, was now
the head of DEFA. His unfinished *Protokoll eines Lebens* was published by
Henschel, East Berlin in 1980.

728 To Suhrkamp   1 July 1953
Suhrkamp was clearly concerned about the many damaging reports in the
Western media as to his friend's attitude.

Erna Dorn: Brecht mistakenly wrote 'Eva Born', which has been corrected
by his German editor. The former concentration camp guard's activities were
reported in *Neues Deutschland* on 26 and 27 June, after she had been condemned
to death.

RIAS = Radio in the American Sector (of Berlin), then a significant factor in
the not-so-Cold War.

According to Mittenzwei's account, Brecht spent the second half of the

morning of 17 June walking with Strittmatter and Rülicke down to the
Brandenburg Gate, where the red flag had been torn down, and saw the Soviet
tanks approaching along Unter den Linden, the crowd withdrawing to the other
(West Berlin) side of the Gate, and the tanks then turning back. The Potsdamer
Platz and the Warschauer Brücke, which the letter also mentions, are respectively
just south of the Gate and some 3 to 4 kilometres away to the East, near the
Schlesische Bahnhof.

Brecht's sensitivity to Nazi survivals in both East and West is very evident in
his Journal and his poems; see the Journal entry for 7 July 1954 and the poems
'Still at it', 'Eight years ago' and 'The one-armed man in the undergrowth' in
the Buckow Elegies sequence (*Poems 1913–1956*, pp. 438–45). Note too his
reaction to the singing of 'Deutschland über Alles', today once again the
national anthem of the greater part of Germany, which had led him and Eisler
to write their 'Children's anthem' (ibid., p. 423), and particularly its third verse.

*729 To Walter Victor   10 July 1953
Victor was editor of a series of 'Readers for Our Time', and Brecht had undertaken
to write a preface for the Shakespeare reader. He now begged to be excused.

730 To Grotewohl   12 July 1953
Wolfgang Harich, Marxist Philosophy Professor at the Humboldt (Berlin)
University, pupil of Ernst Bloch and husband of Isot Kilian, had become one of
the government's most persistent critics. After Brecht's death he would be tried
and imprisoned, claiming in his defence that Brecht had agreed with him. This
was certainly so as regards cultural policy, where the two men launched an open
attack on the Commissions in July–August 1953. Helene Weigel however
would deny that it went further. After some years Harich would be released and
move to the Federal Republic. Kilian remained in the GDR.

731 To Weigel   Mid-1953
Weigel was holidaying at Ahrenshoop (Note 642) while Brecht remained at
Buckow, working on his last play *Turandot* and writing the Elegies.

Hill = Hainer Hill the designer, a protégé of Neher's.

Ulrich = Luise Ulrich from Weigel's office.

The flat – on two storeys – was at 125 Chausseestrasse, where the Brechts
remained till after Weigel's death. The building now houses the Brecht and
Weigel Archives, the Brecht Estate secretariat, the Brecht-Zentrum and the
Brecht bookshop.

Apart from *Coriolanus* the programme would be realised, but over a period of
two years.

Mutter = Anna Mutter, the Buckow housekeeper.

732 To Paul Wandel   Aug. 1953
Wandel, though deprived of responsibility for Culture in August 1951 (Note
665) was still Minister for Education, and Brecht still saw him as an ally in what
had become a conflict between the Academy and the Commissions. Brecht
emerged as the former's spokesman in his article 'Cultural Policy and Academy
of Arts' in the Party paper for 12 August 1953 (translated with notes in *Brecht on
Theatre*, pp. 266–70).

An earlier draft of this letter, dated 4 August, is quoted in Mittenzwei's *Das
Leben Bertolt Brechts*, vol. 2, p. 561.

*733 Ditto   Mid-Aug 1953
Not sent. The poem in question is 'The truth unites' in the Buckow Elegies, and
the letter says that this truth is 'that [the workers] are in mortal danger of being
dragged into a new war by the revival of fascism; that they must do all they can
to bring the petit-bourgeois elements under their leadership'.

*734, *735 To Burri   c. Autumn 1953
Telling him that both Wien-Film (Austrian) and DEFA want to film *Puntila*
with Curt Bois (who had taken the stage part over from Steckel at the end of
1951). Would he write the script for one or the other? Would Liebeneiner [a
successful director under the Nazis] be good?
   Brecht and Bois knew the artistic director of Wien-Film, Hans Winge, from
California. The firm was under Soviet management.

736 To Hans J. Leupold   20 Aug. 1953
Answer to a query about the sets for the original Paris production of *Señora
Carrar's Rifles*. Were they influenced by Dada or the Proletkult?

*737 To Wilhelm Girnus   29 Aug. 1953
Girnus was on the Party paper's editorial committee, and had been discussing
its theatre reviews with Brecht. The letter recommends four younger critics.

738 To H. O. Münsterer   29 Aug. 1953
Walter Nubel was a devoted collector and bibliographer of all publications to
do with Brecht. His invaluable bibliography was published in the *Sinn und Form*
special Brecht number of 1957. The long withheld 'Augsburg Sonnets' are now
included in the *Gedichte aus dem Nachlass*, pp. 193–9.

739 To Renata Mertens-Bertozzi   Autumn 1953
Hans and Renata Mertens were Zurich friends (Note 559). She helped arrange for
an Italian edition of Brecht's theoretical writings to be published by Einaudi
(Turin).

*740 To Comrade Wenk   Sep. 1953
This comrade cannot be identified by the Brecht-Archive, but was evidently a
reader of *Neues Deutschland* who thought he had detected a number of stylistic
faults in Brecht's article (Note 732 above). Some of these, like the use of Latin-
derived words such as 'quality', would likewise have pained the Nazis.

*741 To Berlau   Aug. 1953
Berlau had gone to Copenhagen to help in the Royal Theatre's production of
Mother Courage. Brecht warns her to be tactful in her comments at rehearsal, and
tells her that the Walchers are at Buckow and Palitzsch has left for Malmø.

742 Ditto   Aug. 1953
Brecht now spoke of asking Astrid and Barne Henning-Jenson to direct the
Courage film. Neu-Babelsberg was the location of the old UFA studios near
Potsdam.

743 Ditto   Sep. 1953
Penguins: paperback detective stories. The authors referred to are Anthony
Berkeley (*The Case of the Poisoned Chocolates*) and John Dickson Carr, both, like
the publishers, British.
   Hans Garbe: see Note 706. In the second half of October Brecht and Eisler

discussed collaborating on a work about him 'in the style of *The Decision* or *The Mother*, with a whole act about 17 June' (*Arbeitsjournal* entry for 15–30 October 1953). They planned to write this in March and April. The play was to be called *Büsching* (name of a character in the unfinished *Fatzer* of pre-Hitler days) but all that remains is fourteen typescript pages from before 1953, a sketch of November 1954 for an 11-scene structure, and Käthe Rülicke's preliminary reportage entitled *Hans Garbe erzählt* which had been published by Rütten und Loening (Potsdam) in 1952.

744 Ditto   Sep. 1953
The German text of the 'short chronicle' has not come to light, but a Danish version appeared in *Politiken*, Copenhagen 7 October 1953.

*745 Ditto   Sep. 1953
To say he has returned to Buckow from Berlin.

746 To Suhrkamp   17 Sep. 1953
Suhrkamp was worried about possible correction costs. The Prologue (or First Act) to *The Caucasian Chalk Circle*, being set in contemporary Soviet Georgia, was liable to be cut for various reasons, both West and East of the Iron Curtain. The rest of the letter, here omitted, deals with the publication of the first two volumes of plays and of the *Versuche* (where Brecht then envisaged including *Fear and Misery of the Third Reich* in *Versuche 14*). It is dated from Helene Weigel's office near the Deutsches Theater.

*746x To Erwin Leiser   ?
Cited in his essay 'He who said No' in *Bertolt Brecht*, published by Inter Nationes, Bad Godesberg 1966 (i.e. by the West German cultural relations service).

*747 To Suhrkamp   Nov. 1953
Congratulating him on the first two volumes of plays, Brecht suggests continuing in the same format rather than republish the earlier *Versuche* volumes. Enclosing also 'a few Buckowlic Elegies for your private reading'.

*748 To Helen Weigel   Early Nov 1953
The Brechts had been in Vienna for the Scala's production of *The Mother*, directed by Wekwerth with Weigel as Pelagea Vlassova. It opened on 31 October. Brecht, who had returned early to Berlin, asked Weigel if she had been able to meet Gielen of the Burgtheater, apparently so as to be able to ask him for Neher's costume designs for *Julius Caesar*, which had just been staged there.

749 To Pablo Picasso   13 Nov. 1953
This was a draft, and it is not known whether the letter was either sent off or answered. The Ensemble in fact used two versions of the Picasso dove, a monochrome drawing on the theatre curtain and the other, originally designed as a coloured scarf for the 1951 World Youth Festival, for publicity.

750 To Becher   11 Dec 1953
Ulbricht had proposed on 25 November that an all-German committee be set up to decide what publications should be banned as militarist and anti-humanist. He had not mentioned the Academy in this connection, nor had there been a response from the West Germans on government level. The Berlin Conference was a meeting (to be held in Berlin from 25 January–18 February) of the

Foreign Ministers of the four occupying powers to discuss the reunification of the country and the holding of free elections. There was no agreement.

The Open Letter. See Notes 673 and 685–6.

751 To Ulbricht   12 Dec. 1953

A draft which may not have been sent off. The omitted words were a handwritten and reputedly unreadable reference to Helmut Holtzhauer of the Commission for Art Affairs. These commissions would be abolished on 7 January 1954 – i.e. within a month – and replaced by a Ministry of Culture under Becher.

The German term rendered by 'the world of letters' is 'Schrifttum', a Nazi expression which Ulbricht must have used unwittingly and Brecht with conscious irony. Compare this letter with Galileo's letter to the Archbishop in scene 14 of the play.

752 To Leo Kerz   18 Jan. 1954

Kerz (see Note 491) was a New York stage designer and director who had written about a plan to produce the play on Broadway. The letter is in English.

753 To Becher   2 Feb. 1954

Becher's play *Winter Battle* had been produced in Leipzig in 1954. The Berliner Ensemble now planned to stage it in a production by E. F. Burian, a leader of the Czech theatrical avant-garde before the Nazi takeover and thereafter in a concentration camp.

In the past Brecht's references to Becher's writing had been less complimentary.

754 To Suhrkamp   8 March 1954

This was the flat mentioned in Letter 731.

*755 To Harry Buckwitz   13 March 1954

Buckwitz, formerly at the Munich Kammerspiele, where he directed *The Threepenny Opera* with Albers as Macheath (Note 578), became Intendant of the Frankfurt City Theatres.

Brecht says he recently talked again to Kortner about playing Galileo. (Buckwitz would stage the play in 1961, but with another actor.) And he enclosed a script by Peter Hacks which he liked but found too recondite for the Berliner Ensemble.

756 To the German Academy of Arts/Otto Nagel   6 April 1954

Nagel, a 'proletarian' painter close to Käthe Kollwitz, was head of the Academy's fine art section. Karl von Appen, who like him had belonged to the pre-Hitler Association of Revolutionary Artists (ARBKD), had become the Ensemble's principal stage designer after Neher decided he must give up working in East Berlin at the end of 1952.

*757 To Martin Pohl   24 April 1954

Telling Pohl that his translation of a poem by Christine de Pisan would be used in the adaptation of Anna Seghers's *Trial of Jeanne d' Arc*.

*758 To Class 9b of the August Bebel High School, Leuna   26 April 1954

Answering queries about *Señora Carrar's Rifles*. This uncharacteristic but comparatively naturalistic work was then much the most frequently performed of Brecht's plays in the GDR.

759 To Joris Ivens   7 May 1954
Ivens, who had Eisler as his composer for *Song of Heroes*, the film about
Magnitogorsk which he and Tretiakoff made in 1932, had now asked Brecht to
write the theme song for *Song of the Rivers*, a film for the World Federation of
Trade Unions, for which Vladimir Pozner wrote the script and Shostakovich
was to write the music. Though Semyon Kirsanov had translated poems by
Brecht, the suggested reverse collaboration did not take place. The première
was in Vienna on 11 October 1954.

760 To Anton Ackermann/Ministry of Culture of the GDR   21 May 1954
Miracle in Milan was directed by Vittorio de Sica. Ackermann had become
Secretary of State and headed the film section in the new ministry.

761 To Hans Henny Jahnn   May 1954
Written for a volume produced by the Hamburg Academy for Jahnn's sixtieth
anniversary. He was a north German playwright and organ-builder who received
the Kleist Prize in 1920 for *Pastor Ephraim Magnus*. Official organ consultant to
the city of Hamburg, he was sacked for 'political unreliability' by the Nazis,
emigrated to Denmark where he bred horses, then returned and died in
Hamburg in 1959.

762 To Suhrkamp   May 1954
See Note 746. On 26 May 1954 Suhrkamp had written that he did not agree that
each of the 'Buckow Elegies' should have a page to itself, and that he found the
Prologue (or first Act) of *The Caucasian Chalk Circle* embarrassing and the
transition into the story proper too abrupt. Both the poems and the play were in
Versuche 13, whose publication he was preparing.
   The 'short story' was 'The Augsburg Chalk Circle'.

*763 To Ekkehard Schall   May 1954
About Eilif's sword dance in *Mother Courage*, which Brecht describes as much
the same terms as in his notes for the 'Model-book' (translated in *Collected Plays*,
5ii, p. 112).

*763x To Reyher   ?
Covering note to the latest *Versuche* volume (containing *The Good Person of
Szechwan*) which he was sending as 'a slight sign of life'. Reyher did not respond.

*764 To Emil František Burian   19 June 1954
Welcoming Burian's collaboration on *Winter Battle* (see Note 753), regretting
that he himself has to be at a PEN meeting in Amsterdam, and hoping to
outline the proposed cuts on his return.

*765 To Raimund Schelcher   Mid-1954
To say that the company were pleased with his work in *Katzgraben* and the
Chinese play *Hirse für di Achte*, and that they would delay the premières till his
health had improved.

*766 To Benno Besson   15 July 1954
Apologising for failing to introduce him as the director of *Dom Juan* when
addressing a conference at the First Paris International Theatre Festival.

767 To Grotewohl   19 July 1954
RIAS = The American radio station in West Berlin.

Brecht's suggestions for making the People's Chamber an organ of liaison between people and government are in *GW 20*, pp. 329–30.

768 To Eisler   July 1954
From the writing of the GDR national anthem in 1949 to the *Johannes Faustus* débâcle and his consequent shift from Berlin to Vienna, Eisler was collaborating rather more with Becher than with Brecht. By 1953 however the old alliance had been revived, and it was Brecht who persuaded him to write music for Becher's play. Comparatively traditional in orchestration, it would be made into a *Winterschlacht Suite* for orchestra.

*769 To Therese Giehse   4 Sep. 1954
Asking her if she would like to be Intendant in Leipzig. She answered on 28 September 1954 that she was most unsuited.

*770 To Johannes Berndt   18 Sep. 1954
Thanking him for the conversion of the stage and lighting system at the Schiffbauerdamm. He was an employee of the Institute for Cultural Installations.

771 To Emil František Burian   20 Sep. 1954

772 To Vladimir Pozner   6 Oct 1954
A Russian-French writer who had been in Hollywood in the 1940s and was now resident in Paris. The figure of Matti in the finished film (see Notes 734–5 and 791) was vulgar and cliché-ridden. Brecht had originally wanted the director to be Joris Ivens, for whose *Song of the Rivers* (Note 759) Pozner had written the script, but accepted Alberto Cavalcanti instead. Curt Bois played the lead and Eisler wrote the music.

773 To Burian   Oct./Nov. 1954
Part of the case for West German rearmament was that the East German People's Police was already a militarised force. It would now be joined by a People's Army in response.

774 Ditto   Dec. 1954
Burian, who by then had directed a Czech production of the play for an anti-Nazi, if not anti-German public, started rehearsing the Berlin actors in October and abandoned the task in December. Brecht and Wekwerth then took over, and the play opened on 12 January 1955.

*775 To Ernst Busch   23 Dec. 1954
To say that he could not come to the Christmas-Day opening of Langhoff's *Faust Part I* production, in which his old friend was playing Mephisto.

776 To Ernst Schumacher and family   Dec. 1954
Schumacher, a literary scholar from Munich, had done a doctorate at Leipzig University under Ernst Bloch and Hans Mayer. He had seen Brecht in connection with his dissertation on the early plays and its revision to make the book *Die Dramatischen Versuche Bertolt Brechts 1918–1933*: the first serious study of Brecht's work. Later he would emigrate to the GDR, become a professor at the Humboldt University and emerge as the leading East Berlin theatre critic after the death of Jhering.
Paulaner is a Munich beer.

*777 To Irene Schiller   4 Jan. 1955
She was the widow of the leading Warsaw director Leon Schiller, who had
written an article on the Berlin theatre in *Pamietnik Teatralny*, Warsaw, 1953,
no. 3. Brecht considered that in the discussion of his own work his theory of
Alienation should have been given a more central place and his breaking of the
play's flow by means of poems and songs been treated not as so many 'bridges'
but as integral parts of the dramaturgy with a value of their own. He found it
'terrible' that their discussions should have been so abruptly cut off.

778 To the International Stalin Prize Committee/D. V. Skobeltsyn   4 Jan. 1955
Stalin had died on 5 March 1953. These awards had been founded after 1945 as
alternatives to the supposedly 'non-political' Nobel Prizes and were given 'for
peace and understanding between peoples'. Brecht's was announced on 21
December 1954, and he went to Moscow to receive it on 25 May 1955.
Retrospectively it is often referred to as a 'Lenin Prize', but it was not bestowed
as such.

*779 To Becher   5 Jan. 1955
Thanking Becher for 'unfreezing a beautiful car'. This was a West German
BMW, for whose purchase by Brecht Becher had obtained permission.

780 To Wolfgang Harich/Aufbau-Verlag   5 Jan. 1955
Harich (see Note 730) was compiling a Festschrift in honour of Georg Lukács's
seventieth birthday. It is not clear whether such a telegram was sent.

*781 To Suhrkamp   5 Jan. 1955
Suggesting a small volume of 'Political Poems' which Brecht (and, presumably,
Hauptmann) had selected and planned as a warning for the future. Suhrkamp
rejected this in favour of a short general selection to be made by himself. (This
he would publish in 1956.)

782 To Grotewohl   20 Jan. 1955
Lucebert-Swaanswijk (better known perhaps as an artist) and Peter Hacks both
settled in the GDR during 1955 on grants from the Academy.

*783 To Georg Mayer   1 Feb. 1955
Mayer was the Rector of Leipzig University, some of whose students had seen
the Ensemble's production of *The Caucasian Chalk Circle* (première on 7 October
1954) and met its dramaturgs. Their ignorance, wrote Brecht, suggested that his
work must be being misinterpreted by their teachers, so why should these not
come and find out more about it?

784 To Elisabeth Bergner   1 Feb. 1955
Their last recorded contact was in 1946 (Letter 547). Bergner and Paul Czinner
were living in London. She was now about fifty-seven. She had played the lead in
the prototype *Chalk Circle* in Klabund's adaptation at the Deutsches Theater under
Reinhardt in 1925. None of Brecht's suggestions was taken further.

785 To Geneviève Serreau   9 Feb. 1955
Madame Serreau had written a short book on Brecht for his French publisher,
Robert Voisin of L'Arche. *Der Monat*, edited by Melvyn Lasky, was financed by
the CIA-backed Congress for Cultural Freedom, along with its stable-mates
Preuves (Paris), *Encounter* (London) and *Tempo Presente* (Rome). Herbert Lüthy's

article 'Of Poor BB' (1952), which appeared in more than one of these, attacked Brecht on the grounds of his Austrian citizenship, his Swiss bank account and his failure to settle in the USSR.

*786 To Arthur Pieck/GDR Government Administrative Office   17 Feb. 1955
To the President's son, Piscator's old lieutenant (see Note 618) to suggest that the Academy decide how and where to make use of unwanted sculptures commissioned by the State.

*787 To Hermann Henselmann   17 Feb. 1955
Henselmann, said to have been trained at the Bauhaus before 1933, was the architect of the Stalin-Allee (subsequently renamed Karl-Marx-Allee). Brecht appealed to him to preserve the Friederichstrasse flats lived in by the Herzfeldes, Elisabeth Hauptmann, the Hills, Iva Besson, Hurwicz and others connected with the Ensemble.

*788 To Werner Heisenberg   18 Feb. 1955
Asking the eminent physicist to speak to the PEN Centre in Hamburg about the effects of experiments with nuclear weapons. Heisenberg answered saying that Brecht was concerning himself with the symptoms of the world's sickness and not the causes.

*789 To Grotewohl   18 Feb. 1955
Telling the GDR premier that the Academy, the Kulturbund and other bodies had collected about 200,000 signatures against the Paris Agreement (23 October 1954) ending the occupation of West Germany and allowing its remilitarisation.

790 To Wien-Film AG   20 Feb. 1955
This letter appears to have been edited for inclusion in the notes in *Texte für Film II* (1969), which are translated in the Methuen *Collected Plays*, volume 6iii, pp. 124–7. The other script writer beside Pozner was Ruth Fischer-Meyenburg (pseudonym Ruth Wieden).

*791 To Slatan Dudow   21 Feb. 1955
About a film *Buon giorno, elefante* directed by Gianni Franciolini and featuring Vittorio de Sica. Dudow (who had worked with Brecht and Eisler between 1930–32 on *The Decision* and *Kuhle Wampe*) was now established as a director and writer for DEFA.

792 To Harry Buckwitz   1 March 1955
For Buckwitz see Note 755. He staged *The Caucasian Chalk Circle* in his Kleines Haus on 28 April 1955, with Reichel (one of Brecht's last lovers) as Grusha and Hanns Ernst Jäger as Azdak. The Schleswig Landestheater meantime had asked for Buckwitz's help with their production of *The Good Person of Szechwan*, which opened on 7 April.

The difficulty of Dessau's music for the former was due largely to Brecht's own requirements, which in Hanns Eisler's view had been unreasonable. By Eisler's account (in *Fragen Sie mehr über Brecht*, pp. 240–42) Brecht in 1944 had asked for oriental-type music such as might accompany an interminable verse epic. This he refused to provide, leaving it to Dessau to 'do so to the best of his ability'.

793 To Dessau   2 March 1955
Iva Besson was the Ensemble's répétiteuse and voice coach.

*794 To Erich Franz   3 March 1955
About his performance in a secondary rôle in Becher's *Winter Battle*.

*795 To Leonhard Frank   18 March 1955
Asking the author of *Karl und Anna* and *Der Mensch ist gut* to join the German
East and West PEN Centre. Frank, then aged seventy-two, was living in
Munich and honoured in both halves of Germany.

796 To Ernst Schumacher   12 April 1955
See Note 776 about Schumacher, the Paulaner and his book. 'Bargan gives up'
is in *Short Stories* (Methuen, London and New York 1983, pp. 3ff.).

797 To the Nordmark-Landestheater/Horst Gnekow   18 April 1955
This is the Schleswig theatre and director referred to in Note 792. The 'Song of
the Eighth elephant' is in scene 8 of *The Good Person of Szechwan*.

*798 To Ruth Fischer-Meyenburg   21 April 1955
She was the Wien-Film dramaturg working on the *Puntila* script. Brecht writes
with four detailed suggestions.

*799 To Karl Kleinschmidt   22 April 1955
Kleinschmidt was one of the cathedral clergy at Schwerin in north Germany.
He had written a short book on Luther and, when Brecht commented
approvingly, wondered if he was being ironic. Brecht replies: no, not at all.

800 To Berlau   24 April 1955
About Buckwitz's Frankfurt production (see Note 792).

801 Ditto   7 May 1955
Hanne = Brecht's daughter Hanne Hiob. Hans Schweikart's Kammerspiele
production opened on 30 June 1955 with Erni Wilhelmi in the part after all.
The sets were by Neher, who now met Brecht again – apparently for the first
time since 1952.

   Trumpets and Drums was the Ensemble adaptation of George Farquhar's *The
Recruiting Officer*, which was being directed by Besson. The Paris publisher was
Robert Voisin of L'Arche. The *Organum* notes, with their new emphasis on
'dialectical theatre', are in *Brecht on Theatre* pp. 276–81.

*802 To Walter Meusel   12 May 1955
Meusel appears to have been an animator of folk music in Karl-Marx-Stadt (the
former Chemnitz). Brecht was interested in his views on the relevance of the
Alienation principle to children's acting.

*803 To Franz Reichert   14 May 1955
Reichert was involved with the Wuppertal company, whose production of *The
Good Person of Szechwan* had been well spoken of, prompting this letter of
congratulation.

804 To the German Academy of Arts   15 May 1955
In little more than a year's time Brecht's instructions would be followed.

*805 To Raimund Schelcher   16 May 1955
Asking him to rest his voice until Brecht's return.

*806 To Kurt Palm   16 May 1955
Palm was the company's costume designer. Brecht wanted a less feminine-
looking uniform for Regine Lutz in *Trumpets and Drums*.

*807 To Lothar Bellag   17 May 1955
Since *Winter Battle* was due for extra rehearsals because of a cast change, Brecht
asked that attention should be paid to aspects of Ekkehard Schall's
performance.

808 To Bernhard Reich   19 May 1955
Asja Lacis was directing a theatre in the Latvian SSR (at Valmiera or Wollmar)
when she and Reich heard that Brecht was coming to receive his Stalin Prize.
They wrote, provoking this answer, then came to Moscow for their first
meeting with Brecht and Weigel for fourteen years. Reich's account in his *Im
Wettlauf mit der Zeit* describes how Brecht asked Pasternak rather than Kirsanov
to translate his speech of thanks, how he was coolly received except by Fedin
and Okhlopkov, what he thought of Ranevskaya and other Soviet actors, how
he feared that *Trumpets and Drums* might clash with the recruiting of the new
People's Army, and further interesting details. Brecht also made inquiries about
Carola Neher and Margarete Steffin, and 'intervened emphatically on my behalf',
says Reich, 'in order to speed up my request for rehabilitation'.

809 To Nikolai Okhlopkov   21 May 1955
Okhlopkov was a noted actor and film director who directed the Moscow
Realistic Theatre briefly in the early 1930s in some remarkable 'in the round'
productions before it was closed. The Berliner Ensemble would visit Moscow
in 1957, the year following Brecht's death.

*810 To Faina Ranevskaya   24 May 1955
To the Soviet actress to say how much he hoped she would play Courage.

*811 To Tadeusz Kulisiewicz   31 May 1955
This excellent Polish draughtsman had agreed to make drawings based on *The
Caucasian Chalk Circle*. Brecht hoped that he could deliver them before the
company went to Paris. In the event some of them could be shown in the foyer
of the Théâtre du Châtelet, and the series were published by Henschel-Verlag as
a book with an introduction by Brecht in 1956.

*812 To Hans Henny Jahnn   3 June 1955
Jahnn had written on 18 May offering the Ensemble his play *Thomas Chatterton*,
but Brecht wrote regretting that they had not got the right actors for it.

*812x To Fritz Kortner   ?
Kortner had been asked by Neher if he would direct *Courage* or *Galileo* in
London. Brecht thanks him for his quick and affirmative response. But he fears
that Theatre Workshop (who are performing *Courage* at a festival in Devon)
have no resources, though Littlewood herself is said to be a good actress. If
prospects improve he will let Kortner know.

*813 To Harry Buckwitz   6 June 1955
Buckwitz had told Brecht on 4 June that the Ruhr Festival at Recklinghausen
might cancel its invitation to the Frankfurt company to bring their production
of *The Caucasian Chalk Circle*, apparently on the ground that Brecht had accepted
a Stalin Prize. Brecht replied that any such breach of contract must be fought,
and hoped that Buckwitz had read his Moscow speech (which stressed the need
to see things 'from below'). In the event the invitation was maintained.

814 To Vassili Osipovich Toporkov   8 June 1955
Toporkov was author of a book of recollections called *K. S. Stanislavsky at Rehearsal* of which Henschel-Verlag had published a German translation in 1952.

   Galileo was being translated by the Soviet Germanist Lev Kopelev, who later emigrated to West Germany.

   Ilya Fradkin, the former Soviet Theatre Officer in Berlin, is a leading Russian authority on Brecht.

815 To Joan Littlewood   22 June 1955
Miss Littlewood, the founder and leader of Theatre Workshop, had been asked to stage *Mother Courage* (in a mongrel translation) for Ronald Duncan's Barnstaple (Taw and Torridge) Festival in June 1955. Carl Weber, an assistant director from the Ensemble (now a professor at Stanford University, California), had been sent to advise, but reported to Brecht that another actress, Catherine Parr, was taking over the part of Courage and he himself being barred from rehearsals. At the première Miss Littlewood played the part after all, but the critical reception was not good enough for Brecht to allow a transfer to London. (Note Brecht's appreciation of the Engish pejorative 'boring'.)

816 To Henri Magnan   26 June 1955
Written to a French critic just after the Ensemble's triumph at the Paris International Theatre Festival.

*817 To Liselot Huchthausen   June 1955
The writer was a classicist who asked why, in 'Socrates Wounded', Brecht had called the battle of Delion a victory over the Persians when it was really a defeat by the Spartans. Brecht replied that he would see if he could change it, but (as in other such cases) he never did.

*818 To Hermann Duncker   c. Mid-1955
An evasive answer to the old Marxist, who had complained about Brecht's allowing West German theatres (like Buckwitz's at Frankfurt) to cut the Prologue (or first Act) of *The Caucasian Chalk Circle*.

819 To Ernst Bloch   6 July 1955
The article has not been identified, but the poem is surely 'The way the wind blows' (*GW* 1037) which was written for this occasion and set to music by Eisler. (It is on EMI's recording *Robyn Archer Sings Brecht*).

*820 To Isot Kilian   ?
Saying that he was reading detective stories brought back from Paris, thought that Max Lingner should have a National Prize for his 'Peasant War' painting (now in the East Berlin Museum for German History), and sometimes missed her. Lingner was given a prize. Kilian died in 1986.

821 To Wolfgang Staudte   July/Aug. 1955
The French actor Bernard Blier had now been cast as the Cook in the DEFA *Mother Courage* film. Staudte was about to start shooting.

822 To Hans Schweikart   7 Aug. 1955
See Note 801. The Ensemble would perform *Trumpets and Drums* at the Munich Kammerspiele from 10–12 June 1956, but the Kammerspiele's proposed visit to East Berlin never took place. *The Good Person* would therefore be performed at

the Theater am Schiffbauerdamm only in 1957, and then by the Ensemble in Besson's production, with Reichel as Shen-Teh/Shui-Ta.

*822x To Caspar Neher   nd
Neher had written from Salzburg asking Brecht to send twenty of his drawings for *The Tutor* which the Arts Council of Great Britain were wanting to buy.

Brecht answered that Neher could not have them, since they are 'what we have left of our happy collaboration'. Brecht in fact had retained hundreds of Neher drawings, some of which had clearly been gifts.

823 To Albert Wilkening/DEFA   13 Aug. 1955
As Wilkening was on holiday, his superior Hans Rodenberg answered this letter, confirming Brecht's right of veto and saying (somewhat cryptically) that he had 'never doubted for one instant that the film is being made because it has to be made'.

*824, *825 To Berlau   26, 27 Aug. 1955
About the new edition of *Antigonemodell 1948* which Henschel were publishing. Berlau had been taken to St Joseph's Hospital in Berlin following what appear to have been drunken aggressions. As a result Brecht persuaded her to leave Berlin for Copenhagen, where he found her a flat and asked friends to help her settle down. Her effort to do so lasted till early in 1956.

826 To Berlau   ?
On the same subject. Brecht wanted her to concentrate on photographic and editing work.

*827 To Yüan Miau-tse   ?
A brief letter of thanks to Yüan, who translated the play *Hirse für die Achte* for the Ensemble's production of 1 April 1954, and had now written out the Chinese text of Mao Tse-tung's poem on flying over the Great Wall, which Brecht thereafter kept hanging in his flat. Brecht's version of the poem is in *GW*, p. 1070.

828 To Wolfgang Staudte   Aug./Sep. 1955
Re the *Courage* film, on which Brecht's disciple Manfred Wekwerth was an assistant. Wekwerth later became artistic director of the Berliner Ensemble.

829 To Rodenberg (DEFA)   5 Sep. 1955
With a copy to Staudte. Willi Teichmann was in charge of production. Mrs Roth was Sigrid Roth, a last-minute casting as Kattrin. There the matter ended, since Weigel refused to work under the proposed schedules and Therese Giehse (Letter 833) would not agree to replace her. Shooting, which had begun at Neubabelsberg on 18 August (according to Klaus Völker's chronology), was broken off and the project cancelled, to be eventually replaced by a wide-screen monochrome filming of the Berliner Ensemble production, directed by Wekwerth and Palitzsch in a big studio after Brecht's death.

*830 To the Henschel-Verlag (for its chief editor Karl Heidkamp) 13 Sep. 1955
Complaining about the proposed publication of two works by Theodor Bahrisch, whose aesthetic writings struck him as too metaphysical and redolent of 'eternal laws'. This should be discussed with members of the Academy.

831 To the Members of the Berliner Ensemble   27 Sep. 1955
This appears to relate to Besson's very brilliant direction of *Trumpets and Drums*.

832 To Lion Feuchtwanger   28 Sep. 1955
Feuchtwanger and Laughton both lived in Pacific Palisades (Los Angeles).
The English Stage Company took over the Royal Court Theatre in April 1956,
altered the face of the London theatre with John Osborne's *Look Back in Anger*
(première on 8 May) and produced *The Good Woman of Sezuan* (Bentley's
translation) with Peggy Ashcroft and sets by Teo Otto under Devine's direction
that October. The 'guest performances' must have been those of some other
company, since the ESC had not yet got going, while the National Theatre and
Royal Shakespeare Companies were founded only in the 1960s.

Laughton's response was that, while 'a great devotee' of Brecht, he would
under no circumstances perform in London.

833 To Therese Giehse   5 Oct. 1955
Last of the story in this correspondence. Staudte complained that Brecht did not
understand the cinema.

*834 To Tadeusz Kulisiewicz   6 Oct. 1955
Further to Note 811, an invitation to come to Berlin.

*834x To Julius Raab, Austrian Federal Chancellor   11 Oct. 1955
To thank him for an invitation to the reopening of the Vienna Burgtheater. His
shaky health will not allow him to come. (Cited by Kurt Palm in *Vom Boycott
zur Anerkennung*, p. 92.)

*835 To Carl-Emil Binkenstein   17 Oct. 1955
Not identified. Three lines about what constitutes a novella.

*835x To Berlau   31 Oct. 1955
A letter printed in Mittenzwei *Das Leben Bertolt Brechts*, vol. 2, p. 555, in
which B. advises her to be moderate and regular in her eating and drinking.

*836 To Paul Wandel   26 Nov. 1955
Saying he tried to simplify a text sent him by the Central Committee for the
Dedication of Youth. Did Wandel approve? The committee evidently did
not, since it wrote on 13 June 1956 to say that his version could not be used.

837 To Berlau   Nov./Dec. 1955
She was still in Copenhagen.

The 'Chinese farce' (not very funny) opened on 8 November. Palitzsch and
Weber were joint directors.

The *Coriolanus* study, written in dialogue form, is in *Brecht on Theatre* pp. 252–
265.

838 Ditto   Nov./Dec. 1955
Busch seems to have been something of a last-resort casting for *Galileo*, and
this, along with Brecht's poor health, made for a long drawn-out rehearsal
period. It began on 14 December 1955.

*839 To Kulisiewicz   8 Dec. 1955
The artist had written on 6 December to thank Helene Weigel for his Berlin
visit and ask if Brecht would write something for the catalogue of his forthcoming Warsaw exhibition. Brecht's letter says apologetically that he is on a
course of digitalin and feels considerably worse than he doubtless looks.

840 To Berlau   14 Dec. 1955
She had taken some film of the New York *Galileo* in 1947, as well as 35 mm
colour transparencies. What 'list' is referred to is not clear.

841 To the GOKS, Tbilisi   21 Dec. 1955
Directed by Michel Saint-Denis, the Centre Dramatique de l'Est (now the
Théâtre National de Strasbourg) had asked the Rustaveli company to help with
designs for a planned production of *The Caucasian Chalk Circle*.

Hugo Huppert was an Austrian poet who became a Soviet citizen in the 1930s
and was Mayakovsky's principal German translator. In 1945 he returned to live in
Vienna.

842 To Wolf von Beneckendorff   27 Dec. 1955
Beneckendorff, a cousin of the former President Hindenburg, was the doyen of
the Ensemble actors. In the production he would play the Very Old Cardinal,
while Norbert Christian was the Inquisitor.

***843** To Dieter Knaup   27 Dec. 1955
Brecht suggested that, as Plume in *Trumpets and Drums*, Knaup was not
sufficiently able to make the audience laugh at, rather than with him, and so
would fail to bring out the narrow self-interest which characterises Lodovico in
Galileo (evidently a part he had hoped to play). Cf. the following two letters to
Knaup's fellow-actors.

***844** To Axel Triebel   27 Dec. 1955
To say that Galileo's clerical and other enemies must be portrayed 'positively'
(in other words, seriously and without caricature) if his task is not to appear
unduly easy. Triebel played 'The Individual'.

***845** To Ralf Bregazzi   27 Dec. 1955
Lodovico must not appear comic.

846 To Berlau   31 Dec. 1955
The Stepdaughter opened on 12 December 1955, with the Mexican actress Rosaura
Revueltas in the lead. Angelika = Hurwicz.

***847** To the members of the Berliner Ensemble   14 Jan. 1956
To say that the Lusatian peasants on whom Strittmatter had based his *Katzgraben*
had built a local arts centre and were inviting the Ensemble to come and
perform the play there.

***848** To Julius Hahn   18 Jan. 1956
A short letter of encouragement to a senior Frankfurt city official who had been
sacked and arrested for 'pro-Communist activity'.

848x To Berlau   20 Jan 1956
She had announced her intention to return to Berlin, telling Brecht that she was
still 'his creature' and found everyone else boring.

Of the women mentioned by Brecht, Hilde Eisler was Gerhart Eisler's wife;
Christine Gloger a young actress who married Besson's assistant Guy de
Chambure. Brecht's own daughter Barbara (pseudonym Barbara Berg) was now
acting with the company, for whom she played Pegeen Mike in Synge's *Playboy*.
Brecht's letter did not make Berlau change her mind.

It is printed in Werner Mittenzwei: *Das Leben des Bertolt Brecht* oder der

Umgang mit den Welträtseln, vol. 2, pp 556–8. Aufbau, East Berlin and Weimar, 1986: Suhrkamp, Frankfurt-am-Main, 1987.

849 To Friedrich Siems   21 Jan. 1956
The Nuremberg production directed by Siems opened on 26 May 1956. It was the play's German première.

*850 To the 'Lalka' puppet theatre, Warsaw   28 Jan. 1956
Welcoming a plan for them to do *The Caucasian Chalk Circle* (which was unrealised).

*851 To Louis Fürnberg   1 Feb. 1956
Fürnberg, a poet who later became GDR ambassador to his native country of Czechoslovakia, had worked in agitprop before 1939. The genre was returning to cultural-political acceptability, particularly once Alfred Kurella had become head of the Politburo's Cultural Committee. Brecht is writing to say that he had arranged a meeting with cabaret artists and 'young satirical writers' at his flat on 13 February.

852 To Rudolf Engel/German Academy of Arts   4 Feb. 1956
The volume would be published by Volk und Welt in 1959, but contain no translations by Brecht. Hikmet wrote in Turkish.

853 To Peter Huchel/*Sinn und Form*   4 Feb. 1956
The translator of Halldór Laxness's play *Silfurtúnglid* (Silver Moon) sent it to Brecht apparently without the author's agreement. Laxness was the Icelandic novelist and winner of the Nobel Prize for literature in 1954.

*854 To Ekkehard Schall   5 Feb. 1956
Advising him not to exaggerate Eilif's drunkenness in scene 2 of *Mother Courage*.

855 To Suhrkamp   9 Feb. 1956
Günter Gläser thinks that this letter may not have been sent.

856 To Berlau   11 Feb. 1956
Brecht had gone to Milan with Elisabeth Hauptmann and his daughter Hanne Hiob for the première of Giorgio Strehler's *Threepenny Opera* production at the Piccolo Teatro on 10 February.

857 To the Piccolo Teatro, Milan   27 Feb. 1956
The director of the theatre was Paolo Grassi, who later headed La Scala.

*858 To Martin Strauss   27 Feb. 1956
Strauss, a Berlin physicist, had read of Brecht's intention to write a play about Einstein, and sent him some articles. Brecht thanks him, but finds them difficult.

*859 To Oscar Lewenstein   27 Feb. 1956
Lewenstein, formerly of the Marx Memorial Library in Clerkenwell, was partner of Wolf Mankowitz in presenting the Blitzstein version of *The Threepenny Opera* at the Royal Court Theatre in February 1956. He had visited Brecht in Berlin. The same letter went to the play's director Sam Wanamaker and to Jean Vilar, Paolo Grassi and half a dozen other Swedish, Polish and Israeli theatre people, to appeal for their support in protesting against the proposed closure of the Communist-run Scala Theatre in Vienna by the city authorities. This theatre had been in some measure the heir to the wartime Zurich Schauspielhaus, since it

was where *Mother Courage*, *The Mother*, the Nestroy *Höllenangst* with Eisler's music, and other important works had been performed under Wolfgang Heinz's management. Its last production was of *Galileo* in the Hollywood version, directed by Heinz, with Paryla in the title part. It closed on 30 June. See Kurt Palm: *Vom Boycott zur Anerkennung*, pp. 121ff.

860 To Paul Wandel   15 March 1956

*861 To Eugen Schaub   22 March 1956
About proposed cuts in Schaub's production of *The Caucasian Chalk Circle* at the Erfurt (GDR) city theatre.

862 To Fritz Selbmann   28 March 1956
Selbmann, who spent the Nazi years as a concentration camp prisoner, had been head of East German economic affairs and later emerged as a writer. Brecht will have needed these data in connection with his Garbe (or *Büsching*) project with Eisler. (See Note 743.)

*863 To Erich Engel   31 March 1956
Thanking him for conducting the *Galileo* rehearsals. Brecht had been taken ill with a high temperature while rehearsing in March, and would go into the Charité hospital (close to the theatre, the Academy and his flat) in May, taking with him the documents about the Soviet Communist Party's 20th Congress and Khrushchev's attack on Stalin.

*864 To Bernhard Reich   4 April 1956
Hoping that he will get leave from the Soviet authorities to come to the Ensemble for a season.

865 To Paul Patera   21 April 1956
Patera had asked for the rights for a production at the Uppsala Kammarteater in Sweden. Ever since 1945 the play had been interpreted in the West as a brutally inhuman work, anticipating (if not actually explaining) the attitude of the victims of Stalin's show trials during the Great Purge. It was quoted in Brecht's Un-American Activities Committee hearing and printed in a mangled translation in Ruth Fischer's book *Stalin and German Communism* as evidence that he was what she called a 'minstrel of the GPU'. Unlicensed performances in the US and elsewhere, given without the essential Eisler music, had been (and still are) staged so as to reinforce this view, and since the Party critics too had from the first raised objections to the work, Brecht effectively withdrew it. Even today the present letter is quoted as a reason for not licensing it, though Brecht's enemies go ahead and perform it without licence, while Brecht himself in those last months of his life would be seeing it as the model for *Büsching*, and telling Manfred Wekwerth that it was in this type of play that he saw the future of the theatre.

*865x To Kurt Kläber   21 April 1956
Mittenzwei quotes a sentence from this otherwise unpublished letter of 21 April, expressing Brecht's pleasant memories of his stay at Carona (in Italian Switzerland) twenty-three years earlier.

866 To Boris Pasternak   25 April 1956
According to Gerd Rüge's pictorial biography, it was only after Brecht's death

that Pasternak came to realise he was a great poet, because the East German
selection he had previously looked at (presumably the Aufbau *Hundred Poems* of
1951) had been predominantly 'political'. In any case he did not respond.

*867 To Ernst Busch   30 April 1956
Apologising for the postponement of rehearsals just as Busch was starting to
create 'a splendid figure'. Engel did not want to complete the production on his
own.

868 To Feuchtwanger   3 May 1956
Written from the Charité. Feuchtwanger had told Brecht on 5 April that Norman
Lloyd was interested in a New York production of *Simone Machard*, but said he
himself realised that it might be better if Brecht staged the play in Europe first.

The première would be on 8 March 1957 at Frankfurt, with music by Eisler, sets
by Teo Otto and Buckwitz as director.

869 To Pasternak   9 May 1956
Once again, nothing resulted.

*870 To Bruno Henschel   17 May 1956
Henschel-Verlag were to publish the *Galileo* model-book, with the Laughton
material being supplemented by a section on the Ensemble's production with
Ernst Busch. Brecht's letter apologises for the delay due to his illness.

871 To Becher   22 May 1956

872 To the German Academy of Arts
Georg Maurer is a respected East German poet.

Voelkner's novel, published in 1956, was called *Die Leute von Karvenbruch*.

*873 To Wolfgang Heinz   4 June 1956
Regretting that he cannot get to Heinz's *Galileo* at the Vienna Scala, with Paryla
in the title part. This was opening on 9 June. He would like Heinz to work with
the Ensemble when the Scala folds. (Heinz replied that his first commitment
was to the Deutsches Theater – whose Intendant he eventually became.)

*874 To Karl Paryla   4 June 1956
Similar regrets. Would Paryla and Hortense Raky perform Tolstoy's *The Living
Corpse* with the Ensemble next season, possibly with Heinz as director? (This
scheme fell through.)

*875 To Hans Schweikart   8 June 1956
Regretting that he cannot join the Ensemble on their visit to Munich (Note
822), but would Schweikart come and direct 'the Dürrenmatt' (i.e. *The Visit*)
for them, with Giehse as the old lady? (This did not materialise either. And
according to a note by Käthe Rülicke the letter was not sent.)

*875x To Alexander Abusch   11 June 1956
About Brecht's foreign royalties. Item 18812 in the Brecht-Archive catalogue.
Abusch was deputy Minister of Culture.

*875xx, *875xxx To Isot Kilian   June 1956
Two letters referring to his hospital treatment, cited by Mittenzwei in his *Das
Leben Bertolt Brechts*, vol. 2, p 659.

876 To Reich   26 June 1956
Extracts from the play would appear in *Inostrannaja Literatura* 1957, no. 2. The

'Collected Plays' materialised as a volume of nine plays published by Isskusstvo in 1956.

'Prussian Switzerland': Buckow is in a hilly area known as 'die Märkische Schweiz'.

877 Ditto   28 June 1956

878 To Nina Polyakova   24 July 1956
Her essay was none the less included as a postscript to the volume.

879 To Suhrkamp   25 July 1956
Johann Ludwig Schmitt was some kind of 'alternative' doctor in whom Brecht had long had faith (see Note 153). Munich, like East Grinstead, was a centre of alternative thought.

*879x To Eulenspiegel-Verlag (Comrade Seydel)   25 July 1956
Thanking S. for information about the poor sales of the *Kriegsfibel* epigrams which had at long last been published. Christiane Bohnert (see Note *640x) cites B's offer to write to schools, libraries and other institutions to recommend the book, since 'our mad suppression of all facts and judgements about the Hitler years and the War has got to stop'. The book appeared in November 1955 in a printing of 10,000 and had sold 3,400 by the time of Seydel's letter.

*880 To Erich Franz   31 July 1956
Franz was an excellent small-part actor with the Ensemble. Brecht suggests that he and Harry Gillmann, another such, should help make a more varied-looking crowd in the Prologue to *The Caucasian Chalk Circle*, which 'must aim entirely for optical solutions. (Most of the audience can't understand the language anyway.)'

*881 To Walter Meier   2 Aug. 1956
Thanking the theatre's all-important technical director for his work in the past season, and for seeing technical problems 'absolutely with the eyes of an artist'.

882 To the members of the Berliner Ensemble   5 Aug. 1956
A notice for the bulletin board dated 5 August 1956 with advice for the forthcoming season at the Palace Theatre, London.

*883 To Kulisiewicz   6 Aug. 1956
See Note 811. Brecht thinks it will be a splendid book, but will send a list of suggested omissions.

884 To Paul Dessau   8 Aug. 1956
Professor Theodor Brugsch was head of the Charité's Medical Clinic no. 1.

*885 To Max Schroeder   8 Aug. 1956
Telling him to get well, because he is needed. Schroeder was chief editor of the Aufbau-Verlag. He died in 1958.

886 To Iskusstvo Publishers, Moscow   9 Aug. 1956
Brecht began writing an introduction ('For Soviet Readers', in *GW SzT*, p. 952), but did not get beyond the first paragraph. Accordingly the publishers prefaced the volume with the poem 'On everyday theatre' (translation by Edith Anderson Schroeder in *Poems 1913–1956*, pp. 176–9), which is evidently the one referred to by Brecht.

887 To Theodor Brugsch   13 Aug. 1956
Dictated to Isot Kilian on 13 August, the day before Brecht's death, and not sent.

Book list

The following is a select list of works, other than Brecht's own, that have helped us to understand and annotate the Letters.

Ernst Josef Aufricht: *Erzähle, damit du dein Recht erweist*. Propyläen Verlag, West Berlin 1966.

Walter Benjamin: *Understanding Brecht*. Translated by Anya Bostock. New Left Books, London 1973.

Eric Bentley: *The Brecht Commentaries*. Grove Press, New York and Eyre Methuen, London 1981. (Contains account of 'The Brecht-Bentley Correspondence'.)

—— *The Brecht Memoir*, new edn. Carcanet Press, Manchester 1989. (Contains seven letters to Brecht and illuminating recollections.)

Elisabeth Bergner: *Bewundert viel und viel gescholten* . . . Elisabeth Bergners unordentliche Erinnerungen. C. Bertelsmann, Munich 1978.

Ruth Berlau: *Brechts Lai-tu*. Erinnerungen und Notate. Edited by Hans Bunge. Luchterhand, Darmstadt 1985.

Albrecht Betz: *Hanns Eisler* Political Musician. Cambridge University Press, 1982.

Walter Brecht: *Unser Leben in Augsburg, damals*. Suhrkamp, Frankfurt 1984.

Arnolt Bronnen: *Tage mit Bertolt Brecht*. Die Geschichte einer unvollendeten Freundschaft. Desch, Munich 1960.

David Drew: *Kurt Weill*. A handbook. Faber, London 1987.

Manfred Durzak (ed.): *Die Deutsche Exil-Literatur*. Philipp Reclam jun., Stuttgart 1973.

Hans Bunge: *Fragen Sie mehr über Brecht*. Hanns Eisler im Gespräch. Rogner & Bernhard, Munich 1972.

Harald Engberg: *Brecht auf Fünen*. Exil in Dänemark 1933–1939. Wuppertal 1974.

Exil-Literatur 1933–1945. Ausstellung der Deutschen Bibliothek, Frankfurt am Main 1965.

Werner Frisch and K. W. Obermaier (eds.): *Brecht in Augsburg*. Erinnerungen, Dokumente, Texte, Fotos. East Berlin and Weimar, 1975.

Patrick Goode: *Karl Korsch*. A Study in Western Marxism. The Macmillan Press, London 1979.

George Grosz: *Briefe 1913–1959*. Edited by Herbert Knust. Rowohlt, Reinbek 1979.

Ludwig Hoffmann, Wolfgang Kiessling, Eike Middell and Werner Mittenzwei (eds.): *Kunst und Literatur im antifaschistischen Exil 1933–1945* in sieben Bänden. Reclam, Leipzig 1979.

Joachim Lucchesi and Robert K. Shull: *Musik bei Brecht*. Aufbau, E. Berlin and Weimar 1987, Suhrkamp, Frankfurt 1988.

James K. Lyon: *Bertolt Brecht in America*. Princeton U.P., Princeton, 1980. Methuen, London.

—— *Bertolt Brecht's American Cicerone*. With an Appendix Containing the Complete Correspondence Between Bertolt Brecht and Ferdinand Reyher. Bouvier-Verlag Herbert Grundmann, Bonn 1978.

Werner Mittenzwei: *Das Leben des Bertolt Brecht* oder Der Umgang mit den Welträtseln. Two volumes. Aufbau-Verlag, East Berlin and Weimar 1986.

—— *Das Zürcher Schauspielhaus*. 1933–1945 oder Die letzte Chance. Henschel, East Berlin 1979. (Series 'Deutsches Theater im Exil'.)

Hans-Otto Münsterer: *Bert Brecht*. Erinnerungen aus den Jahren. 1917–22. Verlag der Arche, Zurich 1963. (English language edition in preparation.)

Erika Munk (ed.): *Brecht*. Bantam Books, New York 1972.

Yurii Oklyanskii: *Pov'est' o malen'kom soldat'e*. Sov'etskaya Rossiya, Moscow 1978. (Fictionalised account of Margarete Steffin, based on her papers held by the Union of Soviet Writers.)

Kurt Palm: *Vom Boycott zur Anerkennung*. Brecht und Österreich, Wien-München, 1983.

David Pike: *German Writers in Soviet Exile, 1933–1945*. University of North Carolina Press, Chapel Hill 1982.

Bernhard Reich: *Im Wettlauf mit der Zeit*. Erinnerungen aus fünf Jahrzehnten deutscher Theatergeschichte. Henschel, East Berlin 1970.

Ernst Schumacher: *Leben Brechts*. Reclam, Leipzig 1984. (Fourth edition of picture biography first published by Henschel, East Berlin 1978.)

Klaus Völker: *Brecht-Chronik*. Daten zu Leben und Werk. Hanser, Munich 1971.

John Willett: *Caspar Neher*. Brecht's Designer. Methuen, London and New York 1986.

—— *The Theatre of Erwin Piscator*. Eyre Methuen, London 1978.

—— *The Theatre of the Weimar Republic*. Holmes and Meier, New York 1988.

Hella Wuolijoki: *Und ich war nicht Gefangene*. Memoiren und Skizzen. Edited by Richard Semrau. Hinstorff, Rostock 1987. (Much shortened from Finnish originals.)

Monika Wyss (ed.): *Brecht in der Kritik*. Kindler, Munich 1977. (Reprints contemporary reviews of the plays.)

Carl Zuckmayer: *Als wär's ein Stück von mir*. S. Fischer, Frankfurt-am-Main 1966.

List of common abbreviations

AMG Allied Military Government (for administration of occupied
  enemy territories)
APO Army Post Office
BE Berliner Ensemble, the company founded by Brecht and Helene Weigel in
  1949 and now located in the old Theater am Schiffbauerdamm in East Berlin
BMW Bavarian Motor Works, makers of quality cars before and after the War
BPRS Bund Proletarisch-revolutionärer Schriftsteller. Communist writers'
  association (1928–33) to which Brecht did not belong
CC Central Committee
CP Communist Party
CPSU Communist Party of the Soviet Union
DDT Powerful insecticide much used by AMG for disinfestation
DEFA East German film monopoly, founded in 1946 with Soviet participation
DT Deutsches Theater. East Berlin theatre, formerly Max Reinhardt's principal
  Berlin stage (1905–33)
DWK (East) German Economic Commission, precursor of the GDR
ECCI Executive Committee of the Communist (or Third) International (the
  Comintern)
FBI Federal Bureau of Investigation, headed for many years by J. Edgar Hoover
FDJ Free German Youth. Communist youth organisation post-World War 2
FRG German Federal Republic (West German state, founded in 1949)
GDR German Democratic Republic (East German state, founded in 1949)
GOKS The Georgian State Theatre (Rustaveli) in Tiflis
IAH International Workers' Aid, a Comintern agency headed by Willi
  Muenzenberg between 1921 and c. 1939
IL International Literature (German edition), a Moscow literary journal c.
  1930–45
KPD German Communist Party 1919–33 and in emigration 1933–45
MASch The Marxist Workers' School, Berlin, suppressed in 1933
MGM Metro-Goldwyn-Mayer
MORT International Organisation of Revolutionary Theatres, a Comintern
  body with headquarters in Moscow in the first half of the 1930s
NDB Neue Deutsche Blätter. Literary magazine published by Wieland
  Herzfelde from Prague, 1933–35
NYC New York City
OSS Office of Strategic Services. US wartime espionage and sabotage
  organisation, a precursor of the CIA

OWI Office of War Information, a Second World War propaganda
  organisation, based in Washington
PAG An unidentified journal of the 1930s
PEN Poets, Essayists and Novelists, an international writers' organisation with
  headquarters in London
POW Prisoner of War
PT Physical Training
RGO Rote Gewerkschafts-Organisation. The breakaway German Communist
  trade union grouping, c. 1928–33
RIAS Radio in the American Sector (of occupied Berlin after 1945)
SA Sturm-Abteilungen, the Nazi brown-shirted stormtroopers of the 1920s
  and 30s
SDS Schutzverband Deutscher Schriftsteller, (left-wing) German Writers'
  Defence organisation. See Note 558
SPCA Society for the Prevention of Cruelty to Animals
SPD German Social-Democratic Party
SPÖ Austrian Socialist Party
SS The Schutz-Staffel, black-uniformed Nazi bodyguards commanded by
  Heinrich Himmler and embracing the SD (or Sicherheitsdienst) and the
  Gestapo security services. A military wing, the Waffen-SS, was formed in
  World War 2
TRAM Theatre of Revolutionary Working Youth. An Association of Soviet
  agitprop type companies of the late 1920s and early 30s
TsGALI Central State Literary and Art Archives, Moscow
UCLA University of California, Los Angeles campus
UFA Universum-Film: principal German film company before 1945, long headed
  by the Nationalist Alfred Hugenberg
US(A) United States (of America)
USSR Union of Soviet Socialist Republics
VEGAAR Foreign Workers' Publishing House, Moscow
VIP Very Important Person
VOKS The All-Union Society for Cultural Relations with foreign countries
WDR Westdeutsche Rundfunk. The West German (regional) radio

Index

References to the editorial introduction and interludes are given by page numbers in italics (*1, 2* etc). Otherwise Letter numbers are used. The Letters *addressed to* the particular correspondent are distinguished by their numbers being in bold type (**364** etc). References within the Letters or the Notes to them are identified by Letter numbers in a lighter type (e.g., 256). Both Letter and Note should then be consulted. Where *only* the Note and not the Letter is referred to, (or where the actual Letter is omitted from our selection) the number is preceded by a small 'n'. Biographical or other elucidations will normally be found in the Note to the first number given. Where the item seems particularly relevant to its subject its number is asterisked (*).

Abraham, Pierre 397
Abusch, Alexander n580, n875x
Ackermann, Anton, **760**, 833
Adamic, Louis *Dynamite* 250
Adaptation 455
Adler, Stella 444
Agitprop 310, 313, 709, n851
Albers, Hans 567, 570, 578, n**609**, n613
Alexander, Elias 168, 218
Alienation *159*, n777, 816
Allert de Lange 180, 192, **199**, **212**, 336
   Proofs and publication of *Threepenny Novel* **217–25**, 230
Alpári, Gyula 380
Aman, Marie Rose 7, 12, 15, 18, 22, 23, 24, 25, 28
American Academy of Arts and Letters **559**, 560
American Guild for German Cultural Freedom n**363**, **369–70**, **389**, **415**, And see Löwenstein
American Play Company 82
Andersen, Mrs 340, 342

Andersen-Nexö, Martin **329**, 349, **354–5**, 390, 420
Apletin, Mikhail *309*, **420***, **427***–**9***
Appen, Karl von 756
Arbeiterzeitung 167
Aristophanes 401, 535
Arrests, 305, 307, 347, 375, 454
Art and beauty 739
Artists 8
Ashcroft, Peggy *313*, 832
'Asphalt literature' 211, 213
Atkinson, Brooks 552
Atom bomb, The 510
Auden, W. H. **297**x, 316–8, *312*, **478**, 489–91, **492**, 498–501
Aufbau (New York) n440a
Aufbau-Verlag (East Berlin) n680, 699, **780**
Aufricht, Ernst Josef *92*, n146, 151, 172, 245, 332, 397, *438*
   In US *310–11*, n451, 454, 456–8, 461, 465, 468, 472
Augsburg 523
   Brecht's youth in *12*
   Haindl paper works *12*, 62

Aurora (publishing house, New York) 484, 503
Austria 560
 Defeat of Socialism n620
 Citizenship 567, 583, 591, 597–9
 Federal Chancellor n834x
 See Salzburg, Vienna

'Babylonian confusion of languages' 688
Bachmann, Ida 450
Bacon, Francis
 Novum Organum 411
Baden-Baden 122, 126, 148–9
Bärensprung, Horst, 480, n530x
Bärwald, Professor 480–1
Bahr, Hermann
 Das Konzert 2
Bahrisch, Theodor n830
Banholzer, Paula ('Bie', 'Bittersweet', 'Paul') *13, 14,* 5, 7, *18–25,* 28, 29, **31,** *33–36,* **37,** 38, 47, **60, 254**
 Blanka n40
 Frank n37, 231, 254*, *311*
Banyai, Tommy 344
Barbusse, Henri 263
Barlach, Ernst *436*
Barlog, Boleslav 634
Barnowsky, Victor n69, n101,
Bartel, Kurt. See Kuba
Bartók, Béla 464
Bartosch, Sandor 323
Basel Carnival 584
Bauer, Otto 195, 200
Bassermann, Albert 482
BBC n205
Becher, Johannes R. 58, n140, **173,** 177, *157,* **263*, 264*, 291,** 297, **314,** 420, *433, 435, 438,* **580,** n656, n707, n727, **750,** 833, **871**
 Winter Battle 428, **753,** 768, 771, 773–4
Beggar's Opera, The 111, 138
Belgium 190
Bellag, Lothar n807
Beneckendorff, Wolf von 842
Beneš, Edvard 368
Benesch, Harald n647
Benjamin, Walter 153, **194,** *150, 153,*

n203x, **204,** n205, **210, 247, 258, 289–90, 302, 325–6**
 'Eduard Fuchs, the collector and the historian' 326
 'The Work of Art in the Era of Technical Reproducibility' 302, 310
Bentley, Eric *313,* 498, 501, 504, **513,** 515, 520, **521–2,** 525, n609x, 610, **616–7,** 784
Bergner, Elisabeth *90, 310,* 464, 468, 478, 481–2, 485, 502a–3, **512,** 527, *434,* **784**
Berlau, Ruth *157,* 253, 362, 384, 388, *307, 311–14,* 404, **444–6, 450–9, 461–9, 472–6, 483–9,** 494, **498– 501,** 543, **548–9, 552, 554–5,** n611, **612, 637, 639,** n696x, n741, **742–4,** n745, 791, **800–1, 808, 826, 837–40, 846, 848x**
 Birth of 'Michel' *312,* n489x
 Breakdown 1945/46 *313,* n511x-xx, 512
 Contribution to B's work 419, 848x*
 Moves to East Berlin *434,* 595
 Stay in Copenhagen n824–5, n835x
 Any animal can do it 445
Berlin *14–16,* 45–48, 60, *89–95, 434–5,* 548–9
 Admiralspalast 724
 Brecht's return, 1948 566–8
 Brecht and daughter to, arrangements 1949 591–603
 Cabaret 'Grössenwahn' n54
 Cabaret 'Wilde Bühne' n67
 Chausseestrasse 125, flat 731, 754
 Deutsches Theater 60, 71, 90, *89f,* 508, 514, *432,* 571, 586, 614, **721,** 724
 Erich Reiss Verlag 60
 Gurlitt Gallery 61
 Hebbel-Theater 571
 Hotel Adlon 571–2, 586
 Junge Bühne, Die *14,* n81, *91,* 117ff
 Komische Oper 579
 Lessing-Theater 69, 70

'Möwe' club 585
Satire, plan for a theatre of 724
Schlosspark-Theater 634
Siemens-Plania works 706
Staatsoper 724
Staatstheater 64, n89, *89f*, 97,
    104, 106, 135
Theater am Schiffbauerdamm
    n146, 311, 533, 543, n575,
    432, *438*, 570
    Brechts expect (1949) 575–
        7, 724*, 743–4
Theater in der
    Königgrätzerstraße n117,
    n141,
Volksbühne *91*, 579, 724
Berlin Airlift *435*, n591, n597
Berliner Ensemble, Plans *433–4*, 570,
    575ff, 586, 588*, 590*, 724*, 726,
    809
    1953–54 programme 731
    Notes to the company **831**, n**847**,
        882
    Adaptation of *Der Tag des grossen
        Gelehrten Wu* 837
    Ditto *Hirse für die Achte* n765,
        n827
Berndt, Johannes n770
Bernstein, Leonard n551
Bernstein, Sam **440**
Berstl, Julius **69**
Besson, Benno *438–9*, n**766**, n831, 846,
    868
Besson, Iva 793
Bezold, Otto ('Bez') 21
Bienert, Gerhard n105
Bibesco, Princess Elisabeth **234**
Bihalj-Merin, Otto ('Otto Biha', 'Peter
    Thoene') 173, ?181, 198
Bildt, Paul 571, 639
Billiards, 340, 342
Binkenstein, Carl-Emil n**835**
Blacks 491, 510
    Threepenny Opera project n435x,
        n439x, n441x-xxxx
Blaue Reiter, Der 11
Blier, Bernard 821
Blitzstein, Marc *160*, n288, n859
Bloch, Ernst n**261**, **262**, 606, **819**

Bloch-Erben 137, **174**, n344, 347–8*,
    n380x, n530x, 570, 578, n604xx-
    xxx, n609x
'Bloomsbury, Lord' n222
Boenheim, Felix 480
Boetticher, Hermann
    Friedrich der Grosse 43
    Die Liebe Gottes n43
Bohemian Forest 37
Bois, Curt 535, n575, 724
Bolihn, Sture 404
Borchardt, Hans (Hermann) 188, *161*,
    163, 211, n275, **330–1**
    Expelled from USSR 307–8
    In US *310*, 431
Bork, Otto **297**, **301**
Bourgeois morality, society etc. 522
BPRS 140
Branting, Senator George 384
Braun, Alfred 128
Braunschweig 633
Braunthal, Julius 167
Brecht, Bertolt ('Bert', 'Bidi', 'Biti')
    'Dark times' *162*, *311*
    Death wishes 804
    Difference with Hanns Eisler
        267–8
    Emigration from Nazi Germany
        167–70
    Emigration from Europe 380,
        307ff, 408–31
    'Establishment' recognition *435–6*
    Health of 5, 30, 72, 74, 76, 138,
        212, 215–6, 340, n609, 698,
        n834, n863, 868ff, n875xx-
        xxx
    Housing 167–71, 187, *157*, 388,
        467, 543, 731, 744, 754
    and Lukács (qv) 780
    Moves to Sweden 388
    Moves to Finland 403
    'Positive' writings. See also
        Optimism
    Reading poems 144, 447
    References 599
    Return to Europe 506, 533–6,
        548*–9*,
    Revision of plays 509
    Solidarity with GDR 724, 728

Stockholm lectures 384
Trips to New York 476
Versuche booklets 180, 183–4, 228, n569, n746, n747
War service 28
Writing block 1941 n439x
Main films:
Kuhle Wampe n158
Mother Courage (abandoned) *438*, 619, 639, 645, 688, 698, 716*, 742, 821*, 823–33 passim
Puntila 438, n734–5, 772, 790*, n798
Threepenny Opera n155, 295
    Stories for 231. See also under Films below
Plays:
Alexander and his Soldiers (project) 9
Antigone (after Sophocles and Hölderlin) *431*, *434*, 553*–60 passim, n674
    Model-book 848x
Ares's Chariot (revue project) 532, 535*, *432–3*, 567, n613
Aus nichts wird nichts (project) 151
Baal 26, 27, 32, 34, 41–7, 62, 64, 71, 81, 86, *84*, 101b
Büsching (project) n743, 796
Caucasian Chalk Circle, The 312, 481, 485–92, 498–501, 504, 506, 520–2, 529, 532 *538–9*, 668, 784, 832, 841, n861
    Frankfurt 1955 792, 800–1, n813
    Music (Dessau qv) n705, 710–11
    Prologue 746, 762*, n818, n880
    for Salzburg n646
Collected Works (1937) 336, 364, 369. Third volume pulped 380, 383
Dan Drew (project) 151
Days of the Commune, The (music Eisler, qv) *433*, *436*, *439*, 582–91 passim, 593, 596, 615, 617, 625, 639

Drums in the Night 14–16, 67*, 68–72, 75, 76, 79, *92*, 104
Duchess of Malfi (adaptation) See Webster
Einstein (project) 801
Eulenspiegel (project) 596
Exception and the Rule, The 190, 865
Fat Man on the Swingboat, The (project) 39
Fatzer (project) *92*, 126, 142, 145
Fear and Misery of the Third Reich 159, *161*, 332, 341, 347, 356*, 364, 369, 375, 383, 394, 397–8, 409, 414, 507, *432*
    Paris production 1938 (*99%*) 357*–60*
    In US 430–1, 442*, 443*, 444–5, 495
    New York 1945 (*The Private Life of the Master Race*) *313*, 498, 501–2a, 503–4
    Basel 1947 *314*
Flüchtlingsgespräche 308
Good Person of Szechwan, The 308, *311–14*, n380x, 397, 411, 415, *434*, n435x, 451, 520, 522, 532, 545, 784, 797
    Munich Kammerspiele 801, 822
    Rostock 846
    Russian translation 876
    US projects 434–5, n476x, 491, 610
Gösta Berling (adaptation with Ellen Karyn) 86, 174
Hannibal (project) 72, 73
Happy End (with Hauptmann and Weill, qv)
Herrnburger Bericht 435, *436*
Horatians and Curiatians, The 158, 267*, 409
In the Jungle (or *Jungle*) *15*, 59a, 61, 62, 64, 70, 79, 83–5, 87, *89*f, 97, 138
In the Jungle of Cities 89
Joe P. Fleischhacker from Chicago (project) *89*, *92*, 151

Julius Caesar (project) *162*, 345*,
   347*. See 'Prose' below
Life of Edward II, The (adaptation
   with Feuchtwanger) 88, 90,
   91, 92, 98, 346, 502a
   Cologne production n105,
      108, 110
Life of Galileo 162, 308, 398, 409,
   486, 508, 520, 522, 531,
   532*, 543, 568, 832, 877
   'Danish' version 372–3*,
      375, 383, 511
   Hollywood version and
      production (music
      Eisler, qv) *311*, 504,
      506–7, 511, 519, 528*,
      543, 550–3
   Berlin version and
      rehearsal (do.) *434,
      438*, 635, 639, 642,
      660, 668, 838, 840,
      842*, n843–5
Lindbergh's Flight 148*, 626*
Mahagonny ('Songspiel', with
   Weill, qv) *91*
Man equals Man (initially *Galgai*)
   89–90, 101a, 106, n113–5,
   177, 184, *313*, 752
   Broadcast 1927, 128;
   Berlin 1928, n132;
   Berlin 1931, 153, 509
Massnahme, Die ('The Decision' or
   'The Measures Taken', with
   Eisler qv) 153, 159, *157*, 287,
   336, 532
   Barred 865*
Mother, The, 190, 193, *157*, 252,
   272–85, 336, 340, *310*, 668,
   n748
   Barred from tour 709*
   Dramaturgy of 274*
Mother Courage 308, 400, 409, 415,
   430, 511, 543, 545, n694,
   784, 877
   Zurich production 1941
      421
   ditto 1948 n571
   Berlin production 1949
      (music Dessau, qv)

432–3, 436, 438, 567,
   571–6, 579, 634
Revised ditto 1951 668
West Germany 594, 644
Scandinavia 742–3
England n8, 12x
Mr Puntila and his man Matti 308,
   454, *432–4*, 594, 624, 639,
   796, 848x
   Zurich production 1948
      n561x, 564, 566
   With BE, 1949 575,
      582–3, 586, 588, 614,
      620, 634
   Authorship 564*, 696
Ocean Flight, The. See *Lindbergh's
   Flight*
Pluto (revue project) 401
Pope Joan (project) 61
Practice pieces for actors 431
*Resistible Rise of Arturo Ui, The
   308*, 435
Rise and fall of the City of Mahagonny
   (with Weill, qv) 336
*Roundheads and the Pointed Heads,
   The* (music Eisler, qv) n160,
   168, 170, 184, *158, 160*, 204–
   10 passim, 227, 231, 245*,
   270, 275–6, 284, 297–304,
   312–3, 336, 353, 409, 532
Saint Joan of the Stockyards 174,
   177, 207, 231, 257, 266, 301,
   336, 340, 353, 419, 521–2,
   574
Salzburg Dance of Death (project)
   432–3, 602, 642, 651, 672
Schweik in the Second World War
   (music Eisler, qv; project
   with Weill, qv) n162, *311–12*
   451–75, n476x, 481, 485
   'Song of the Moldau' 467
Señora Carrar's Rifles 158, 336,
   352, 353, 409, 521, n758
   1937 Paris production 332,
      347, 736
   Prague production 339–41
   1938 Copenhagen
      production 349–50*,
      354, 736

After 1945 704, n711
US translation 364
Seven Deadly Sins, The. See under
    Weill
Story of the Flood, The (project)
    128
Threepenny Opera, The (with
    Weill, qv) n132, 141, 145,
    174, 245*, 286, *314*, n435x,
    486, 489
    Post-war 508, n509x–xx,
        n511, *432*, n561x,
        566–7, 570*, 578*
    In Danish 348*, 352, 362
    In English 168, 273, n859
    In French 332, 337, 347
    In Russian 184, *159*, 508
    Italian 'true rebirth' of
        (1956) 856–7
    Songs 157
    See also under Blacks.
        Rights
Trial of Jeanne d' Arc, The
    (adaptation after Seghers)
    n711, n757
Trial of Lucullus, The (opera
    version by Dessau, qv) *308*,
    436, 642, 652*–61, 668, 697
Trumpets and Drums (after
    Farquhar) 801, n806, n808,
    n831
Turandot n731, 742–4
Tutor, The (adaptation) See Lenz
Visions of Simone Machard, The
    (with Feuchtwanger; music
    Eisler, qv) *310*, 451, 521,
    550–1, 568, 582, 868, 879
Weizen. See *Joe P. Fleischhacker*
Poems:
'Anachronistic Procession, The'
    539
Augsburg Sonnets 126, 738
'Ballad of Mazeppa' (poem) 80
'Ballad of Paragraph 218' 167
'Ballad of the Soldier' n138
'Ballade vom armen Stabschef'
    (Röhm ballad) 351
'Buckow Elegies' n728, n731,
    n747, 762

'Children's Anthem' *435*
'Children's crusade, The' 438,
    448, 470–2, 475, 484, 511
    English translations n438
'Der Führer hat gesagt' ('March
    into the Third Reich') 162
*Devotions for the
    Home (Hauspostille)* 74, *89*,
    91, 101a
'German Satires' *158*, 369
'German War Primer' *158*
'Germany' 452
'Hymn of Baal the Great':
    missing stanzas 701
Kriegsfibel n493, n498, n640x,
    848x, n879x
'Legend of the Dead Soldier' *90*
'Legend of the Origin of the
    Book Tao-Tê-Ching' 392
'Legend of the Unknown
    Soldier' 167
'Lenin Cantata' *158*
'Lenin poems' (?) 869
'Lullabies' ('Songs of Proletarian
    Mothers', with Eisler) 177–8
'Mahagonny Songs' n87
'Manifesto' 494*, 507
'Pied Piper, The' 365
Pocket Devotions (Taschenpostille),
    738
'Pokerfaced girl, The' (from
    Kriegsfibel) 498
'Questions from a worker's
    reading' 399
'Saar Song' 237
'Song of a German mother' 452
'Song of the Brandy Peddler'
    ('Exemplary Conversion of
    a Grog-Seller') 146
'Song of the Hours' 573, n598,
    n601
'Song of the Third Thing' 637
Sonnets 99
Svendborg Poems *161*, 369, 372,
    419, 467, 848x
'The Truth unites' n733
'The way the wind blows' n819
Three Soldiers, The (Versuche vol 6)
    226, 231, 340

'To my countrymen' n659
'To the German soldiers on the
    Eastern front' 485
'To those born later' *163*
Workers' Songs 231
'Zehr und Petschek' 162
Prose:
'Augsburg Chalk Circle, The'
    420, 762
'Bargan gives up' 796
'Is the drama dying?' 104
'Mean Bastard, A'
Me-Ti 161, 304. See Forke
Mr Julius Caesar's Business Deals
    (unfinished) 354, 357, 361,
    369, 397, 400, 415
'Notes to the opera *Mahagonny*'
    395
Notes to *The Threepenny Opera*
    520, 522
'On experimental theatre' n384–8
'On Rhymeless Verse with
    Irregular Rhythms' 394
'Open letter to German artists
    and writers' n673,
    n684–7
'Popular and the Realistic, The'
    365
'Problems of the modern theatre'
    101
'Seven Difficulties when Writing
    the Truth' 288
'Short Organum for the Theatre'
    432, 436, 562, 616–17, 801
'Socrates Wounded' 704, n817
Speech to Paris Writers'
    Congress, 1934, 266
'Stage construction', article 310
'Street Scene, The' 369, 837
Theoretical writings 395*, 409,
    520
'Theory of the Alienation effect,
    The' 369
'Three cheers for Shaw' n111
Threepenny Novel 186, 192, *158*,
    199, 212–25 passim, 236,
    246, 297, 301, 320, 334*,
    336, 373, 400
'Tui novel' 259, 336, 433

Translation:
    Memoirs of Martin Andersen-
        Nexö (with Margarete
        Steffin) 354–5, 390, 394, 420
Brecht, Berthold (BB's father)
    191, **260**
'Brecht collective', The *90*, n117
Brecht, Sophie (BB's mother) 18,
    n55
Brecht, Stefan Sebastian 100, 122, 126,
    138, 142, 167–8, 184, 189, 200,
    230, **233, 283**, 284, 286, 336, 339,
    340, 357, 432, 437, 446, 448, 452,
    473–4, 481, 493, 526, **528, 553**, 610,
    632
Brecht-Schall, Barbara 158, 167, 200,
    283–4, 286, 339–40, 357, 425, 432,
    437, 446, 448, 481, 501, 582, 584,
    591, 848x
Bredel, Willi n156, **366***, n**676**, 833
    Die Prüfung 266
    Gastmahl im Dattelgarten 872
Bregazzi, Rolf n845
Breitenbach, Joseph 339, 342
Brentano, Bernard von n**139**, **140**,
    n**154**, n**155**, 156, n**166**, 168–9,
    185, 201, 214–5, 231, n**240, 241**–
    2, 290, **305**, n**321**
    Deutschland erwache! n214
Brentano, Margo von **169, 235**
Breslau 128
Bressart, Felix 358–60
Brezing, Amalie n1–2
Broadway. See New York
Bronnen, Arnolt **64, 65, 66, 68, 71, 72**,
    74, **76**–**8, 81, 83, 85**–**7**, *86*, 100
    Anarchie in Sillian (Verrat), *15*,
        72, 76–8, 81
    Excesses 78
    Rheinische Rebellen 86, 98
    *Second Flood, The (Robinsonade auf
        Asuncion)* (project with
        Brecht), 64
    *Vatermord 14*f, 65, 76
'Brown Books' 197, 358
Bruckner, Ferdinand *Die Rassen* 208
Brueghel 358, n486
Brugsch, Theodor 884, **887**
Buckwitz, Harry n**755, 792**

Budzislavsky, Hermann ('Butsch')
    450, 480–1, 507
Büchergilde Gutenberg 185
Büchner, Georg
    Danton's Death 584
    Woyzeck 95, 709
Bünger, Wilhelm n197
Burian, E. F. 316–8, 339–40, 342, *438*,
    n764, 771, 773–4
Burri, Emil Hesse *90*, 117–18, 119,
    126, 151, n150, 151, 158, *313*, 509,
    529, 545, 645, n663, 688, n705,
    710, 716, n734–5
    *Amerikanische Jugend (Tim
        O'Mara)* 117–19
Busch, Ernst 332, 359–60, 511, 532,
    434, *438*, 586, 668, 698, 709, 726,
    n775, 846

Cabaret *157*. And see under Berlin
Cain, James M. 383
California 430
    exile community 432–3
    Hollywood 432, 448, 481, 540
    Lake Arrowhead 458–9
    Santa Monica 432
Capri 95f
Carnap, Rudolf n259
Carona 167–71
Cassirer, Paul n61, 68
Cavalcanti, Alberto *438*, 790
Censorship 186
Cervantes 239
Cézanne 61
Chaplin, Charlie n543, 840
    Monsieur Verdoux 537
Chekhov, Anton 510, 525
Chicago 146
Chinese painting described 226, 233
Christensen 263
Chur 553, 558, 560
Churchill, Winston S. 500
Clair, René n397
Clark, Barrett O. **82**
Clown Gottes, Der 81
Clurman, Harold *314*, 444
Cologne n105, 108, 128, 633, 657
Comintern (Communist International)
    158–9, 202

Communist Party See KPD
Concentration Camps 309, 507
    Eisler project *160*
Conferences, Congresses etc.
    BPRS (1928) 140
    Kharkhov (1929) n173
    Soviet Writers (1934) *159*
    Seventh Comintern (1935) *158*
    First Paris Writers (1935) *159*,
        258–66
    London Writers (1936) 294
    Madrid and Paris Writers (1937)
        329
    PEN Stockholm (1939)
        396
    All-German committee (project)
        750–51
Congress for Cultural Freedom
    Der Monat 785
Contracts
    Berliner Ensemble 590
    Collected Plays 1952 701
    Duchess of Malfi n527
    Good Person of Szechwan, The 472
    Mother Courage 421
    *Roundheads and the Pointed Heads,
        The* 174
    Saint Joan of the Stockyards 174
    Schweik with Weill 455, 462;
        without Weill 489
    Threepenny Opera 174*, 286
    Works in English 504
Cook, Ellen 278. See also Henry,
    Helen
Copenhagen 846
Council for German Democracy 480*,
    481–2, 495*, 498, 505, 507
Crime stories 112, 400, 743
'Cultural heritage', doctrine of *161*
Curjel, Hans n553*, **556**, 599
Czinner, Paul 311–13, 464–5, 482, 515,
    527*, 544

Dada n124, 736
Dammert, Hans 231
Darmstadt *86*
Darwin 339
'*Das Wort*'. See *Wort*
Daumier 358

DEFA 577, 589, **645, 688, 698,**
    727, 730, **823, 829,** 833
Defregger, Franz 3
De Gaulle, General Charles 496
De Lange, Gerard **186**
Democracy 200
Denmark invaded *308*
Desch, Kurt 564, 594, 696, n**723**
Dessau, Paul 452, *433–4, 436*
    Caucasian Chalk Circle music 792,
        793
    Mother Courage music 532, **573**
    Trial of Lucullus, opera 654–7,
        695, 697
Devine, George 832
Dialectics 140, 179, 185, 200, 380, 411,
    619, 782
'Dialectical realism' 522
'Diderot Society', project for *159*,
    316–23
Diebold, Bernhard 144
Dieterle, William *309*, n424x–xx, 428–
    9, 482, 532, **547**
Diktonius, Elmer 404
Dimitrov, Georgi *158*
Dinamov, S. S. 173
Dnepropetrovsk 270
Döblin, Alfred *91*, n123, **144**, 167–9,
    184, 192, 244, **256, 265, 367,**
    (birthday tribute)
    In US 433, 466, 482, 508–9
Domke, Martin **344–5, 361, 397**
Donath, Ludwig 535
Doone, Rupert 316–18
Dorn, Erna 728
Dreiser, Theodore *An American
    Tragedy* 282, 295
Dresden State Theatre **624**
Dressler, Bruno **390**
Dubislav, Walter 304
Dudow, Slatan 158, 177, *158, 161,* 198,
    201, 253, 258, 295, **332–3,** 340,
    356
    And DEFA 589
    'Grenzbestimmungen'
        (Demarcations) 332–3
Dürrenmatt, Friedrich *The Visit* n875
Dumas jeune, Alexandre
    Camille 85

Duncker, Hermann 615, **625,** n818
Dunkirk 191
Durieux, Tilla 61
Dymschitz, Alexander *432*, 585

Ebert, Carl *91*
Ebinger, Blandine 76, 77, 79
Eddington, Sir A. 333
Ege, Friedrich n696
Ehrenberg, Carl 31
Ehrenburg, Ilya 48
Einem, Gottfried von *431, 433,* **561,**
    597–600, n**601, 636,** 642, **646,**
    672
    The Trial (opera) 598
Einstein, Albert 358, 482, 599, n**715**
Eisenach, Landestheater n677, n690
Eisenstein, S. M. 316–17
Eisler, Gerhart *158, 314,* n551, 620
Eisler, Hanns *157–60, 155,* **160,** 167,
    177, 190, 193, **208,** 212, n229,
    231, 269, 274–87 passim, 295,
    316, 318, 353, *310, 314,* 421, 430–
    1, 444, 448*, 453–4, 466, 469, 485,
    488–9, 509, 621
    After World War 2 *433, 435, 589,*
        n**671, 706, 768,** 838, 860
    'Ballad of the Soldier' n1138
    Days of the Commune (music) 589
    Galileo (music) 849
    Gegen den Krieg, op. 55 *158*
    Horatians and Curiatians, The
        (failure to collaborate) 267–8*
    Johannes Faustus (opera text) *436,*
        669, n**670, 706,** 718*
    Koloman-Wallisch Cantata **620**
    Lenin Requiem op. 59, *158*
    Lukács attacks 365
    'Lullabies' 177–8
    Die Massnahme (with Brecht, qv)
        153, 159. See also Patera
    'Opera' project 312
    Schweik (music) 472
    Simone Machard (music) 451–2,
        551, 868
    Weissbrot-Kantate 620
    Winterschlacht (music) 768, 773.
        See also Becher
Eisler, Hilde (Mrs Gerhart E.) 828x

Eisler, Lou 207, 364, 435
Eklund 404
Eliot, T. S.
    Old Possum's Book of Practical Cats
        679
    Sweeny Agonistes, n229
Elsner, Martin **102**
Empathy 311, 395
Encyclopaedia project *159*, 236, 255,
    224
Engel, Erich *15*, 79 84, 87, *90*, *92*,
    n106, **131–2**, 135, n138, n141,
    608, **619**
    Relations supended **133***
    Their resumption after 1945 *432–
        3*, *438*, 571, 573
    With the BE 575ff, 583–4,
        n863
    Film 639, 645
Engel, Rudolf 607, **804**, **852**
Engels, Friedrich 347, 494, 506
    Dialectics of Nature 153
Engels, capital of the Volga German
    Republic, qv
English, Brecht and 304, 440
    phrases or words 141, 245, 259,
        288, 311, 383, 415, 430, 437,
        442, 443, 445, 450, 458, 459,
        461, 472, 475, 481, 485, 487,
        490, 494–5, 497x, 498, 503,
        512, 516–17, 519, 525, 536–
        7, 543, 552–3, 567, 577, 579,
        583, 585, 591, 603, 617, 620,
        669, 784, 826, 868
    songs 94, 96, 162
    letters in 439, 492, 497
    Chicago dialect 464
    See also under Translation
English Stage Company 832
Entertainment and Instruction 395,
    520, 522
Epic
    acting 341, 556
    literature 367
    science 558
    singing 486
    theatre *90*, 245*, 311, 313, *313*, *431*
Erpenbeck, Fritz n298, 346, 365, 366,
    375, **394**, *436*

Essen n121, 212
Eulenspiegel-Verlag n879x
Euripides 718
European Books Ltd n218
European Film Fund *309*
Evans, Ernestine **353**, **364**, 454
'Exile literature' 517
Existentialism 532, *431*
Experiments 149, 831

Faber, Erwin 79, 84
Fabian, Dora n265
Fabig, Paul **704**
Fadeyev, Alexander n429
Faktor, Emil n111
Fall of the Commune See Brecht: *Days of
    the Commune*
Farmer, Virginia 519
Fascism 200, 312
    Archive for study 193
    Popular Front against *160*; its
        collapse *162*
    Differentiated from Communism
        241–2
    Persistence after 1945 728
    See also National Socialism;
        Silone; Sternberg
FBI, The *312*
Fedin, Konstantin n808
Fehling, Jürgen n89
Feilchenfeldt, Walther 68
Felsenstein, Walter *432*, 642
Feuchtwanger, Lion *14*, 41, 47, 62,
    n82, 88, 91, 92, n117, 158, 167,
    183, *160*, **244**, **334**, 337, n338x
    346, 415, n415x, n420x,
    n424x–xx*, 482, **832**
    Birthday tribute **213**
    Helps the Brechts *309*
    Moscow in 1937 **327–8**
    At Pacific Palisades *310*, 445, 447,
        509
    Falsche Nero, Der 334
    Jew Süss 209
    Josephus 346
    Kalkutta 4 Mai 138
    Moscow 1937 332, 334
    Simone 868
    Success 327

Vasantesena 209
Fields, Joe 475
Film
    Brecht's involvement 290, 295,
        310
    Plans and projects 270, 282, 295–
        6, 315, 466, 508, 537
    'The children's crusade' 438
    Galileo project 560
    Hangmen Also Die 310, n445
    King's Bread, The 519
    Overcoat, The 647
    'Potato Jones' 323
    Schweik 323–4*
    Tales of Hoffmann 576
    See also under Brecht: Main
        Films
Finland *308*
    arrival in 404
    Finnish People's Theatre 406
    Marlebäk *308*
    Petsamo route 411
Fischer, Ernst 706, 852
Fischer, Franz Theodor
    Auch Einer 49
Fischer-Meyenburg, Ruth n798
Fleisser, Marieluise n678
Folk stories 790
Foreign Workers' Publishing House.
    See VEGAAR
Forke, Alfred, translation of Me-Ti
    251
Form and Content 652*
Formalism *159*, 312, 332 366*, *437–8*,
    655, n670, 684, n709
Forster, Rudolf 138
Fradkin, Ilya 814
Fränkel, Mary 342
Frank, Bruno 482
Frank, Leonard 433, 509
Frankfurt
    Institute for Social Research 247,
        n432–3, 448. See
        Horkheimer, Pollock etc.
    Radio 155
Franz, Erich n880
'Freedom' as slogan 728
French, Samuel, agency 472, 489–90,
    506

Frey, Alexander Moritz n232
Friedman (?) 454
Frisch, Max **562, 629**
Fürnberg, Louis n691, 833, n851
Fürst, Manfred 359–60
Fyn (Fünen) 161

Gábor, Andor *161*, n312
Ganghofer, Ludwig 433, 666
Garbe, Hans 743
Gasbarra, Felix *92*, **123**, 124–5, 231
Gaugler, Hans 556, 583, 628, n708
Gehweyer, Fritz 16, 17, 37
Geiger, Rod 543
Geis, Jacob **41, 48**, 83, 84, 122, 529, 545,
    432, **564**, n**565**, 578, 647, n**663**, 716
Gelsted, Otto 208
George, Heinrich 71, 231
George, Manfred n440a
George, Stefan, Brecht's view of 136
Gera. See Reuss
Gerhardt, Karl 401
Germain, André 149
German Democracy. See Council
German Democratic Republic
    Academy of Arts *435–6*, *438*,
        607–8, 621, **667**, 693, n**719**,
        726, n726x, **727**, 732, 750,
        756, **804**, **852**, **872**
    Advanced drama class project
        665, 782
    Central Committee for the
        Dedication of Youth n836
    Central Institute for Pedagogy
        666
    Cultural bureaucracy n700, 709,
        732, 751
    Education policy 621, 756
    Kulturbund zur demokratischen
        Erneuerung Deutschlands
        433, 580
    Ministry of Culture *438*, 732, 751,
        760
    National Prize, scepticism and
        recommendations 872
    People's Chamber *437*, 767
    Propaganda 684
    Riots of 17 June 1953 *437*, 725–
        7, n726x, 728*

Socialist Unity Party n640x, **712**, 728, 732, 860
Teaching of literature 666–7
German Federal Republic
 Rearmament 771, 773
German Freedom Radio *158*, 346
'German Misère' *436*, 638, n718
German Writers' Defence League. See SDS
Germany
 Allied Occupation (zones and sectors) *434–5*, n502a
 Ditto (policy) n563
 Impact on modern theatre 311*
 Nazi survivals n728
 Postwar 495–6, 505
 Question of Brecht's return 506, 548
 Reunification 701
 Theatre plans 529–37
 Wartime democratic opposition 477*
Geschonneck, Erwin *434*, 668, n**717**
Geyer, Georg 21, 23, 29, 36
Gide, André 236, 263
 Return from the USSR 302
Giehse, Therese *434*, 575, 577, 582ff, 642, 644, 647, n**664**, n769, **833**
Gielen, Joseph 588
Gielgud, John 832
Gillmann, Harry n880
Girnus, Wilhelm n**737**
Gitermann, Valentin 583–4
Glaeser, Ernst 290
Glaeser, Günter *1*
Glaser, Kurt 480
Gloger, Christine 848x
Gnass, Friedrich 801
Gnekow, Horst **797**
God 8, 16, 23, 38, 330, 354
Goedhart, Gerda 551
Goering, Hermann 195
Goethe 25, 213, 328
 Faust 3, 502a, 718, 721
 Götz von Berlichingen 709
 Urfaust 434, 436, 669, 721
Gog, Gregor: League of Tramps n399
GOKS **841**
Gold, Käthe 577, n646

Goldbeck, Eva (Mrs Blitzstein) 288
Gomez, Manuel 274
Gorelik, Mordecai (Max) *160*, n272, 293, **310***, 311, 316–7, **318**, 323, *310*, 474–5
Gorky, Maxim **285**, 328, *434*
 And *The Mother* 709
 Vassa Zhelesnova 575, 582–90 passim, 628
Gottron, Heinrich 138
Goya 10
 Disasters of the War and Brecht's *Fear and Misery* 356
Graf, Oskar Maria *159*
Granach, Alexander 60, 69, **75**, **89**
Grass n40
Grassi, Paolo, n857, n859
Greenburger 282
Greid, Hermann 403
Greisle, Felix 503
Gresshöhner See Osten
Gretler, Heinrich 332
Grieg, Nordahl 316–7
 The Defeat 433, 579, **582***, 584
Grossmann, Stefan 65, 76, n112
Grosz, George ('Böff') n123, 124–5, *160*, **211**, **226**, **245**, **263**, **269**, 283, **307**, *310*, 323, 336, 431, **539**
 plan for San Francisco show 465
Grotewohl, Otto **724***, 730, **767**, **780**
Grouping (blocking) etc. 245, 414
Grünberg (?) 339
Grünberg, Karl n**650**
Gründgens, Gustaf **574**
Grzesinski, Albert 480–1
Guilbeaux, Henri 149
Guilbert, Yvette 347
Gullberg, Hjalmar 404

Haas, Dolly? 535
Haas, Willy **112**, **136**
Hacks, Peter n755, 782
Hagen, Friedrich 480–1
Hagg, Heinz **4**, **14**, **40**
Hahn, Julius n848
Hale, Robert **320**
Hambleton, T. E. 552–3
Hamsun, Knut 5
Hanisch, Herta (Steffin's sister) **541**

Harcourt Brace n513
Hardt, Ernst n105, 108, 128, 148, n149
Harich, Wolfgang 730
Harris, Jed n486
Hart, Moss n476x
Hartmann, Rudolf 37, 518, 522
Hartung, Gustav 185, 514
Hase, Annemarie 67
Hašek, Jaroslav n691
    The Adventures of the Good Soldier Schweik 93, 324*
Hasselbach, Steen n249
Hauptmann, Elisabeth *90*, *91*, 126, 135, 158, 169, *157*, 247, 275, 383, *309*, 430, 434, 469, 472, 475, 501, 513, 515, 517, 522, 553
    Return to Europe *434*
    In East Berlin 596, 701, 746, 762, 848x
    Happy End n132, ?133, 146*, n150, 174, n397
Hauptmann, Gerhart 3, 149, 621
    The Weavers 127
    Driver Henschel 127
    The Beaver Coat and *The Red Rooster* 644, 649*
Hay, Julius (Gyula) *161*, 312–5, 313, 328, 333, 366
Hays, H. R. *309*, *310–12*, n421x, 430, 435, 438, n439x, 454, 464, 485, 515
    The Medecine Show (with Oscar Saul) *310*
Hearst, W. R. 288
Heartfield, John 608
Hebbel
    Herodes und Mariamne 103–4
Hegel 606
Heidelberg 138, 514
Heine, Th. Th. 212
Heinz, Wolfgang n859, n873
Hellberg, Martin n627
Helpmann, Robert *313*
Hemingway, Ernest n715
Henning-Jensen, Astrid and Barne n742
Henschel, Bruno n870
Henschel-Verlag (East Berlin) n830

Hergesheimer, Joseph
    Tampico 126
Hermlin, Stephan 606, 852
Hertz, Paul 480–1
Herzfelde, Wieland 181, 266, 269, 336, 339, 354, 372, 375, *308*, *310*, 380, 393, 465, 484, 539, n641. See also Aurora-Verlag, Malik-Verlag
Herzog, Wilhelm 123
Hesse, Hermann 699
Hessel, Franz 155
Hesterberg, Trude n67
Heymann, Stefan n640x
Hikmet, Nazim 852
Hill, Hainer 731
Hilpert, Heinz n72
Hindemith, Paul *91*, *93*, n148, 149, 238*
Hinz, Werner 571, 639
Hiob, Hanne 87a, 96, 100, 101a–b, 138, 260, 276, 339, 554, 566, 801
Hirschfeld, Hans 480
Hirschfeld, Kurt 582, 583, n602, n604, n617
Hitler 81, 87, *90*, 215
Hodann, Traute 339
Hodler, Ferdinand 32
Hölderlin *431*, 558
Höllering, Franz 282
Höllering, Georg 168
Hofer, Johanna (Mrs Kortner) 502a
Hoffmann, Camille 231
Hogan, Edward 509, n509x
Hohenester, Max 5, 13, 16, 17, 35
Hold, Mari 172, 188, 227, 230
Holländer, Felix 79, *89*
Holtzhauer, Helmut n700, 709, n751
Homolka, Florence 481
Homolka, Oskar 89a, 100, *310*, 435, 438, 489, 502a, 532, 535, 634, 668
Honecker, Erich 703
Horace 701
Horkheimer, Max 433, 437, 482
Horwitz, Kurt 599
Huchel, Peter 571, 606, 853
Huchtheusen, Liselot n817
Huebsch, Ben 445
Hüttner, Dr 121, 134
Hugo, Victor 184

Huppert, Hugo 297, 841
Hurwicz, Angelika *438*, 837–8, 846

Ibsen 510
   Peer Gynt 43
Iceland 400
Illés, Béla n178, 184
Illustrierte Rote Post 162
Infeld, Leopold n**713**
Ingenohl, Oscar 571
Intellect and feeling 395*
Intelligibility 652–4, 740
International Association of Writers
   for the Defence of Culture **294**
Internationale Literatur (Deutsche
   Blätter) n173, 177–8, *163*, 214,
   366, 420, 876
International Music Bureau *158*
International Workers' Aid
   (IAH) *158*. See also
   Mezhrabpom, Münzenberg
Isherwood, Christopher 316–8, 438,
   489
Iskusstvo publishers **886**
'it' 34, 35, 36
Ivens, Joris 195, **759**

Jacob, Heinrich Eduard 64
Jacob, Kurt 347
Jacobsohn, Edith **129**
Jahnn, Hans Henny n**812**
   Pastor Ephraim Magnus n87, **761**
Janka, Walter n680, 699
Jaray, Karl n187, 231
Jerome, V. J. **273**, 280, **288**, 353
Jessner, Leopold 62, *89*, *90*, **104**, **106**–
   7, 109, 482
Jews, the. See Racism, Zionism
Jhering, Herbert *14–15*, 64, **70**, **73**, **74**,
   79, **80**, **84**, **88**, **91**, **92**, *85*, *86*, **98**,
   108–**110**, n**113**, **119**, **125**, **145**,
   153, 201, *313*
   Rôle after World War 2 509, *432*,
   573, 585, n776
Johnson, Alvin n**410**, 424
Johst, Hanns 41, **43–45**
   Der Einsame 43, 44
Juchacz, Maria 480
Jugend 11

Kästner, Erich n129
Kaiser, Georg 61, 621
Kalser, Erwin 579
Kanter 126
Kantorowicz, Alfred n**115**, 239, 241,
   264, 480
Karin, Ellyn 86
Kasack, Hermann 64, 72, 514
Kasprowiak, Ilse 585
Katz, Otto ('André Simone') **197**, 332,
   568
Katzenellenbogen, Ludwig 245
Kaufman, George and Ryskind,
   Morrie *Of Thee I Sing* 603
Kautsky, Karl 200
Kawerau or Kawenauer? 309
Kazan, Alfred 501, 519
Kerr, Alfred n157, 378
Kertesz, Andrew 282
Kerz, Leo n476x, **491**, **752**
Kesser, Hermann 201
Kesten, Hermann **180**, **192**, 198, 290
Keynes, J. M. 236
Kiepenheuer, Gustav 59, n64, 71, 86,
   119, 168, 180, **228**, 231
Kilger, Heinrich 823, 828–9
Kilian, Isot n726, n730, n**820**,
   n875xx–xxx
'Kinner, Karl' 429
Kipling, Rudyard 7, *91*, n138
Kirsanov, Semyon n312, 759, n808
Kisch, Egon Erwin n140, **378**
Kitsch, as subject of study *436*, 666,
   693
'Klabund' (Alfred Henschke) 60, *312*
Kläber, Kurt 167–9, 173, 181, 193,
   198, **202**, 215, 231, n865x
Klammer, Karl **157**
Klecha, Herbert n**720**
Kleinschmidt, Karl n**799**
Kleist, Heinrich von *The Broken Jug*
   668
Kleist Prize 64
Klemperer, Otto *91*, 502a, 577, 579
Klöpfer, Eugen 71, 72, 81
Knaup, Dieter n**843**
Knorin, Vilis *152*
Knutzon, Per 208, **209**, 227, **299**, 316–
   8, **348**, 352, 362

Koch, Carl n121, 126
Königshof, Kaspar n690
Koltsov, Mikhail 173, *159–60*, **255**,
    346, 375*, *309*
Korsch, Karl ('the professor') 168,
    184–5, 188, **195**, *157*, *160–1*, **200**,
    206–7, 215, **258**, 265, 275–6, 290,
    303–4, 347, 357, **380–1**, **432–3**,
    436–7, **449***, **481**, **493–4**, 553, **558**
    Karl Marx 380–1, 436
    *Kernpunkte der materialistischen
        Geschichtsauffassung* 494
    Marxismus und Philosophie n206
Kortner, Fritz 100, **103**, 135, 244, *310*,
    n**377**, 469, 482, 494, 502a, 509,
    535, n540x, *434*, 579, 628, **635**,
    660, n755, n**812x**
KPD 170, 173*, 188, *157–8*, 242
    See also under German Democratic
        Republic: Socialist Unity
        Party
Kraus, Karl **175–6**, ?187, 231
    Die Fackel 176
    The Last Days of Mankind 89a
    Krise und Kritik project 155
'Kuba' (Kurt Bartel) 589, n676
Kuckhahn, Heinz n538, 573, 624,
    n627
Kühl, Kate 511
Kuhn, Hedda ('He') 56
Kulisiewicz, Tadeusz n**811**, n**834**,
    n**839**, n**883**
Kun, Béla 270
Kurella, Alfred **365**, n851
Kultur und Volk, publishers n390
Kutscher, Arthur *13*, 13, 21, 39
Kyser, Hans 65

Lacis, Asya (Mrs Reich) n74, 188, *309*,
    n427, 808
Lagerlöf, Selma 86
    Gösta Berling 174
Lagerqvist, Per 317
Lanchester, Elsa 499
Landauer, Walter 218
Landshoff, Fritz 180, 199
'Lane, Dorothy' 146 (pseudonym for
    Hauptmann)
Lang, Fritz *309*, *310*, 445–6, 448, 482

Langen, Albert n47
Langerhans, Heinz 432, 448
Langhoff, Wolfgang *432*, **721**
    Die Moorsoldaten 266
Language, 176
    'Babylonian confusion' 688
    Abuse of 'concrete' 796
    foreign-derived words 390, 740
    Intelligibility 740
    'Operative phrases' 179
    See also under English;
        Translation
Lania, Leo *92*, n229
    Konjunktur 92, n123
    'Seashells from Margate' n123
Larsen, Aksel **352**, **362**
Lasker-Schüler, Else 129
Laté, Lilli *309*, 445, 465
Latouche, John 434
Laughton, Charles 207, *312–4*, 483,
    485, 499, 502a, 504, 506, 511,
    513–9, 525, 536, 543, **544**, 549,
    552*, 556, 832
Laurin 464–5
Lauter, Hans 655
Laxness, Halldór 853
Lazar, Maria 172, 194
Legal, Ernst *91*, *313*, 509, *432*, 577, 642
Lehrstück, Lehrgedicht 149, n153, *158*,
    268
Leibelt, Hans 79
Leiser, Erwin n746x
Leistikow, dancer 25
Le Lavandou n153, 158
Lenin 140, n149, 242, 380
Lenya, Lotte (Mrs Kurt Weill) *91*,
    n122, n169, *311*, 452, 455, 462,
    570, 578
Lenz, J. M. R. *The Tutor 436*, 628, 632,
    634, 638*, 639
Leonardo da Vinci 28
Lerski, Helmut 608
Leschnitzer, Frank n214, 215
Lessing 213, 311
Leupold, Hans J. **736**
Leventhal, Jules n481, 489, 506, 515
Lewenstein, Oscar n**859**
Lewis, Sinclair *309*
Lieb 339–40

Liebeneiner, Wolfgang n734–5
Lieber, Max 383
Lindberg, Per 316, 318
Lindemann, Walter 753
Lingen, Theo n149
Lingner, Max n820
Linkskurve, Die n140, n155, n173
Lipmann, Heinz 64
Lips, Julius 480–1
Literarische Welt, Die 112
Littlewood, Joan n812x, **815**
Living Marxism 437
Ljungdal, Arnold **411**
Löwenstein, Prinz Hubertus zu 334,
    n**335**, n**371**, n**379**, n**389**, n**393**
London *157*, 882
    visit 1934 235, 256
    Savoy Hotel 234
London, Jack
    Martin Eden 126
Lorca, Federico García *434*, 579
Lorre, Peter 452, 458–9, 461, 466,
    471–2, 502a, 508, 518–9, 535, *434*,
    628
    Problems 536
Los Angeles *309*
Losey, Joseph *314*, 526, 536, 549
Lotar, Peter 550
Lourdes (film) 432
Lucebert 782
Lucretius 494
Ludwig, Emil n45, 481
Lüthy, Herbert 785
Lugano 167–8
Lukács, Georg **156**, *161*, 332, 366,
    780*
Lutz, Regine 583, 668
Lyon, James K. *309*

Mackeben, Theo n146
MacLeish, Archibald 316, 318, 434, **439**
Magic Flute, The 502a
Magnan, Henri **816**
'Mahagonny' 87
Malik-Verlag 336, *308*
Malraux, André *Man's Hope* film 537
Mamoulian, Rouben 501
Mann, Heinrich 184, 259, 263, n**382**,
    447, **480**, 481–2, 498, 509

Mann, Klaus 112
Mann, Thomas 112, n139, **165**, *307*,
    394, 432, 477, 480
Mannheim, Dora **49**, **50**, **52–5**
Mao Tse-tung *437*, n827
Marcuse, Herbert 433, 437, 449
Marlowe 88, 502a
Marseilles 135
Marshall, Herbert n560
Martens 744
Martin, Karlheinz n81, n509xx, n511
Martner, Fredrik (Knud Rasmussen,
    'Crassus') n**391**, **392**, **400**
Martov, Yuri Osipovitch 242
Marx, Marxism *89*, 126, 140, 141, 168,
    185, 188, 206, 216, 304, 328, 432–
    3
    And art 144
    Kapital, Das (edited by Korsch)
    168
    Marxist Workers' School n168,
    157
Masereel, Frans n149, 323
Mass und Wert 394–5
Massary, Fritzi 146, *309*
Matray and Sterna, dancers 60, 61
Matisse 61
Matthis, Henry Peter **384–8**, **404**, n623
Mauprey, André 344
Maurer, Georg 872
May, Joe, film producer *14*
Mayer, Götz n**248**
Mayer, Hans **638**, **718***
Medea 190
Mehring, Walter
    The Merchant of Berlin 141
Meier, Walter n**881**
Mei Lan-fang *159*, 250–1
Me-Ti. See Forke; Brecht (prose)
Memphis Belle 489
Mertens-Bertozzi, Renata **739**
Meunier, Constantin 3
Meusel, Walter n**802**
Mexico 307, 315, 403
Meyerhold, V. E. 310
Mezhdunarodnaya Kniga n354, 420
Mezhrabpom Film *161*
Michaelis, Karin 172, 187, 191, n226,
    250, 258, n**441**, 468, 487, 504

Mikhoels, Solomon n270
Milan Piccolo Teatro **857**
Milestone, Lewis 537
Miller, Arthur n715
Miller, Gilbert *162*
Miracle in Milan 760
Mittelgebirge, the 3
'Model-books' 616, 624, 633, 800–1,
　826, n870. See also Photography
Modernism 608
Molière *Dom Juan* n766
Mondsee 96
Money 129, 167–9, 171, 174, 178, 184,
　188, 194, 256, 273, 285, 296, 435,
　481, 632, 699
　Absence of 130
　Advances 465, 582
　American grants 369–70, 415
　and Berlau 468*, 486, 488, 848x*
　For journey to US n415x*,
　　420*, 428–9
　For return to Berlin 568
　As refugees in US *309–10*
　From Collected Works (Malik)
　　372
　From magazines 394
　From *Threepenny Novel* 227, 230
　From translation 394, 420
　Royalties 285, 344–5, 348*, 504,
　　568
　Funds in Switzerland and
　　Czechoslovakia 589, 593,
　　595
Monk, Egon *434–5*, 669
Montage 197
MOPR (International
　Association of Revolutionary
　Writers) n173, **178**
Morgenthau, Henry 496
MORT (International
　Association of Workers'
　Theatres) n173, *158*, *161*, 237, 250,
　295
　Ideas for its proposed magazine
　　243
Moscow *157–9*
　'Hungarian clique' *161*
　Jewish Academic Theatre 270
　Kamerny Teatr *159*

Mostel, Zero 472, 475
Motesicky 189
Moussinac, Léon 316, 318
Müller, Georg. See under Munich
Müller, Gerda (Mrs Scherchen) 68, 72,
　76–8, 81, n149
Müller-Eisert, Otto 7, 9, 21, 47, 62,
　509, 518, 522
Münster 100, 101a
Münsterer, Hans Otto **26**, **27**, **39**, **51**,
　56, **57**, **63**, n**675**, **738**
Münzenberg, Willi n188, n193, n197,
　158, *308*
Müthel, Lothar n105, 108, n117
Munich 646
　Drei-Masken 69, 70
　Georg Müller Verlag 47
　Kammerspiele 46, 76, 644, 801,
　　822*
　Kunstverein 13, 22
　Soviet of 1919 *13*f, n41, 179
　Steinicke Gallery 58
　Under the Empire *9*
　University *13*, 14, 31
　post-Nazi 564, 567
Muse, Clarence n438xx, n441x–xxxx
Mutter, Anna 731
Mynatt, Margaret 235, n336
Myers, Gustavus *The History of the
　　Great American Fortunes* 339

Nagel, Otto **756**
Naples 96
National Socialism, Nazis, etc. 209,
　262, 532, 728. See also Fascism
Nationalverein 10
Naturalism 272–3, 333, 522, *436*, 790*
Neergard, Ebbe n**300**
'Negativism' 718
Negros, See Blacks
Neher, Carola n60, 177, *161*, 199, 251,
　502a
　Brecht's inquiries re 327–8*, 346
　Death of *156*
Neher, Caspar *12–14*, *16*, **3**, **5**, **6–13**,
　15–25, **28–30**, **32–6**, **42**, **46**, **47**,
　58, **61**, **62**, 68, 76–8, *89*, 96, n121,
　126, n132, n138, n141, n146, 158,
　n169

Break in correspondence with
157
Collaboration resumed 313–4,
509, 523, **529*–32***, 431, 435,
548, **557**, n561x, **567**, **572**,
582–5, 608, 645–7, 669, n748
As illustrator 199, 212
As painter 530
Days of the Commune 589
Galileo 846
The Tutor 628
And Salzburg Dance of Death 651
Austrian passports 433, 567, 583,
636, **642**, 672
And Arts Council of Great
Britain n**822**
Neher, Erika 531, 554
Neher, Georg 311, 529–30
Neher, Marianne ('Ma') 42
Nellhaus, Gerhard 515
Neoclassicism 522
Neue Bücherschau, Die n140
Neue Deutsche Blätter 181, 198, 244,
n298
Neue Musik, Die 153
'Neue Sachlichkeit' 91, 262*
Neues Deutschland **696**
cuts Brecht's message n725
Neues Vorwärts 200
Neue Zeit 200
Neumann, Elisabeth (later Mrs
Viertel) 468, 495, 502a, 535, 588
Neurath, Otto 169, **179**
Empirical Sociology 179
New Deal 160, 310
New Statesman and Nation, The 236
New York 3, 157, 160, 310
Brecht visits in 1935 272–88
passim, 430
Amityville Hospital 313
Broadway 282, 529*
'Left' theatres 282*
New School 160, 309, 408–9, 424,
431, 434
Theater Guild 435
Theatre Union 160, 273ff, **277–
81**, 285
Nordmark. See Schleswig
Norman, Dorothy 525, 571

Norris, Frank
The Pit 89, n151
Norway, fall of 308
Nubel, Walter 738
Nürnberg 849

Oberer, Walter n**613**
O'Casey, Sean 434
Odets, Clifford 434
Paradise Lost 288
Waiting for Lefty 160, 288
Office of War Information
(OWI) 311–12, n444
Okhlopkov, Nikolai 159, 310, 316–8,
333, n808, **809**
Oklyanskii, Yuri 9
Olden, Rudolf **396**
Oldenburg 127
O'Neill, Eugene
The Emperor Jones 89a
Opera. See Brecht 'Notes to the
opera'; Dessau; Eisler; Wagner-
Régeny; Weill
Optimism 657
Orff, Carl n705, **710–11**
Oskar 37
Osten, Maria 160, 255, 366, **375***, 309,
428–9, 541
Ostermoor, Alfred 355
Ostrovski, Alexander
The Stepdaughter 837–8, 846
Oswald, Richard 77
Otto, Hans 243
Otto, Teo 162, 784, 792, 800, 856
Ottwalt, Ernst n156, n158, 169, 172–
3, 177 181, 184, 189, 161, 163,
198, 214, 251
Arrest of 305*

Pacifism n645, n655
Palitzsch, Peter 438, n633, n683, n741,
743, 753, 801, 837
Palm, Kurt n806
Papers, permits, passports, visas etc.
231, 265 (Korsch), 403 (Trepte)
1939 384–8, 307
1940 402, 408*, 415, 420*
1941 309, n421x, 424–6, n424x-
xx*, 439, 541, 785

1946 529
1947 537
1948 *432*, 558, 567–8, 572
  (Neher)
1949 583, 588, 591–602 passim,
  785
  Austrian passport 591, 597–9,
    n597x-xx, 614, 636, 646, 672
Paquet, Alfons
  Fahnen 90
'Parable play' 415, 522, 532
Paris 90, 169, 183, 188–92, 195, *157*,
  548
  International Theatre Festival
    438
  Laterne cabaret 325, 359
  Société des Auteurs 344–5
Parmet, Simon 421
Partos, Paul 207, 347
Paryla, Karl 577, n859, **n874**
Pascal: *Pensées* 411
Pasetti, Leo 46
Pasternak, Boris **866, 869**
PEN club 396
Penzoldt, Ernst n673
Peters, Paul **272, 274**
Pfanzelt, Georg ('Orge') 5, 21, 35, 47,
  62, 99, **518, 523**, n**533, 540, 546,**
  n**605**
Pfitzner, Hans
  Palestrina 31
Photography 442, 504, 543, *434*, 826
Picasso, Pablo **749**, 756
Pieck, Arthur n586
Pieck, Wilhelm *161*, *435*, n586, **618,**
  657
Pinker, J. B. agency n**319**, 373
Pinkus, Theo n215
Pirandello, Luigi
  Six Characters in Search of an
    Author 90
Piscator, Erwin
  In Berlin pre-Hitler *90–95*, 123–
    5, **124, 127**, 138, n156, 311,
    434
  In the USSR 177, *159–61*,
    250–2, 269, **270, 293**
  Mid-1930s 298, 310, **316, 322–4,**
    328, 333

New York **282***, *309, 310–11*,
  356, 398, **408–9***, **424**, 430,
  431, 434–5, 457
  And postwar Germany 500,
    534*–**5***, **579**, **586**, 634
  Brecht and the dramaturgical
    collective 123
  Drums in the Night 145
  The Private Life of the Master Race
    356, 502–3
  Schweik in the Second World War
    472
  An American Tragedy (after
    Dreiser) 282*
  War and Peace projects 295
Plärrer 7, 23, 25, 39
Plagiarism 157
Plievier, Theodor *159*
Pohl, Martin n**757**
Poland
  BE tour 1952 709
  Lalka puppet theatre n**850**
Pollock, Friedrich 215, 307, 432–3,
  481
Polyakova, Nina 878
Positano 531
'Positive' writing *435*
Potsdam 669
Pozner, Vladimir **772**
Prague 170, 267, 567–8,
  Carrar production 339–42
  National Theatre **550**, 551
Prestel, Ludwig ('Lud') 21, 24
Productivity 522
Proletariat. See Working Class
Proletkult 736
Proofs and proof-correction 297, 436
  See Brecht – *Threepenny Novel*
Publishing in German. See Allert de
  Lange, Bork, Desch, Henschel,
  Herzfelde (Malik, Aurora),
  Kiepenheuer, Mezhdunarodnaya
  Kniga, Münzenberg, Suhrkamp,
  Ullstein, Vegaar
  In English 497. See Hale; Reynal
    and Hitchcock,
  In Italian 531, n739
  Gesammelte Werke (Malik-
    Verlag) 336

Putz, Leo 3

Race and Racism 209, 245, 312
  See Brecht – *Roundheads and the
    Peaked Heads*
Radek, Karl 173; trial of *163*
Radio 128, 148
  Hilversum 193
  Moscow 193, *159*
  'Psychological warfare' 439, 445
  RIAS (West Berlin) 728
  Stuttgart **626**
  And see German Freedom
    Radio
Rainer, Luise *309*, *312*, n424x–xx,
  489–90
Ranevskaya, Faina n808, n**810**, 877
Ratz, Erwin 167
Realism 239, 520–1, 522. See also
  Naturalism; Socialist Realism
  'Romantic realism' in US writing
    383
Recht 59a
Red Army 267
Red Club 124–5
Reger, Erik 290
Reich, Bernhard 74, *90*, 184, 188, *158–
  9*, **237**, **243**, 295, 310–15 passim,
  312, *309*, n427
  Post-World War 2 589, **808**,
    n**864**, **876–7**
Reichel, Käthe 792, 846
Reichenbach, Hans 432–3, 482
Reichert, Franz n**803**
Reigbert, Otto *15*, 76
Reinhardt, Max *15–16*, 60, *89*, *90*, 244,
  310, 442, **443**, 444–5
Reiss, Kurt, agency **421**, 531–2
Reitter family **1**, **2**
  Fritz 2
Renner, Sophie 7, 12
Renoir, Jean 316, **317**, 318
Rentzsch, Egon **712**
Replansky, Naomi **497**
Reuss, Prince Heinrich xlv n**120**
Reuss, Leo (Lionel Royce) 516, 536
Revue form 532
Rewalt, Lothar 535, 634
Reyher, Ferdinand **135**, **137**, *162*, **373**,

383, *310*, **398**, 501, 508, n511x–xx,
  516, **519**, n524x, **525–6**, **536–7**,
  543, n**696x**, n**763x**
  As translator 458, **479**
  Invited to Berlin n**581**, **603**, n**604**,
    634, n647x
  *Don't bet on Fights (Harte
    Bandagen)* n135, 137
Reynal and Hitchcock 504
  Plan for Brecht's *Plays* 513*,
    515*, 520*–1*
RGO 214
Richter (?Hans) 170
Richter, Trude 173
Rieger, Jonny G. **351**
Rights, Royalties etc.
  Private Life of the Master Race
    translation 501
  Schweik (and translation) 461,
    n691
  Threepenny Opera royalties 347–8*
    362, 578
  Versuche series withdrawn 228
  And see Contracts; Translation
Rilke, Rainer Maria
  Malte Laurids Brigge 217–21
Rising of 1953. See German
    Democratic Republic: Riots
Robeson, Paul n439xx, n441x,
    n441xxxx
Rodenberg, Hans 727, **829**
Roecker, Marie *12*, 61
Rome, classical 347
Rome, Harold *Pins and Needles* 603
Roose, Thorkild **257**
Roosevelt, President, death of 500
Rosa Maria or Rosmarie. See Aman
Rosenberg, Ethel and Julius n715
Roth, Joseph 290
Roth, Ludwig 535
Roth, Mrs 515, 829
Roth, Wolfgang 162, 454
Rothenburg 209
Rowohlt, Ernst 137, 155
Ruehle, Otto 307
Rülicke, Käthe *438*
Ruhr Epic n121
Runa 215
Rundschau 215, 264

Russell, Bertrand 333
Russia 13
Rylands, George *313*

SDS (German Writers' Defence
    League) *158*, *308*, **338**
Salvation Army 146
Salzburg 567, 588, 599, 614, 646, 651,
    668
Salzburg Festival *314*, 502a, *431*, *432–
    3*, 597, 602, 614, 651
Sammlung, Die 247
Samson-Körner, Paul n117, 135
Sanary-sur-Mer 184–6
Santesson, Etti **401**
Santesson, Ninnan 401, 425
Sauerbruch, Ferdinand n161
Savadski, Yuriy 877
Schall, Ekkehard n1763, n1854
Scharrer, Adam 295
Schaub, Eugen n861
Schelcher, Raimund n765, n805
Scherchen, Hermann n148, n149, **695**
Scherfig 848x
Schiller *Wallenstein* 98
Schiller, Irene n777
Schiller, Leon n689
Schleswig Landestheater 792, **797**
Schlichter, Rudolf *91*, 124
Schmidt-Radvanyi, J. L. 168
Schmitt, Johann Ludwig 153, 879
Schneider (?) n374
Schnitzler, Henry 501
Schön, Ernst n205
Schönberg, Arnold 621
Schönlank, Erich 360
Schopenhauer 7
Schrader, Konrad n694
Schreiner, Albert 481, **615**
Schröder, Max 852
Schüfftan, Eugen 519
Schuh, Oskar Fritz n561, 636
Schulz, Alfred n686
Schulz-Dornburg, Rudolf n121, n134
Schumacher, Ernst **776**
    *Die dramaturgischen Versuche
        Bertolt Brechts* **796**
Schurek, Paul n685
Schwab, Sepp **688**, **698**

Schwachhofer, René n**152**
Schwarzschild, Leopold 244
Schweikart, Hans 566, **822**, n**875**
Schwerdt n201
Seeger, Kurt 852
Seeler, Moritz *14*, n117
Seghers, Anna 167–9, 181, 325, *431*,
    438, 548–51, 711
    The Trial of Jeanne d'Arc (radio
        play) For stage adaptation
        see under Brecht: Plays
Selbmann, Fritz **862**
Semyonov, V. S. n726x
Serreau, Geneviève **785***
Serreau, Jean-Marie 868
Shakespeare 7, 312, 431
    Coriolanus 5, *90*, n132, 665, 837
    Hamlet 616–7
    Julius Caesar *92*, n1748
    Macbeth 207, 431
    Measure for Measure 160, 174
        (basis of Brecht's *The
        Roundheads and the Pointed
        Heads*, qv)
    Richard II (or III) 636
    Troilus and Cressida 435, 617
Shanghai Document, A 141
Shaw, George Bernard 7, 197, 236
    St Joan 90
Sherman, Vincent 519
Shubert, Milton 282
Siems, Friedrich **849**
Signoret, Simone n698
Silone, Ignazio
    Bread and Wine 342
    Der Faschismus 201
    Weissbrot Kantate. See Eisler, H.
Simone, André. See Katz, Otto
Simplizissimus *11*, 10, 13
Sinclair, Upton
    Presents William Fox 336
    Singing Jailbirds 127
Sinn und Form 571, **853**
Skobeltsyn, Dimitri V. **778**
Skovsbostrand, Svendborg 187, *157*
Slogans 666, 728
Smoking 93–4, 96, 341, 451, 453, 454,
    459, 484, 489
'Social fascism' n214

Socialist Realism *159*, 243, *437*, n652, 756
Sothmann, Mr 666
Soviet-German Pact, 1939 785
Soviet Union *157–61*
　Brecht visits 177, 250–6, 808f
　Crosses via Vladivostok 420, 425
　Freedom and repression 241
　German theatre in 250–2, 270, 295*
　His reputation there *159*
　Korsch's critique 381, 449
　Steffin visits 163, n226x, n249x, n295–6
　The Great Purge *160*ff
　Twentieth Congress:
　　Khrushchev revelations *438*, n863
　Worries *163*
　Writers' Union helpfulness 427
SPÖ 202
Stage design or consruction 310
　See also Appen, Neher, Reigbert, Roth, Otto
Stalin, Stalinism 206, 236, 328, 437*, *437–8*, n863; Stalin-worship 241
Stalin Peace Prize 778, 808
Standen, Mrs 272
Stanislavsky, K. S. *436–7*, 621, 814
Stanislavsky Method *160*, 296, 310–11*, 525*
State department, The 367
Staudte, Wolfgang 688, 698, **821**, 823, **828**, 829, 833
Steben 2
Steckel, Leonard *423*, **575**, 582–3, 614, 634, n**658**
Steffin, Johanna **542**
Steffin (Margarete, Grete) 160, n161, 162–3, 178, 181, *157*, n226x–xx, n229x–xx, n236x–xx, n247x–xx, n249x, n256x, n289x–xx, 291, 295, 301, 354, 390, *307*, *309*, 398, 400
　Extent of collaboration 409
　Her death 427–9, 541–2
　Short stories 425
　Visa question 408–9, n424x–xx, n425

Steinbeck, John 383
Steinmetz, Hildegard n**662**
Steinrück, Albert 41, 76, 502a
Stemmle, R. A. 619
Stern, James **490**, 491–2, 498–9, 501
Sternberg, Fritz *92*, 124, 138, 141, n144, n145, 168, 215, **271**, 507
　Der Faschismus an der Macht n256, 271
Sternberger, Dolf **697**
Steuermann, Eduard 503
Steuermann, Mrs E. 501
Stewart, Donald Ogden **510**, 548
Stockholm *308*
Storm Petersen, Robert **246**, 342
Strakosch, Carl, agency 348, 362
Strasberg, Lee **287**
Strasbourg 191, 841
Strauss, Martin n**858**
Stravinsky, Igor n543, n551
Strehler, Giorgio 856*
Strindberg, August 33, 796
　A Dream Play 571
Strittmatter, Erwin 706, 743, 872
　Katzgraben n714, n765, n**847**
Strupp, Günther **684**
Suhrkamp, Peter 140, *313*, **509**, *434*, 437, n**569**, n604xx–xxx, **633**, 639, **640**, 647, n**659**, **679**, **699**, **746** n**747**, **762**, **855**, **879**
　As editor of Brecht's *Gedichte und Lieder* 855
Superman 437
Survival 514, 529, 531
Swaanswijk. See Lucebert
Swift 213, 239
Switzerland 529–30, 536–7, *432*ff
　See Basel, Carona, Chur, Lugano, Zurich
Syberberg, Rüdiger n**673**
Symbols, Symbolism 414
　Contrasted with Parables 522
Synge, J. M. *The Playboy of the Western World* n683, n848x

Tagebuch, Das 112
Tagore, Rabindranath 81
Tairov, Alexander 295
Tallon, Ninon 344

Tbilisi 841
Tegernsee 7
Teichmann, Willi 829
Tempo 342
Tetzner, Lisa 202
Theaterarbeit 703
Theatre of All Nations *313*
Theatre Workshop 160, 310, **311***
    (statement), 364
'Third thing, The' 637*
Thompson, Dorothy *309*, 507
Thurø 172–181
Tickhardt, O. E. n674
Tiedtke, Jacob 324
Tillich, Paul *312*, 466, 477, 480–1, **482**,
    505
Todd, Mike *314*, 519
Toller, Ernst 123, *159*, 256
Tombrock, Hans **399, 405–6, n407**,
    **n412–13, 414, n416–18, n422–3,
    425, n630–1**
Toporkov, V. O. **814**
    Stanislavsky in Rehearsal 814
TRAM 310
Translation, Translators 184, 281, 430,
    434–5, 442, 461*, 472*, n476x,
    497*, 513*, 515*
    (a) Into English
    Auden (qv) 297x, 438, 442, 478,
        508, 512*, 513
    Bentley, Eric (qv) 784
    Keene Wallis 364*
    Kreymborg, Alfred 457–79
        passim, **470–1**, 483, 485
    Laughton 499, 506–7, 511, 515–
        16, 519, 526
    Lazar, Christopher 435
    See also Blacks; Hays; Isherwood;
        Peters; Replansky; Reyher;
        Stern; Hans Viertel
    (b) Into Danish 392, 400. See
        also Gelsted
    (c) Into French 397. See also
        Mauprey, Tallon
    (d) Into Russian n312, n814, 866,
        869
        preface to Plays 877, 886
        See also Kirsanov,
            Pasternak

(e) Into Swedish 401. See also
    Martner
(f) Into German 135, 544
    By Brecht and Steffin
        354–5, 390
Trepte, Curt 195, **403**, 408
Tretiakoff, Sergei 158, **170**, **177**, 184,
    188, **193**, *159*, *163*, 250–1, 316–18,
    347
Triebel, Axel n844
'Trojan horse' tactics 313
Trompeter an der Katzbach, Der 666
Tschesno-Hell, Michael 590
'Tuis' 448. See under Brecht: Prose
Tulpanov, Colonel Sergei n532
Turner, Nat 288
Typography, Layout etc. 217–25

Uhu 162
Ulbricht, Walter n594, **652, 654, 725**,
    751*
Ullstein publishers *90*, 100, 109, 126,
    n143, 180
Un-American Activities Committee
    310, 551
Ungar, Hermann
    The Red General 141
United Front policy 214
United States
    American history 526
    Brecht and 135, *163*, 330, 408*
    Colleagues leave for *307*
    Immigration discussed 380
    Journey from Finland 425, 430–1
    Theatre possibilities 409*, 430
    Wish to return to Germany 506
    See also Papers, Passports, Visas
        etc, 1939–41; American
        Guild for Cultural Freedom
Unsere Zeit 239
USSR See Soviet Union
Utting 138, 160, 518, 531

Vakhtangov, Evgeni 621
Valentin, Karl n49, 79
Valetti, Rosa n54
Van der Lubbe, Marinus 197
Van Druten, John 501
    A Tree Grows in Brooklyn 501

Vansittart, Lord 481
Varga, Eugen 214
VEGAAR (Foreign Workers'
    Publishing House, Moscow) *161*,
    297
Verfremdung. See Alienation
Verlaine, Paul 41
Victor, Walter n729
Vienna 99, 100, n164, n167, 181, *157*,
    522
    Burgtheater 588, 636, n834
    Proletarian Theatre **159**
    Scala n571, n748, n859
    Universal-Edition 340, 578,
        n604xx–xxx
Viertel, Berthold *15*, 72, 86, **89a**, 101b,
    114, 438, 442, 495–6, 644, 668
    In US *310*, 482, 499–500, **502a**, **517**
    back in Europe *434*, **571**
    directs *313*, 442, 636
    collaboration with B E *575*,
        577, *582–5*, **588, 628**, 634,
        n648
Viertel, Hans 442, 466, 475
Viertel, Salka *312*, 442
Vilar, Jean n859
Villon 20, 157
Visas. See under Papers
Vishnievski, Vsevolod
    The First Cavalry Army 808
Völker, Wolfgang **661**
Voelkner, Benno 872
Volga German Republic
    (USSR) *159*, 295–6
Voltaire 213
Vorwärts 202

Wälterlin, Oskar 599
Wäscher, Aribert 639
Wagner-Régeny, Rudolf
    *Der Darmwäscher (Persische
        Legende)* 642, **n643**
Waley, Arthur
    The Analects of Confucius 392, 400
Walcher, Jacob 480–1, n741, 743
Wallace, Edgar 153
Wanamaker, Sam n859
Wandel, Paul *437*, 607–8, **621, 653,**
    665, 732*, n836, 860

Wangenheim, Gustav von 251–2, 313,
    n325, 333
War 271, 387
    begins *307*
    turning point *311*
Warburg, Max n308
Warschauer, Frank 45, 60
Weber, Carl *438*, n815
Webster, John *The Duchess of Malfi*
    311–13, 452, 478, 481, *502a–3*,
    527*
Wechsler, Lazar 533
Wedekind, Frank 621
    Funeral 21, 25
Wegener, Paul 47, 64
Weidemann, L. W. 9
Weigel, Helene 90, *90*, **93–97**, 99–100,
    n104, **n116, 122, 126, 138, 142,**
    158, 167–8, 171–2, 183–4, 188–
    91, *157*, **229–31, 250–2, 275–6,**
    282, **284, 286**, 325, **337–43**, 356,
    384, 445, 448, 468, 494, 514, 516,
    518, 531, 540, n622, **n714, 731,**
    n748, 808
    Acts in Denmark 357
    As Señora Carrar 359
    In *Fear and Misery* 360
    Nationality 597
    Return to German theatre 535,
        431, 433, 553, 556, 558, 709,
        711
    Runs Berliner Ensemble (qv) 575,
        577, **582–5, 589–94**, 632
    Rôle in *Mother Courage* 511, 576,
        579
    Rôle in *Mother Courage* film 829
    Russian trip, winter 1933 193,
        201–2
    Steffin upsets **161–3**
Weil, Felix J. 307, 448
Weill, Kurt *91*, 158, 224, 286, n380x,
    n435x, n439xx, n441x–xxxx, **455**,
    486, 529, 531, **570**, n609x
    Happy End (with Brecht and
        Hauptmann) n146
    Lady in the Dark (with Moss Hart
        and Ira Gershwin) *310*, 570
    Mahagonny Songspiel (with Brecht)
        122

One Touch of Venus (with Perelman and Ogden Nash) *311*
'Ruhr Epos' project n121, n134
Schweik project with Aufricht and Brecht 451–75
Schweik without Weill 472, 479
'Seashells from Margate' 123
Seven Deadly Sins, The (ballet, texts by Brecht) 169, 171–2, 419
Szechwan project with Brecht 455, 491
Threepenny Opera (with Brecht) 'new version' 570, 578, n604x–xxx, n609x
Weinert, Erich 586, **587**
Weinert, Li n**722**
Weisenborn, Günter 585
Weiskopf, F. C. 833
    Das Herz – ein Schild 336
    Die Unbesiegbaren 484
Weiss, Ernst
    Olympia 81
Weiss, Peter *Aesthetik des Widerstands 308*
Wekwerth, Manfred *438–9*, n683, n774, 794, 821, 828–9, n865
Welles, Orson *314*, 517
Weltmann, Lutz **101**
Wendt, Erich n680, 699
Wenk, Comrade **740**
Werfel, Franz 244
Werrenreth, Erna 31
Wessely, Paula *314*
Wexley, John *310*
Wiens, Paul 852
Wiktor, Miss 37
Wilder, Thornton n603
Wilhelmi, Erni 801
Wilkening, Albert **823**
Wimmer, Maria 589
Winge, John (Hans) 483, 485, 552, n734–5

Winter, Ella (Mrs Stewart) 548
Wisten, Fritz n575, n634
Witt, Josef n149
Wolf, Friedrich **693**, n**702**, 833
Wolfson, Victor 279
Workers, working class 399
    As audience 577, 579, 588
    As political base 437
    language and 740
    reemergence in GDR *437*
    degree of involvement in 1953 riots 728*
Wort, Das 159, 161, 163, 298, 304–5, 312–15, 321, 328, 332–3, n338x, 346*, 351, 354–5, 375, 394*
    Earnings from *309*, 390
    Suggested series on refugees 365*
    Domination by the 'Hungarian clique' 366*
Wuolijoki, Hella *308*, **402**, **419**, **426**, 454, 506, 696, 790
Woyzeck 95

Yüan Miau-tse n**827**

Ziegler, Lulu (Mrs Knutzon) 299, 352
Zinoviev 242
Zionism 184
Zoff, Marianne *14*, **59a**, 65, 81, 86, **87a**, *90*, 95ff, **101a–b**, 253
Zola 3
Zuckmayer, Carl *89*, 502a
    Cheerful Vineyard, The 91
Zurich 167–9, 332, 530, *431–4*, 548ff, 579ff
    Schauspielhaus 356, 359, *309*, 421, 579, n609, n613
    and the BE 582ff
Zweig, Arnold 184, 244, n**292**, n**306**, 307, **607–8**